Turning 40:

A Year in Haiku

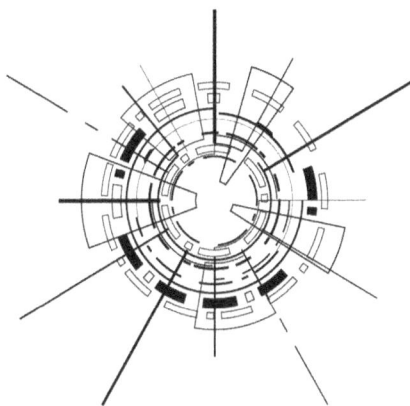

Travis Blunt

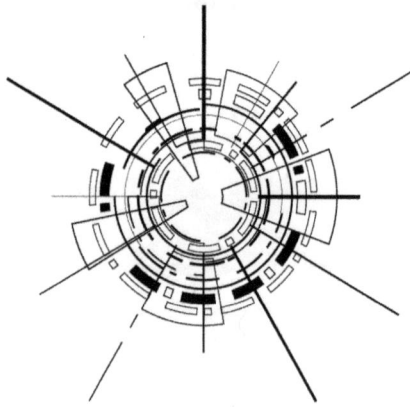

Published by Travis Blunt
and OwlCat LLC

Copyright 2025

ISBN: 979-8-218-86104-9

10 9 8 7 6 5 4 3 2 1

When I decided to start this project, my understanding of haiku was very limited. I realized that all I knew about haiku was what I had briefly learned in elementary school: three lines with a syllable structure of 5-7-5.

Now, in researching proper modern haiku writing I've found that just like everything else on the internet there are too many opinions on what the *actual* rules are. Debates range from run-on sentences, to rhyming, to being abstract in nature, to capitalization, to containing questions and rhetoric, to differences in syllable pronunciation, and so on, and so on.

So I decided I don't care. Fuck it. I am going to write this book however I see fit. So I wrote three lines a day for each day of my 40th year of being alive. That's it. Three lines, no fuss, done.

wrote a poem today
naysayers will always nay
fuck you very much

Maybe you will enjoy this project, maybe not. I don't care. I completed a goal. In the end this is simply a collection of daily thoughts spanning a milestone year in the life of a middle aged man on the front range of Colorado. Some of them are funny, some of them serious, some are pretty clever, and some are just... bad.

Read it aloud in a town square. Read it on the bus or train. Keep a copy in your nightstand. Keep a copy in the bathroom. Burn it in the event that you become stranded and need to start a fire to stay warm. Burn it just because you hate books. Use it as a coaster. Use it to kill a spider. Give it to your grandma. Give it to a racoon. I did my part. It's time to do yours. Enjoy... or don't...

so without ado
i give you turning forty
a year in haiku...

- Travis Blunt

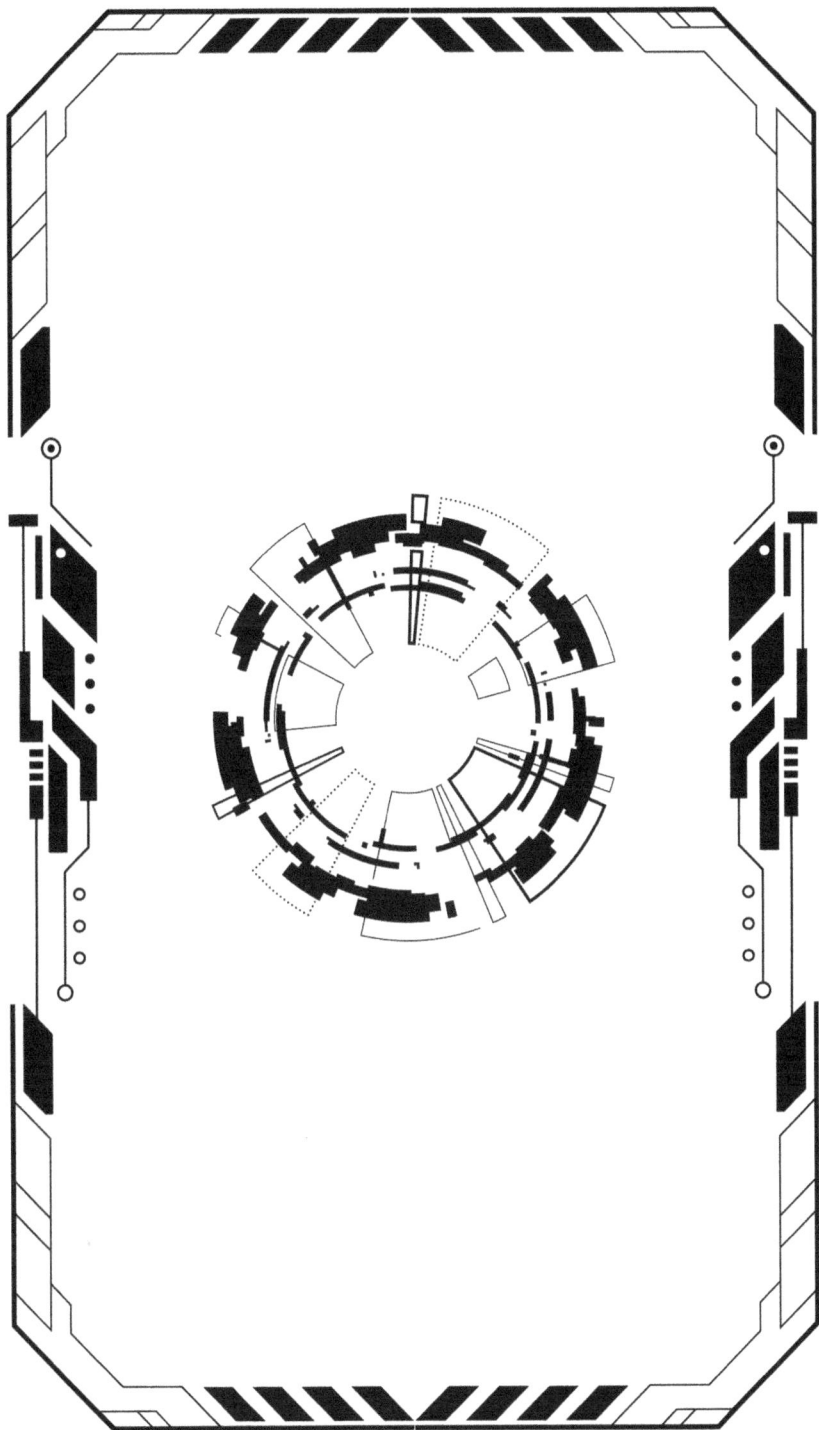

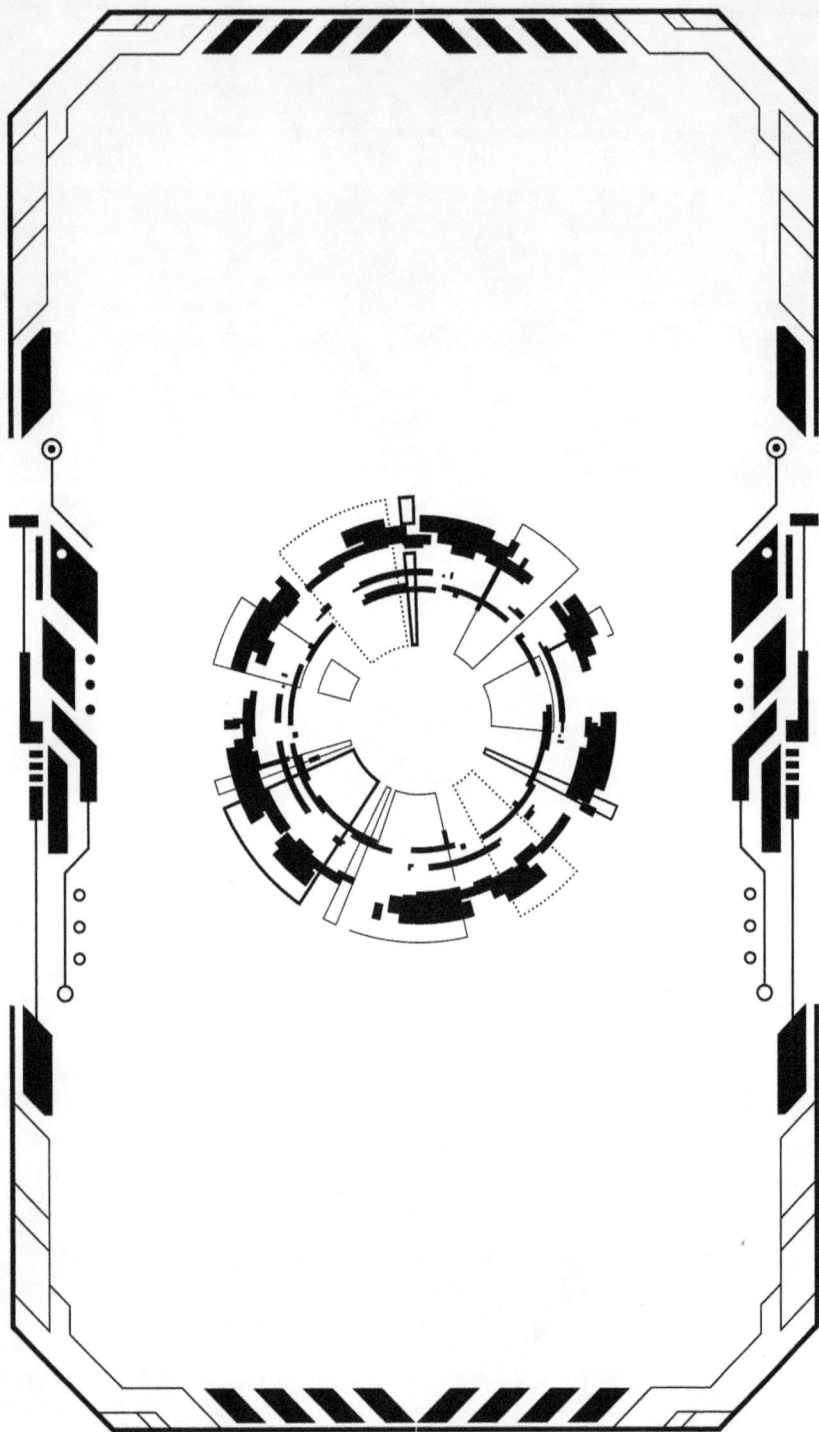

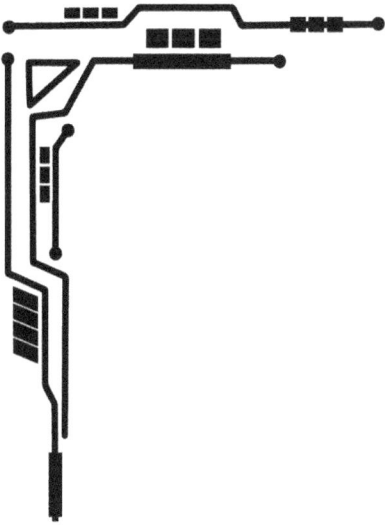

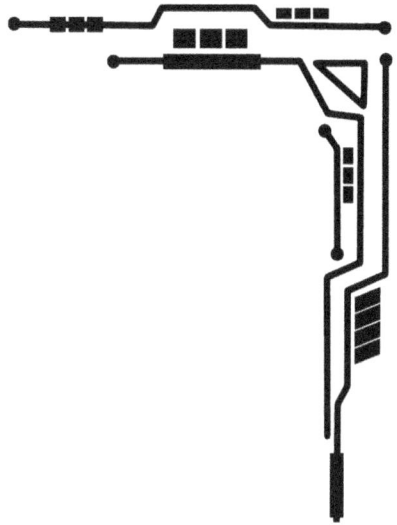

The Beginning.

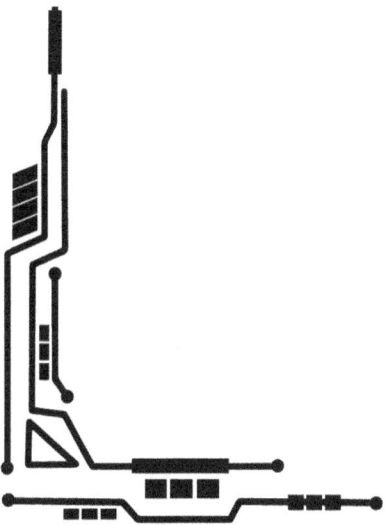

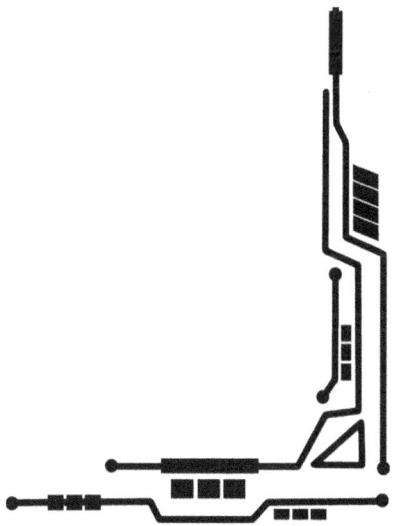

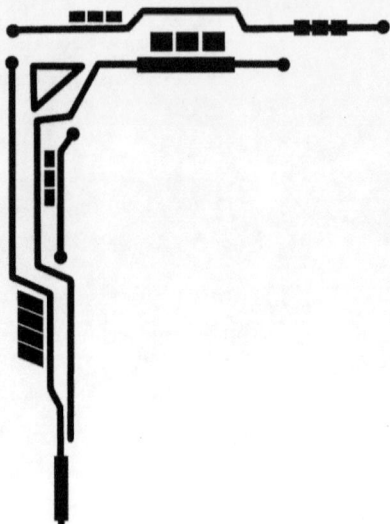

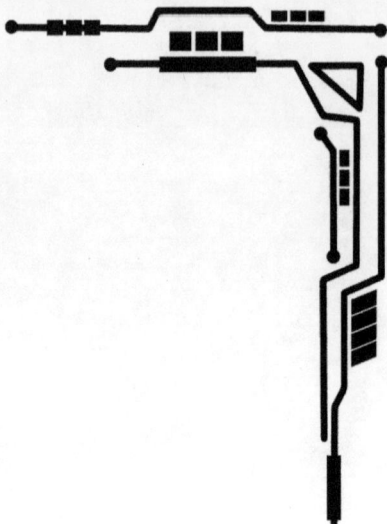

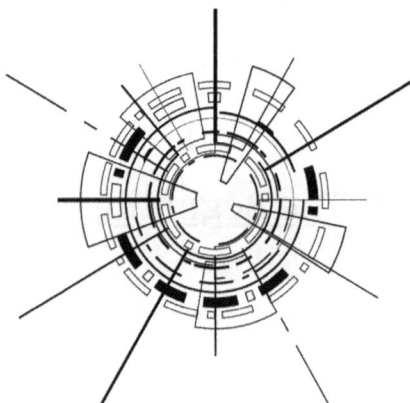

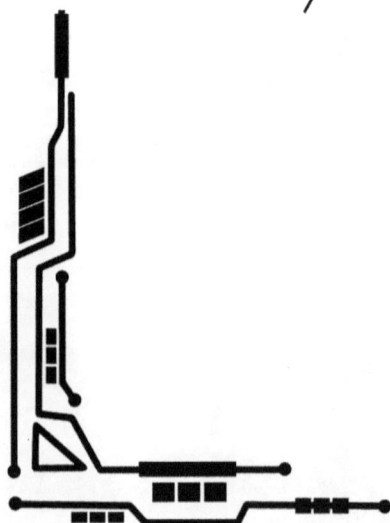

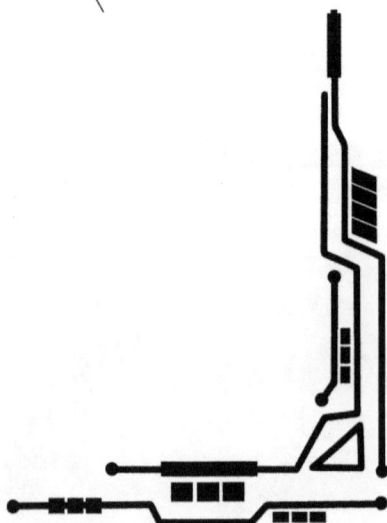

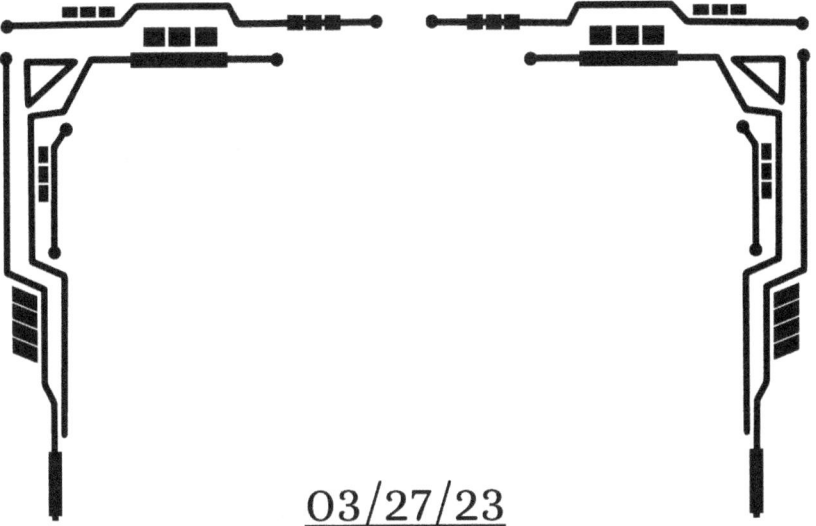

<u>03/27/23</u>

joints and muscles hurt
i guess this is what happens
at level forty

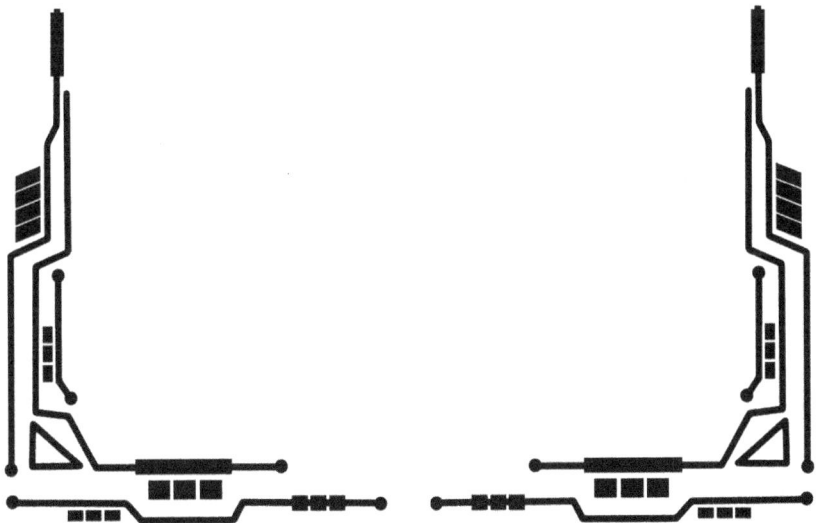

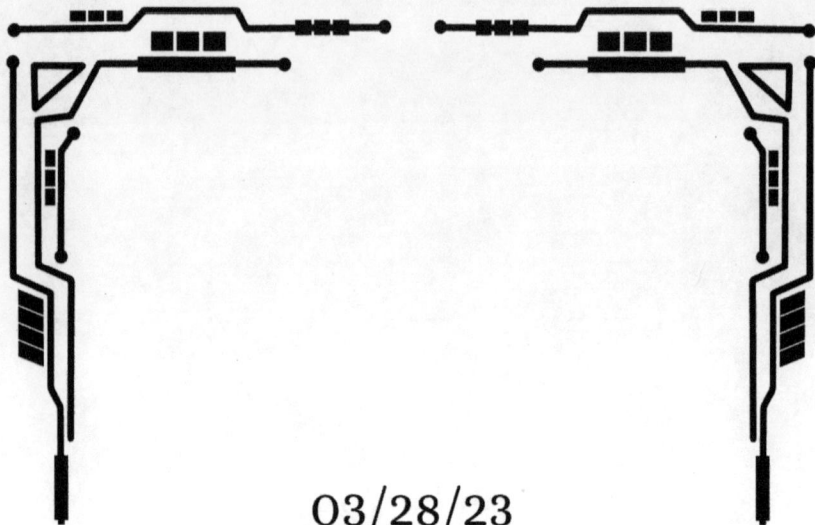

<u>03/28/23</u>

red morning sunrise
before the humans wake up
beautiful silence

<u>03/29/23</u>

decimal points wait
at the end of sentences
you're doing it wrong

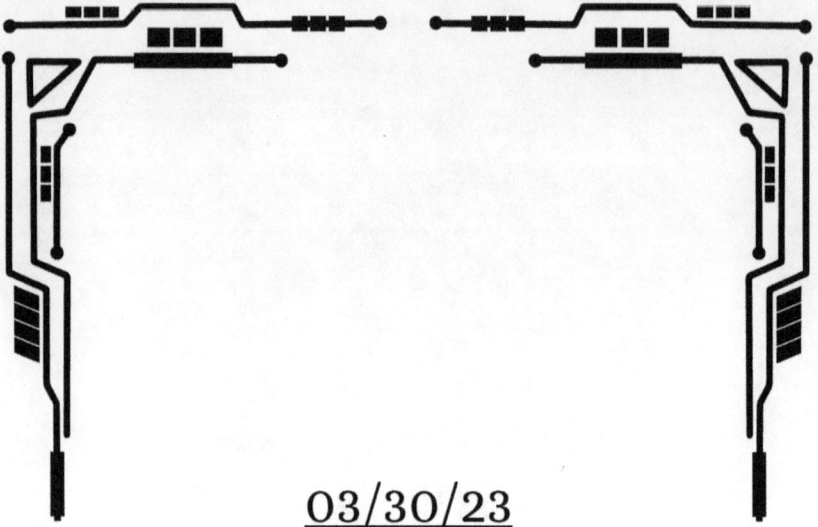

03/30/23

the egg gives a bird
it does its thing for awhile
the bird gives an egg

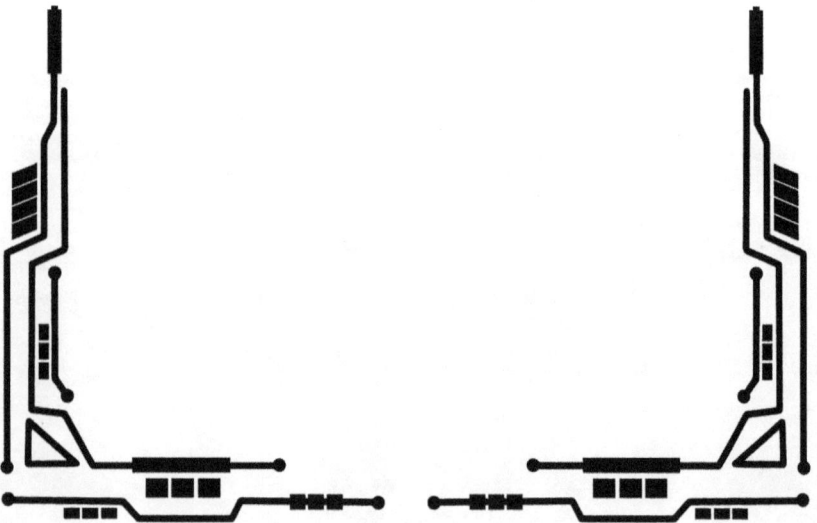

windowsill light beam
illuminating the steam
coffee still too hot

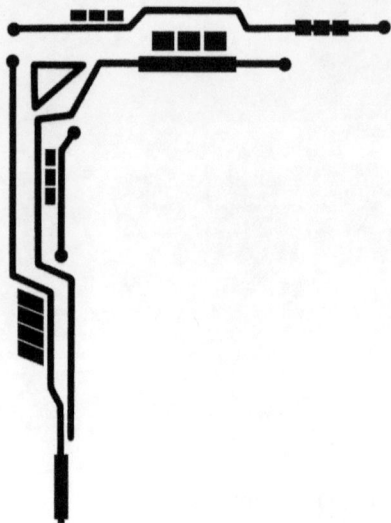

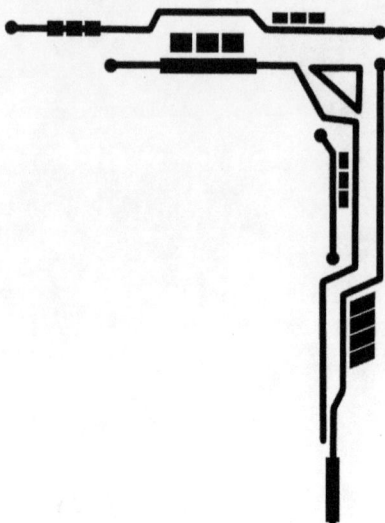

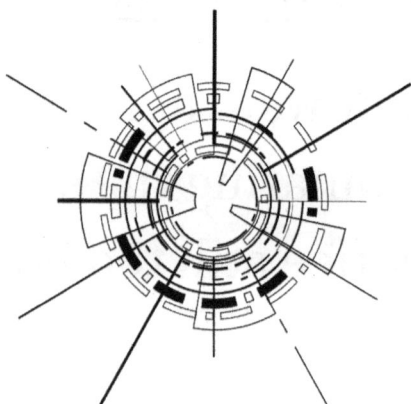

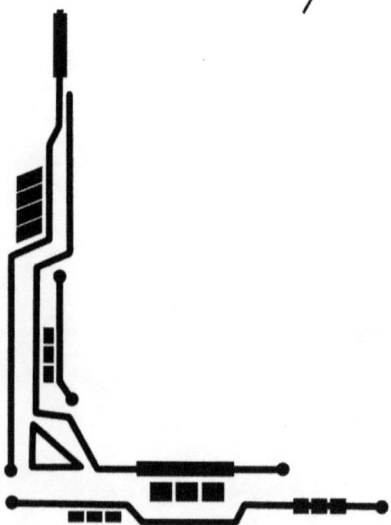

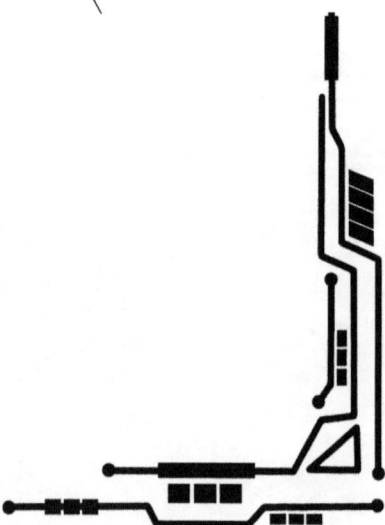

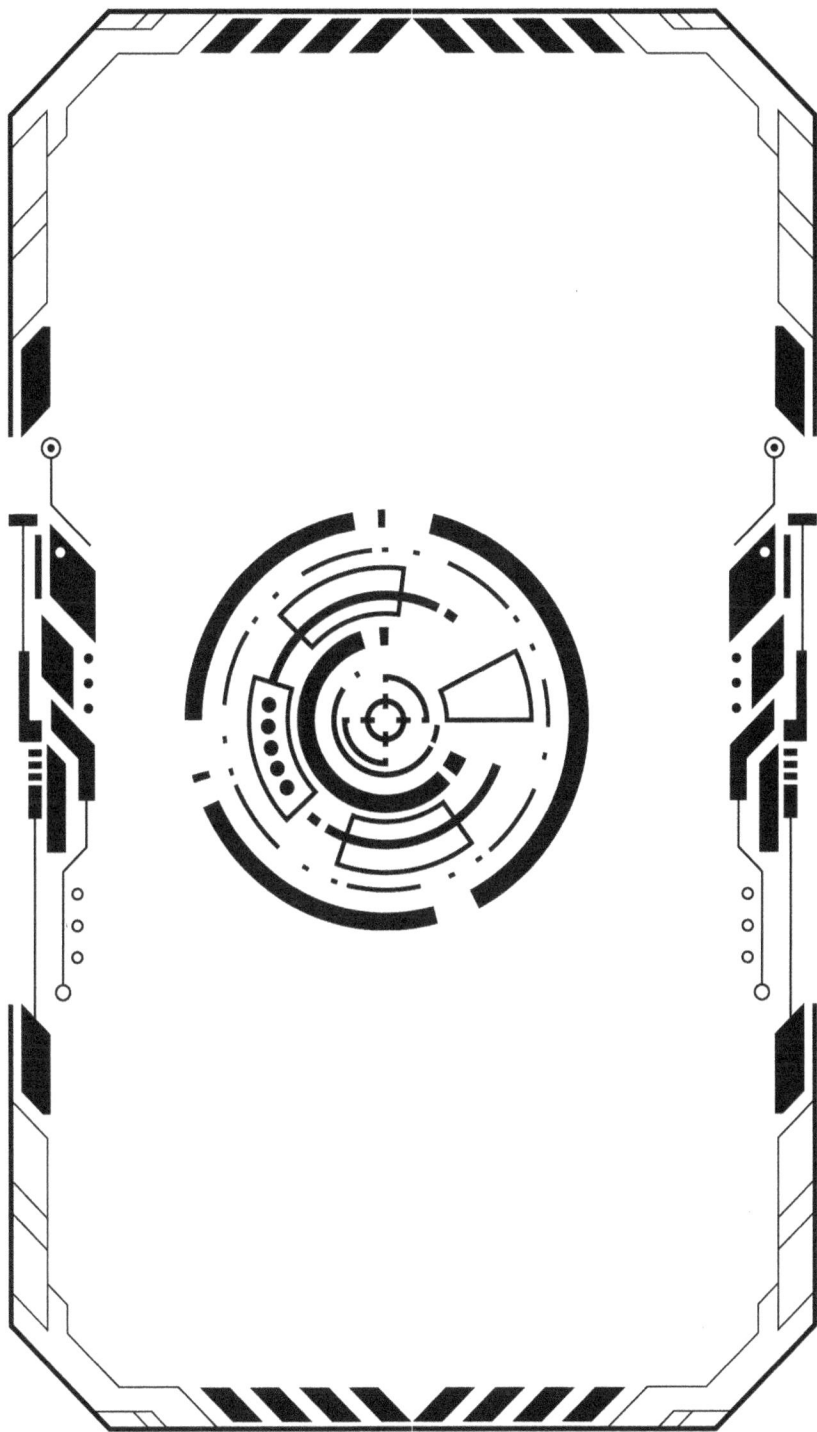

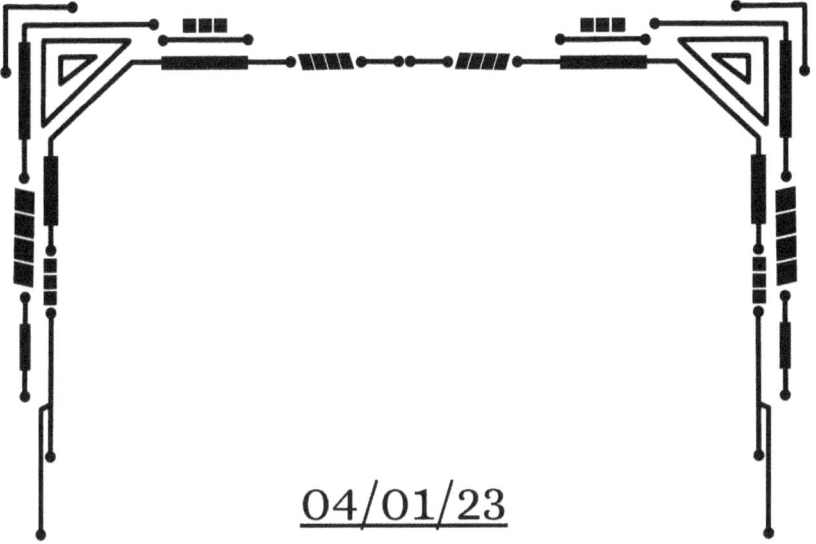

04/01/23

listen to the fence
the grass is not so green here
on the other side

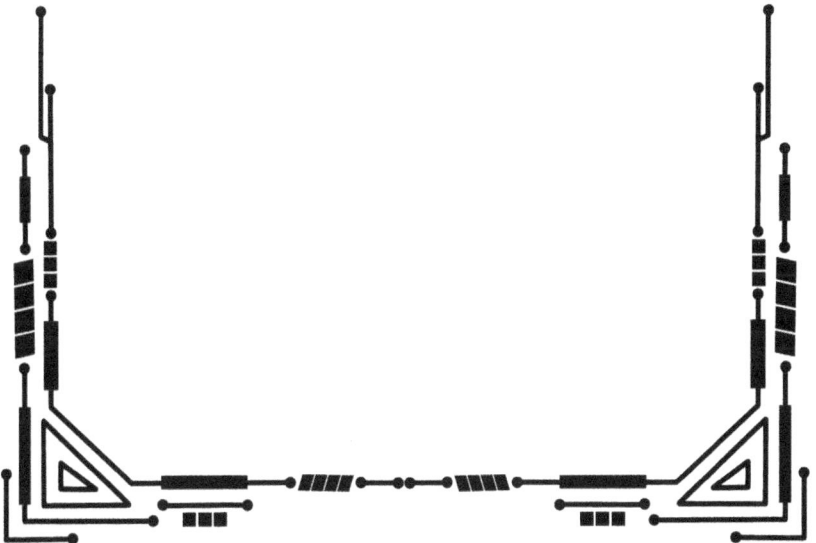

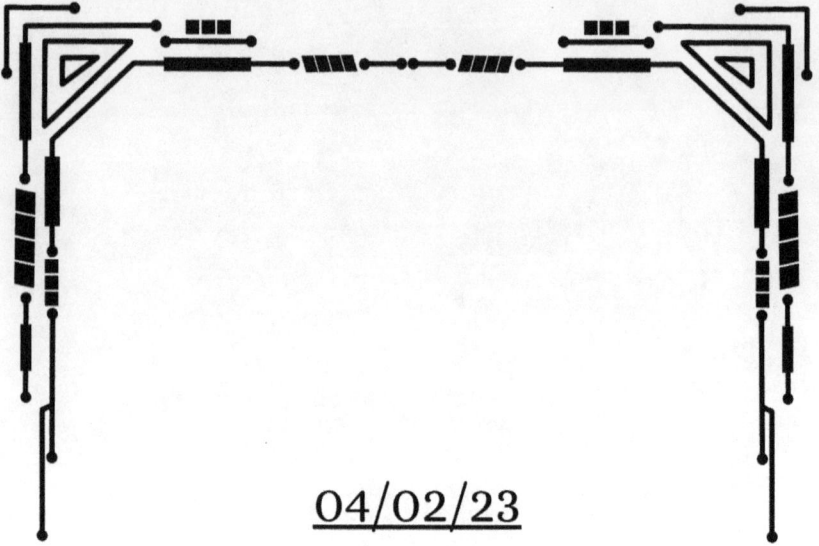

<u>04/02/23</u>

wake up early now
six thirty partly cloudy
dawn is good to write

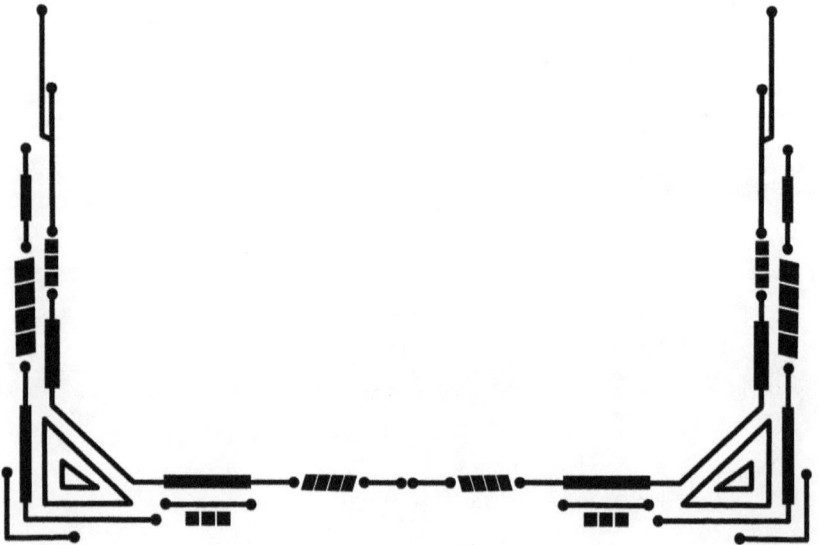

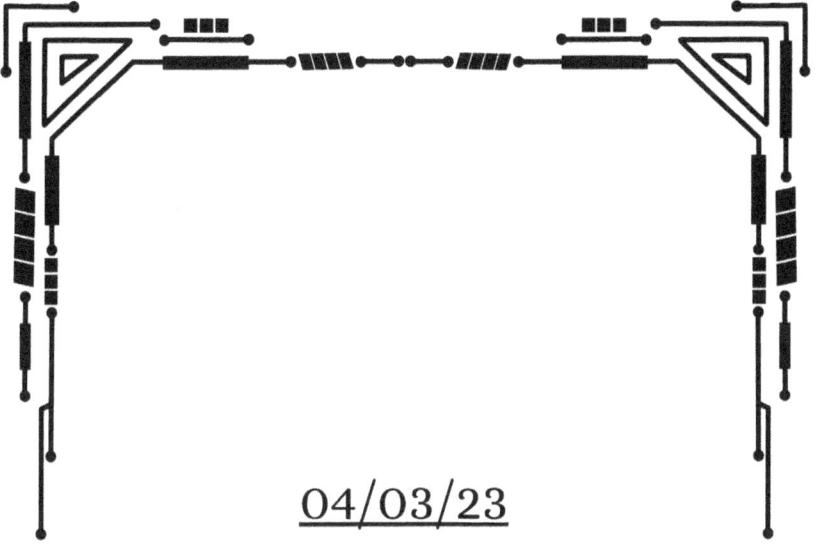

<u>04/03/23</u>

green jacket neighbor
goes to work at eight o'clock
have a good day steve

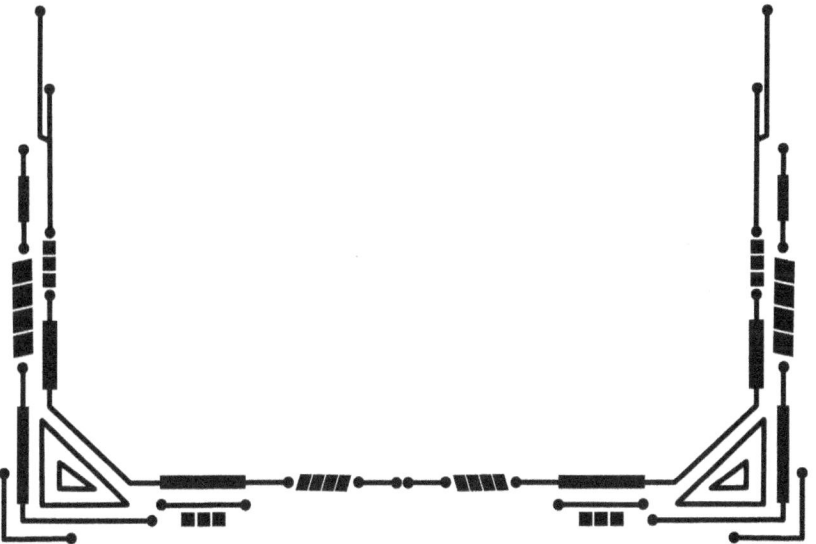

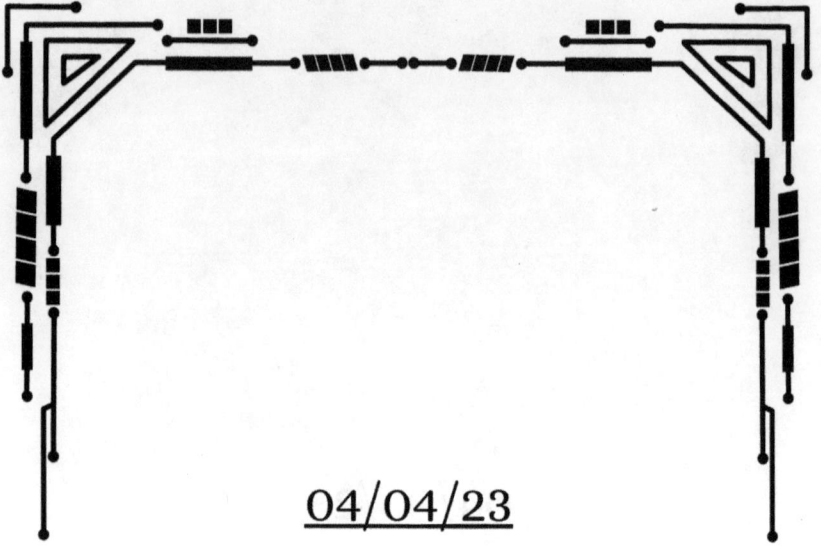

<u>04/04/23</u>

it's cold outside now
thinking about summertime
snow in april sucks

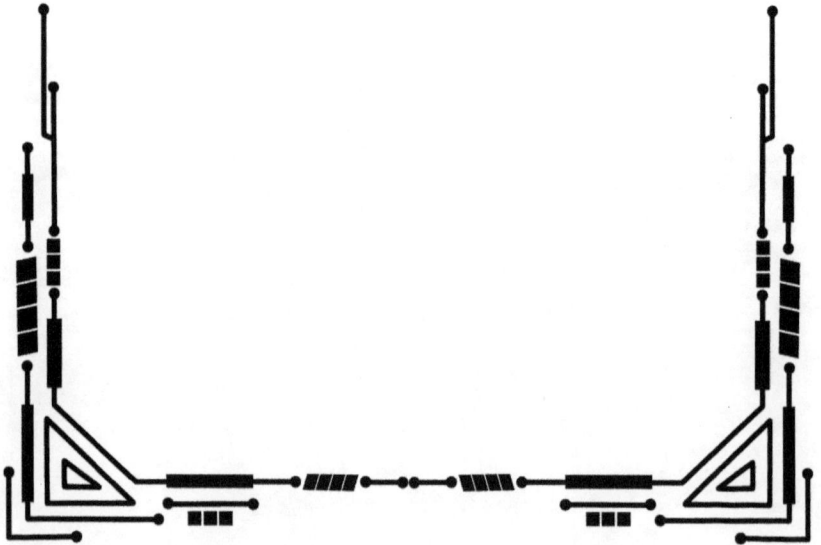

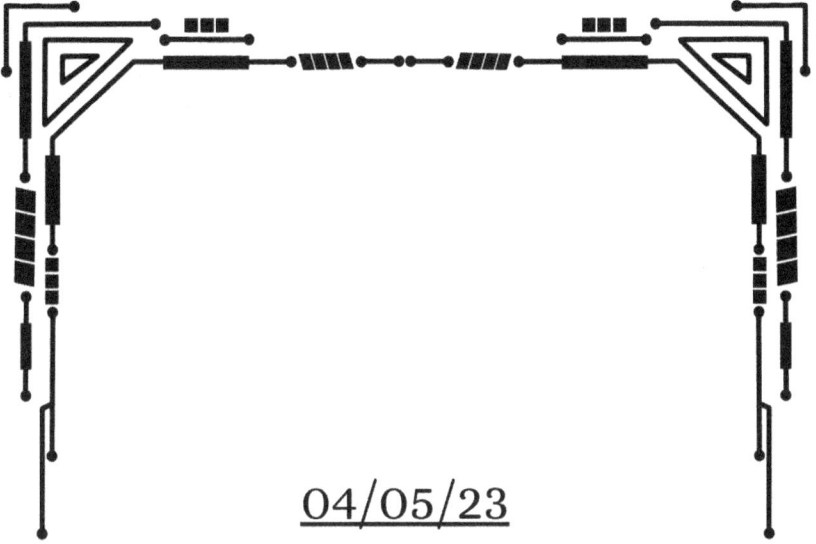

be grateful for home
the cactus doesn't complain
about the desert

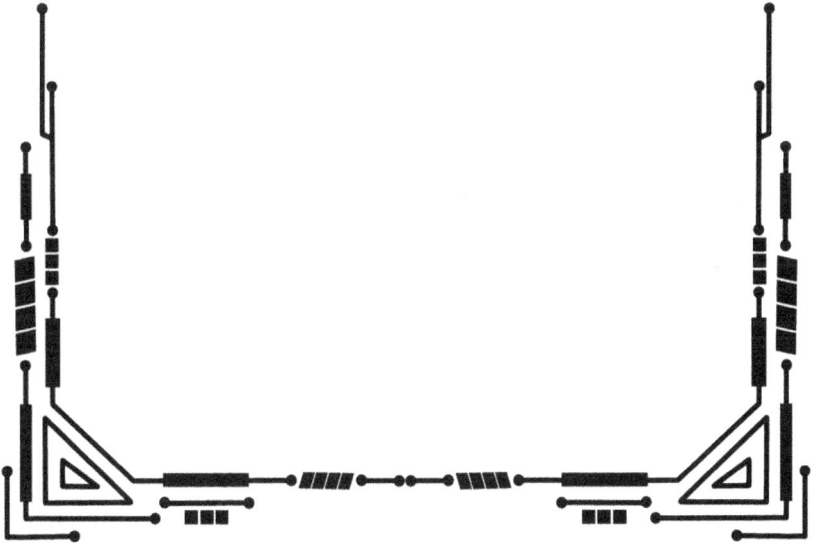

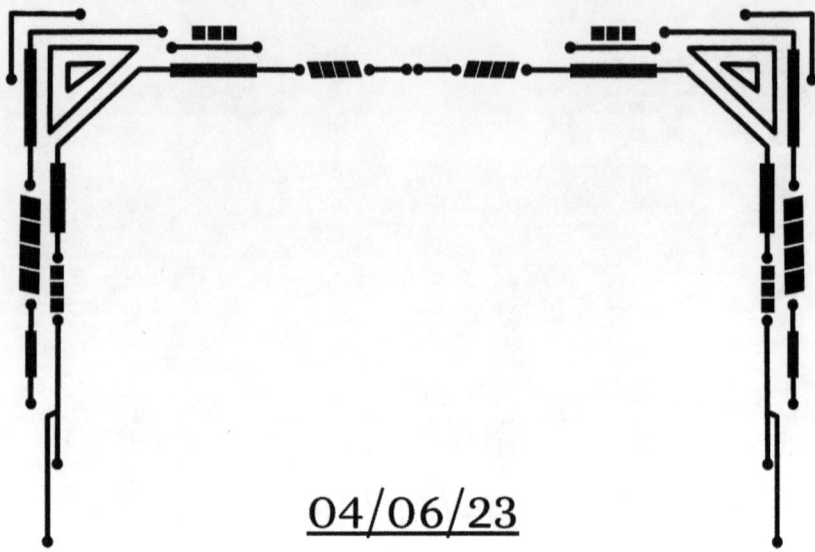

<u>04/06/23</u>

a wetland strip mall
the natural habitat
for pokemon cards

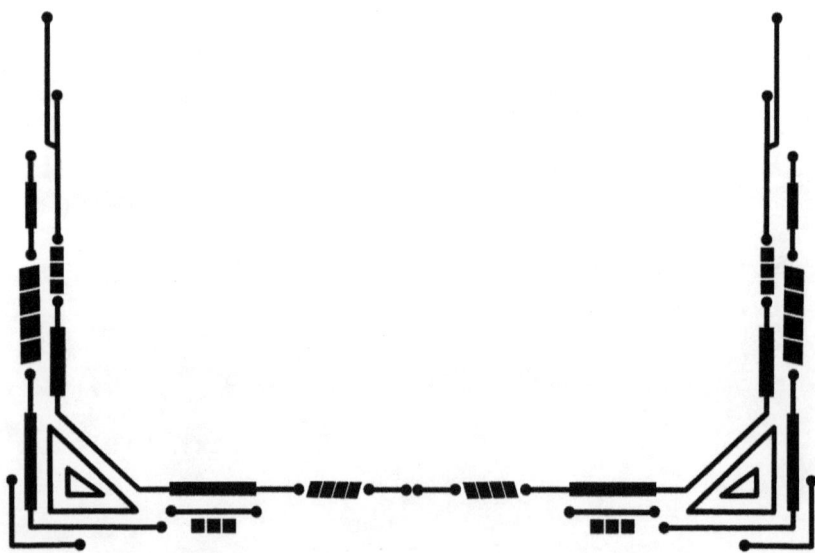

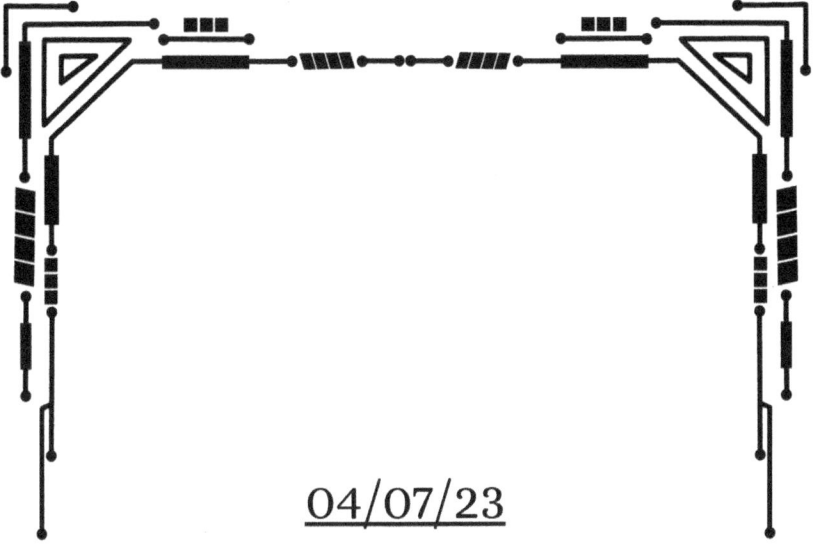

<u>04/07/23</u>

kikkoman soy sauce
let's make sushi rolls my friend
and dip them in it

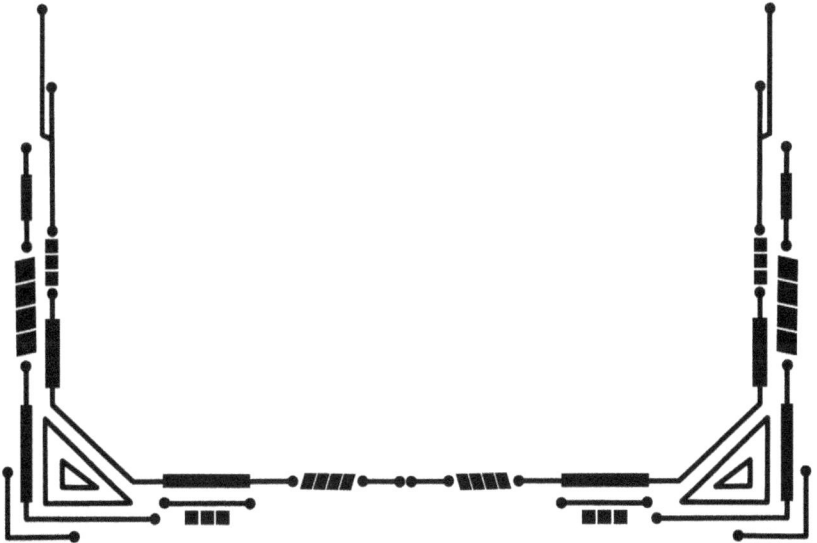

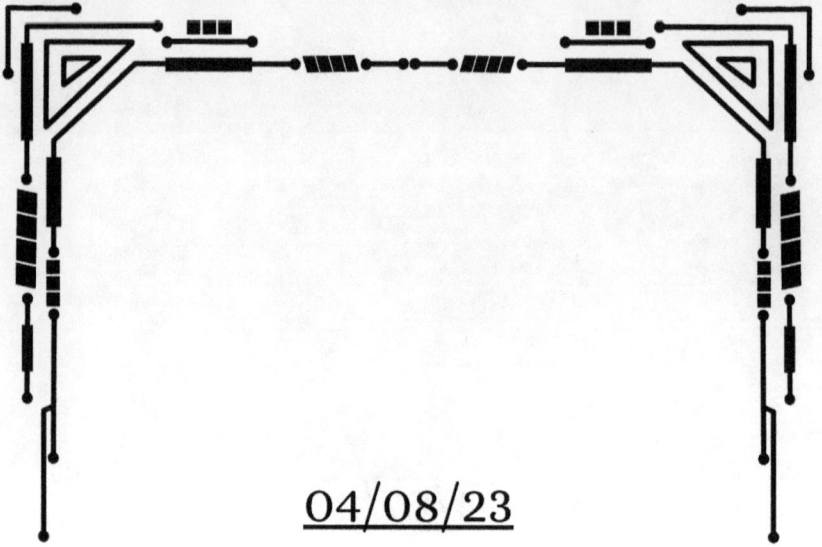

<u>04/08/23</u>

i am really tired
you are also really tired
let's go take a nap

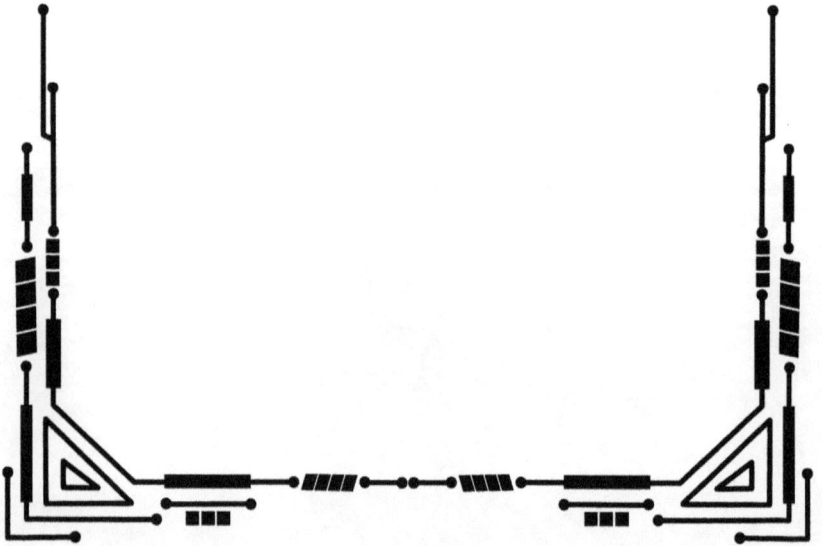

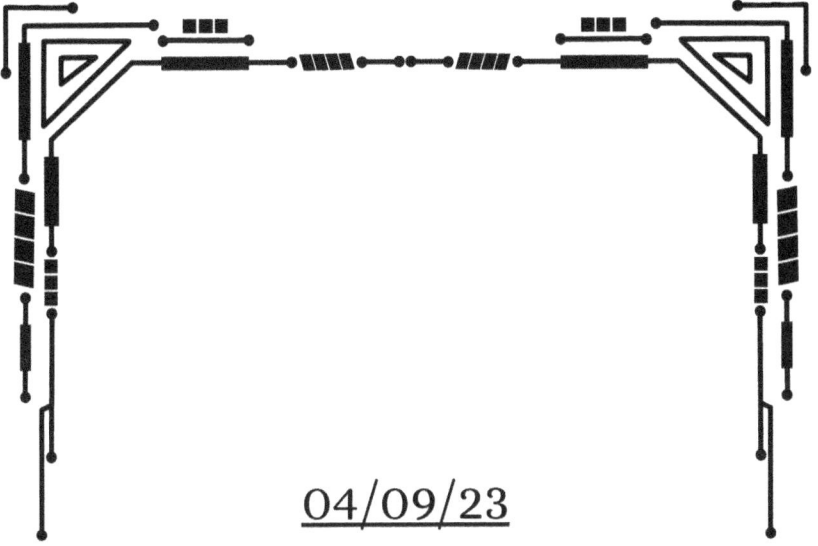

04/09/23

blueberry pancakes
coffee black no sugar please
and eggs benedict

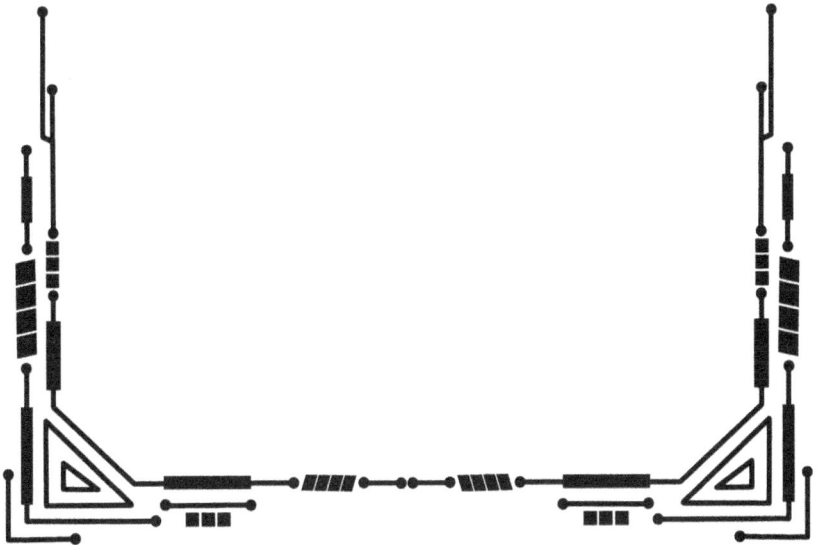

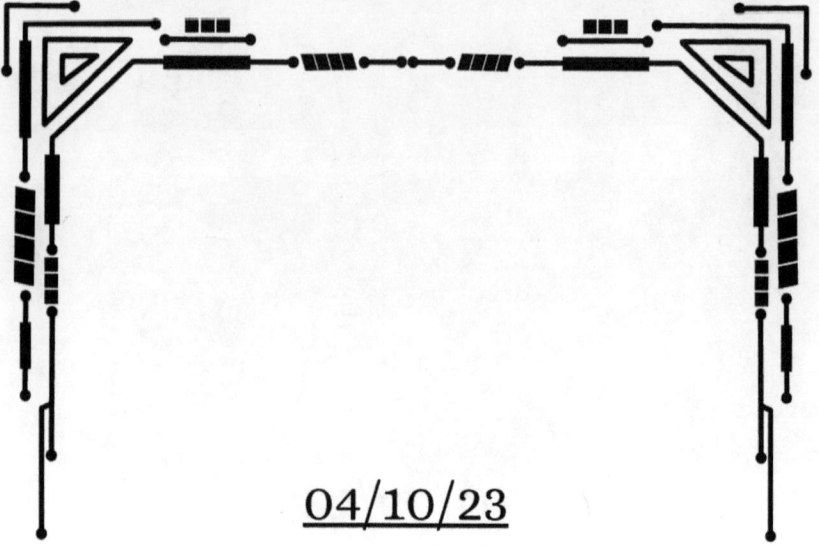

<u>04/10/23</u>

smoking don shula
an excellent sativa
in seventy two

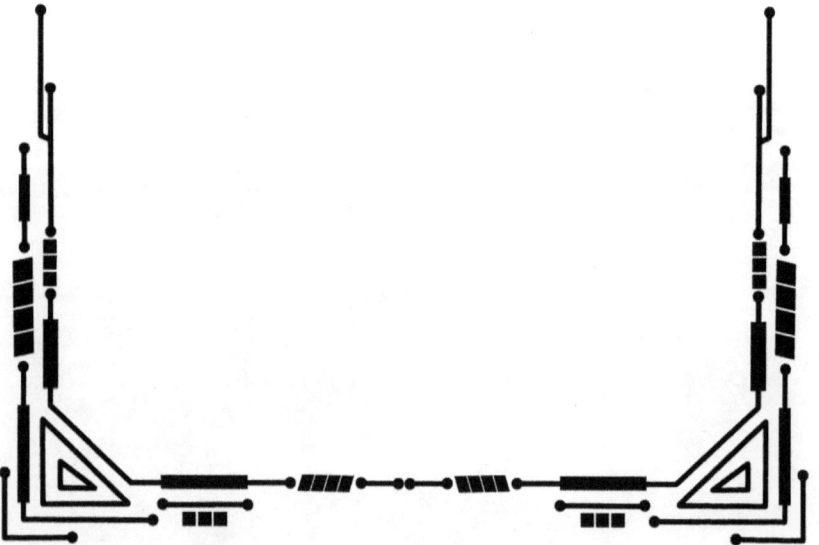

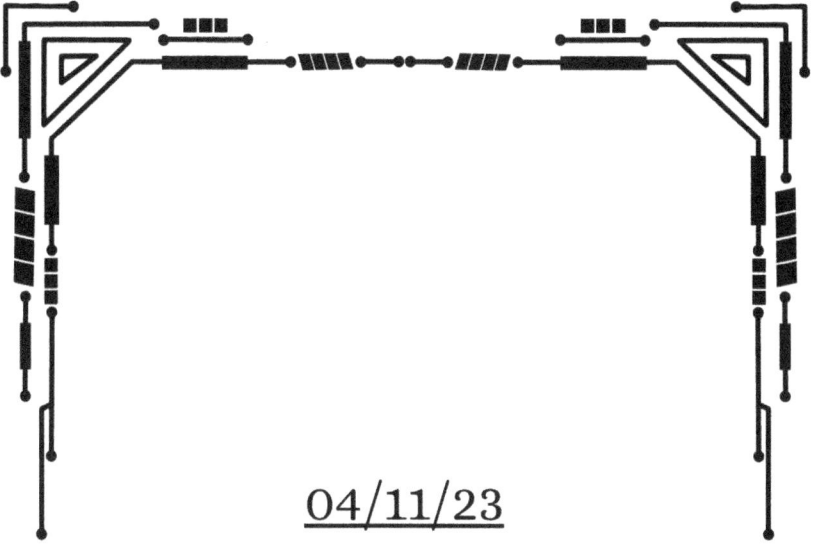

<u>04/11/23</u>

down at the river
fish and snakes and turtles live
i live in a house

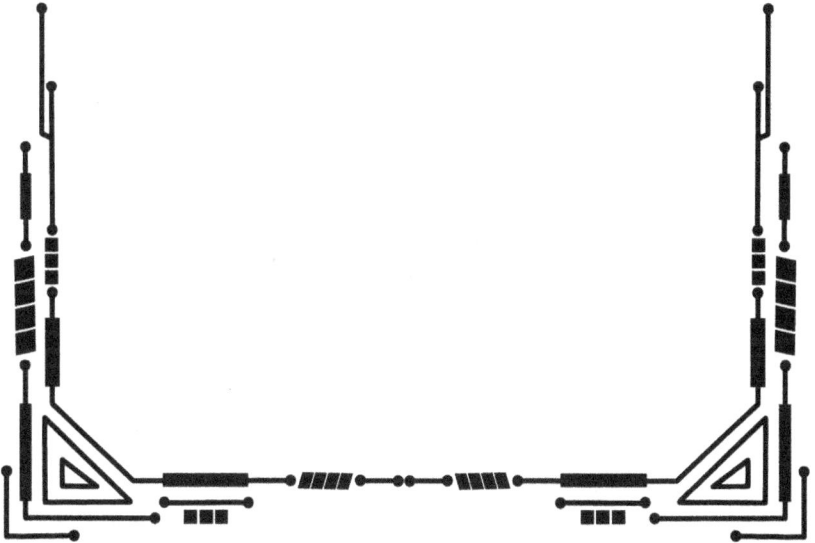

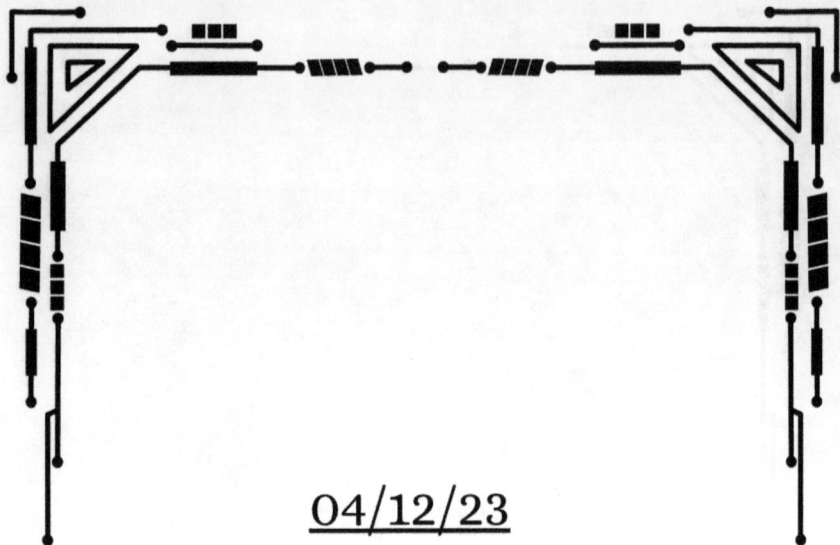

<u>04/12/23</u>

in my neighborhood
smell the burning reefer smoke
and barbeque sauce

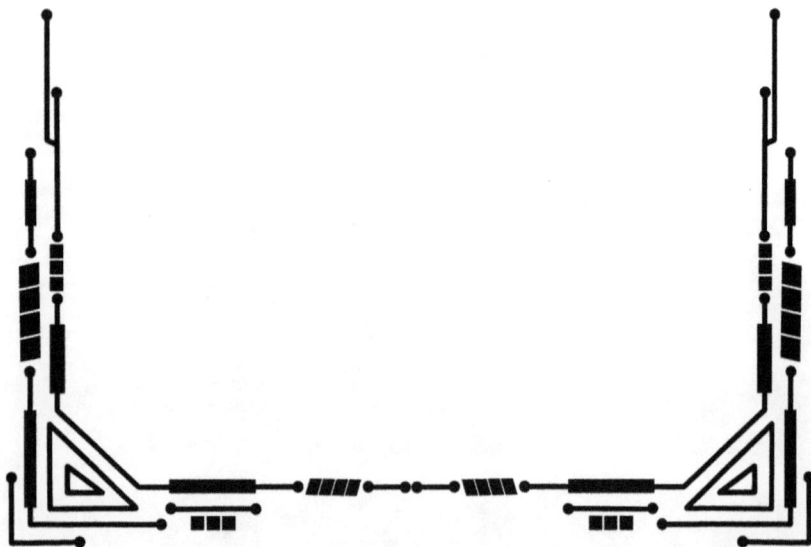

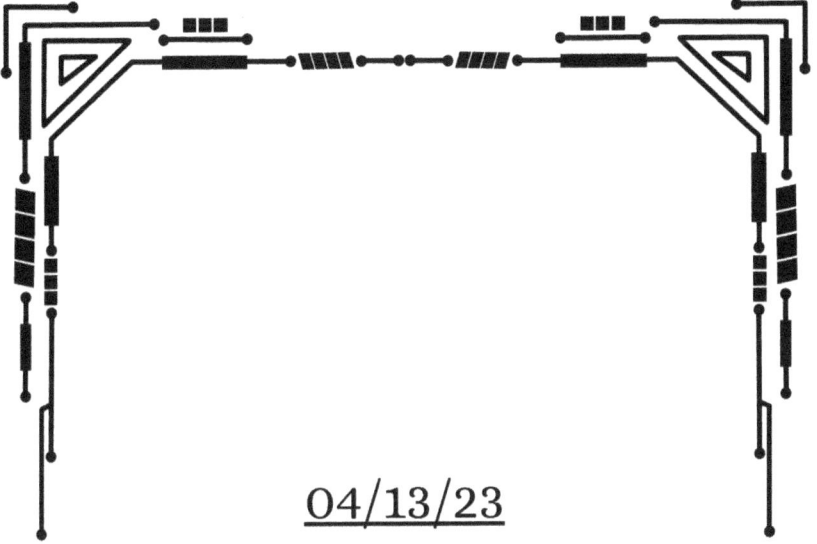

<u>04/13/23</u>

lofting aroma
tempting me with cookie pie
resist temptation

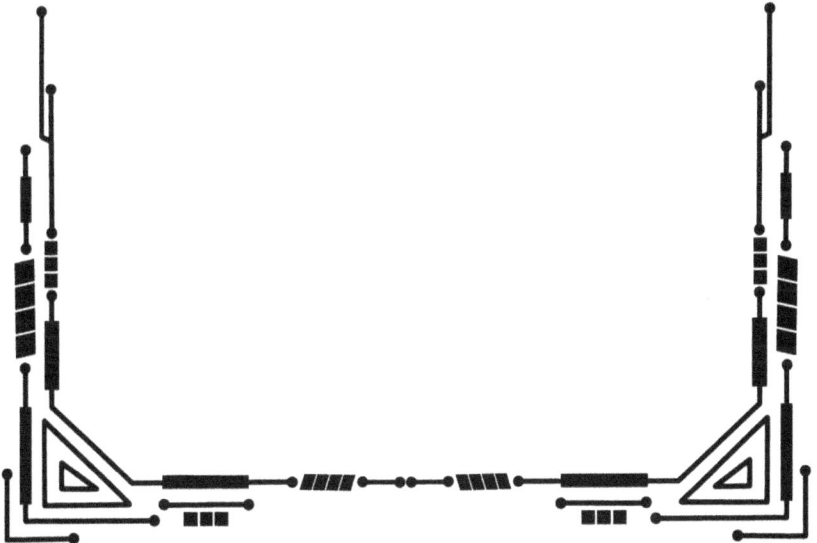

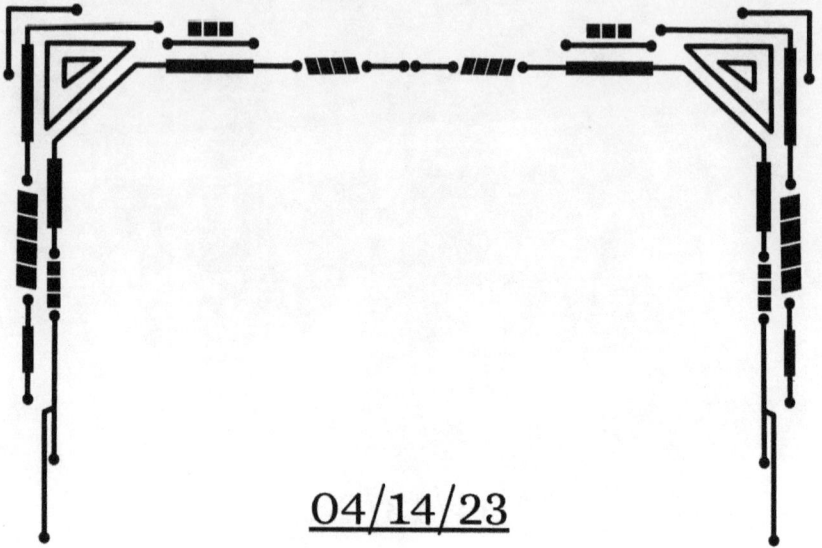

<u>04/14/23</u>

wood metal concrete
styrofoam paper plastic
composite resin

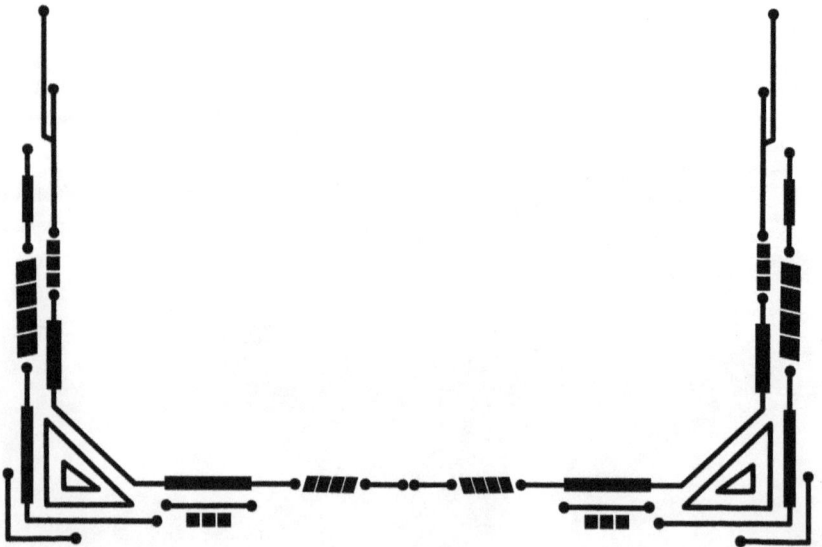

<u>04/15/23</u>

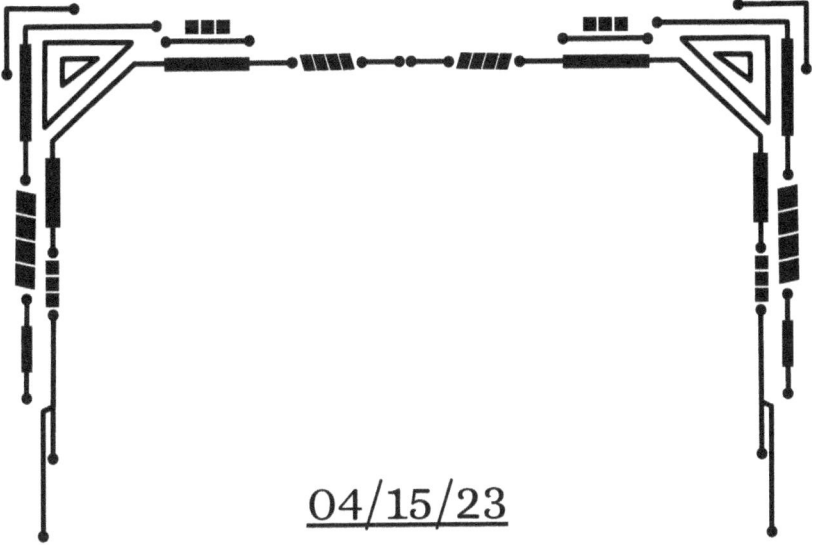

turning the pages
writing the words that i think
small dog shaped balloon

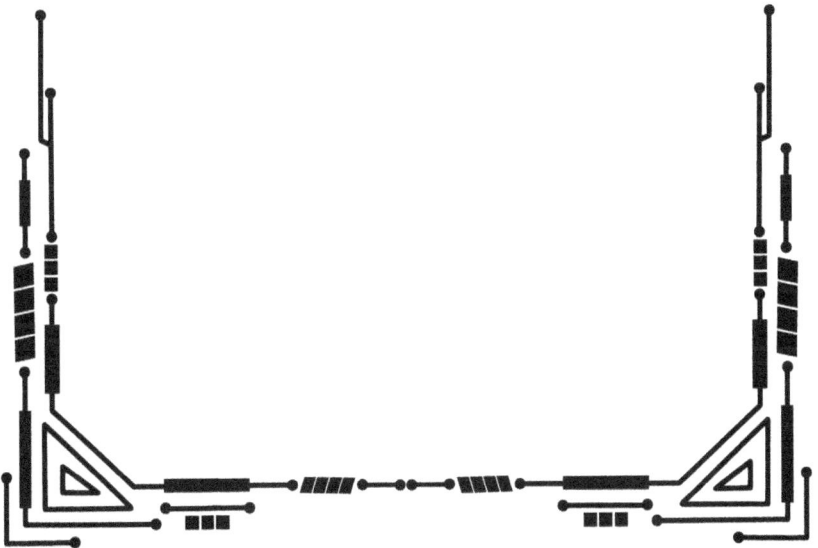

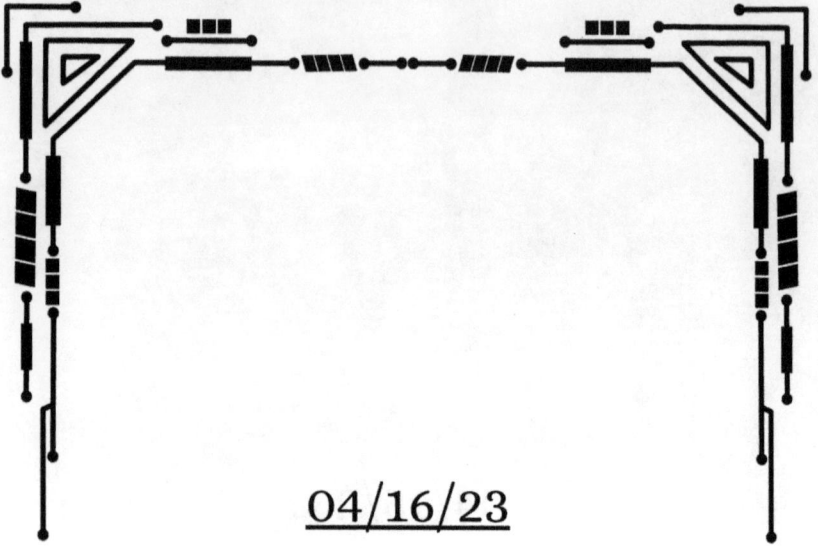

<u>04/16/23</u>

as we walk downstream
looking back to reminisce
a moment upstream

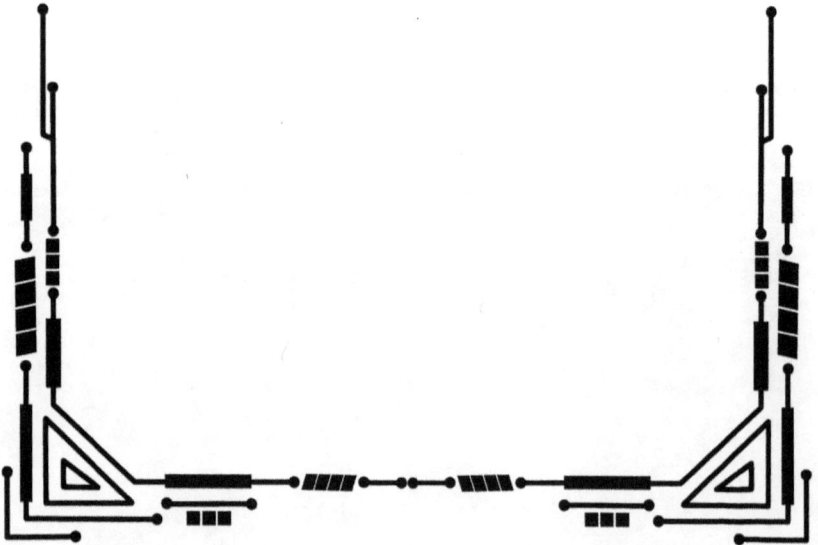

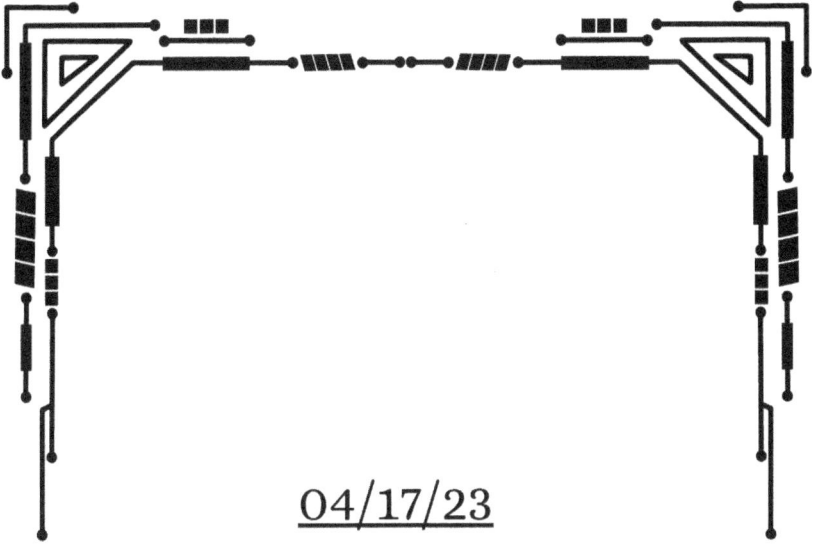

<u>04/17/23</u>

peel off the little
tamper evident sticker
and tamper with it

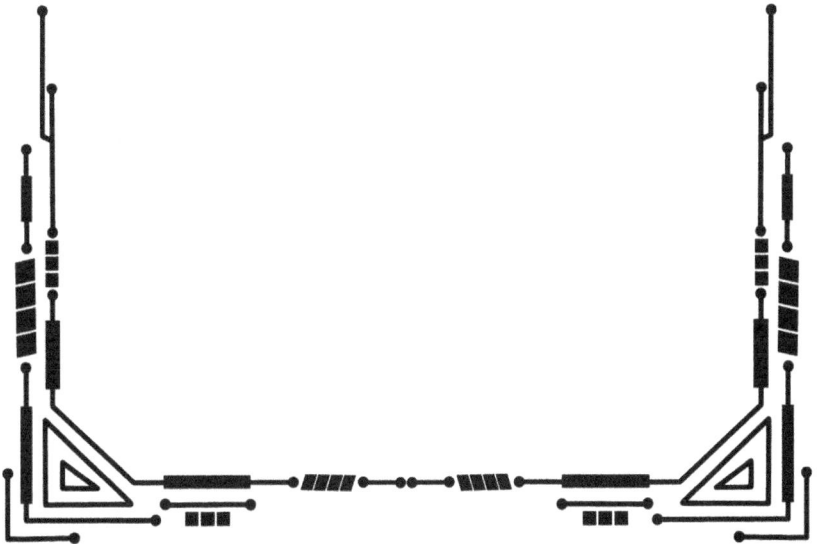

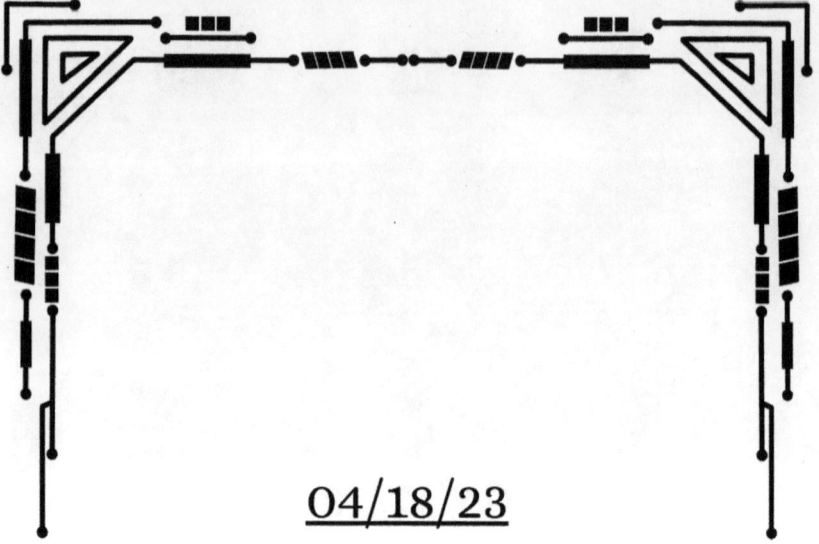

<u>04/18/23</u>

mad as a hatter
weeping in a willow tree
happy as a clam

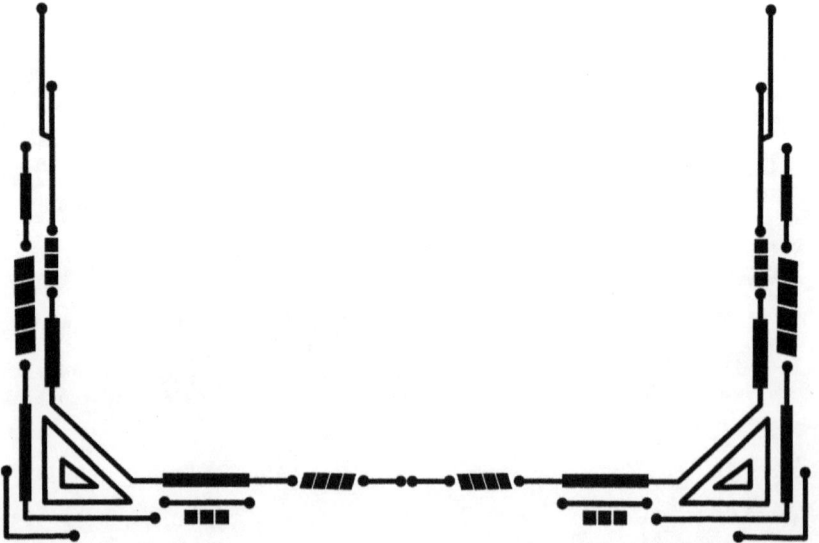

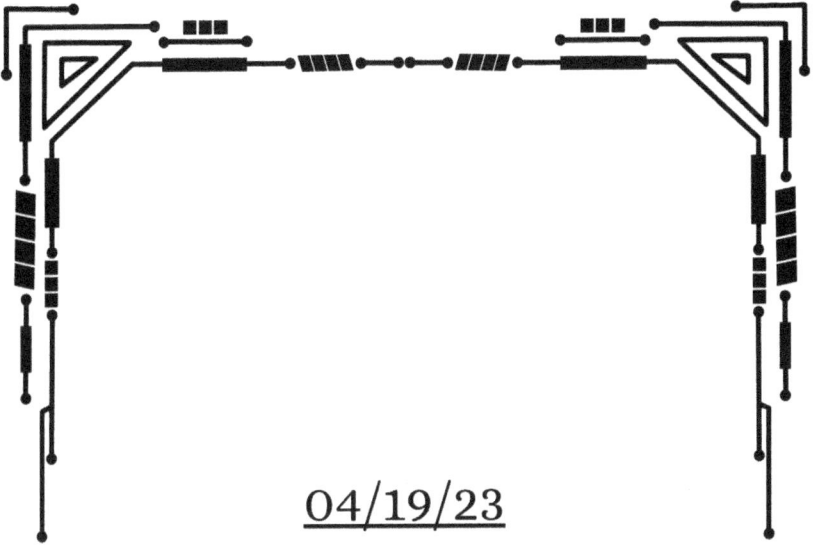

04/19/23

need more sleep today
i don't want to go to work
but i guess i will

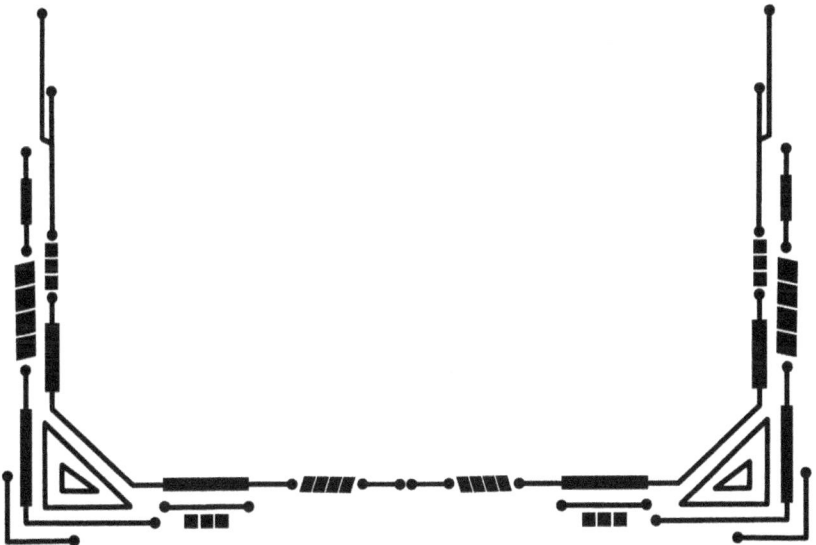

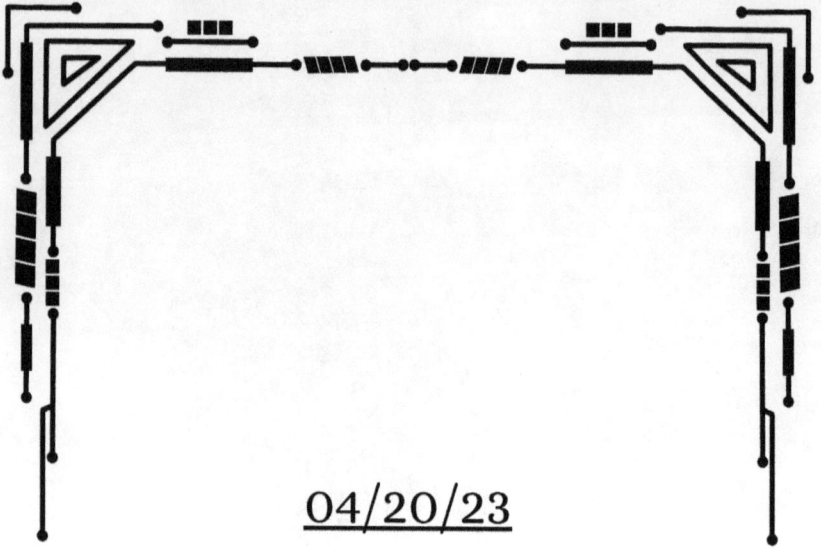

<u>04/20/23</u>

it's four twenty day
the cake is already baked
i will be later

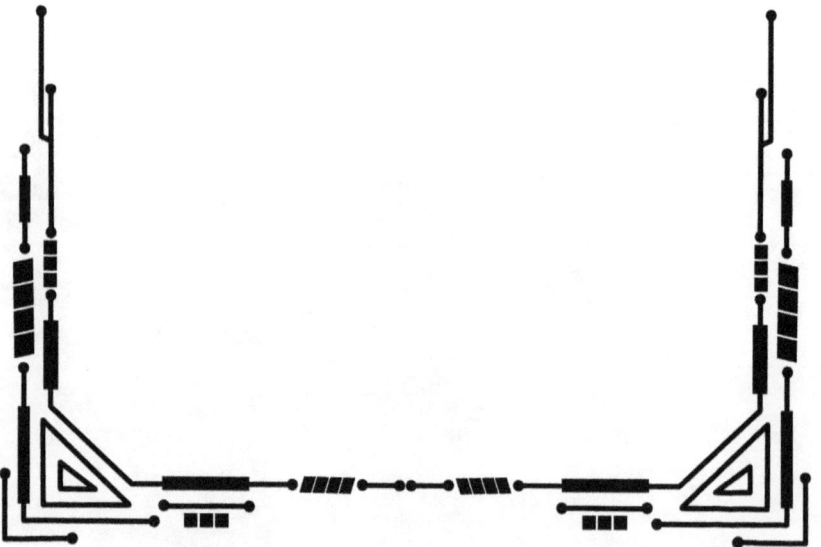

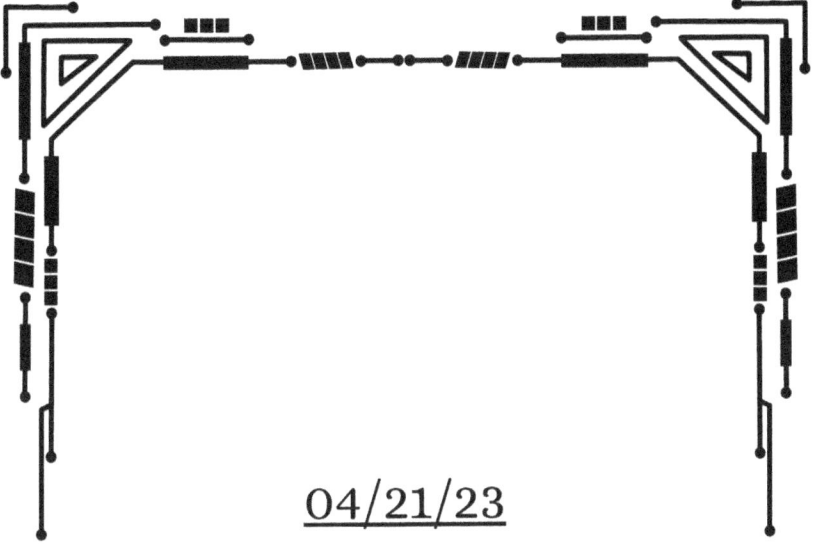

<u>04/21/23</u>

i'm so tired today
not sleeping so well lately
i want cereal

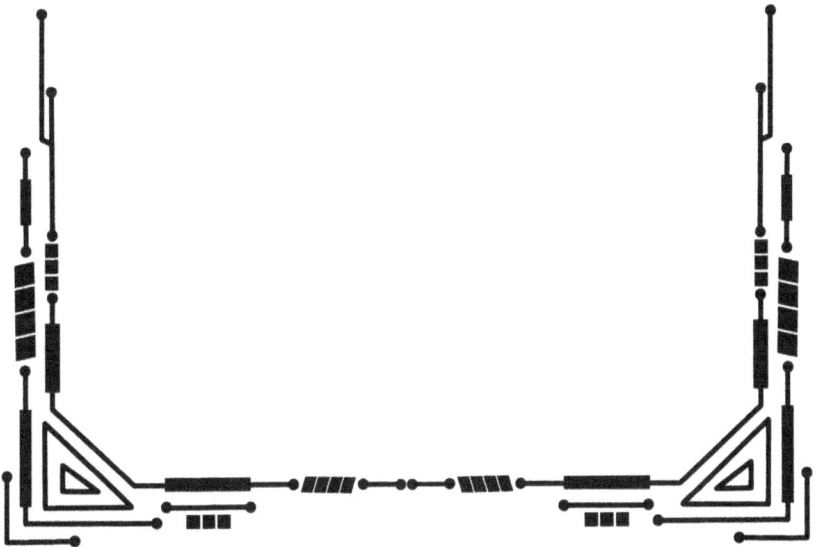

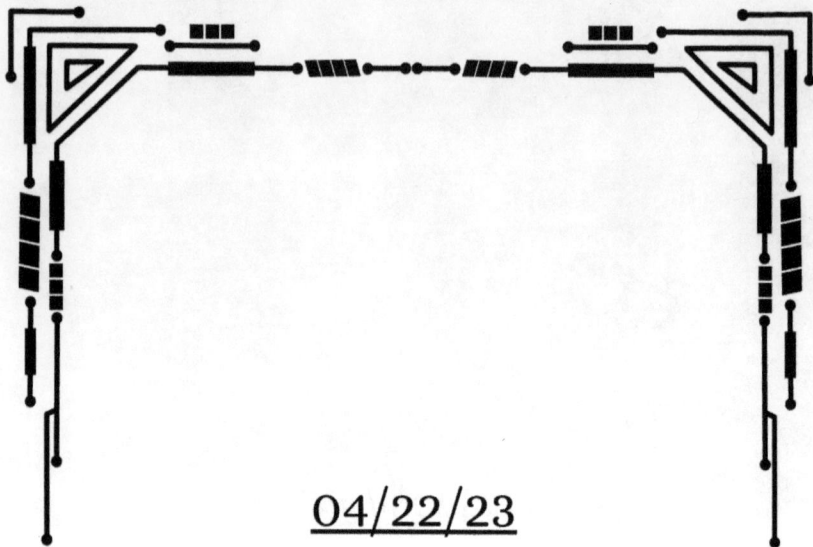

<u>04/22/23</u>

degrees of murder
and the cakes have all been poked
farewell for now meow

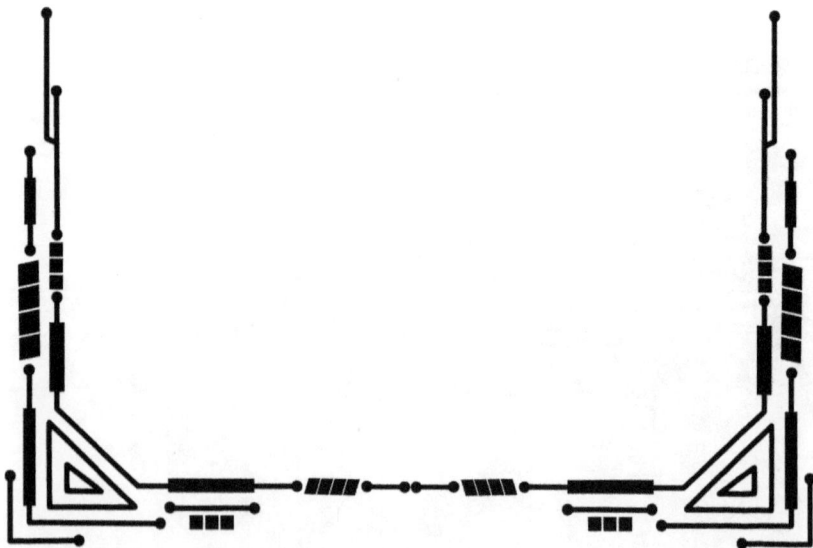

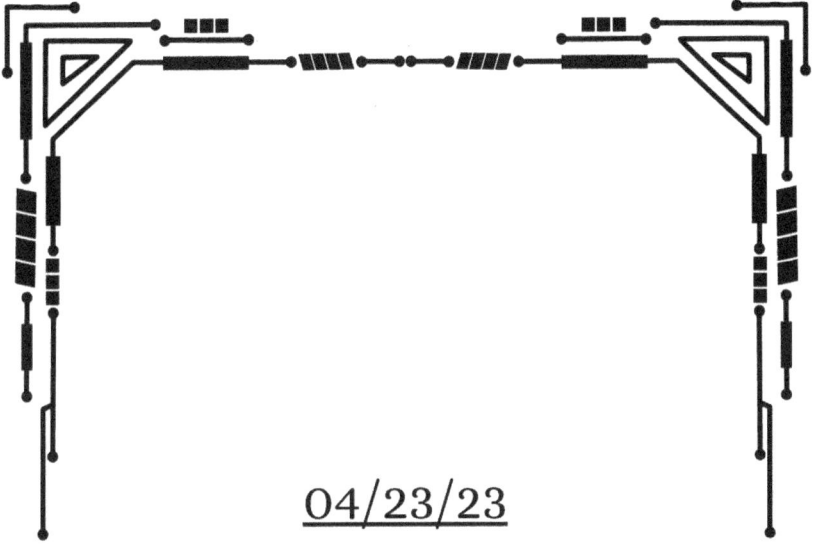

<u>04/23/23</u>

bacon dill swiss melt
only one decision left
spatula whisk tongs

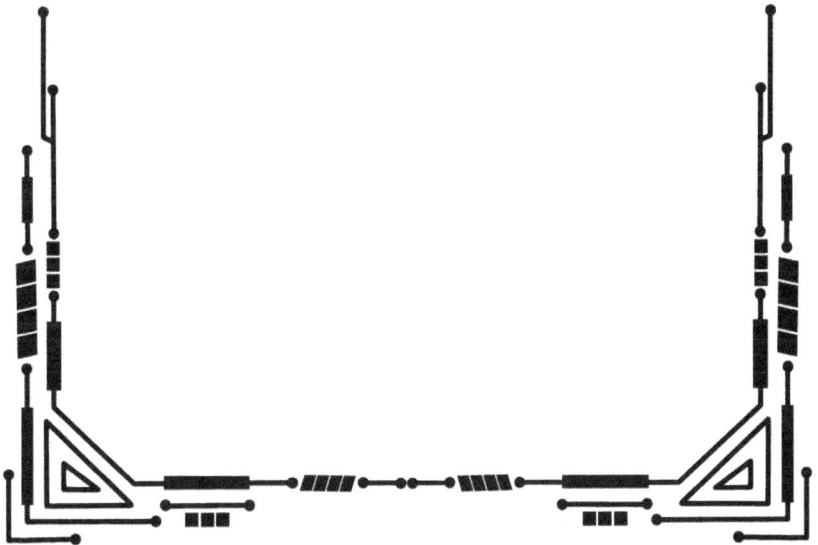

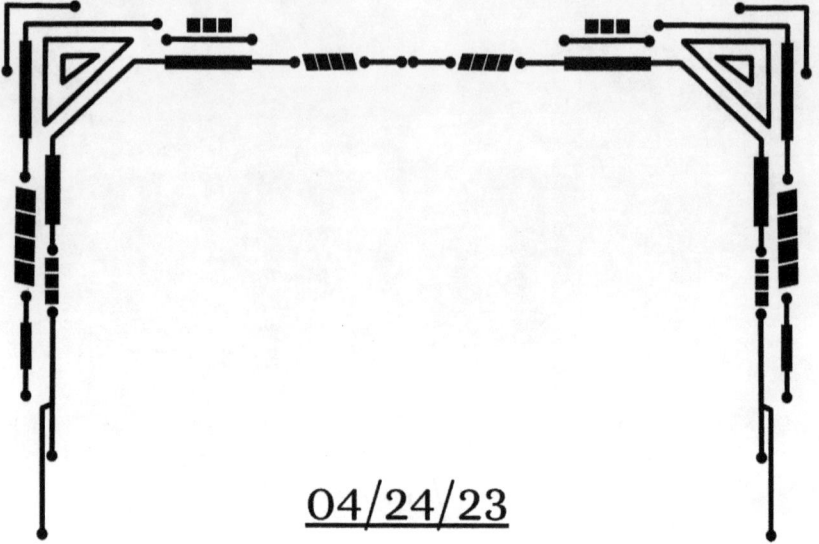

<u>04/24/23</u>

normal is changing
we all need a little weird
maybe more than that

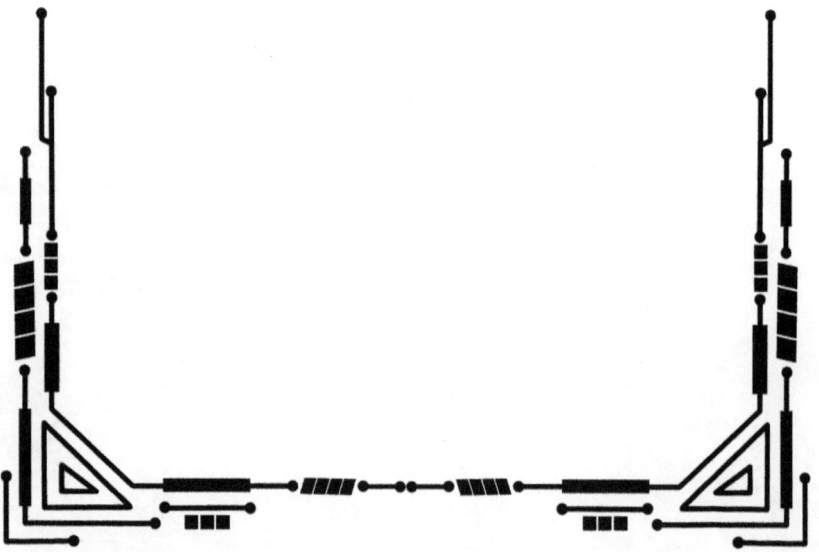

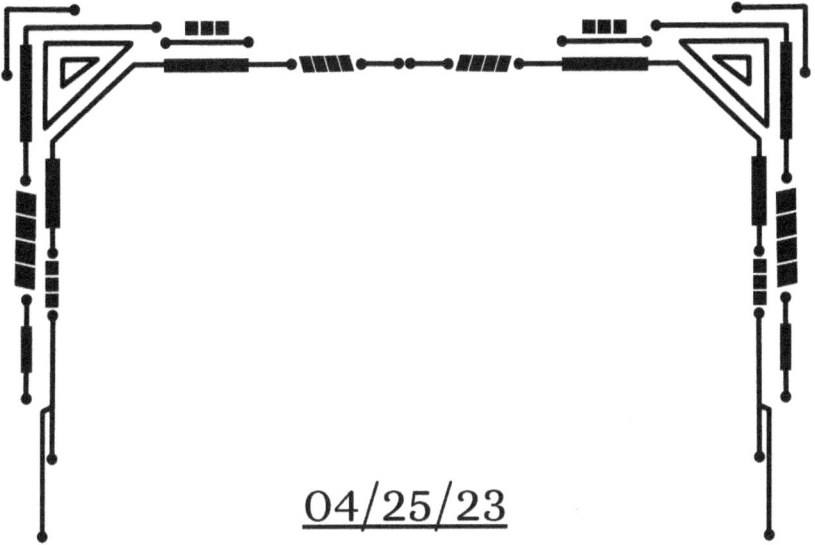

<u>04/25/23</u>

cars and trucks and bikes
make a boring poem with wheels
rolling down the street

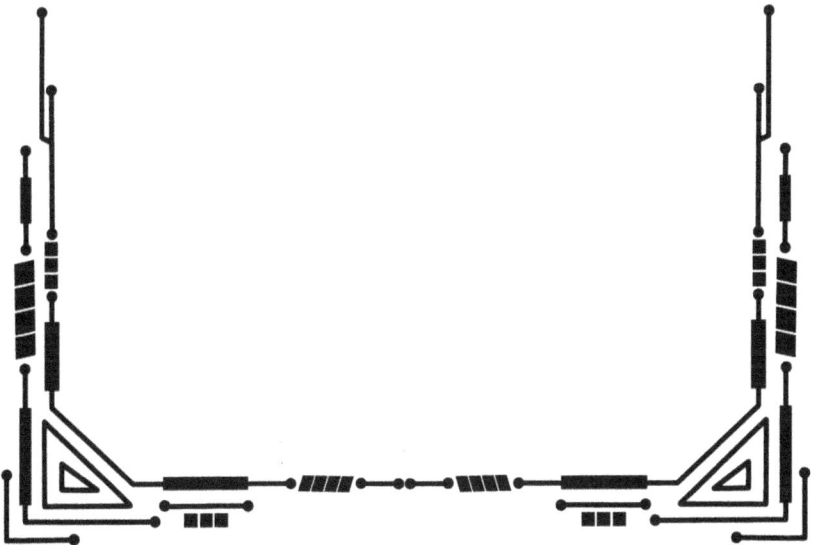

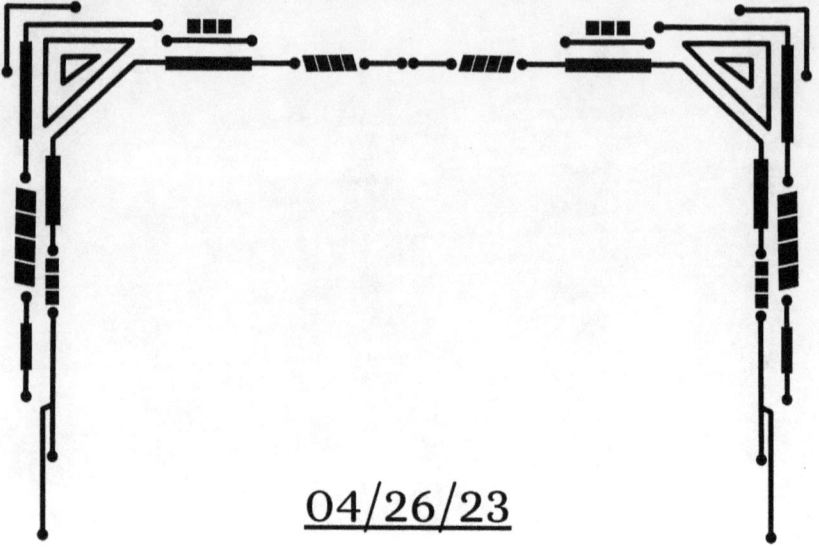

<u>04/26/23</u>

it's expensive here
i don't have enough money
for the good coffee

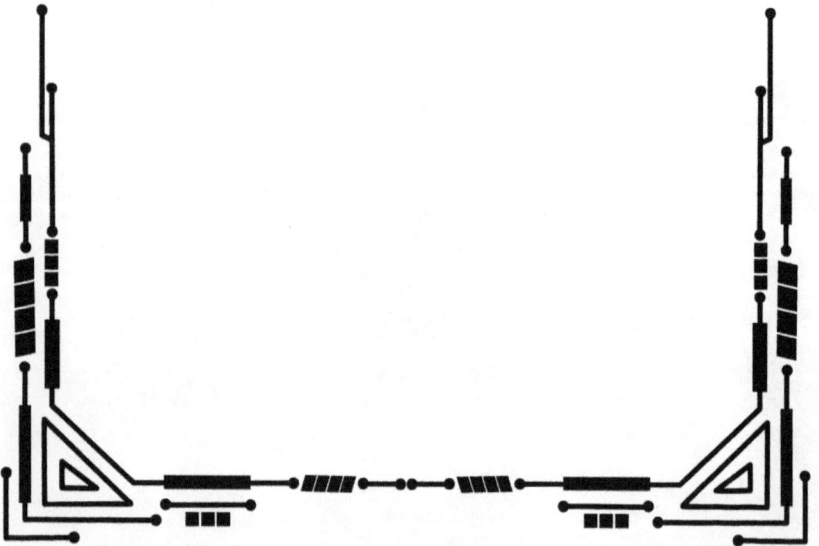

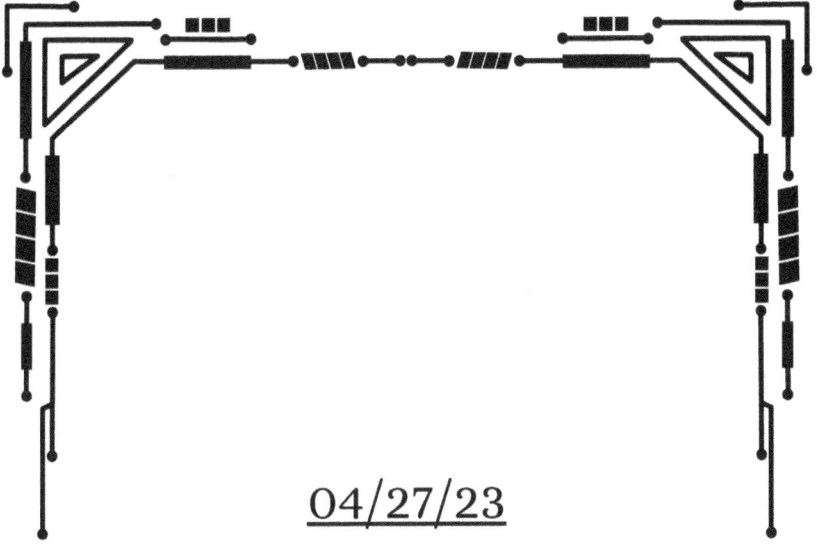

<u>04/27/23</u>

you could eat a bug
i'm not saying that you should
just saying you could

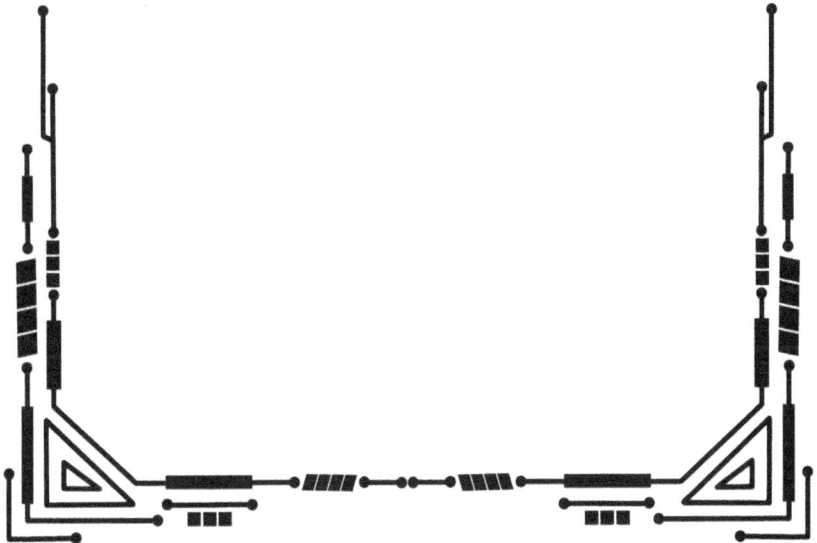

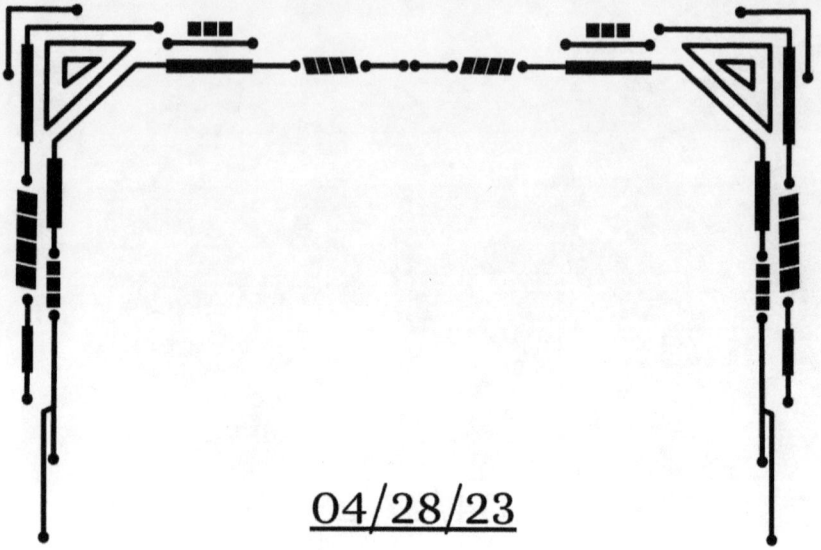

<u>04/28/23</u>

no thank you morning
eggs and pancakes make me tired
and i just woke up

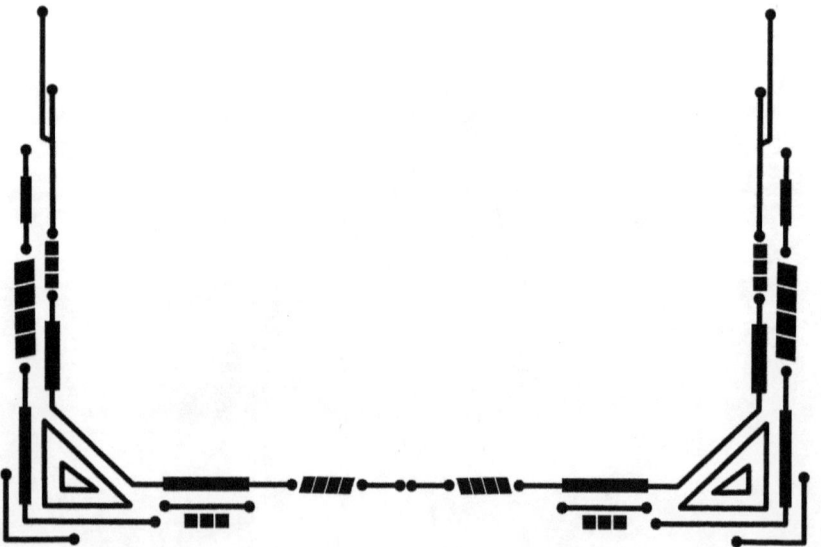

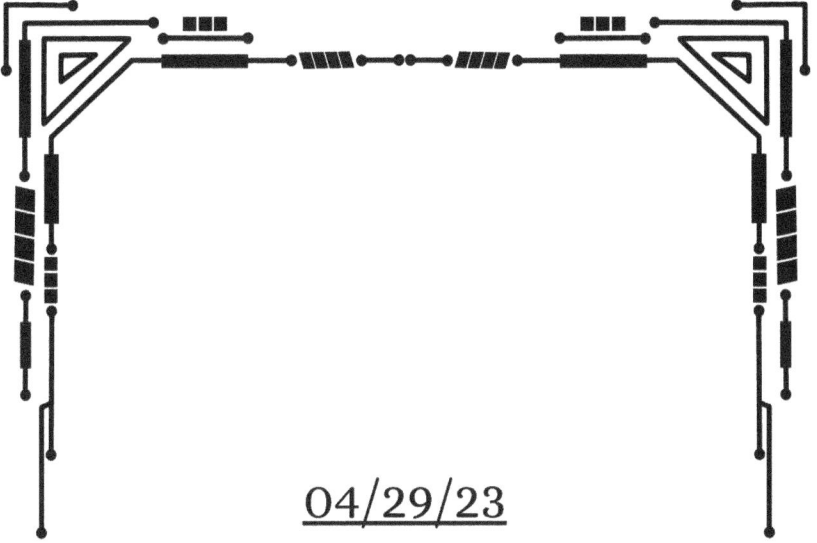

<u>04/29/23</u>

dumb things make dumb poems
and i hate this already
have to keep going

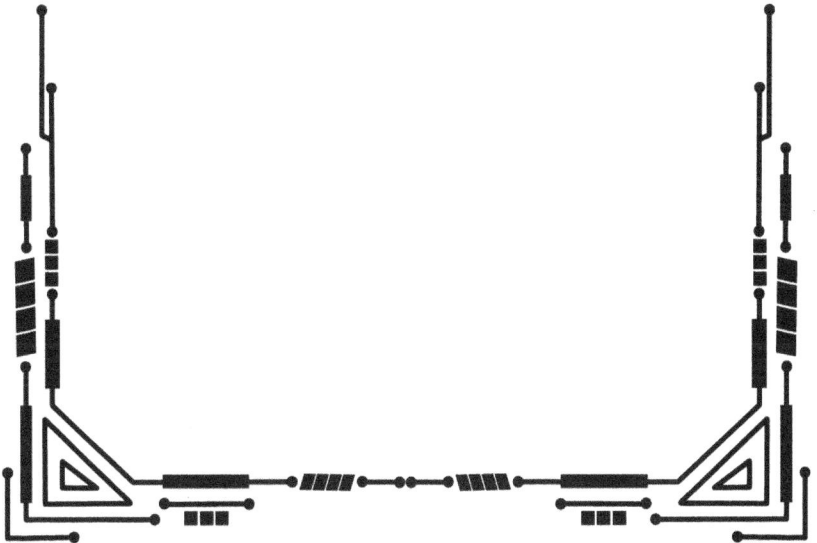

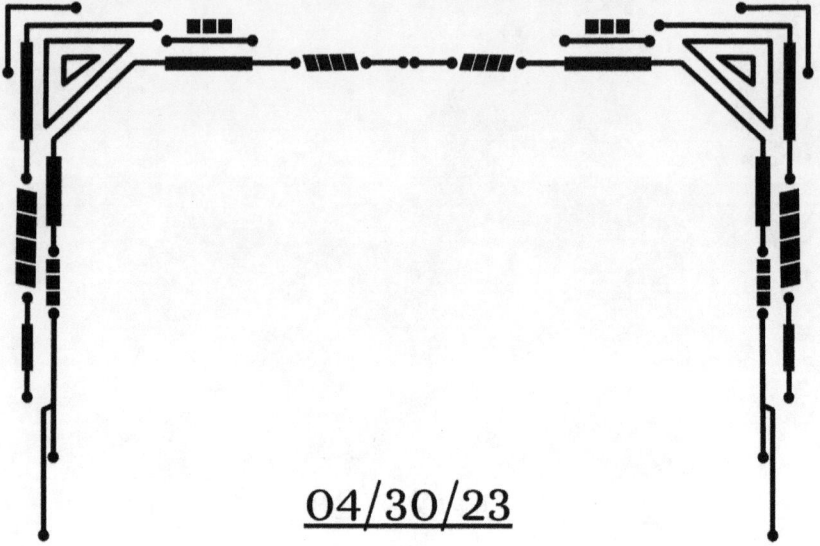

<u>04/30/23</u>

doesn't it seem strange
he blows his nose i suppose
and sneezes freely

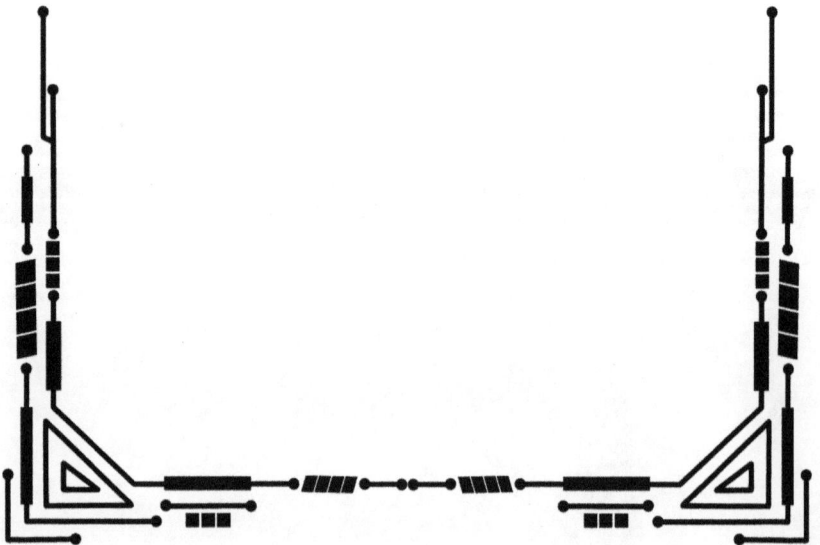

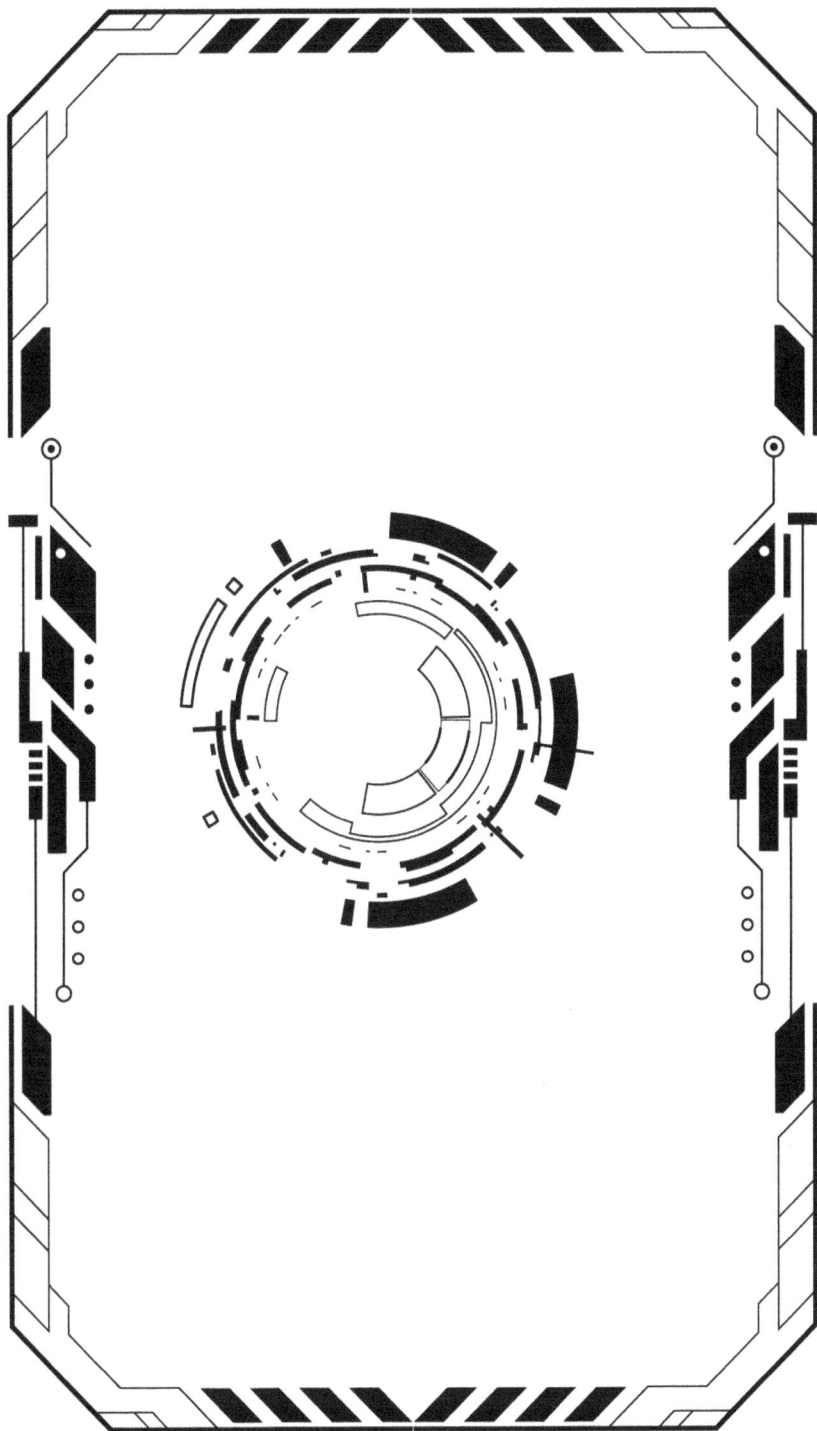

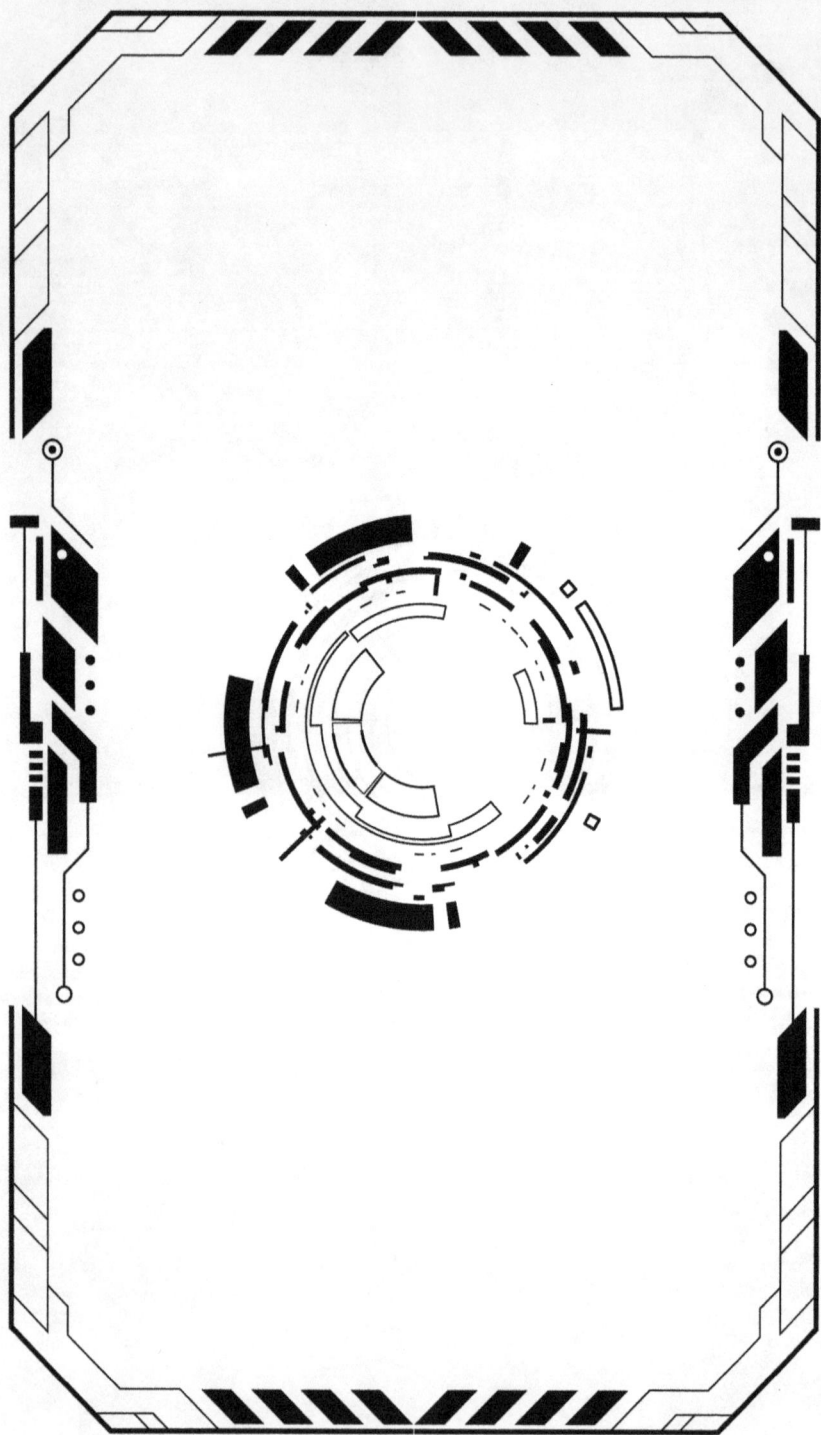

<u>05/01/23</u>

think about breathing
think about how you did that
think about thinking

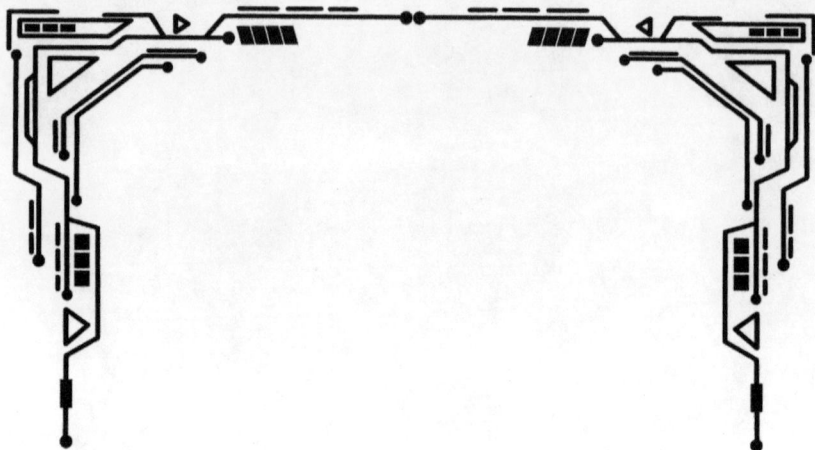

<u>05/02/23</u>

i don't like traffic
i don't like people either
both are annoying

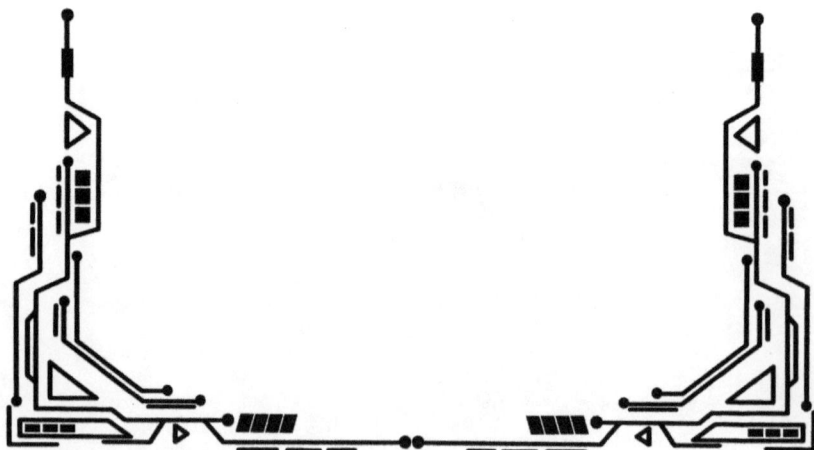

<u>05/03/23</u>

the building is brick
the tree is a conifer
the garbage can smells

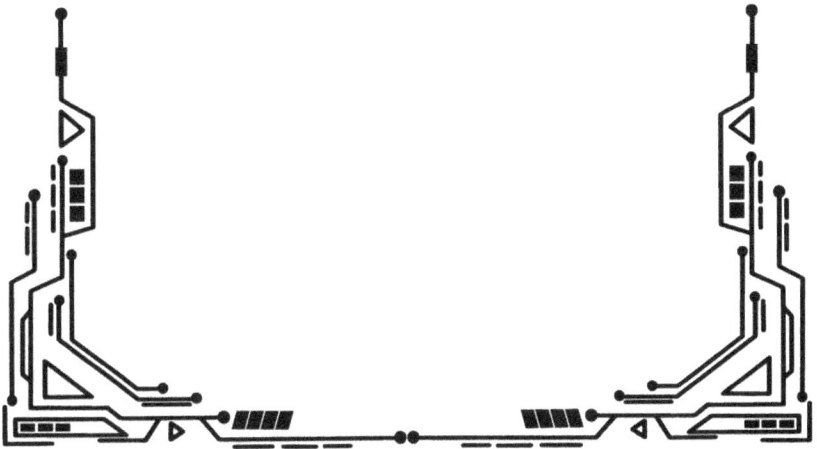

05/04/23

the sky is cloudy
now i hope it rains today
getting wet in may

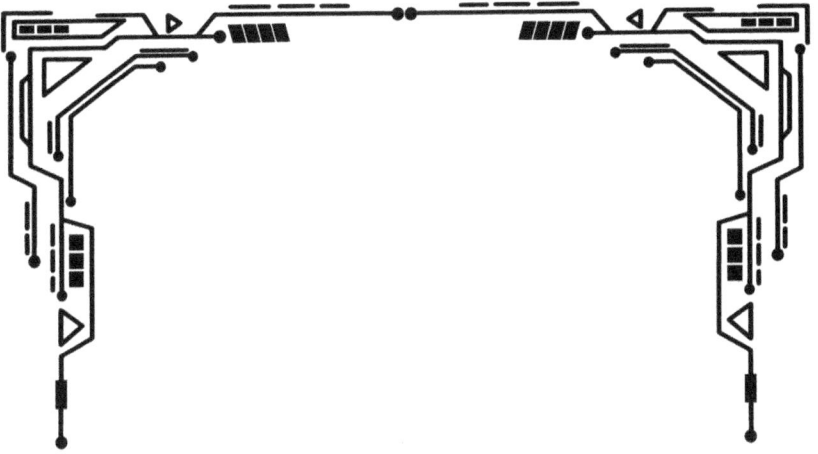

<u>05/05/23</u>

sipping hot coffee
on a cool rainy morning
no milk or sugar

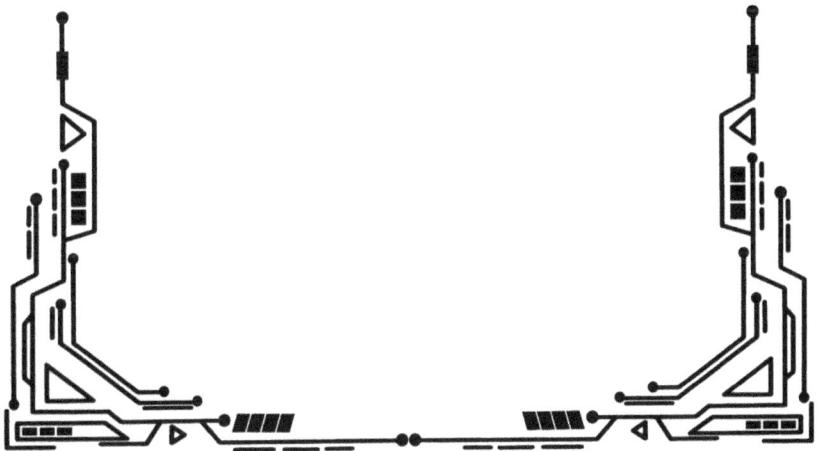

<u>05/06/23</u>

dreaming of the house
again it shows up often
different people though

<u>05/07/23</u>

haikus are boring
gonna write them anyway
my pen fell asleep

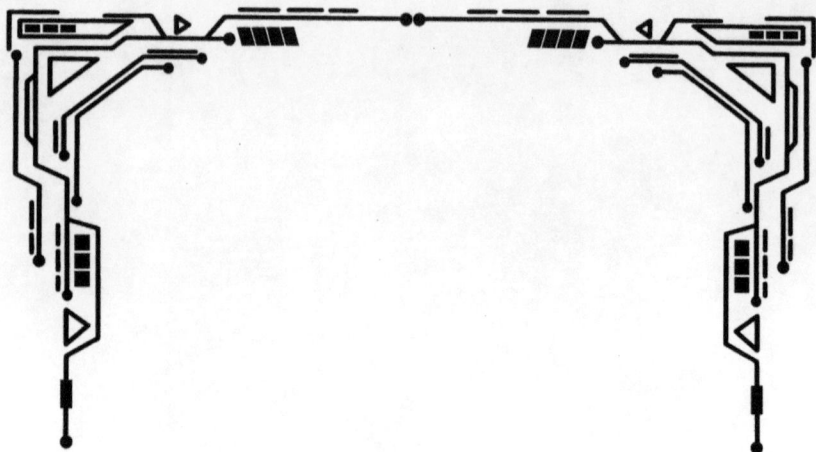

<u>05/08/23</u>

post it sharpie mouse
these are things here on my desk
black tape dispenser

<u>05/09/23</u>

so many boxes
i need a bigger office
and a better chair

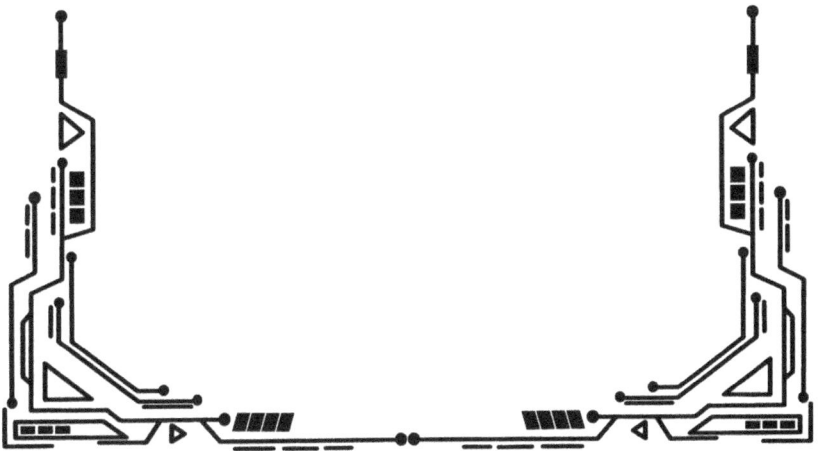

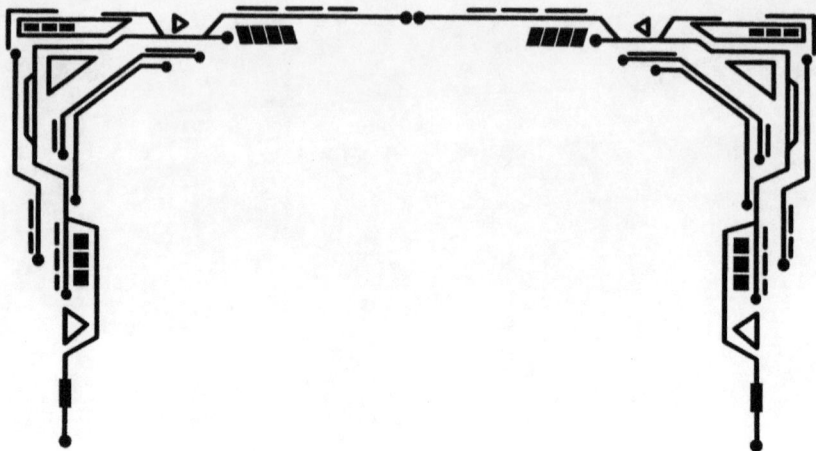

05/10/23

lots of hail last night
a symphony of damage
led by gravity

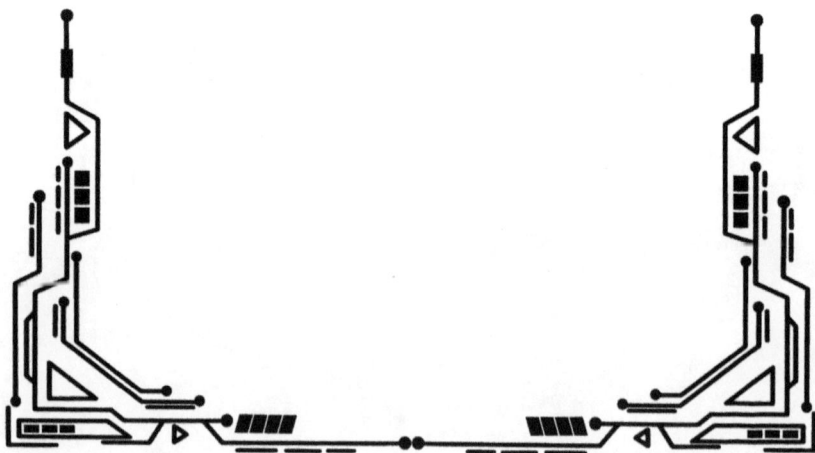

<u>05/11/23</u>

it's thursday morning
five eleven twenty three
the coffee is cold

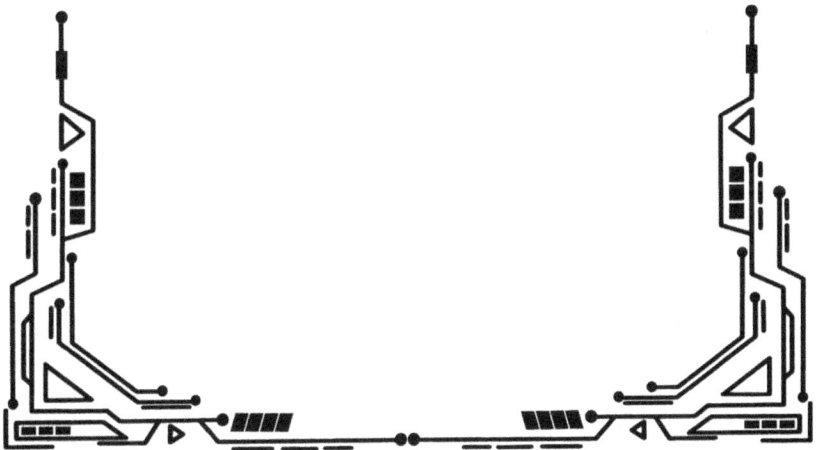

05/12/23

moths will find the light
crickets chirp with rain outside
sneak under the door

<u>05/13/23</u>

satellite tv
from outer space to the dish
then into your brain

<u>05/14/23</u>

some ibuprofen
a multi vitamin and
coffee for breakfast

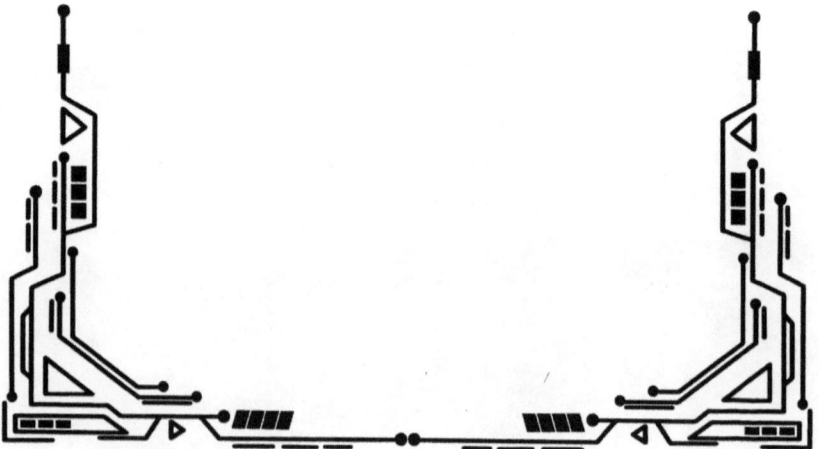

<u>05/15/23</u>

what is that damn noise
i don't want a cheeseburger
fuck you chickadee

<u>05/16/23</u>

now is the time for
smoking a joint on the porch
i just need a porch

<u>05/17/23</u>

plastic wrap bubbles
styrofoam packing peanuts
crumpled kraft paper

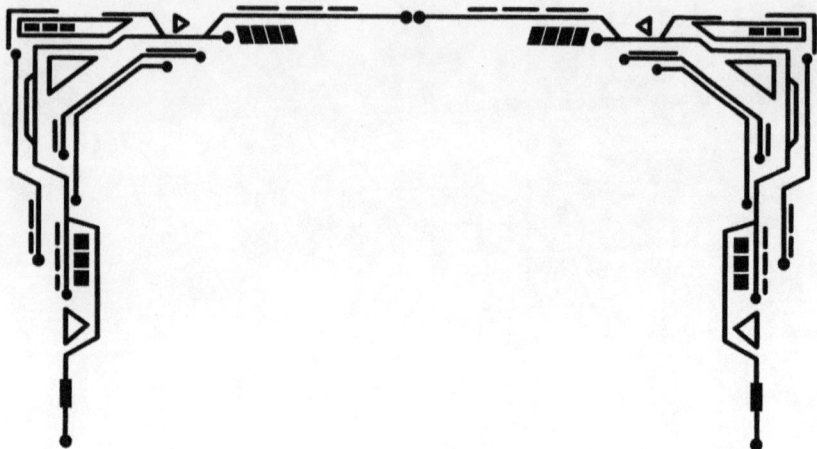

05/18/23

not hungry just yet
what do i want for dinner
smoked salmon tacos

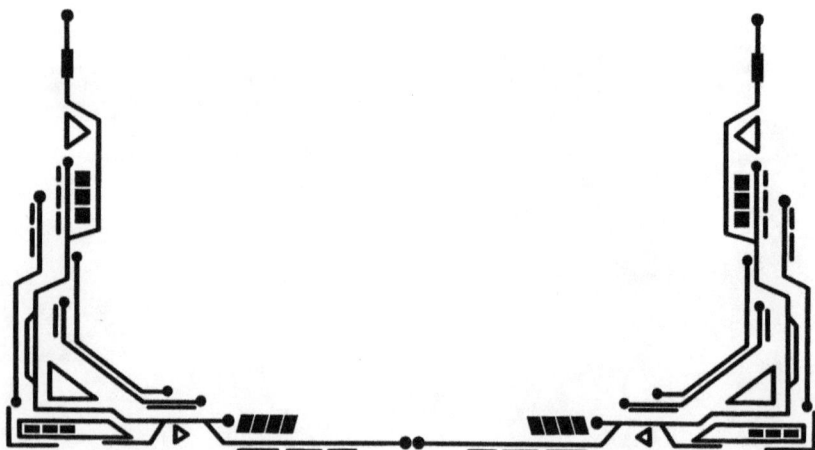

<u>05/19/23</u>

ai server farms
watching out for battle drones
this is the future

<u>05/20/23</u>

blu ray dvds
are much better than streaming
for picture and sound

<u>05/21/23</u>

it's all wet again
magical morning sunrise
down here on the farm

05/22/23

talk to the boss man
time to move on from this town
when summer is done

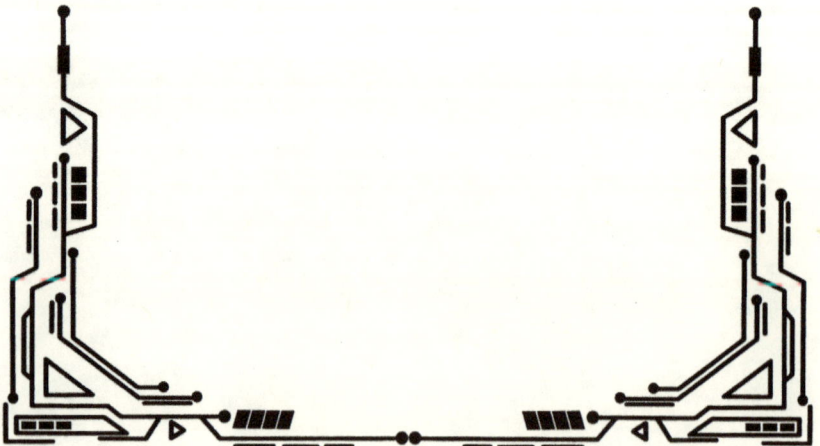

<u>05/23/23</u>

small plastic bottle
it is blue and it holds glue
sticky gorilla

<u>05/24/23</u>

tape measure races
pull it out to sixteen feet
and press the thumb lock

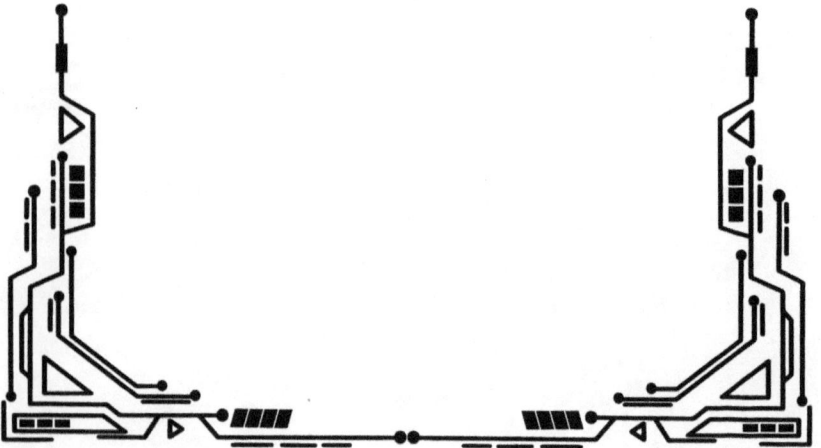

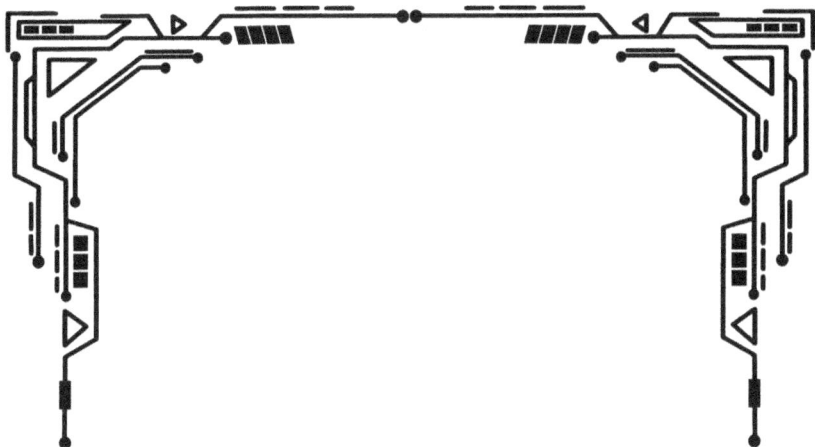

<u>05/25/23</u>

something isn't right
squirrels are walking backwards
acid in the rain

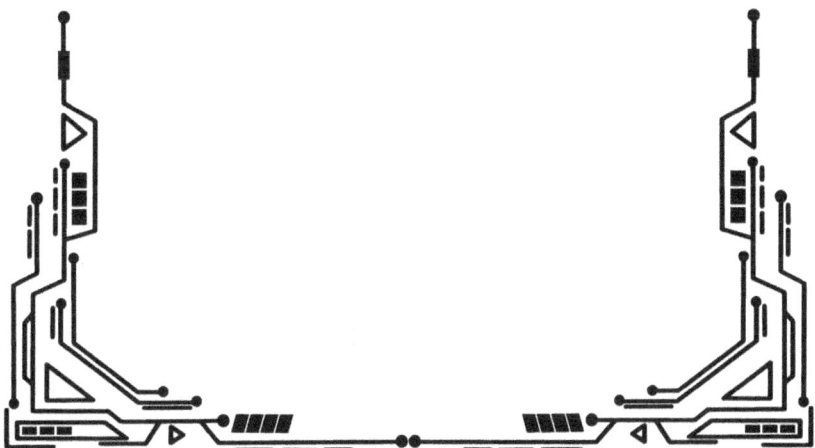

05/26/23

jimmy rode a bike
christopher had a skateboard
donny only walked

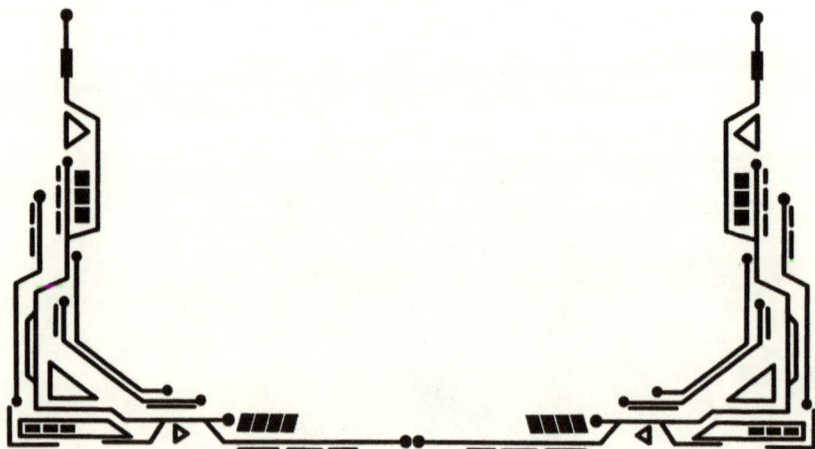

<u>05/27/23</u>

nine in the morning
the sun is out but it is
going to rain today

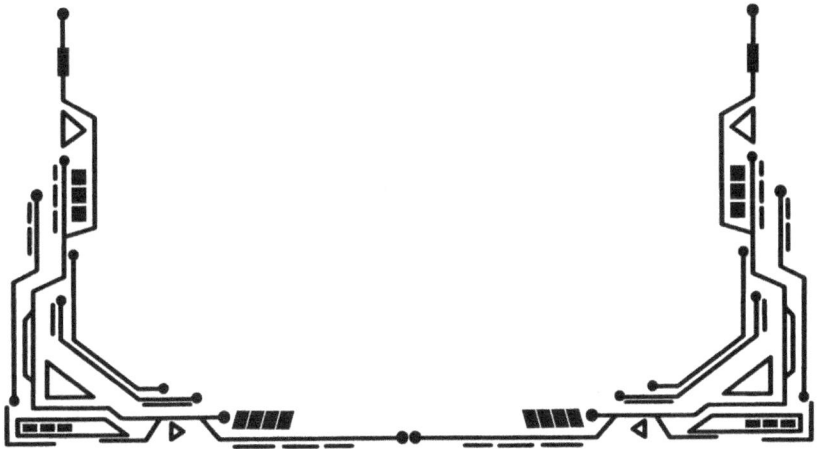

a box of boxes
confuses even the most
foxy of foxes

05/29/23

it's the end of may
the beginning of summer
is upon us now

05/30/23

lady with a dog
picked up the poop with a bag
but left the bag there

<u>05/31/23</u>

turn the page again
updating my resume
go somewhere else soon

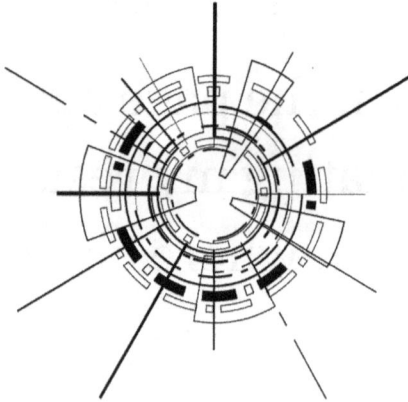

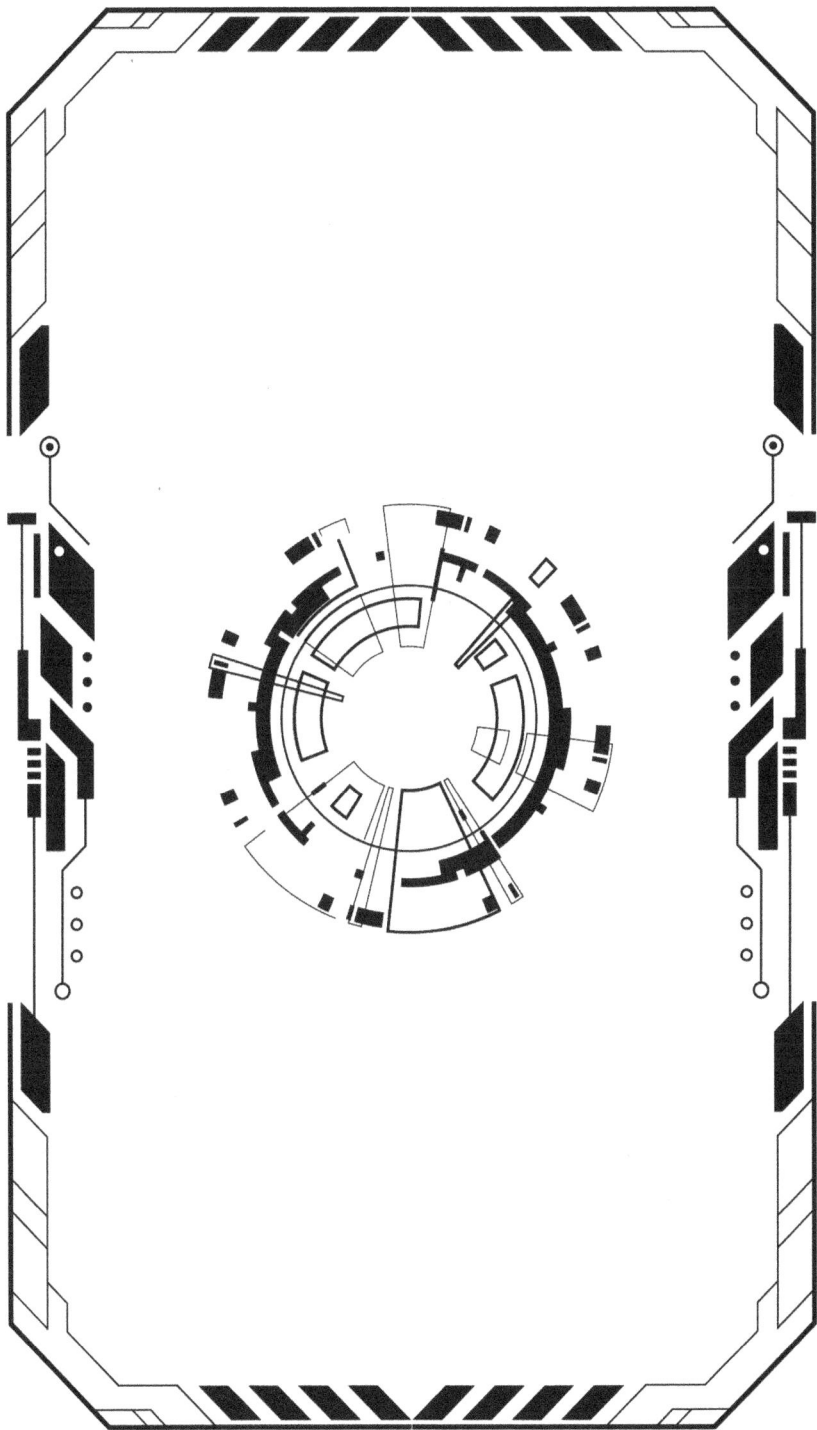

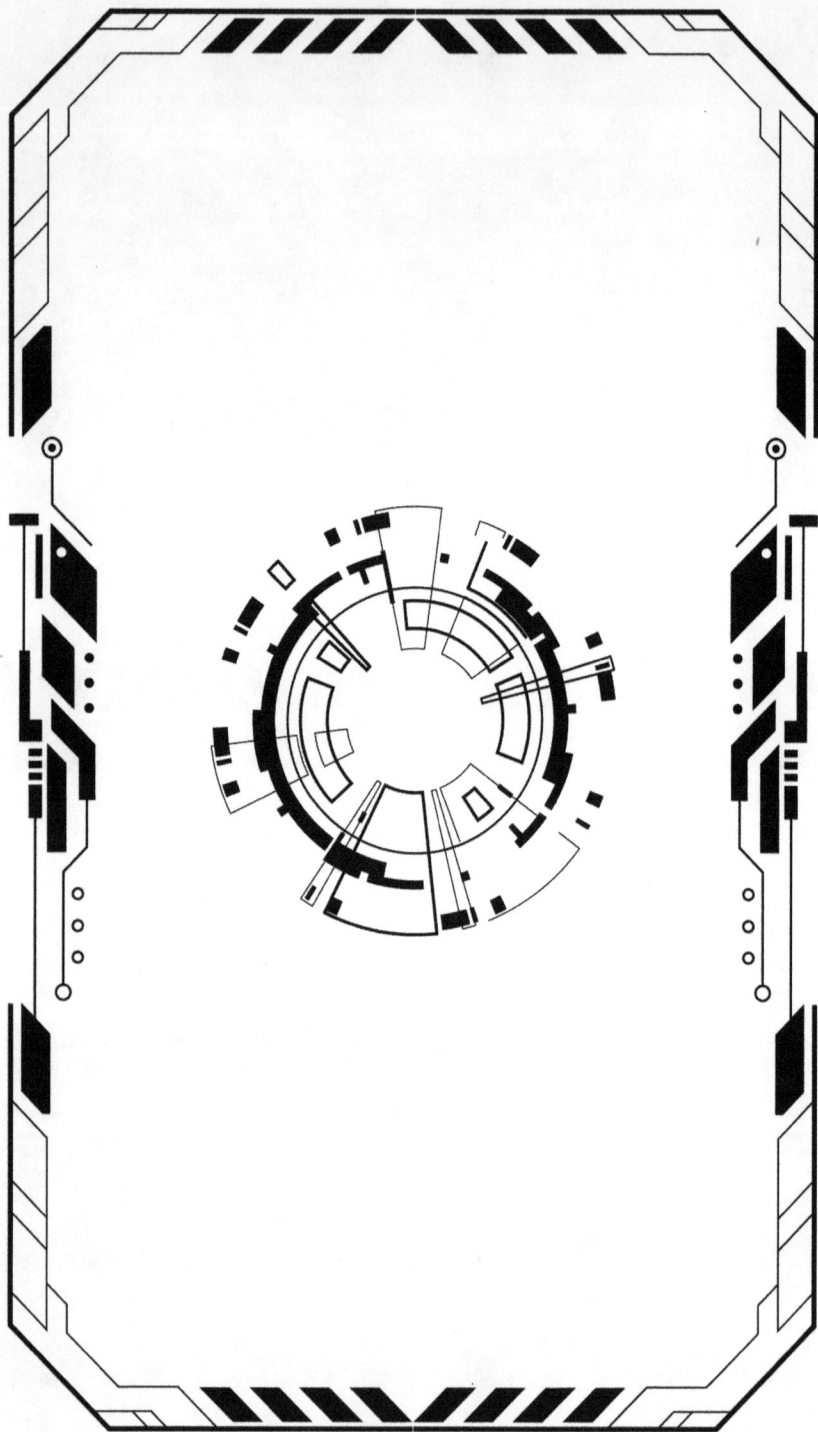

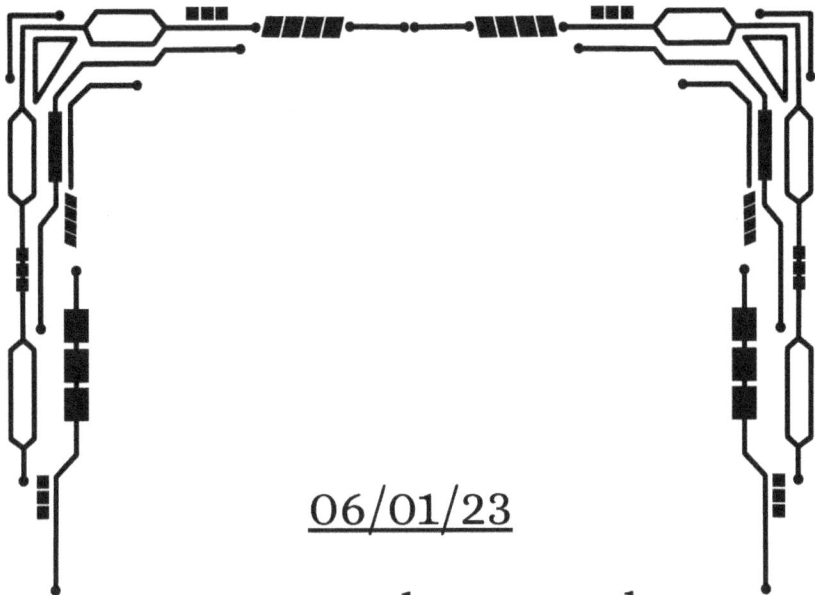

<u>06/01/23</u>

start another month
i'm already bored of this
a year of haikus

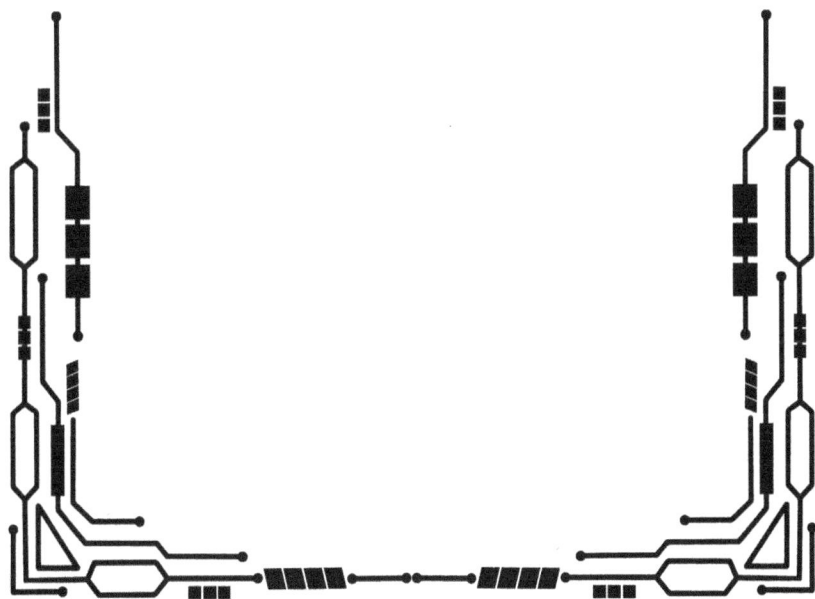

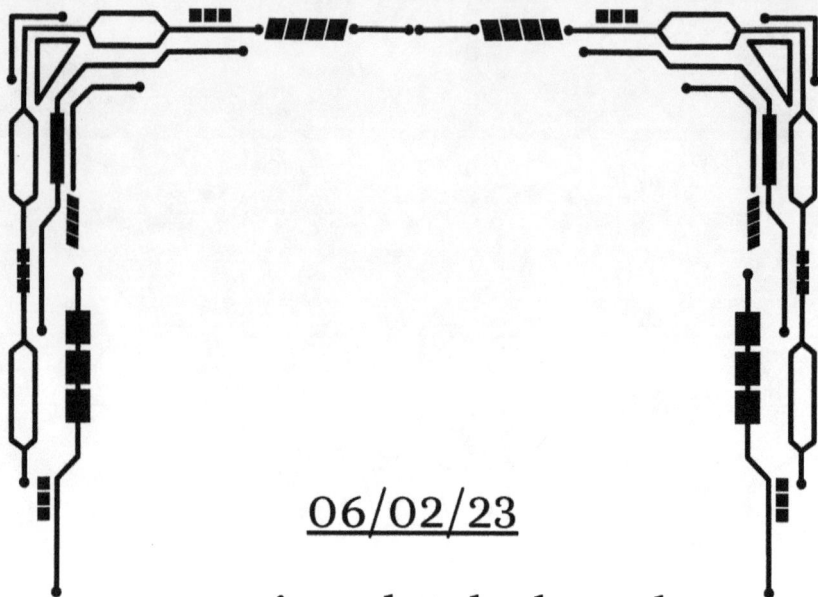

<u>06/02/23</u>

creeping the dark path
no one is safe in their tents
from the zombie crew

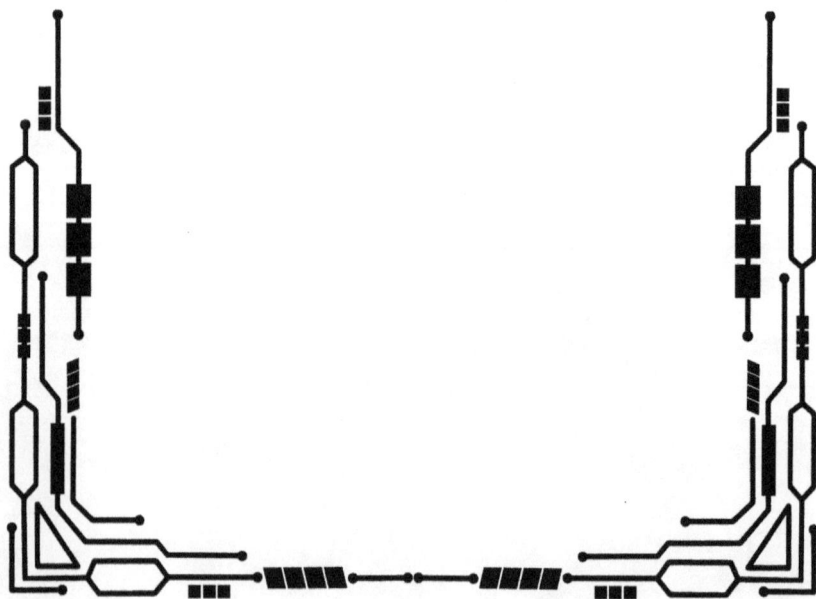

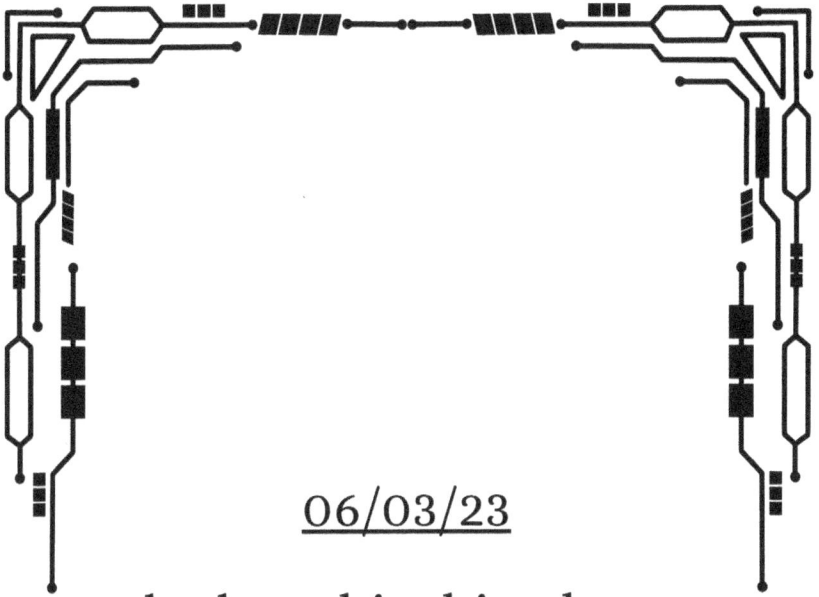

<u>06/03/23</u>

look at this thing here
squeaky and folded like an
origami mouse

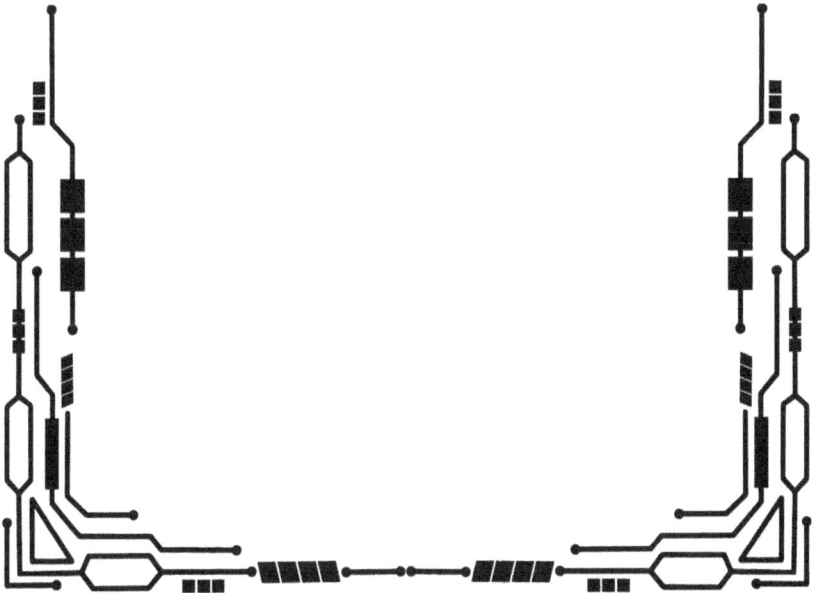

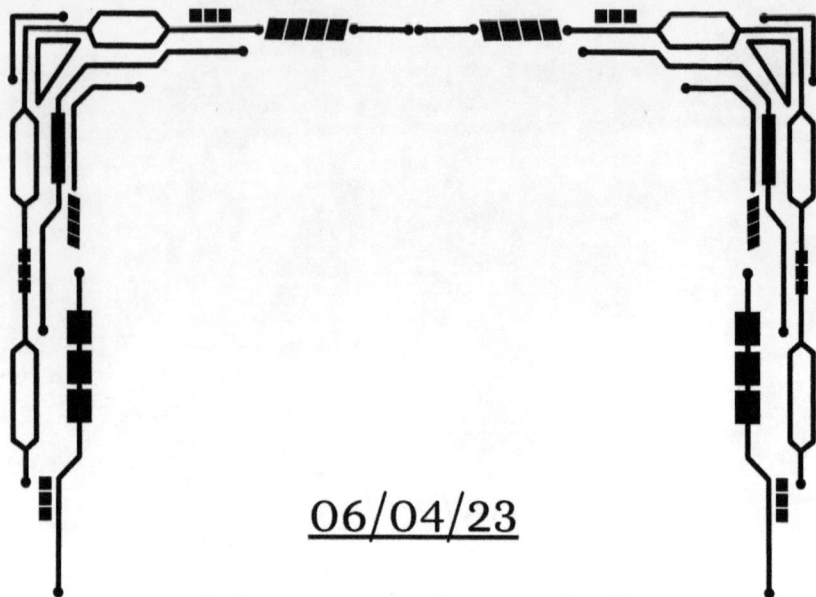

<u>06/04/23</u>

this one takes a left
at the gooseberry bushes
thirteen times a day

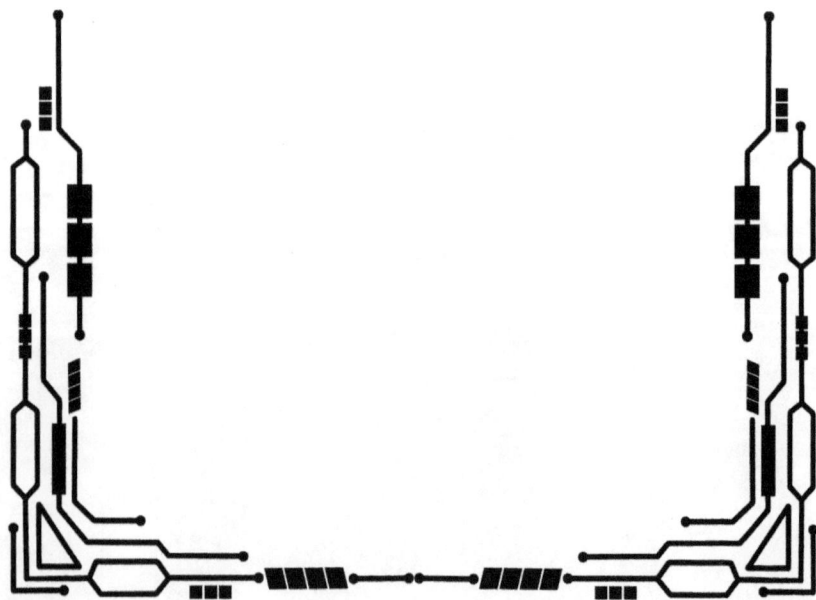

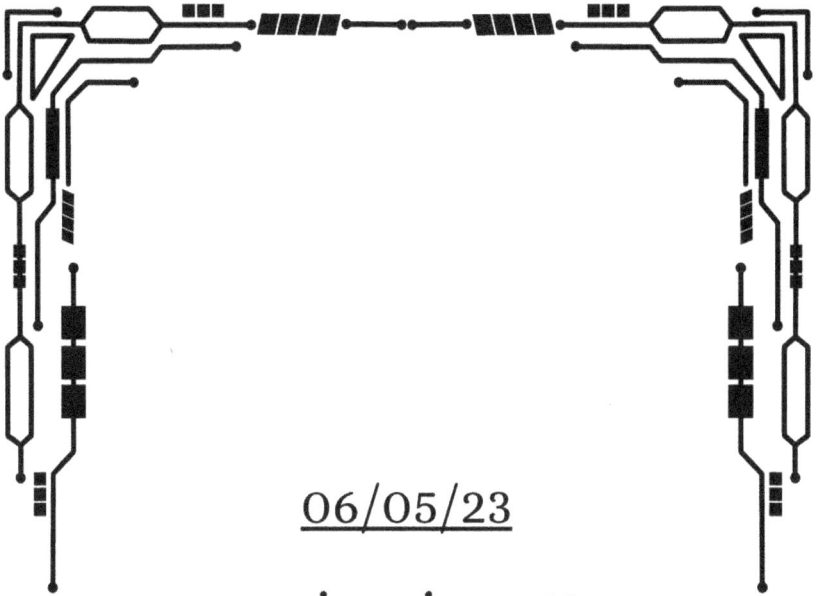

<u>06/05/23</u>

sunrise cigarette
rain clouds rolling in today
both things are good things

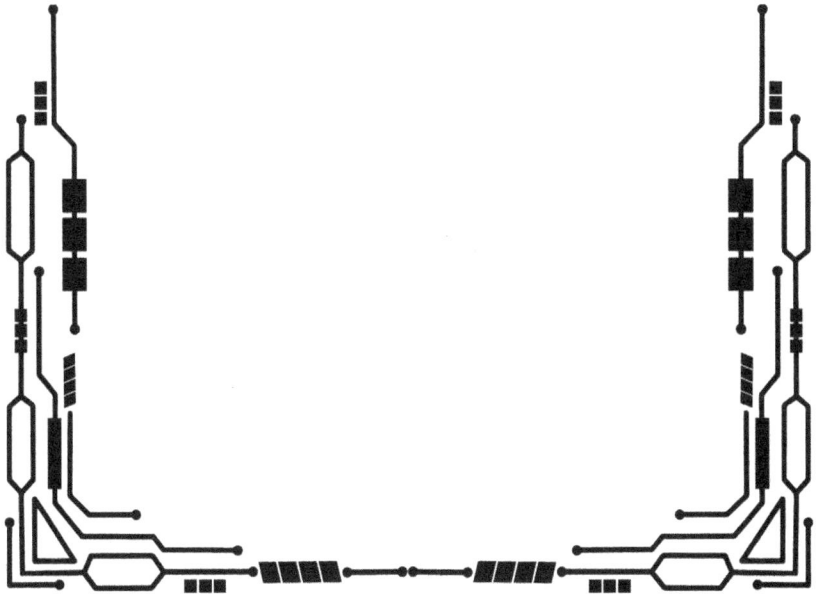

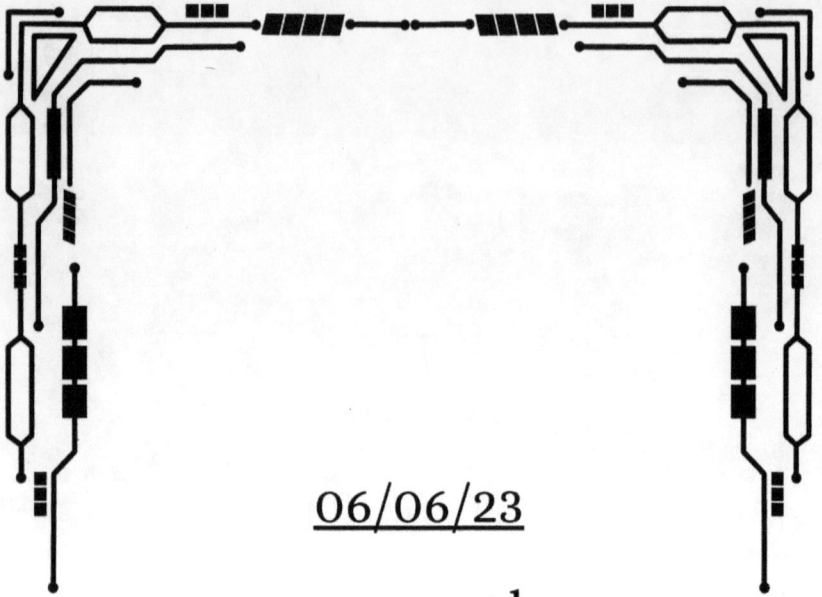

<u>06/06/23</u>

samsung galaxy
amazon 4k fire stick
lenovo thinkpad

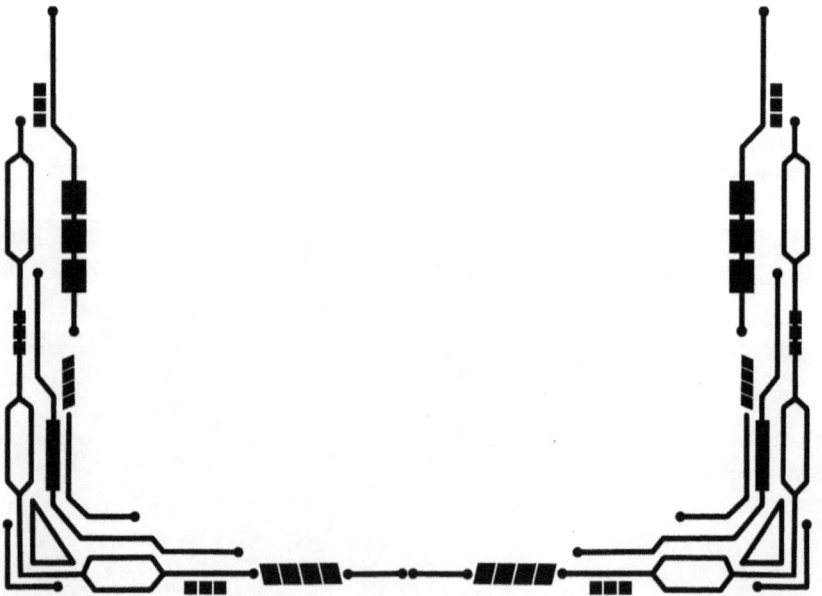

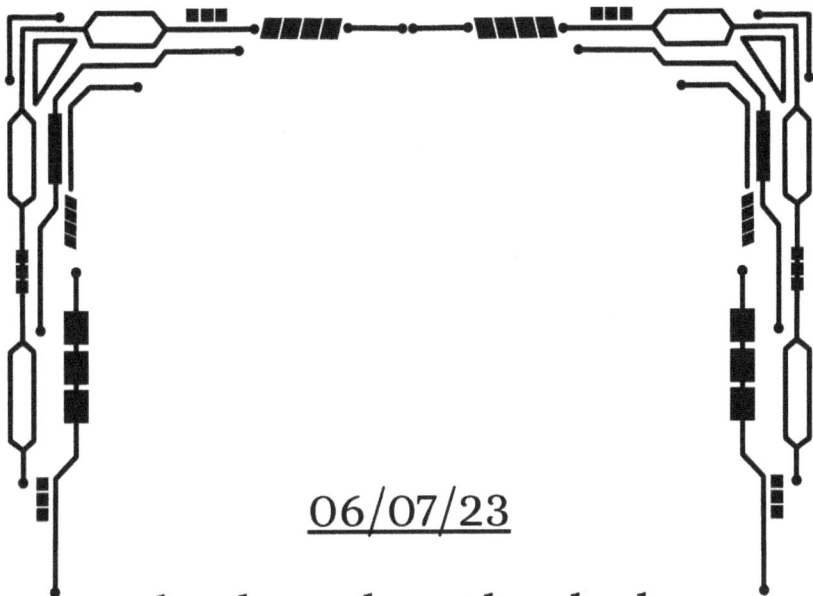

<u>06/07/23</u>

keyboard on the desk
postage on the envelope
travis on the chair

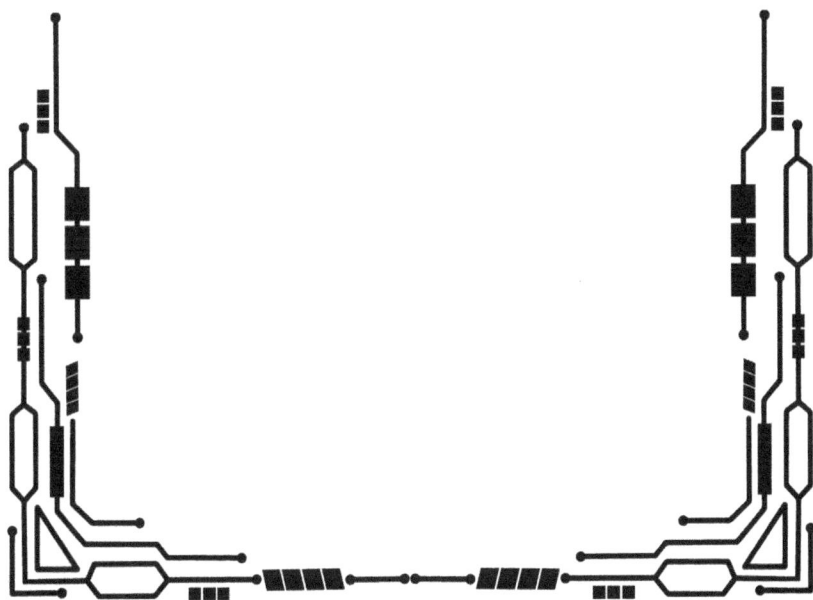

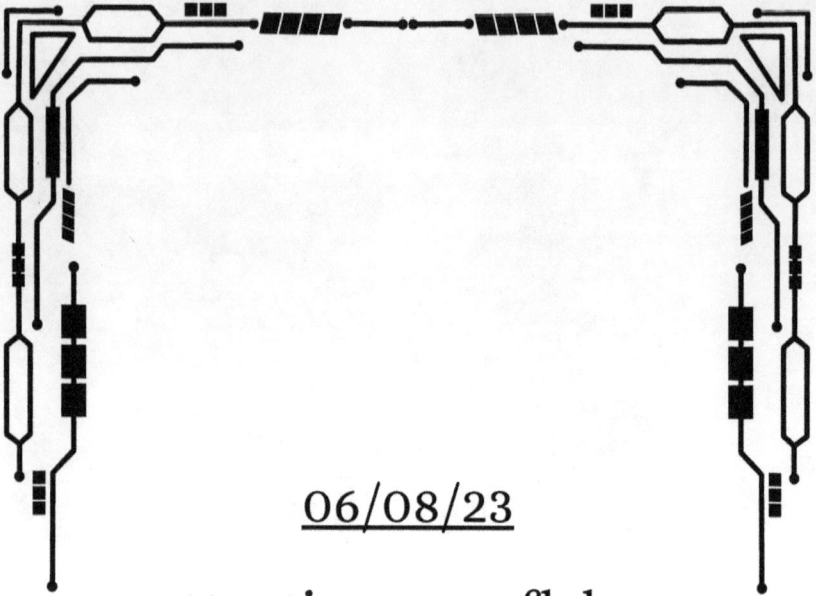

<u>06/08/23</u>

attention snowflakes
seven is the lonely one
where the fuck are we

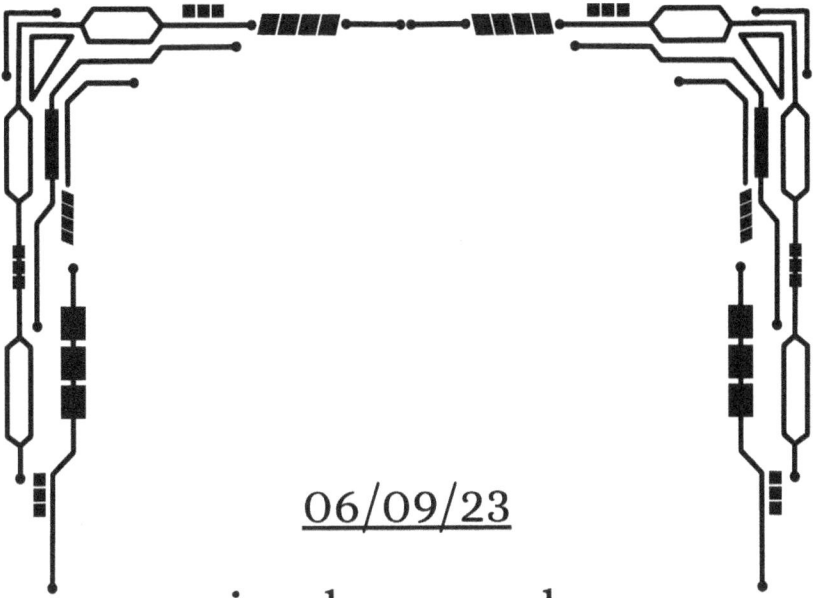

<u>06/09/23</u>

i wake up early
and go to bed really late
never enough sleep

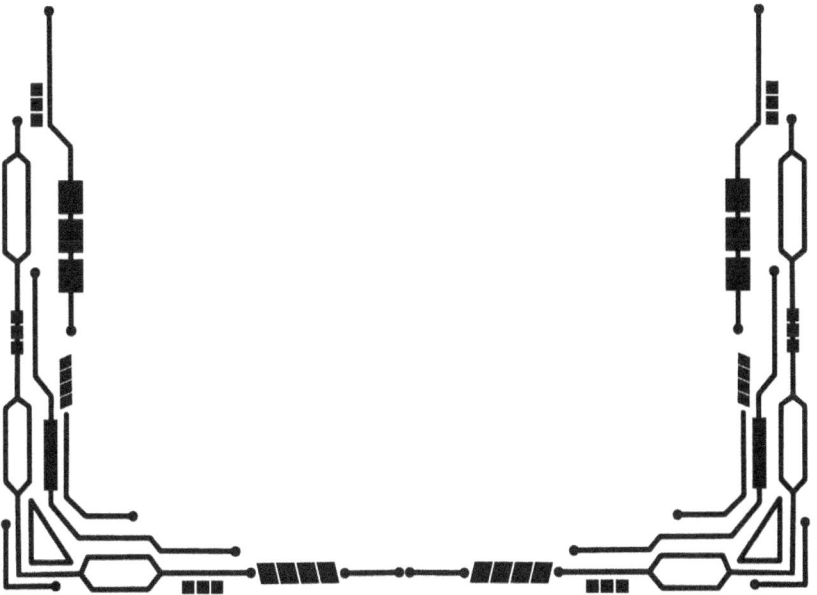

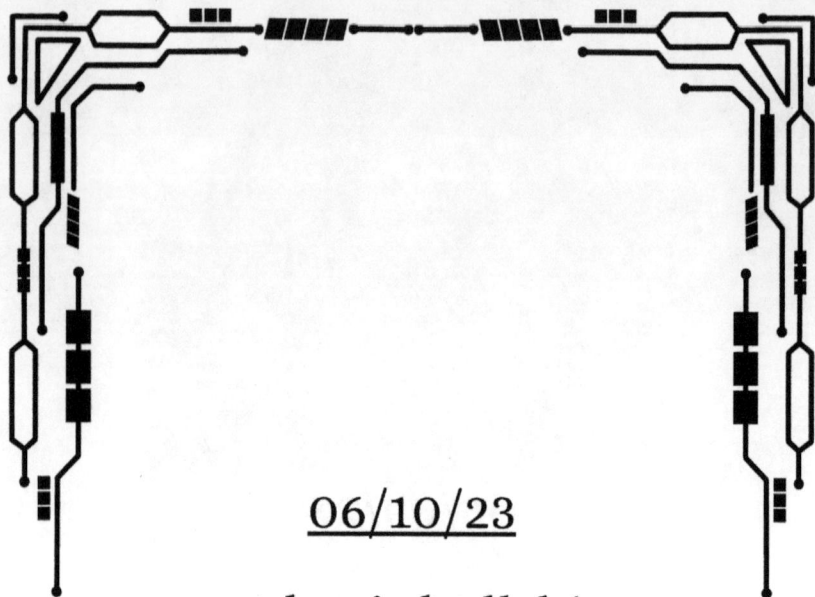

<u>06/10/23</u>

today is bullshit
like a fucking rodeo
after taco night

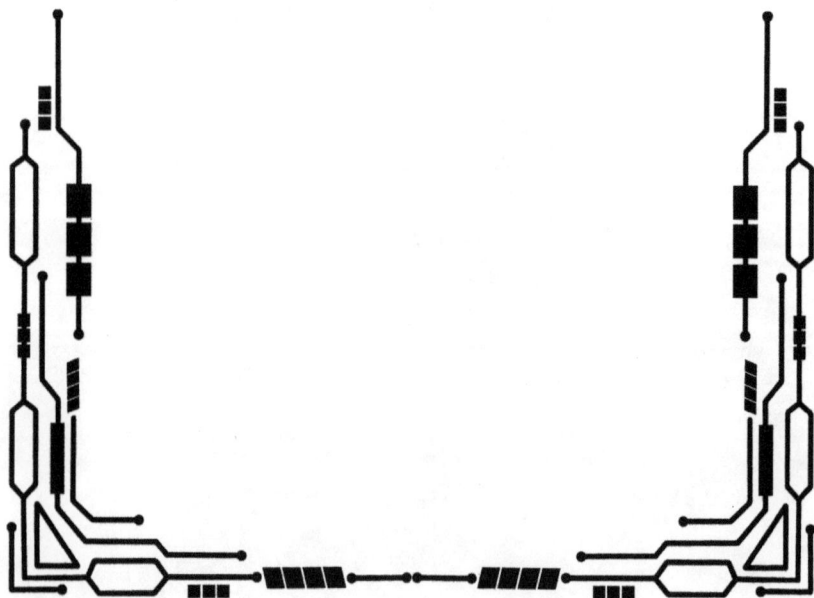

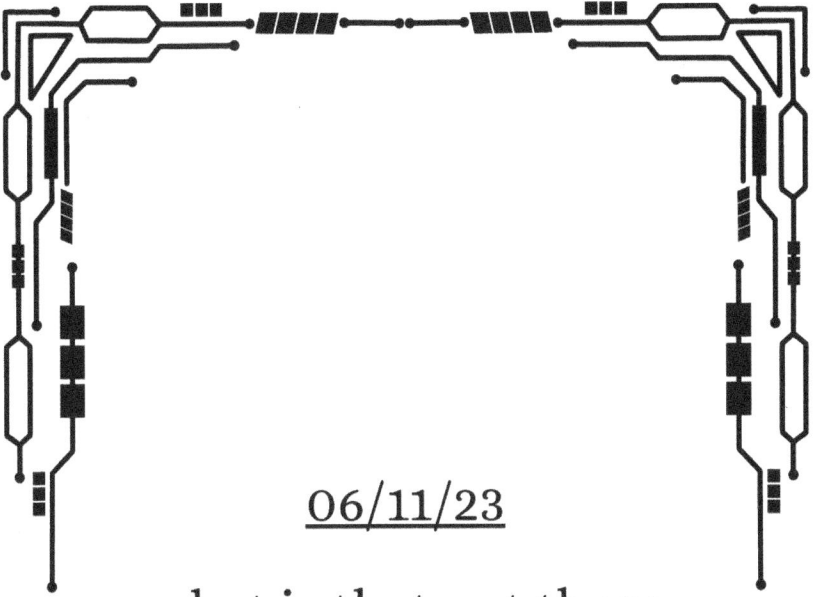

<u>06/11/23</u>

what is that out there
it's too damn early for this
shut up stupid dog

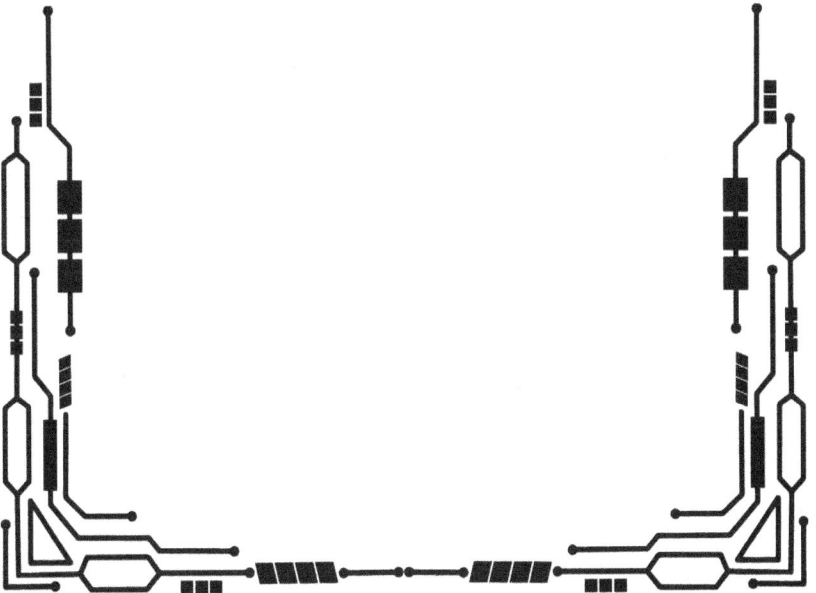

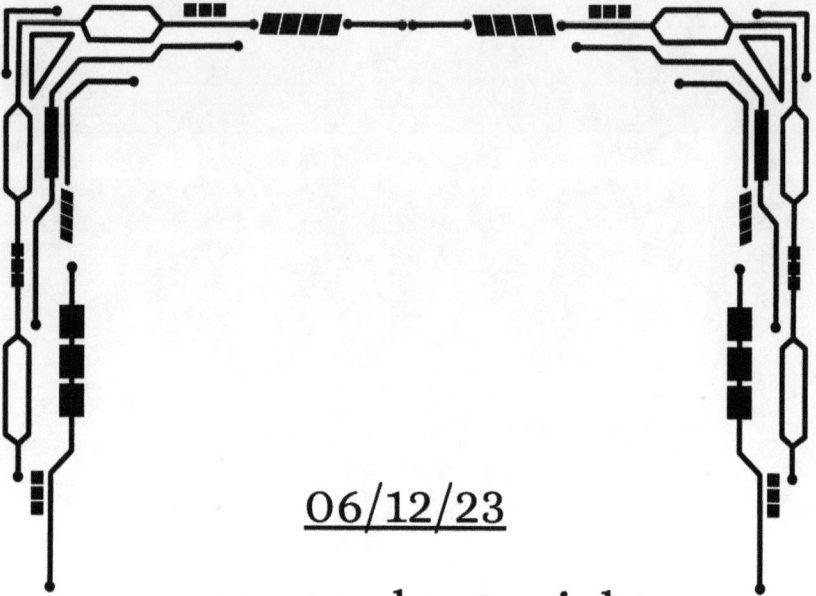

<u>06/12/23</u>

nuggets play tonight
game five to sit court side is
thirty five thousand

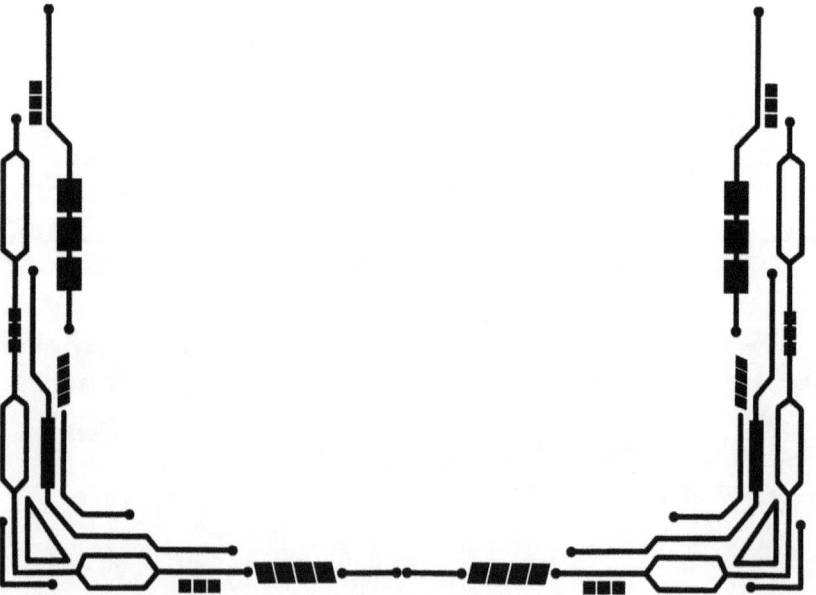

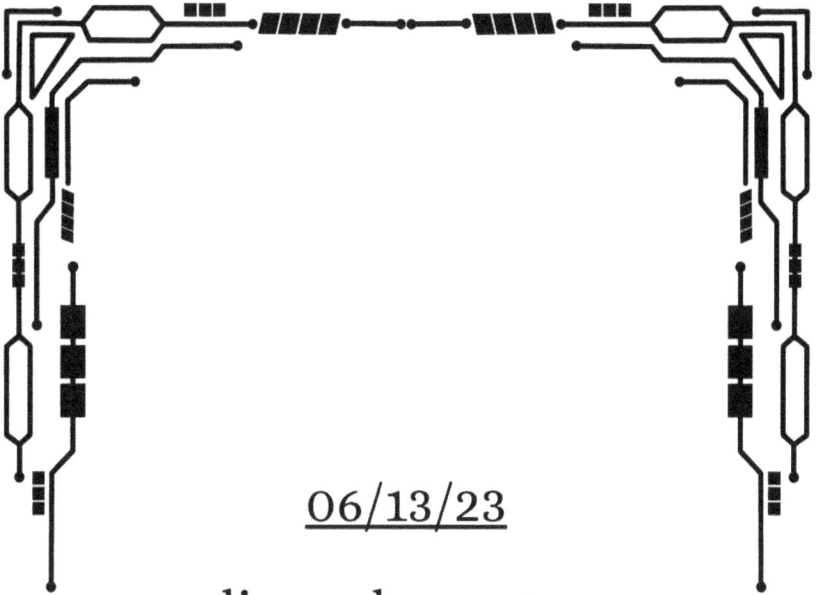

06/13/23

lingonberry tea
peanut butter jelly sauce
dutch oven omelet

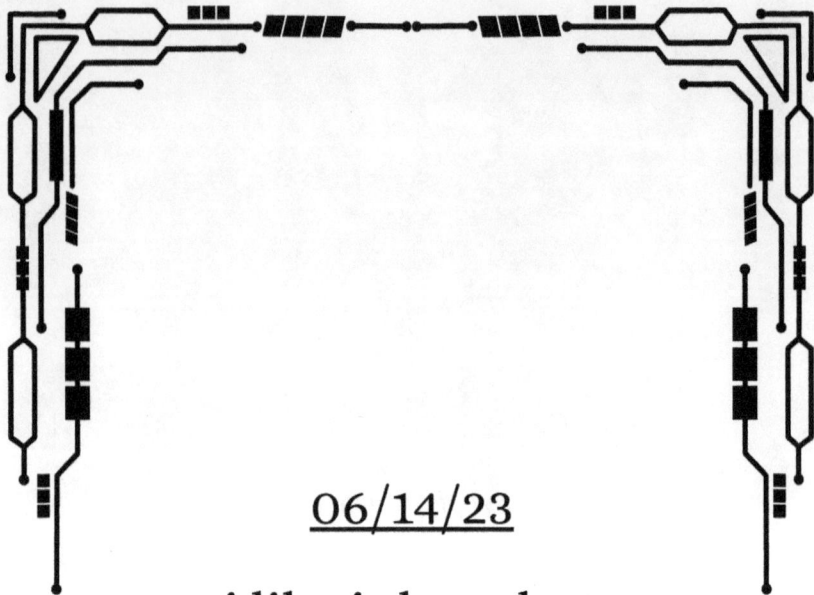

<u>06/14/23</u>

i like it here but
i like it over there too
who has the best deal

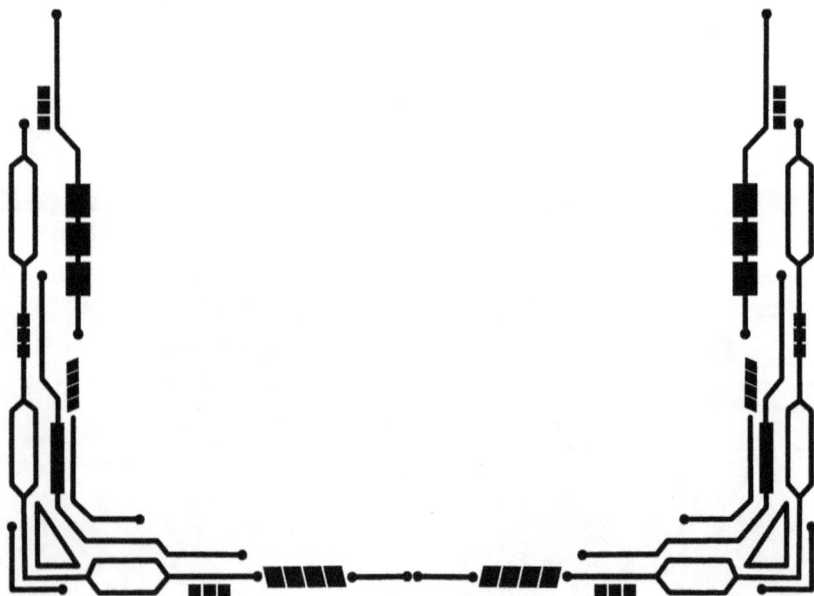

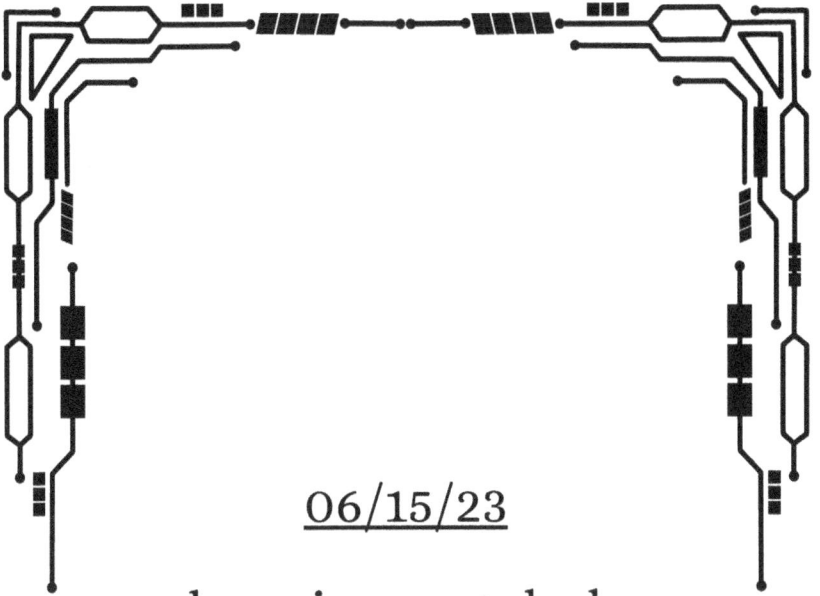

<u>06/15/23</u>

shopping cart derby
lemmings just walk off the cliff
parkour is stupid

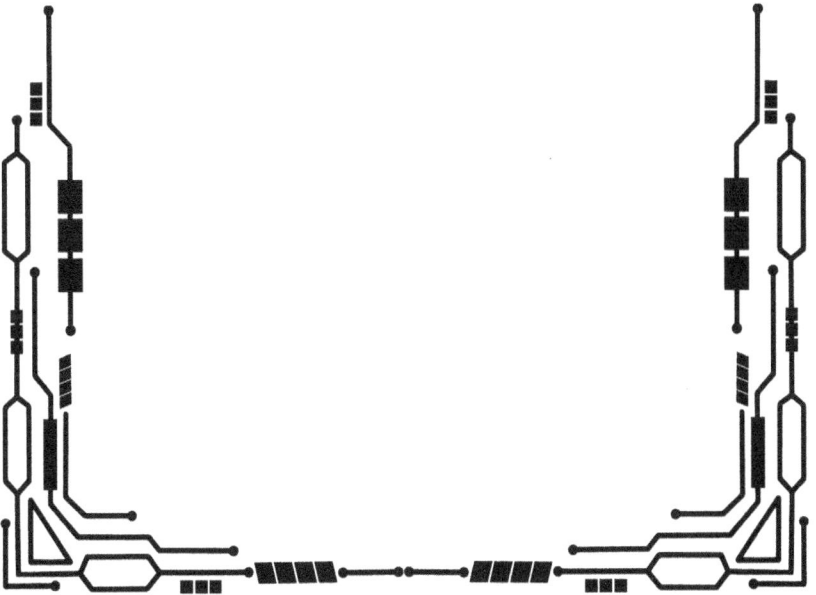

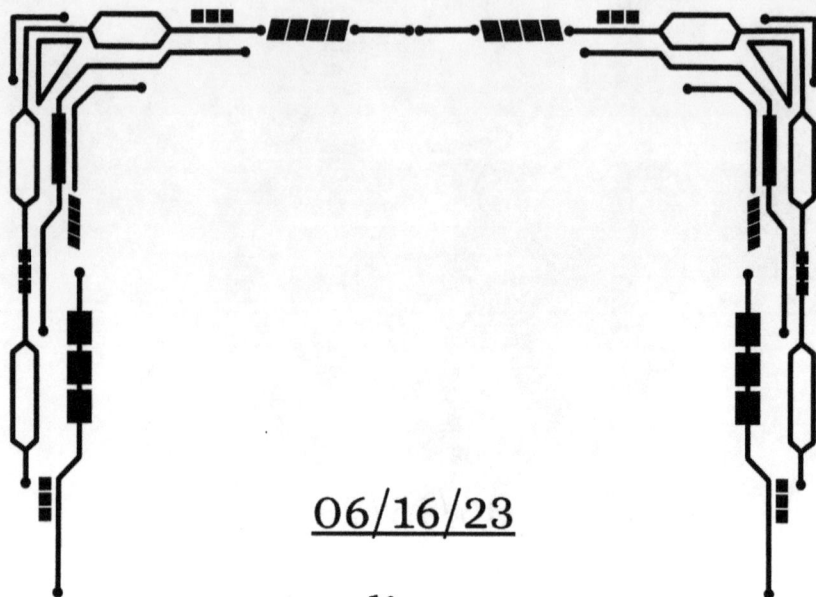

<u>06/16/23</u>

a medium rare
seared filet of dragon loin
with fire salsa please

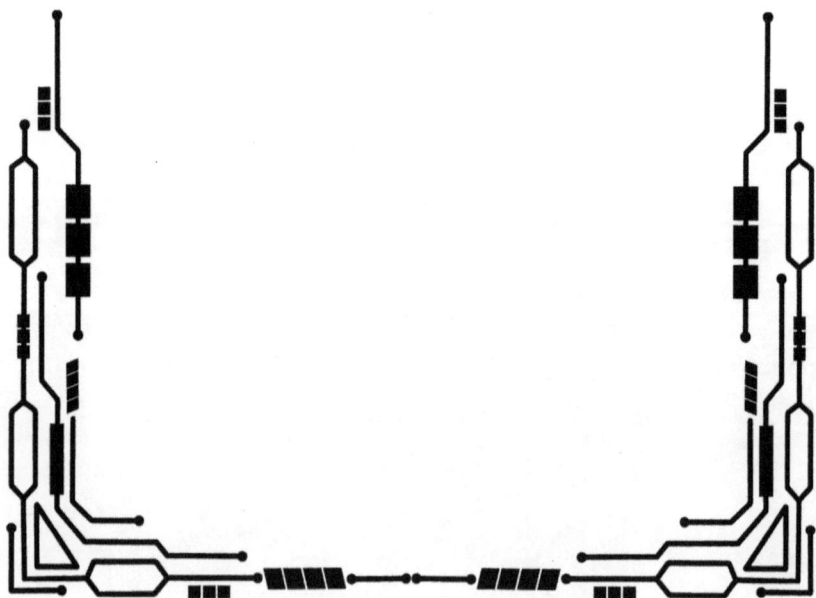

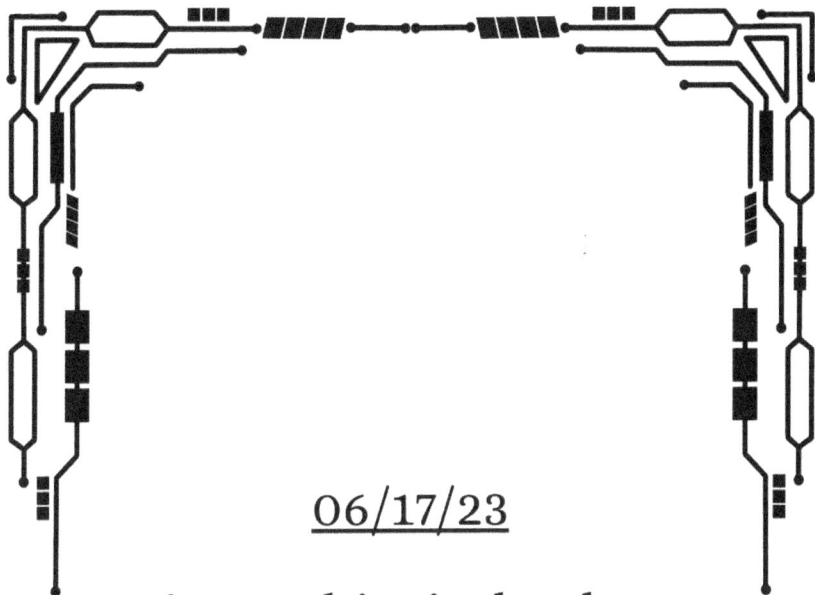

<u>06/17/23</u>

jeans shirt jacket hat
left sock right sock underwear
stir with laundry sauce

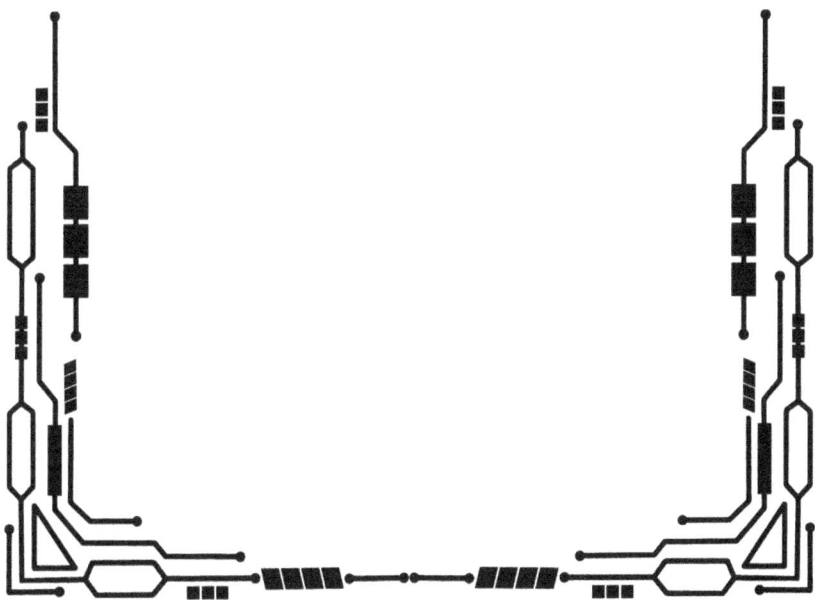

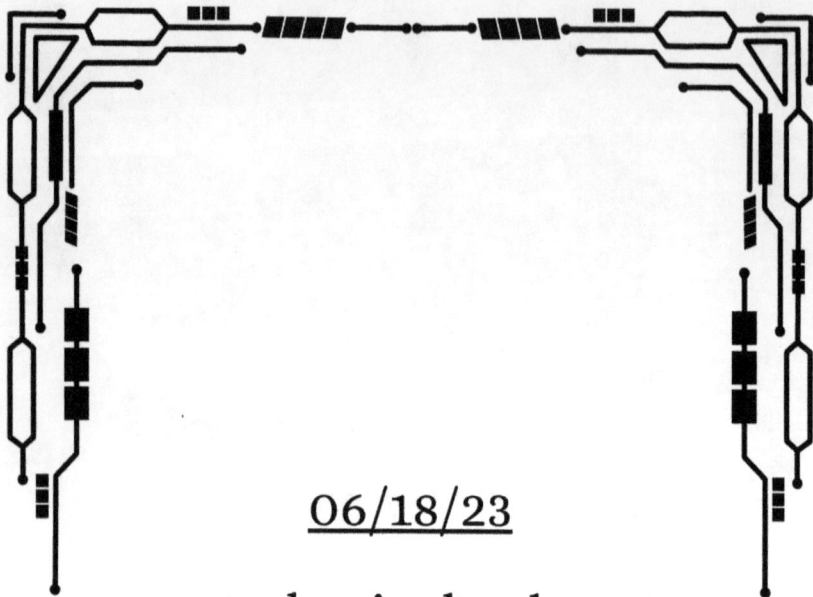

06/18/23

today is the day
put your money on the line
junebug derby race

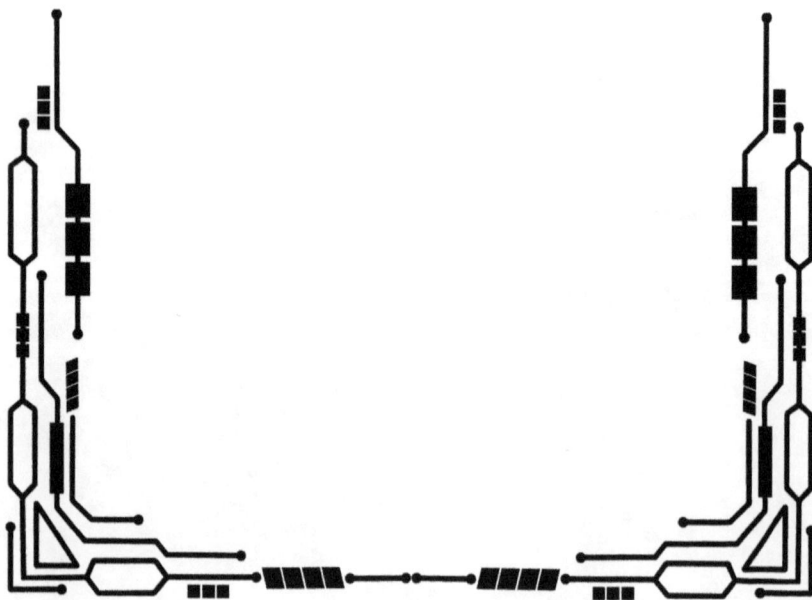

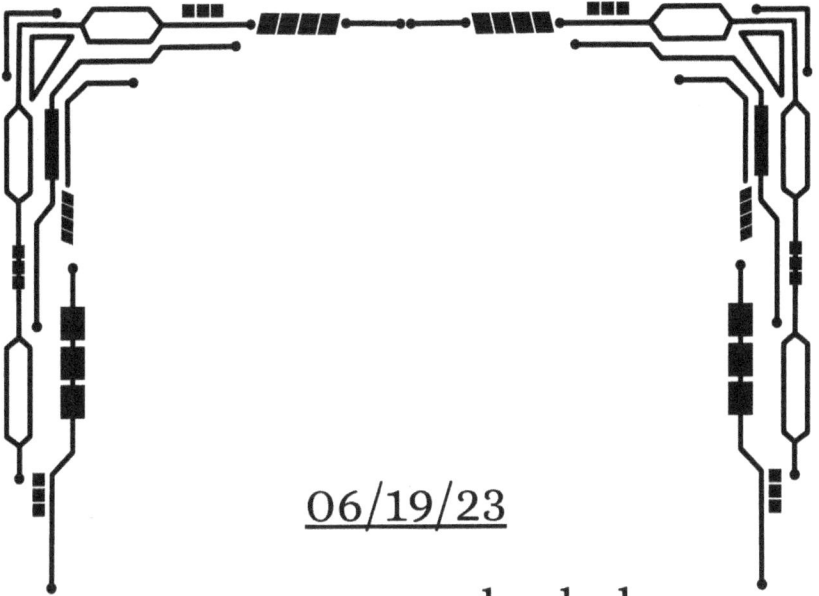

<u>06/19/23</u>

croutons and salad
juice box mixed with cbd
hand carved turkey breast

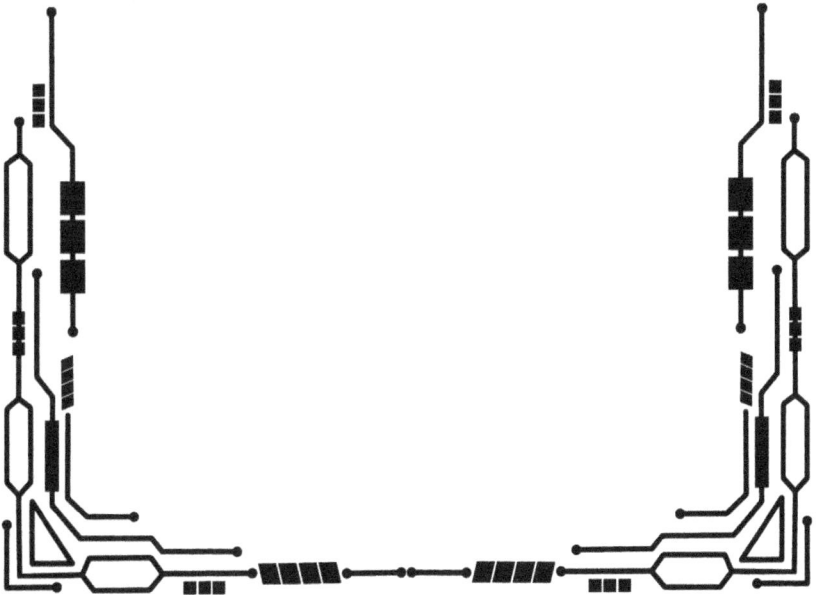

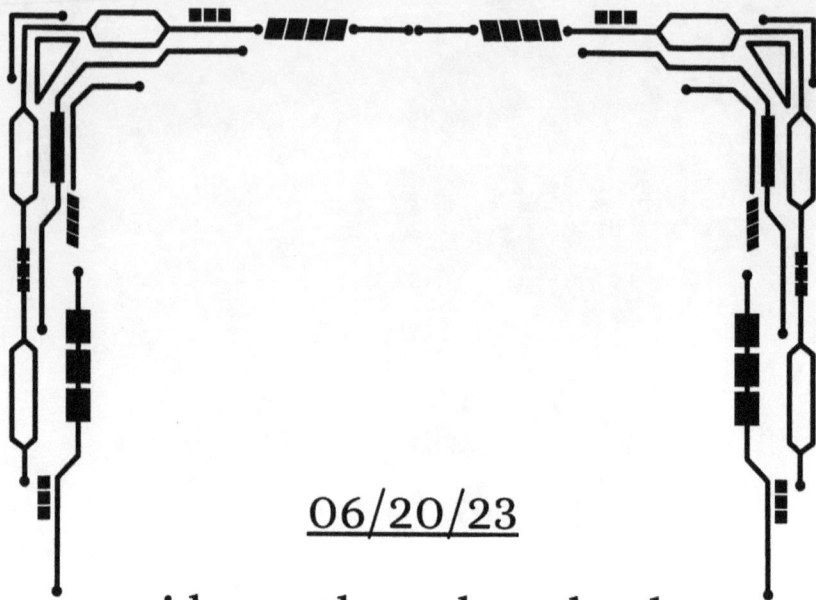

<u>06/20/23</u>

i have three hundred
black sharpies in my office
one brown and one green

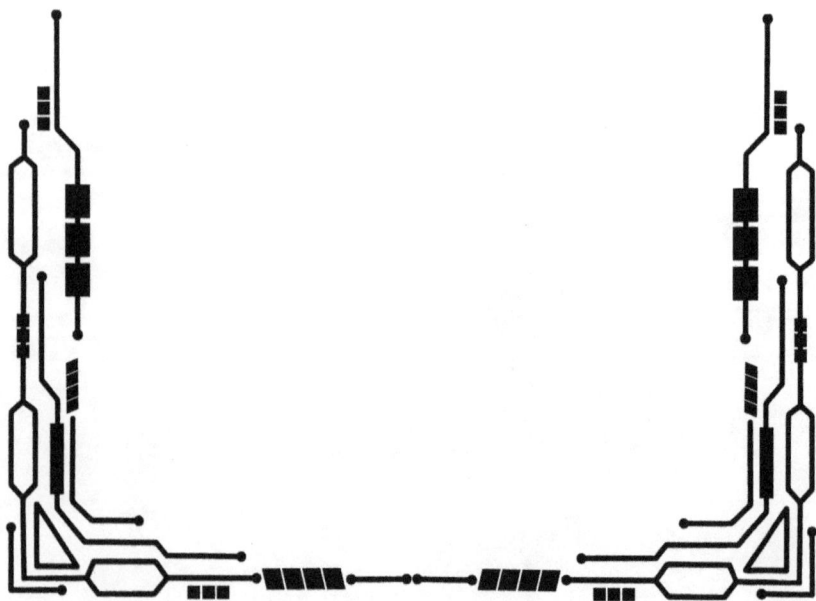

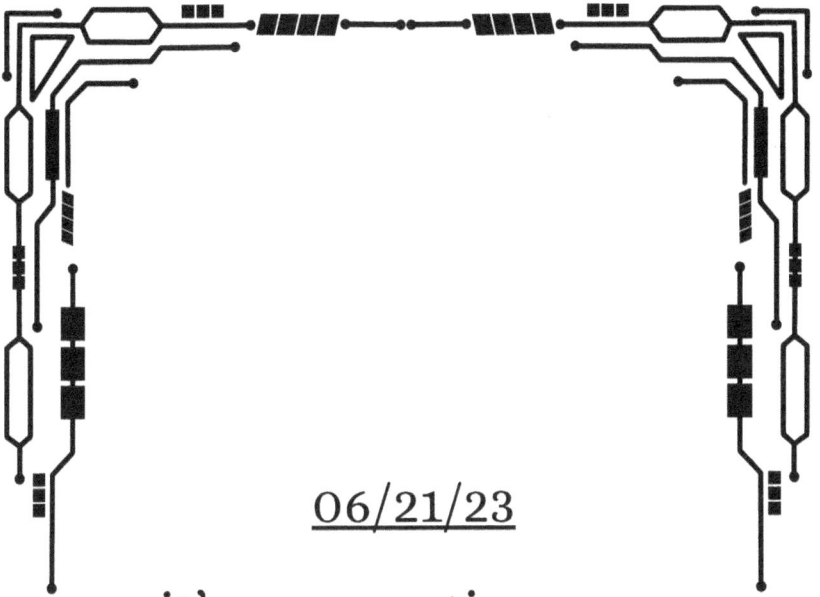

<u>06/21/23</u>

it's summertime now
safeway has a sale on meat
five nineteen per pound

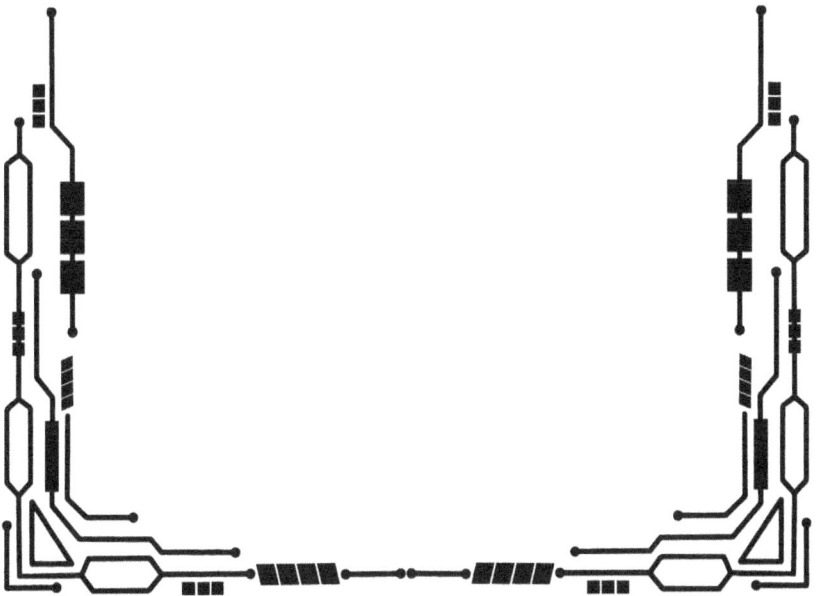

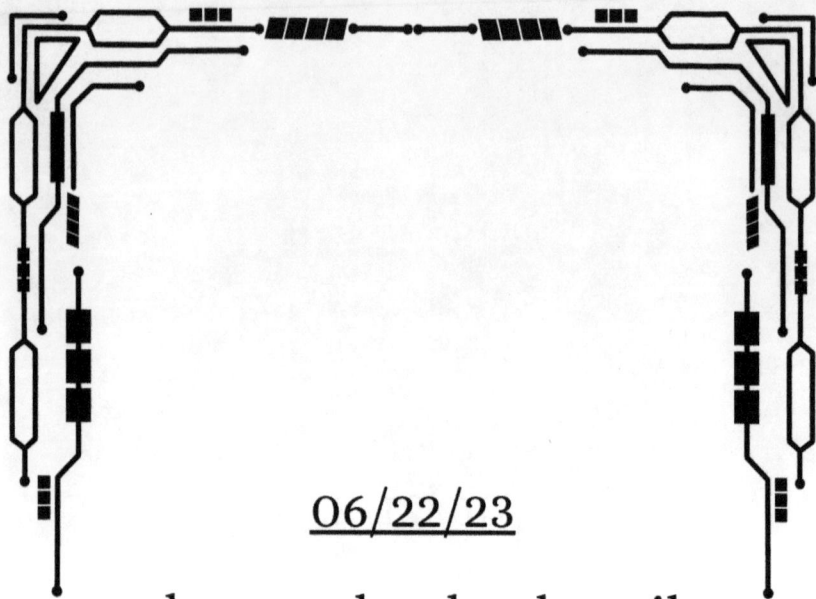

<u>06/22/23</u>

the murder death trail
popper chip popper combos
and broken headlights

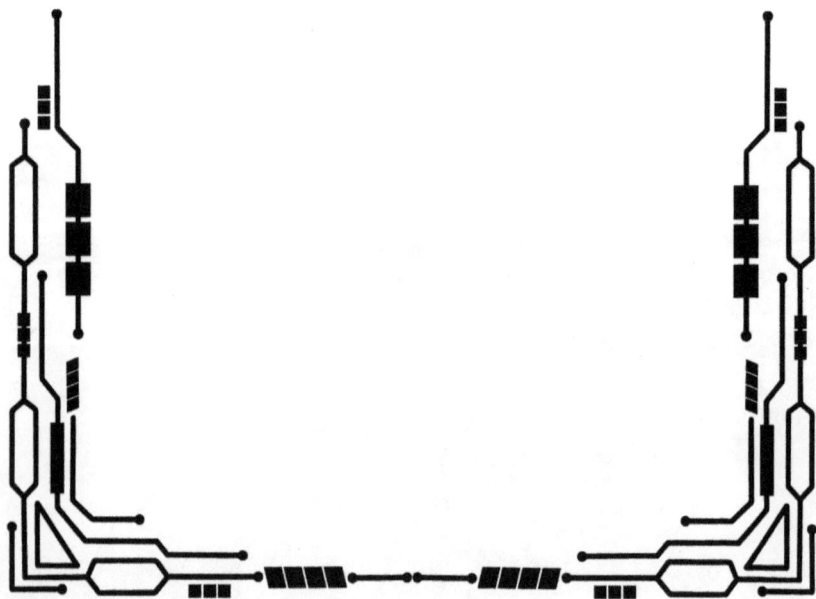

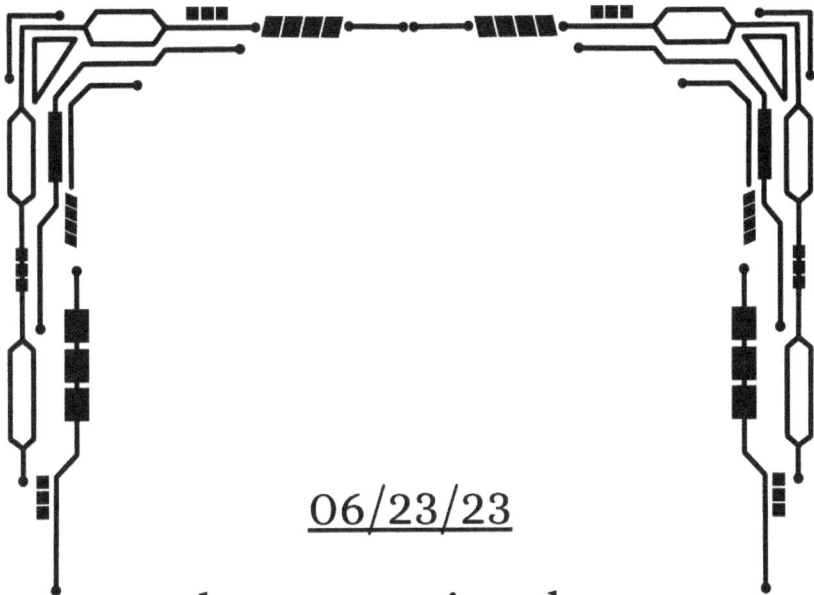

<u>06/23/23</u>

cool summertime breeze
at sunset over longs peak
this is the moment

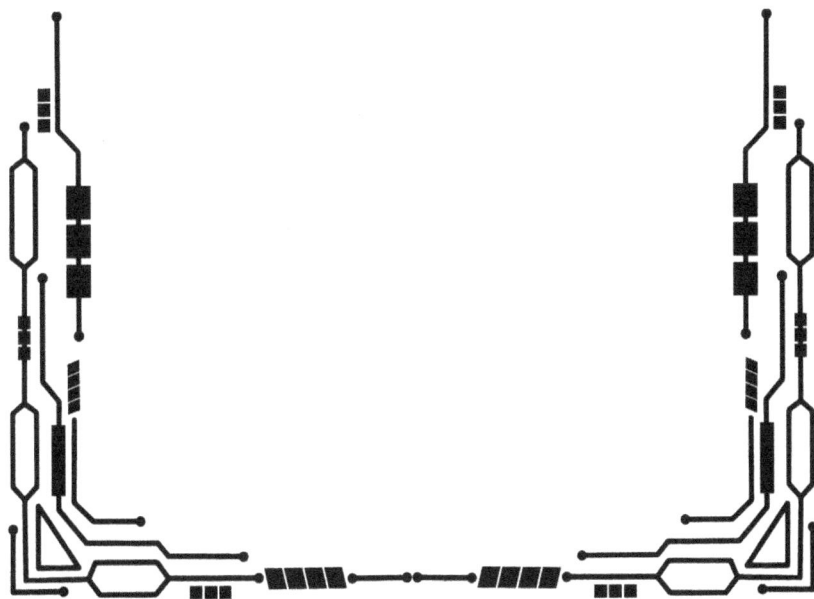

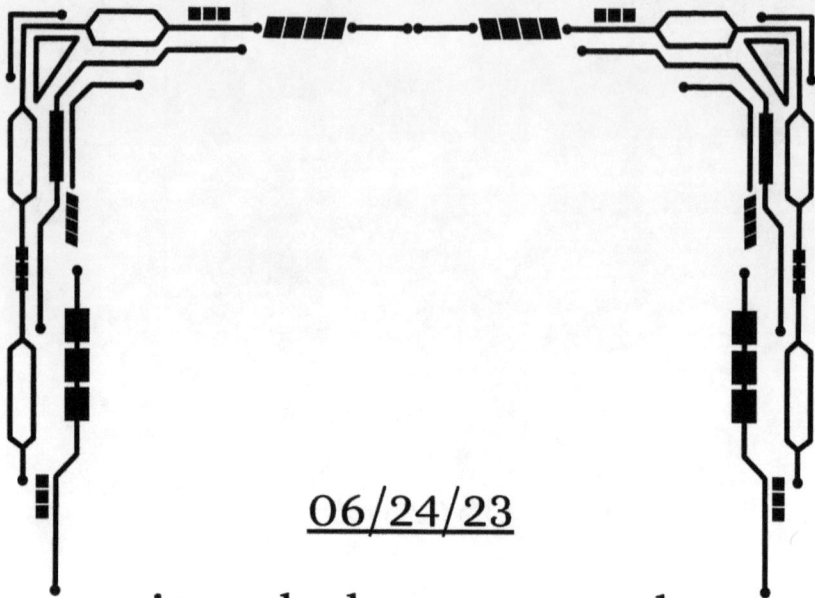

06/24/23

it sucks here now and
it's hot in the alleyway
cigarettes are good

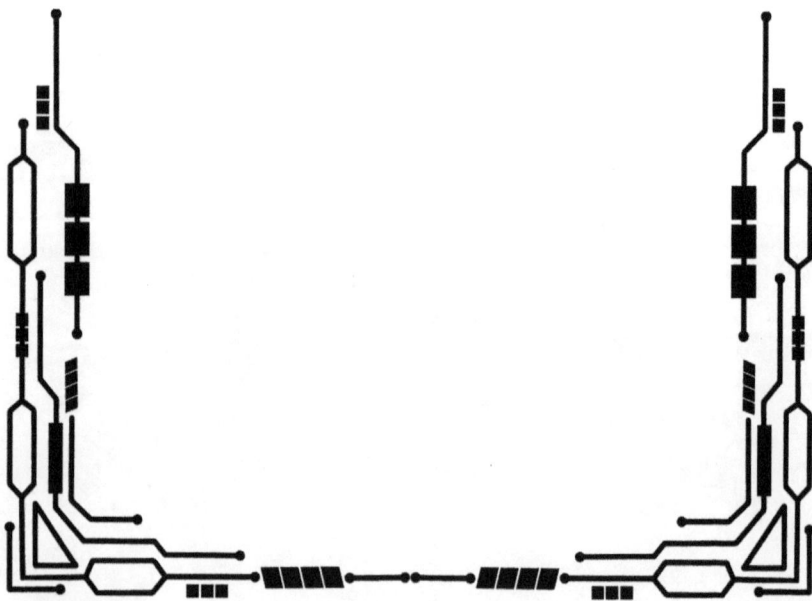

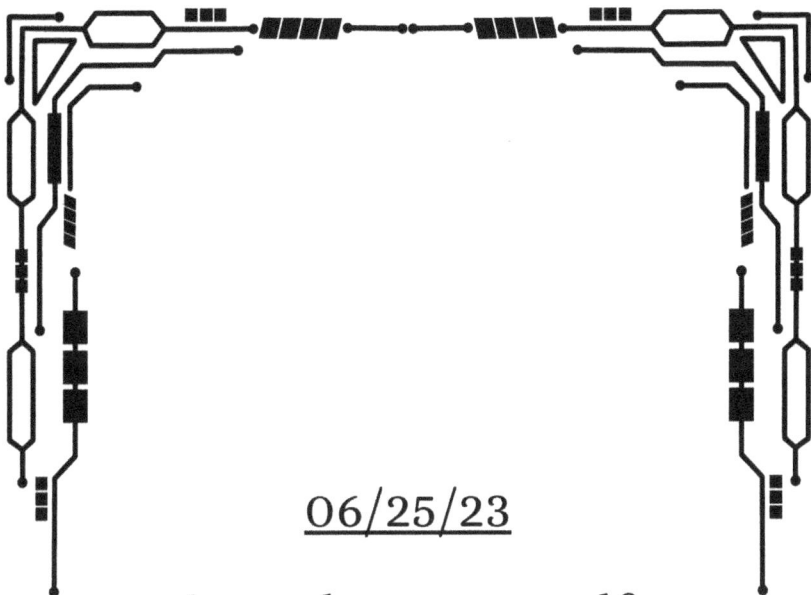

<u>06/25/23</u>

introduce yourself
take off your pants and jacket
now we can have tea

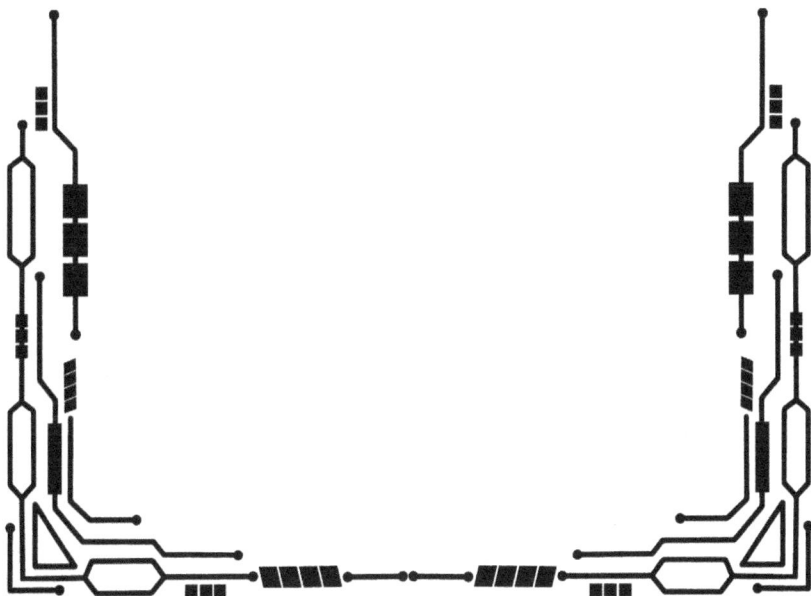

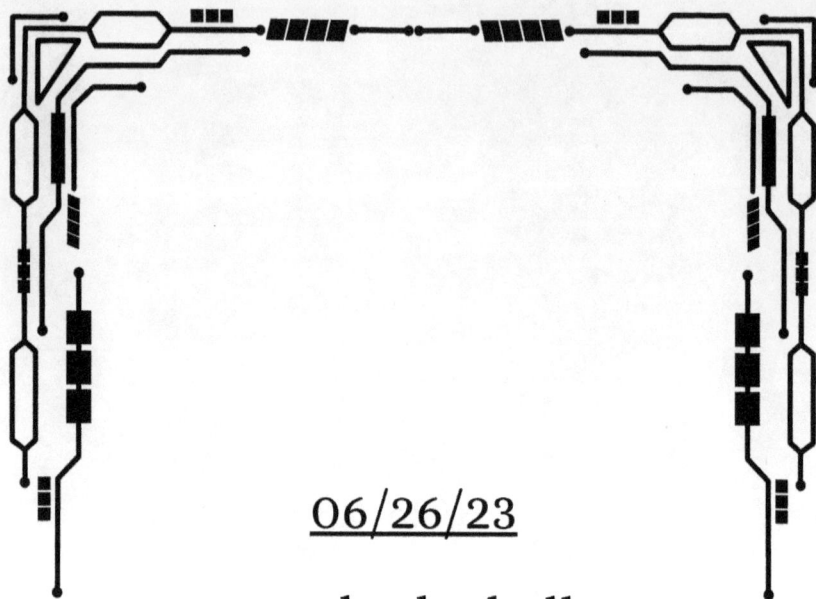

<u>06/26/23</u>

steady the ladle
and spill the sauce on the new
laminate flooring

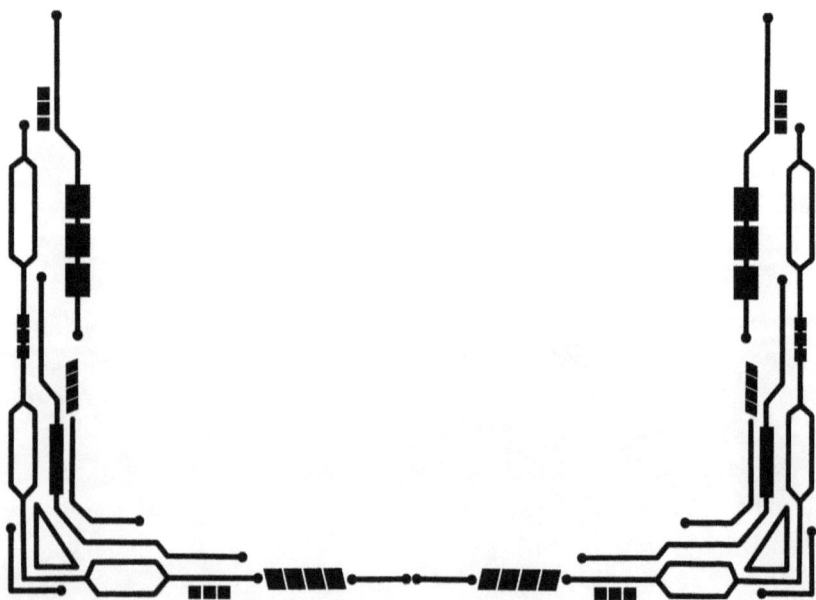

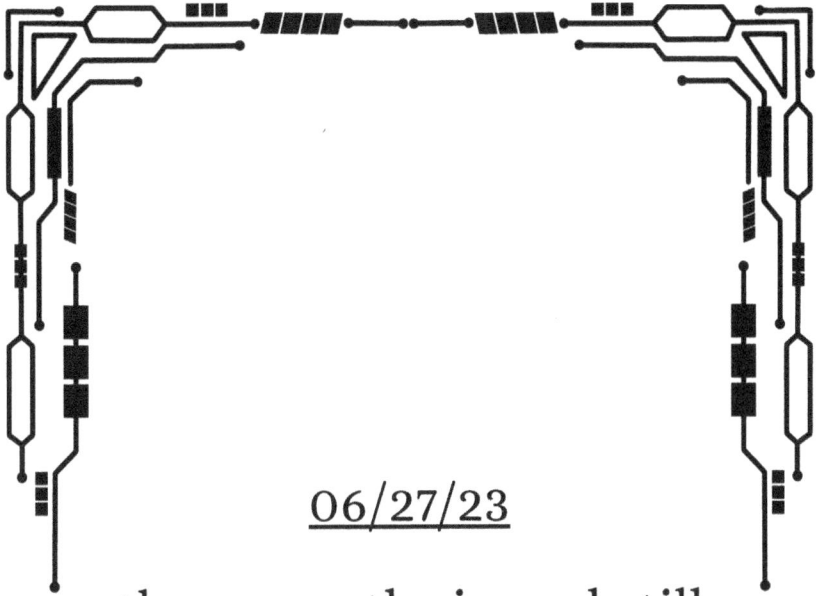

<u>06/27/23</u>

three months in and still
syllables are fillable
three lines at a time

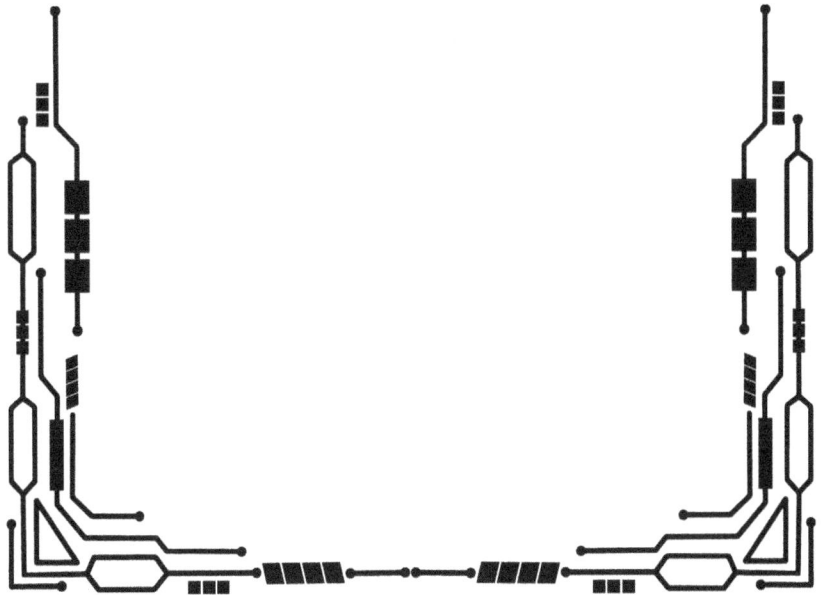

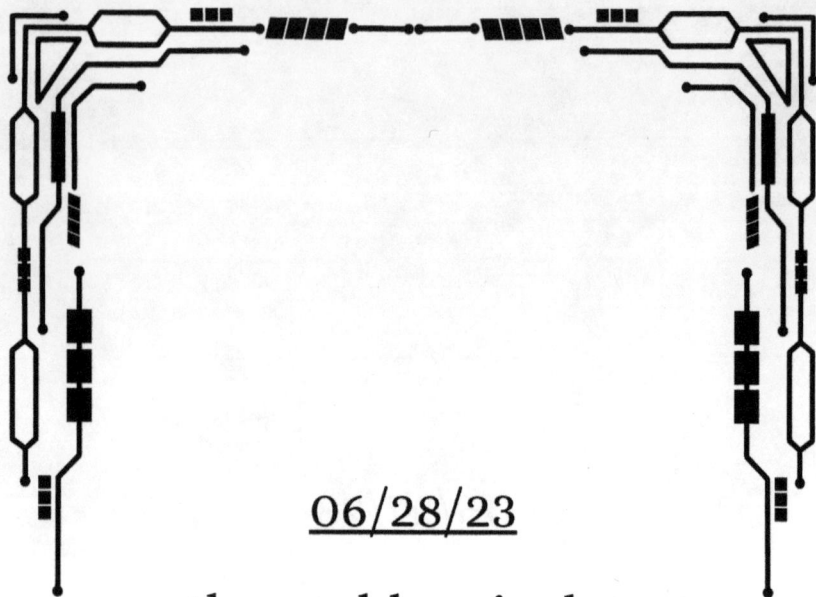

<u>06/28/23</u>

the problem is that
with a shellfish allergy
you can't eat the shrimp

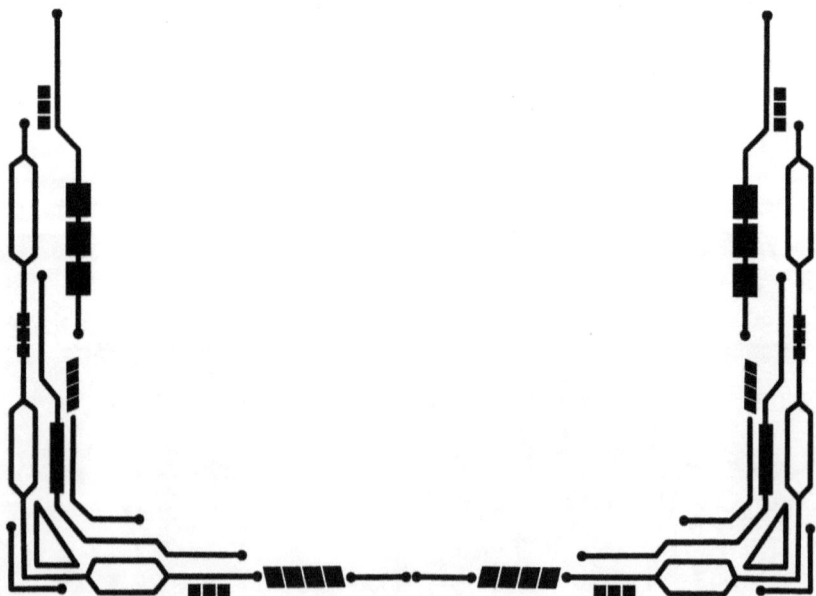

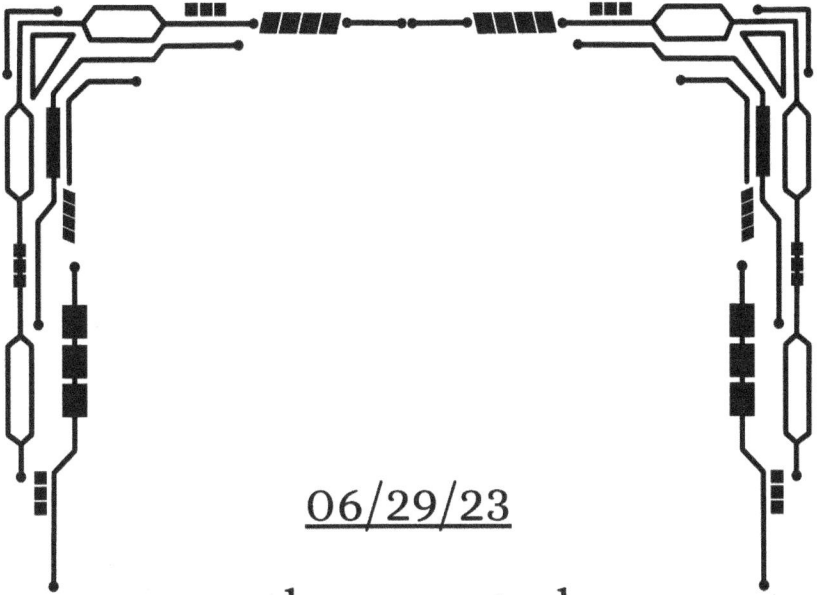

<u>06/29/23</u>

on the news today
an old lady crashed her car
into the storefront

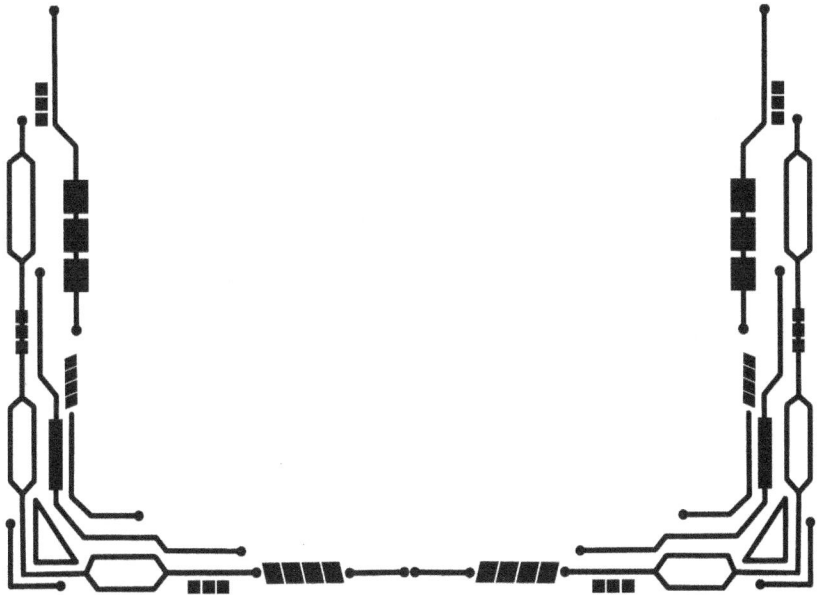

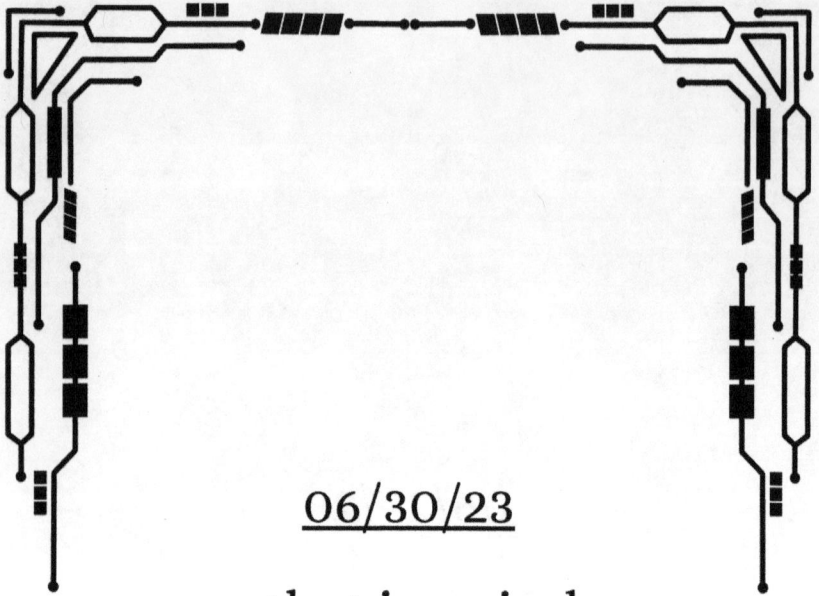

<u>06/30/23</u>

now that june is done
change the menu for july
yellowfin tuna

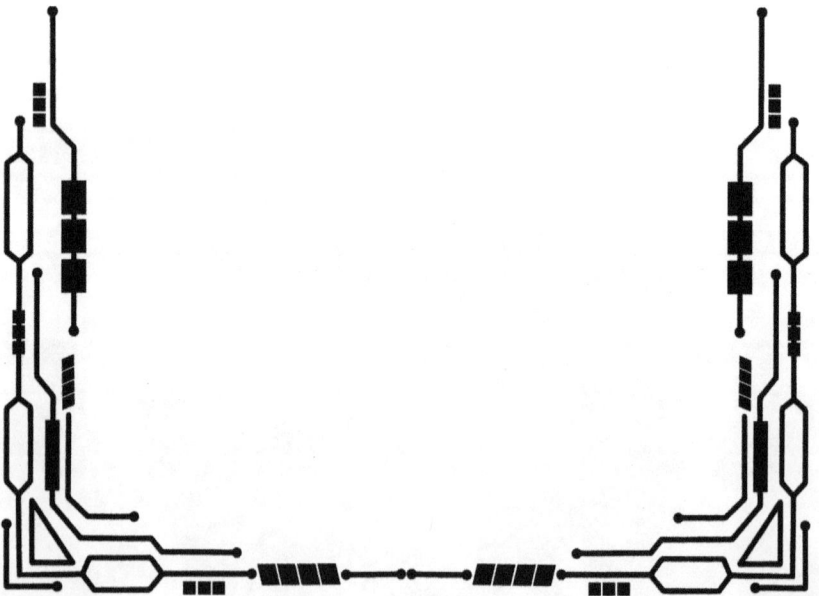

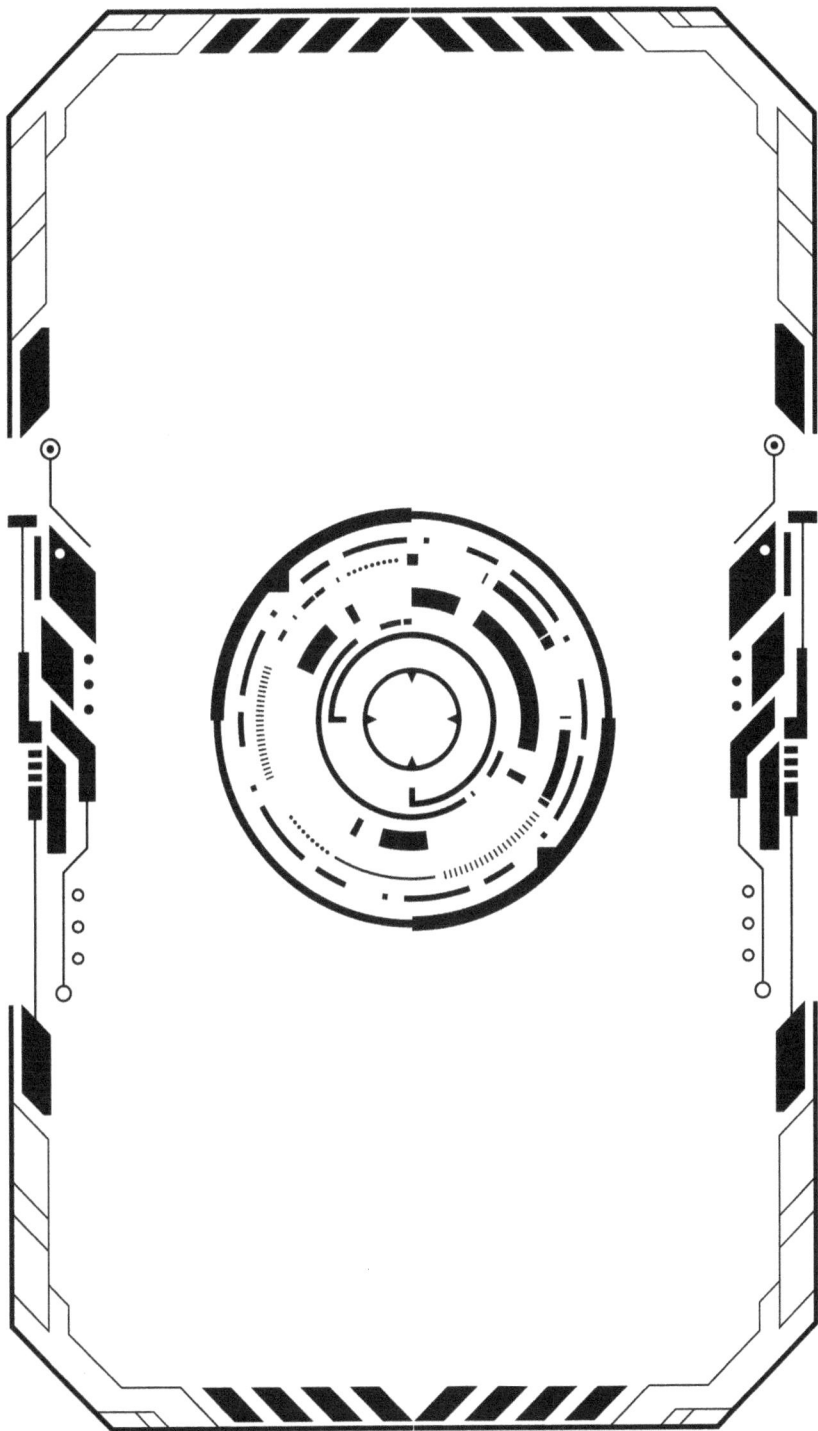

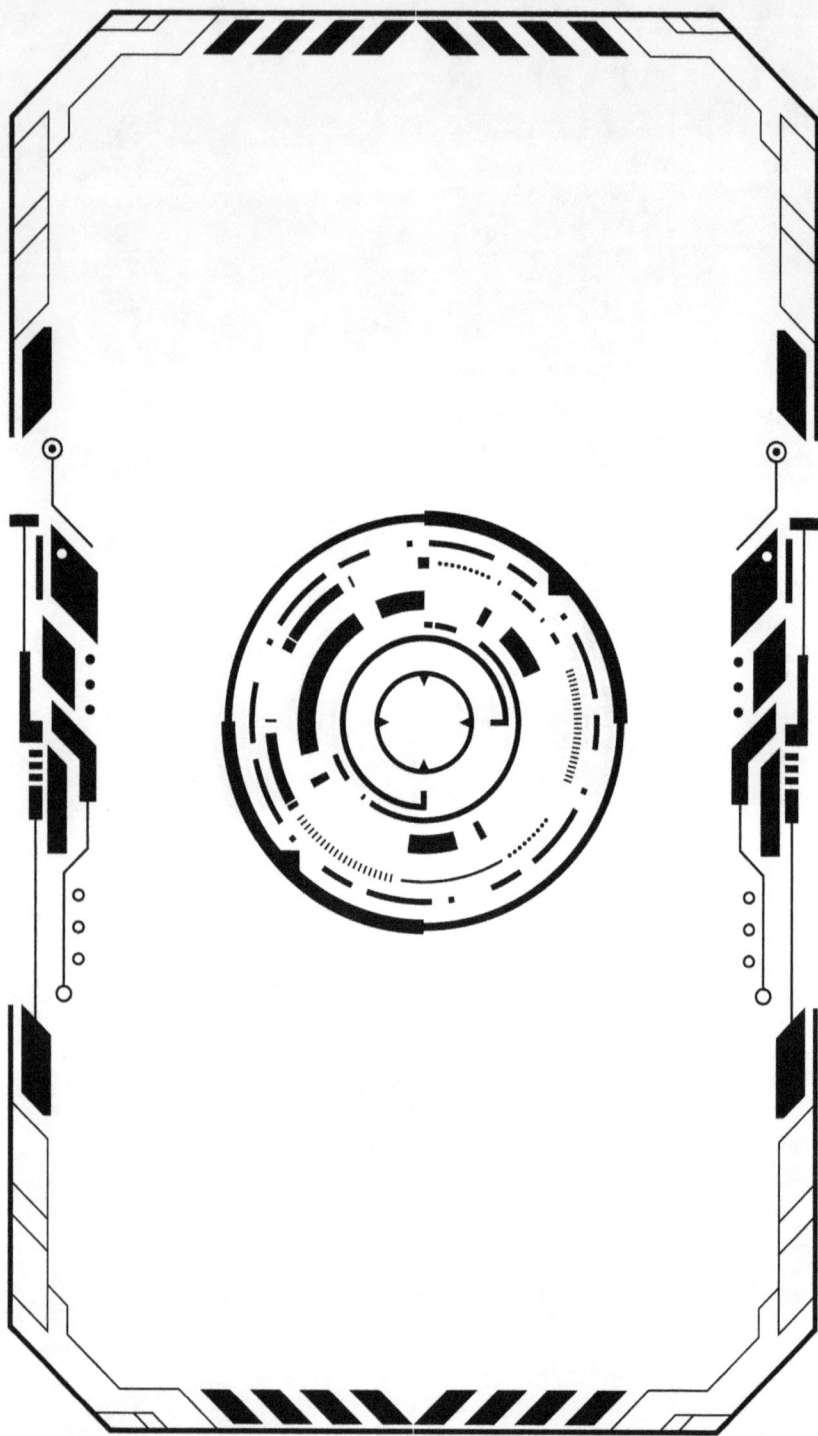

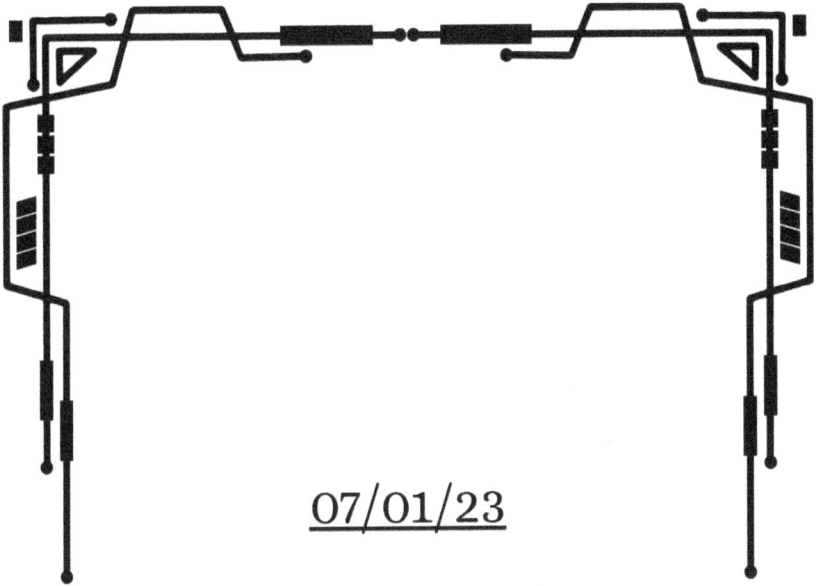

<u>07/01/23</u>

seven twenty three
paychecks are getting sketchy
bluetooth chicken bone

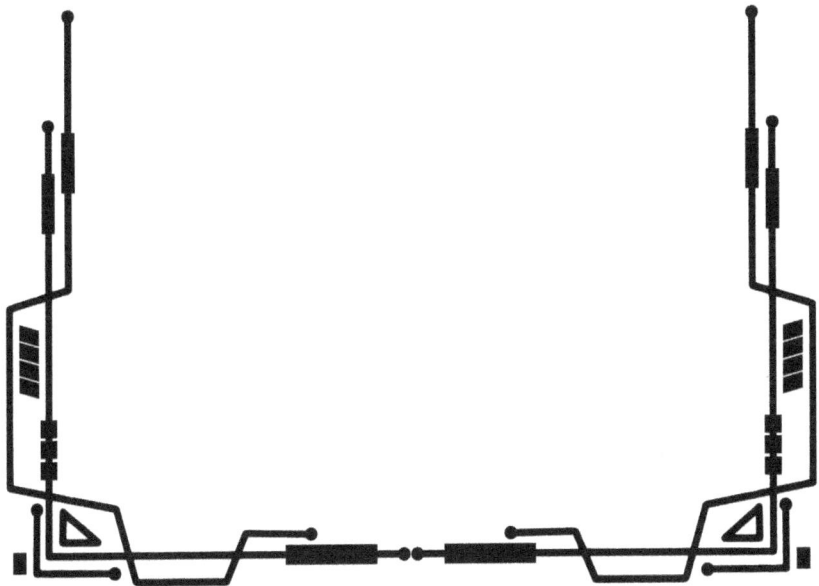

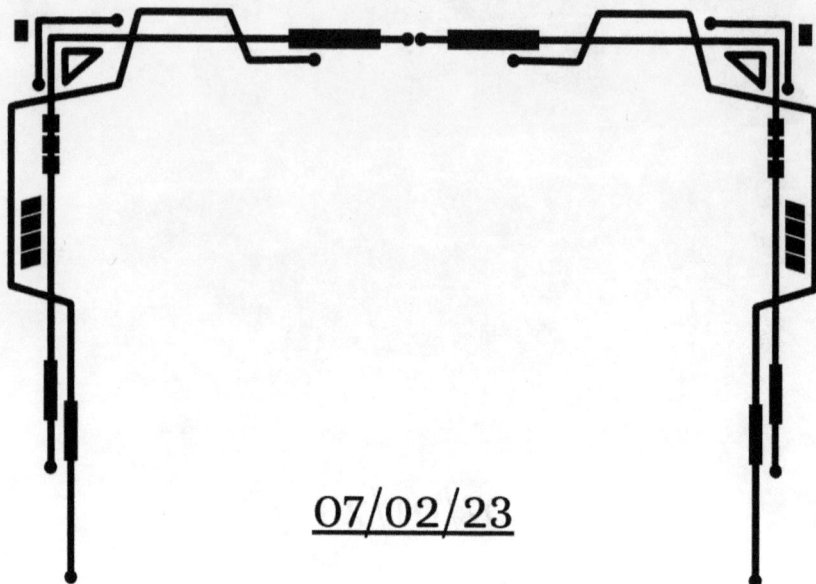

<u>07/02/23</u>

little by little
the coffee pot overflows
hence the towel there

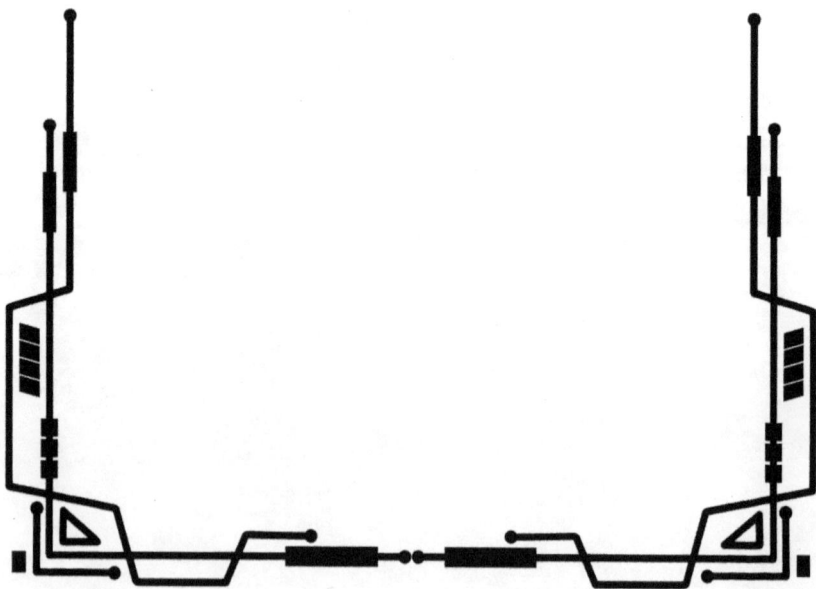

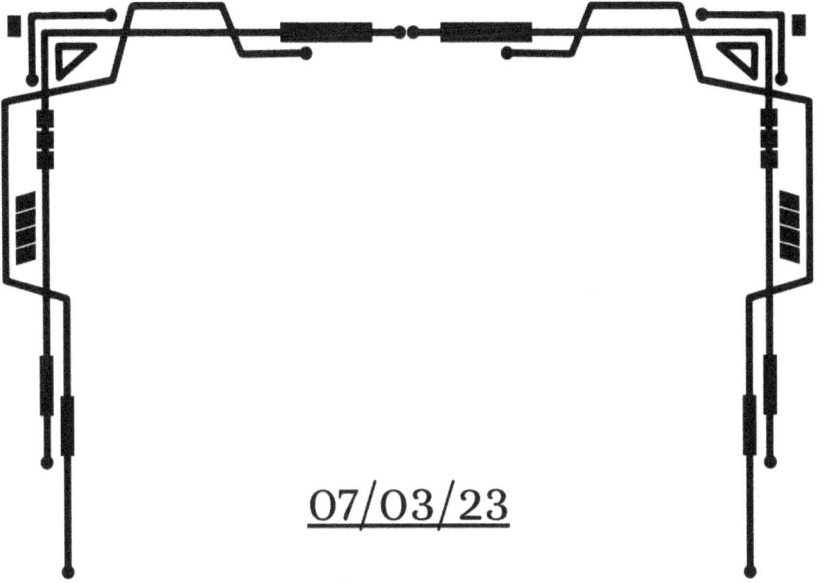

<u>07/03/23</u>

inferno og
is a nice wake and bake for
my only day off

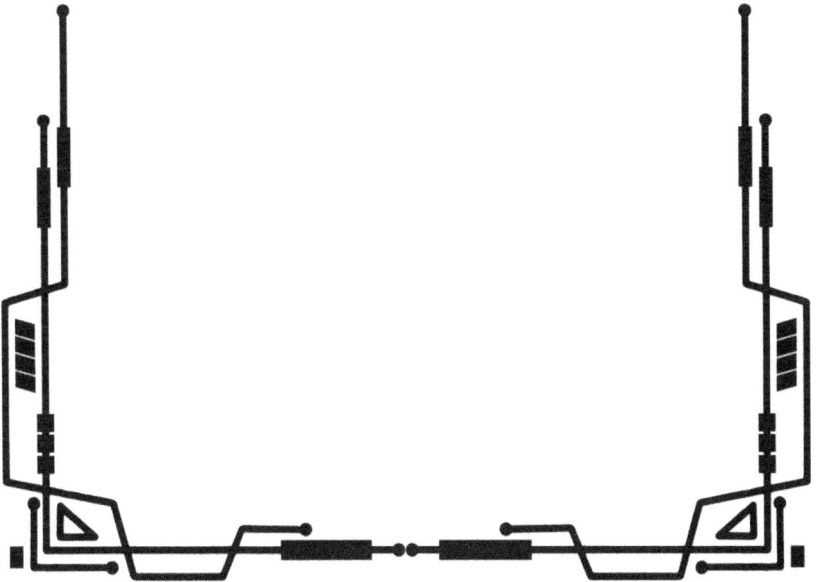

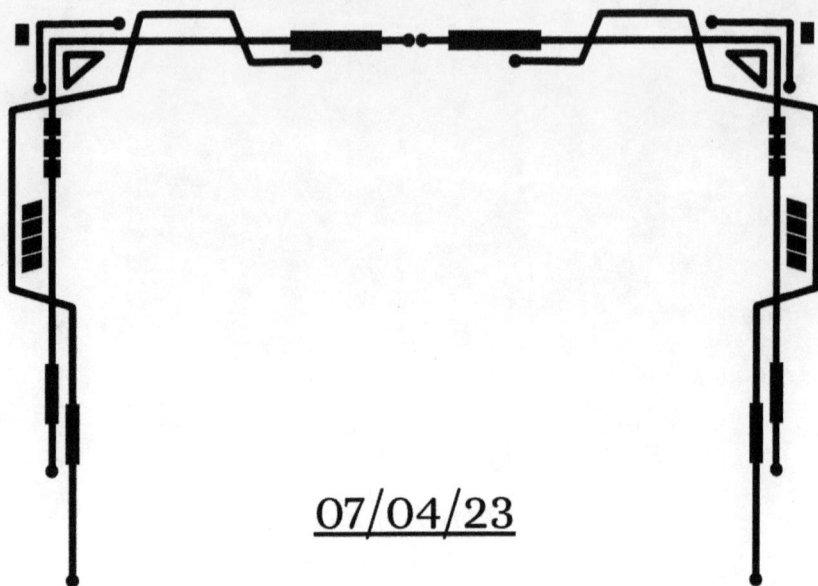

<u>07/04/23</u>

let's celebrate with
prime rib and fireworks tonight
explosions and beef

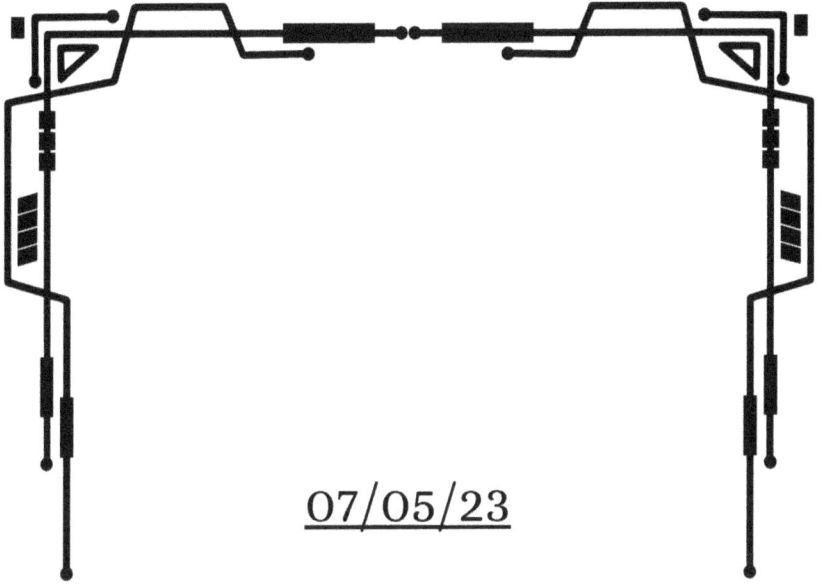

<u>07/05/23</u>

as luck would have it
i found a dollar today
under the table

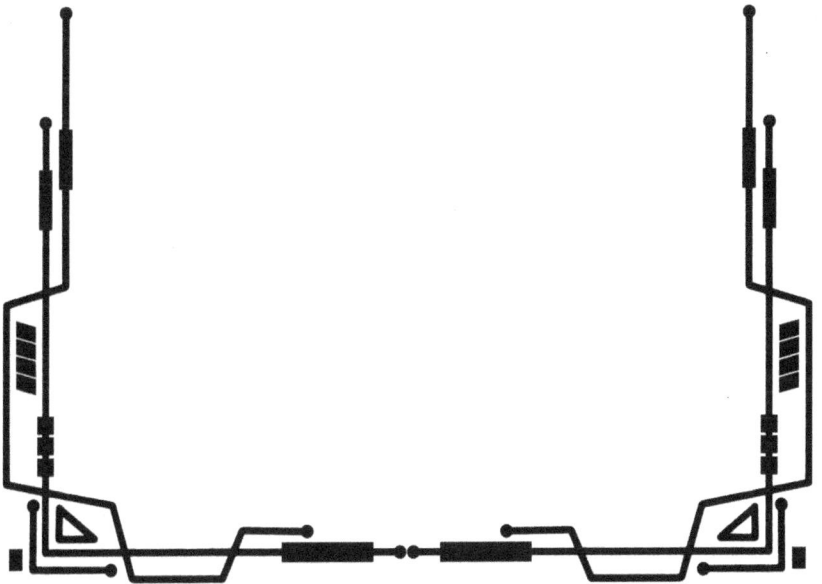

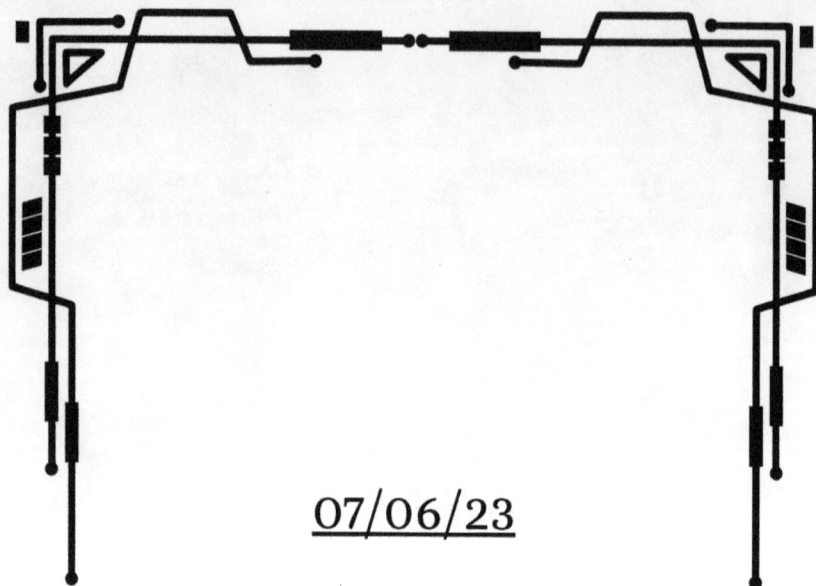

<u>07/06/23</u>

don't make sandwiches
just eat the plain bologna
on your morning walk

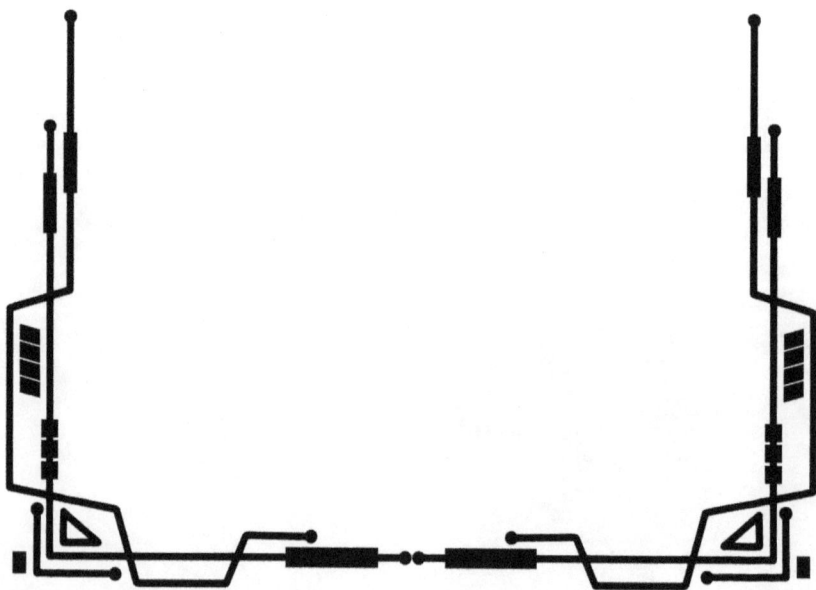

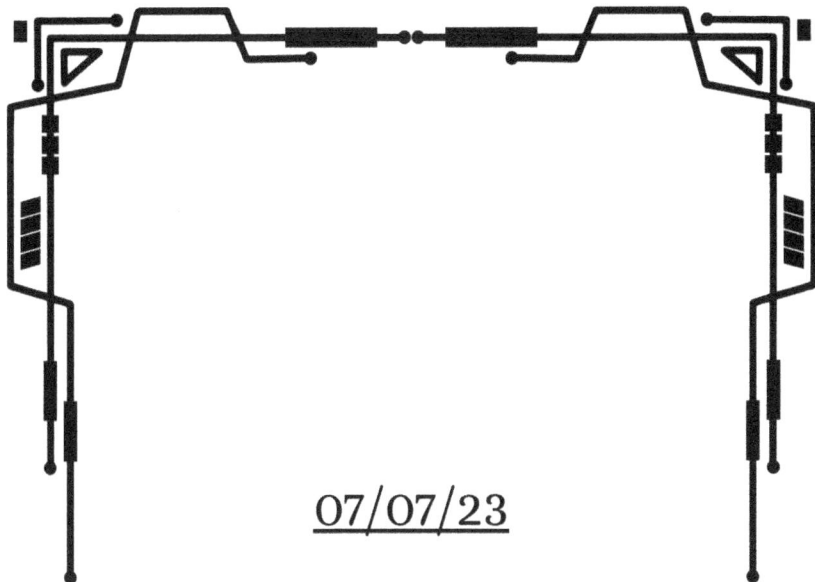

<u>07/07/23</u>

cigarette crisis
there is no more tobacco
only empty tubes

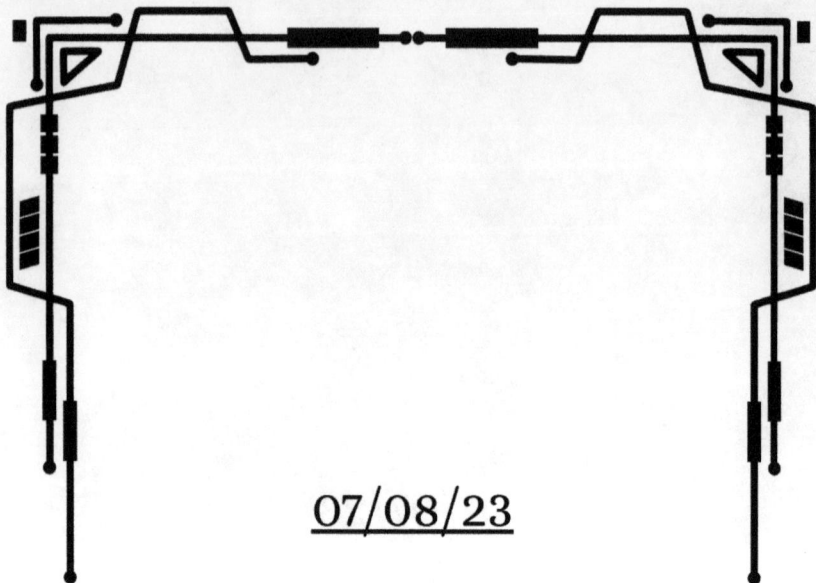

<u>07/08/23</u>

fifteen hours today
fifteen hours tomorrow too
i don't like it much

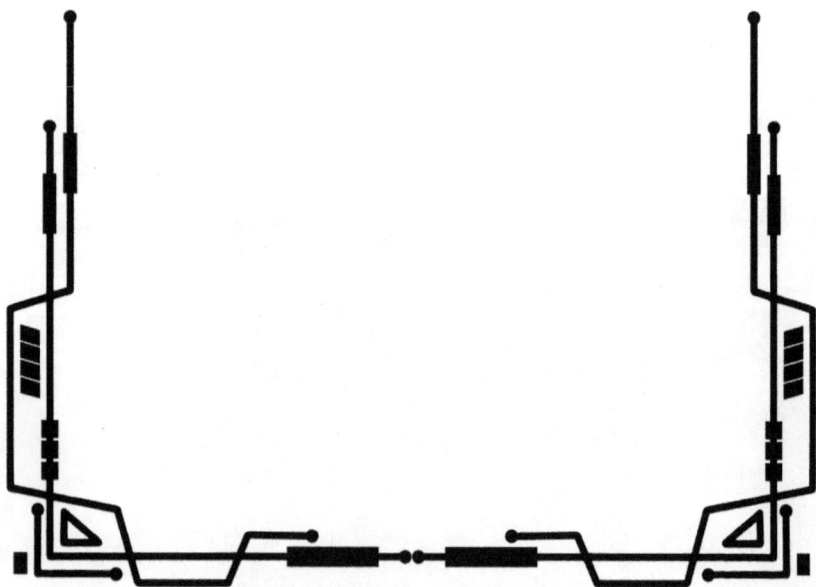

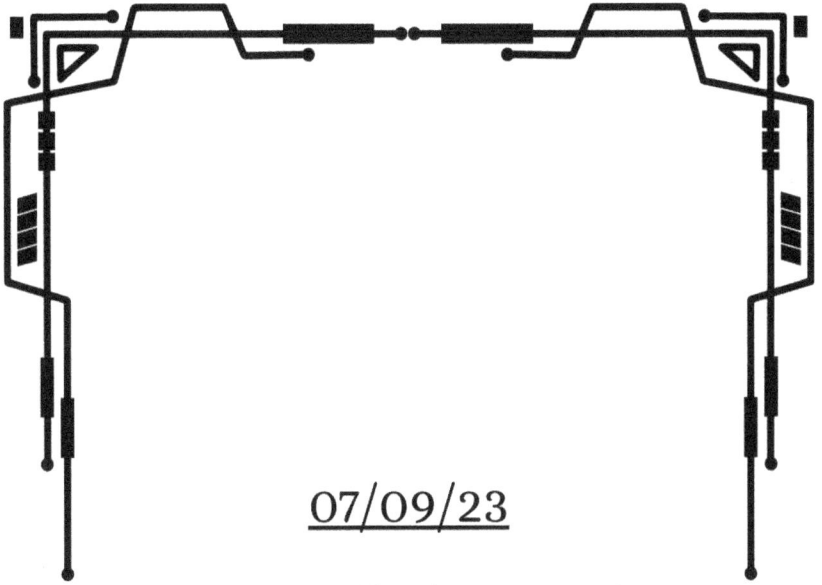

<u>07/09/23</u>

tony called out sick
angel can't make hollandaise
i hate fucking brunch

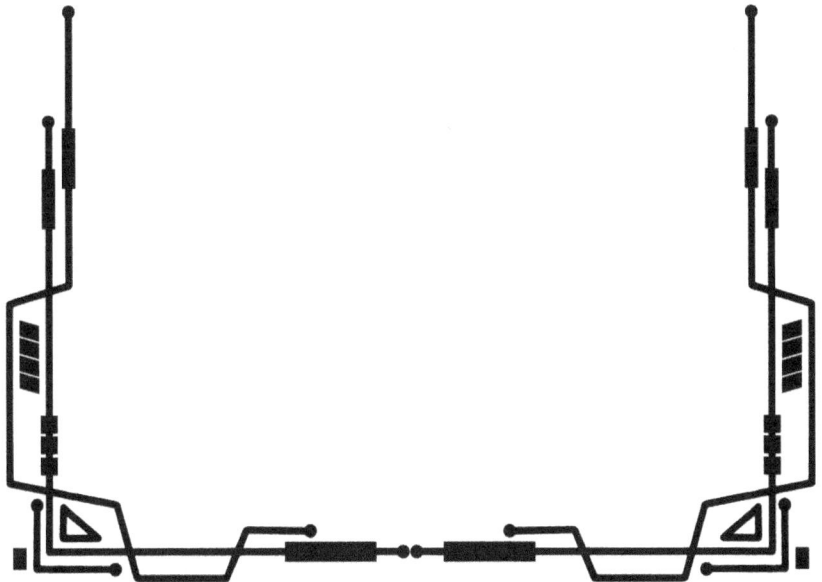

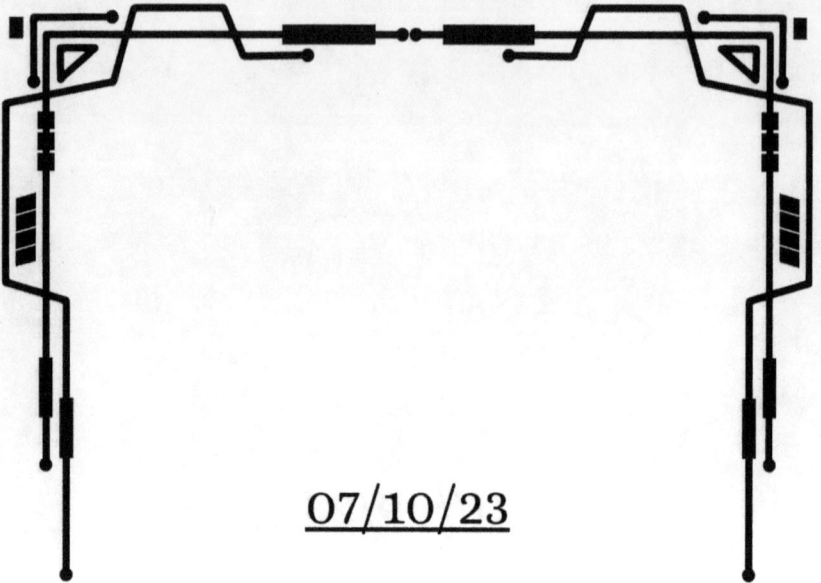

<u>07/10/23</u>

catch a pokemon
with five dollars and some change
maybe get lucky

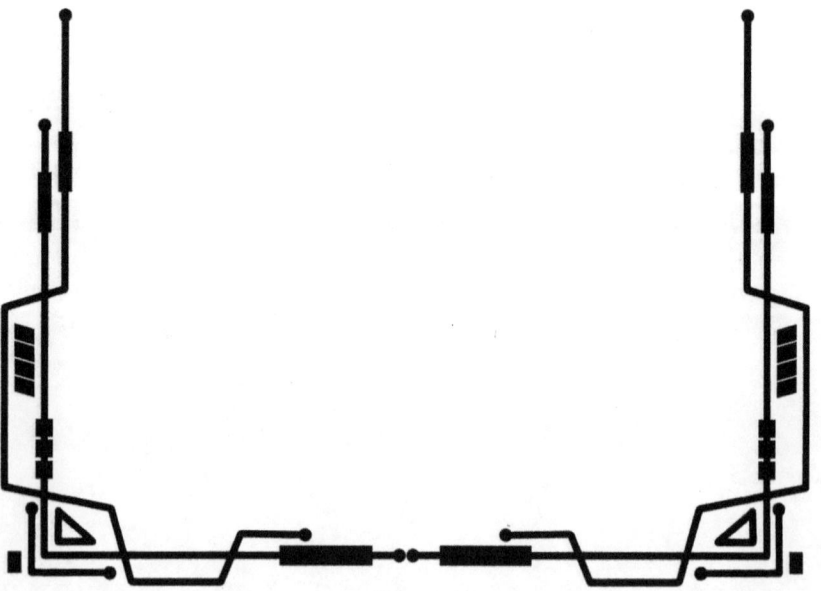

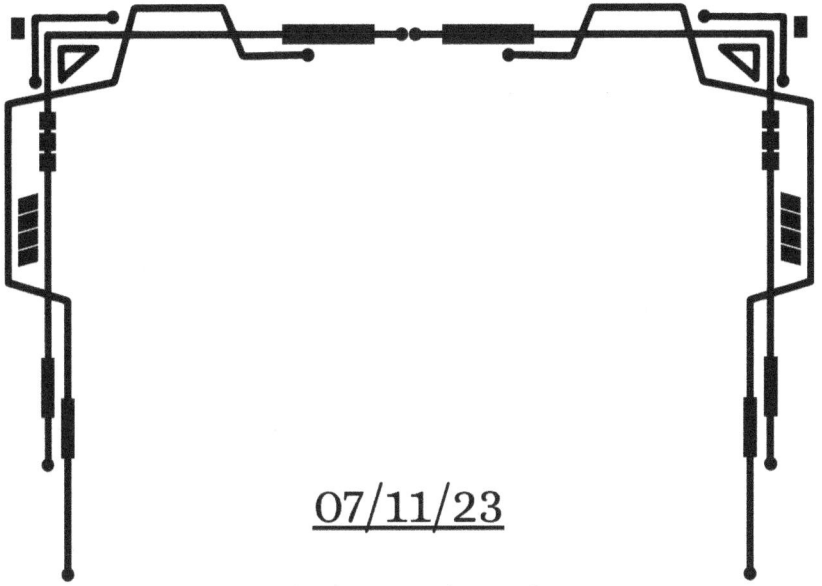

<u>07/11/23</u>

today is the day
to play the lotto at the
seven eleven

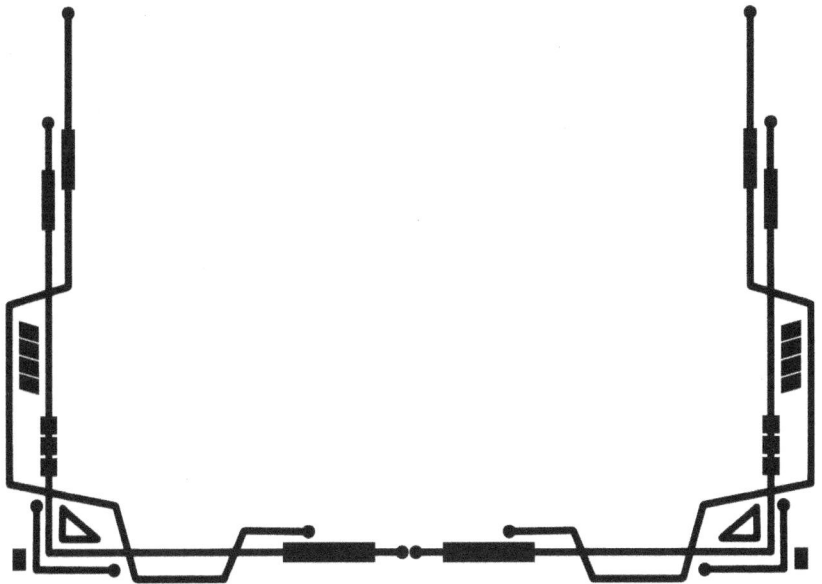

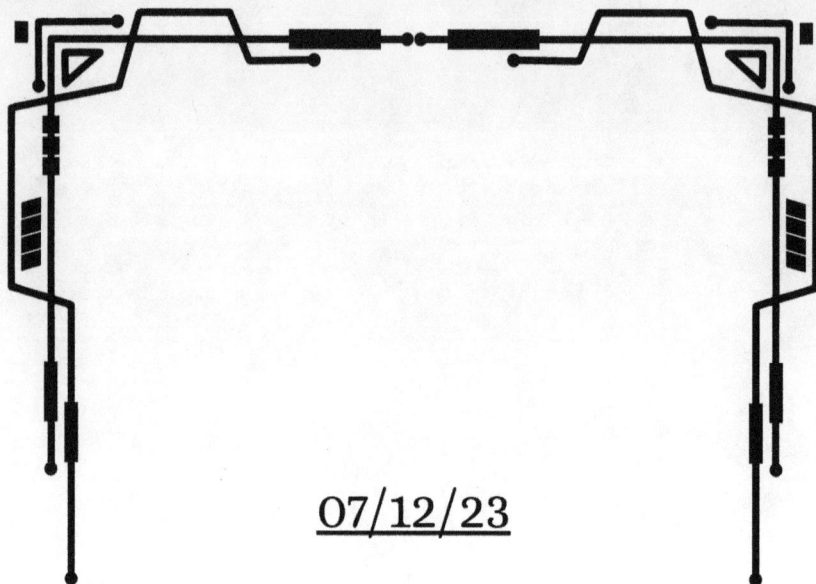

<u>07/12/23</u>

bright early morning
sunshine on the horizon
shut up stupid sun

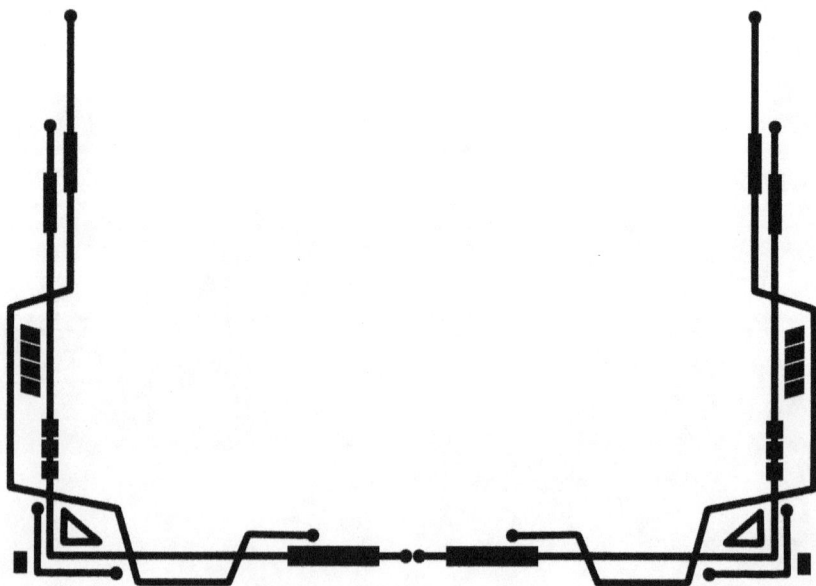

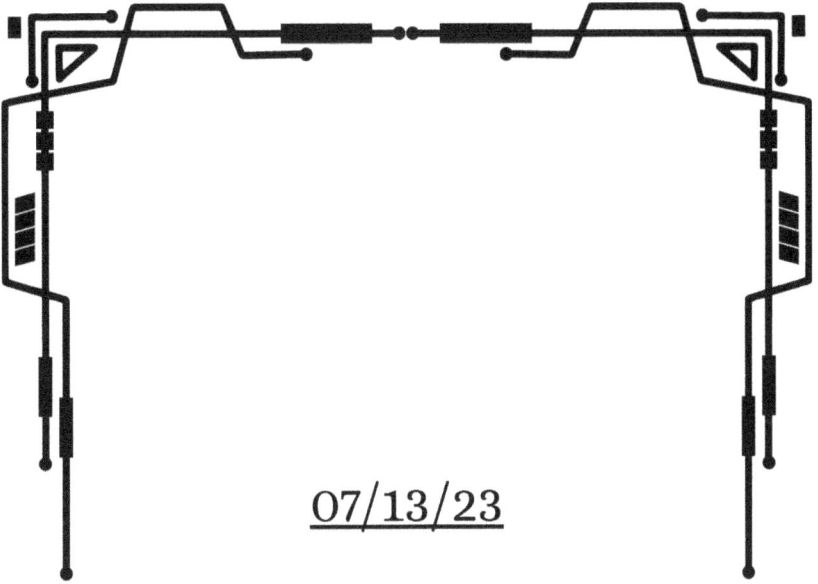

<u>07/13/23</u>

the thing of it is
a little bit is ok
but a lot is not

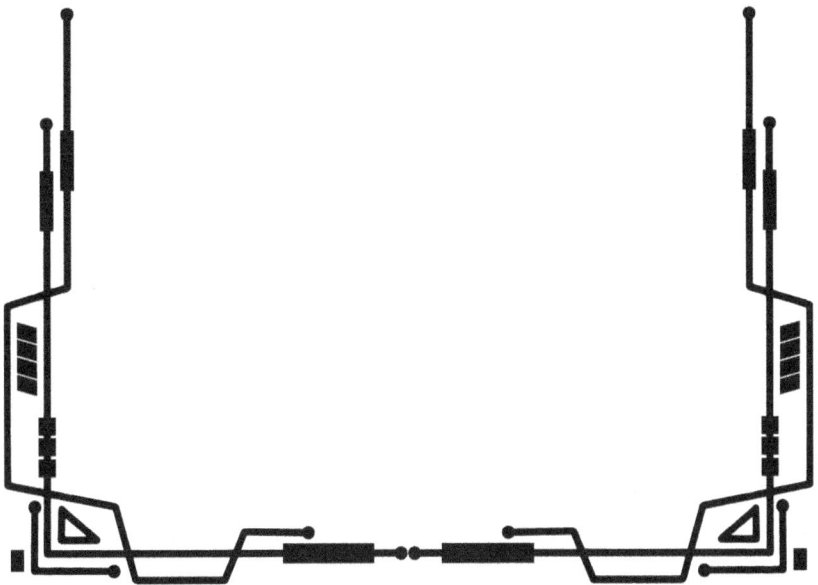

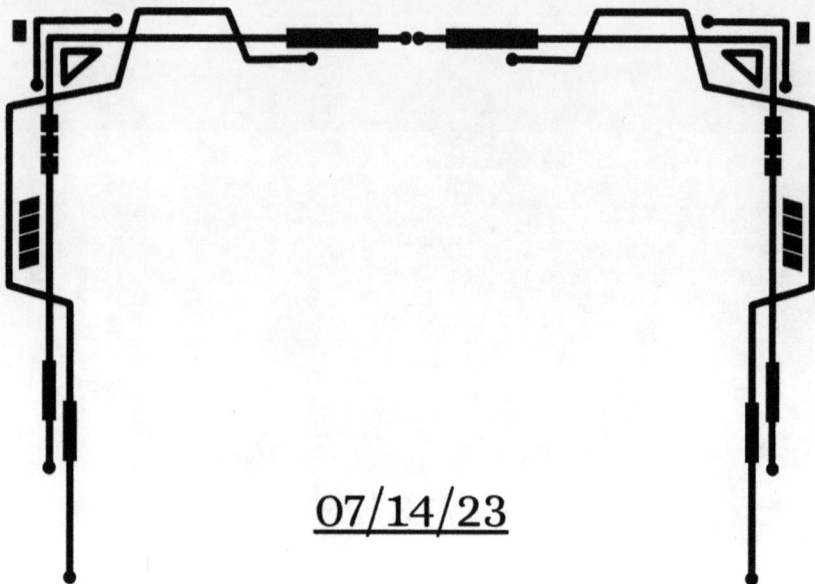

<u>07/14/23</u>

it's unnatural
a beaver with a duck bill
fear the platypus

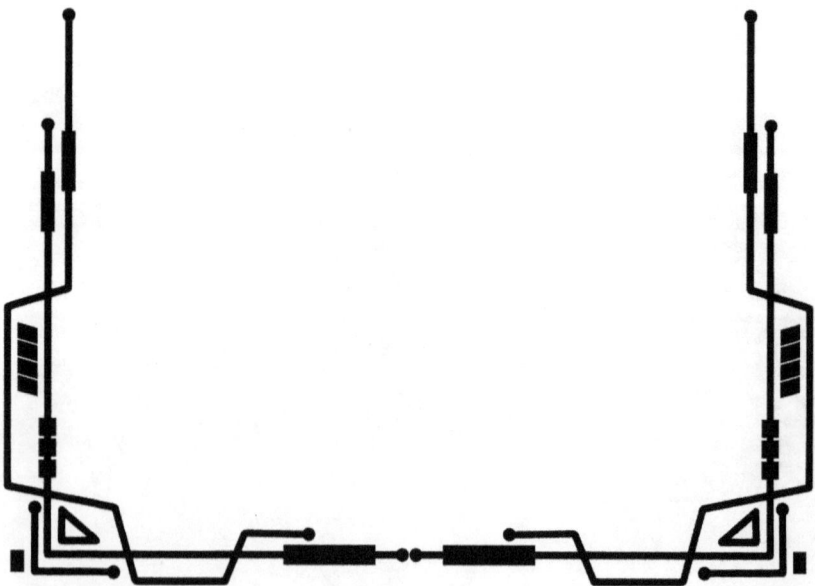

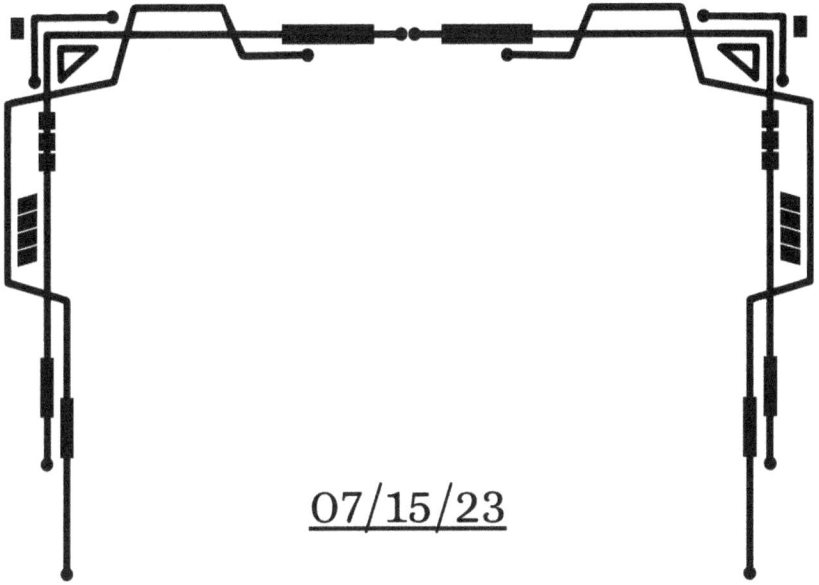

<u>07/15/23</u>

try to find the whisk
this batter needs to be stirred
to stick to the fish

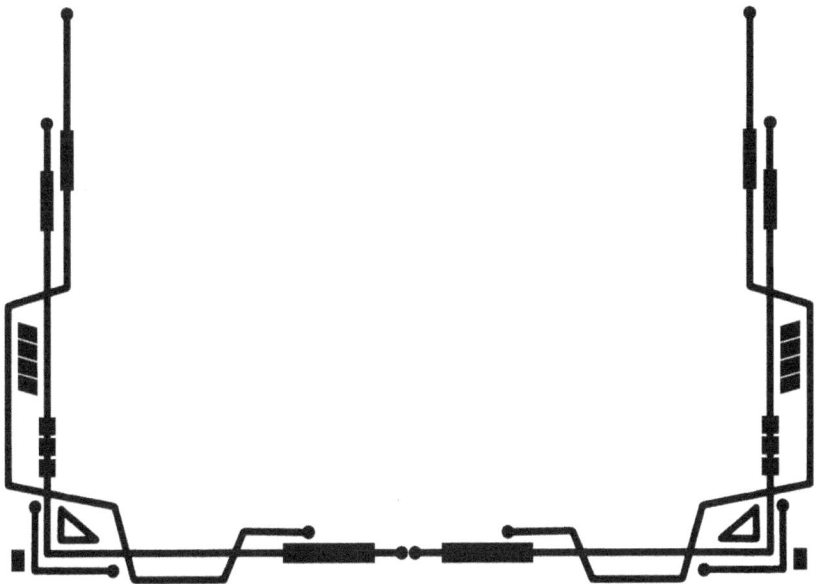

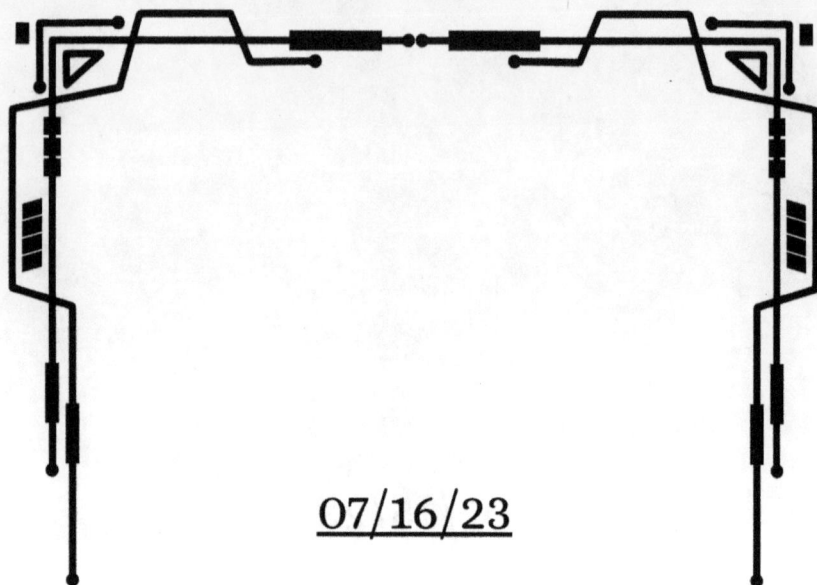

<u>07/16/23</u>

that car is too slow
it makes me late for pancakes
now they are soggy

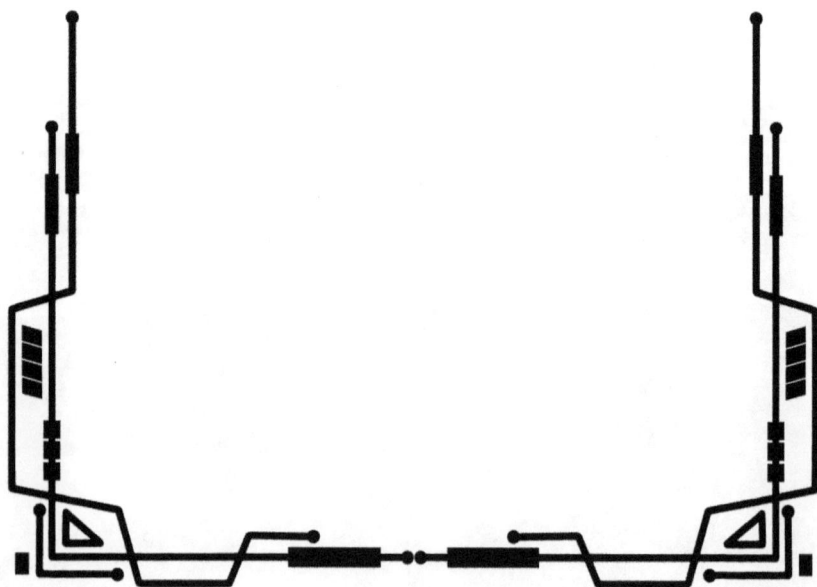

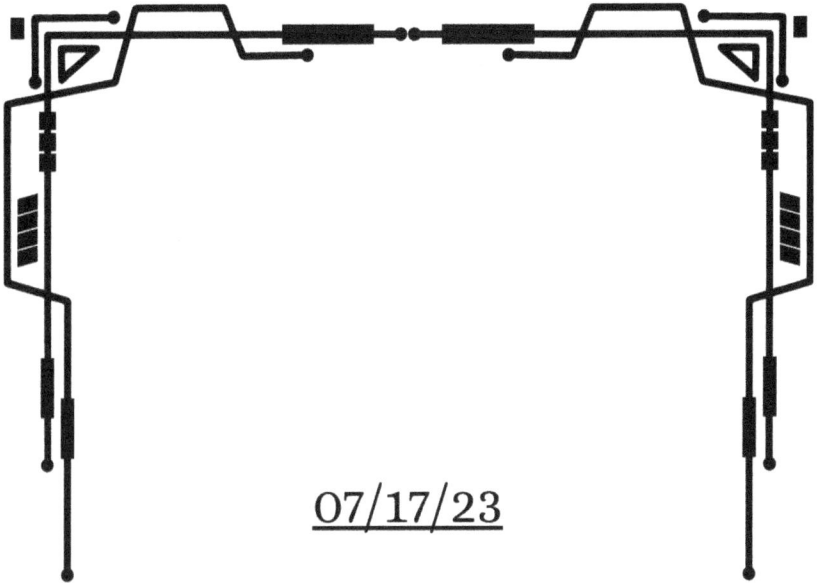

<u>07/17/23</u>

the shade tree is good
for leaning on while smoking
look it's a magpie

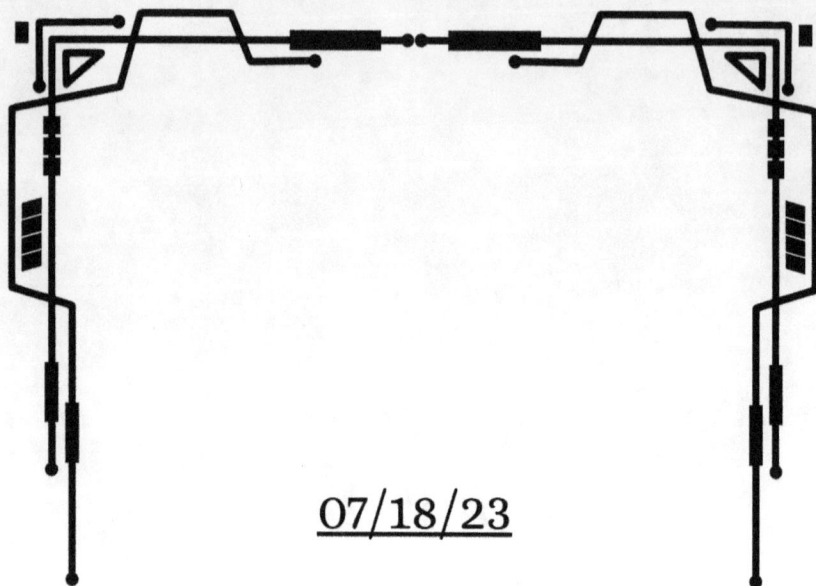

<u>07/18/23</u>

it's dinnertime and
i'm hungry so let's make a
rustic taco pie

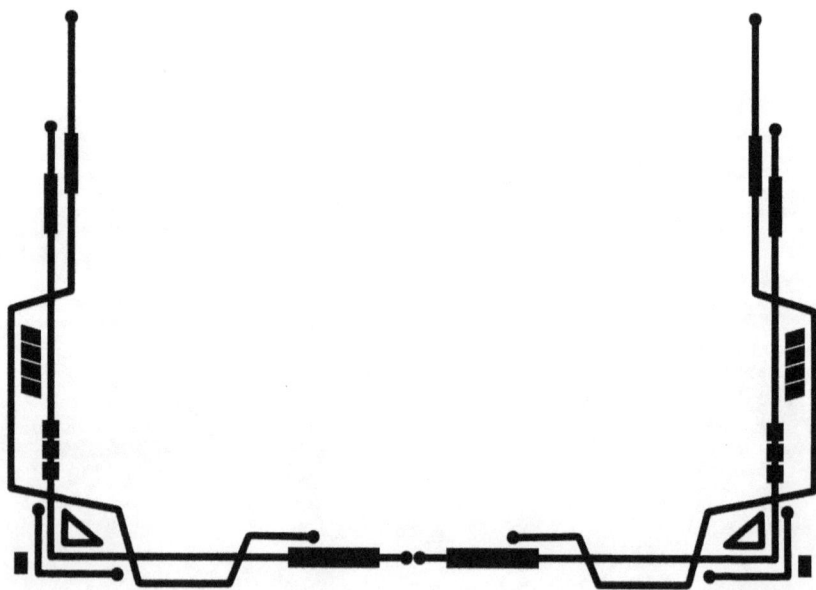

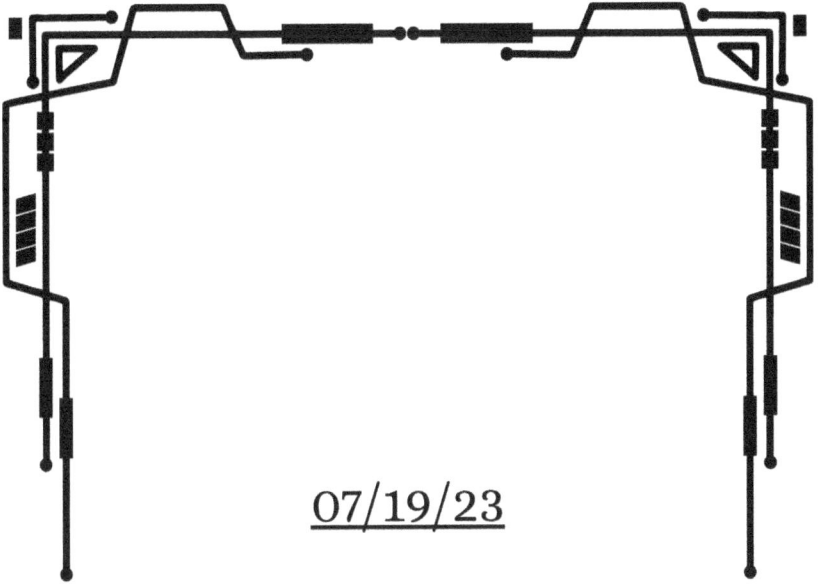

<u>07/19/23</u>

never feed the bear
it's brown and it looks hungry
but they say not to

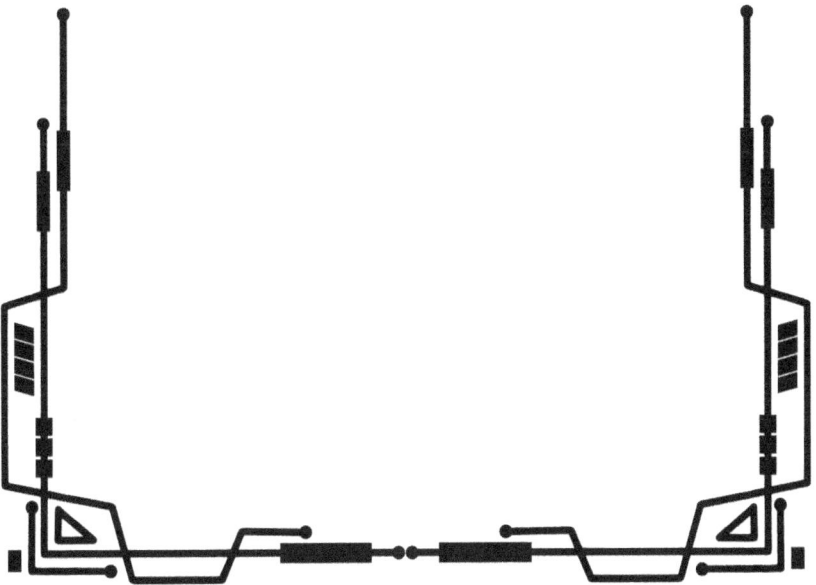

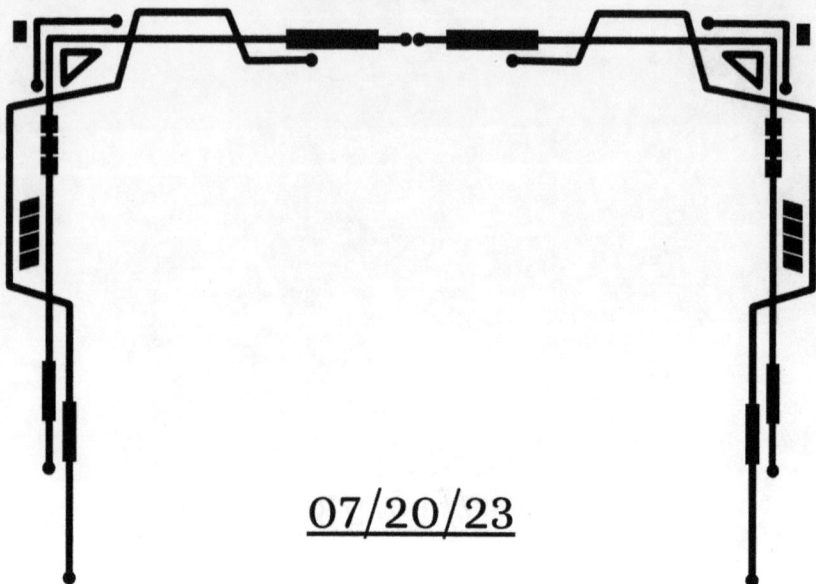

<u>07/20/23</u>

look at that thing there
it wiggles like the jello
i want to touch it

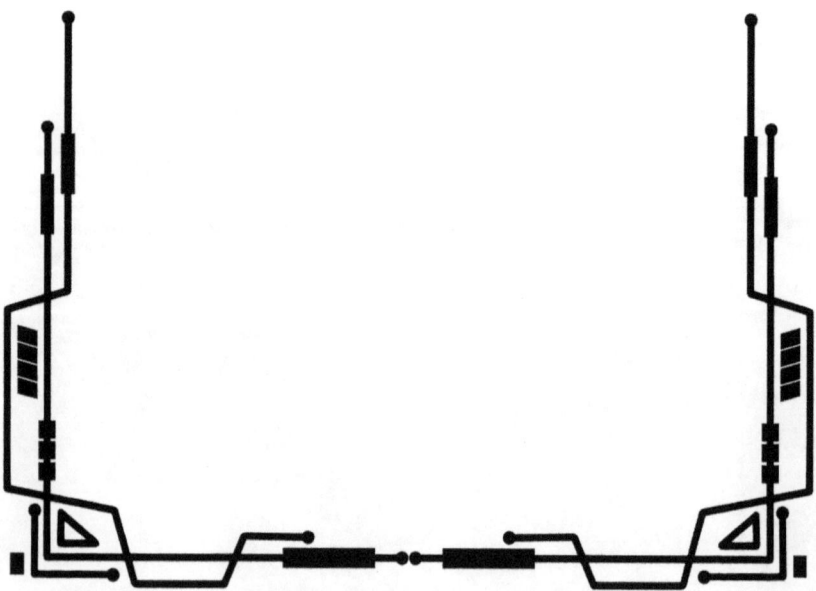

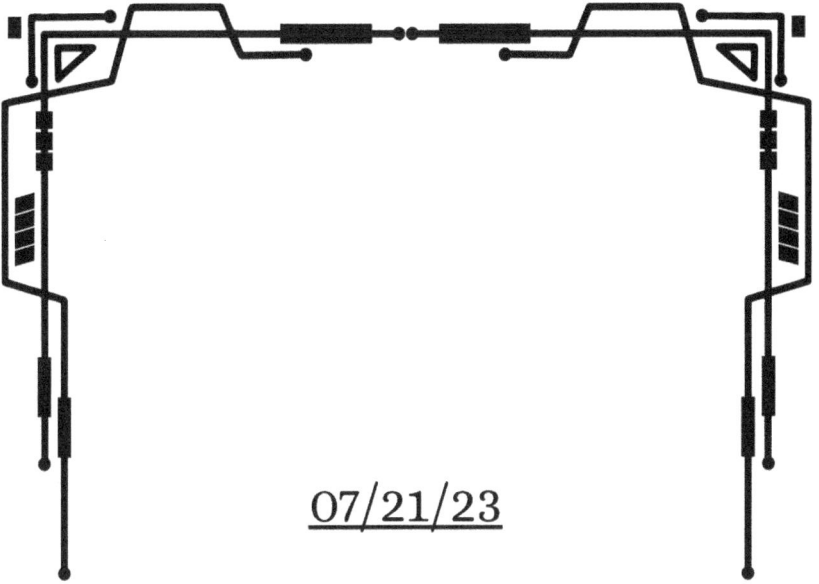

<u>07/21/23</u>

seven twenty one
that's a real good credit score
still can't buy a car

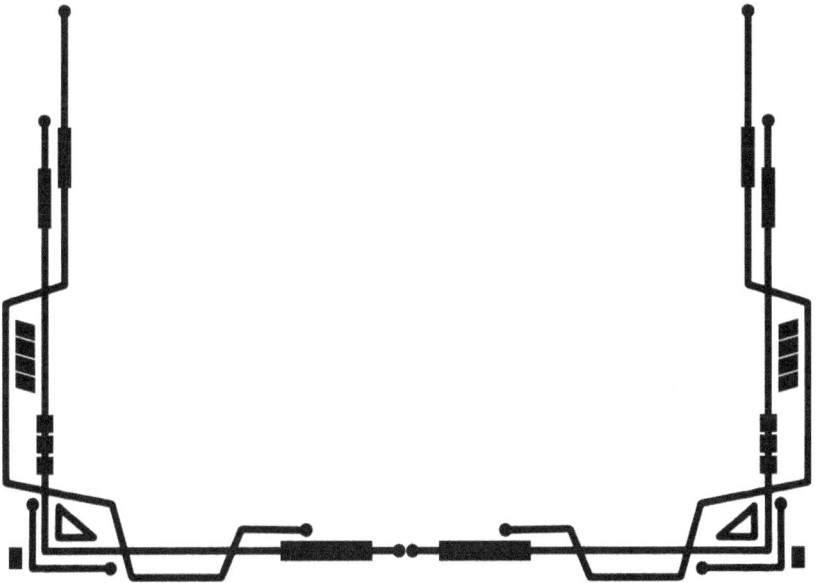

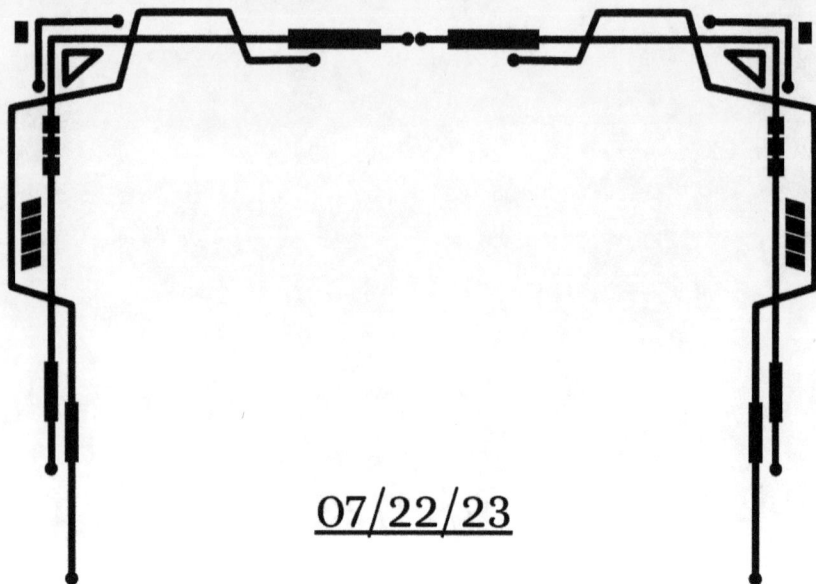

<u>07/22/23</u>

hummingbird physics
it's hot and dry and hazy
here on the front range

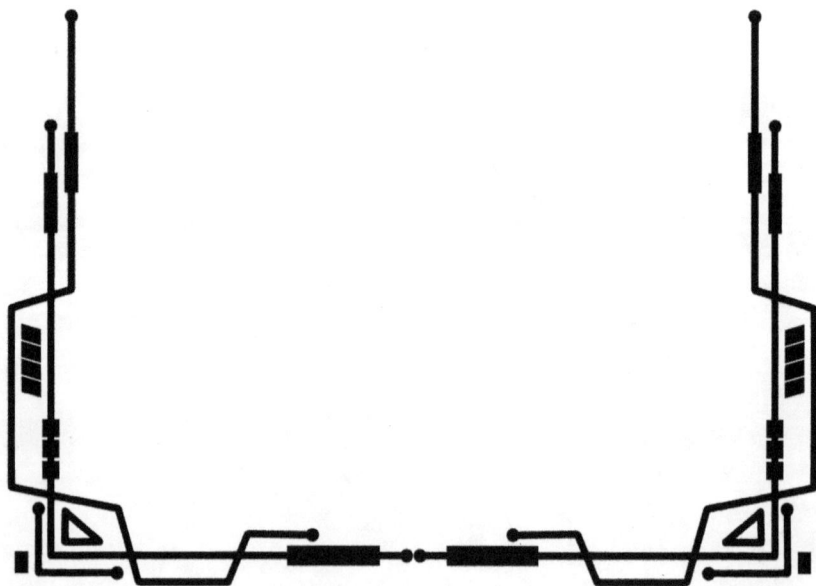

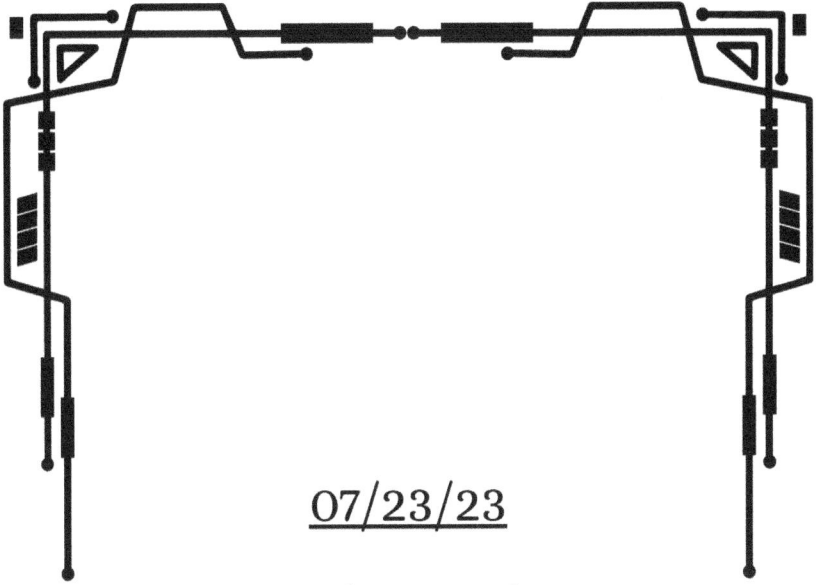

<u>07/23/23</u>

can i have a bite
dip it in the ranch sauce please
thank you now fuck off

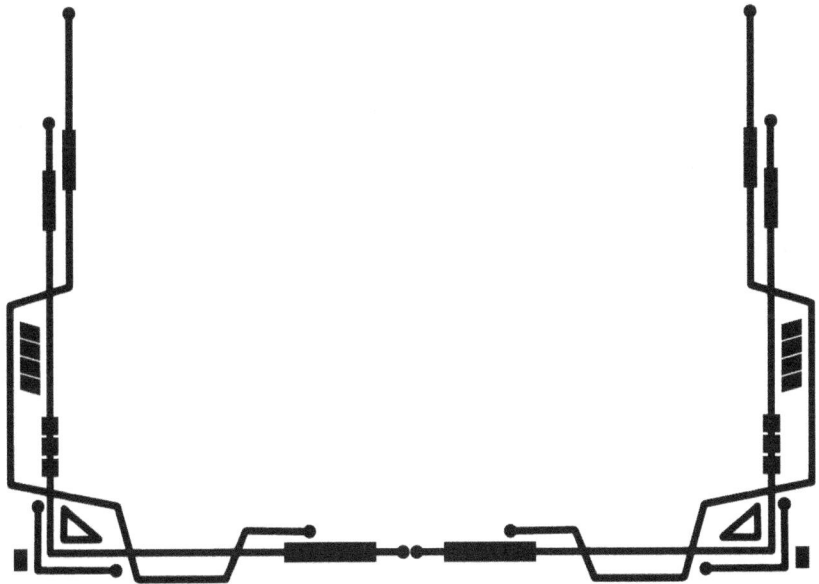

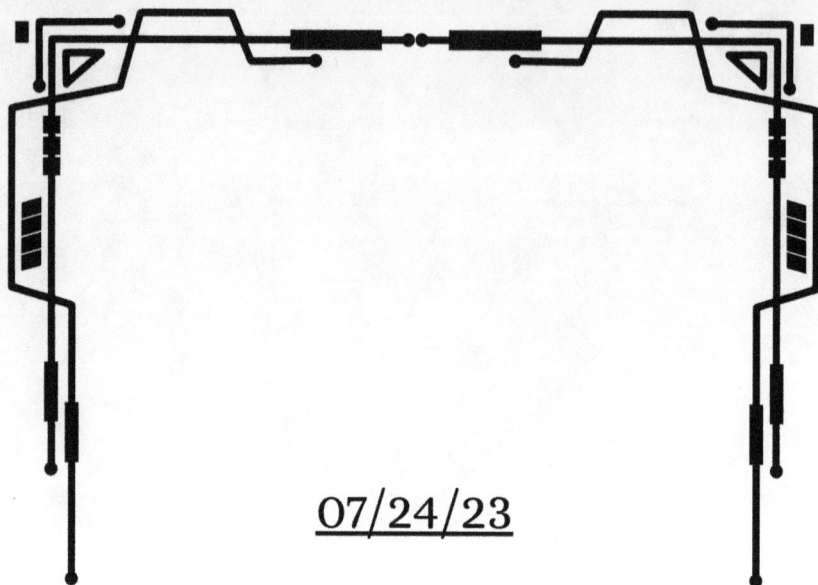

<u>07/24/23</u>

prairie dogs attack
climb up the tree and wait there
until they go home

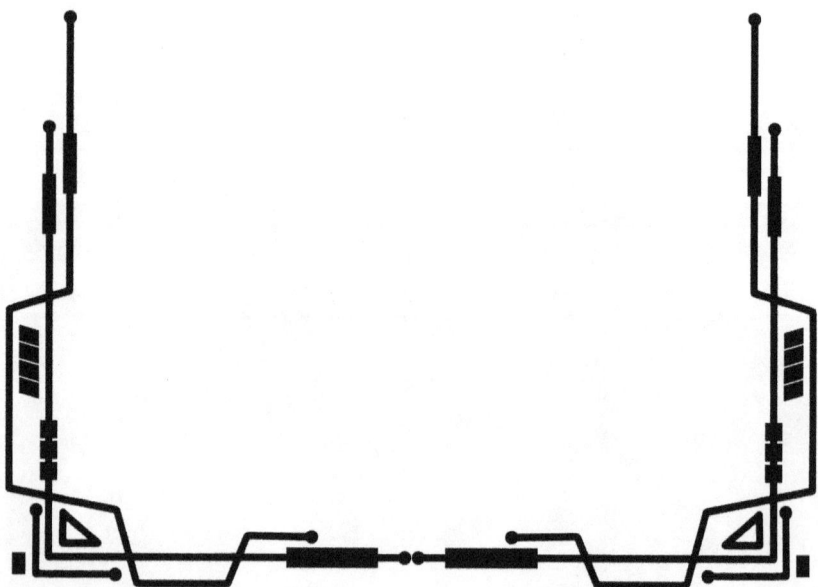

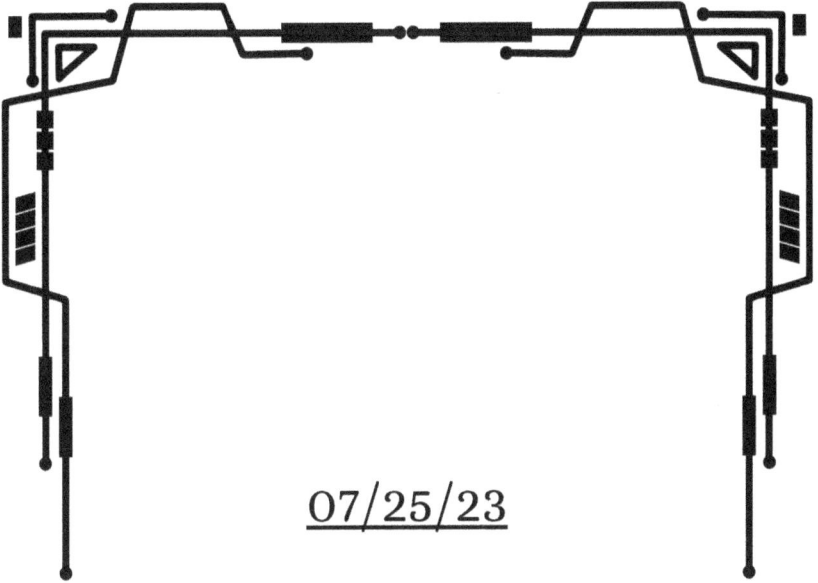

<u>07/25/23</u>

the little cat is
mean to the big cat when there
are treats being had

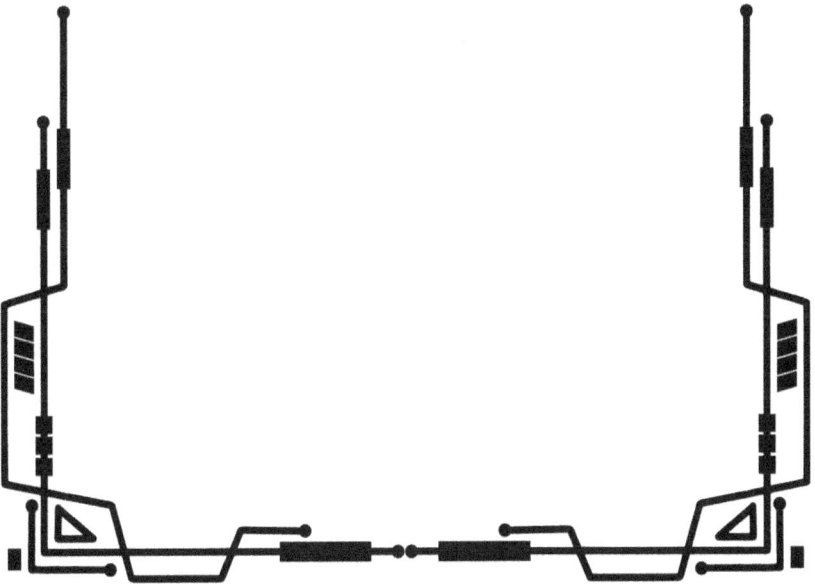

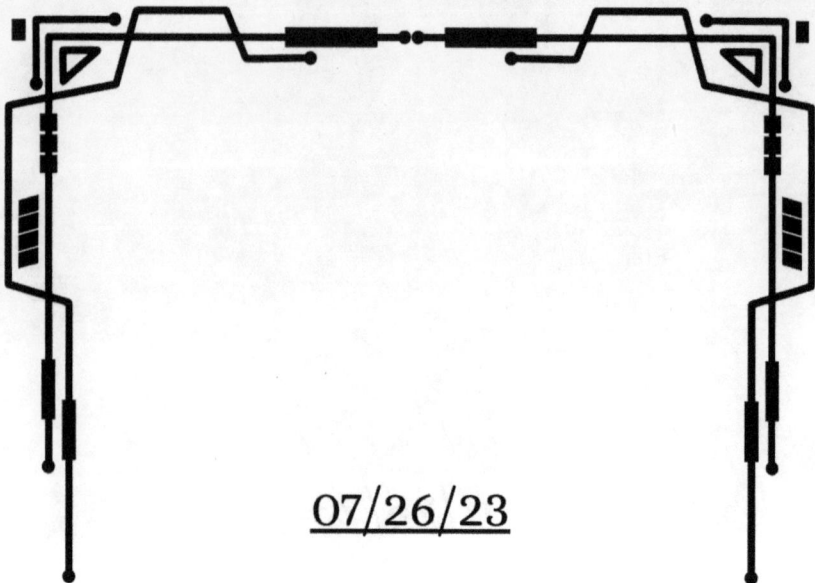

<u>07/26/23</u>

today is the day
it was a very good day
in nineteen sixty

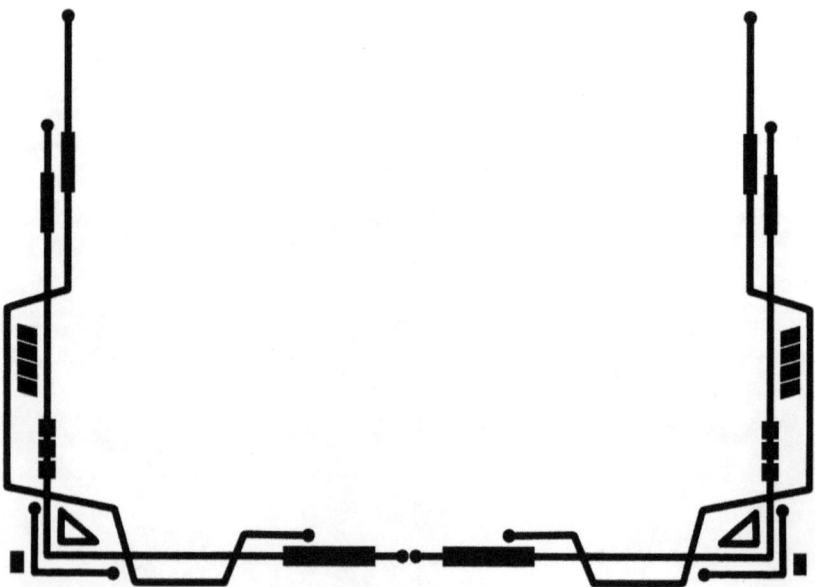

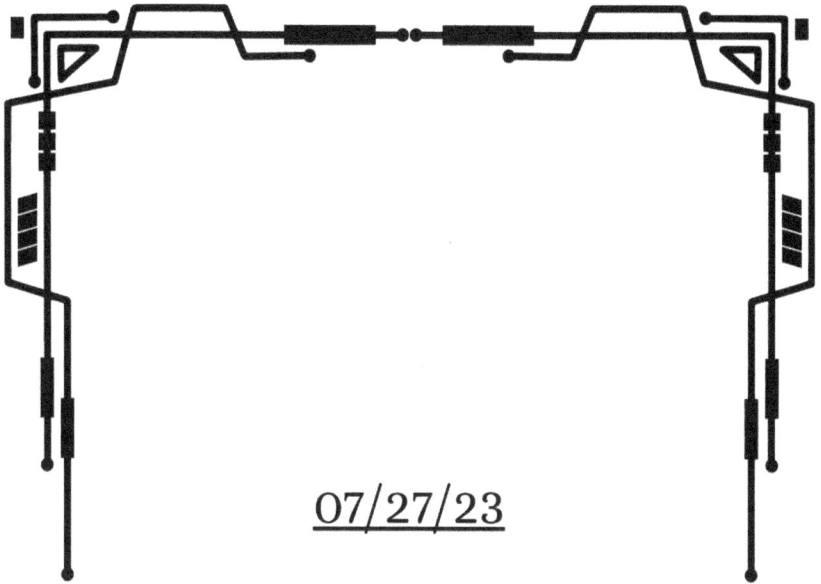

<u>07/27/23</u>

there weren't balls here but
add seventeen percent and
now there are balls here

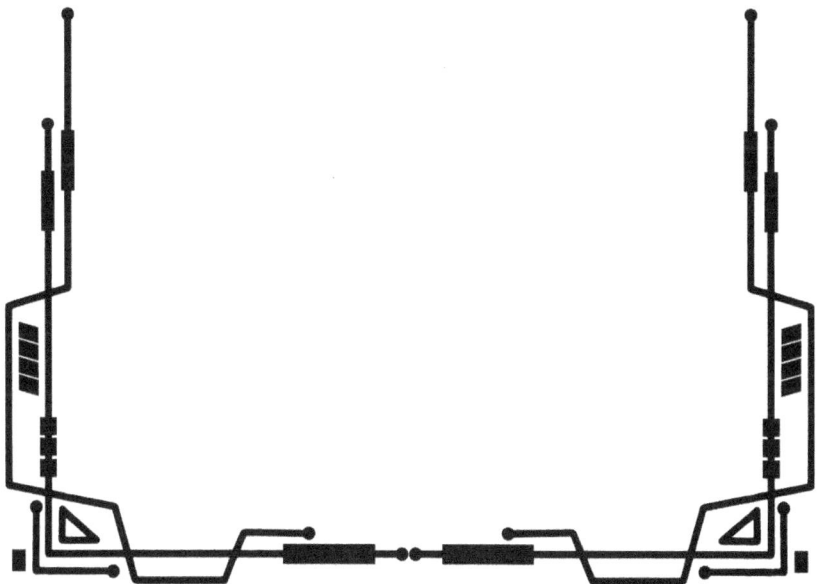

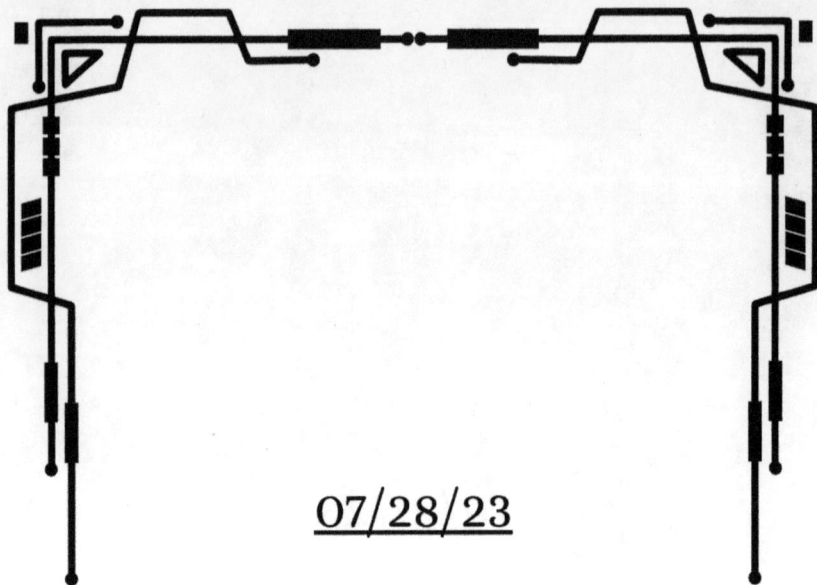

<u>07/28/23</u>

the air is burning
it's sweaty and annoying
because of july

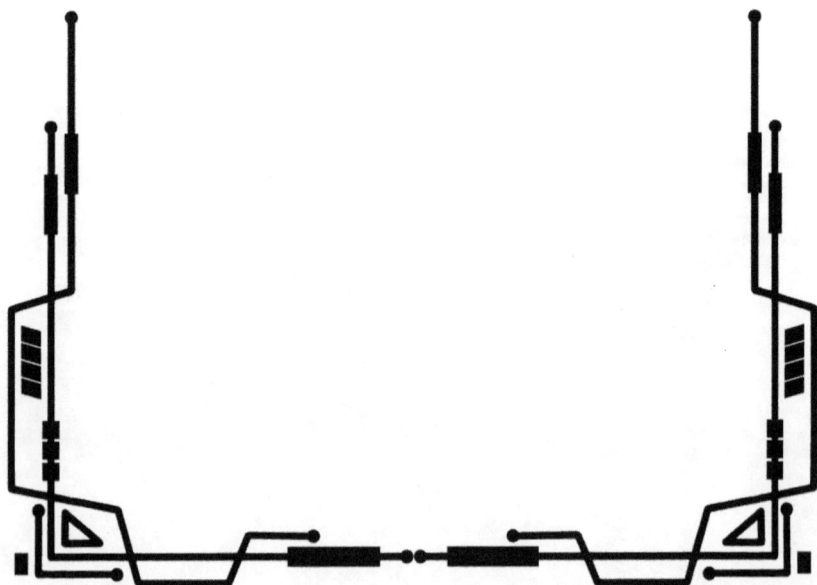

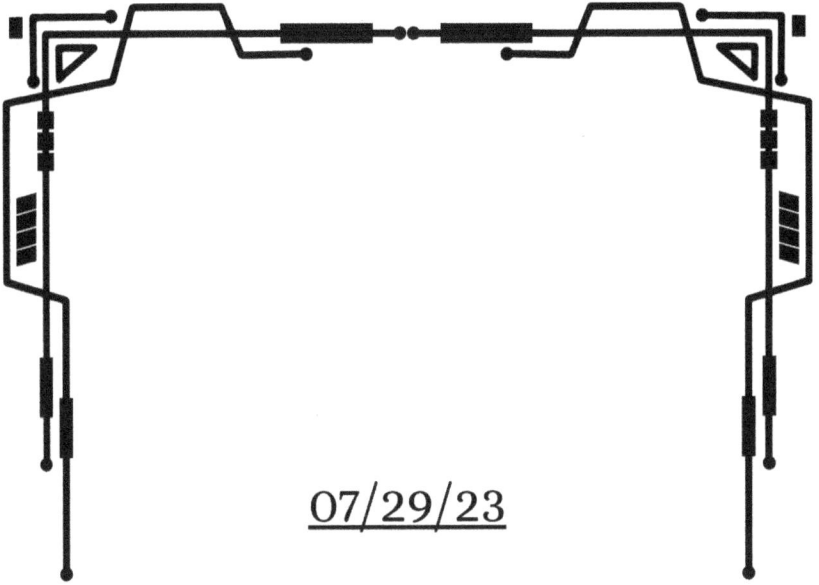

<u>07/29/23</u>

how many more times
will i eat a cheeseburger
without the burger

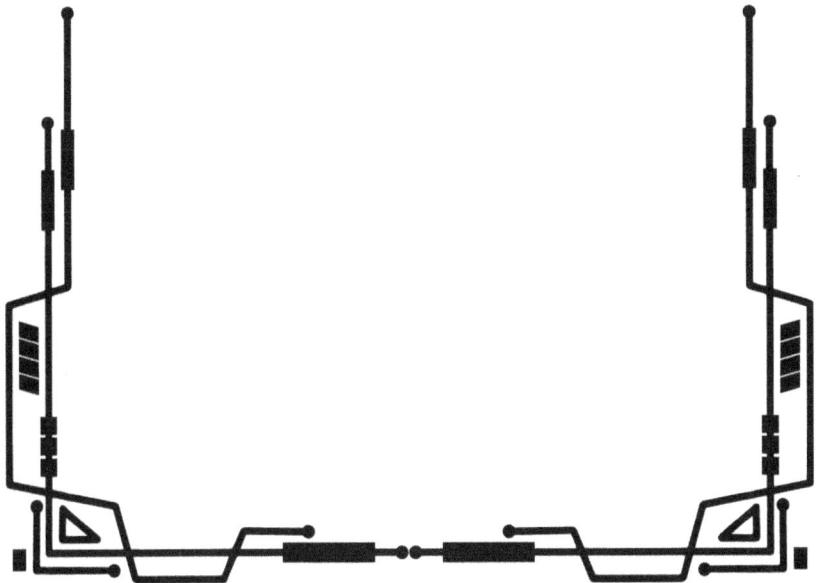

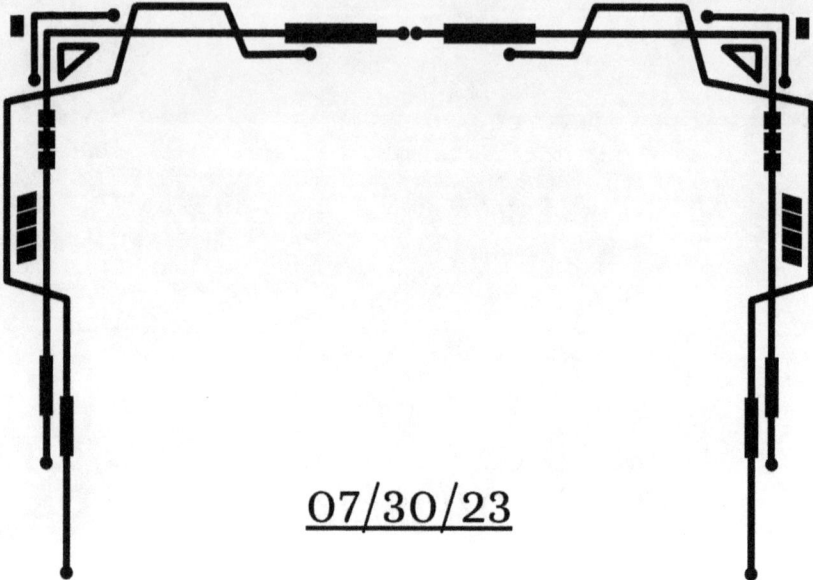

<u>07/30/23</u>

mockingbirds are the archrivals in business to the sincere puffin

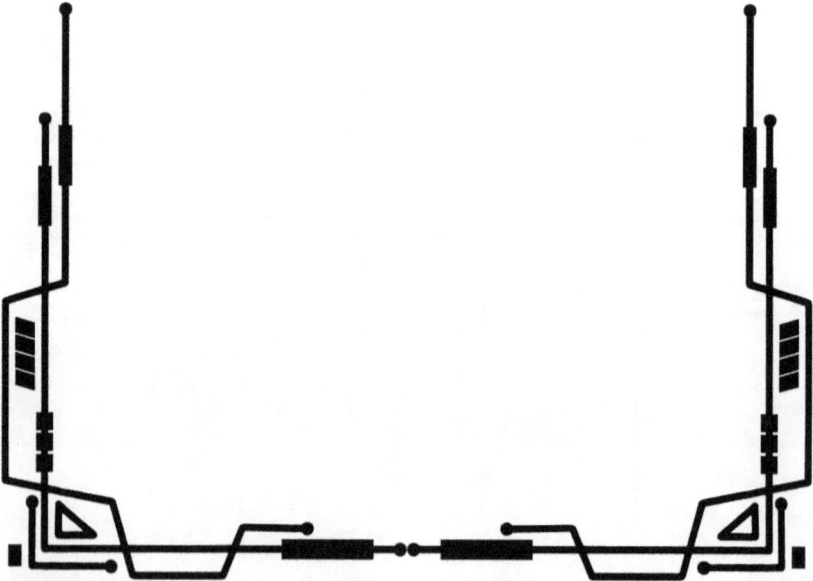

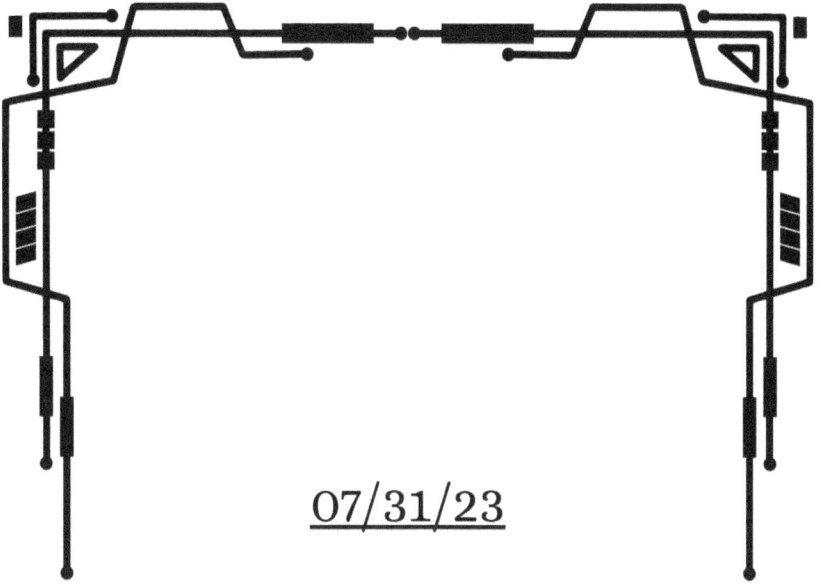

<u>07/31/23</u>

go away now please
it's loud and annoying and
that is just from you

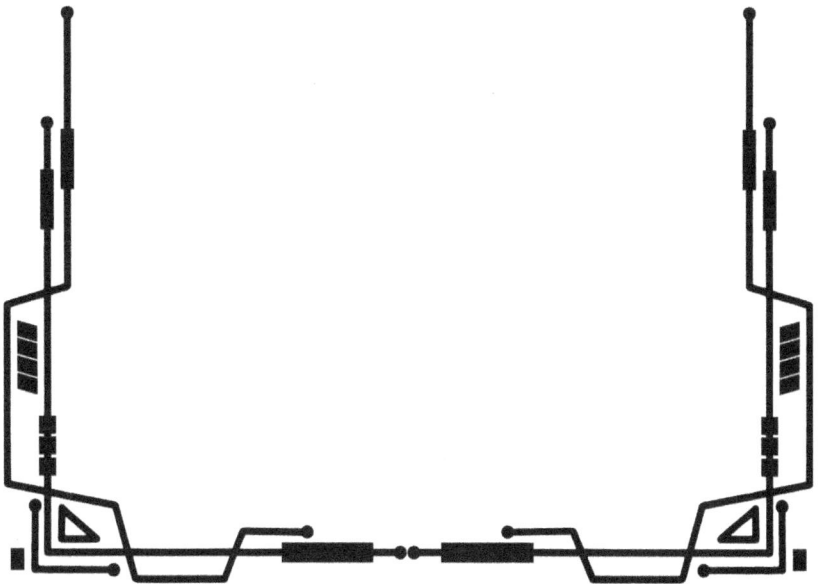

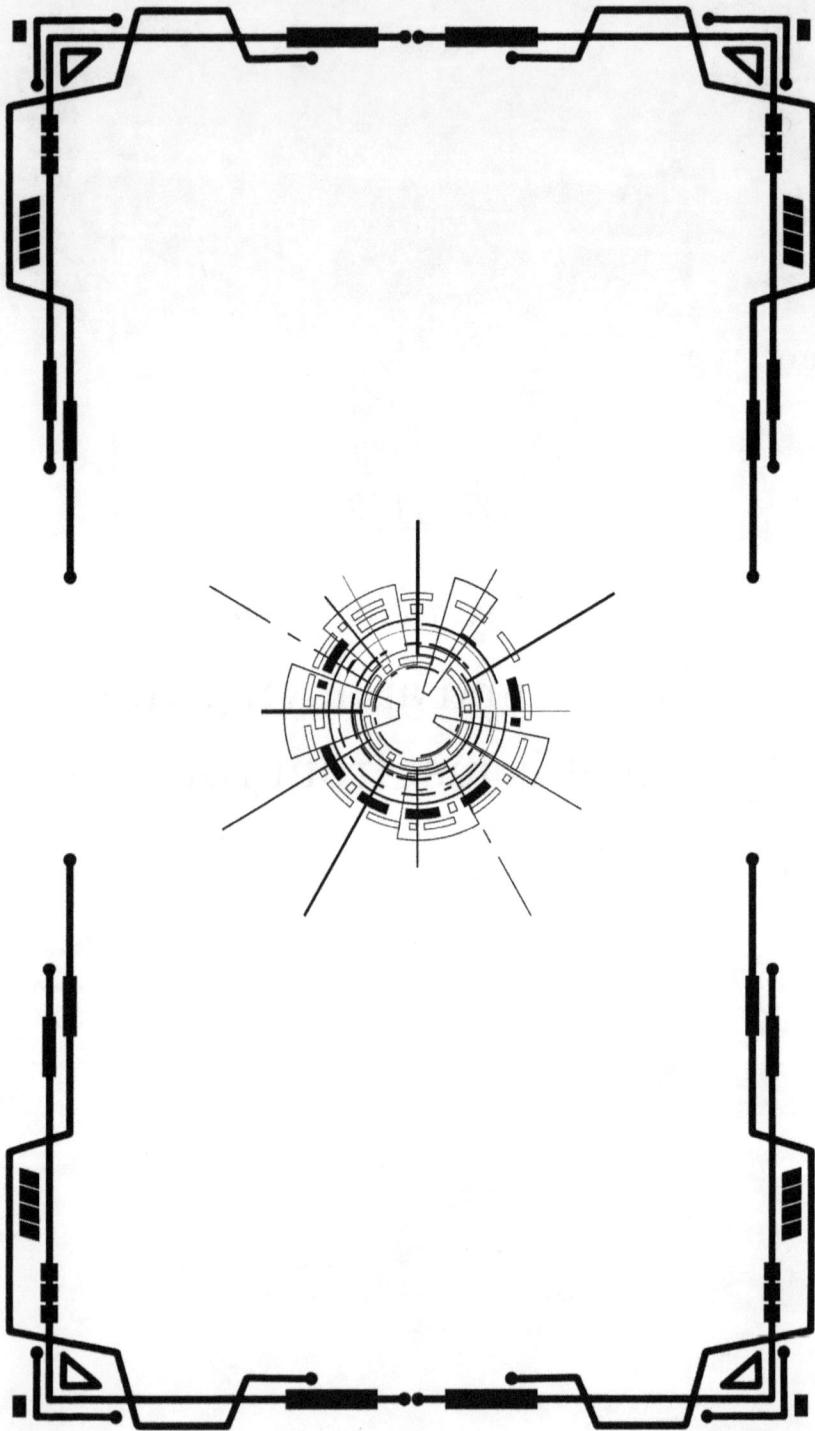

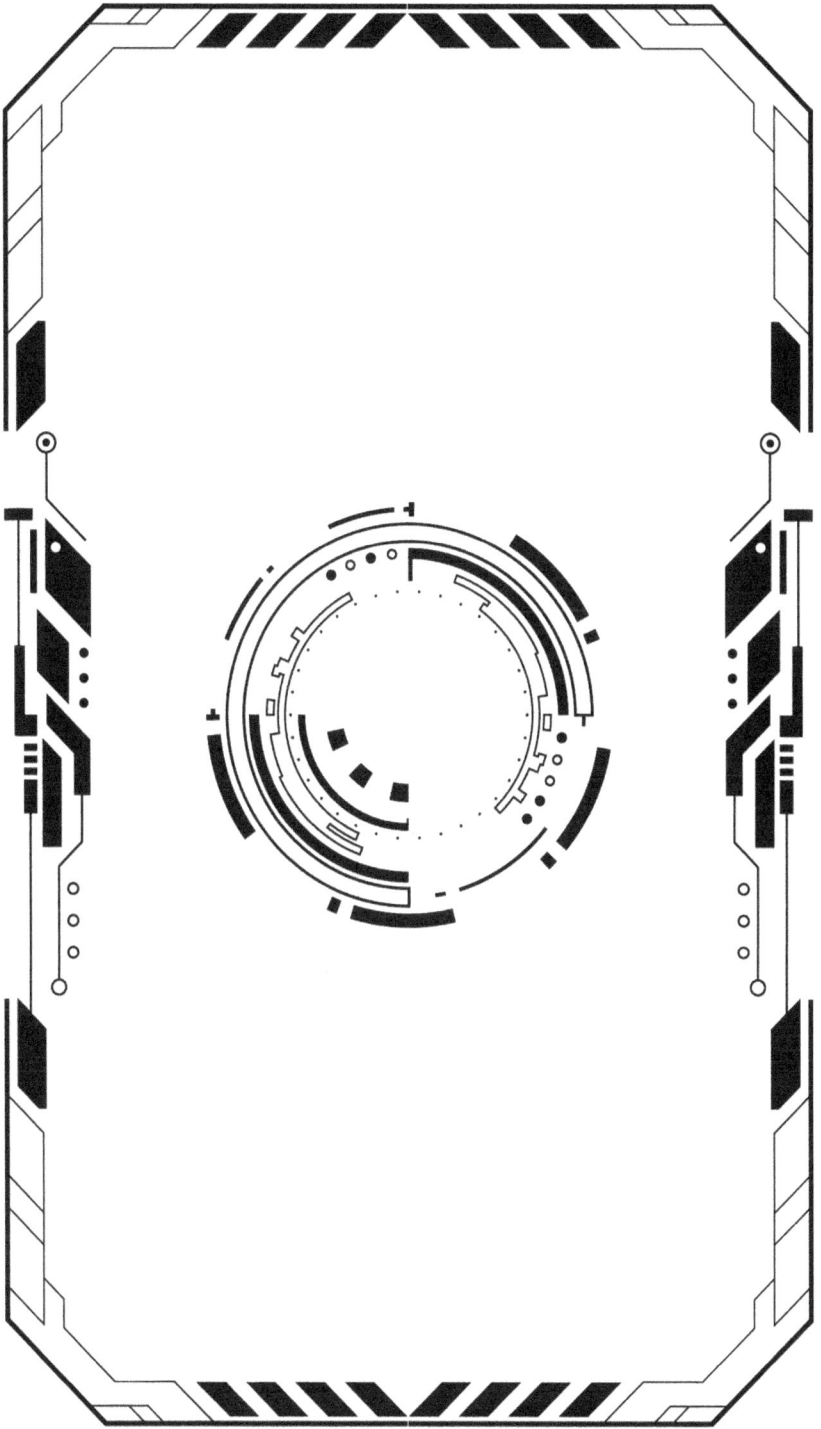

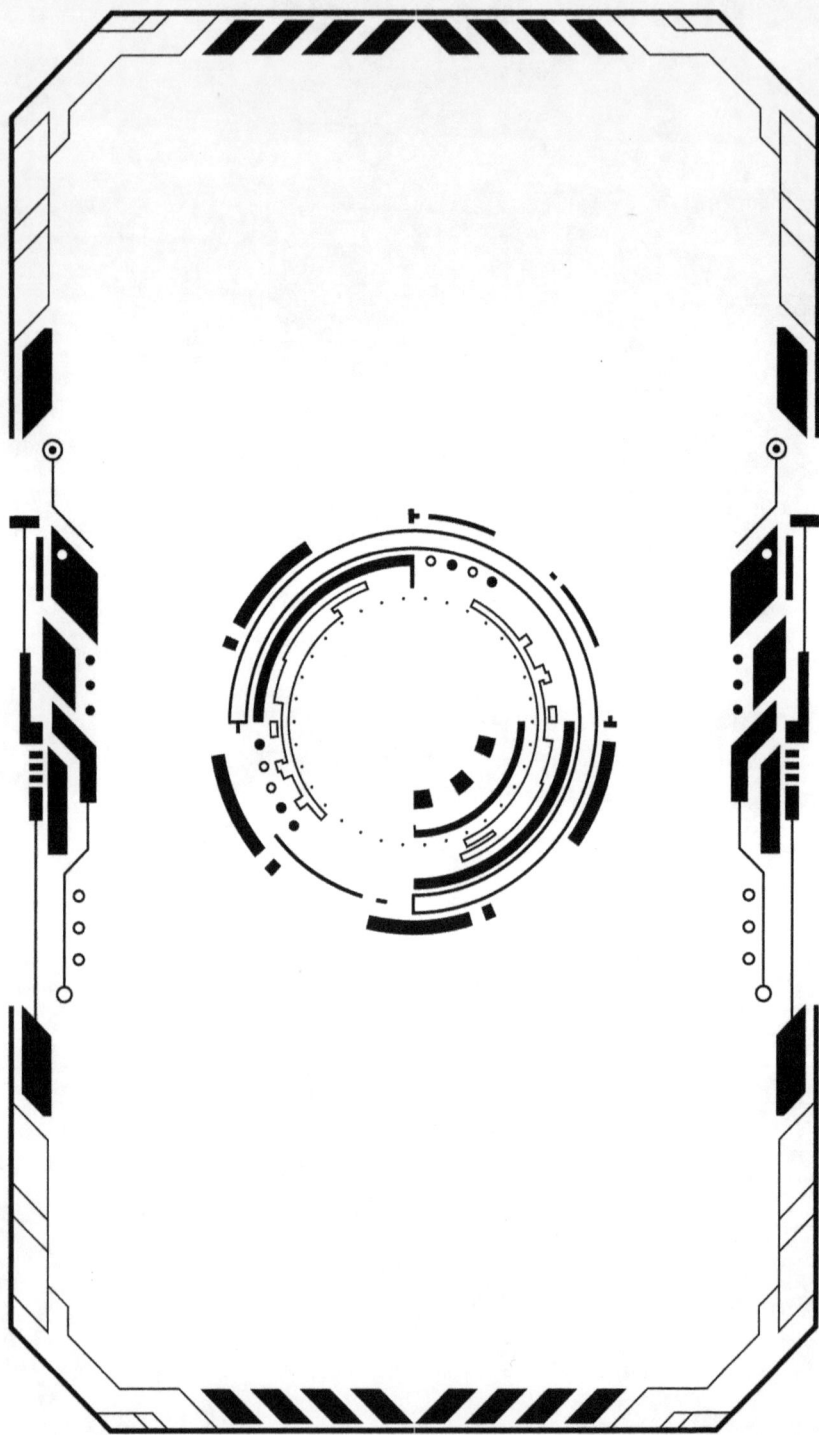

<u>08/01/23</u>

there once was a dude
who made summertime salad
caesar augustus

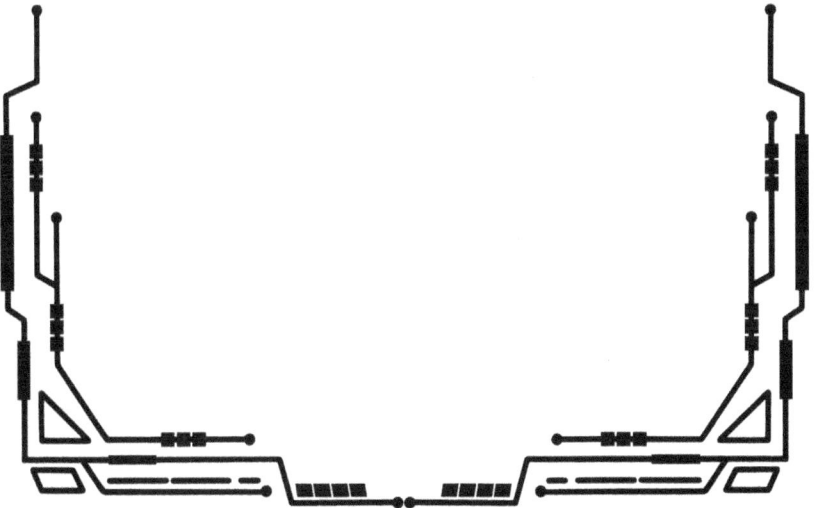

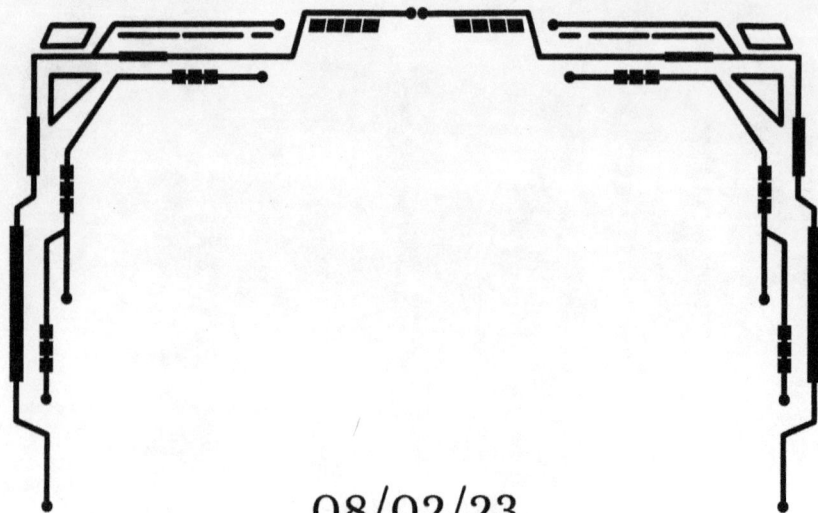

<u>08/02/23</u>

downtown in the rain
the dusty sidewalk settles
and cools down a bit

<u>08/03/23</u>

see that stuff right there
those things are very good things
i like stuff and things

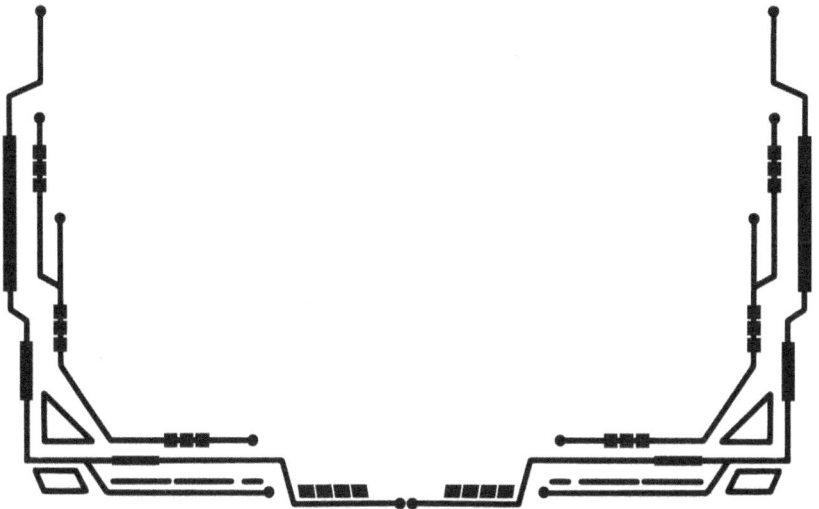

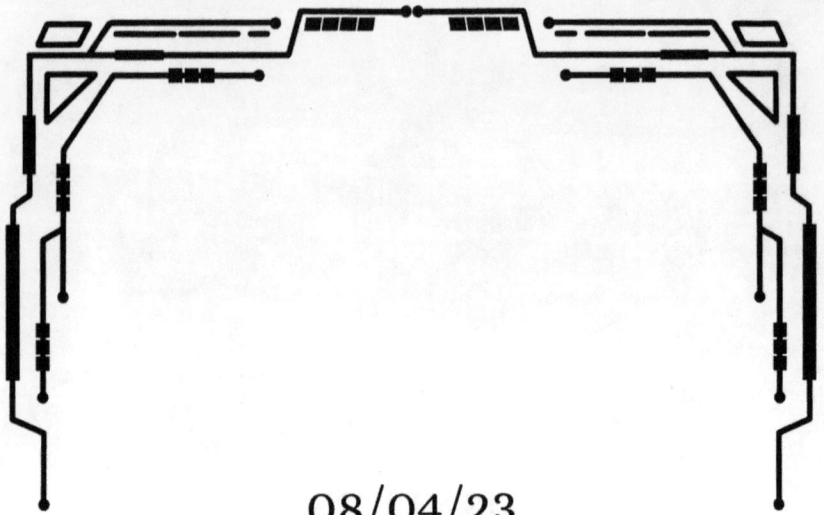

<u>08/04/23</u>

my favorite blanket
it has become unpleasant
i don't like it now

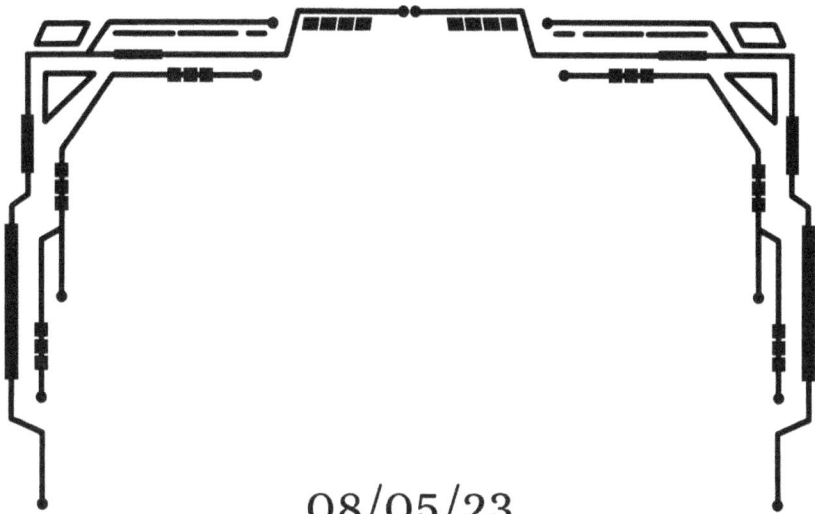

<u>08/05/23</u>

good day my kind sir
i'll have the ketchup platter
and cup of meat please

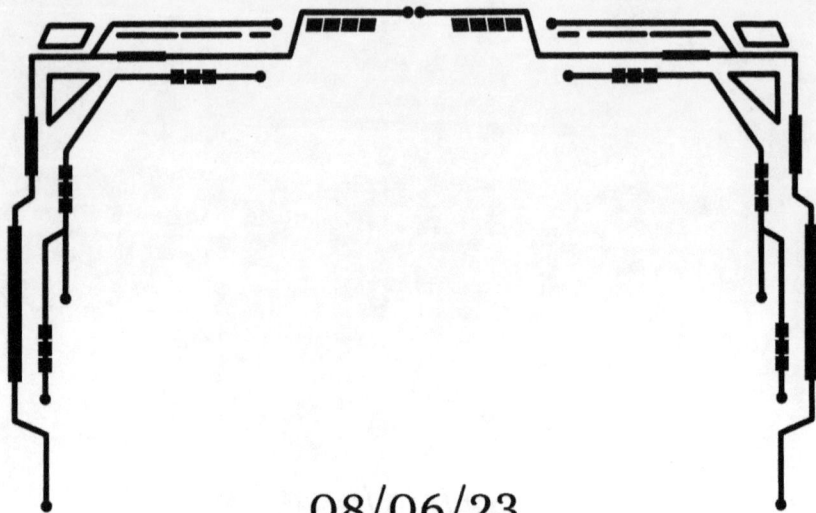

<u>08/06/23</u>

two and a half years
just a couple more weeks now
not soon enough though

<u>08/07/23</u>

i need to sleep now
it's too hot to sleep in here
not a wink of sleep

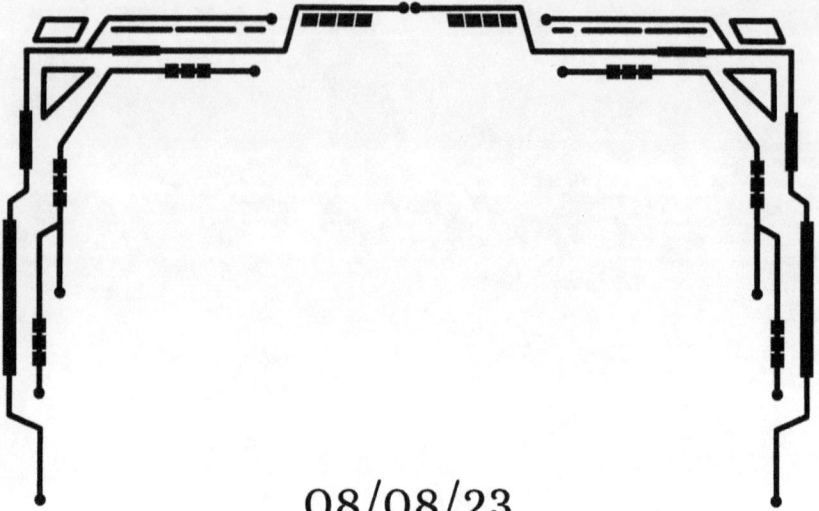

<u>08/08/23</u>

i need more dollars
none of this makes any sense
it's time for some change

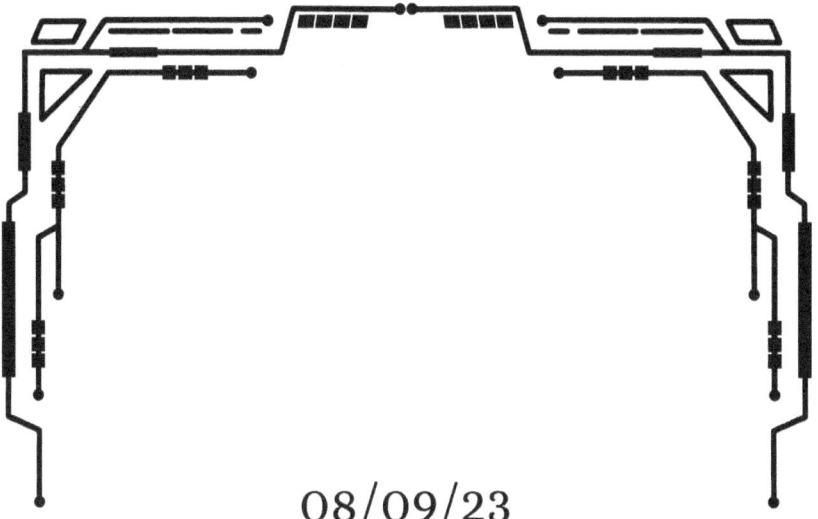

<u>08/09/23</u>

i was going to
write you a letter because
rice cakes are not cake

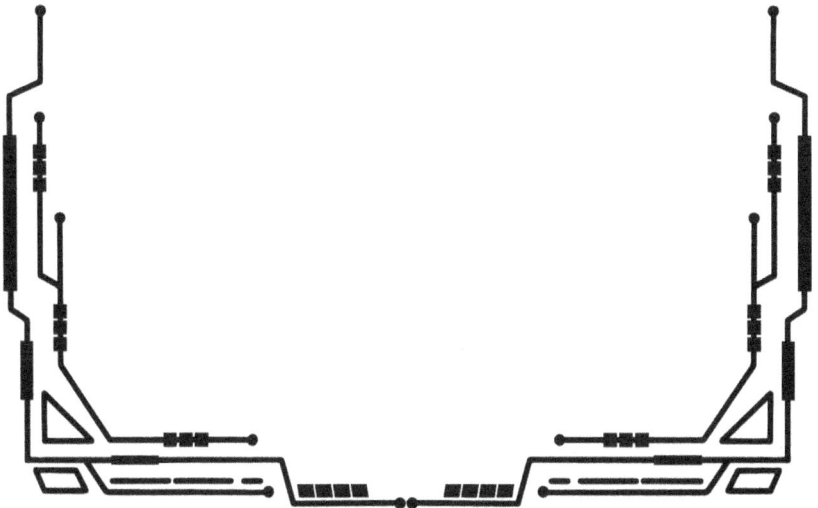

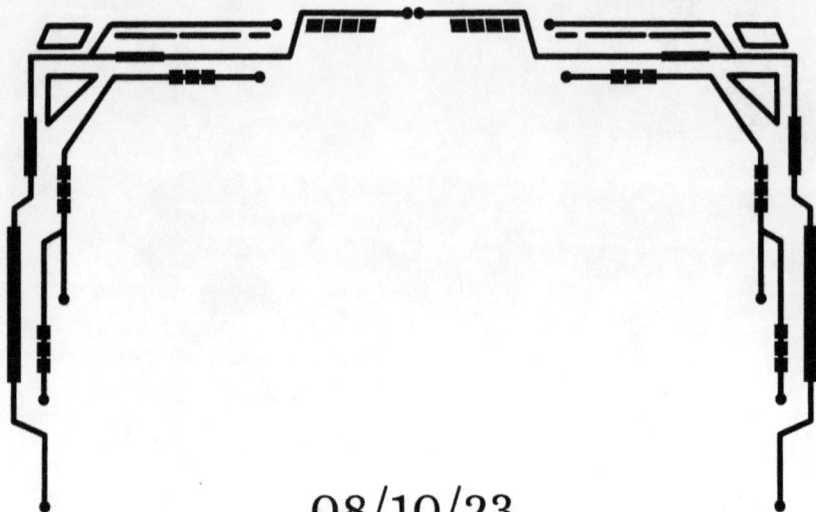

<u>08/10/23</u>

it won't be long now
i think the switch is broken
turn the key and see

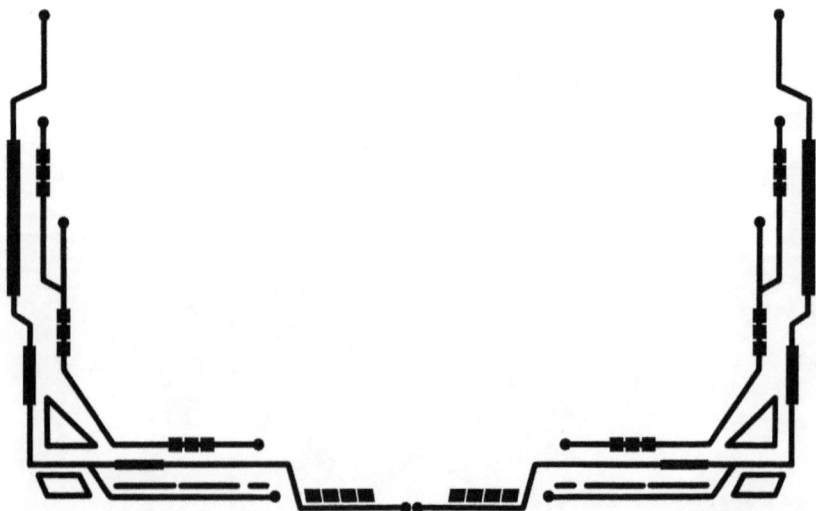

<u>08/11/23</u>

kiwi fruits are the
reptilian aliens
of the fruit species

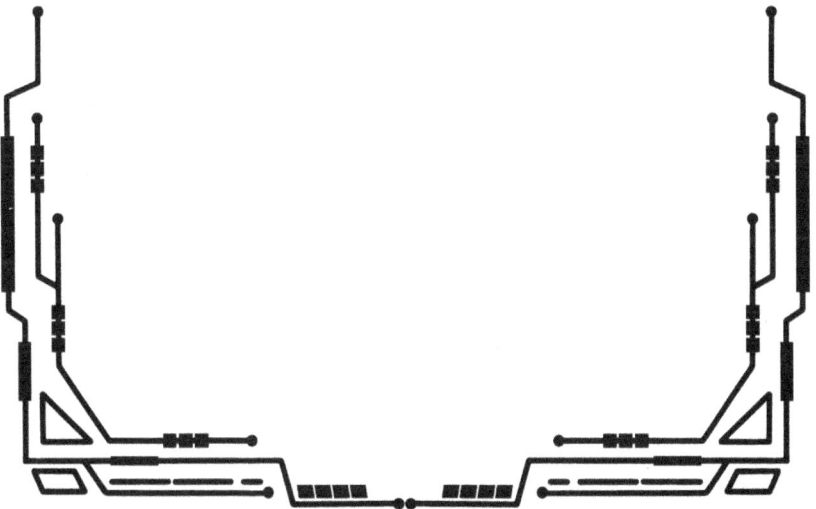

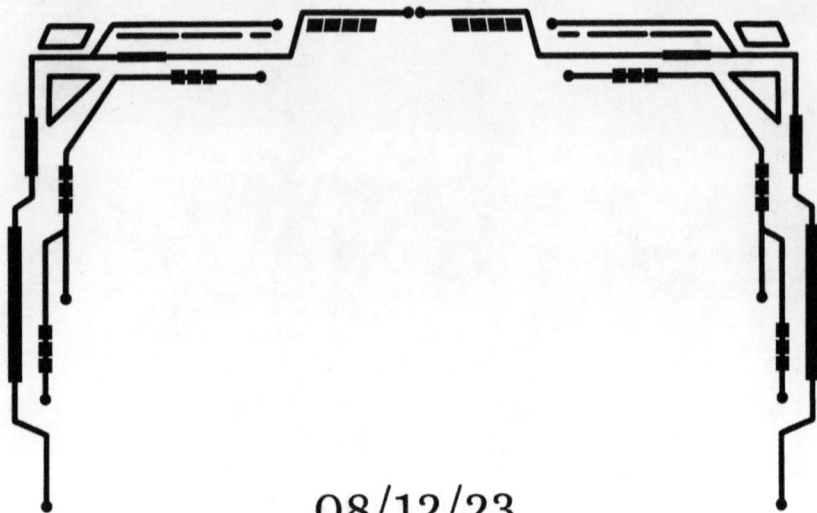

<u>08/12/23</u>

bend the slotted spoon
enough times to give notice
make it official

<u>08/13/23</u>

sunday is for fish
open the tin and eat it
eighteen hours later

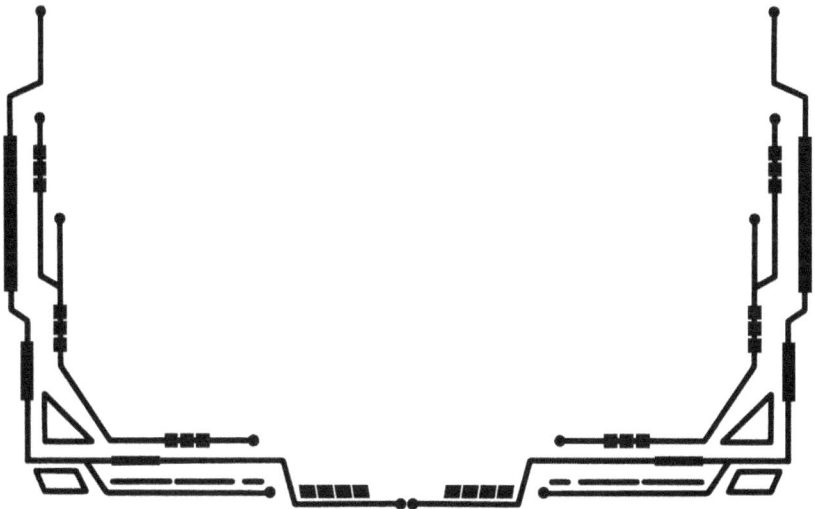

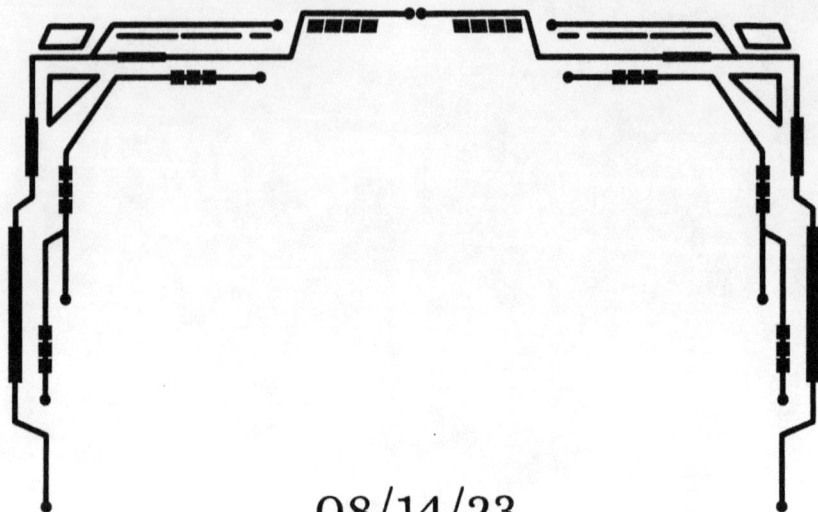

<u>08/14/23</u>

why is there no f
in laughter draught and coughing
enough already

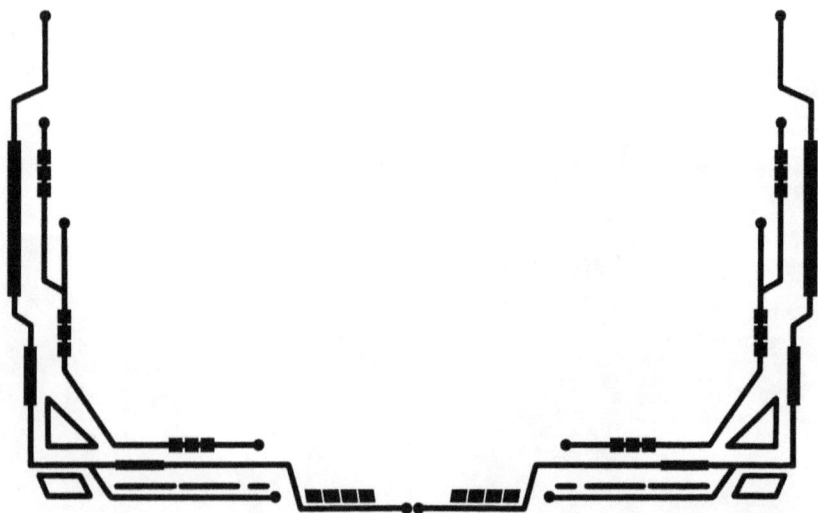

<u>08/15/23</u>

your car has mud flaps
that are way too big for it
that's why it looks dumb

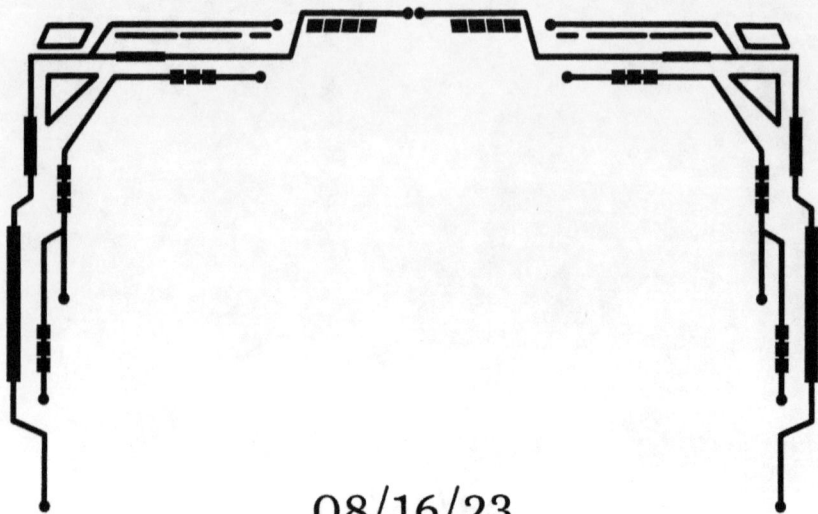

<u>08/16/23</u>

listen here my dudes
sometimes the joint is not lit
and sometimes it is

<u>08/17/23</u>

the clouds are all gone
the reservoir is still now
the air is quiet

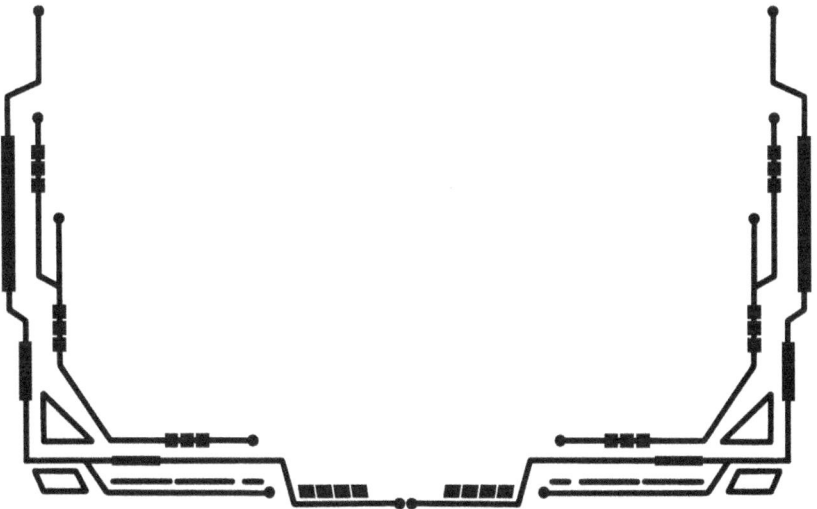

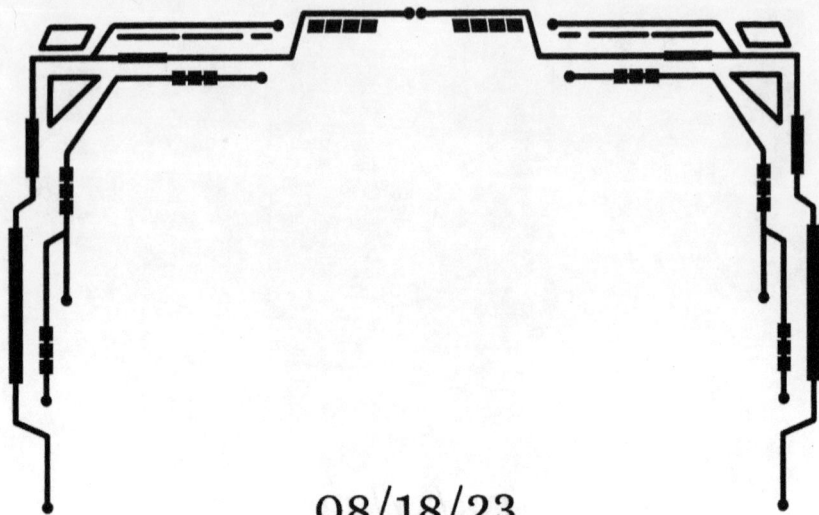

<u>08/18/23</u>

i really like this
he said quite sarcastically
everything is dumb

write a poem about
sad furniture by the couch
coffee table blues

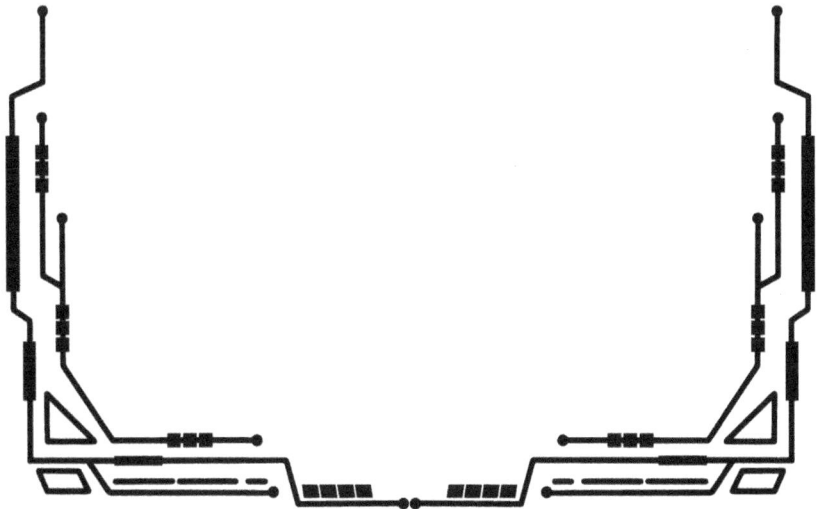

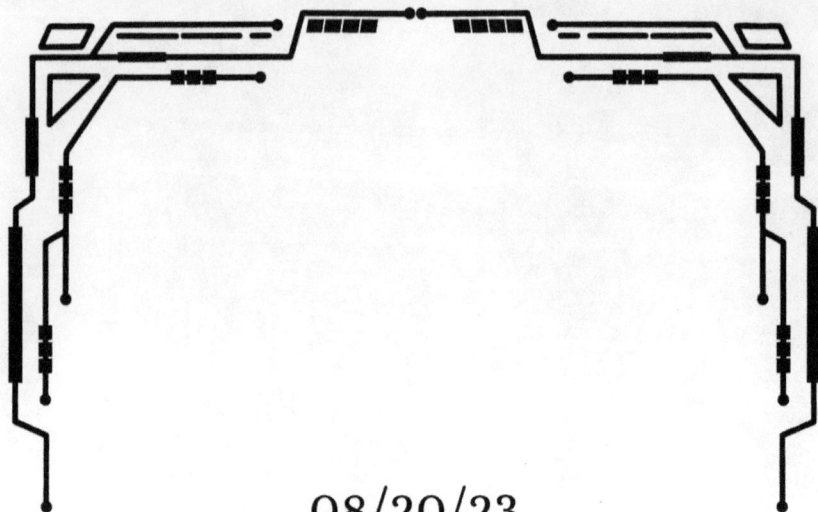

<u>08/20/23</u>

why is that right there
it is too far away now
it should be right here

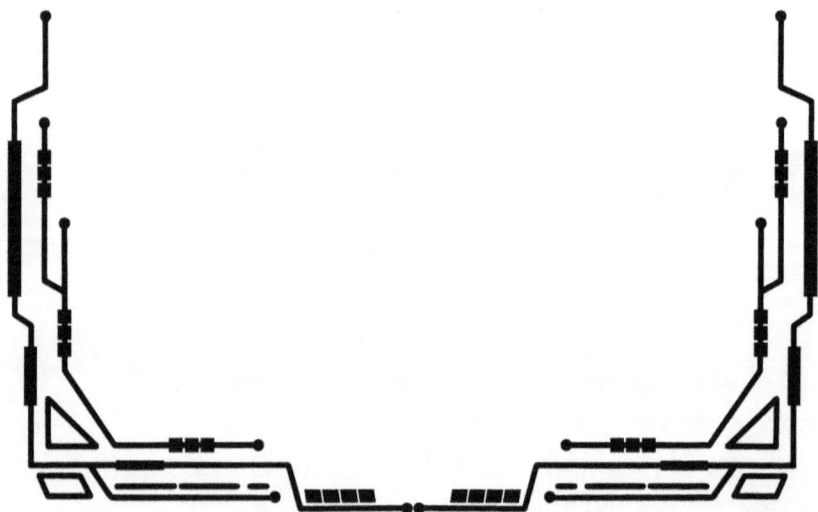

<u>08/21/23</u>

great day for the pool
too many people out here
alligator raft

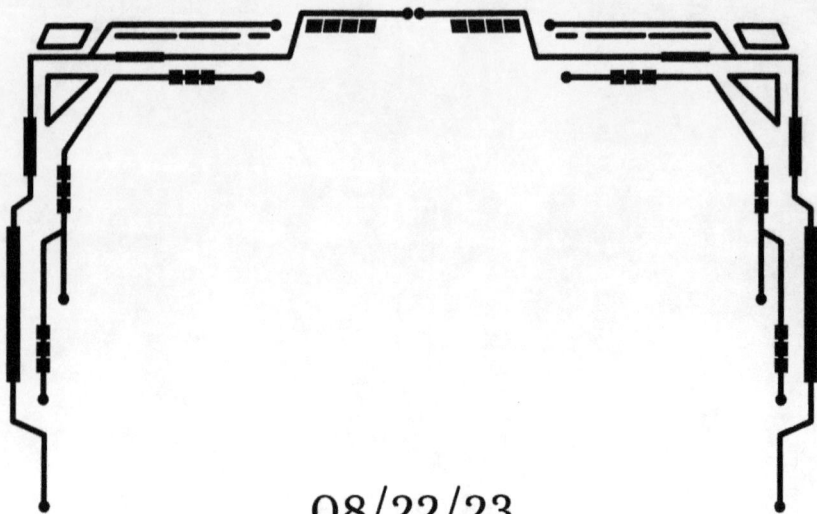

<u>08/22/23</u>

what is she doing
someone tell her to stop it
nobody cares barb

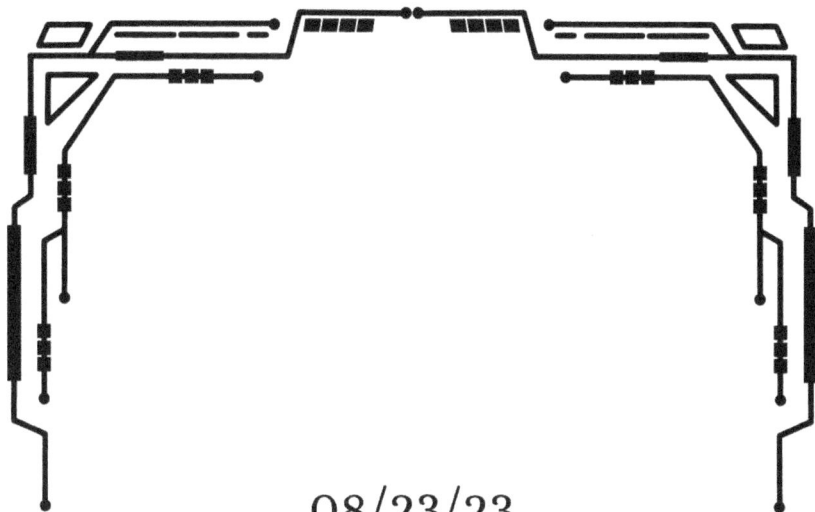

<u>08/23/23</u>

i'm tired and sweating
do you have any ice cream
can't sleep it's too hot

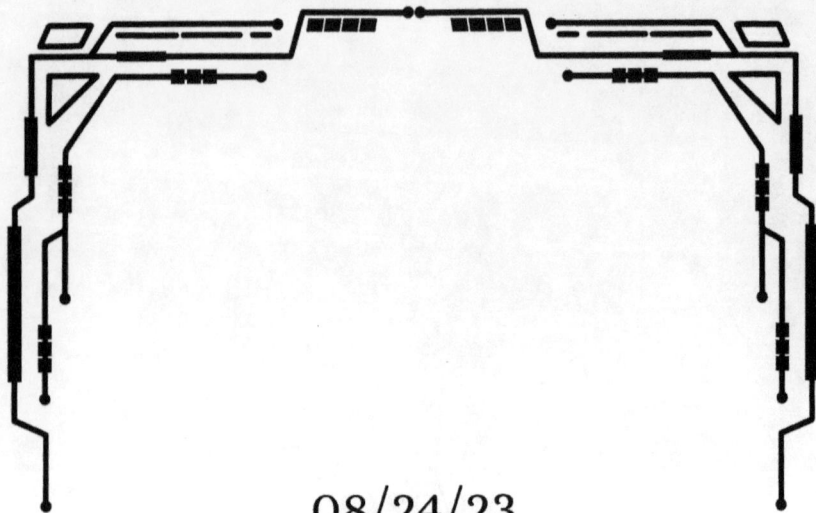

<u>08/24/23</u>

this is it i guess
the beginning of the end
getting out of here

<u>08/25/23</u>

when did this happen
my hands are old person hands
scarred and worn out skin

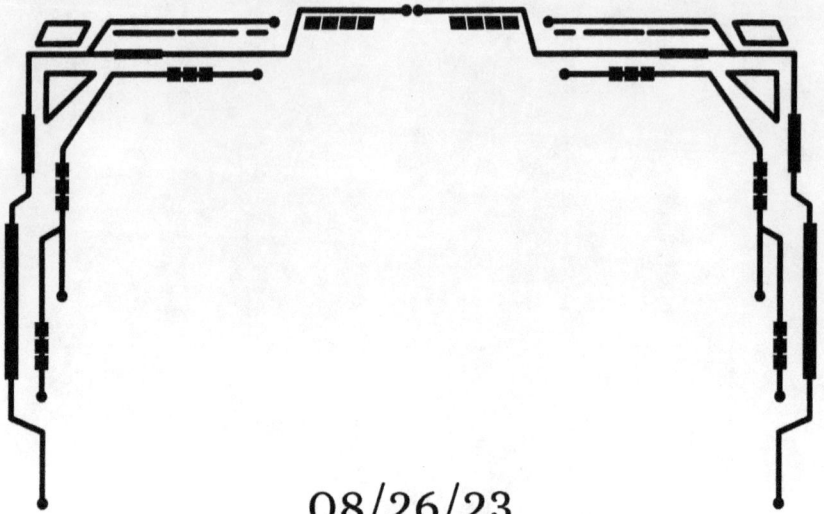

<u>08/26/23</u>

tenderloin filet
with fingerling potatoes
and a béarnaise sauce

<u>08/27/23</u>

it's so hot today
hot tomorrow too i think
been hot for awhile

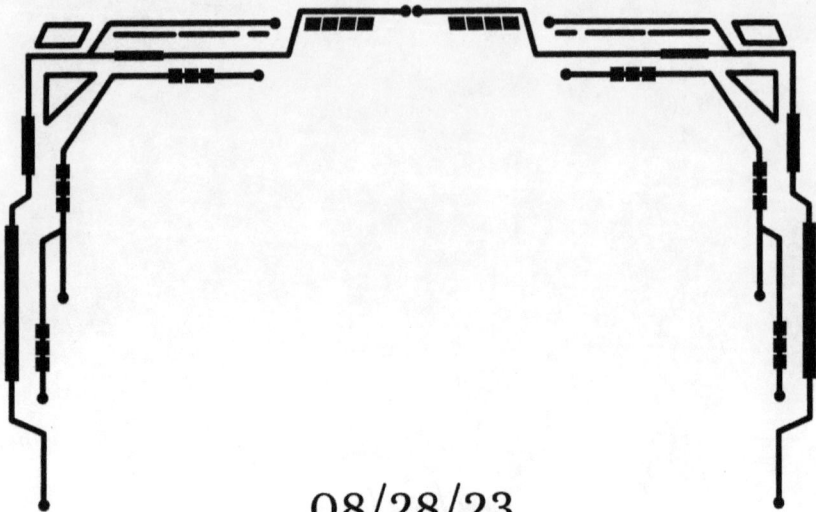

08/28/23

ew gross what is that
crying in the dining room
shut that baby up

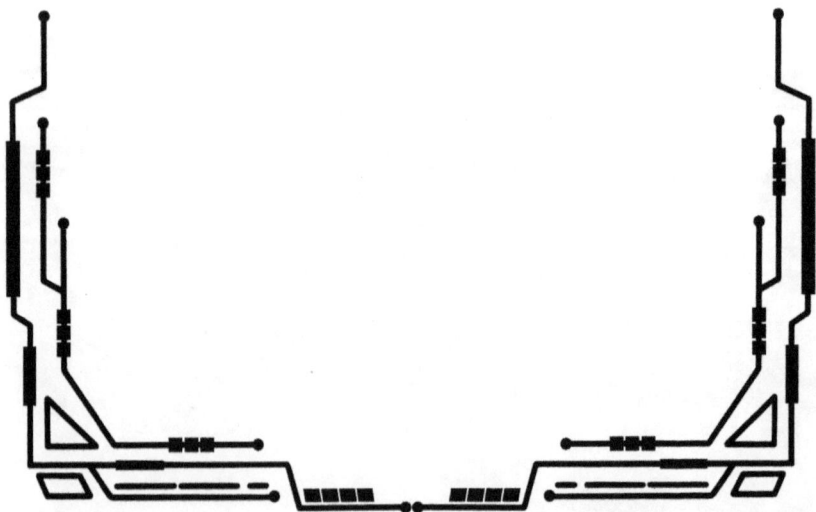

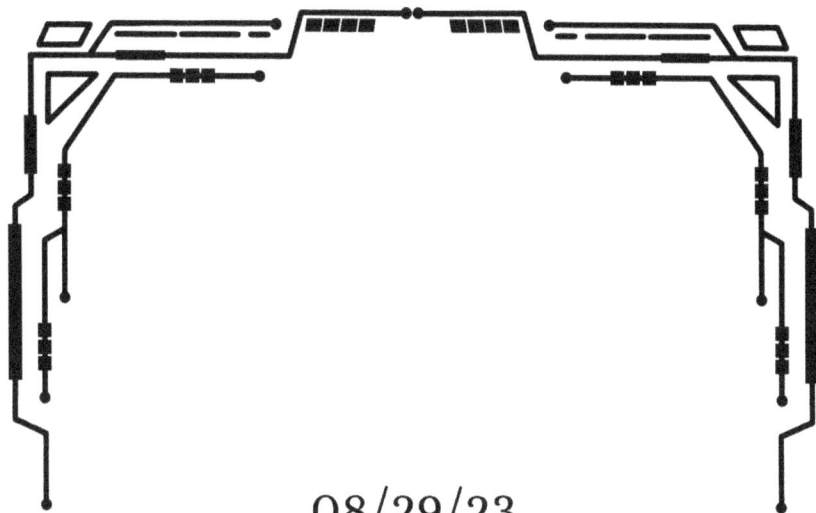

<u>08/29/23</u>

put your money on
eight twenty nine twenty three
thanks for the advice

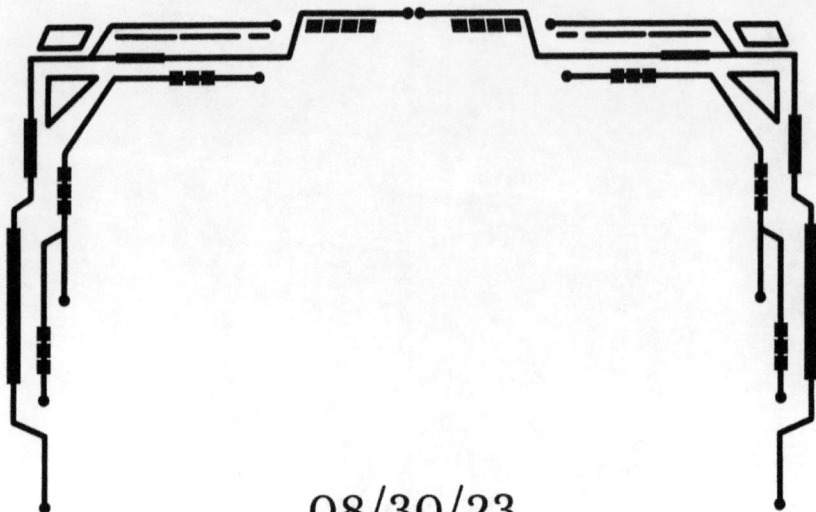

<u>08/30/23</u>

sometimes a little
gatorade from circle k
is all that you need

<u>08/31/23</u>

there was a sandwich
in the alley this morning
it was half gone though

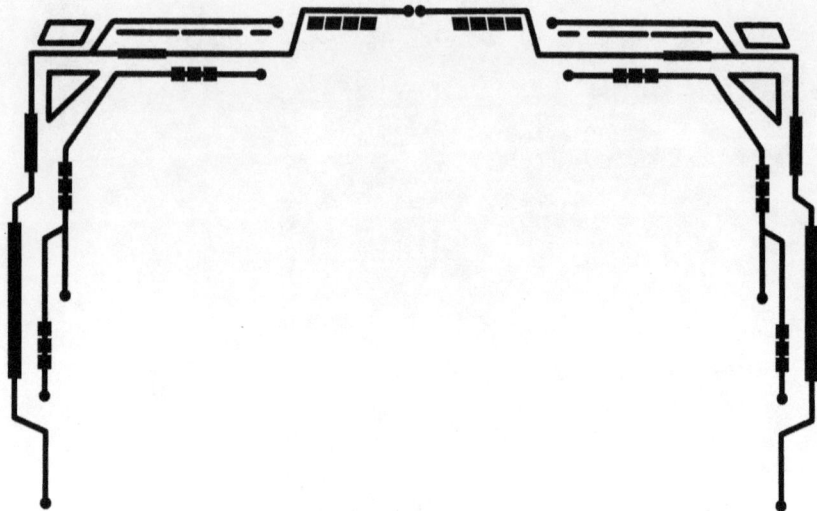

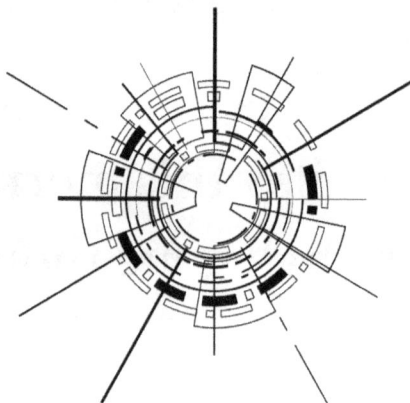

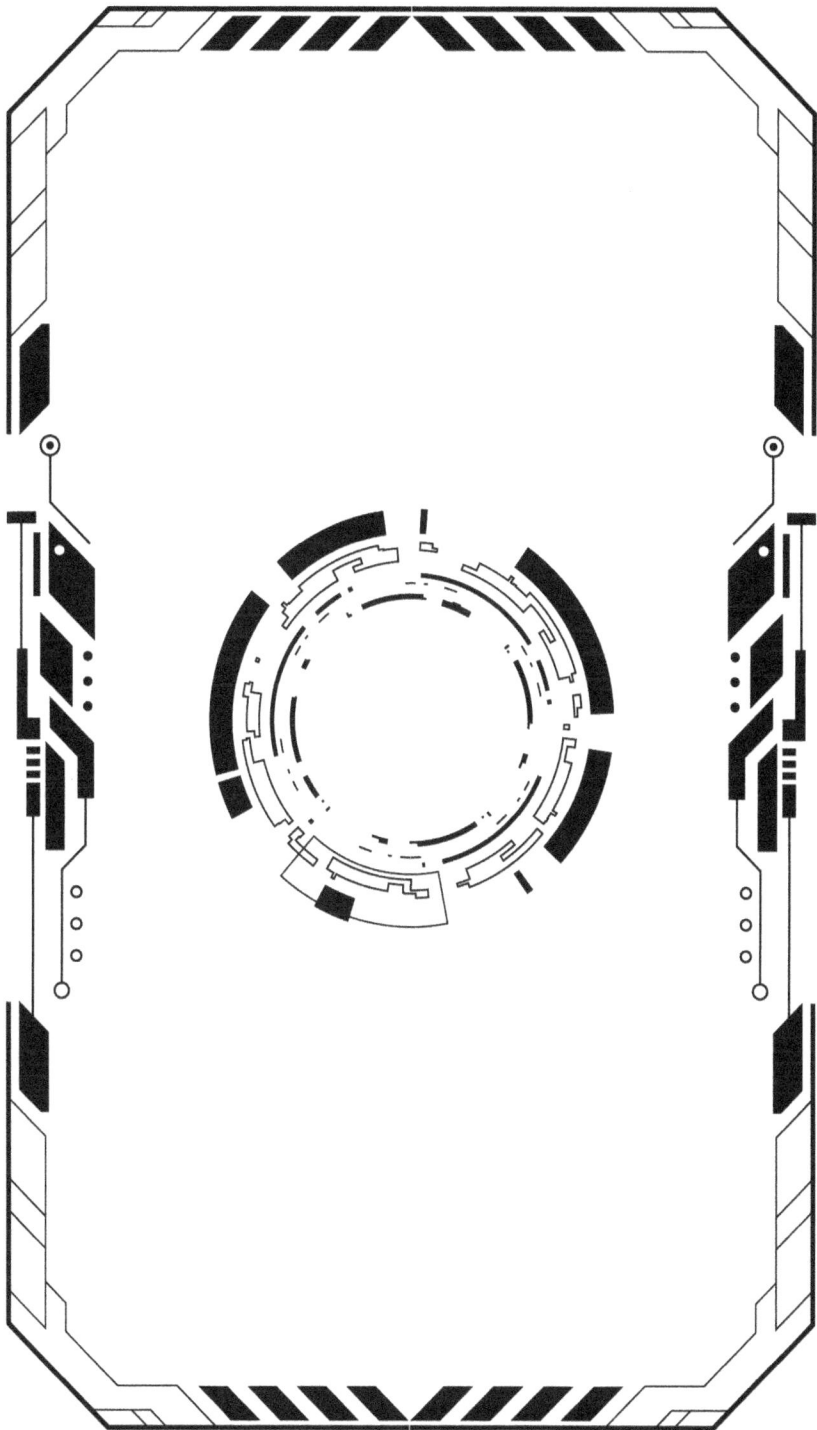

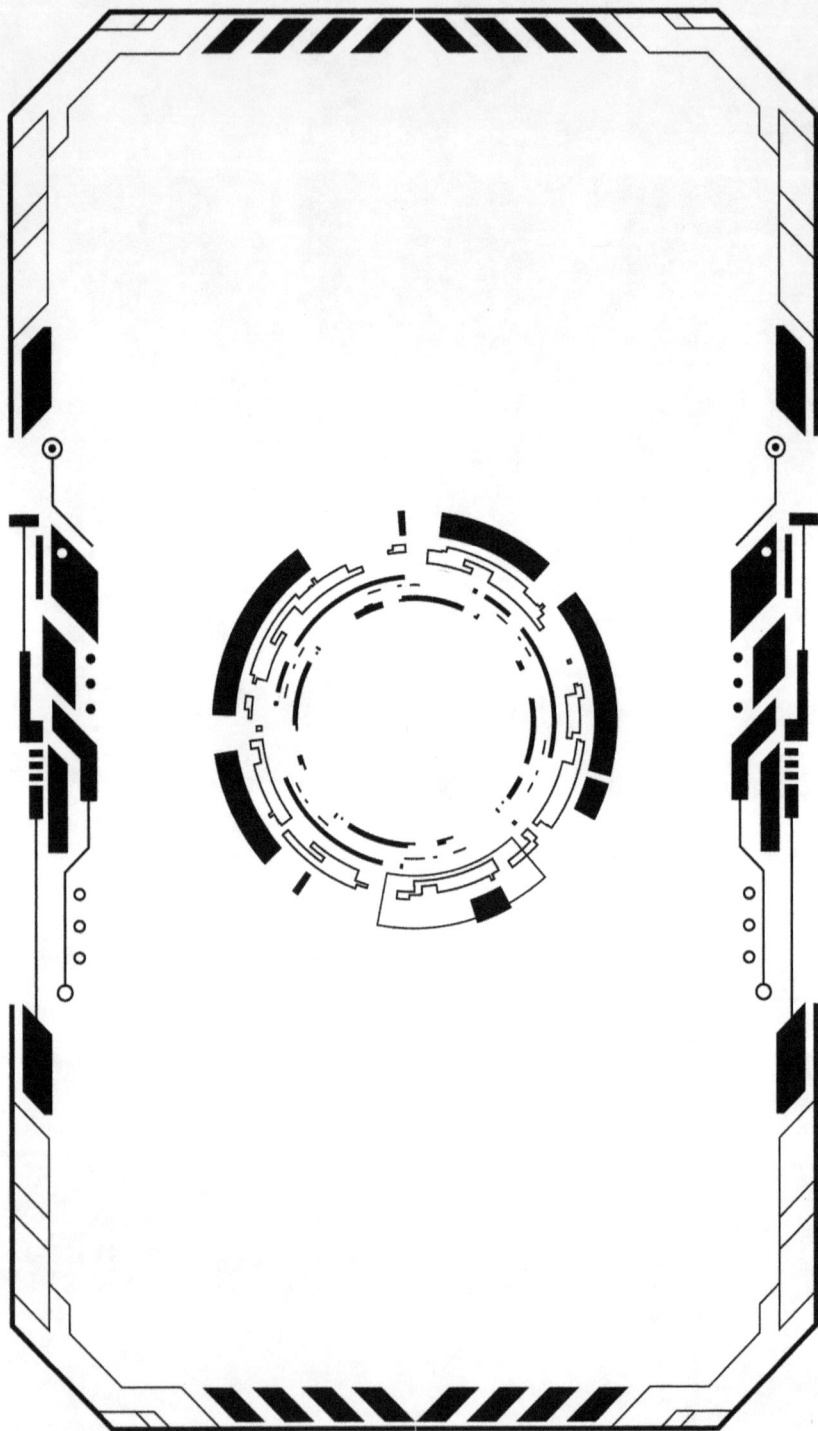

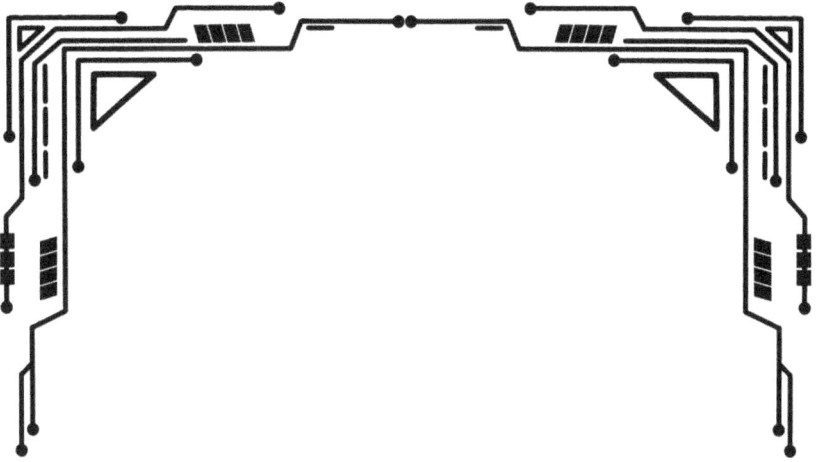

<u>09/01/23</u>

it's almost time now
to get the fuck out of here
it's almost over

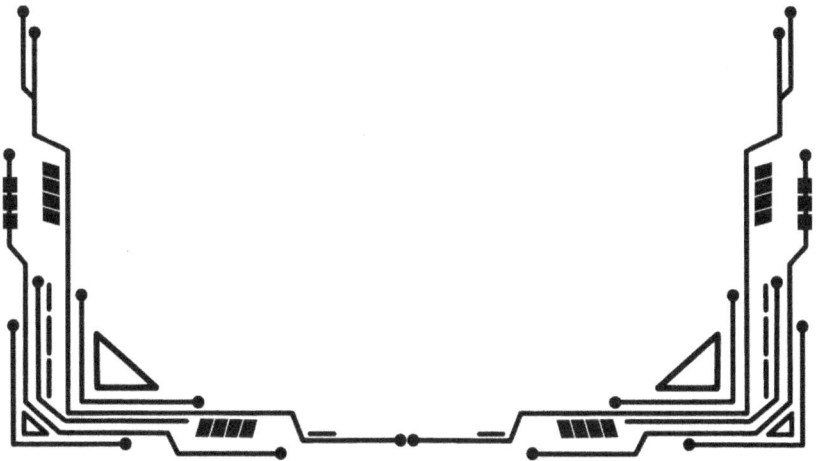

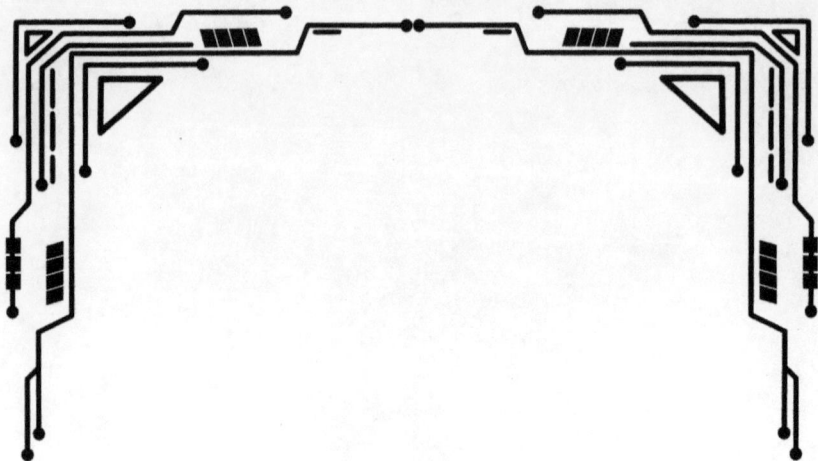

09/02/23

tasty brussels sprouts
oven roasted nut butter
vegetable candy

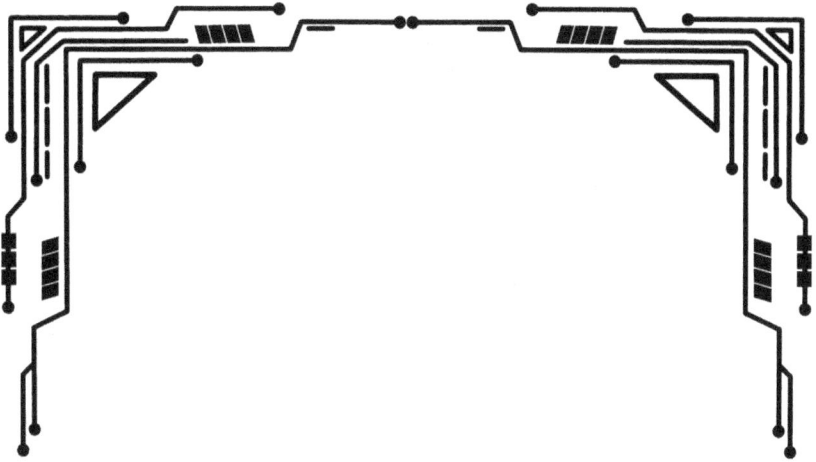

09/03/23

well how about that
closed it down on my last day
whatever i'm done

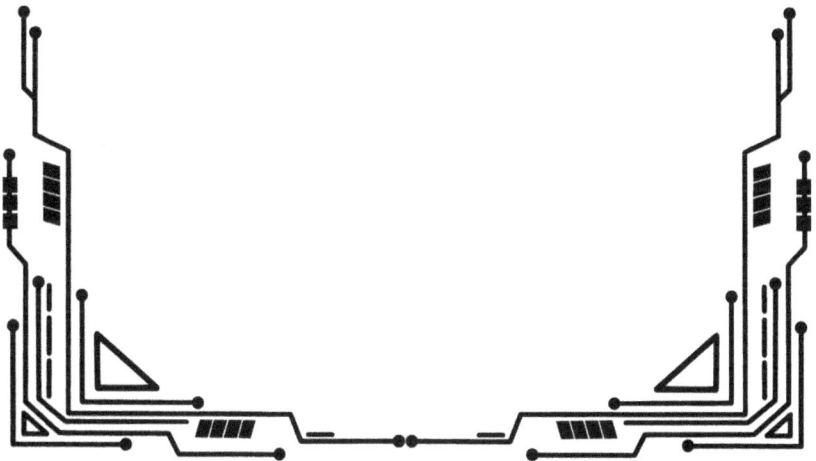

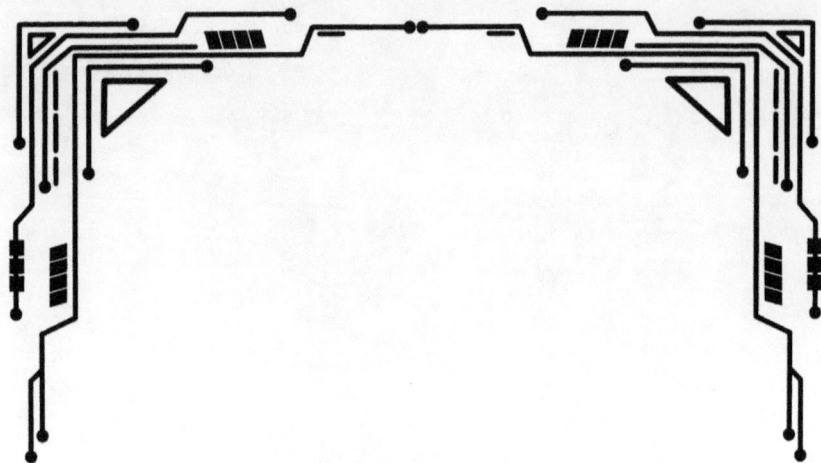

09/04/23

start a new journey
on thursday in the mountains
but first some days off

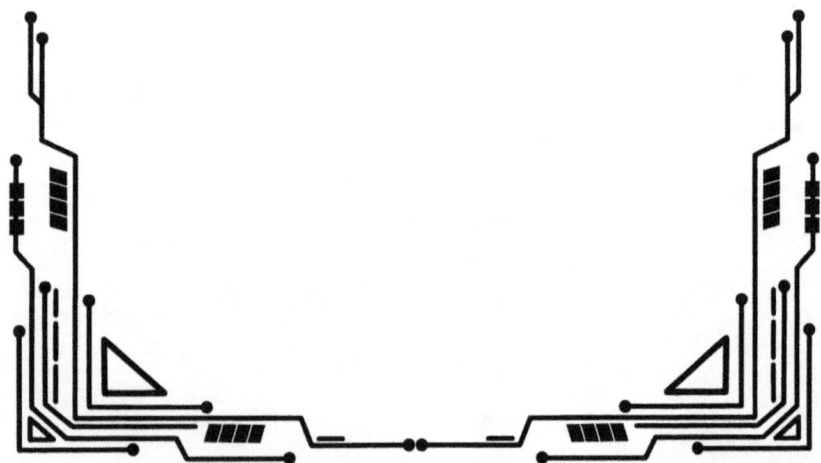

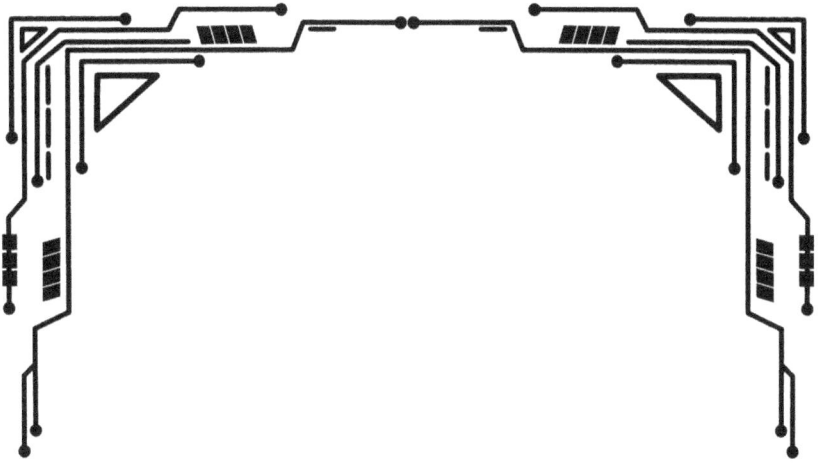

<u>09/05/23</u>

the cheese is missing
that's why we don't trust danny
and keep him outside

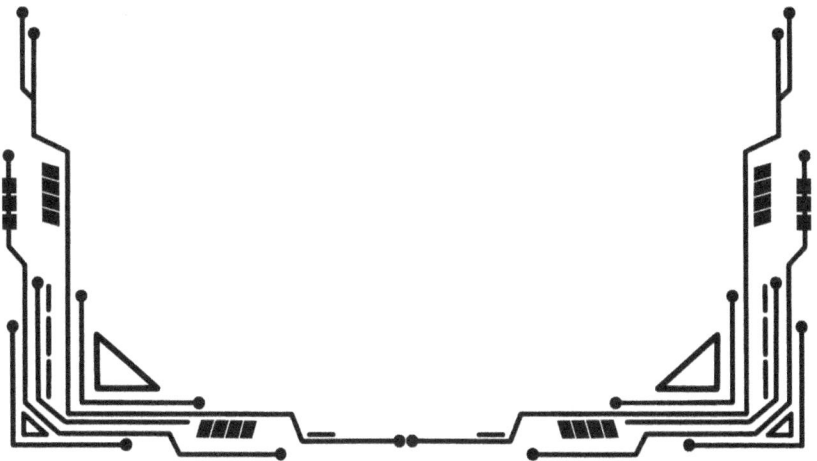

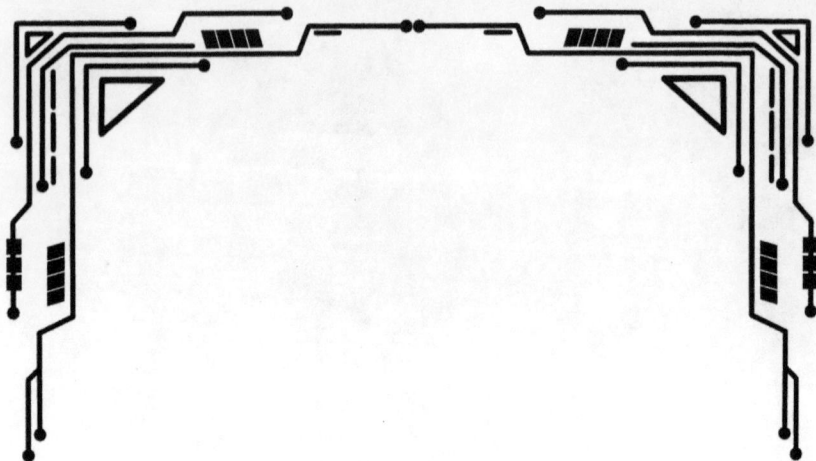

<u>09/06/23</u>

be careful today
it's hot and dry and there is
a red flag warning

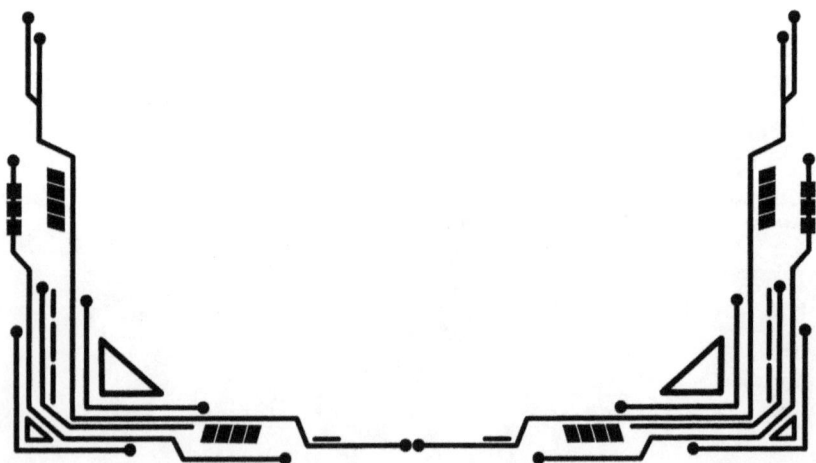

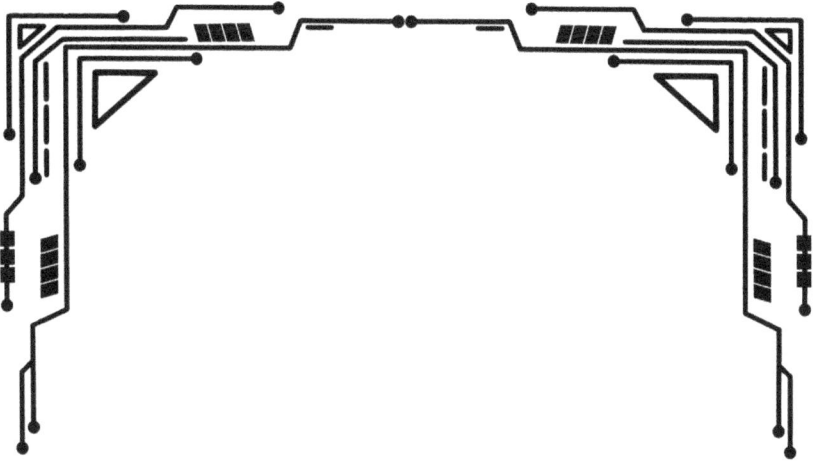

<u>09/07/23</u>

drive up the canyon
meeting the new mountain folks
really good first day

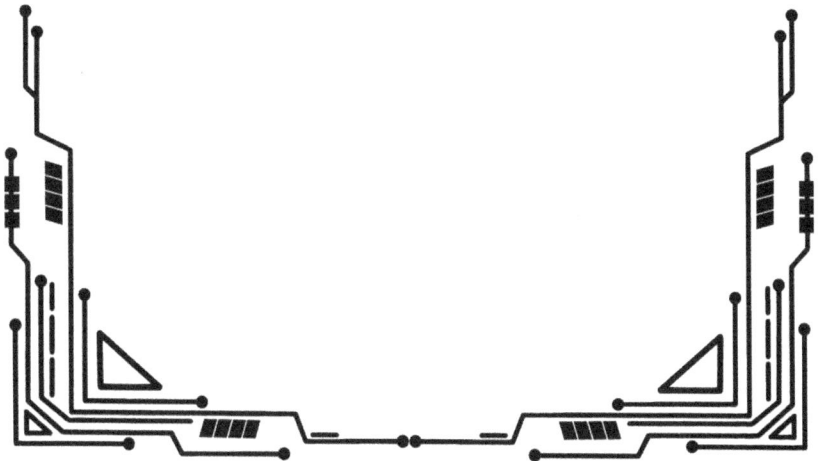

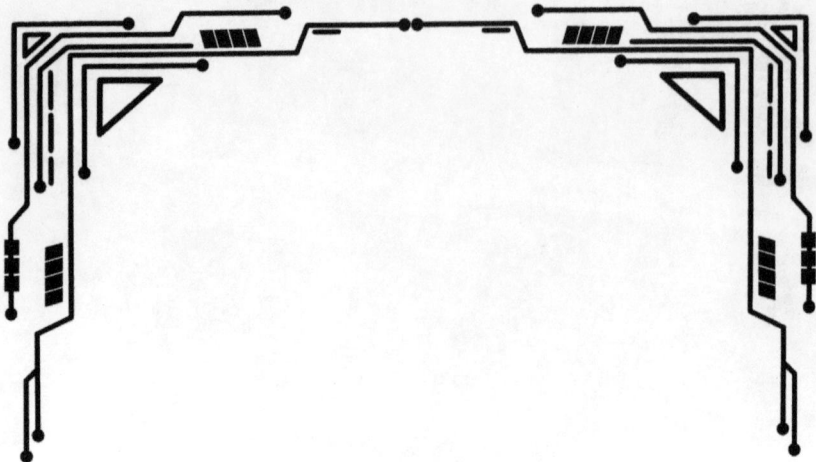

09/08/23

beautiful outside
day one without cigarettes
not too bad so far

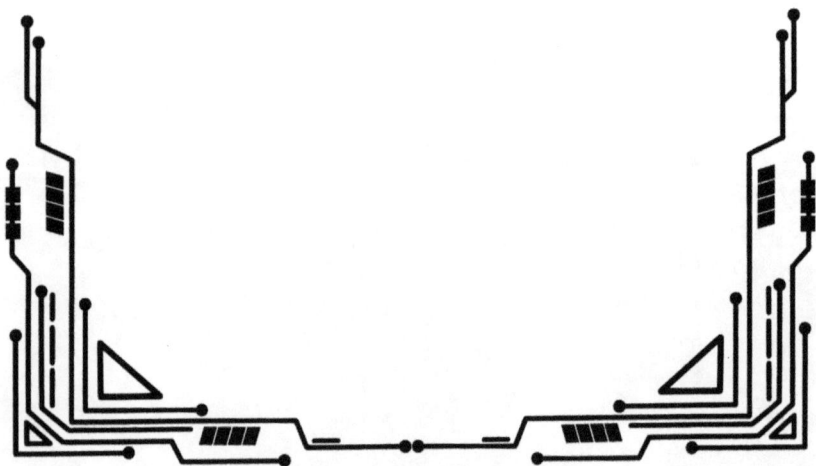

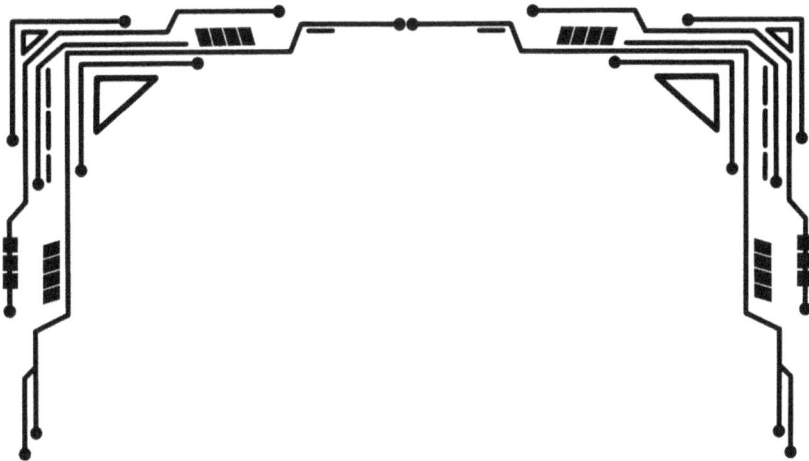

<u>09/09/23</u>

maybe the five spice
beside the tuna wrangler
no no twenty three

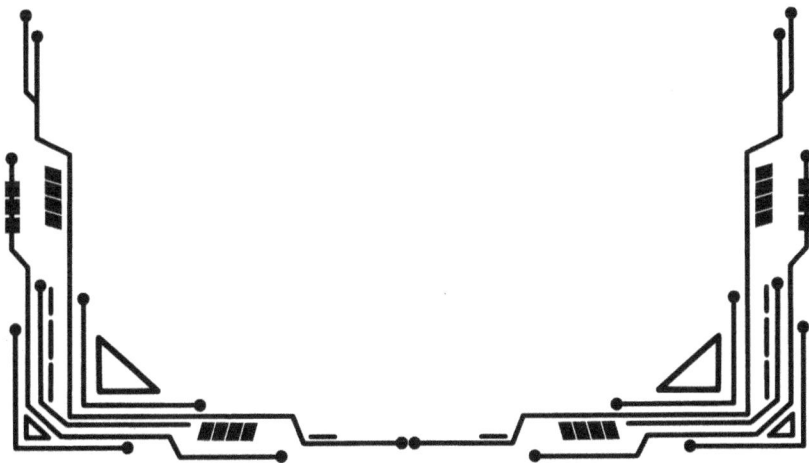

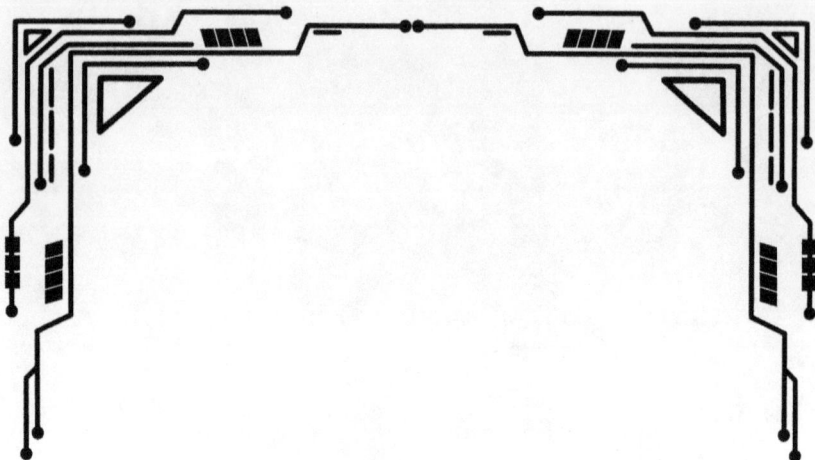

09/10/23

i made a grilled cheese
what else is there to do but
have a bowl of soup

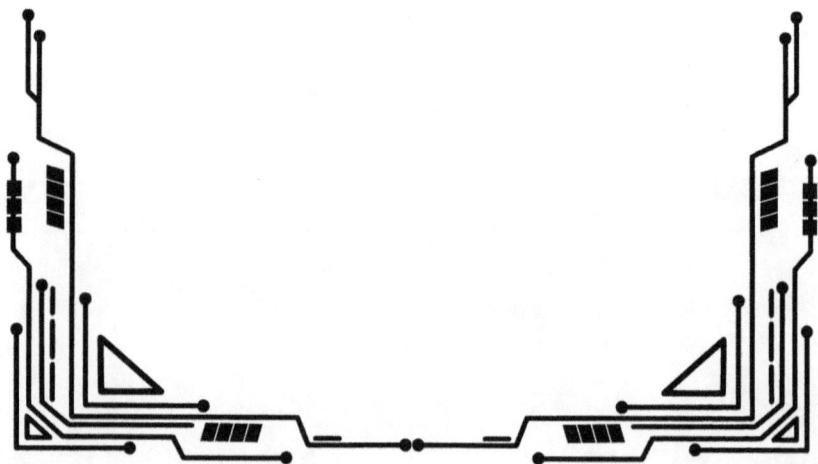

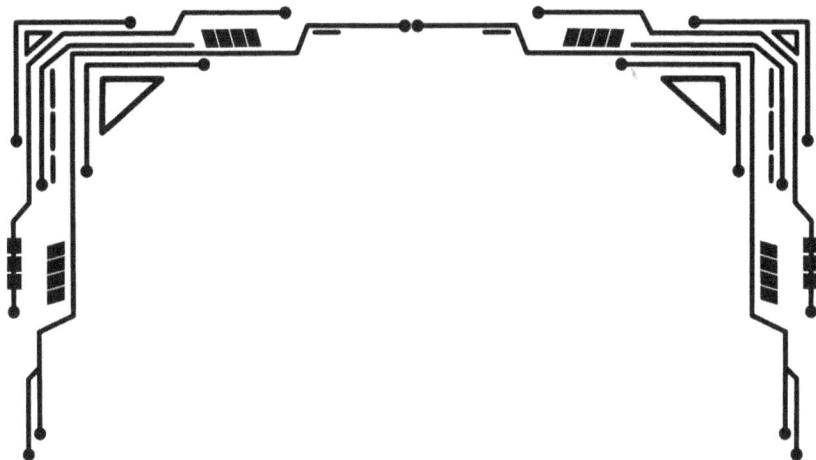

<u>09/11/23</u>

strangeness in the night
dreaming in the house again
over and over

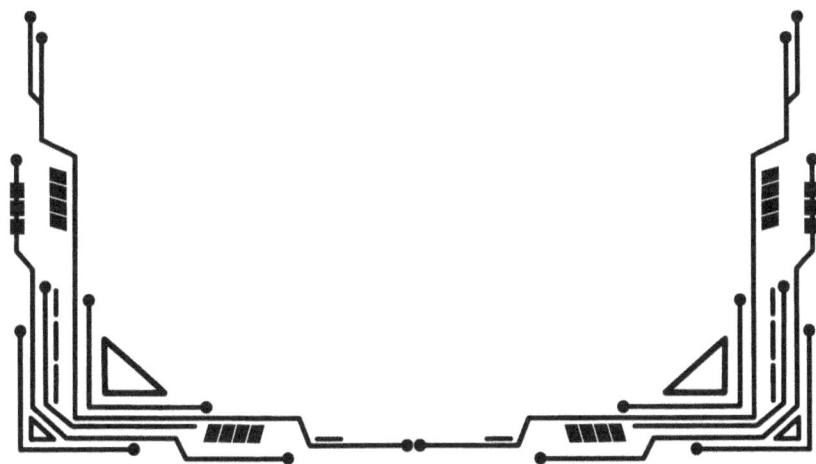

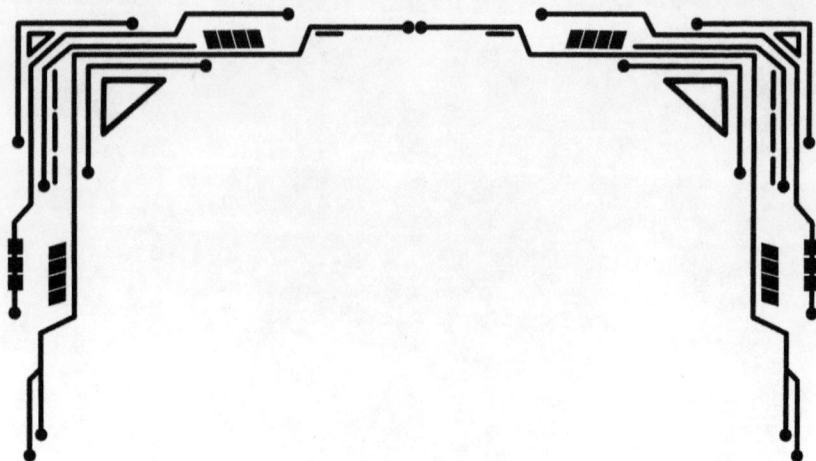

09/12/23

snoopy was a dog
theodore was a chipmunk
felix was a cat

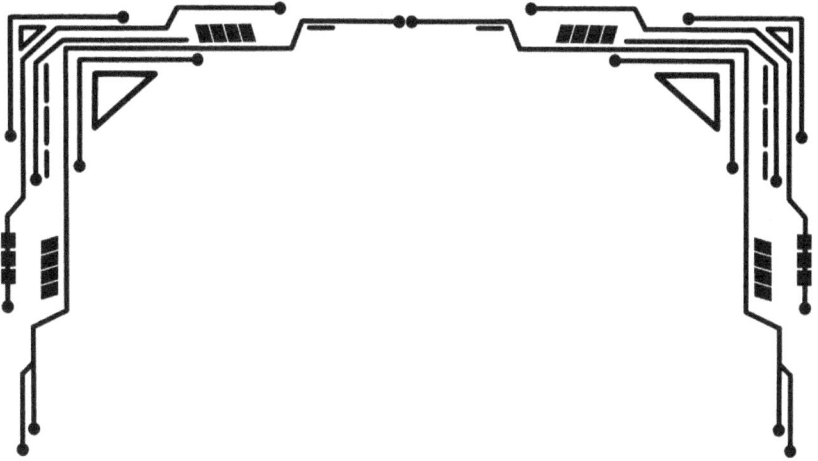

<u>09/13/23</u>

this is not ok
what are all these charges on
my electric bill

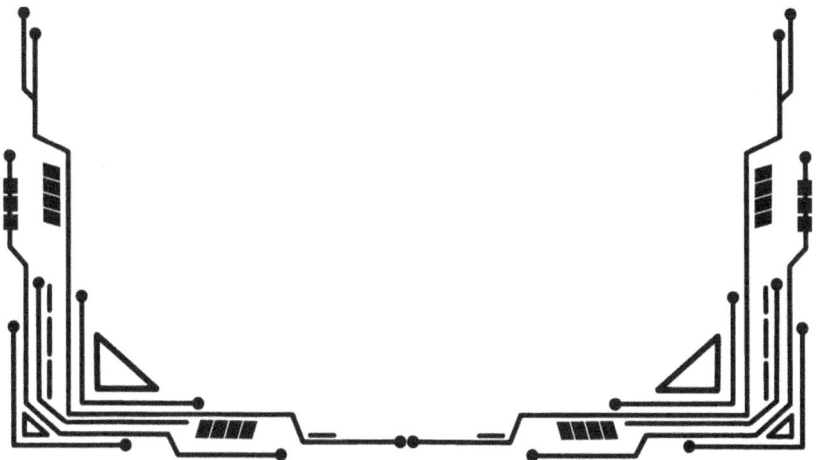

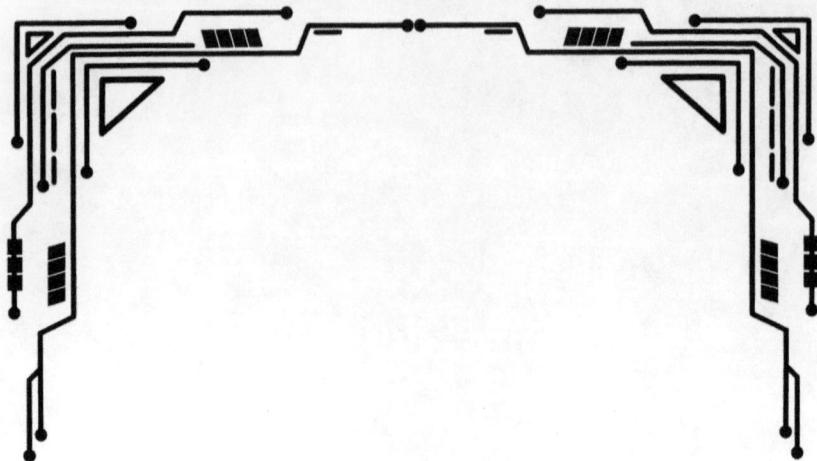

<u>09/14/23</u>

one time there was cheese
it was a very nice slice
atop a cracker

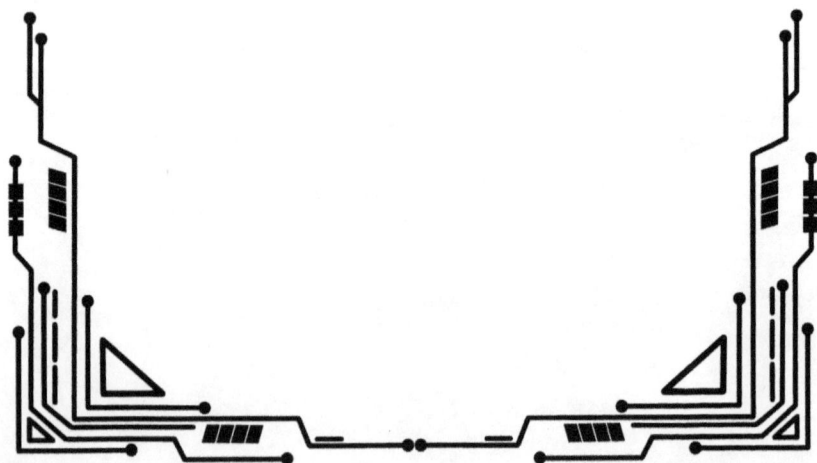

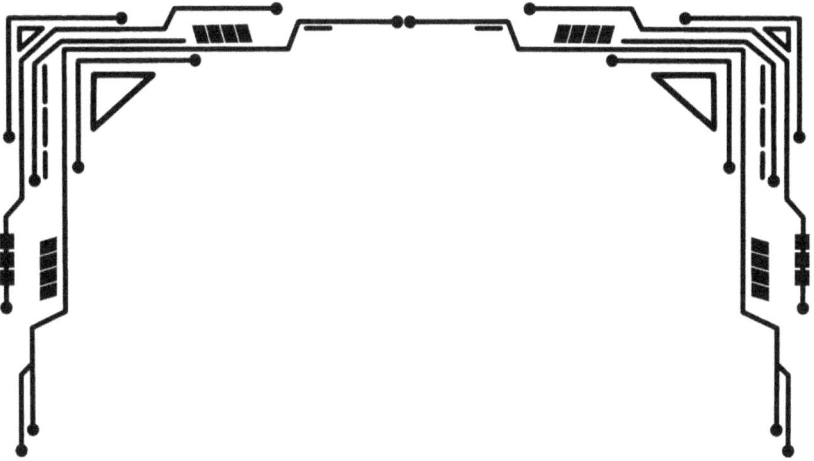

<u>09/15/23</u>

crazy vivid dreams
withdraw from the nicotine
intense things happen

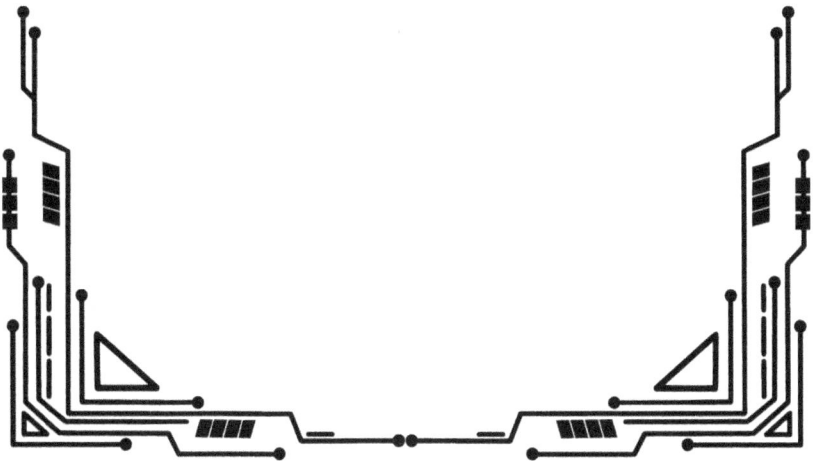

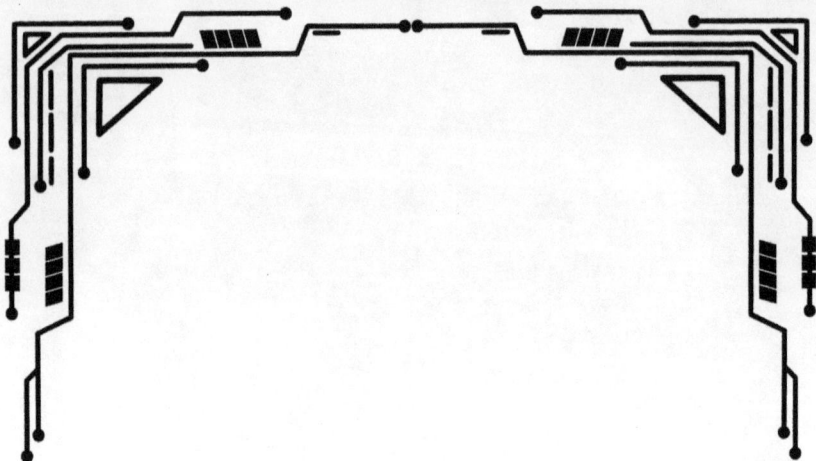

09/16/23

all these one way streets
things are new and i am still
getting used to it

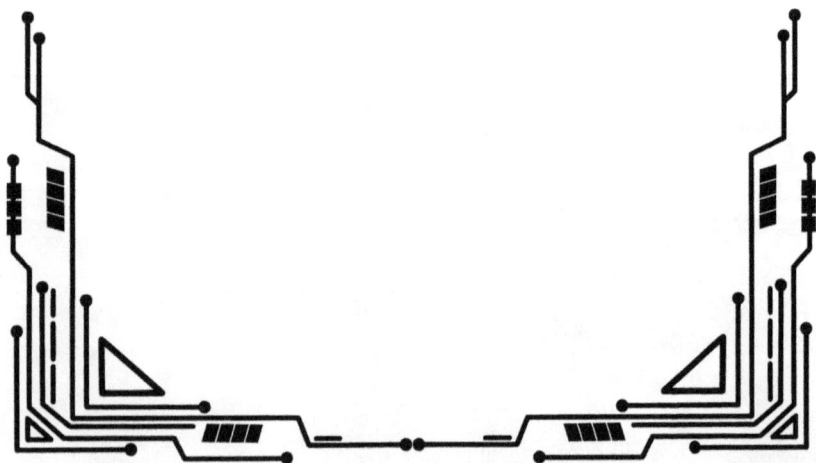

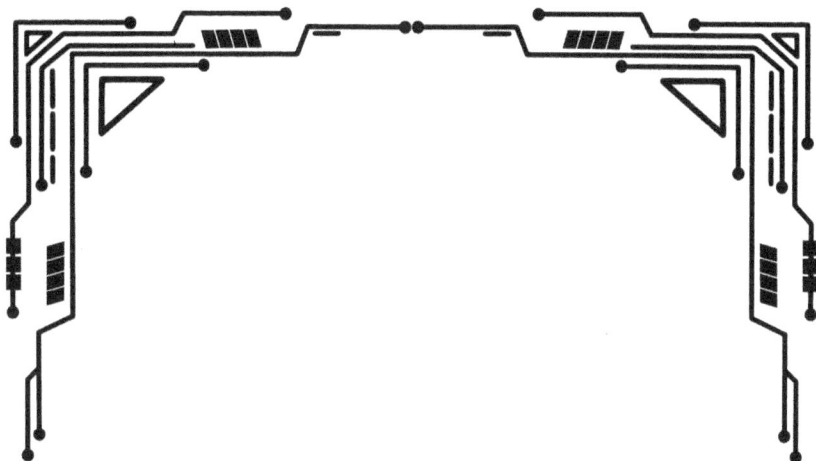

<u>09/17/23</u>

tempting as it is
don't jump in and take a bath
in the mountain juice

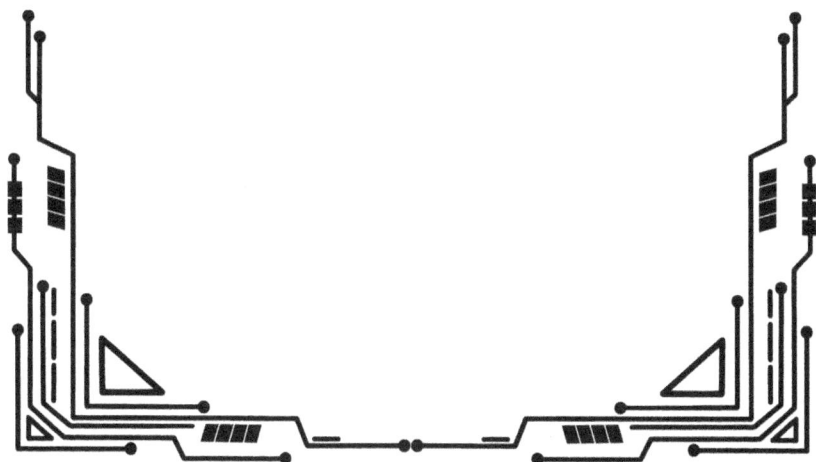

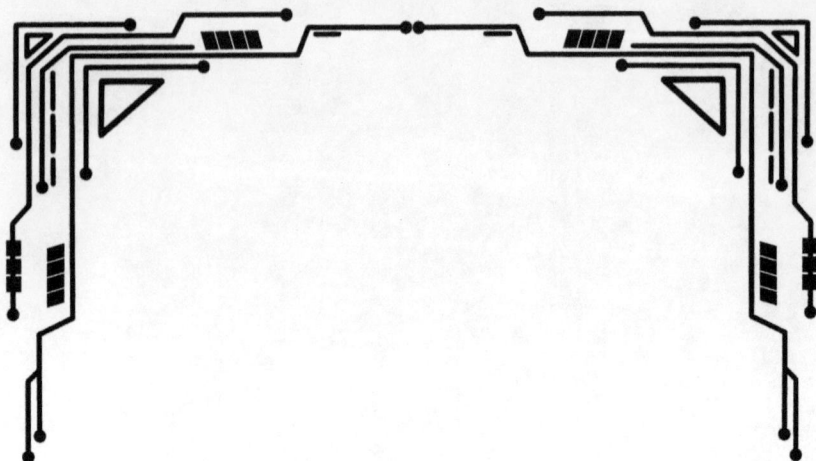

<u>09/18/23</u>

i will be waiting
with a little bit of tea
by the lemon tree

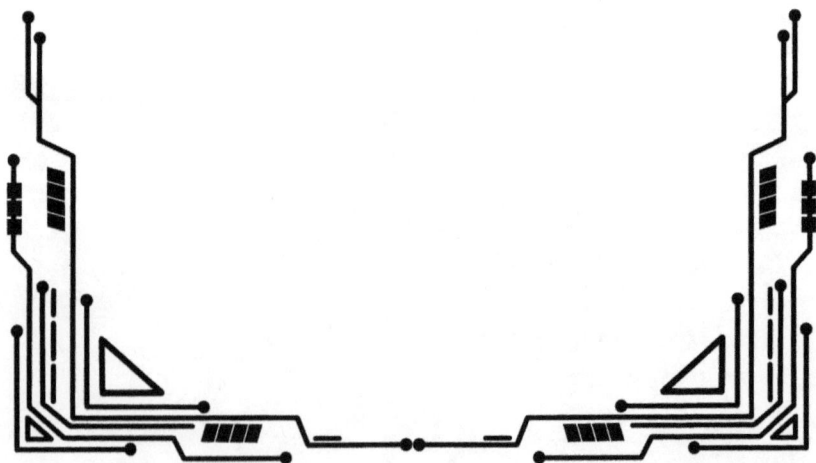

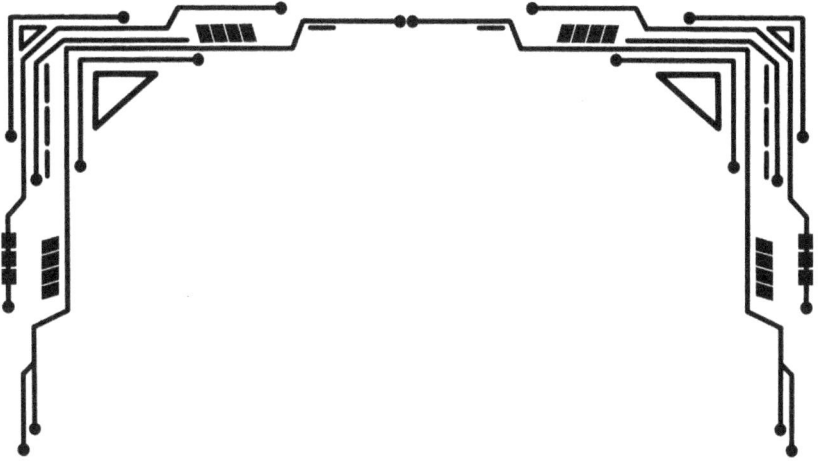

<u>09/19/23</u>

tasty afternoon
done with this banana peel
give it to the fish

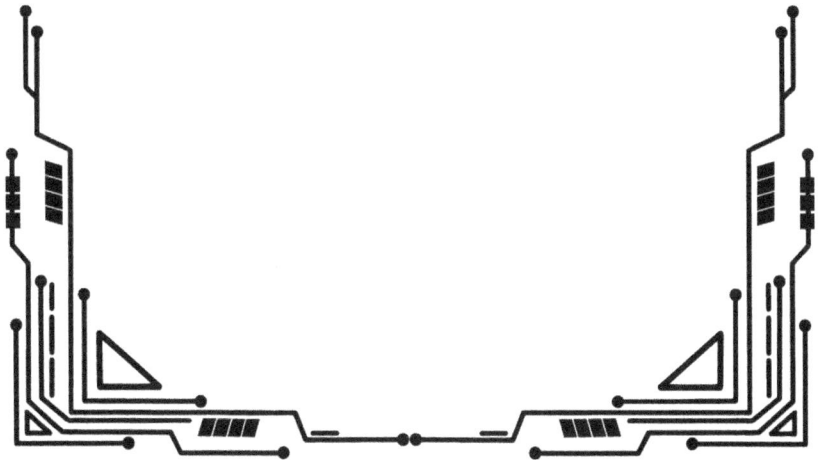

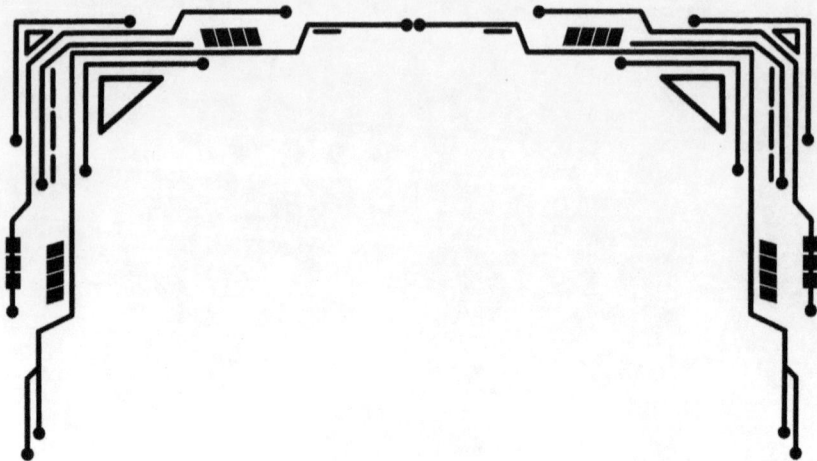

<u>09/20/23</u>

go down to the creek
sit by the water and think
listen to the sound

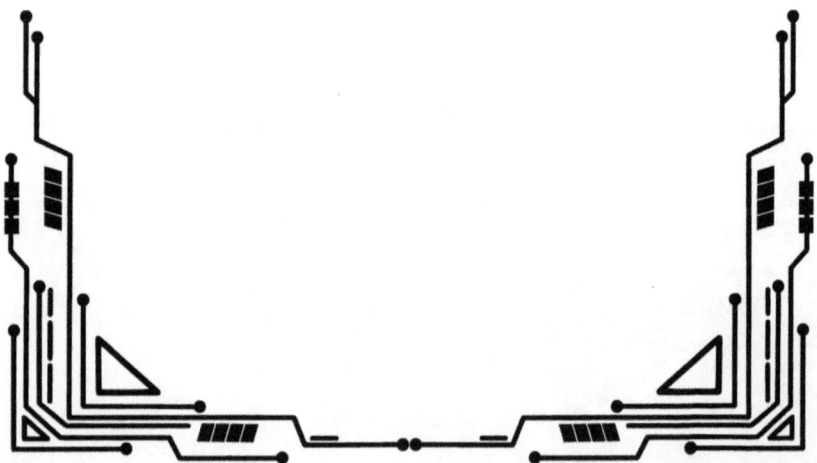

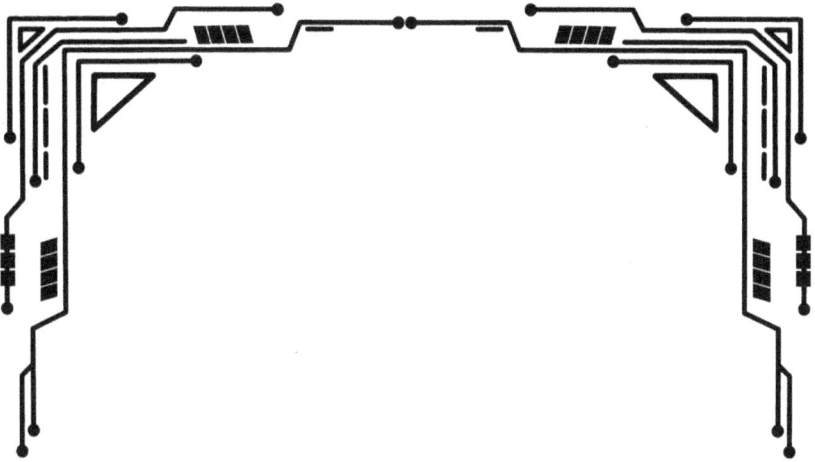

<u>09/21/23</u>

here by the trash can
there is a single flower
waiting for the buzz

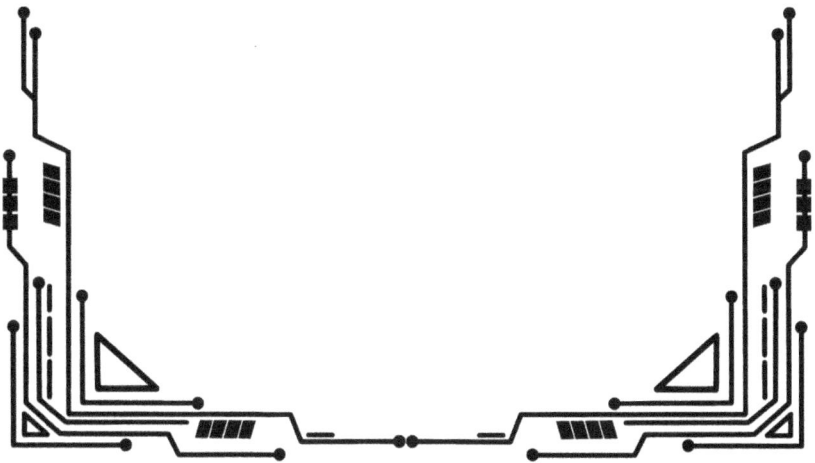

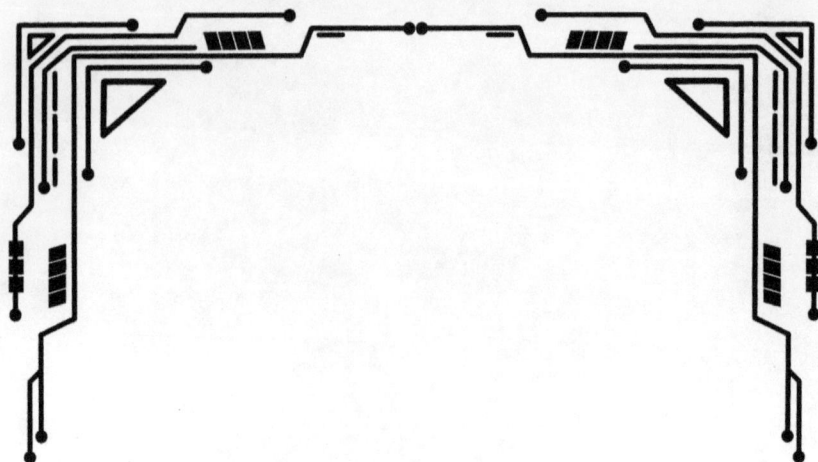

<u>09/22/23</u>

sitting in the sun
waiting patiently for the
cool breeze at night time

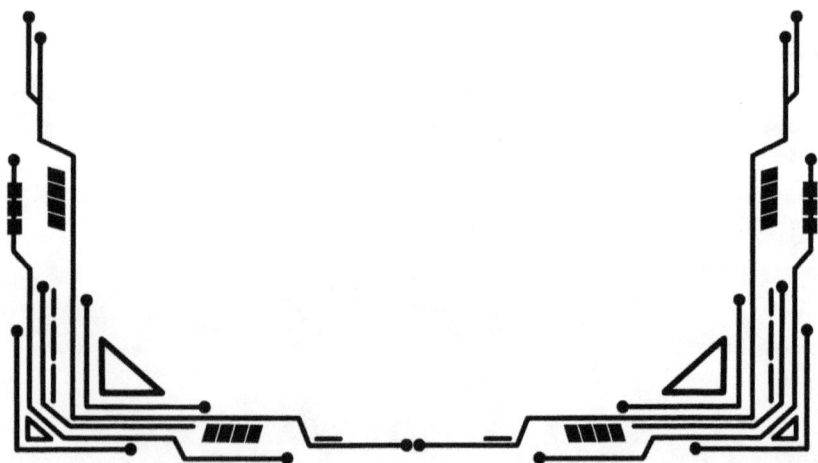

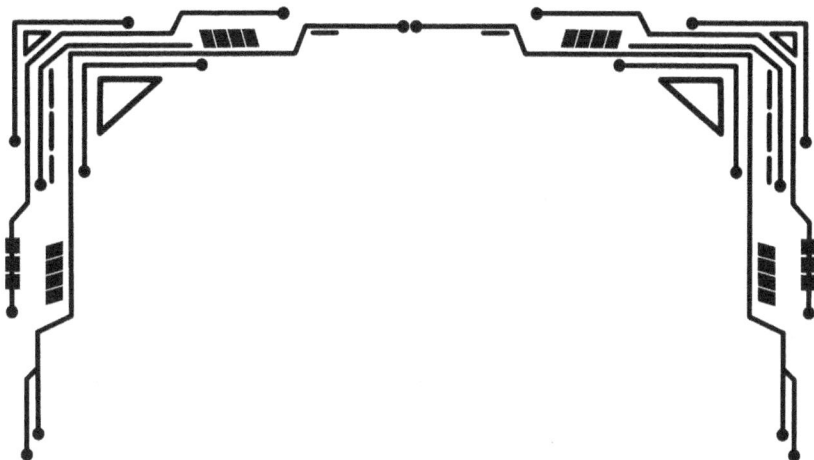

where is the next road
it's a somewhat tricky thing
navigating here

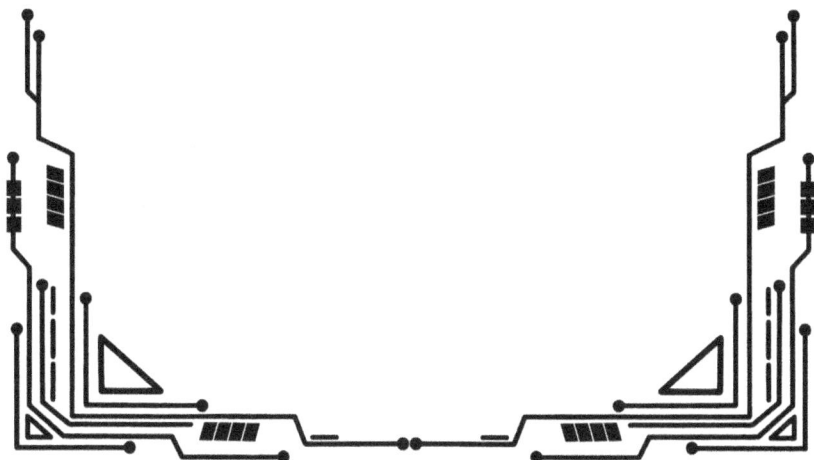

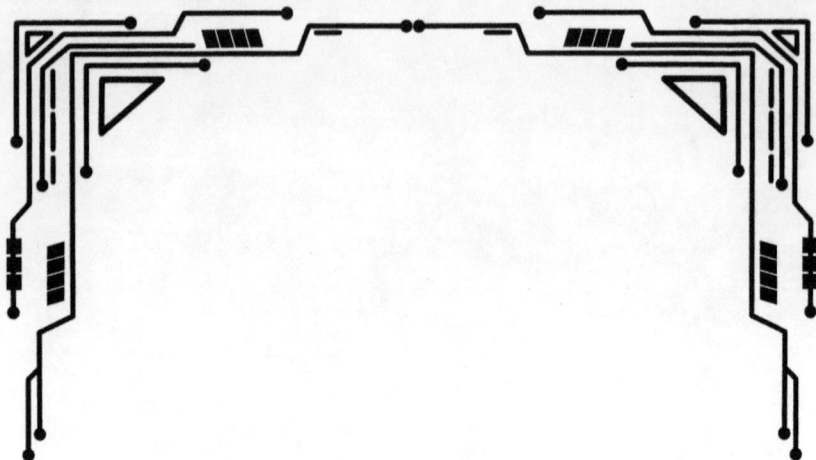

<u>09/24/23</u>

what day is it now
not done with september yet
stay a bit longer

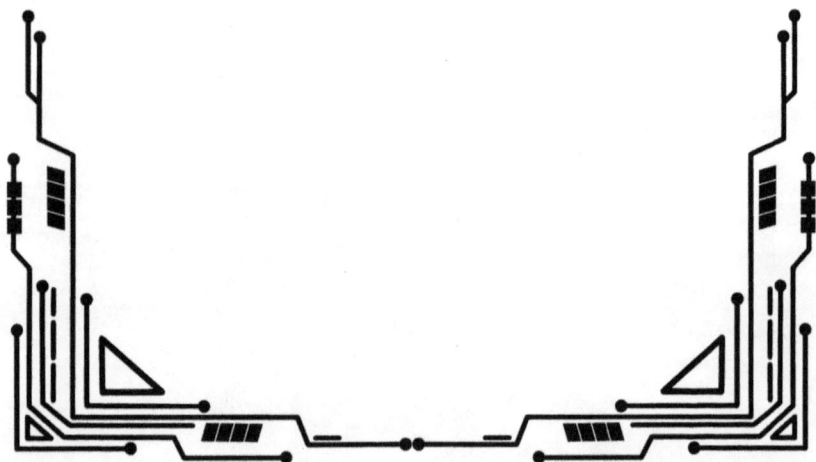

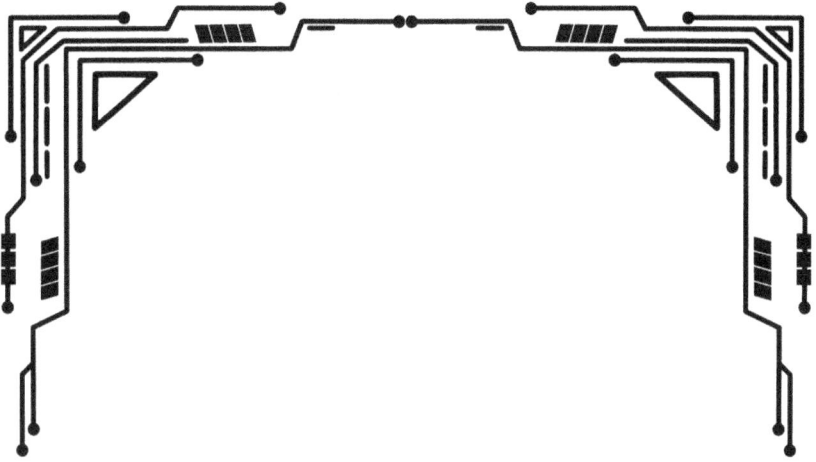

<u>09/25/23</u>

there is a coolness
hanging in the air today
it feels like freedom

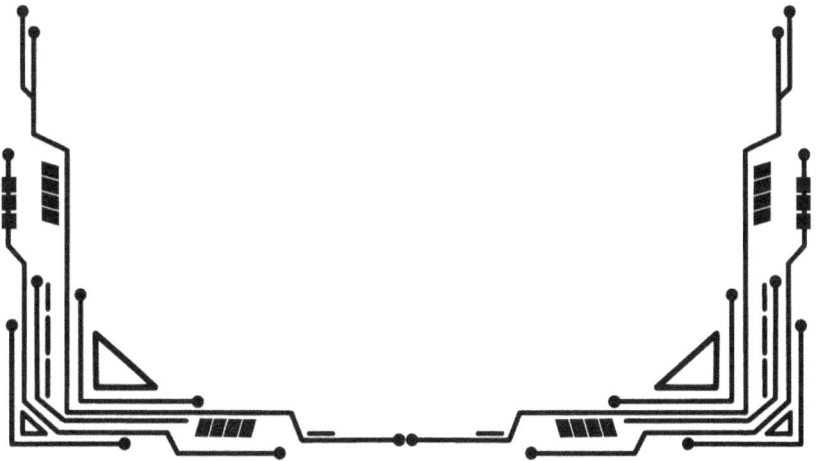

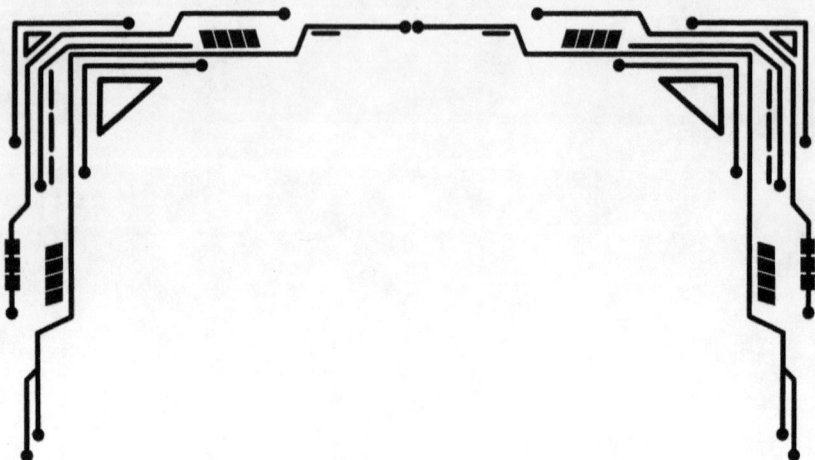

<u>09/26/23</u>

look at the meter
it has the wrong number here
this one isn't mine

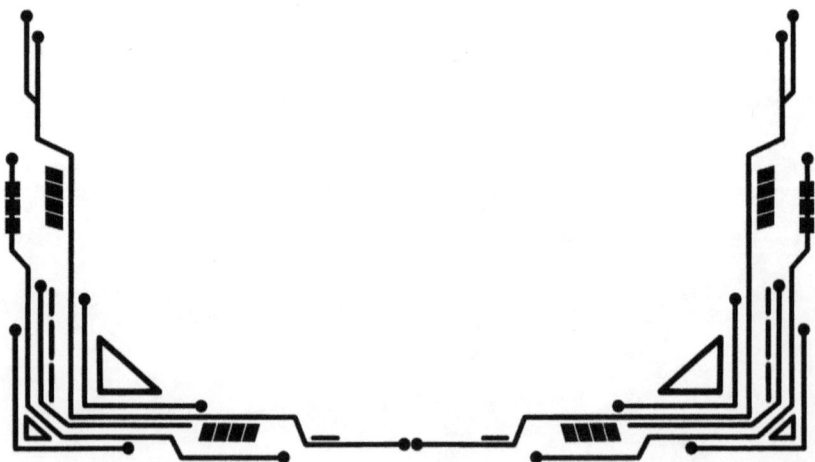

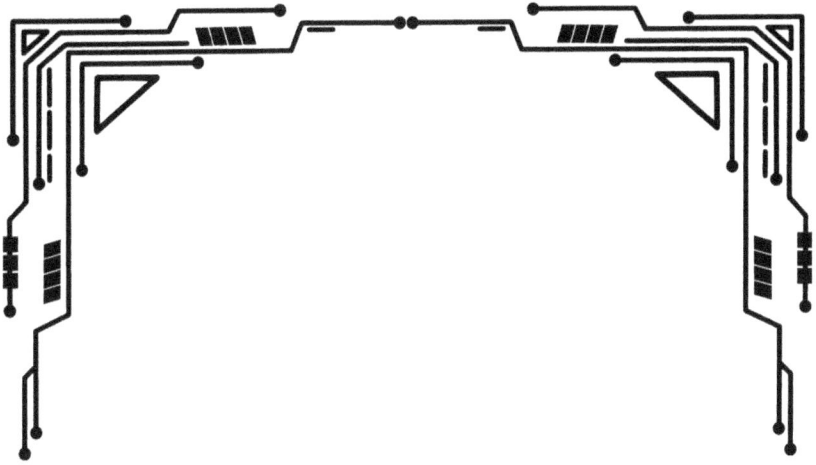

09/27/23

it's been six months now
i hate this and it's stupid
thinking up the words

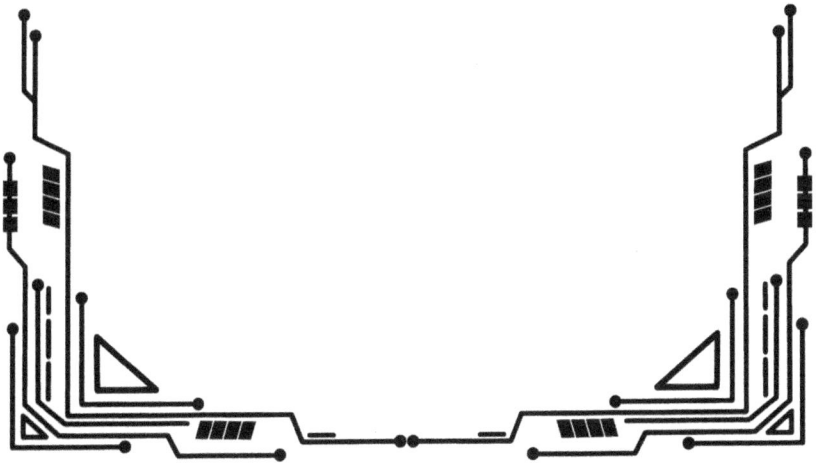

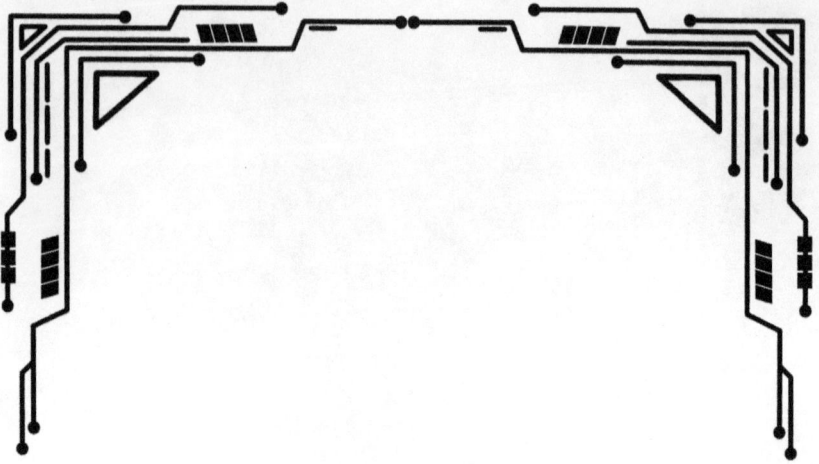

09/28/23

have you seen the news
me neither just wondering
if you would say yes

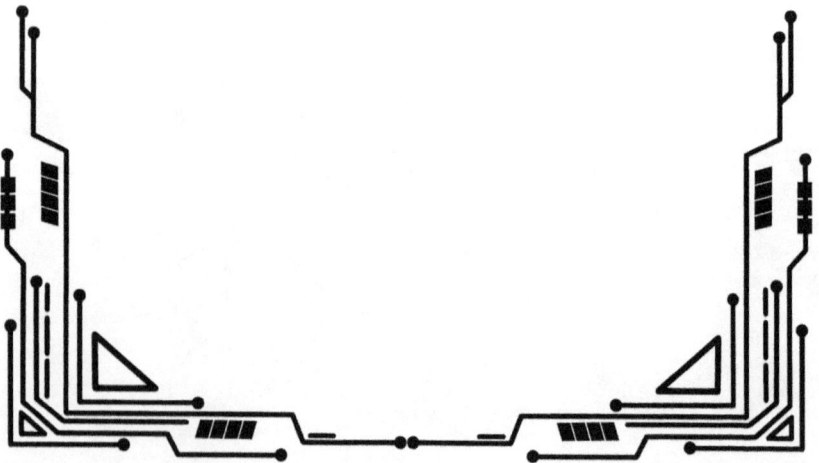

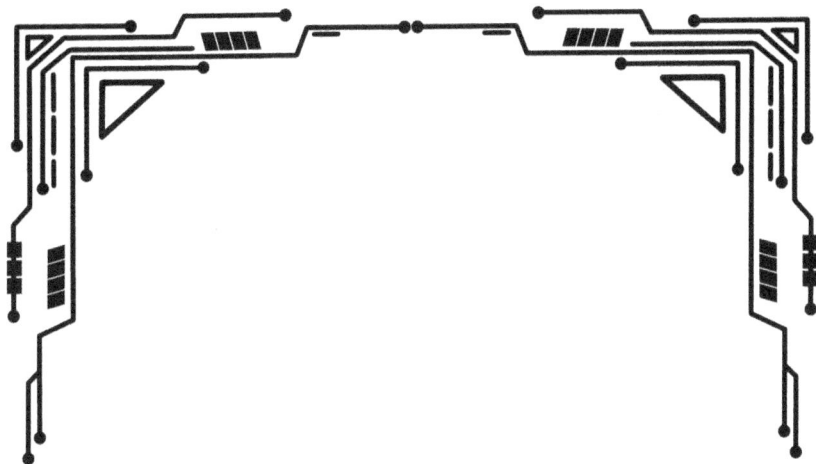

cold water washing
does not work better than hot
you're full of shit todd

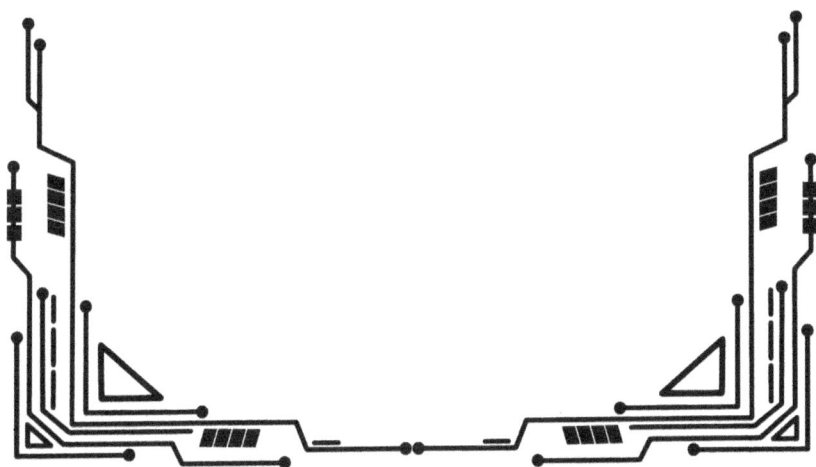

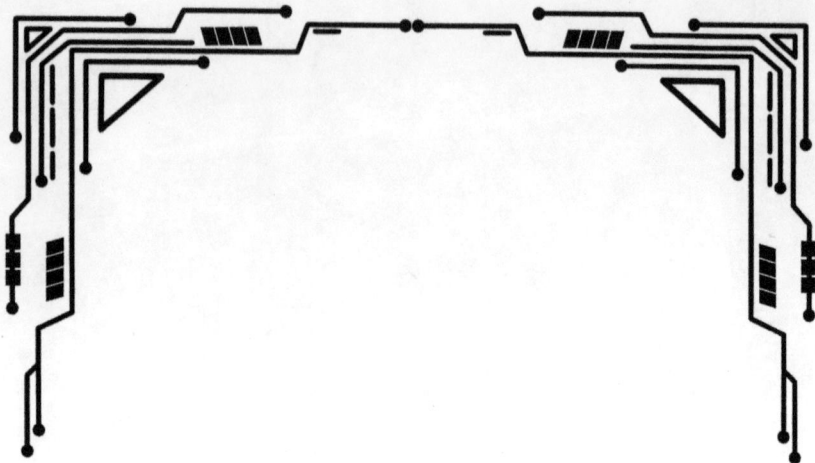

09/30/23

all around my tent
lay the yellow aspen leaves
camping in the fall

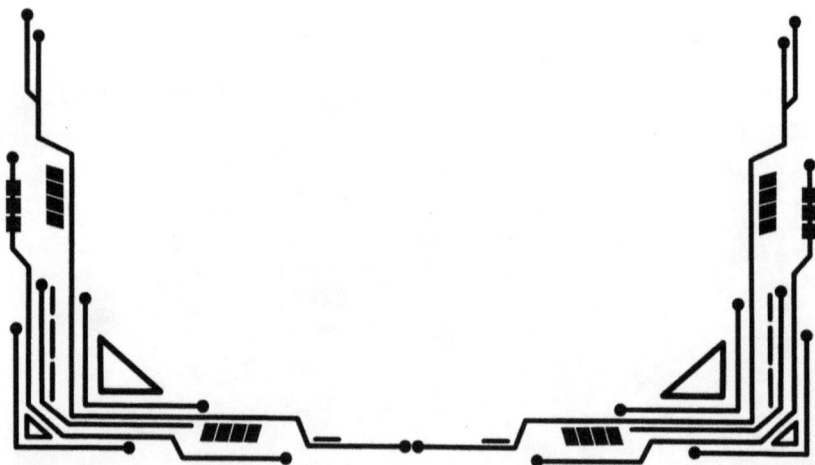

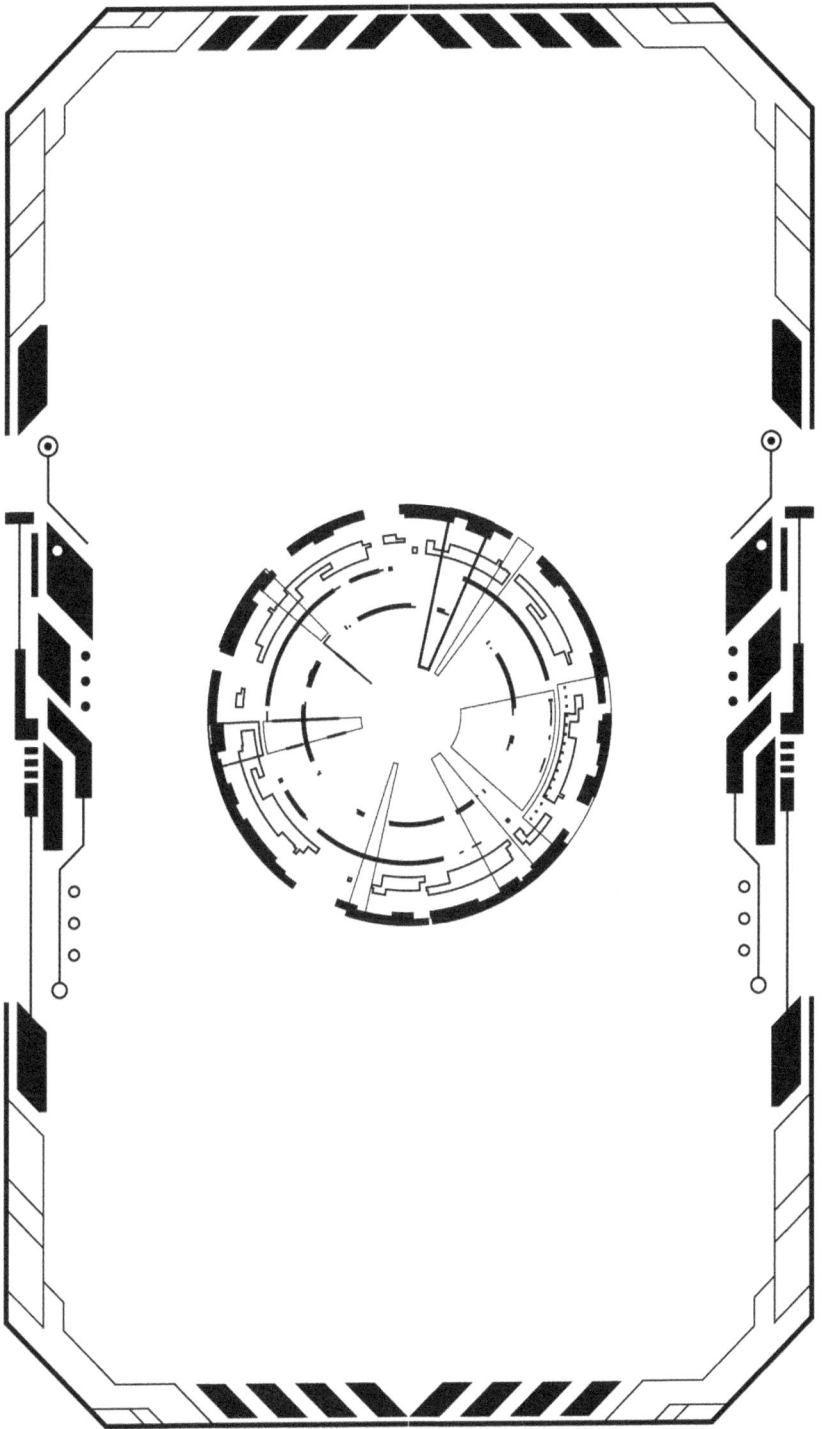

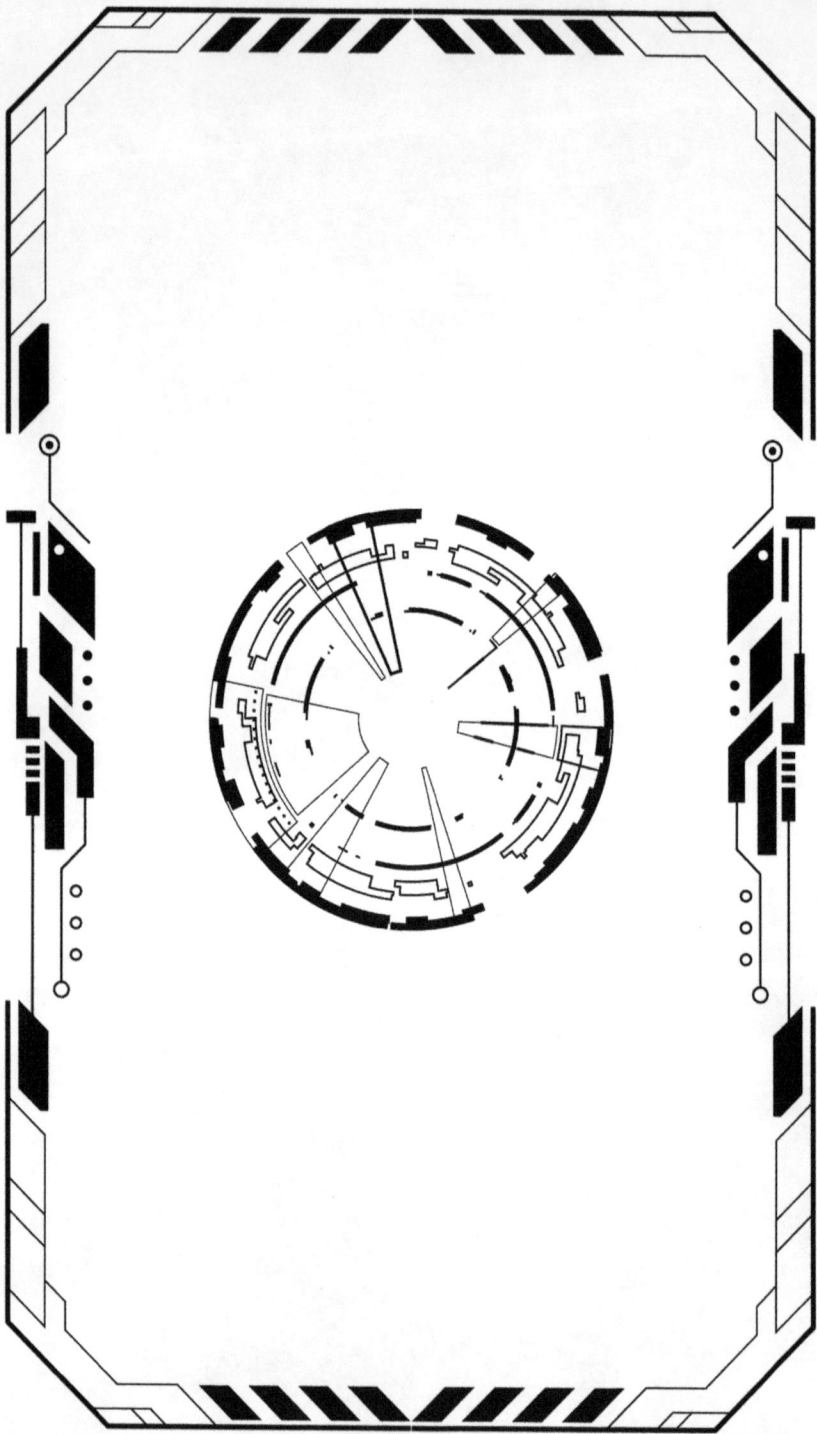

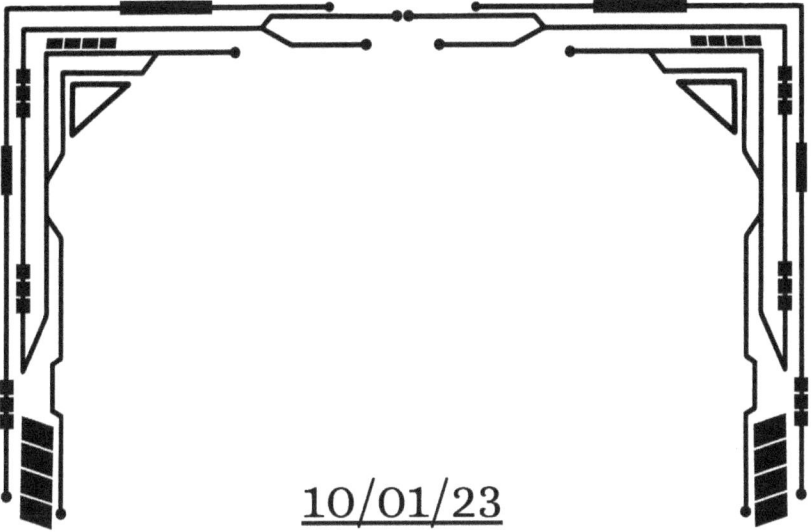

<u>10/01/23</u>

that's the one i want
just like an old murphy bed
gone in the morning

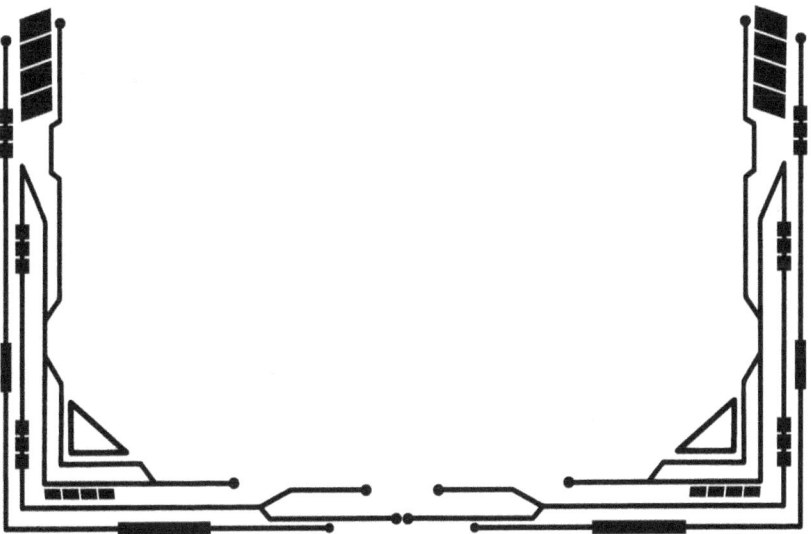

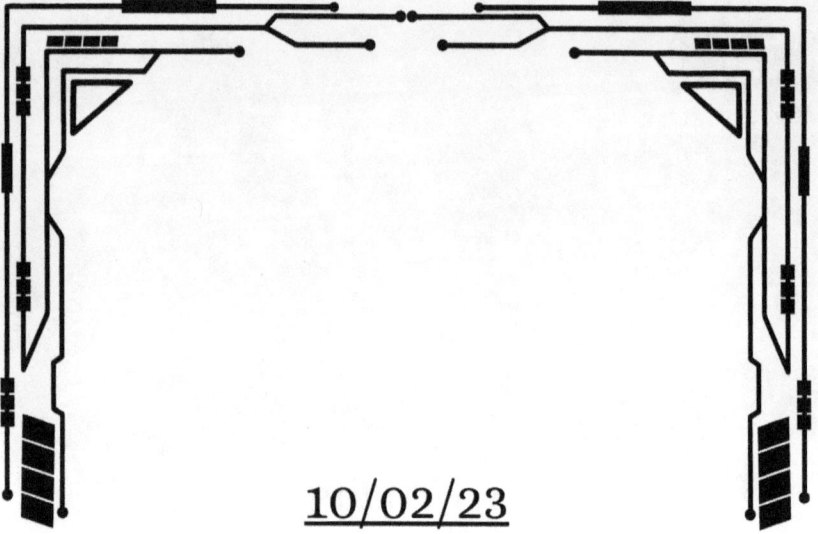

<u>10/02/23</u>

wake and bake today
jasmine thai marijuana
with coffee and toast

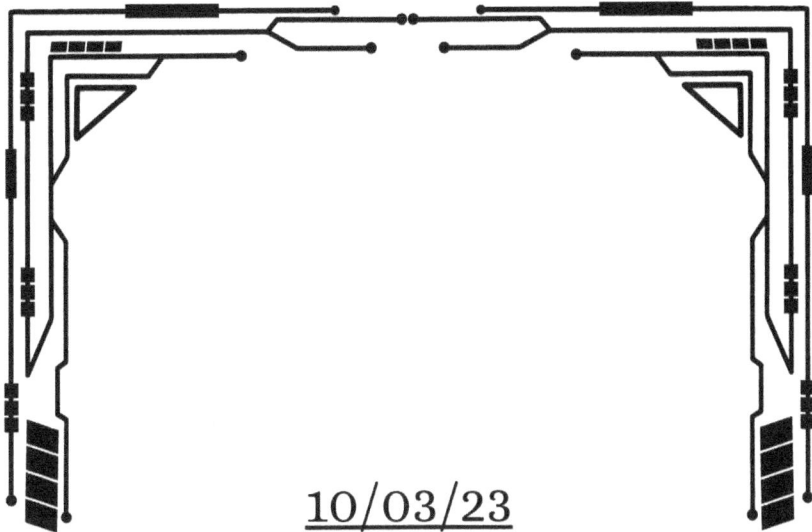

<u>10/03/23</u>

squeaky squeaky wheel
sounds like a lot of money
need new brakes again

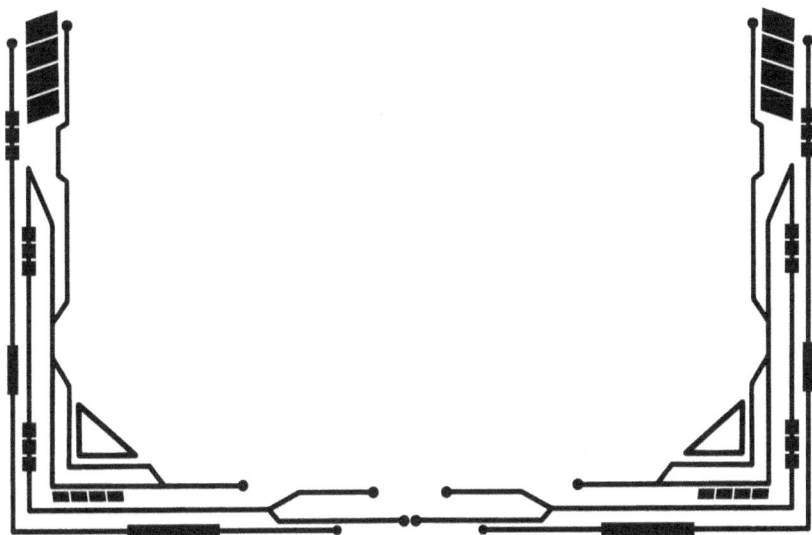

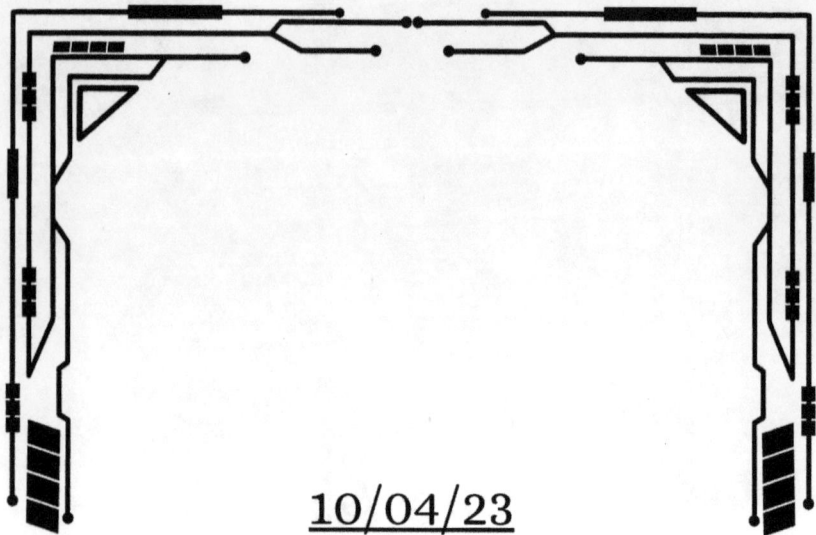

<u>10/04/23</u>

couldn't sleep again
now looking at another
october sunrise

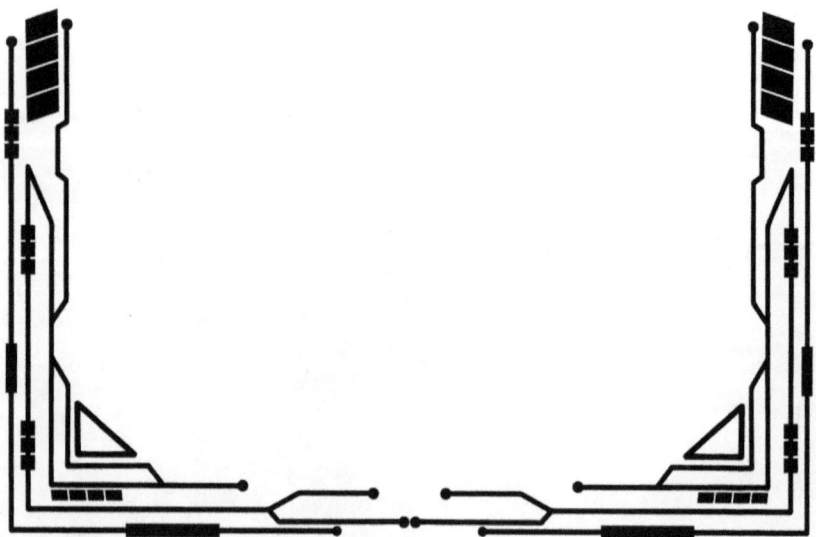

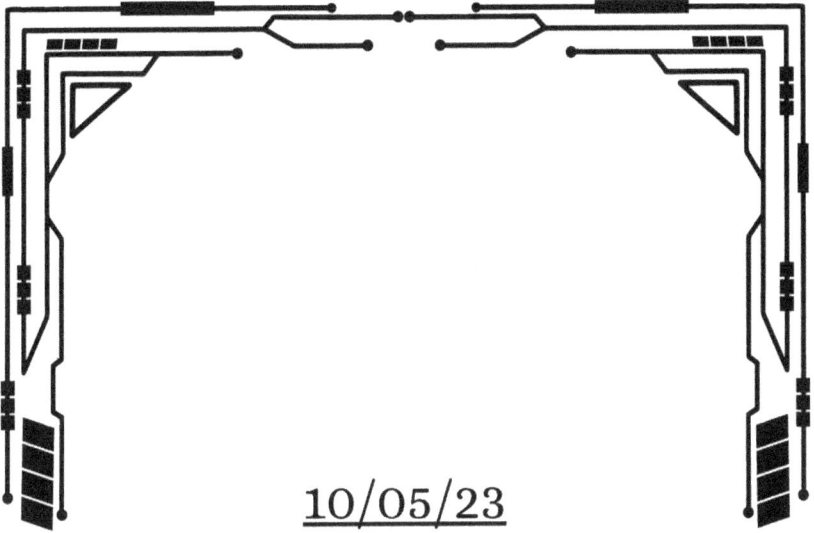

<u>10/05/23</u>

i should have lunch now
that looks like a good pizza
how about a slice

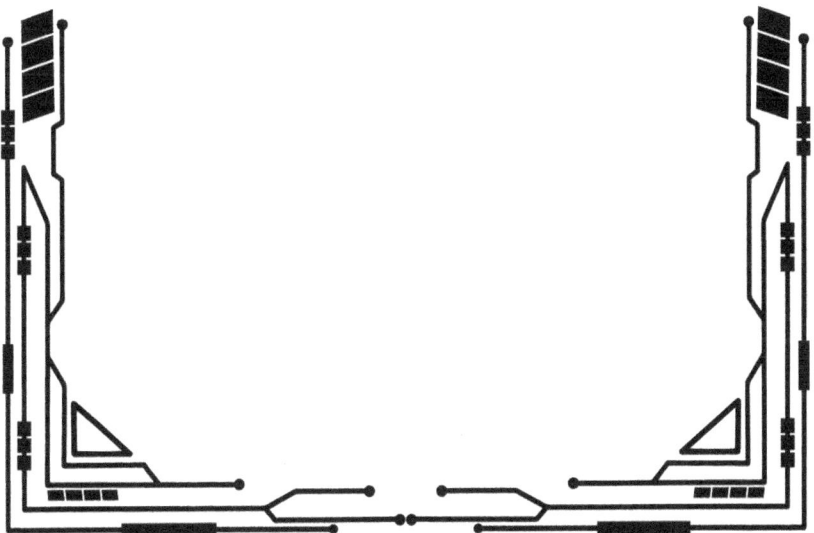

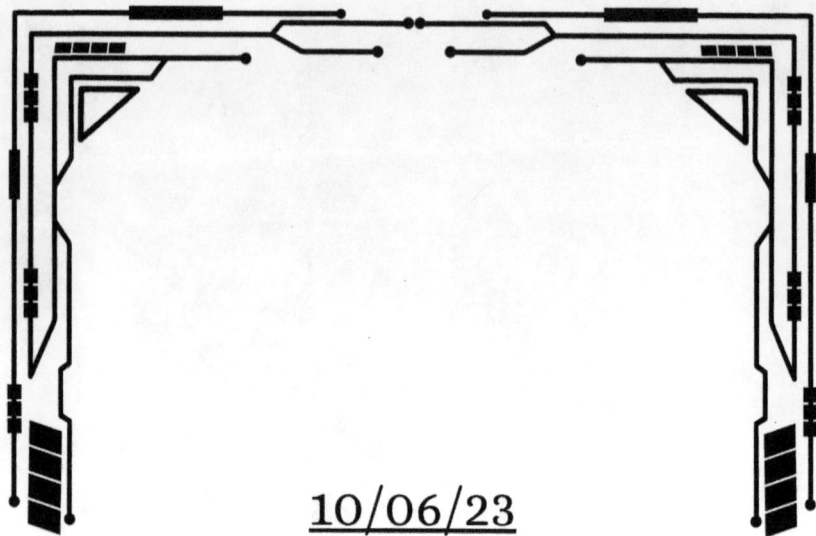

<u>10/06/23</u>

it's today again
a whole year has gone by now
since this day last year

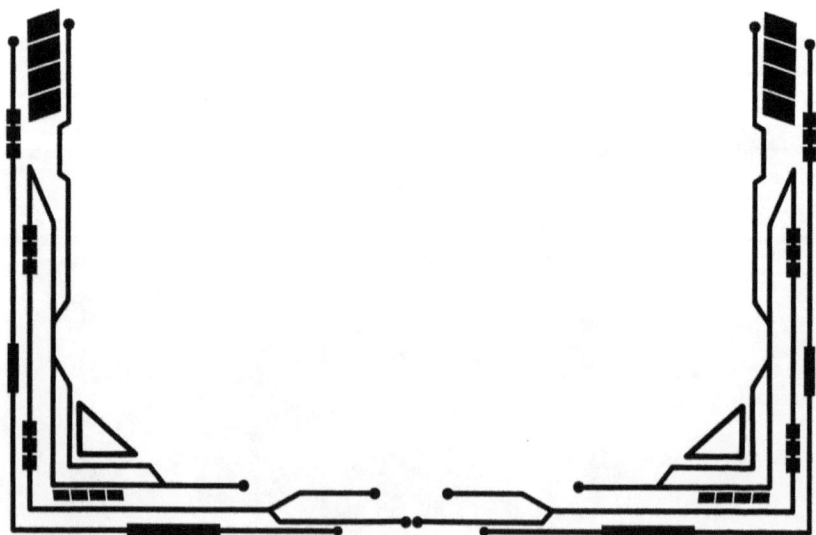

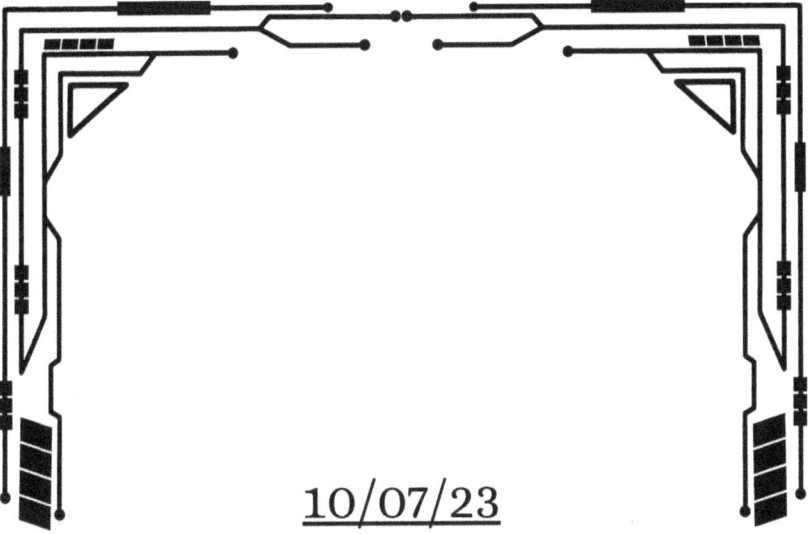

<u>10/07/23</u>

remember the old
electric blue malibu
out in the garage

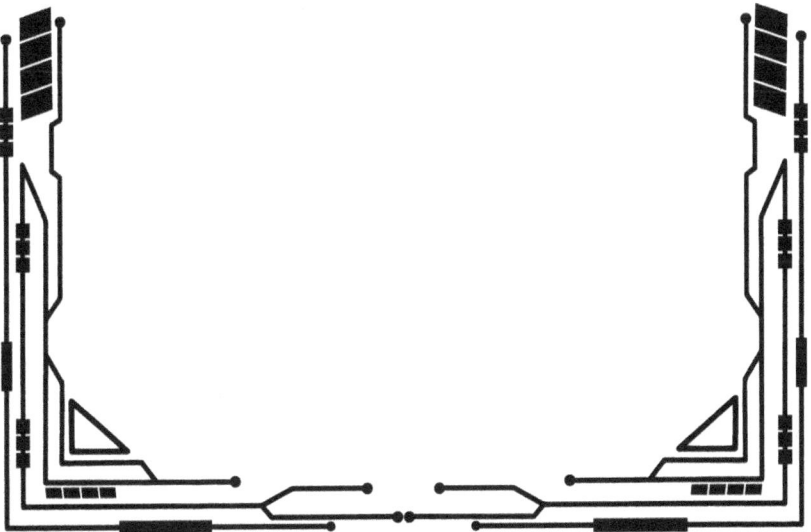

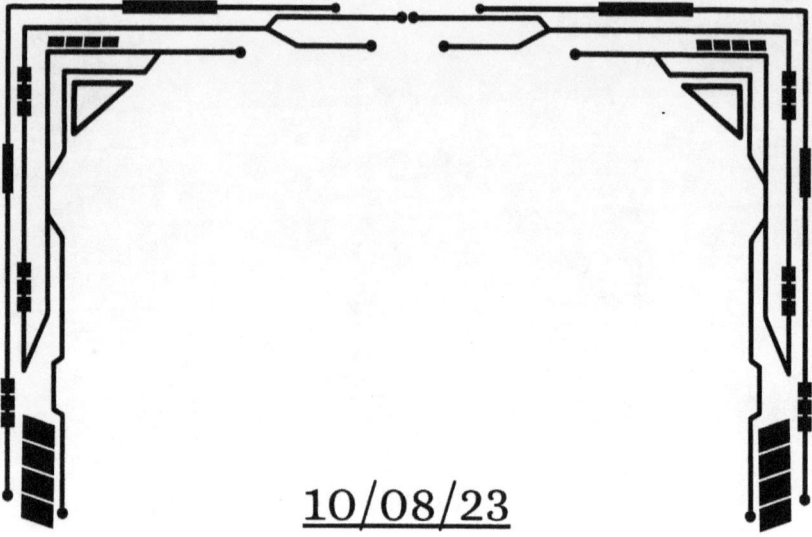

10/08/23

outside this morning
there is a hint of sadness
hanging in the air

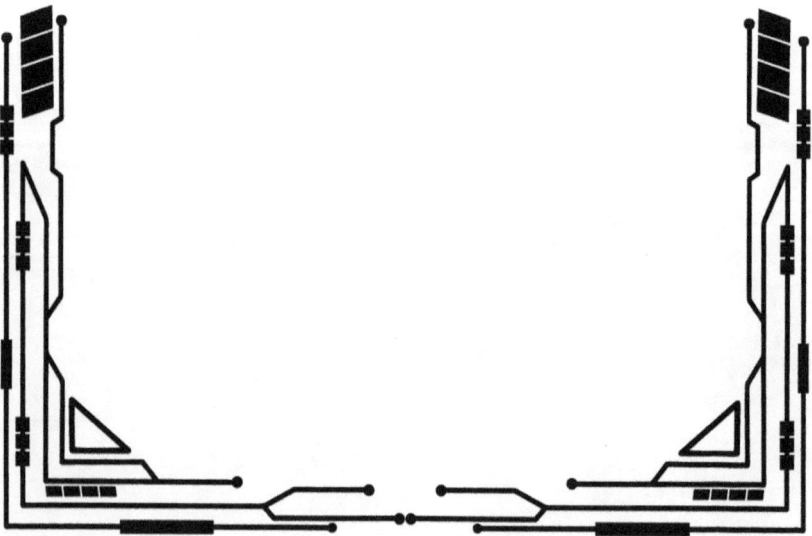

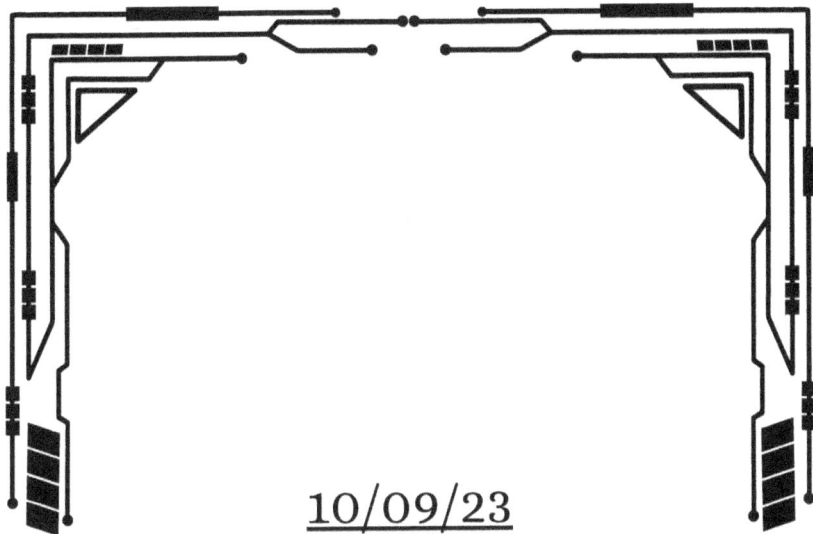

<u>10/09/23</u>

not being able
to reach the peanut butter
i will never know

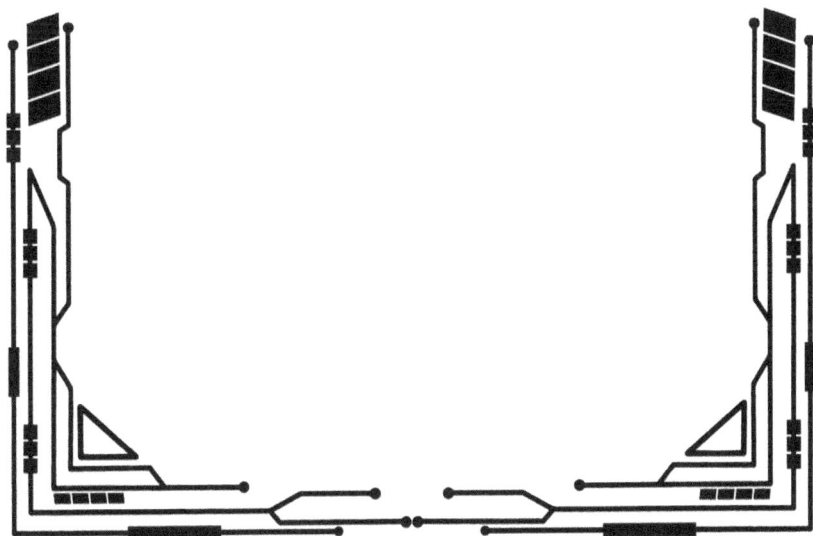

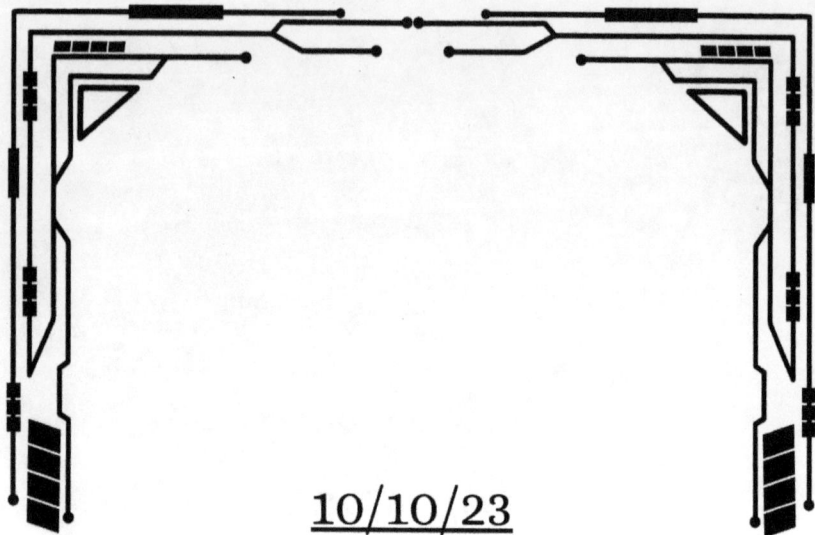

<u>10/10/23</u>

hot mountain coffee
is better in the fall than
cold mountain coffee

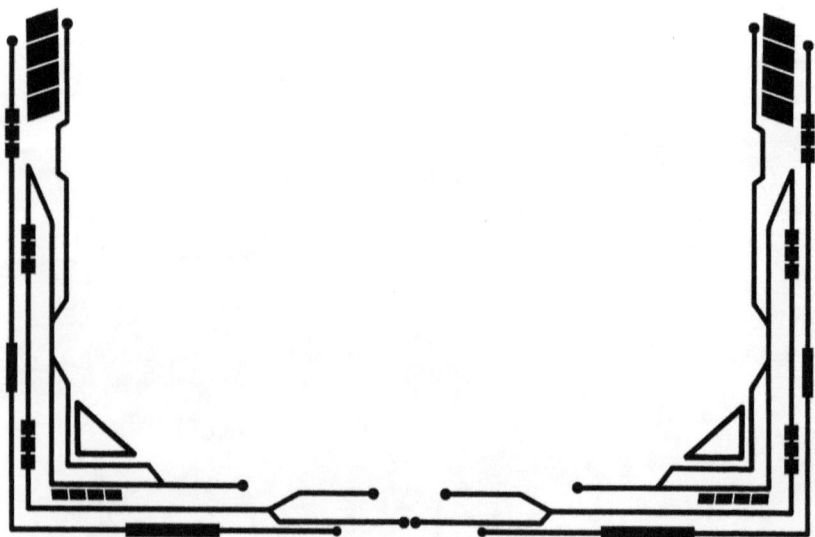

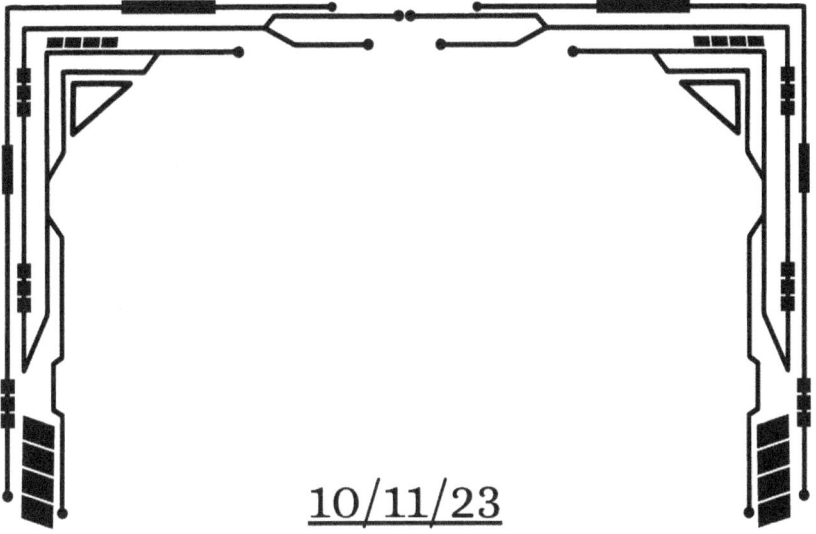

<u>10/11/23</u>

i dropped my sharpie
in a five gallon bucket
full of blue dish soap

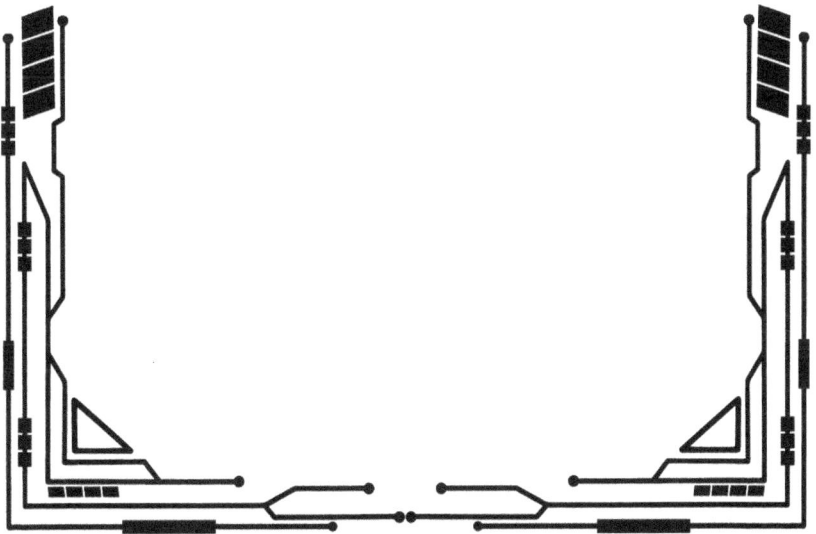

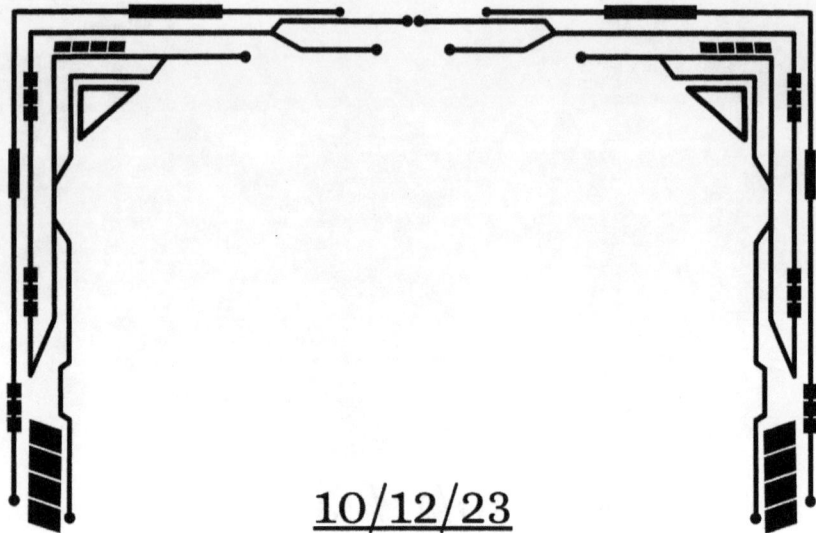

<u>10/12/23</u>

do you remember
what littlefoot saw that day
it was a tree star

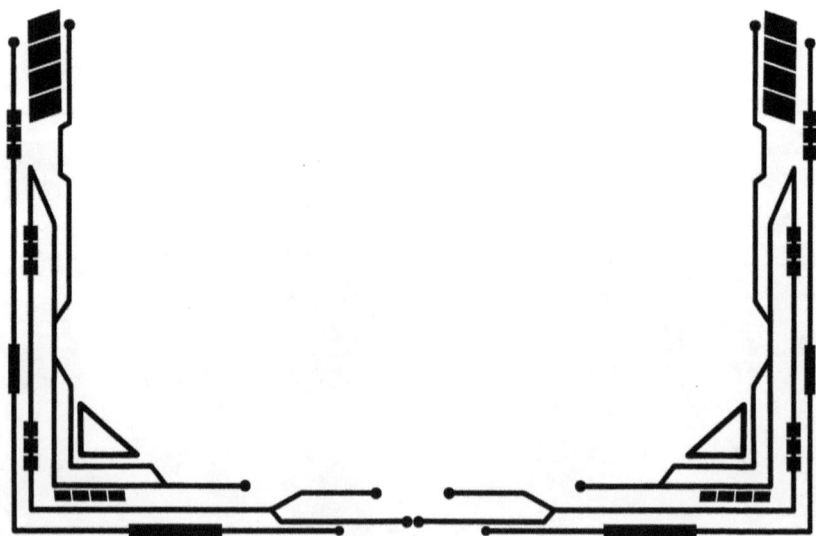

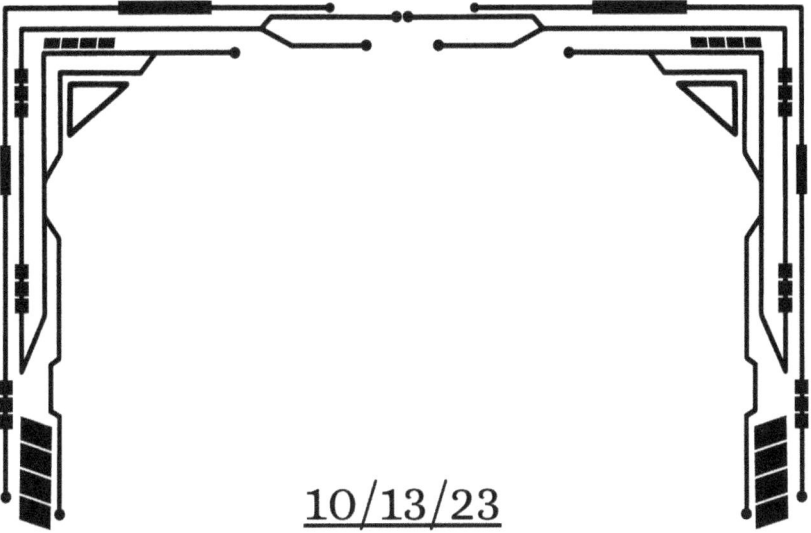

<u>10/13/23</u>

take a look outside
there are no curbs on my street
that dog is confused

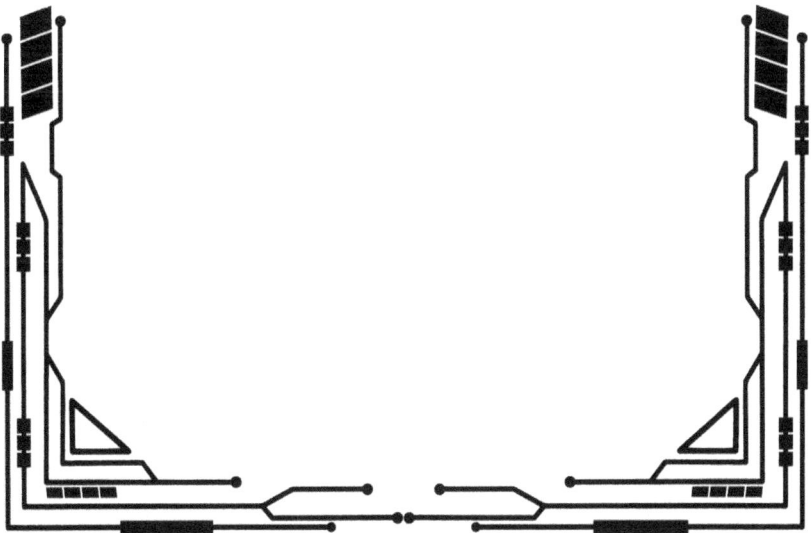

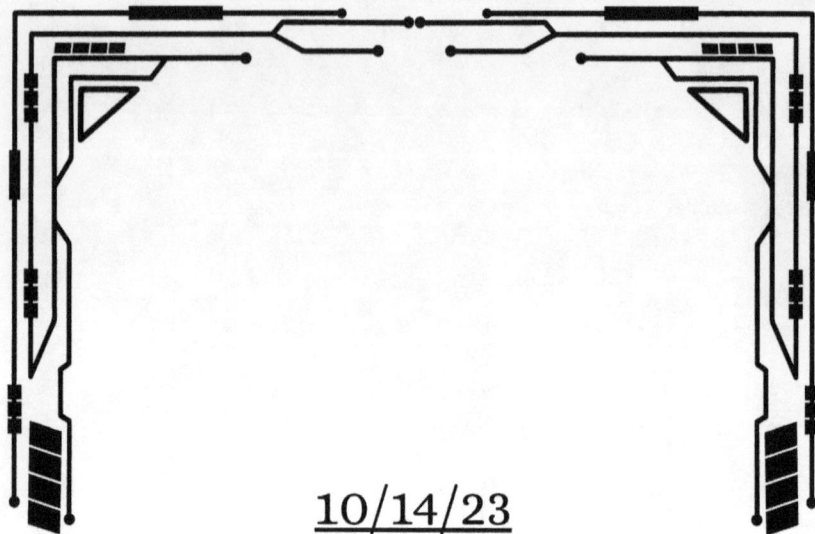

<u>10/14/23</u>

distant memories
of climbing trees in the woods
not so far away

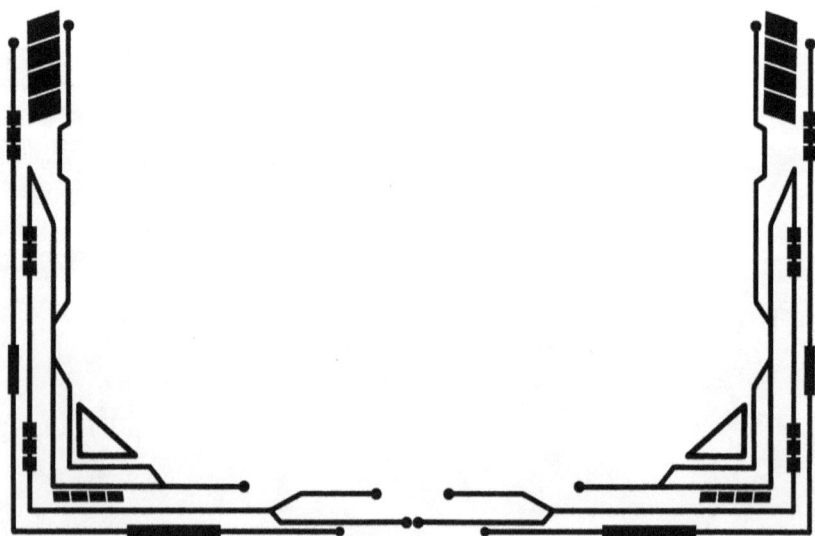

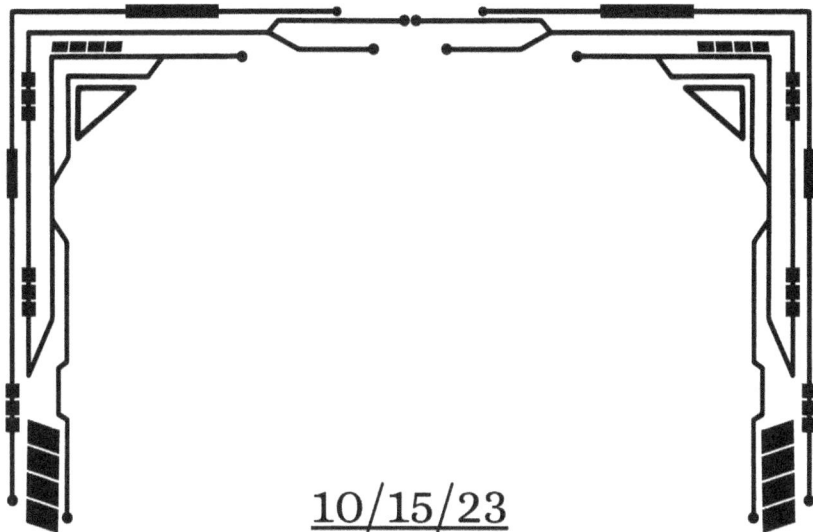

<u>10/15/23</u>

a bit chilly now
and the leaves are almost done
halfway through the month

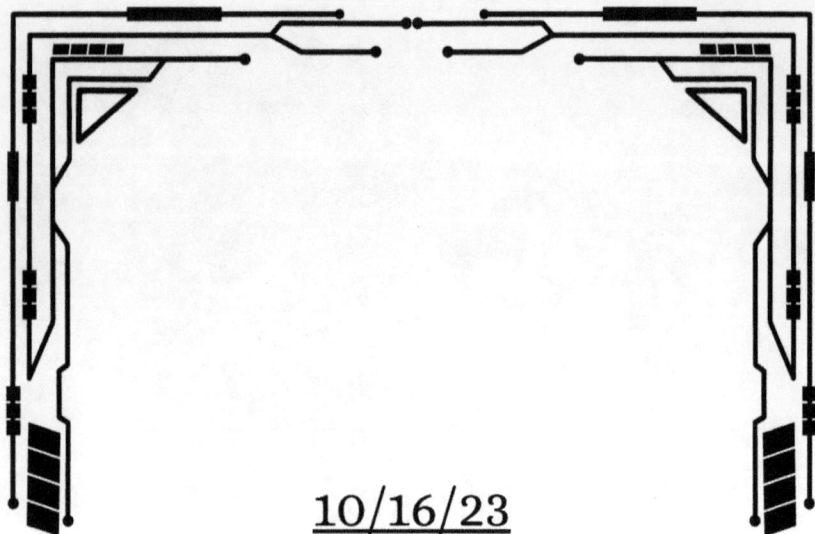

<u>10/16/23</u>

there are too many
dumplings in the dumpling soup
and also it's cold

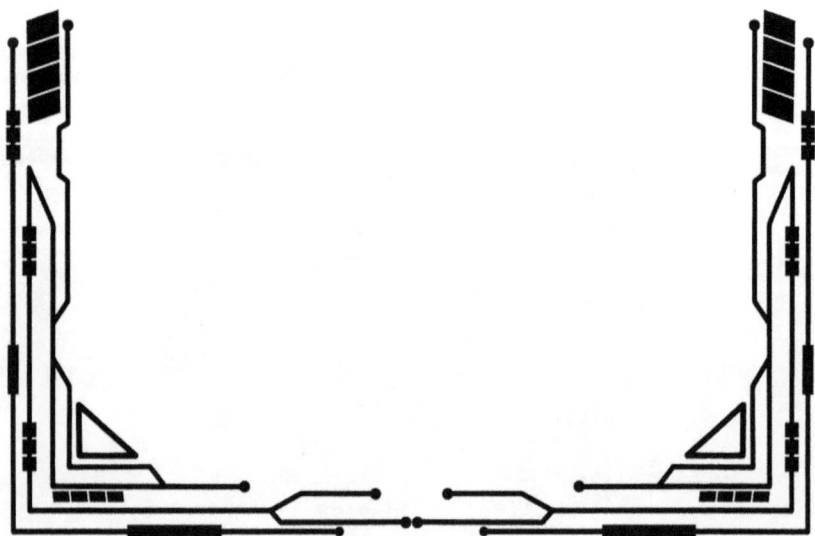

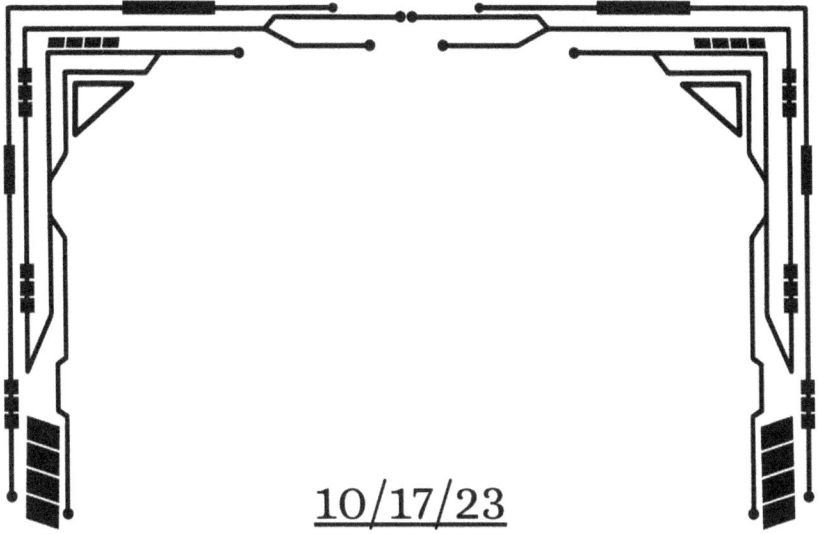

10/17/23

remember the ghoul
who smiles with lsd eyes
i want my soul back

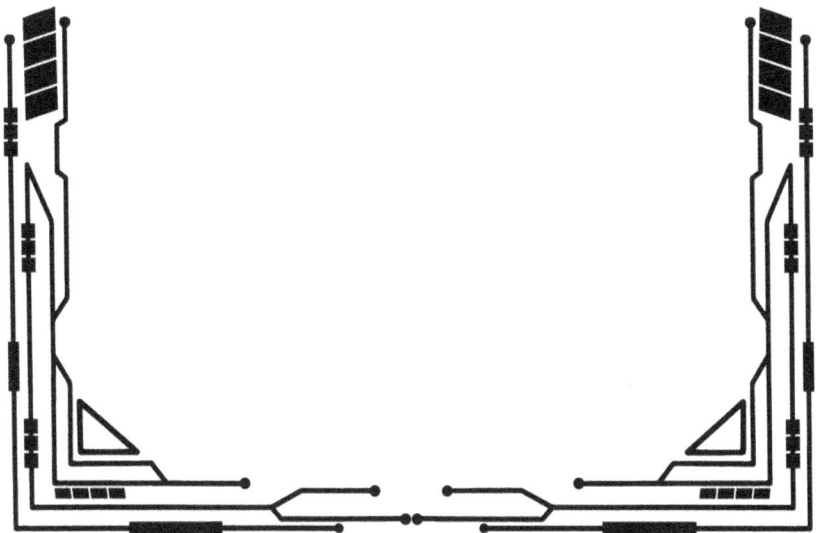

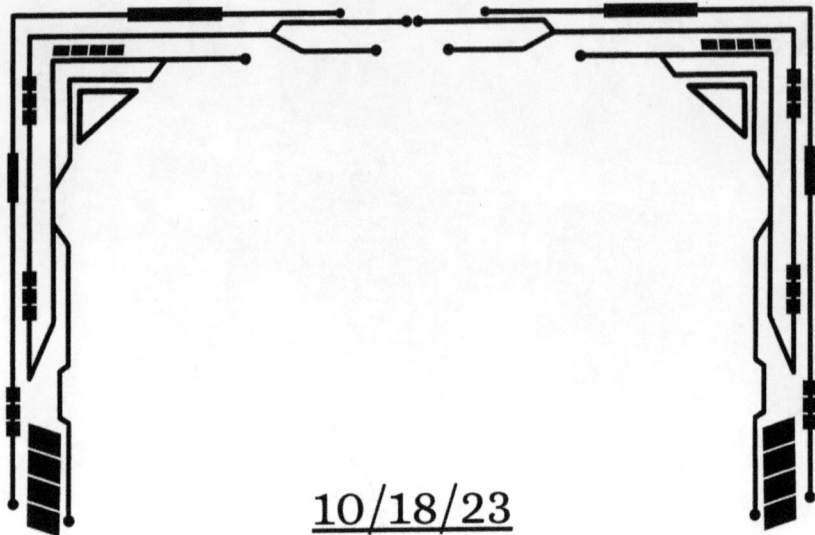

10/18/23

there is a dead glove
on the side of the road here
it is very sad

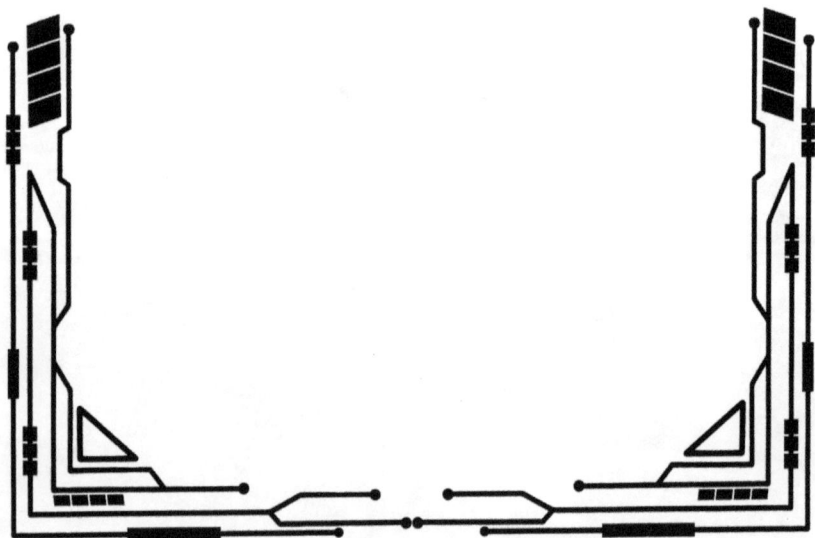

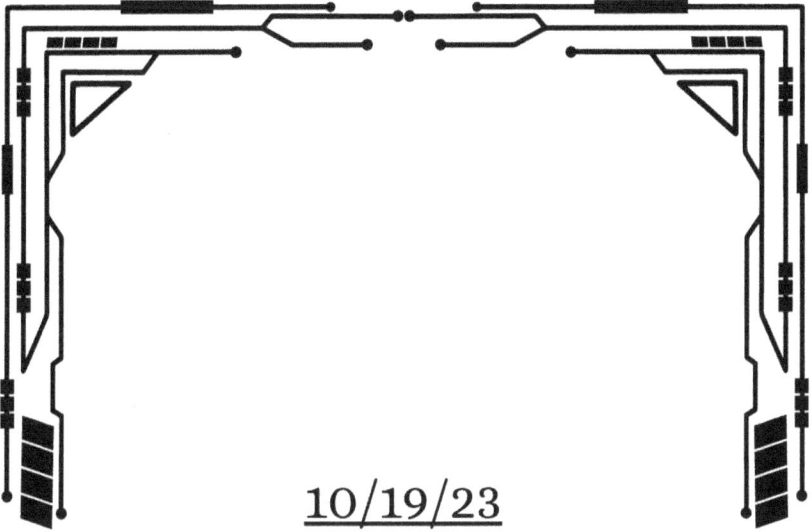

<u>10/19/23</u>

a whole lot of big
a little bit of middle
a tiny bit small

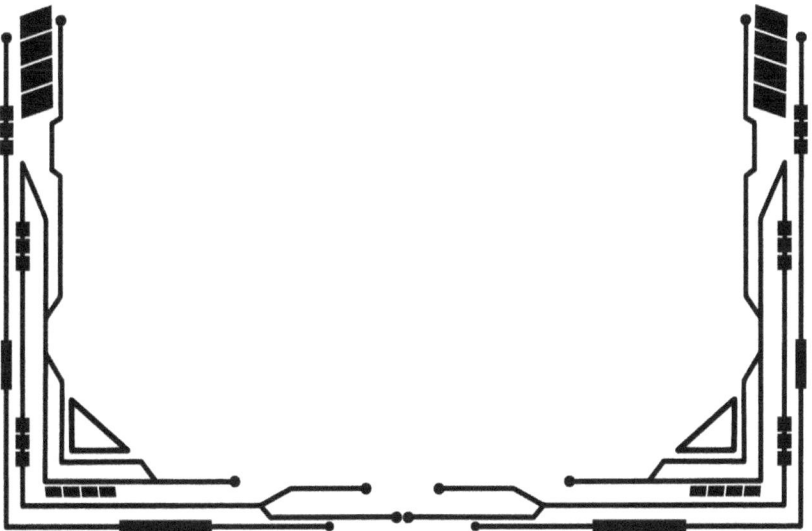

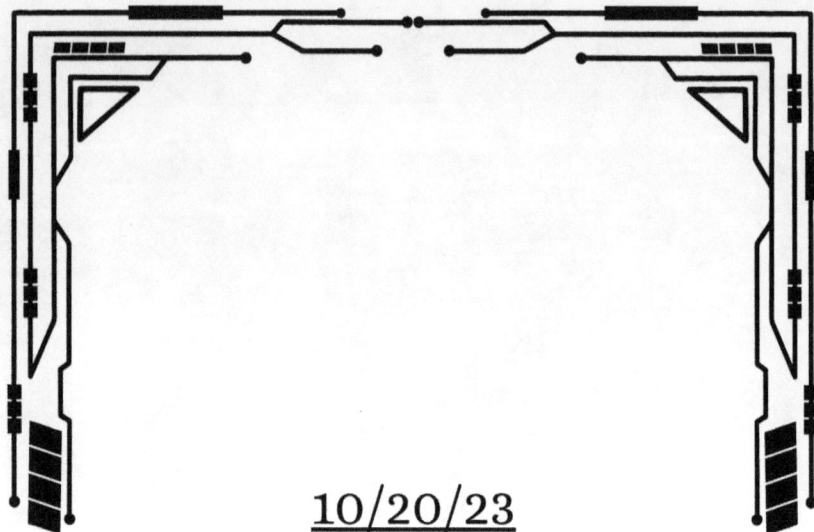

<u>10/20/23</u>

simba was a bitch
my favorite lion is scar
be prepared hombre

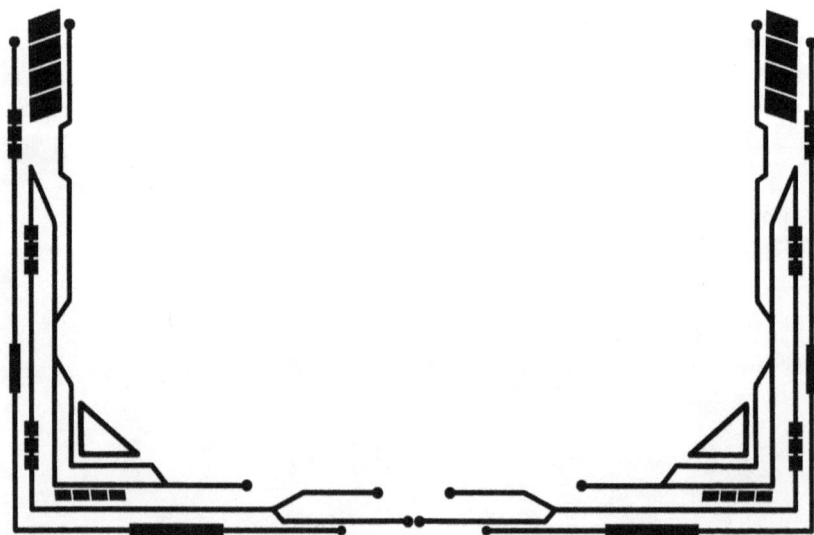

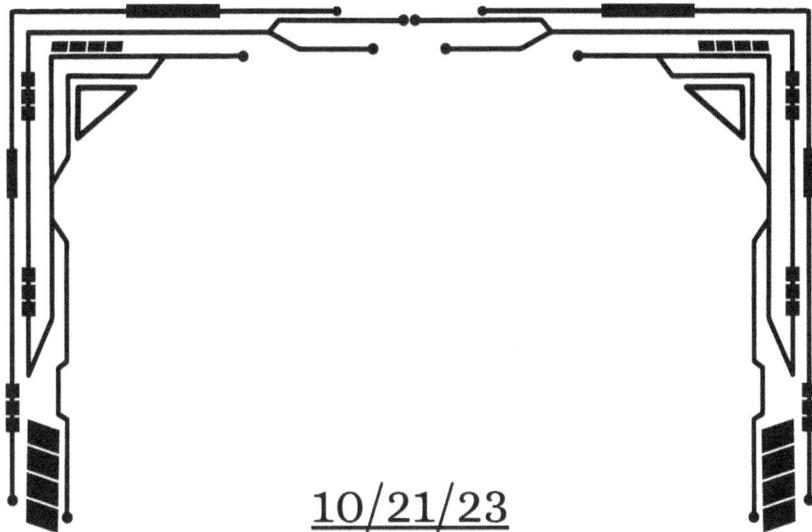

10/21/23

ten two one two three
so many days in a year
i hate this thing now

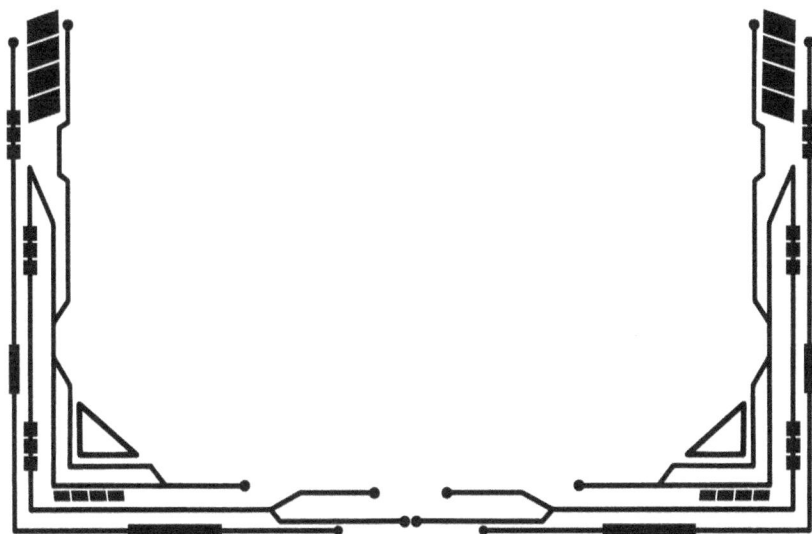

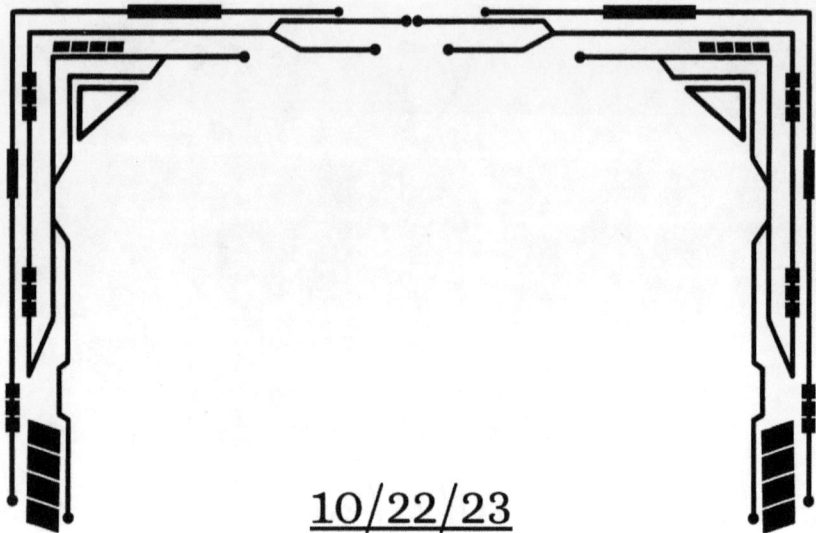

<u>10/22/23</u>

i'm over here but
over on that mountain there
is a waterfall

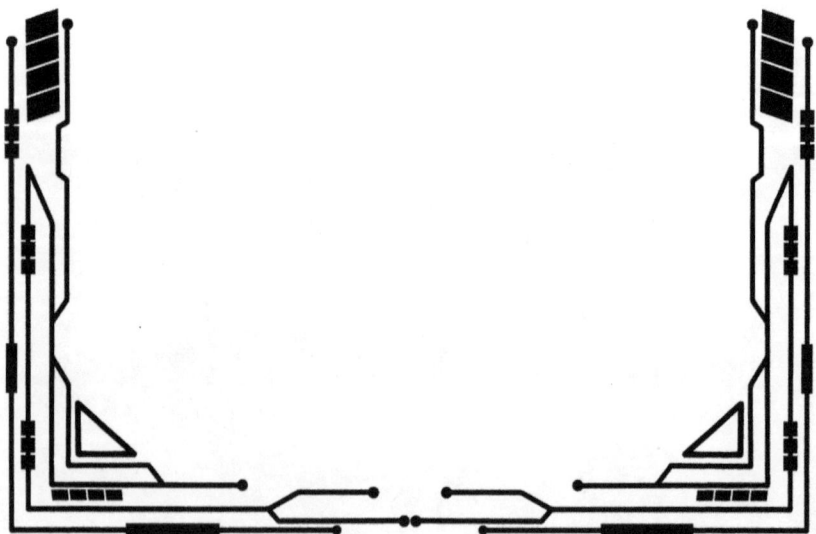

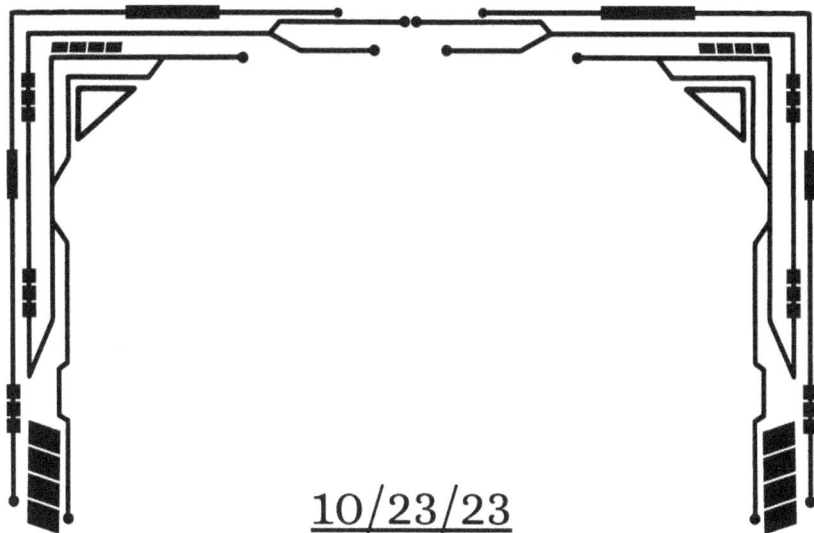

<u>10/23/23</u>

look at the sunrise
listen to the morning birds
live in the moment

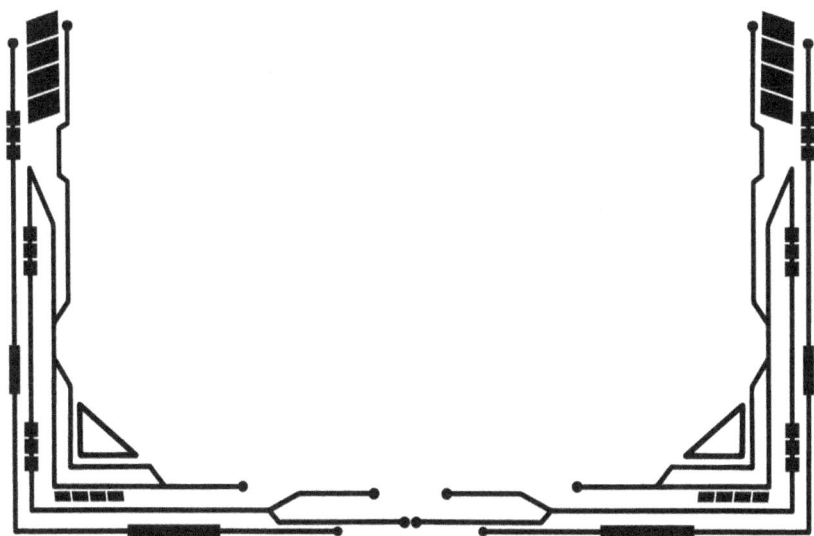

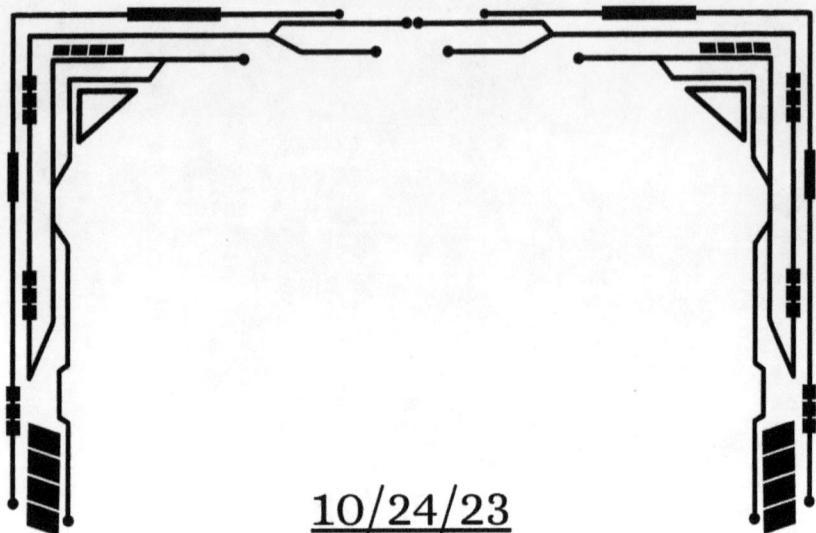

10/24/23

hanging in the tree
a glass bottle and a key
wind chime melody

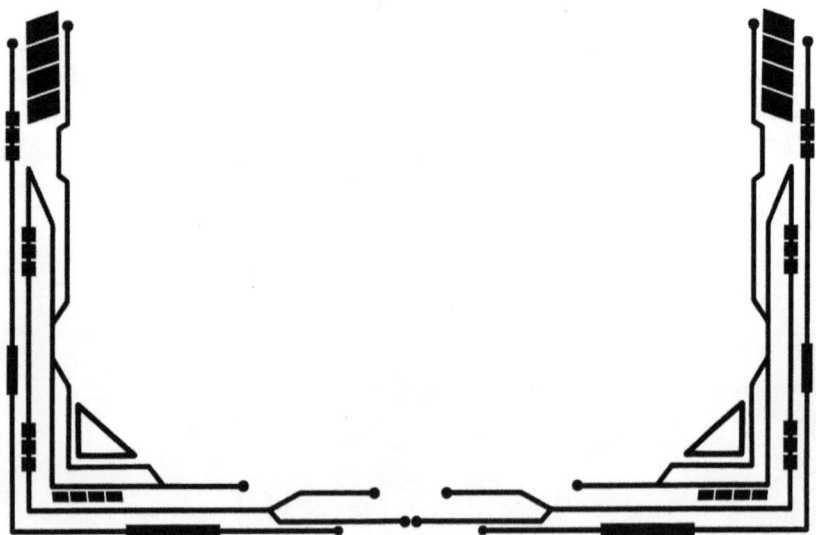

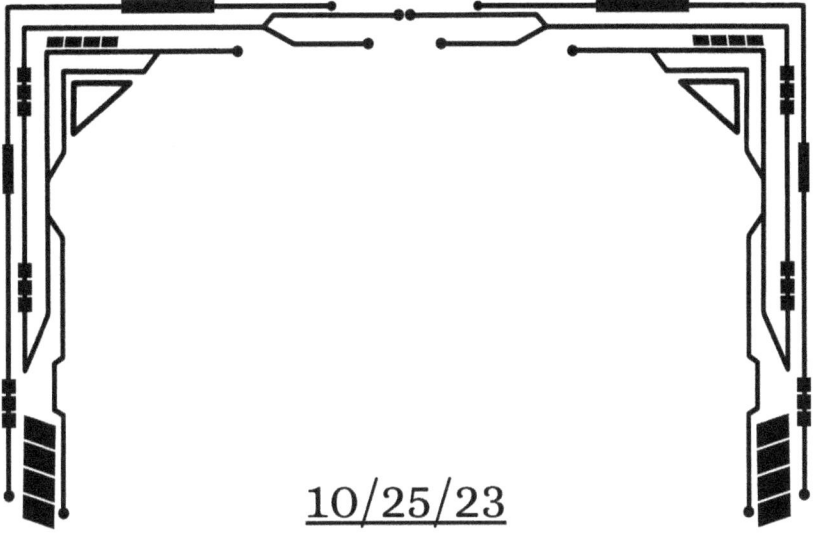

<u>10/25/23</u>

walking on this dark
anonymous forest road
for a long time now

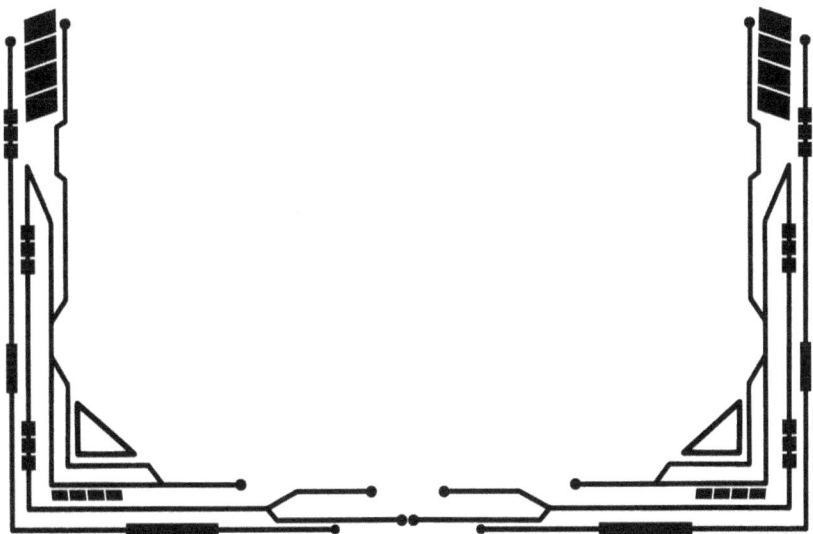

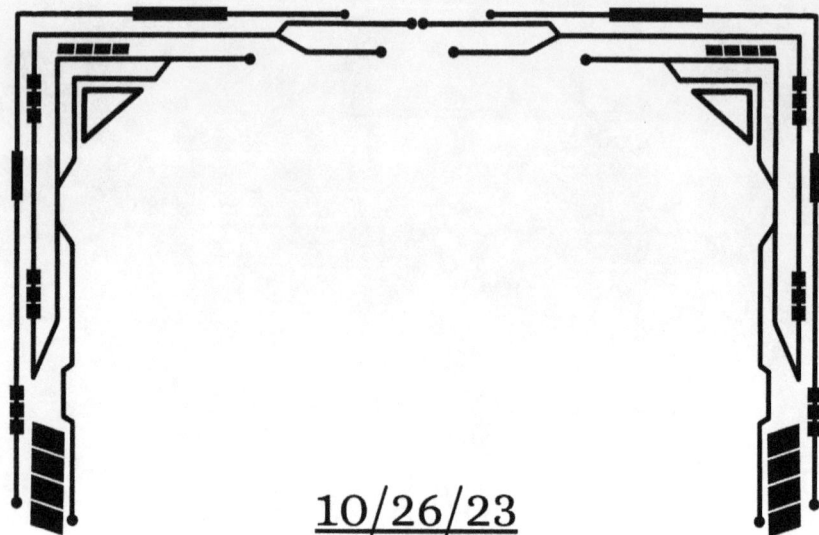

10/26/23

holding on in fear
the final leaf on the tree
let go little one

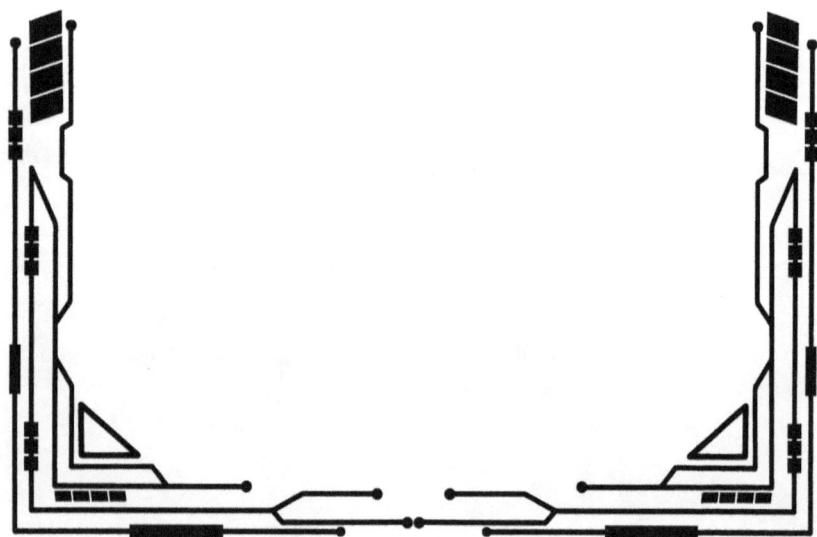

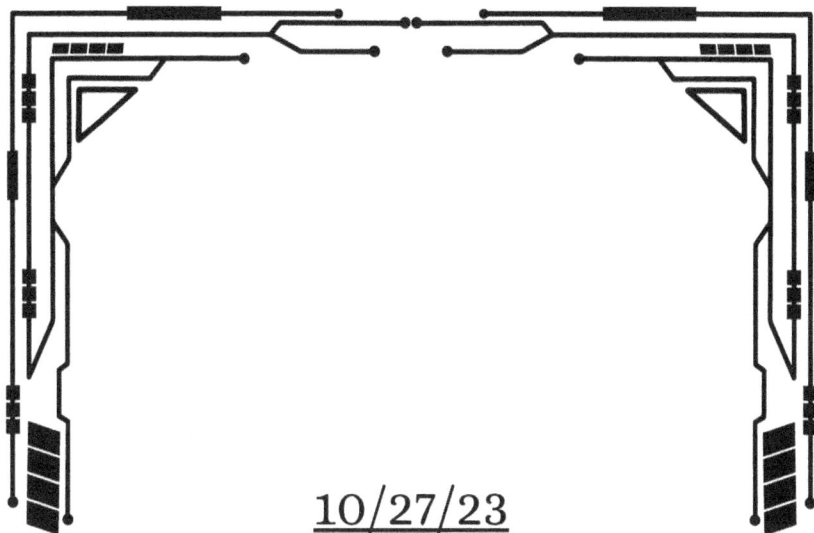

<u>10/27/23</u>

another shot of
warrior kitten juice please
cold brew coffee meow

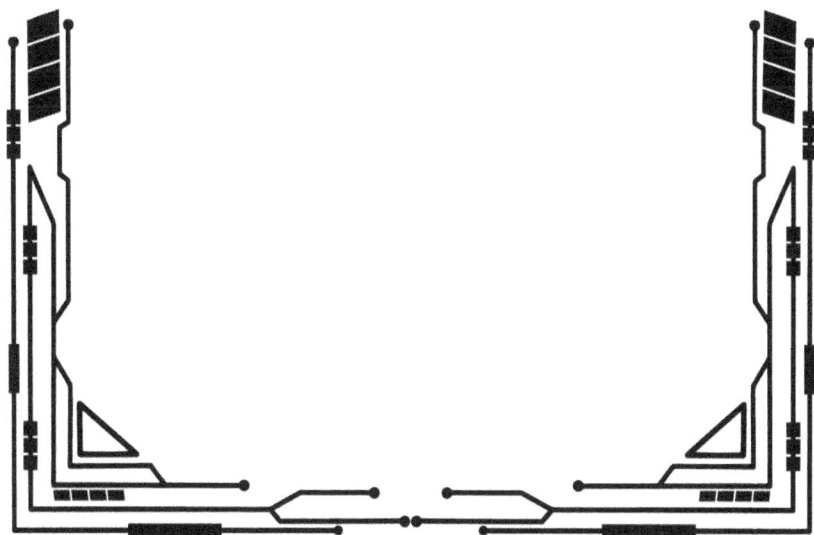

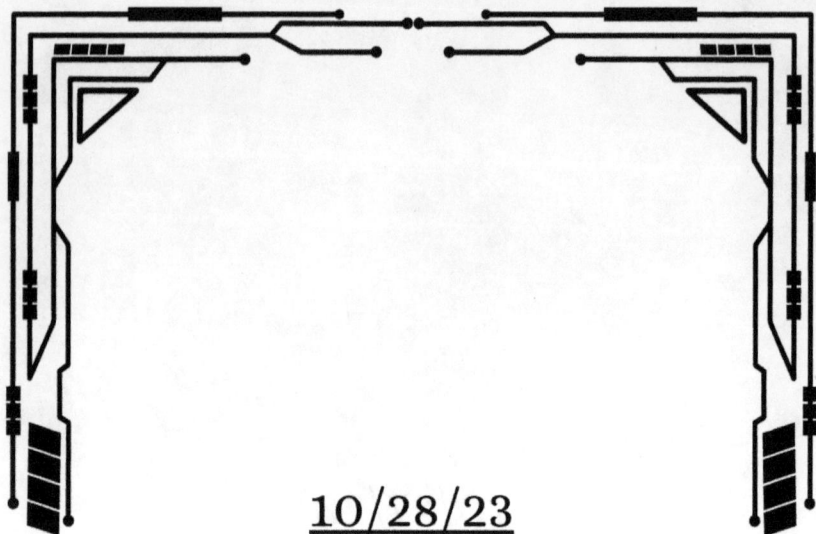

<u>10/28/23</u>

the moon becomes full
with tapioca pudding
once the sun goes down

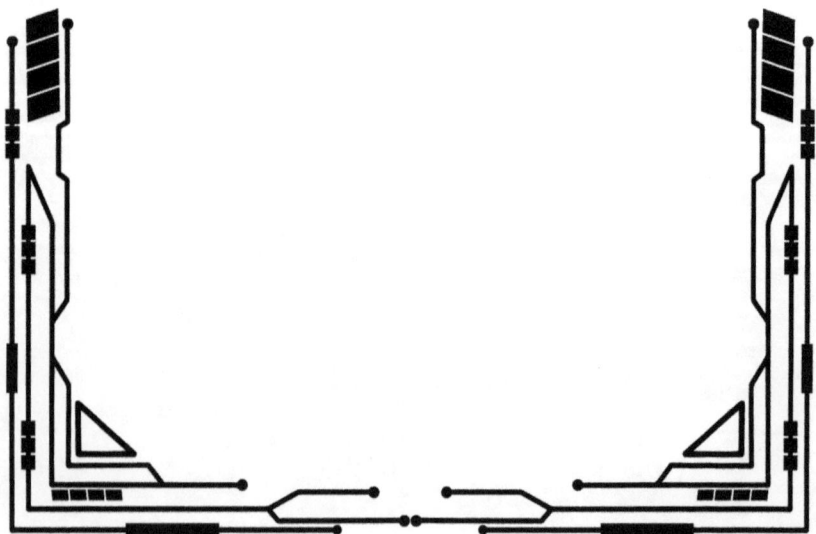

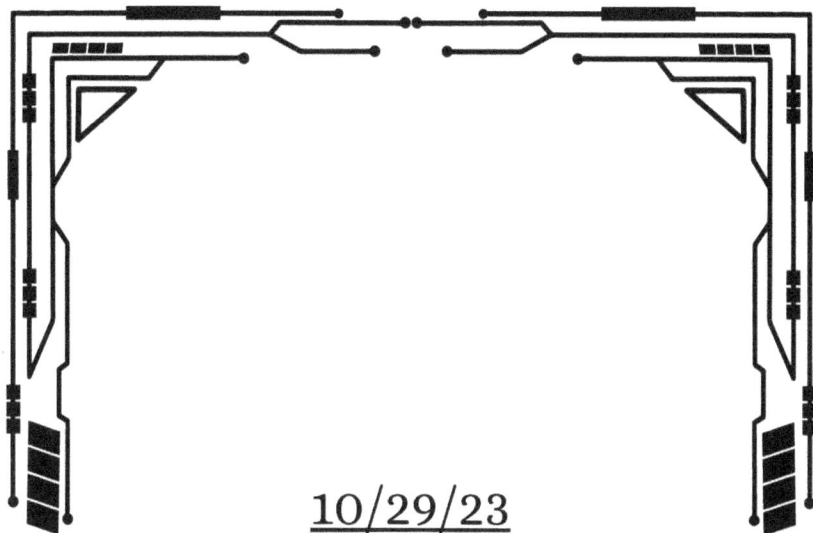

<u>10/29/23</u>

now sing me a song
and i'll tell you a story
we just wrote a play

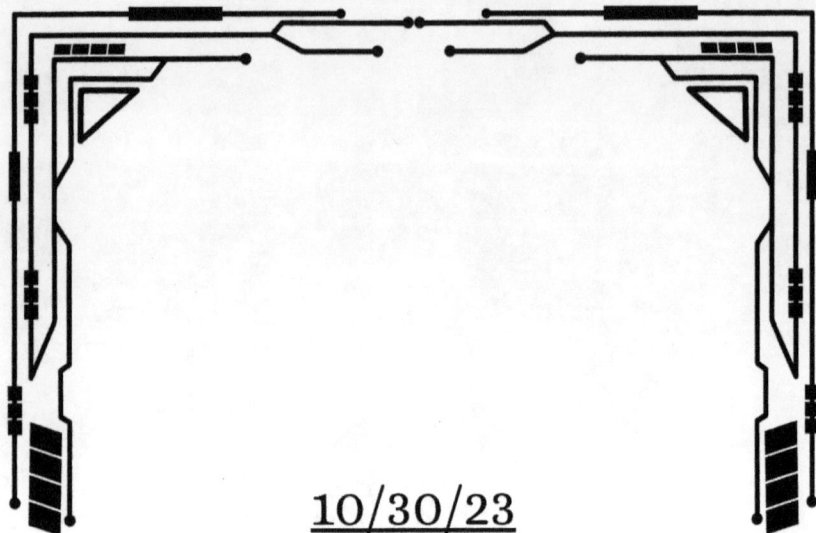

<u>10/30/23</u>

jump over the fence
take it easy and sit here
on a walkabout

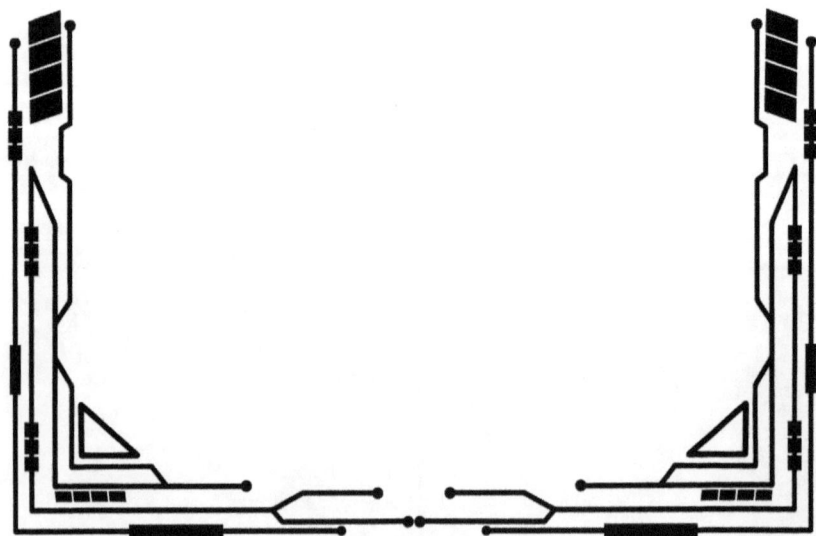

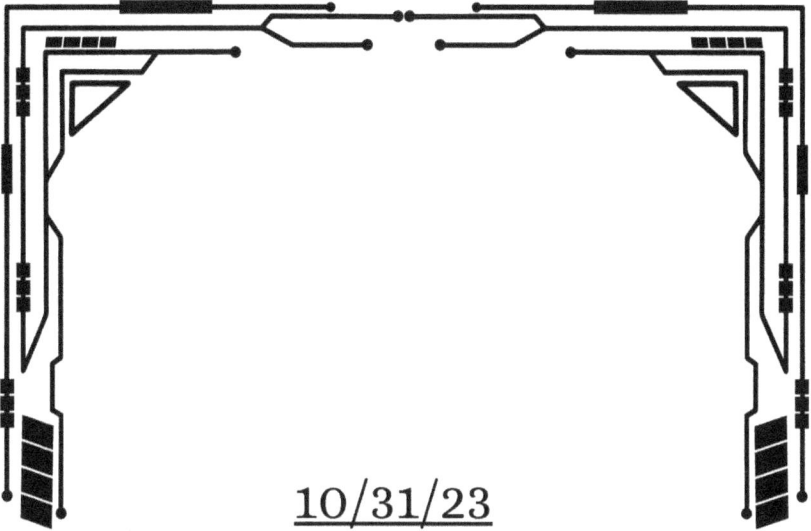

<u>10/31/23</u>

it's finally here
what a joyous occasion
demons and candy

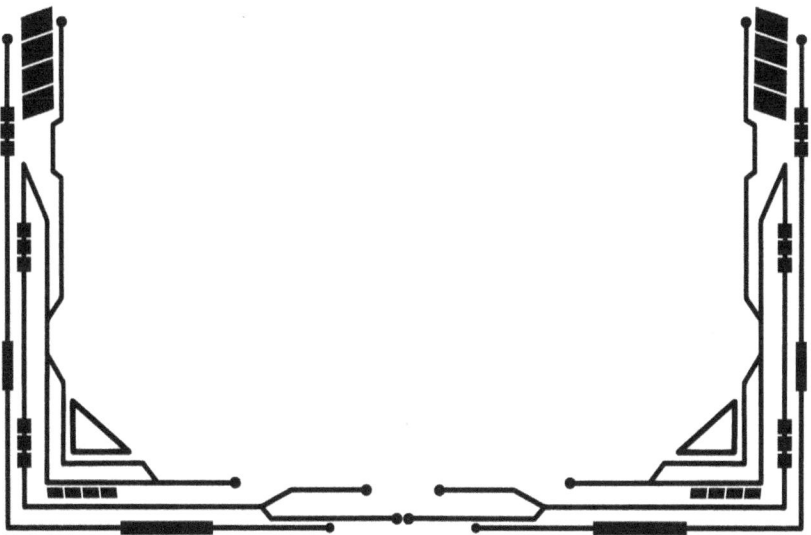

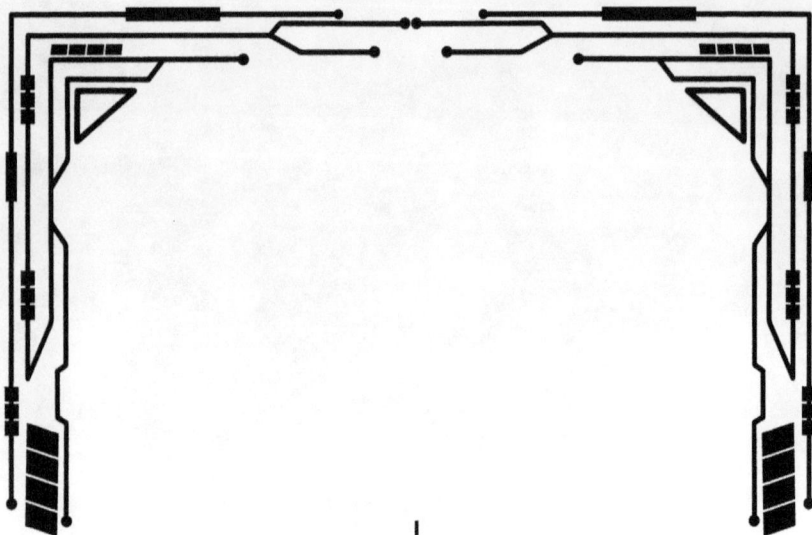

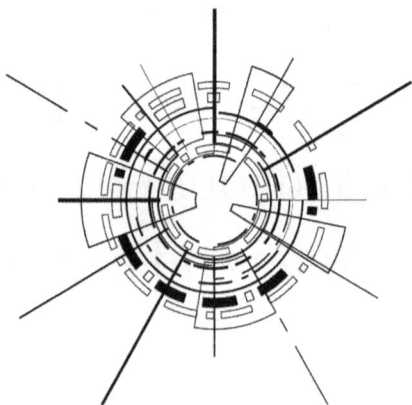

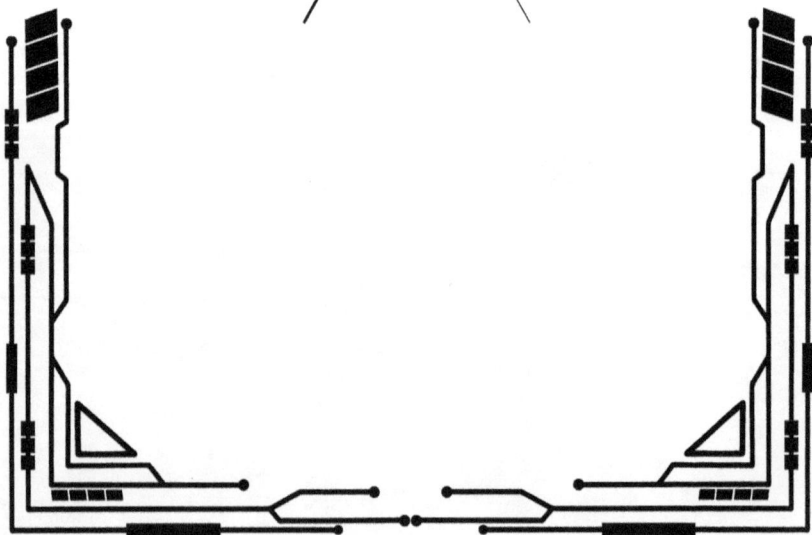

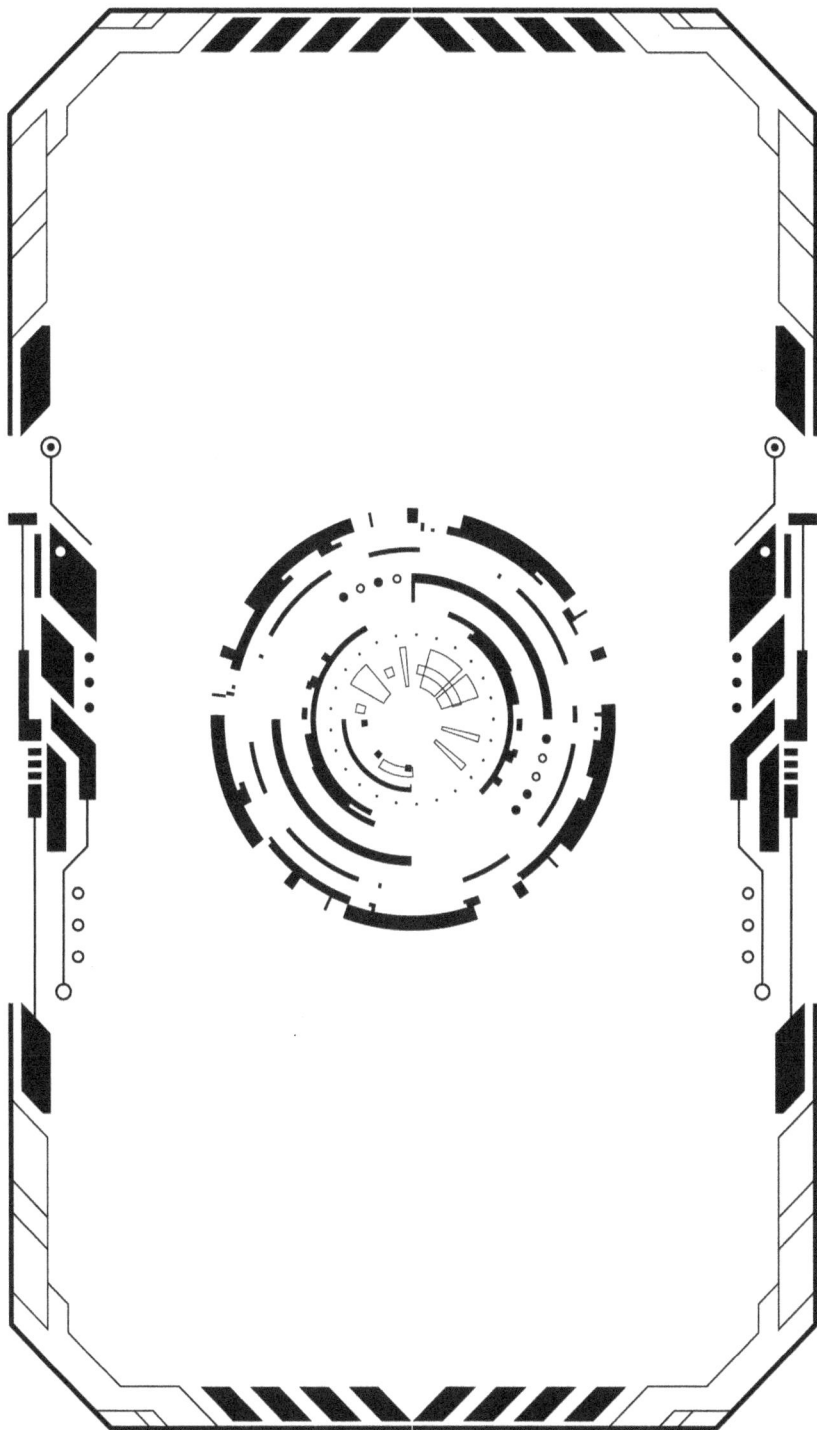

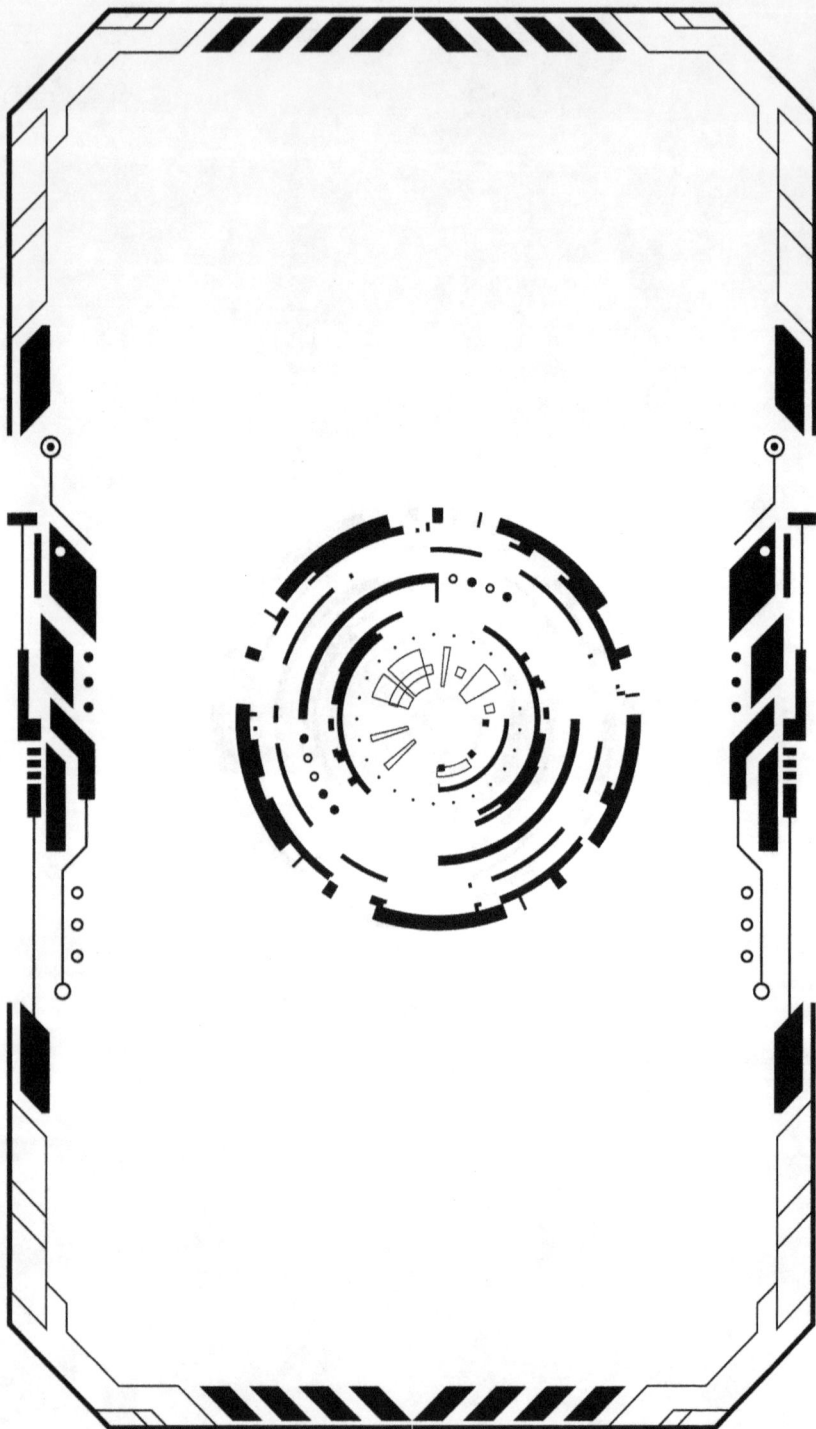

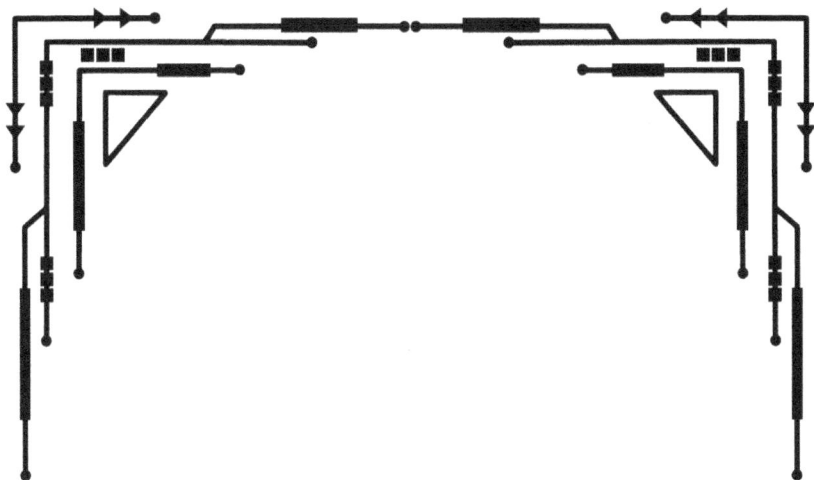

<u>11/01/23</u>

es miercoles
el dia de los muertos
hay mucho dulce

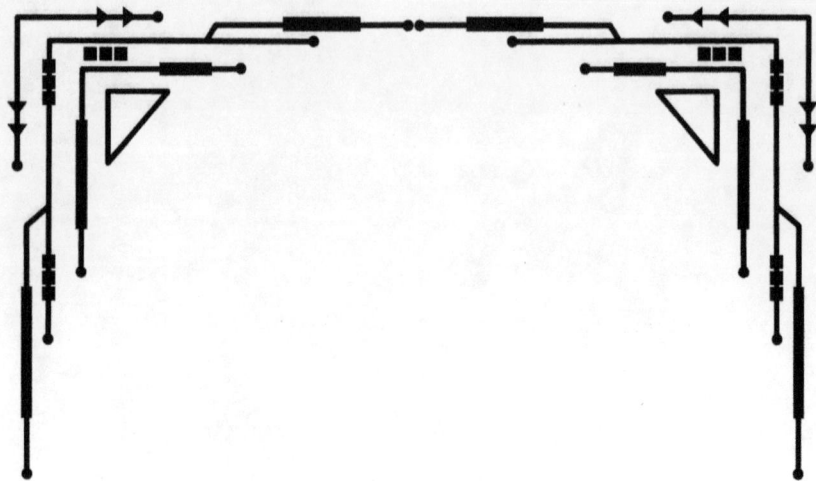

<u>11/02/23</u>

as we travel on
into the eleventh hour
remember the plan

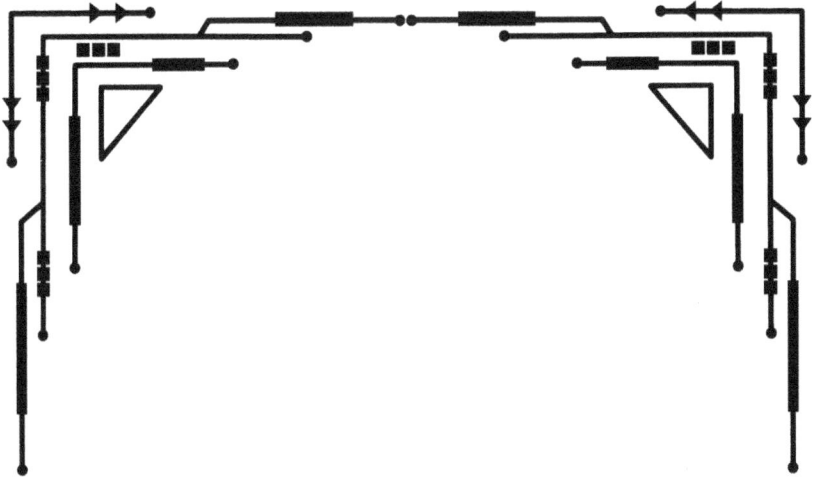

<u>11/03/23</u>

sweet gears and whistles
mechanical orchard fruit
steampunk applesauce

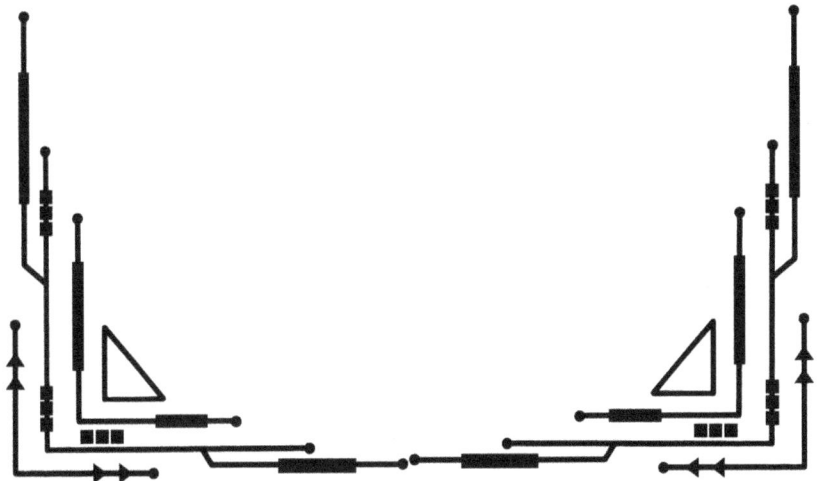

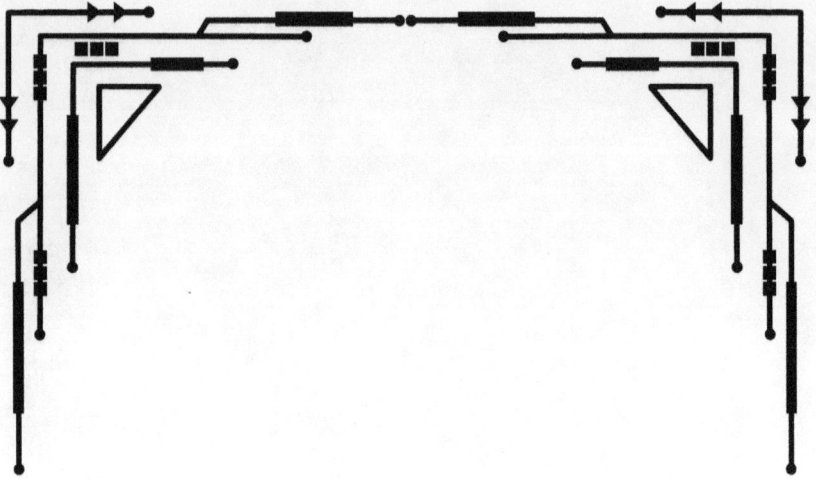

<u>11/04/23</u>

next to the stoplight
there is a guy with a sign
asking for my change

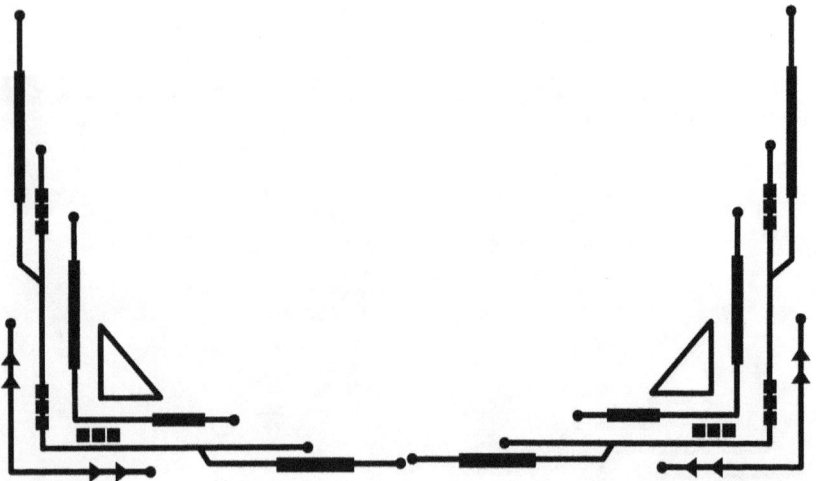

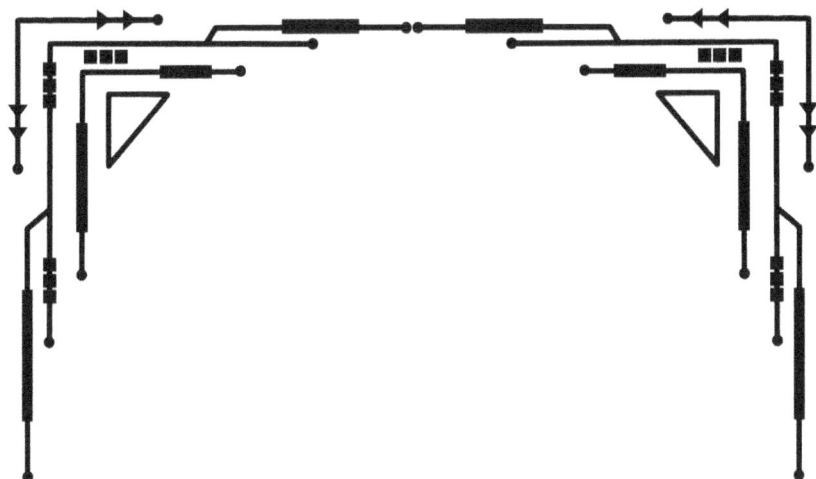

<u>11/05/23</u>

dirty bus stop fork
who eats a denver omelet
at the park and ride

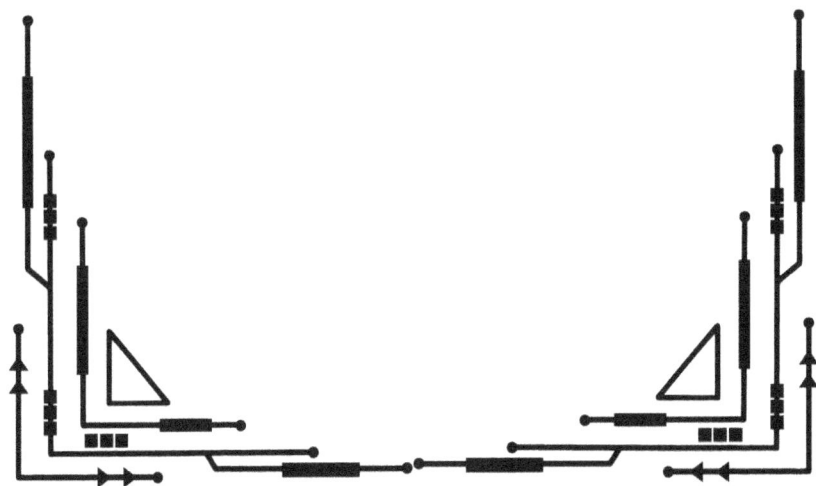

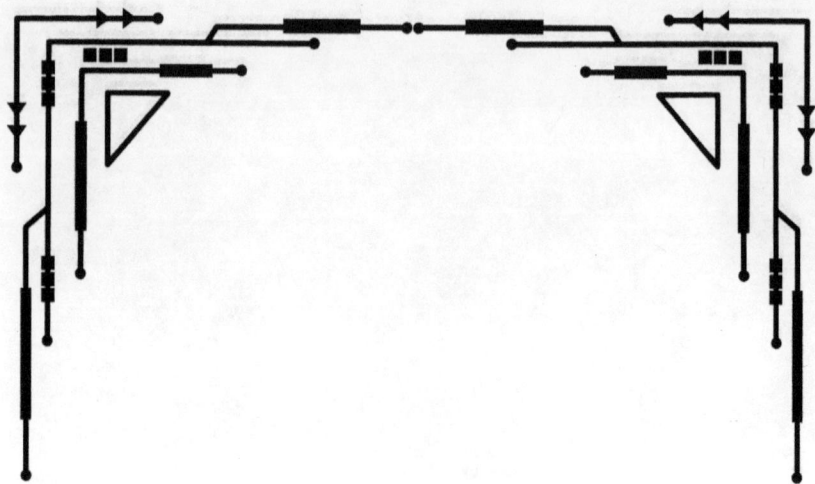

<u>11/06/23</u>

go through the tunnel
take a right at the black bear
and fall off the cliff

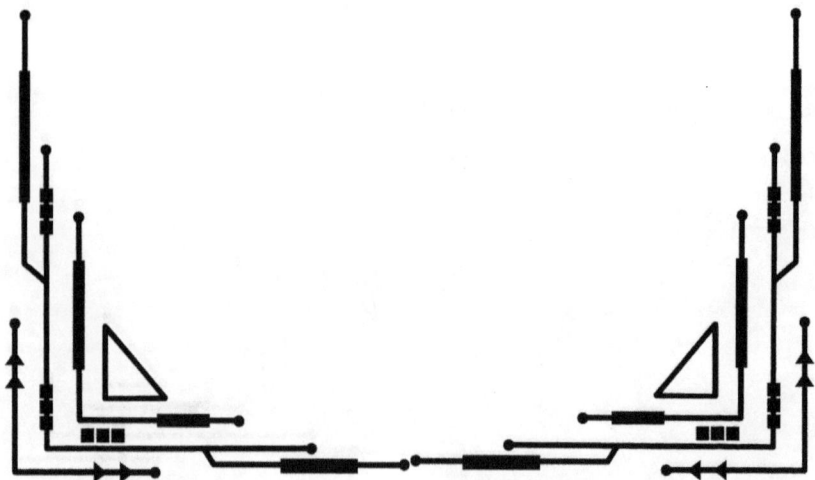

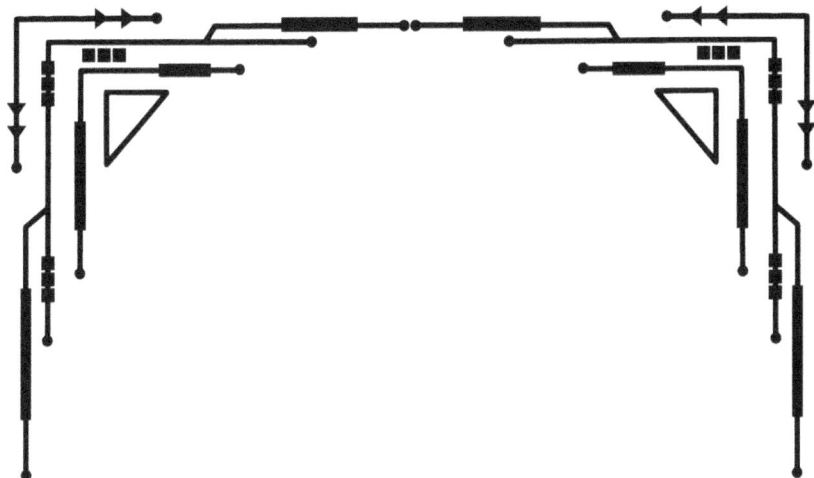

<u>11/07/23</u>

slice the bread for toast
and use all of the butter
one hundred percent

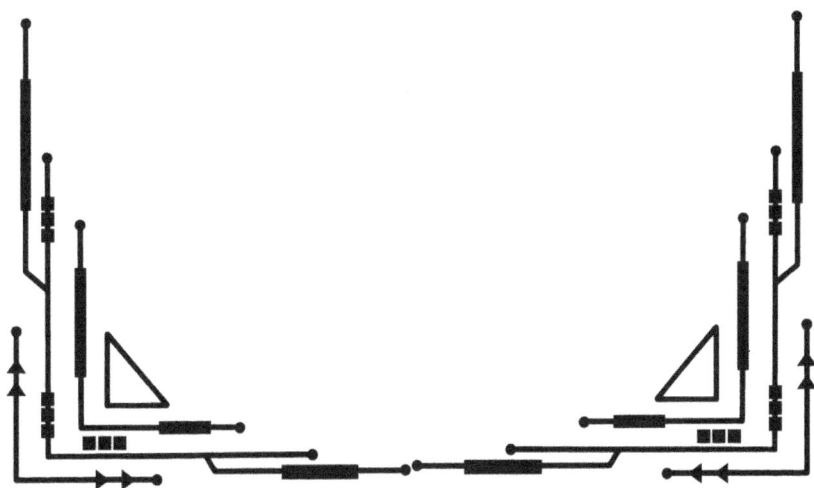

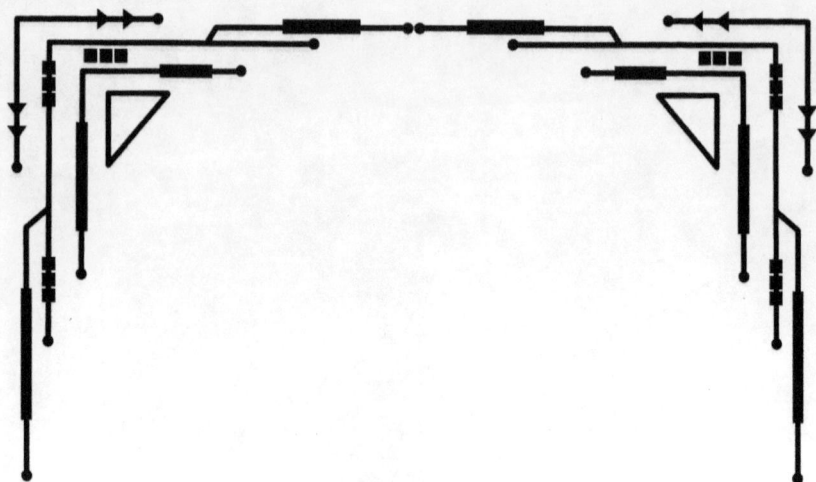

delaware darkness
dreary depressing daytime
dancing dirty dogs

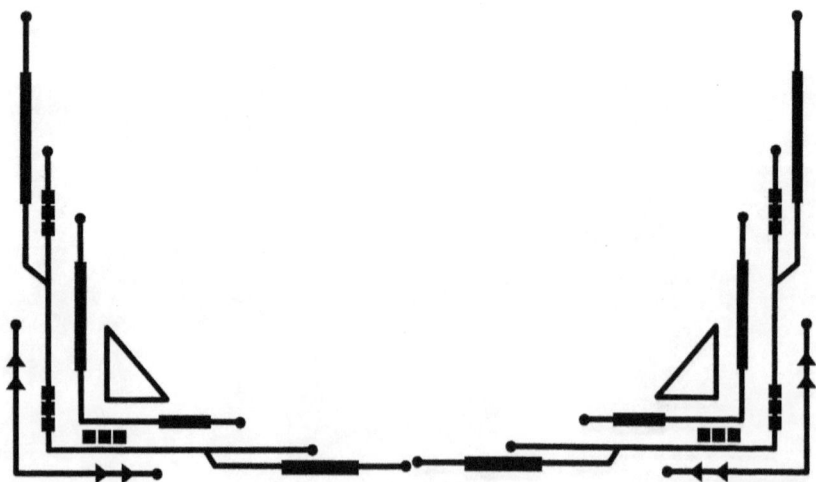

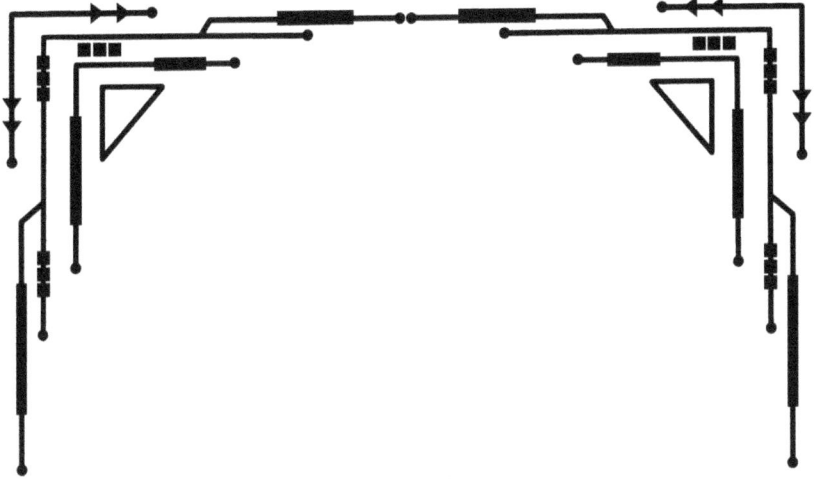

why does that exist
a tumbleweed on my street
you don't belong here

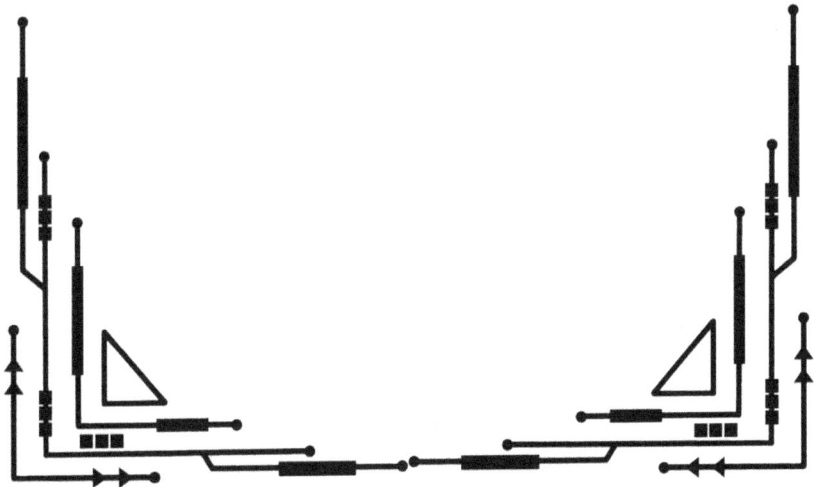

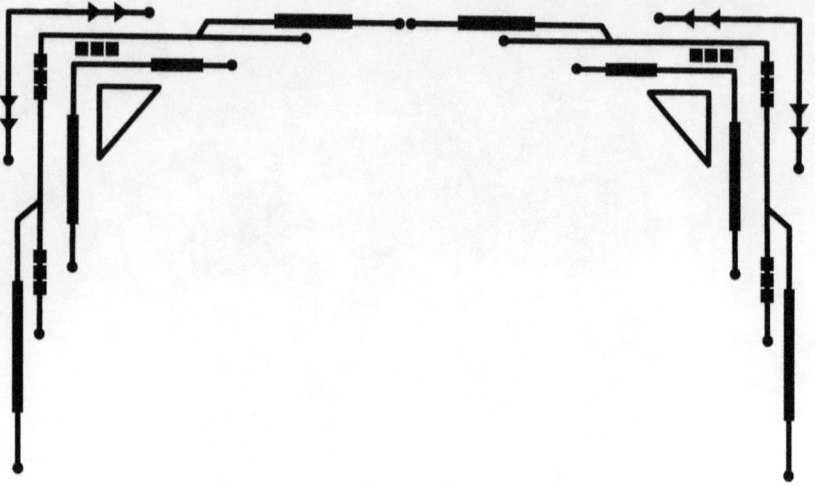

<u>11/10/23</u>

i don't like those ones
and these ones are also lame
this one is nice though

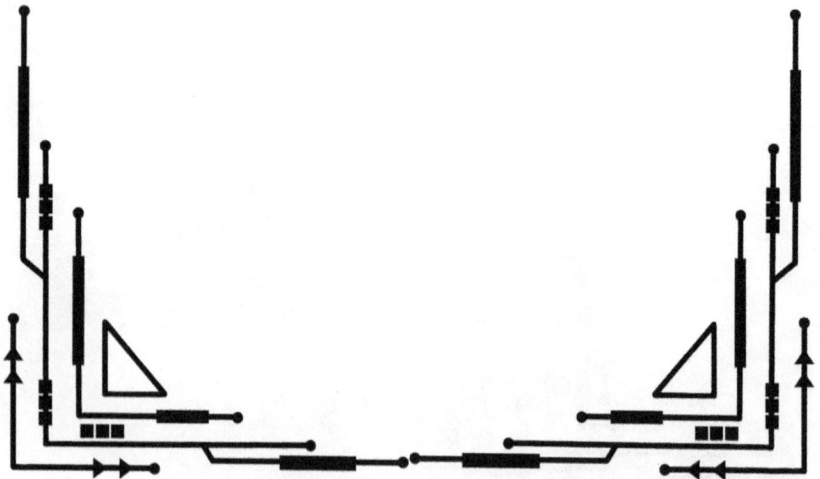

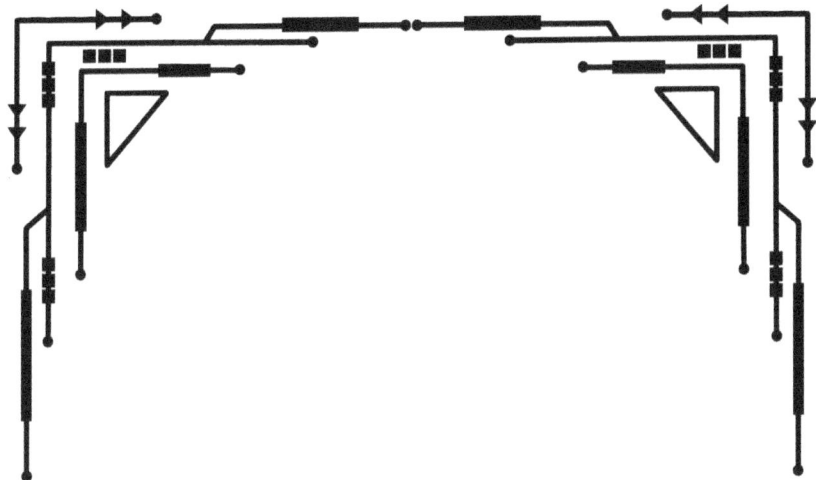

<u>11/11/23</u>

listen to the moon
vibrating in the night sky
ringing like a bell

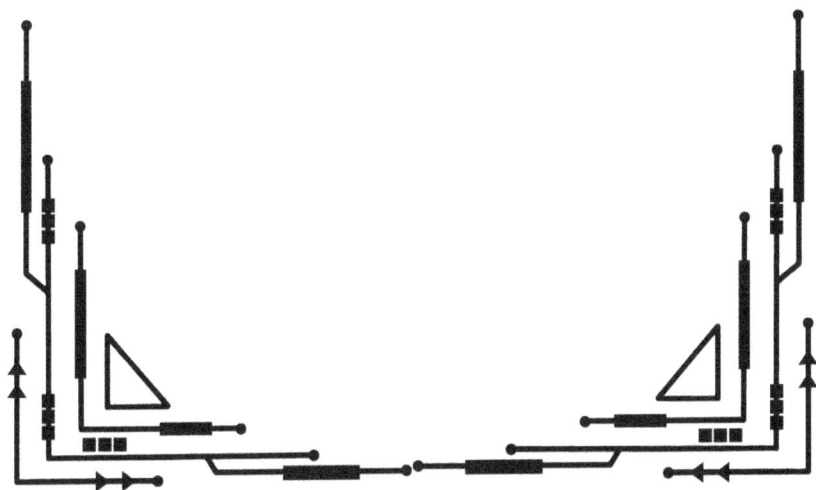

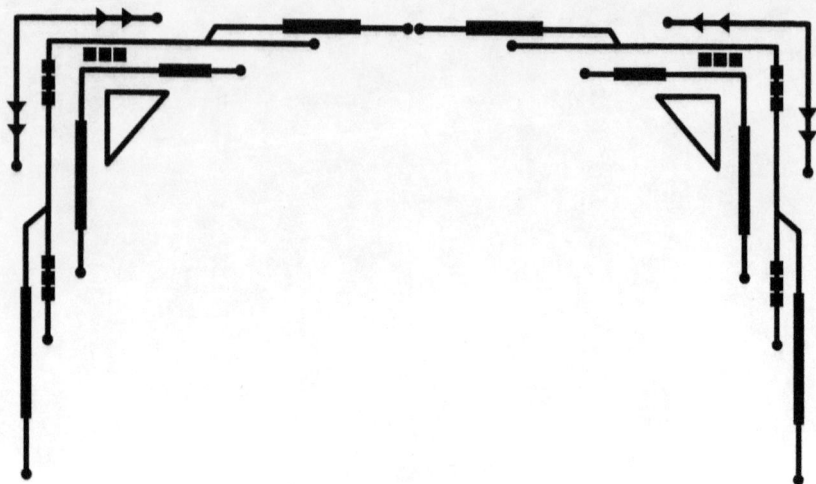

<u>11/12/23</u>

don't use it all up
save a little bit for me
leave it in the fridge

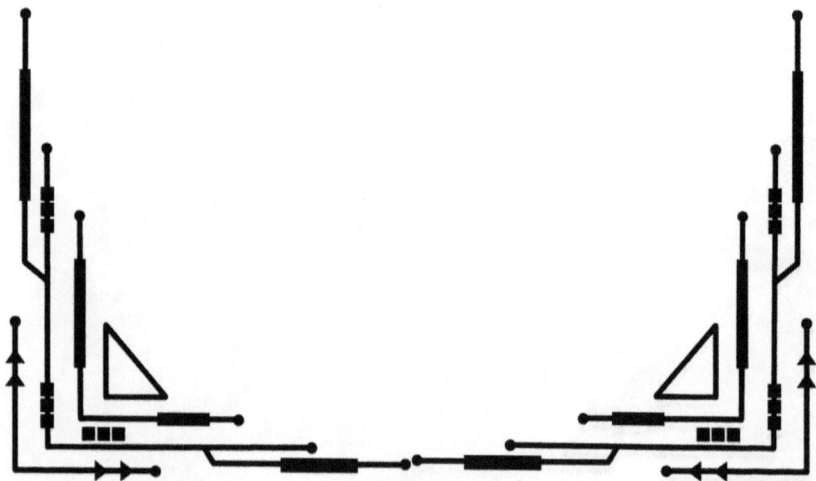

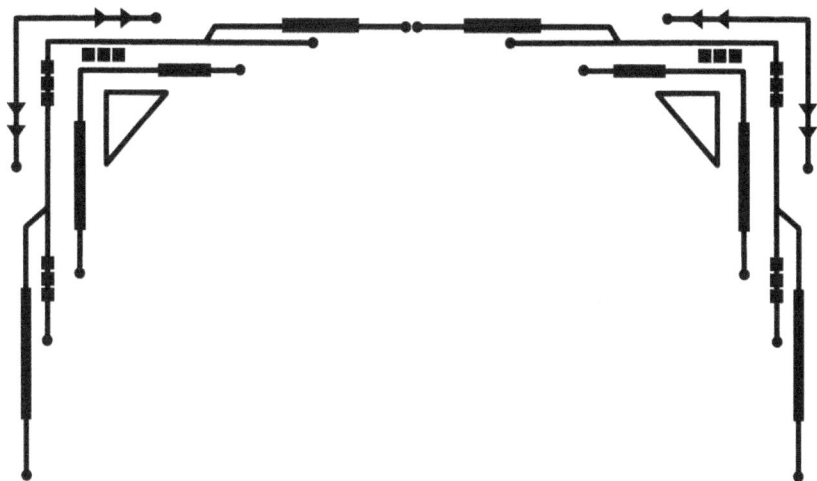

<u>11/13/23</u>

monday the thirteenth
doesn't have the same effect
maybe it's good luck

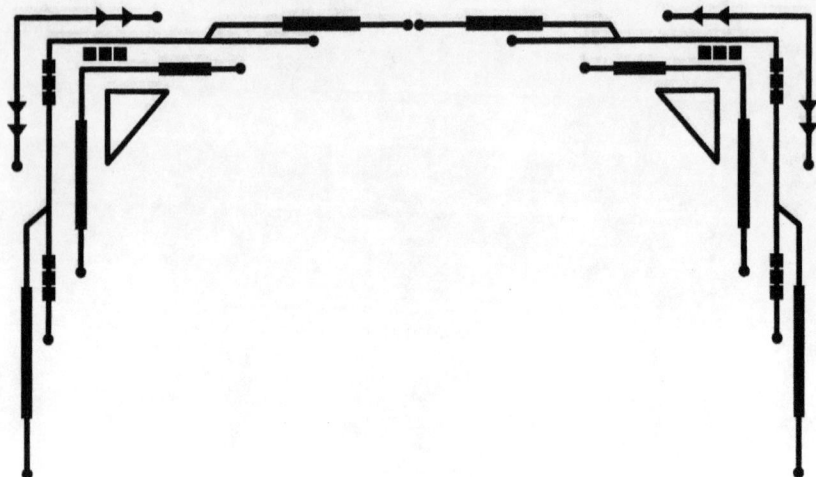

<u>11/14/23</u>

new lenses are nice
crystal clear spectacle glass
i can read the sign

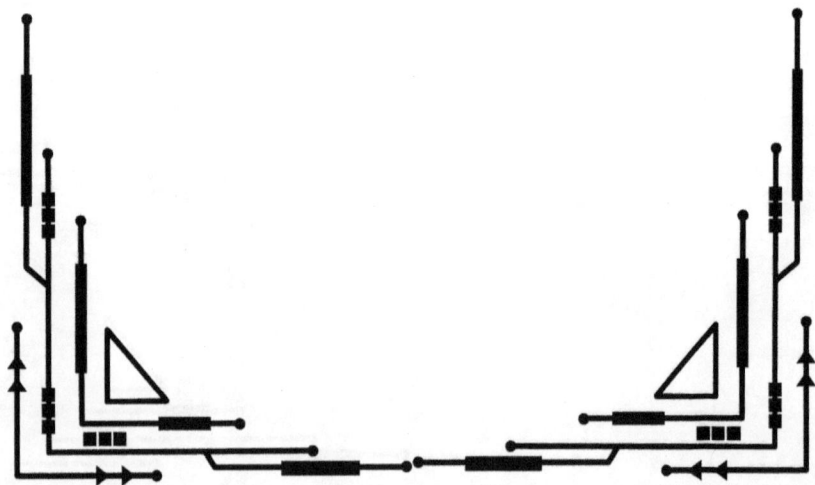

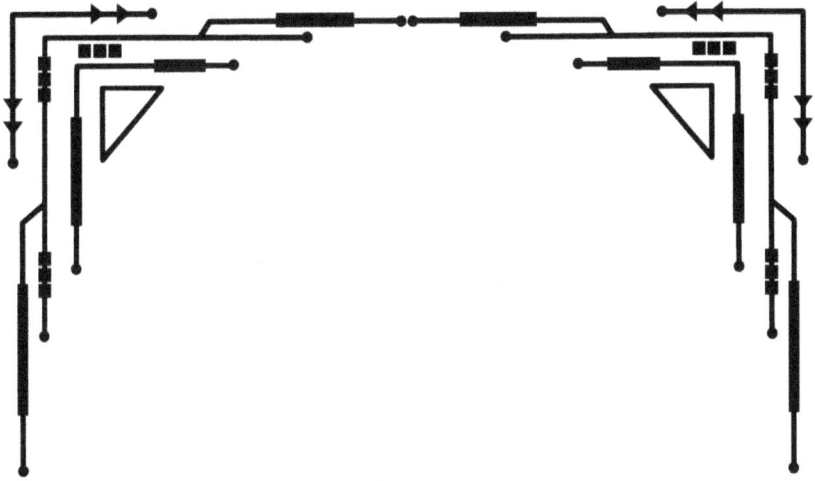

try the og kush
finish it with a spoon of
tangerine sorbet

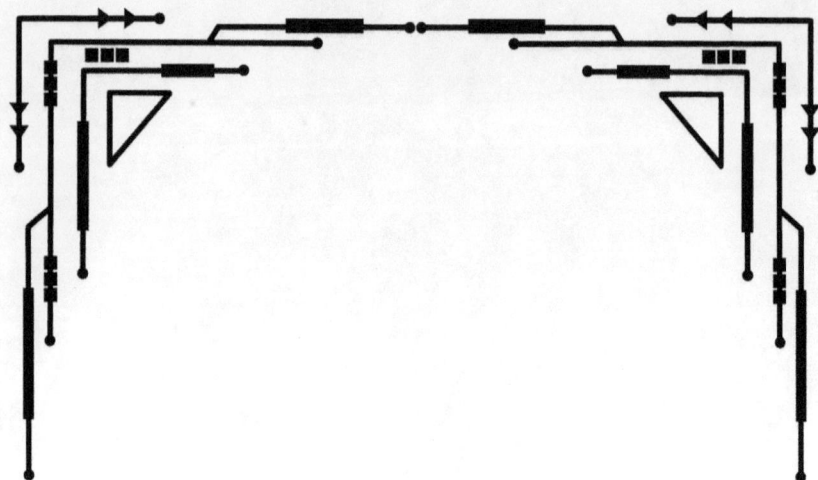

<u>11/16/23</u>

of all the colors
my favorite one in the box
is the black crayon

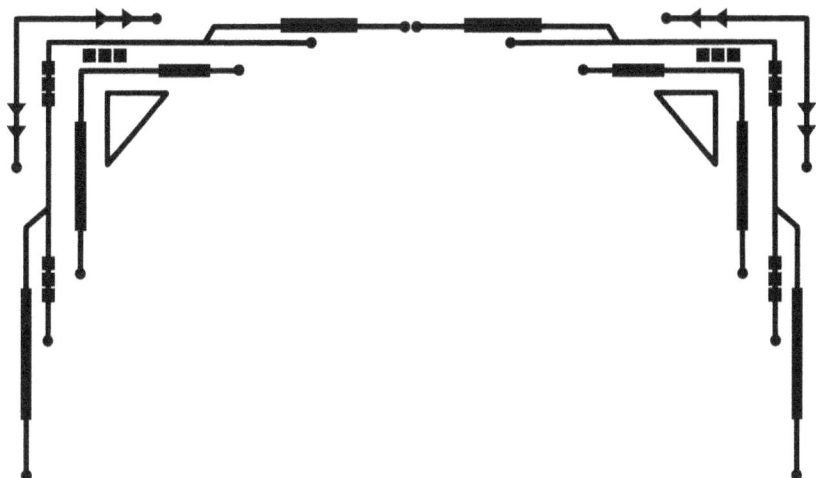

<u>11/17/23</u>

there is so much junk
from the mailbox to the trash
why can't we opt out

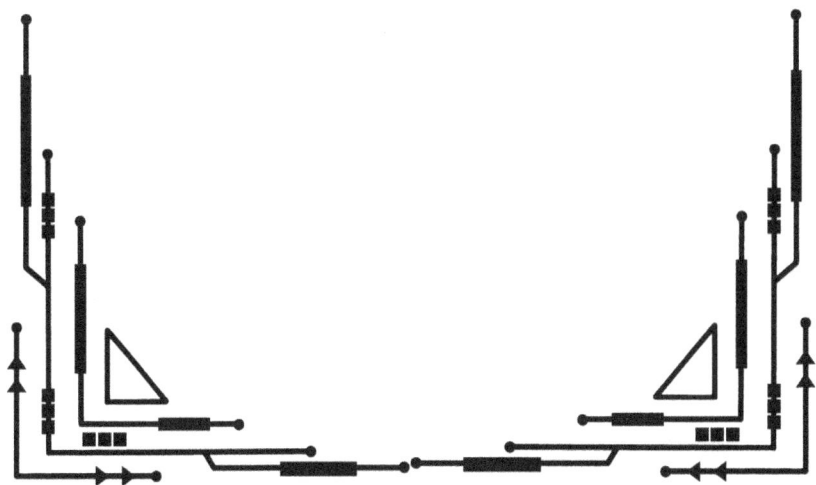

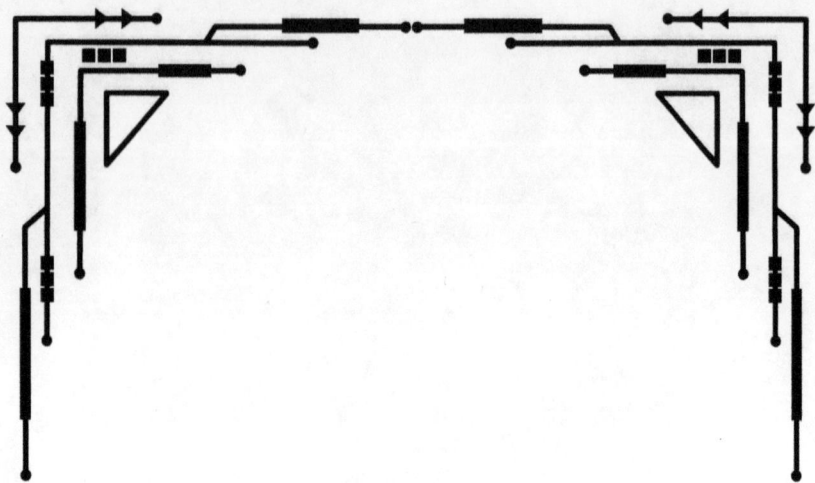

<u>11/18/23</u>

it is a sad day
when the mushroom people fall
into the grinder

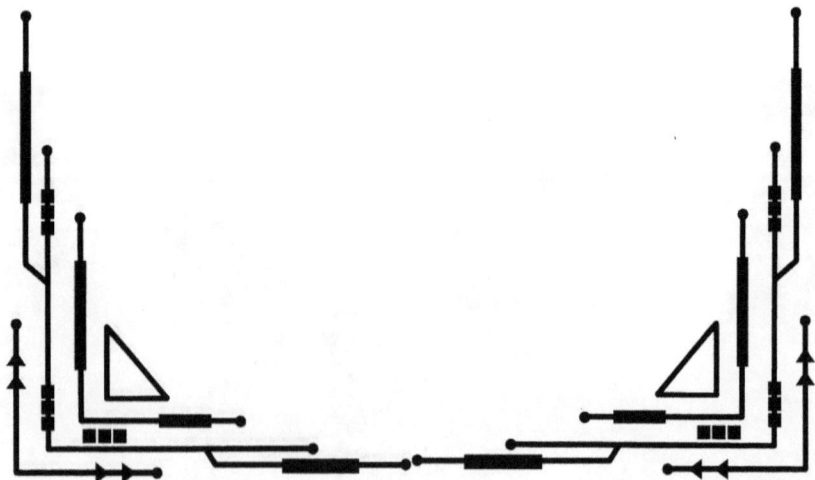

<u>11/19/23</u>

like a full diaper
things need to change around here
today is shitty

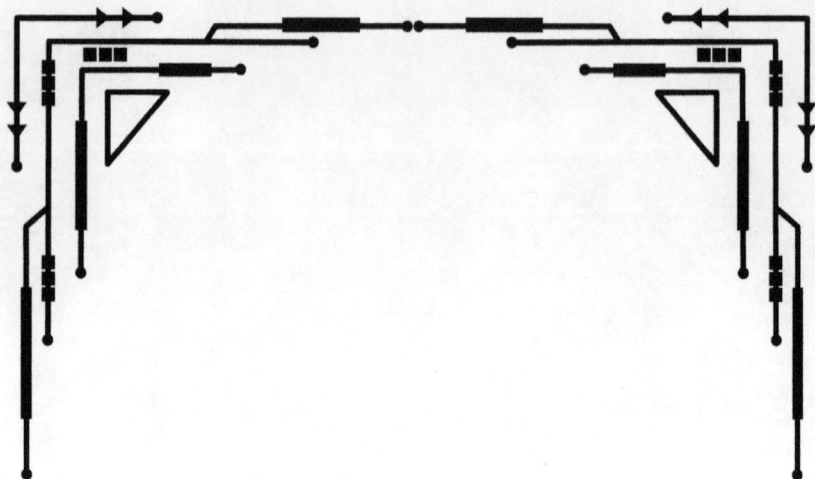

<u>11/20/23</u>

once upon a time
two thirds of nine is the six
triple stamp it please

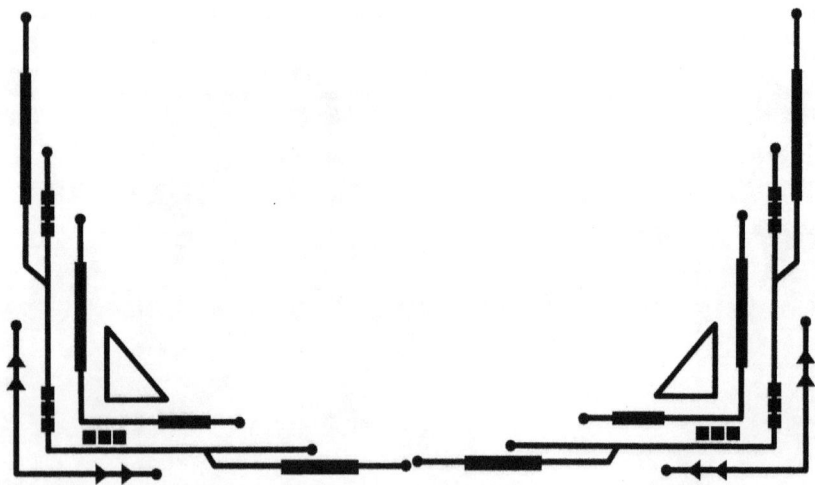

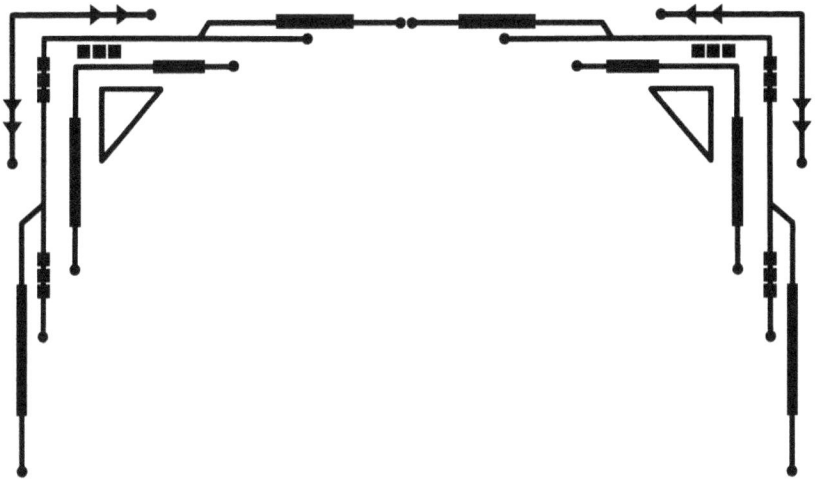

<u>11/21/23</u>

now that we are high
sample some of these cookies
tell me what you think

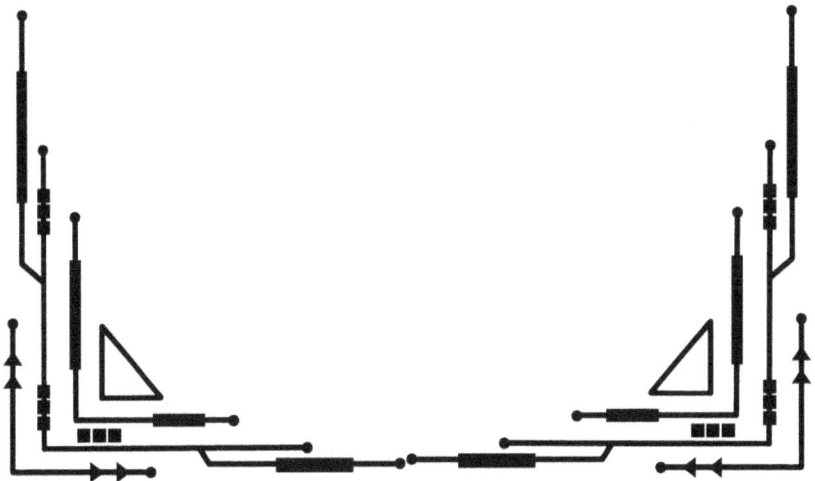

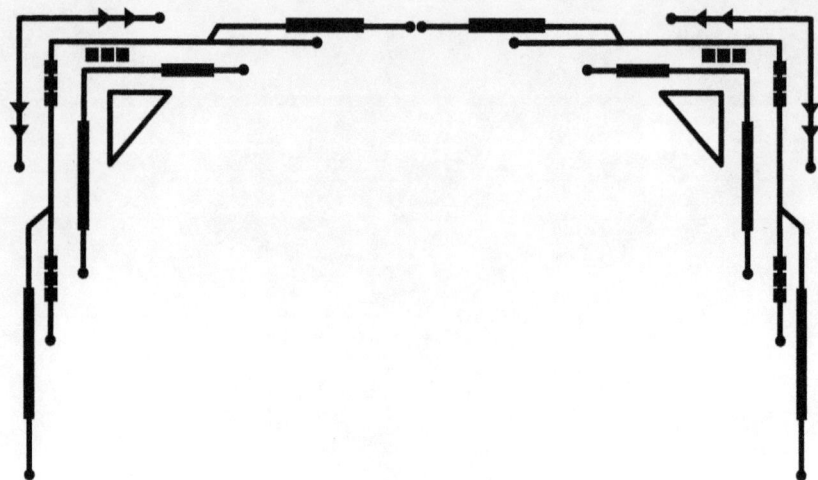

<u>11/22/23</u>

ten years from now is
one one two two three three and
that makes my brain smile

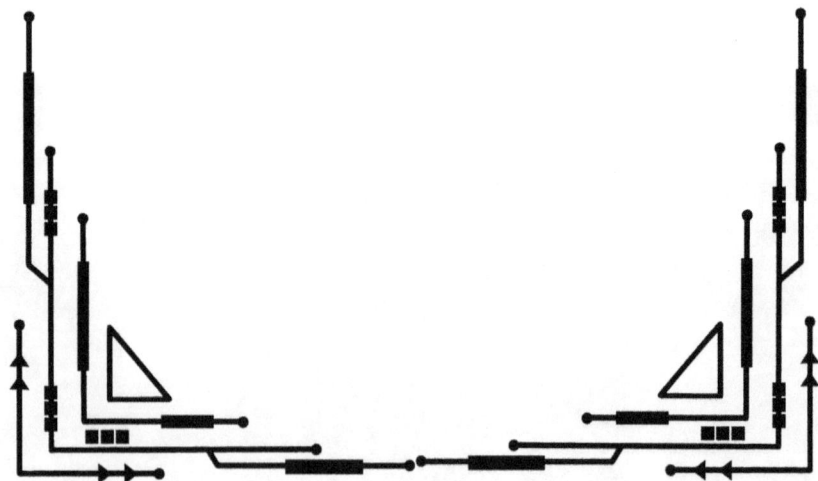

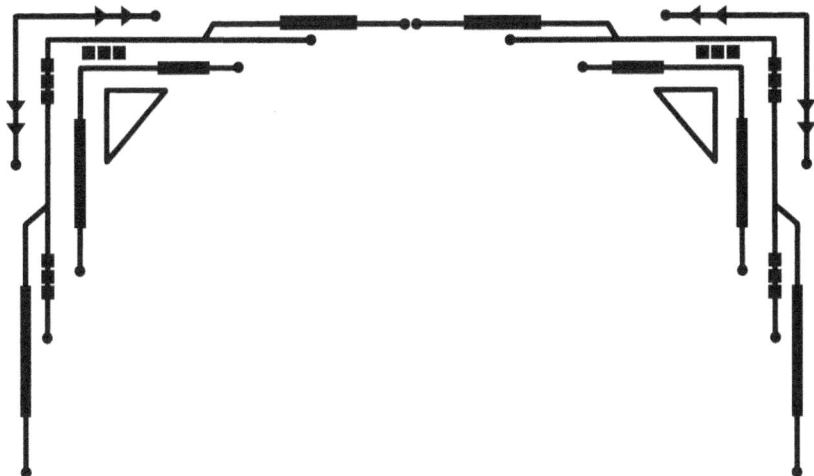

<u>11/23/23</u>

what should we do now
kill the bird and eat its flesh
with gravy and pie

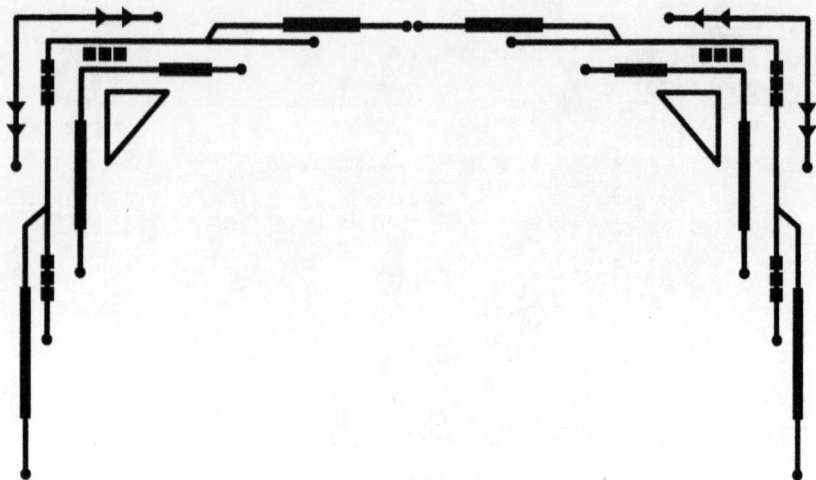

<u>11/24/23</u>

dinner rolls are dry
can i get some butter please
spread it on for me

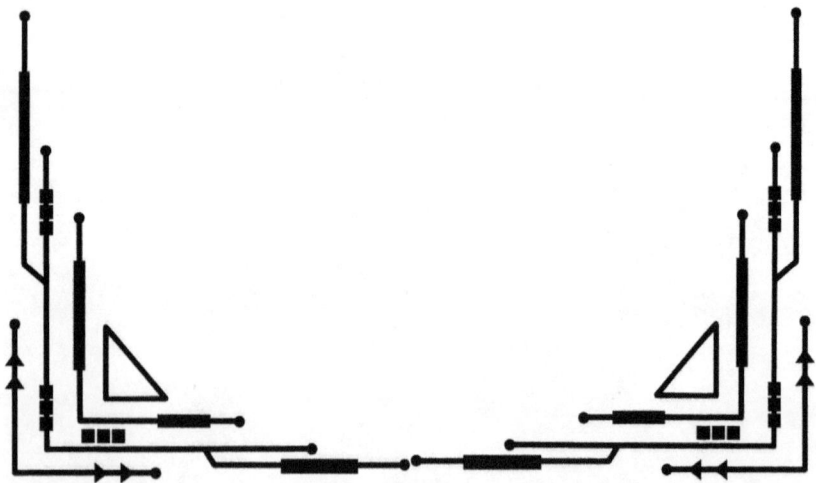

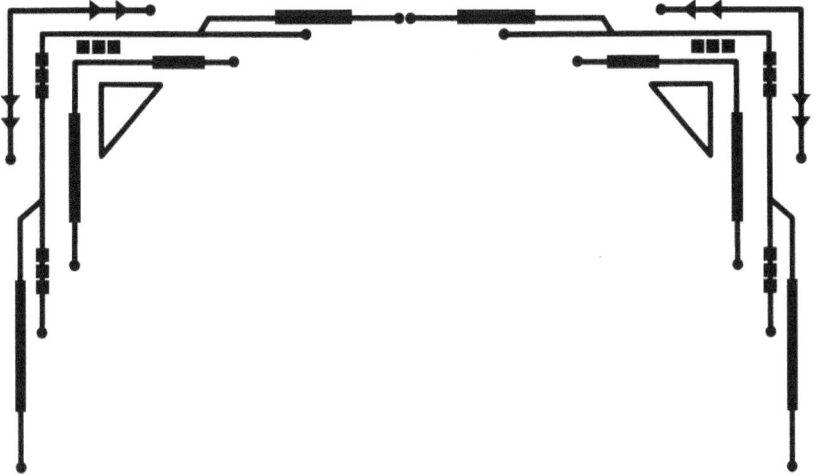

<u>11/25/23</u>

start passing out forks
to the odd starving children
sixty cents a day

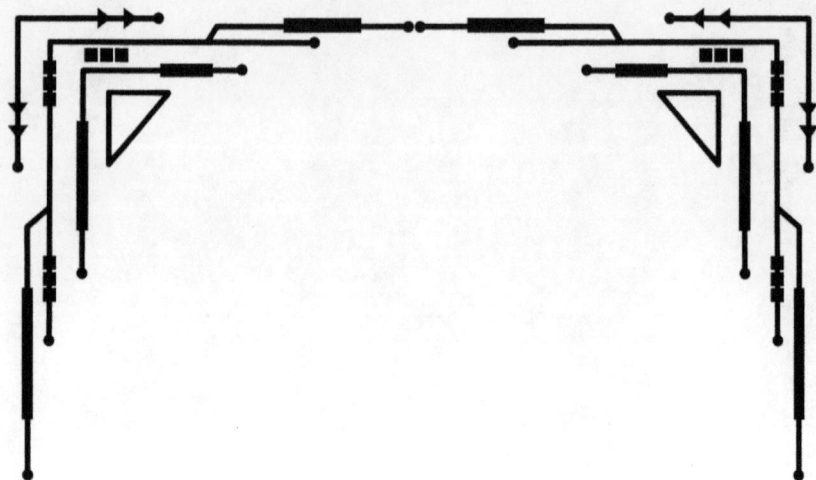

<u>11/26/23</u>

all i see is dark
we're over halfway there now
no light at the end

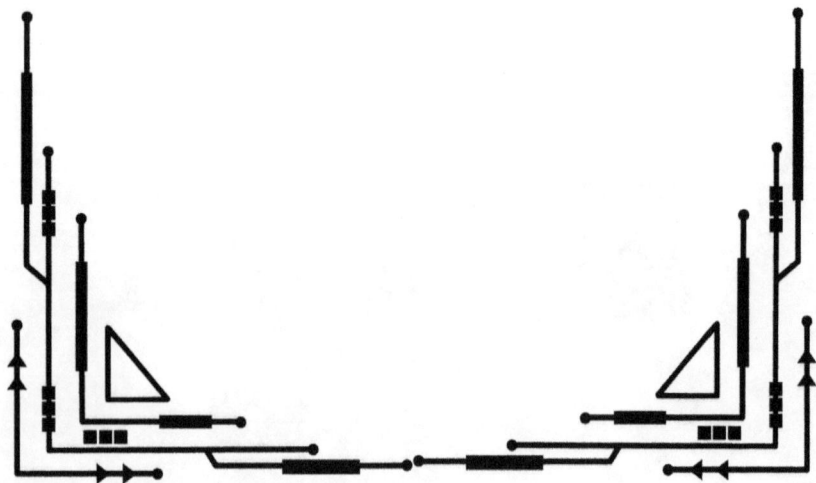

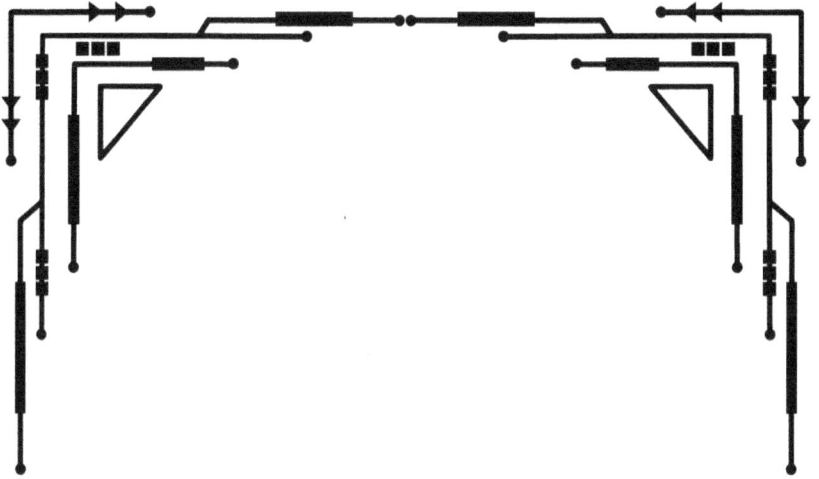

<u>11/27/23</u>

thank you for the pie
yes i will feed your fishes
have a good road trip

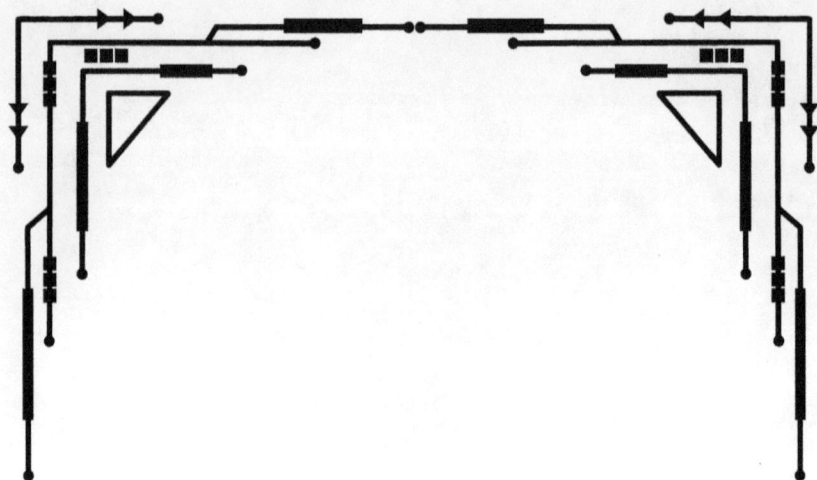

<u>11/28/23</u>

the trees are sleeping
and the leaves have all but left
the bare branches cold

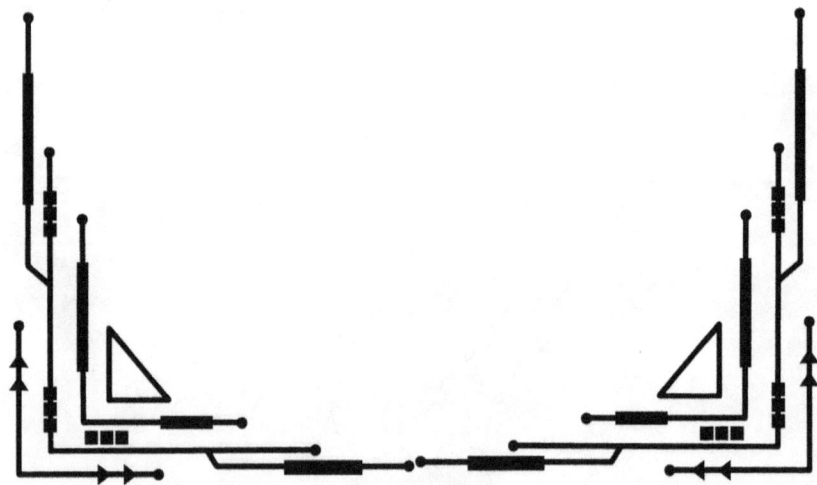

<u>11/29/23</u>

folks in a hurry
it's a busy day in ned
where are they going

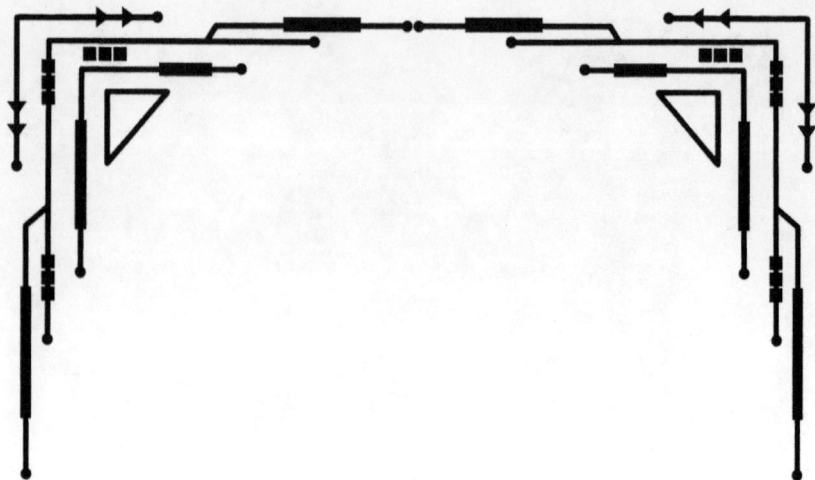

sit down and try this
a sample of all these words
the last eleven

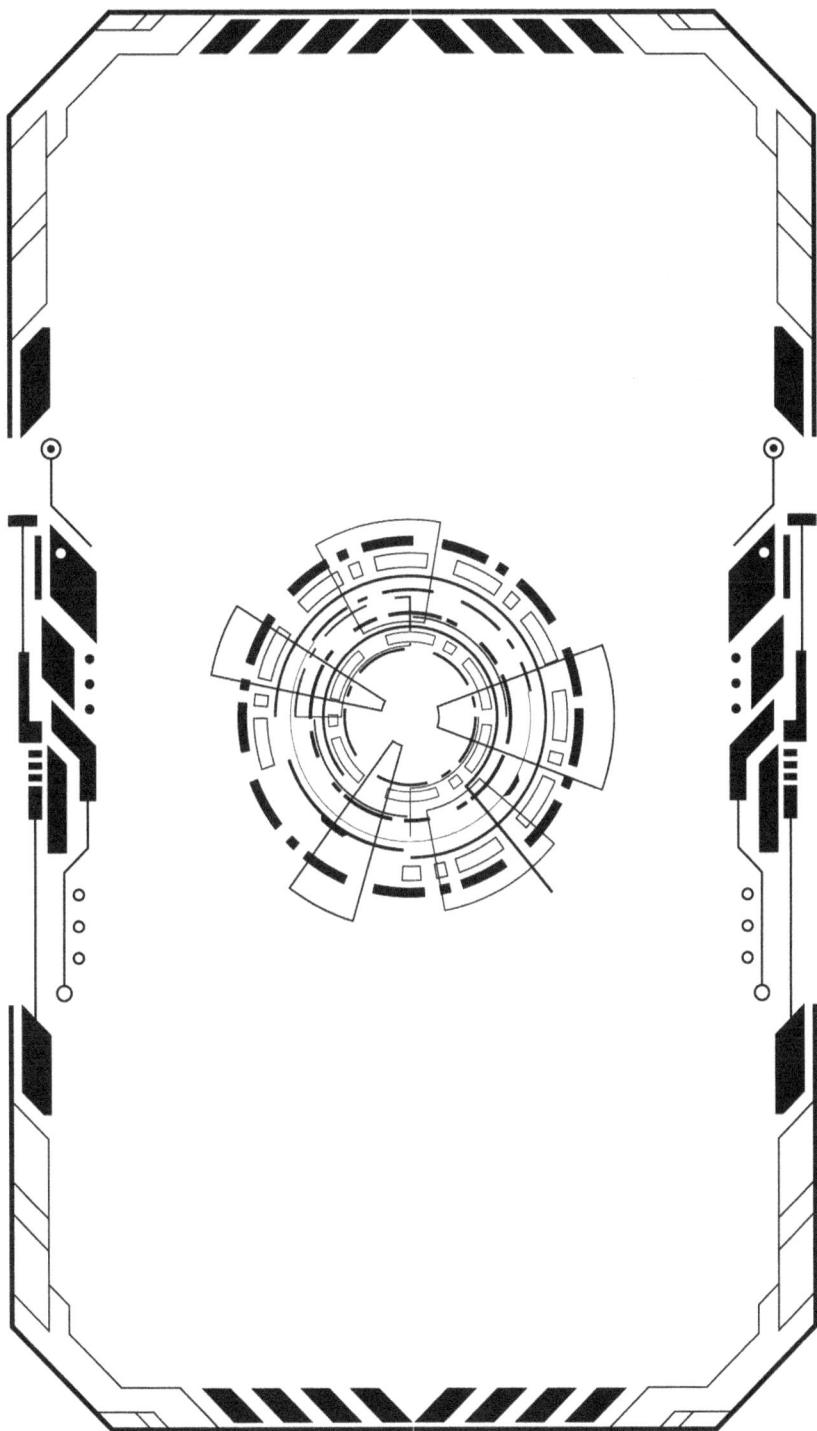

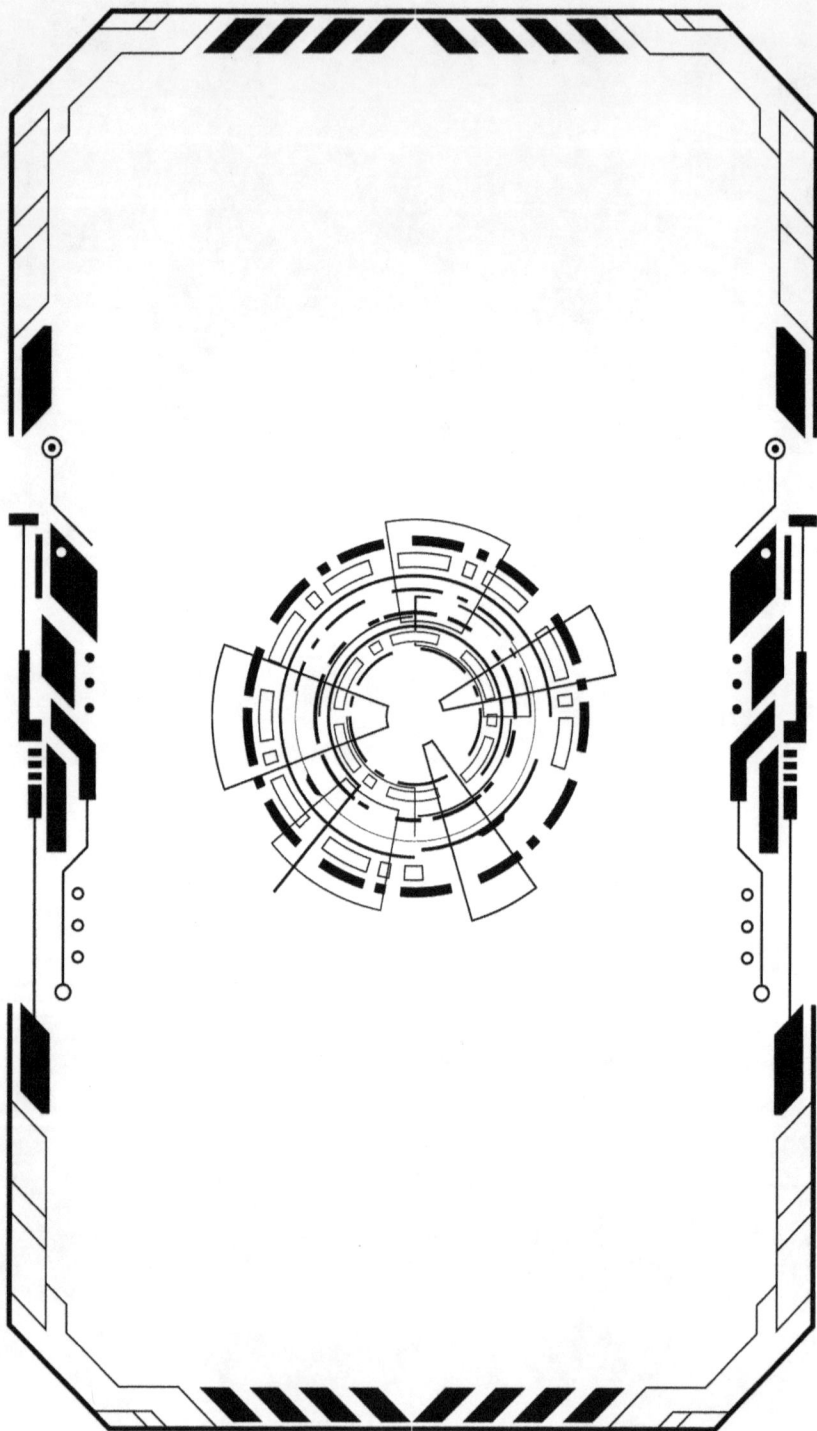

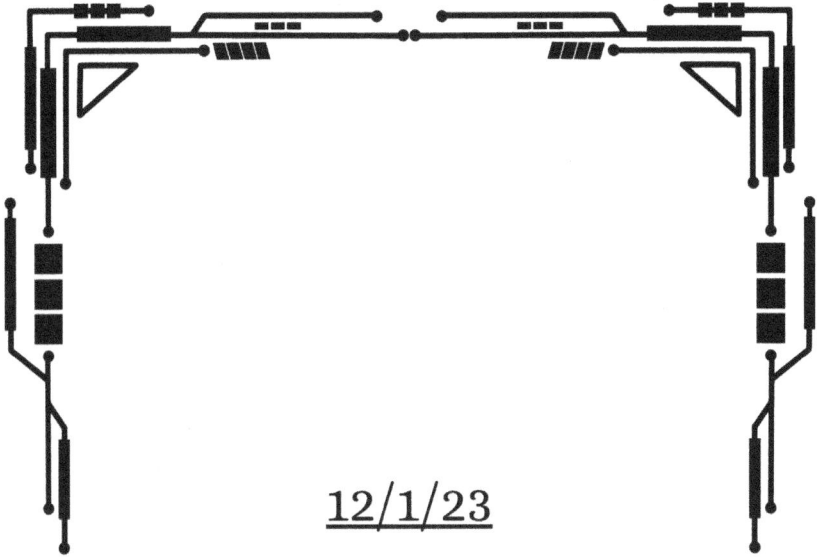

<u>12/1/23</u>

here it is my friend
the end of the calendar
thank you gregory

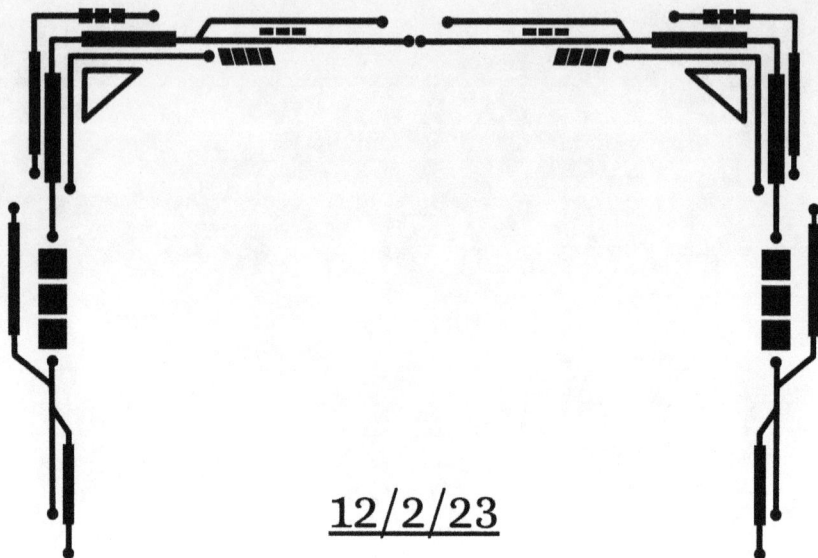

<u>12/2/23</u>

since i work here now
my contract stipulates that
i get a coffee

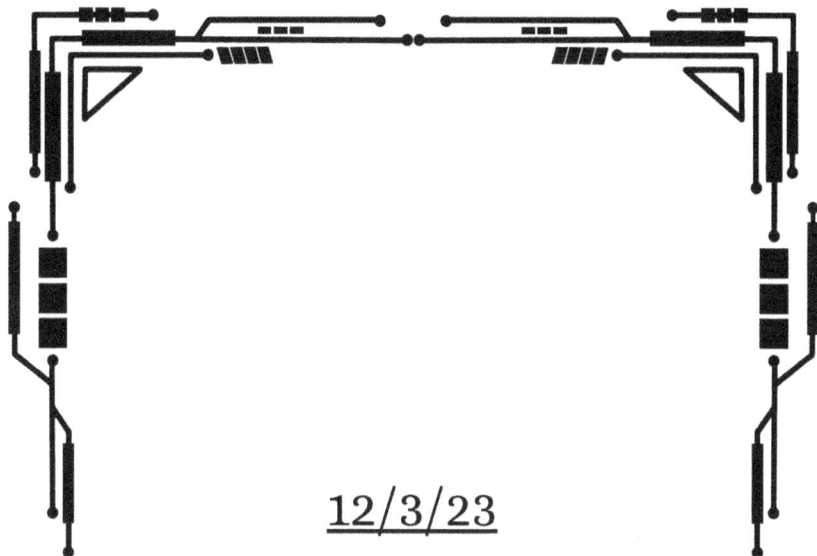

<u>12/3/23</u>

in any language
there are just so many words
put them all in place

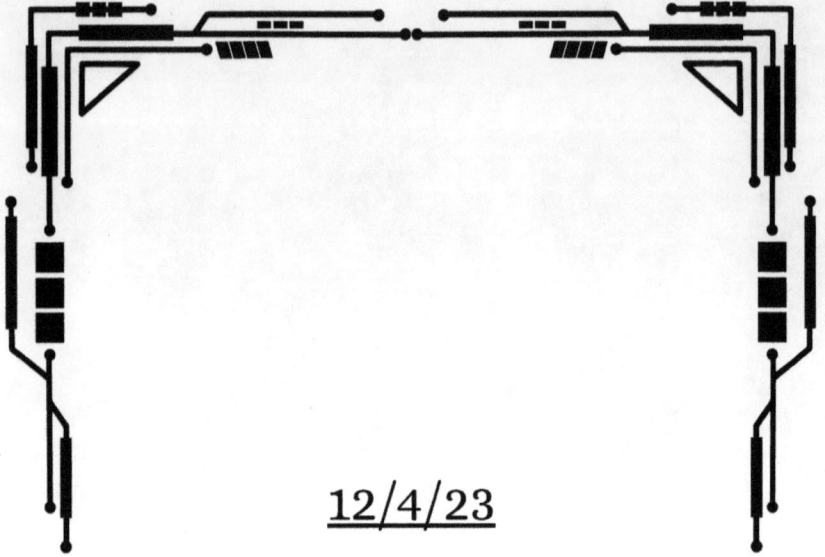

<u>12/4/23</u>

a cowardly mouse
whispering in the desert
is lunch for the snake

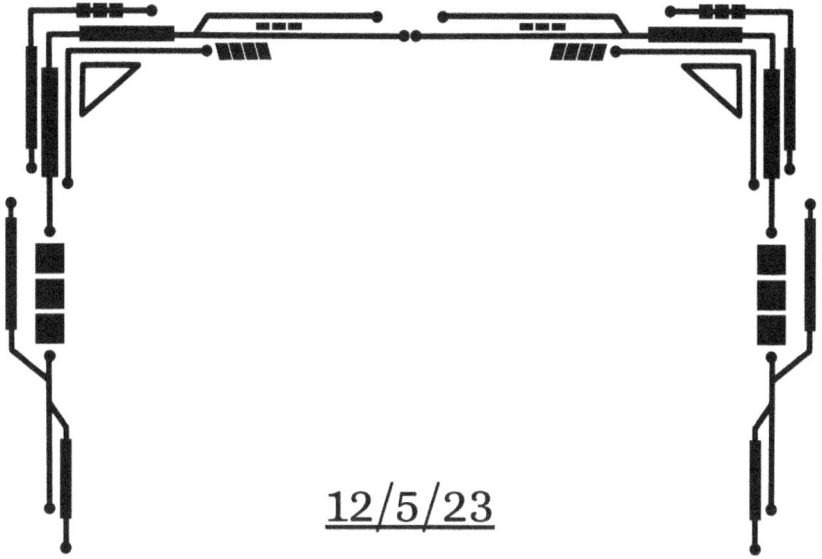

<u>12/5/23</u>

a house of sparrows
living in carol's front yard
my cats are hungry

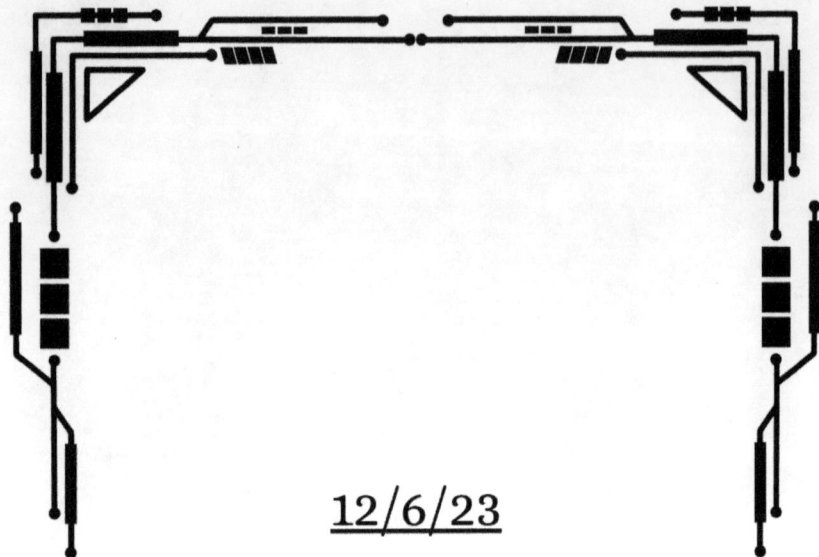

<u>12/6/23</u>

symphonic water
underneath a sheet of ice
three part harmonies

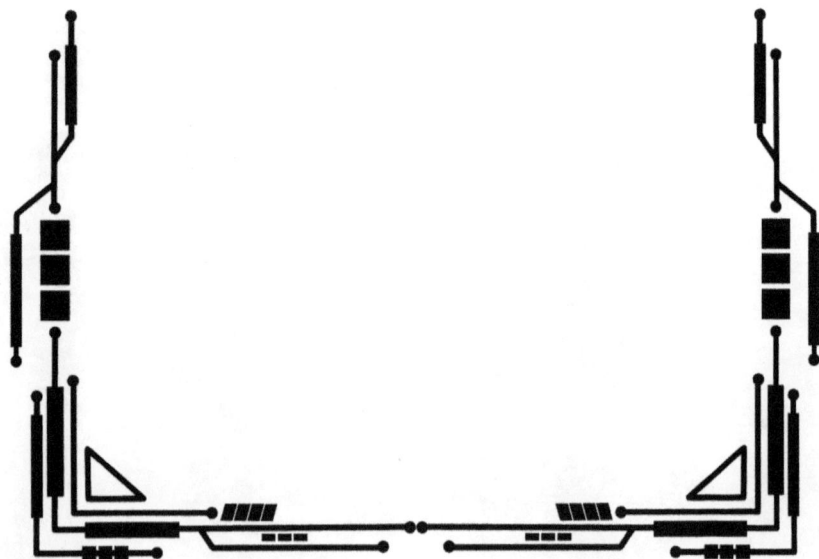

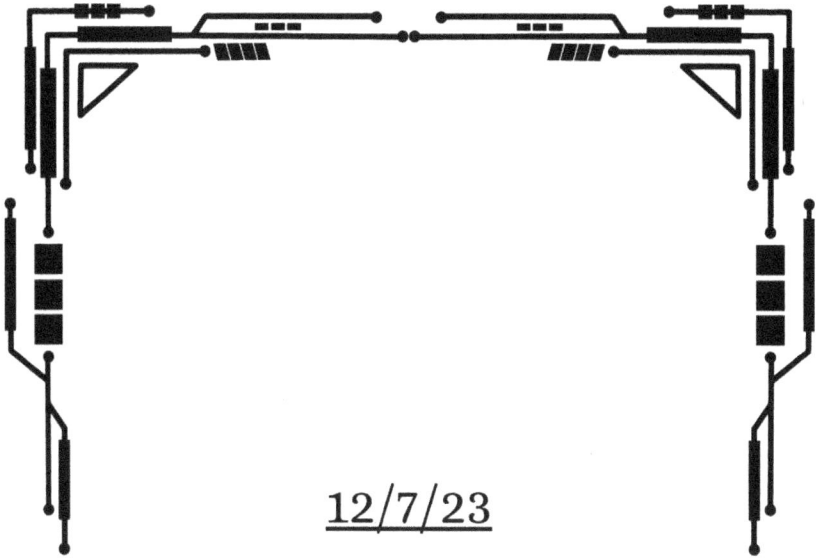

<u>12/7/23</u>

i went to the store
for some bread and turkey meat
sandwiches for lunch

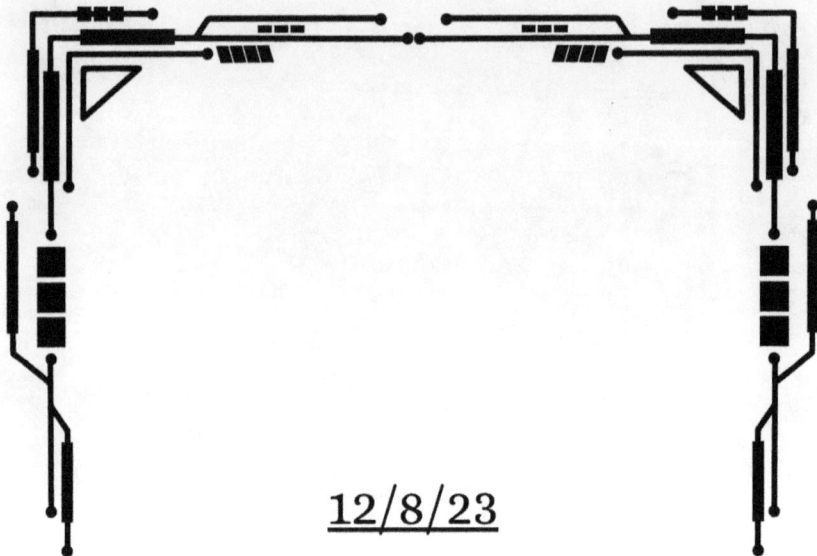

<u>12/8/23</u>

the wolves eat the sheep
the people don't like the wolves
but that's what they do

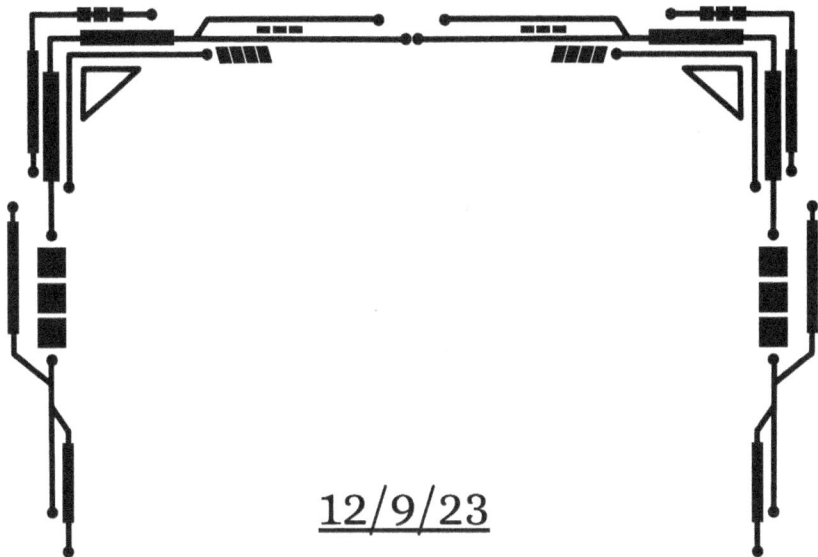

<u>12/9/23</u>

one crystal snowflake
falls and is plowed off the road
it doesn't matter

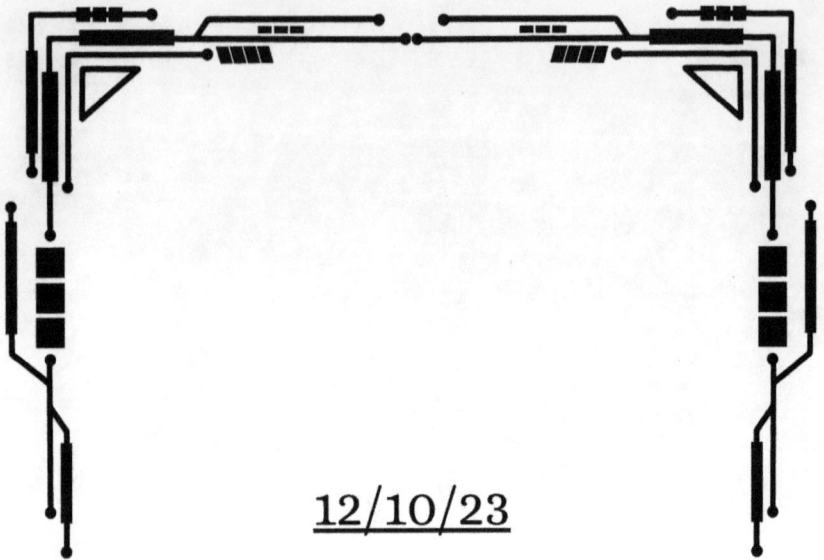

<u>12/10/23</u>

boulder canyon snow
gently clinging to the trees
beautiful morning

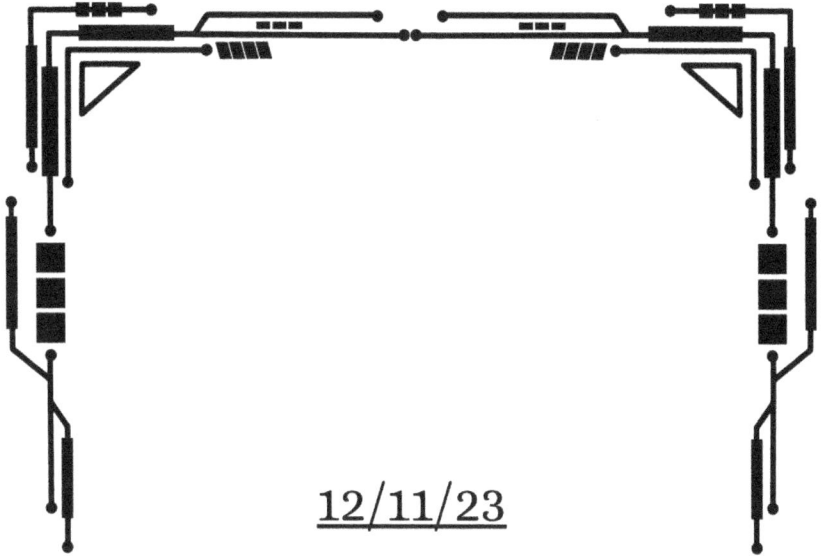

<u>12/11/23</u>

the stars are aligned
confucius is confusing
better call cleo

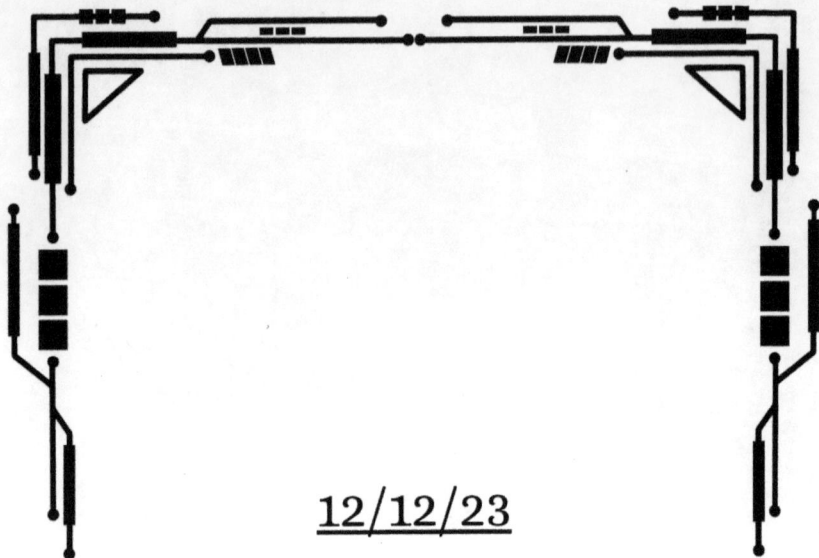

<u>12/12/23</u>

quiet day in town
perfect opportunity
for the garbage bear

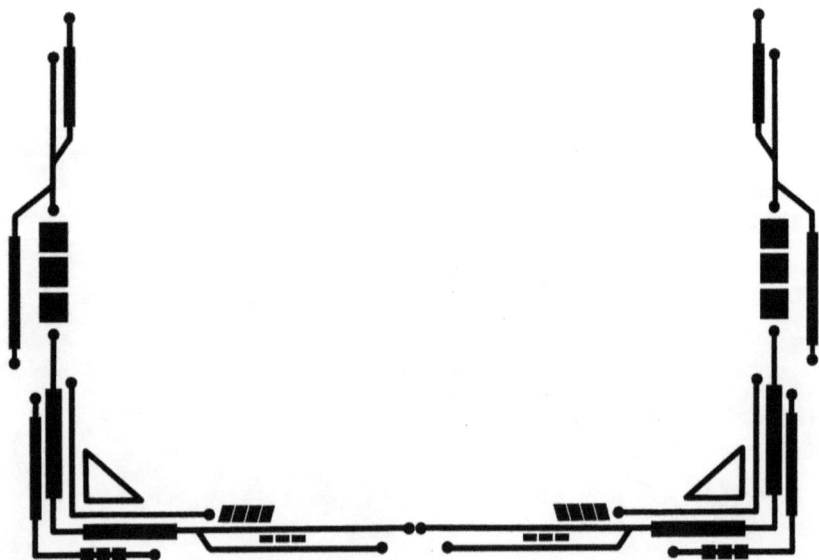

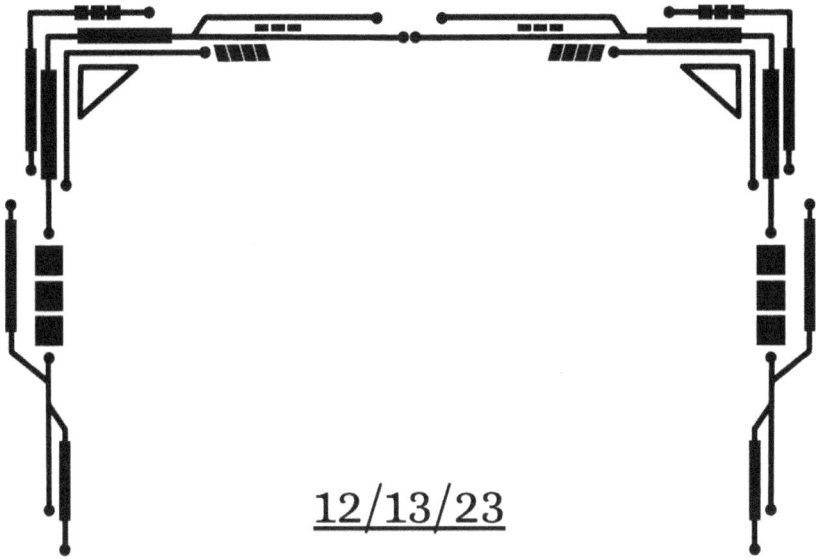

<u>12/13/23</u>

put it in a box
lots and lots of bubble wrap
strips of packing tape

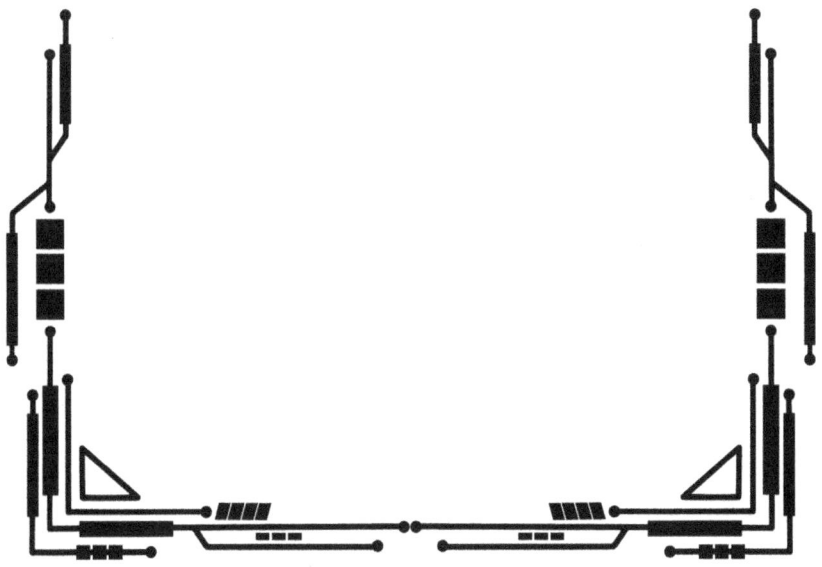

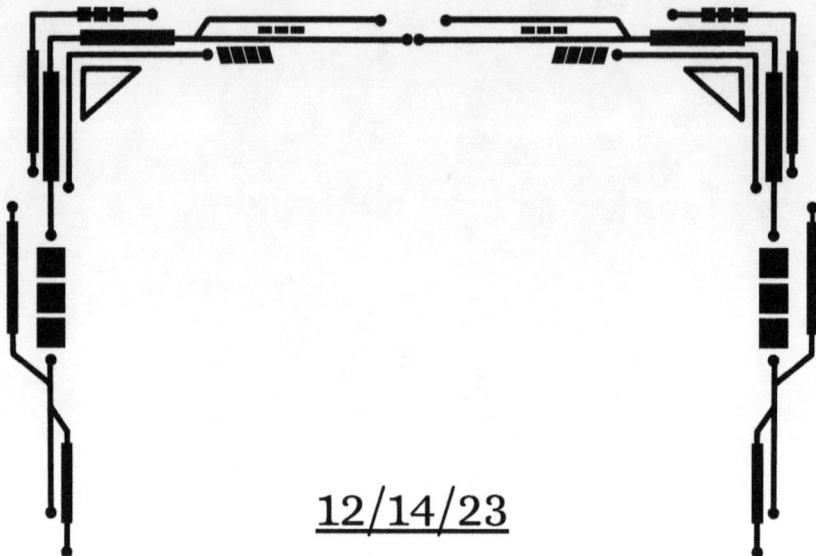

<u>12/14/23</u>

rinse the kidney beans
filter the aqua fava
now i have to pee

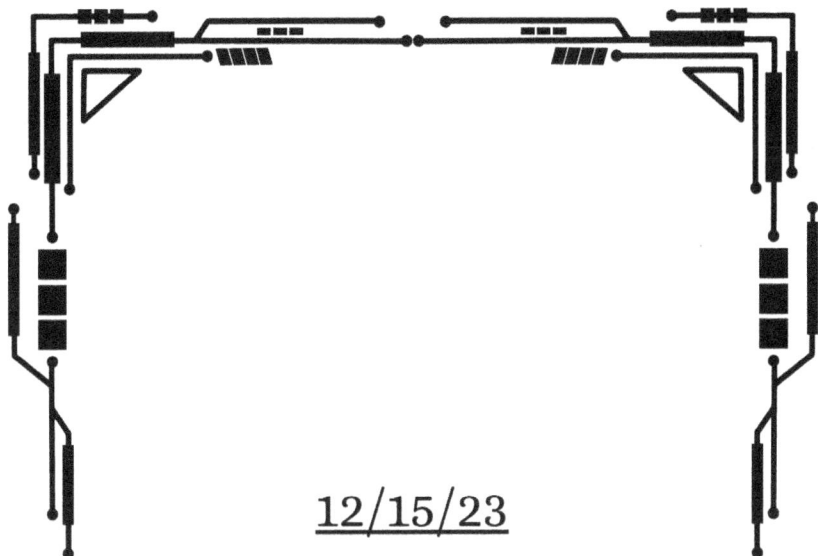

<u>12/15/23</u>

dark to work and home
it's about that time again
so little daylight

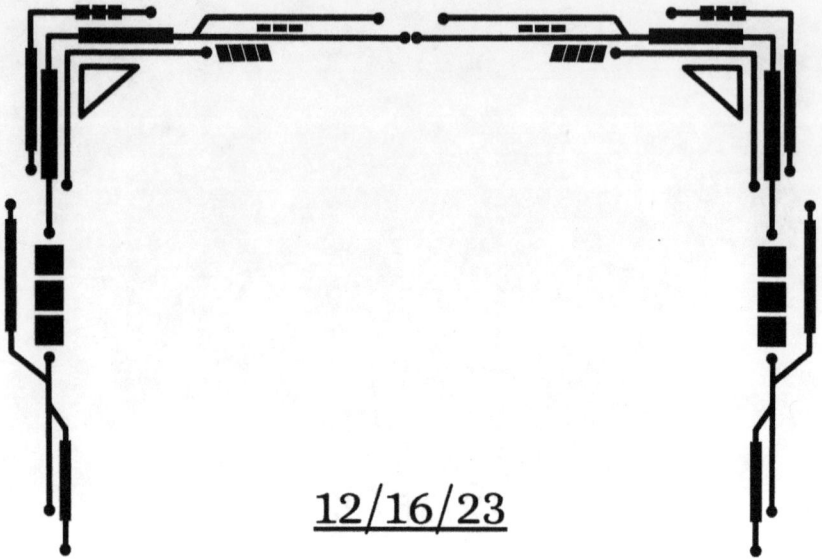

<u>12/16/23</u>

step on the dead leaves
rice krispies in the garden
time to milk the cow

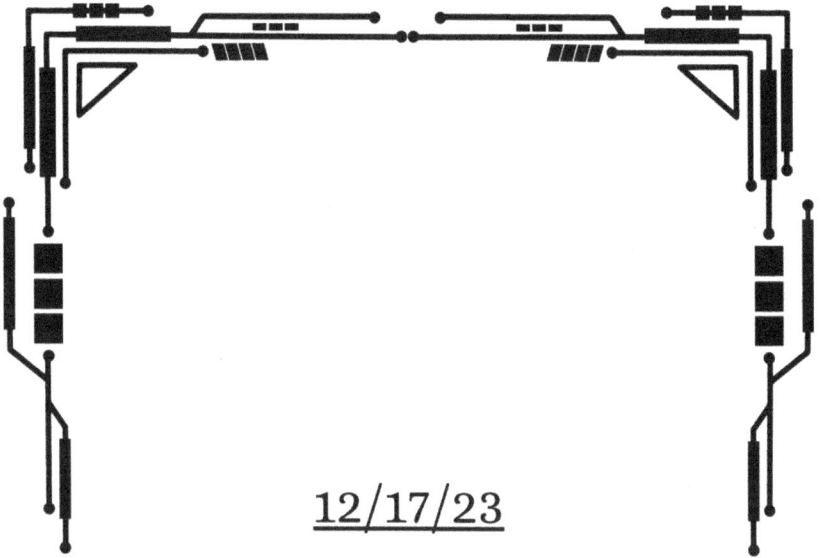

<u>12/17/23</u>

reel to reel and then
betamax and vhs
now discs are extinct

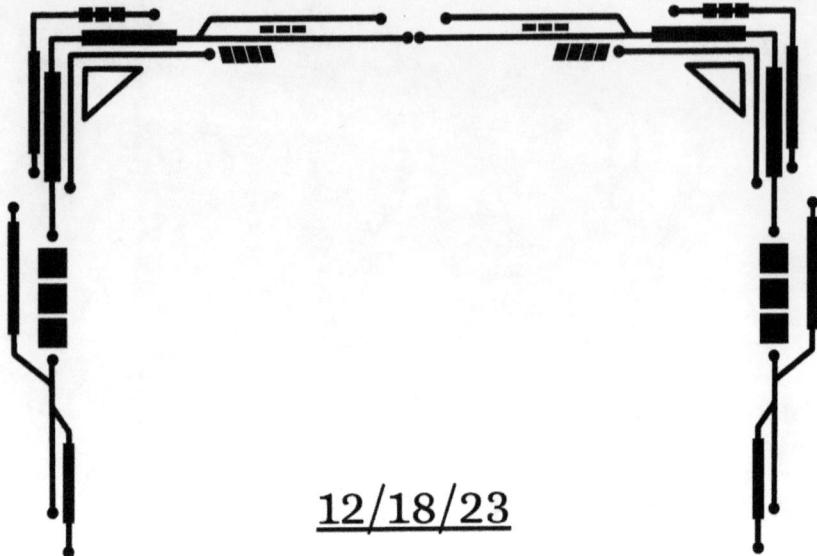

<u>12/18/23</u>

camel toe monday
back in style this holiday
at the post office

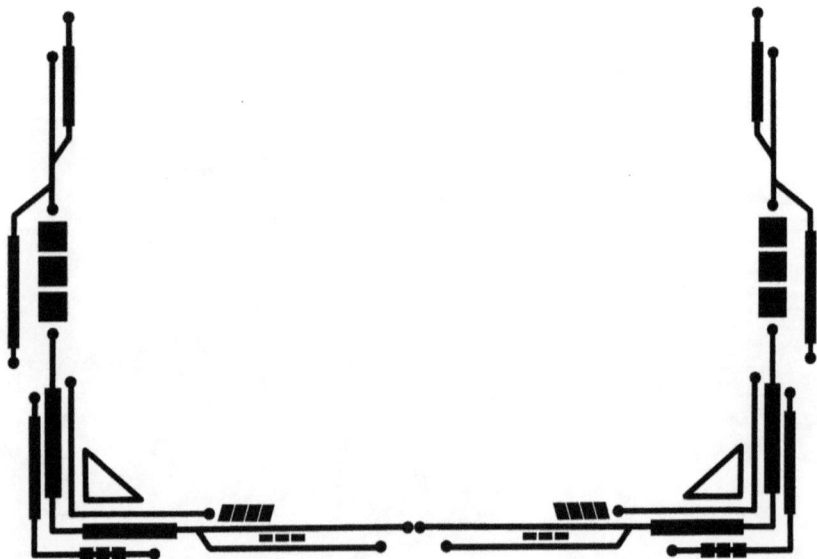

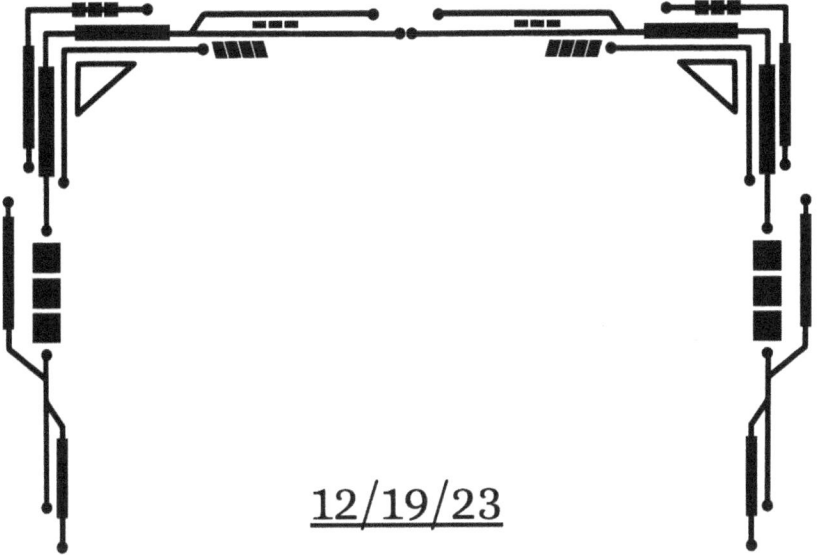

<u>12/19/23</u>

a dinner made by
a shepherd of rodentia
capybara pie

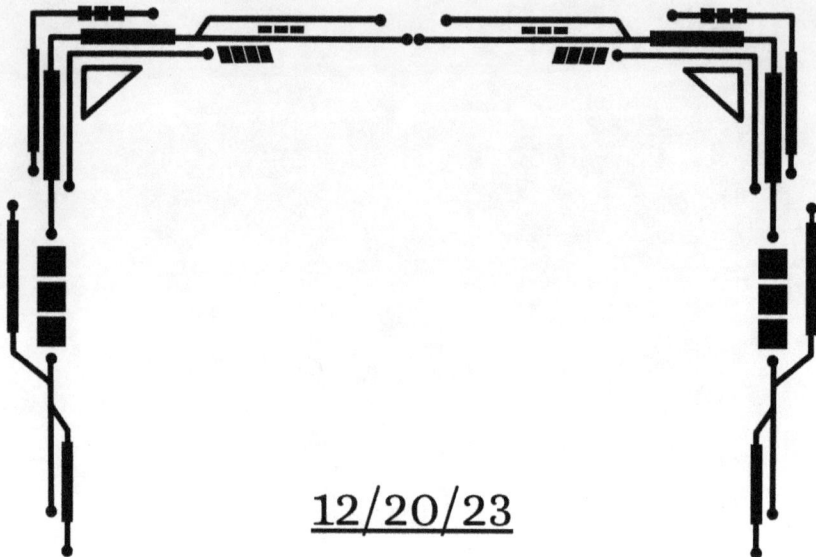

12/20/23

it's warm out today
i think sandwiches for lunch
and also salad

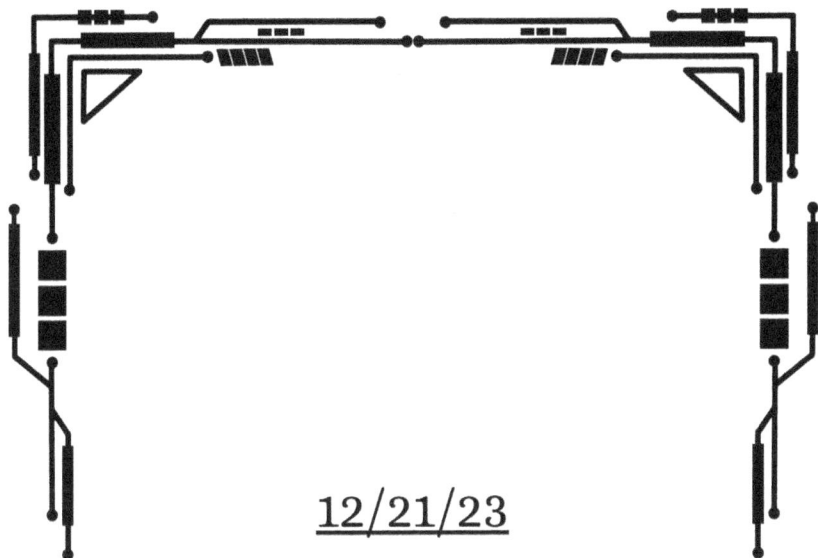

<u>12/21/23</u>

it shall come to pass
winter should be here again
but it's not here yet

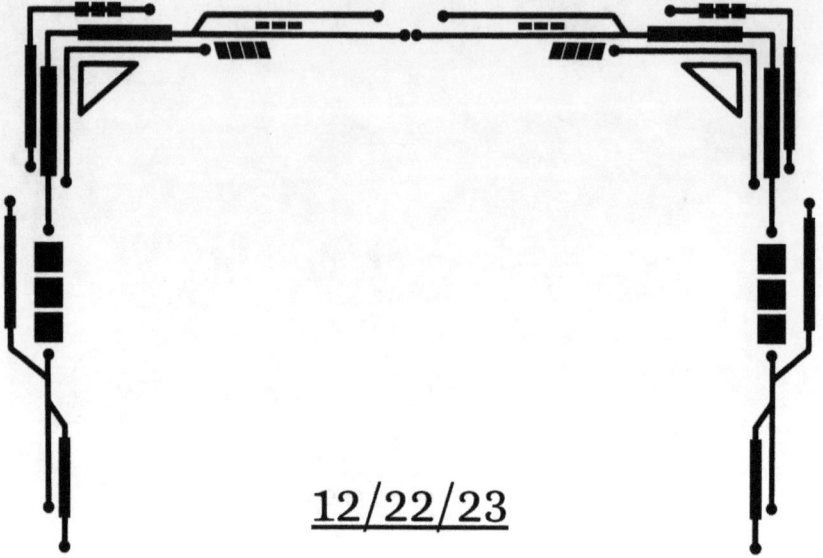

<u>12/22/23</u>

early this morning
a long breath hangs on the air
just for a minute

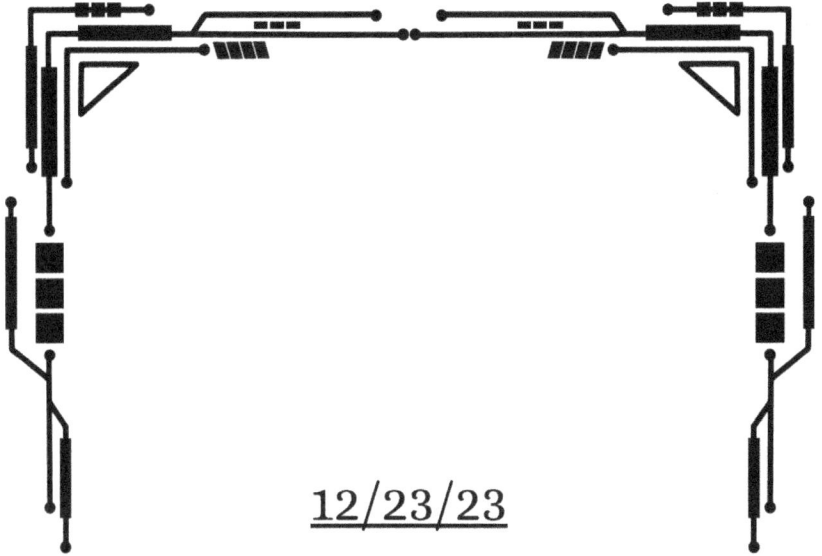

<u>12/23/23</u>

darkness all around
on the eve of christmas eve
because it's nighttime

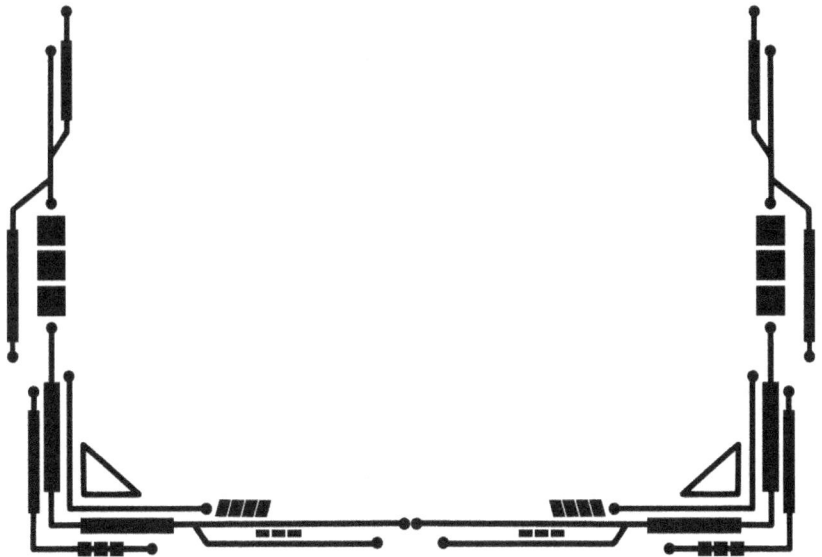

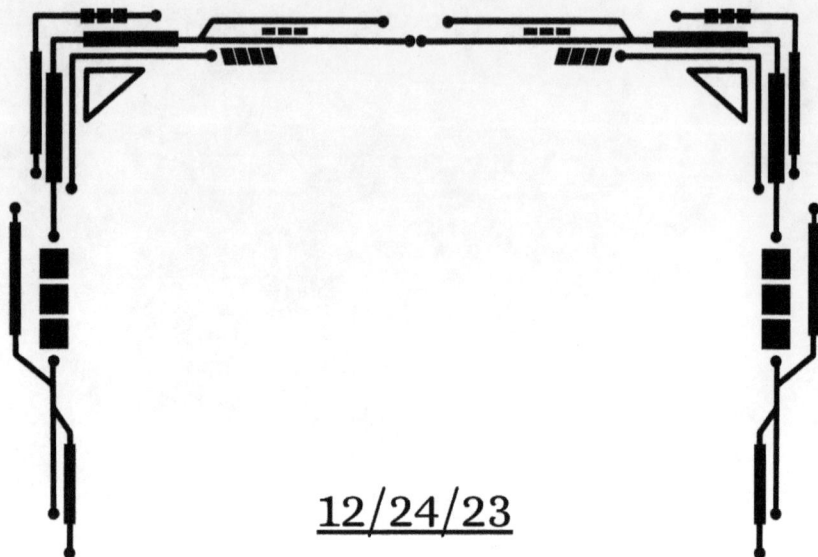

<u>12/24/23</u>

i want some pasta
all the creatures are stirring
the spaghetti sauce

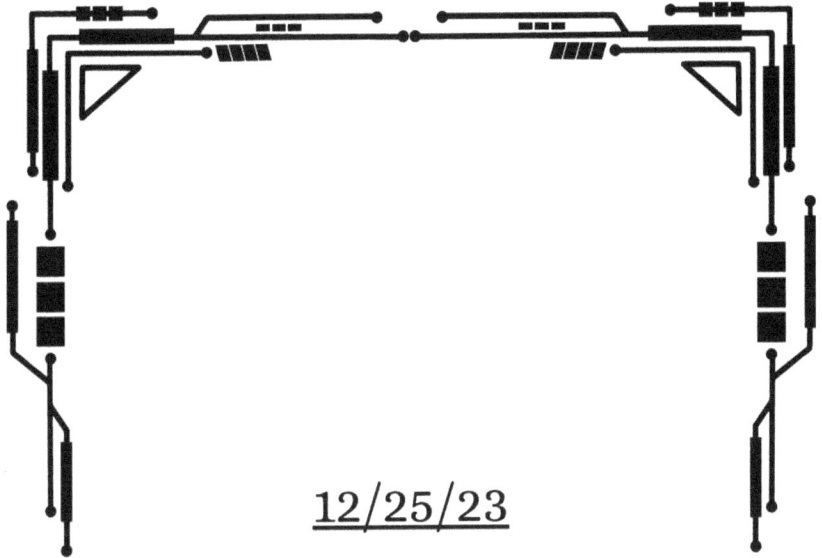

<u>12/25/23</u>

christmas time again
john mcclane won't die easy
yippie ki yay dude

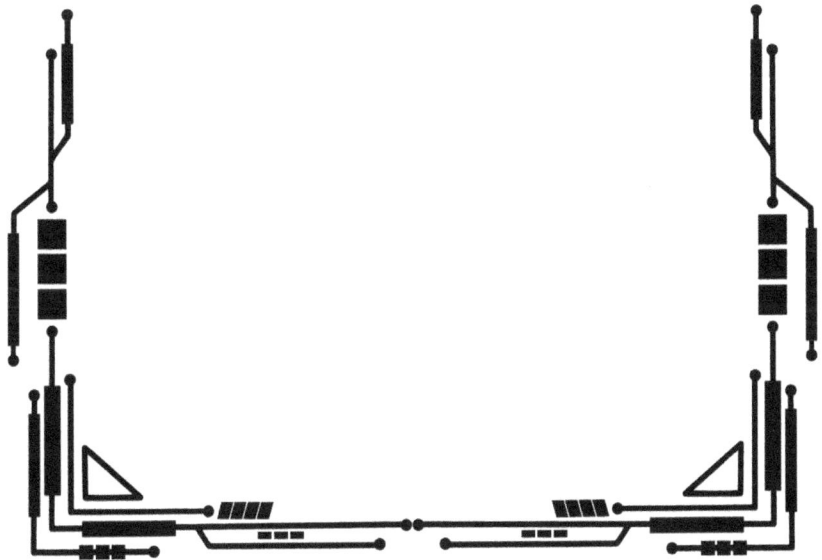

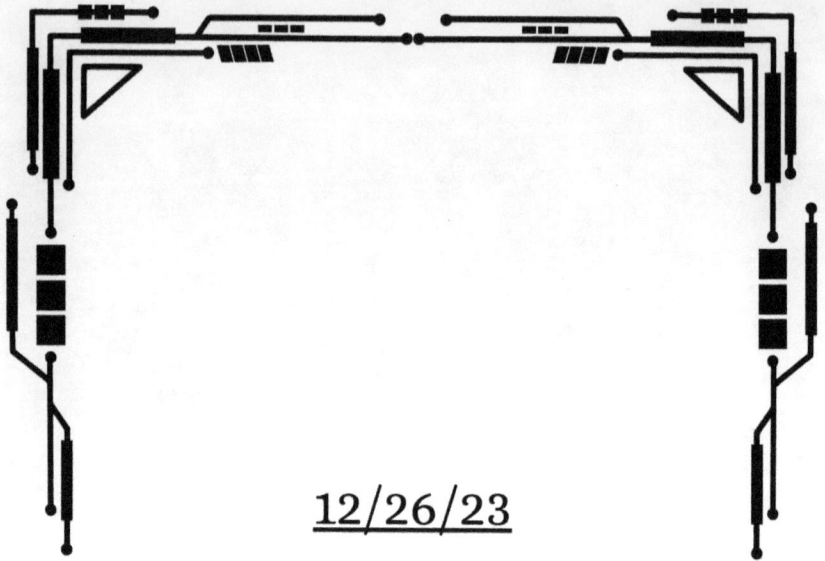

<u>12/26/23</u>

cloudy cold and gray
my least favorite type of day
is what today is

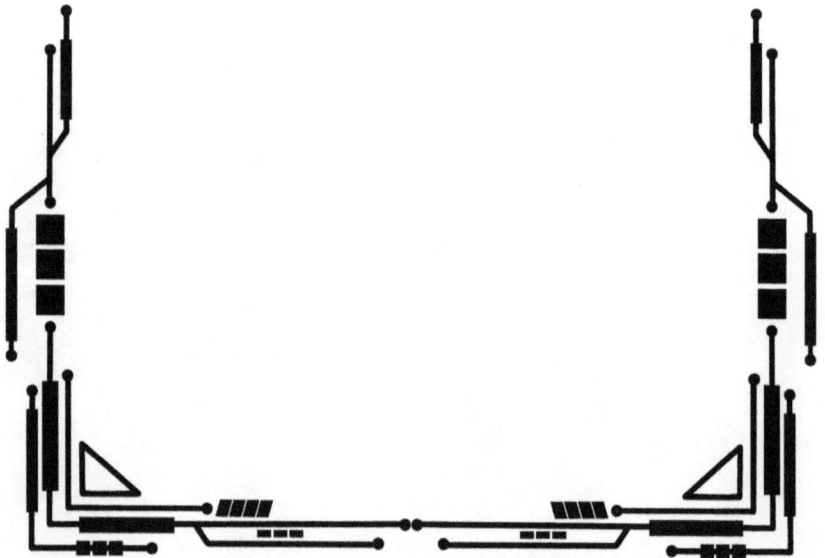

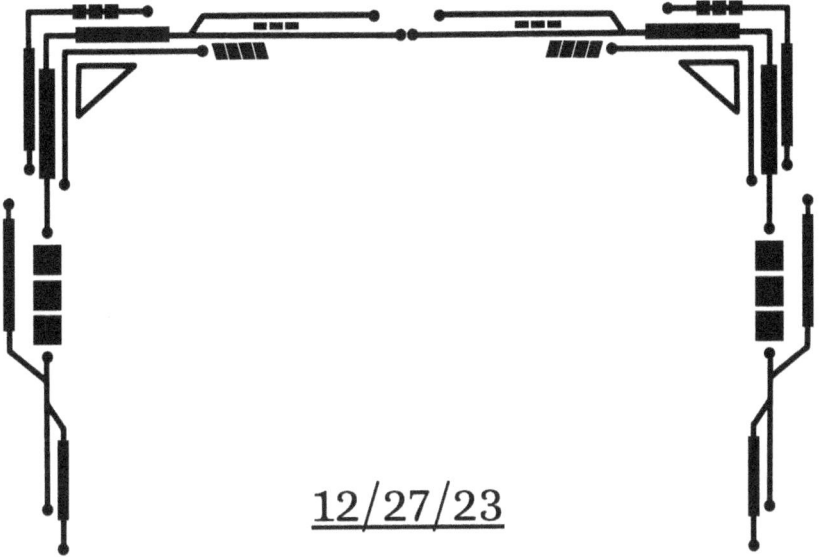

<u>12/27/23</u>

things are darker now
back on this side of the sun
solar system blues

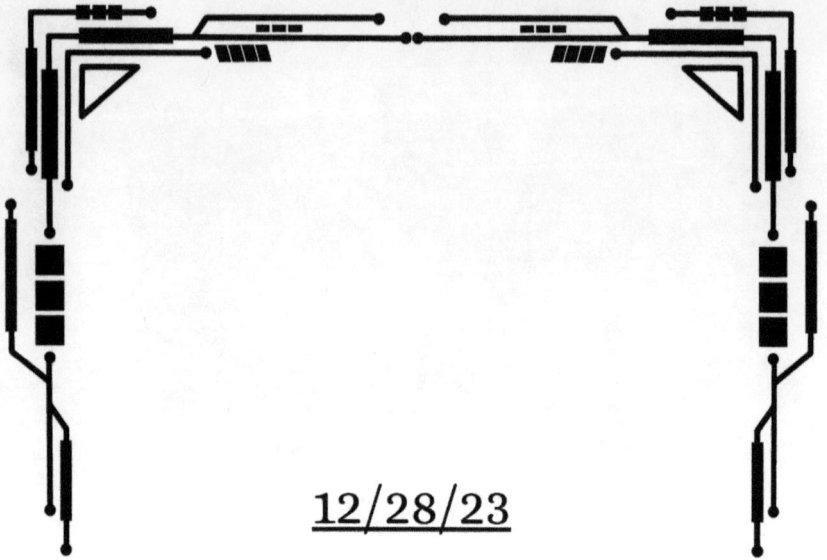

<u>12/28/23</u>

cookies cakes and pies
i don't like this time of year
there's too much sugar

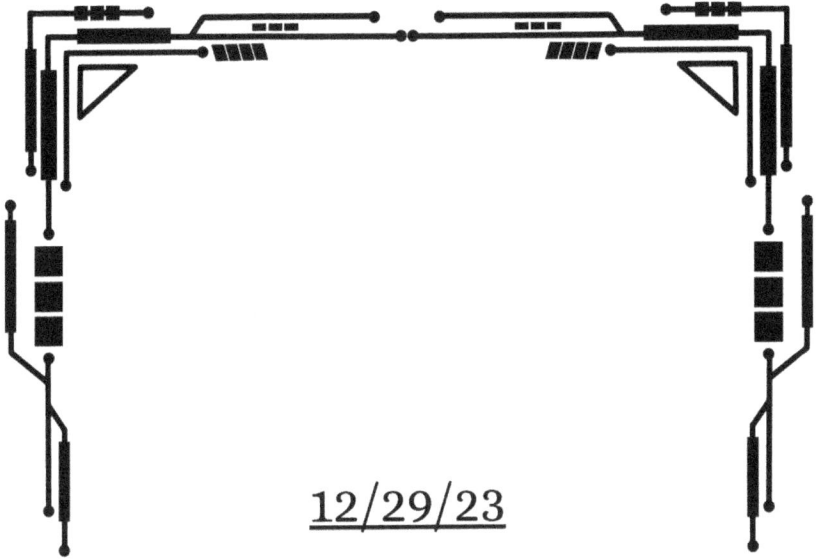

<u>12/29/23</u>

a glimmer of hope
twinkles like the brightest star
on the darkest night

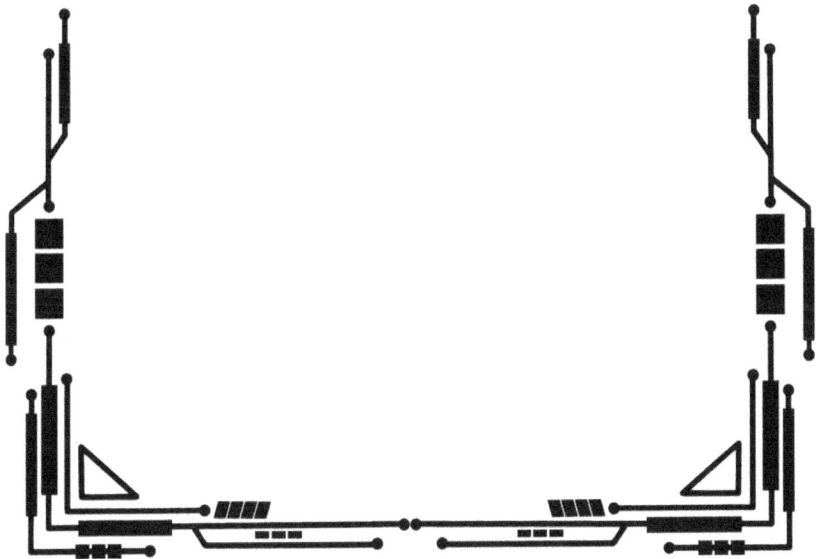

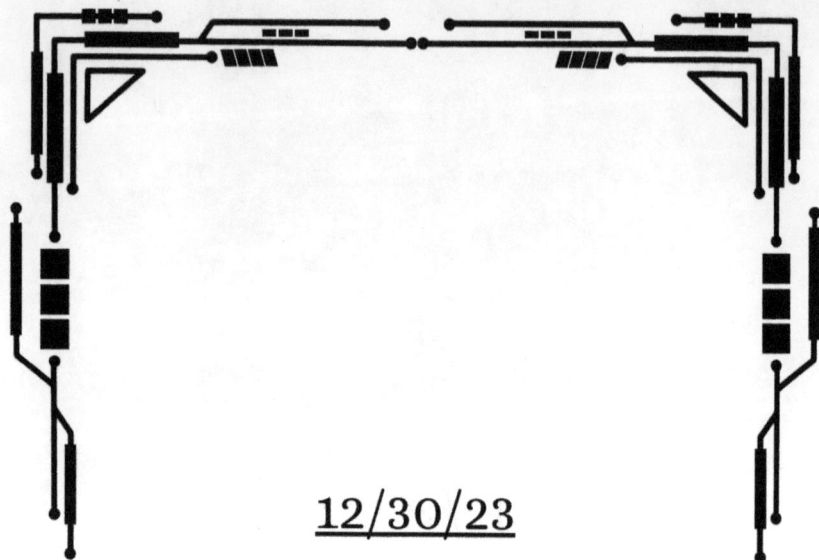

12/30/23

here we are again
i'm all done with twenty three
reset the timer

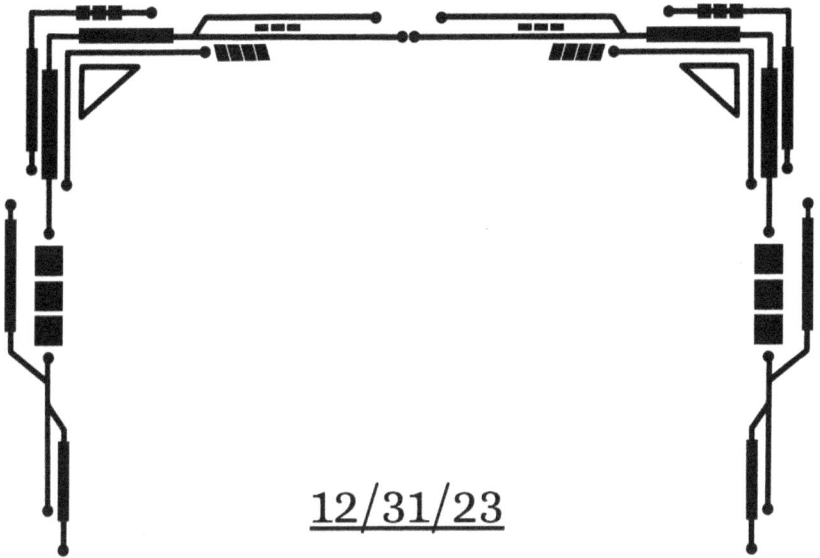

<u>12/31/23</u>

now this is the end
or maybe the beginning
of another end

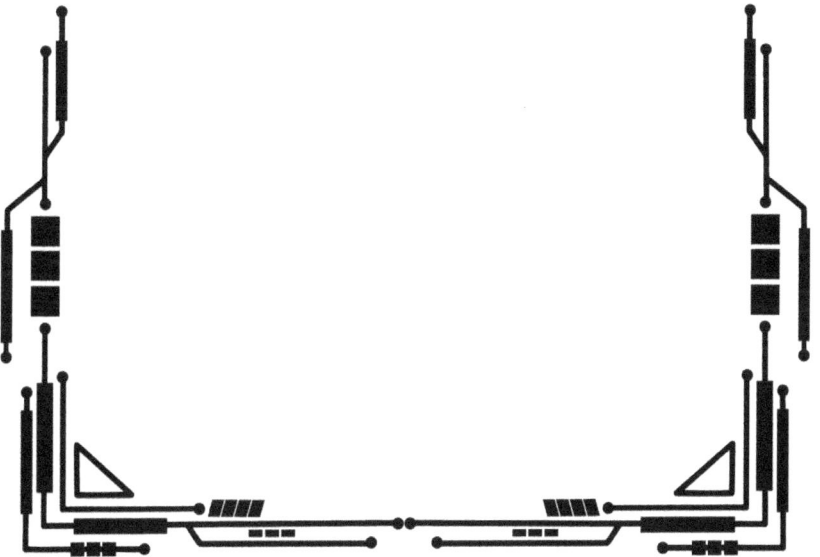

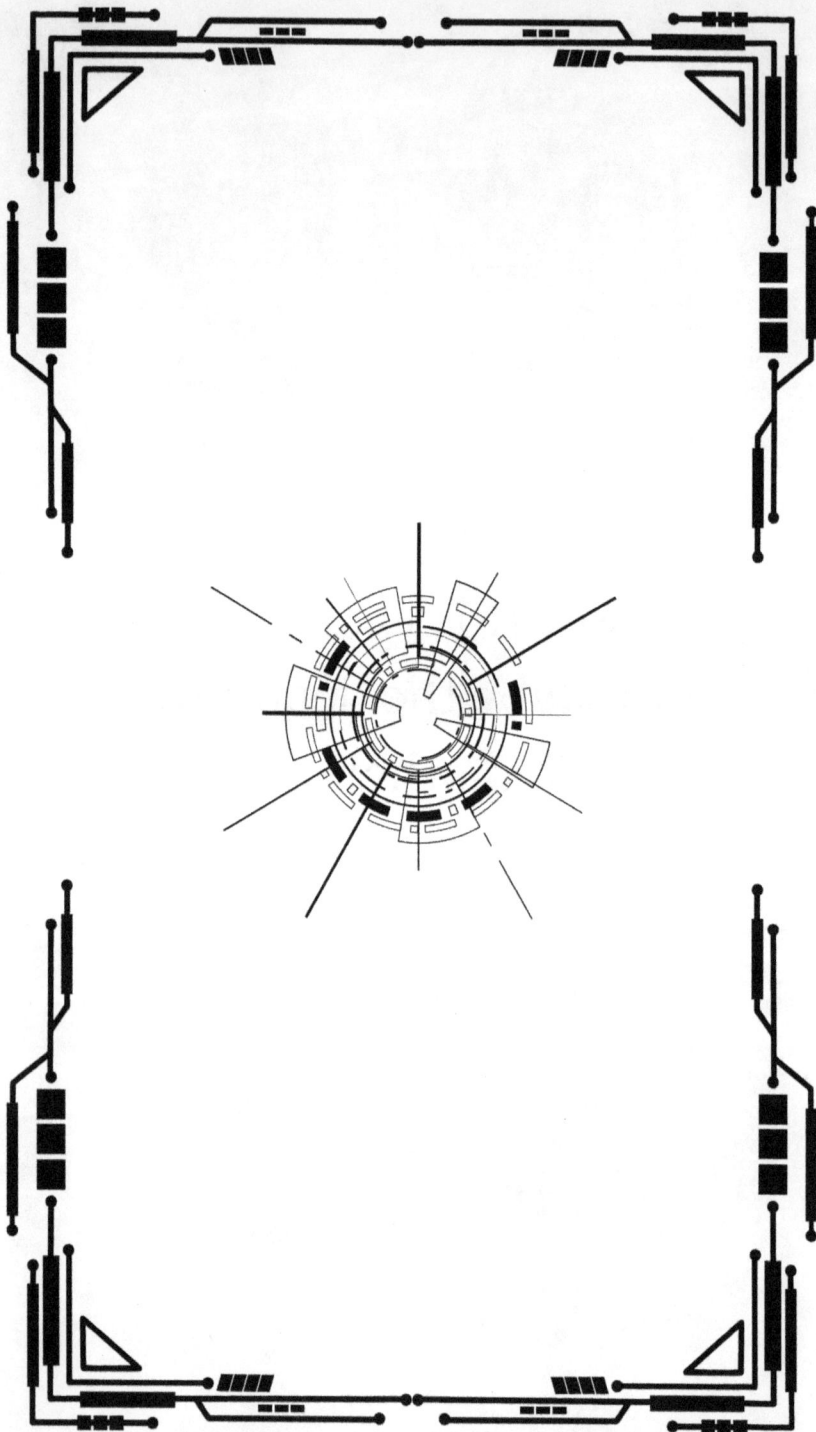

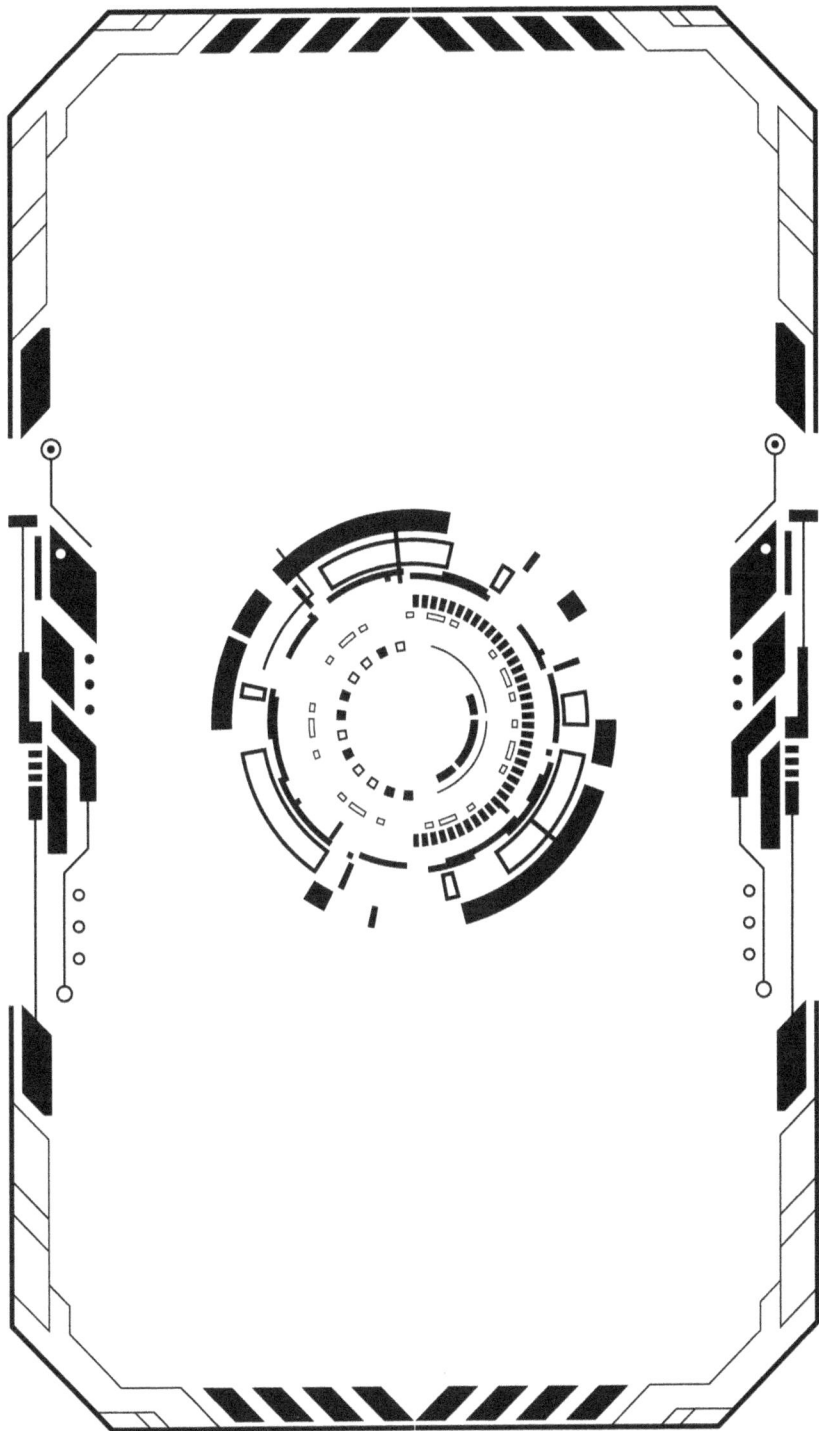

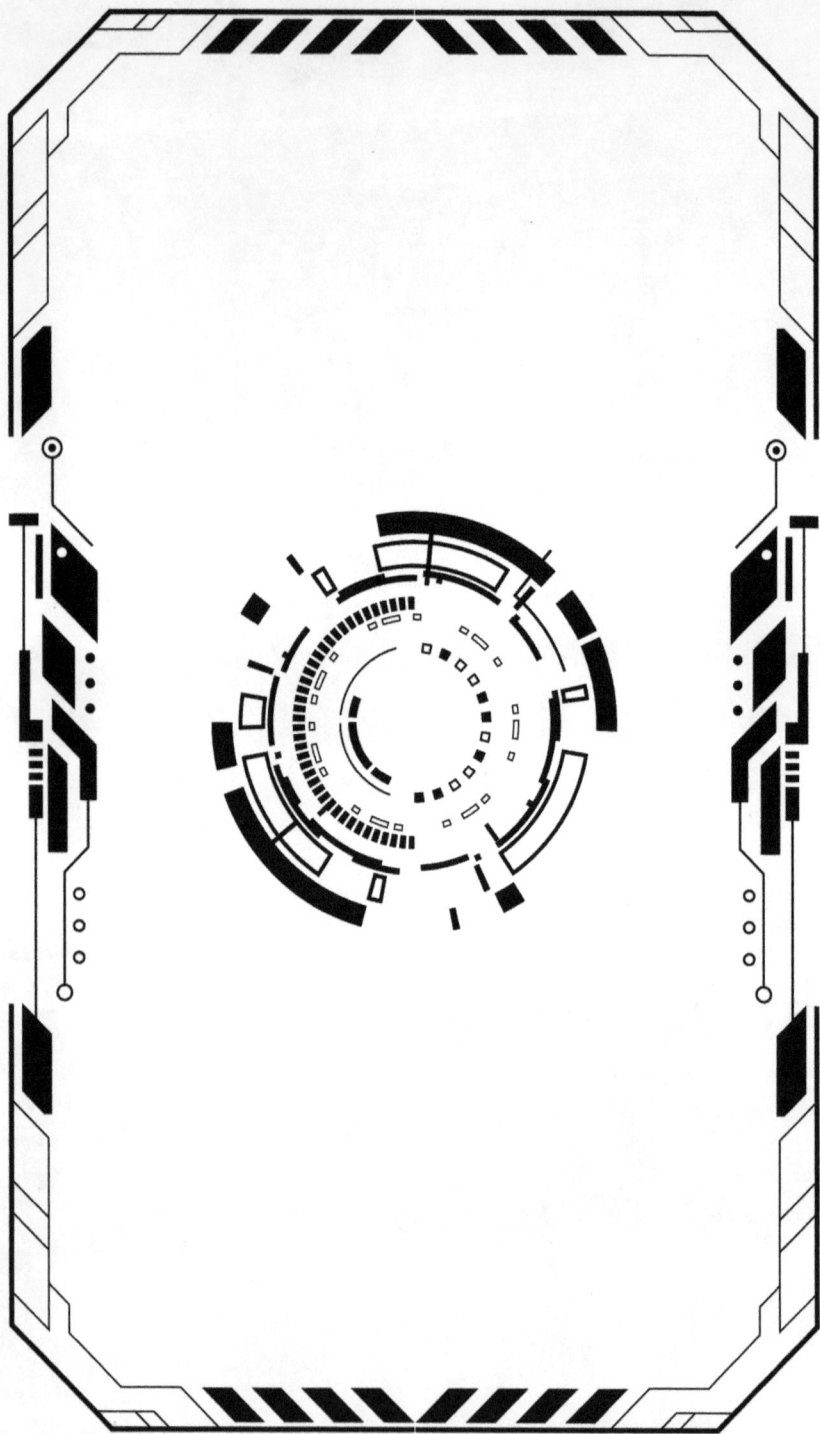

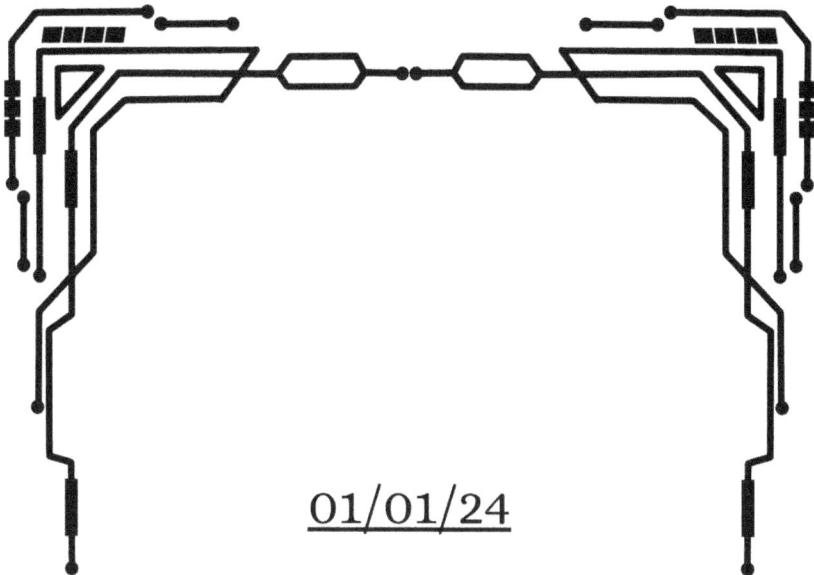

<u>01/01/24</u>

remove the cartridge
blow last year's dust out of it
this time it will work

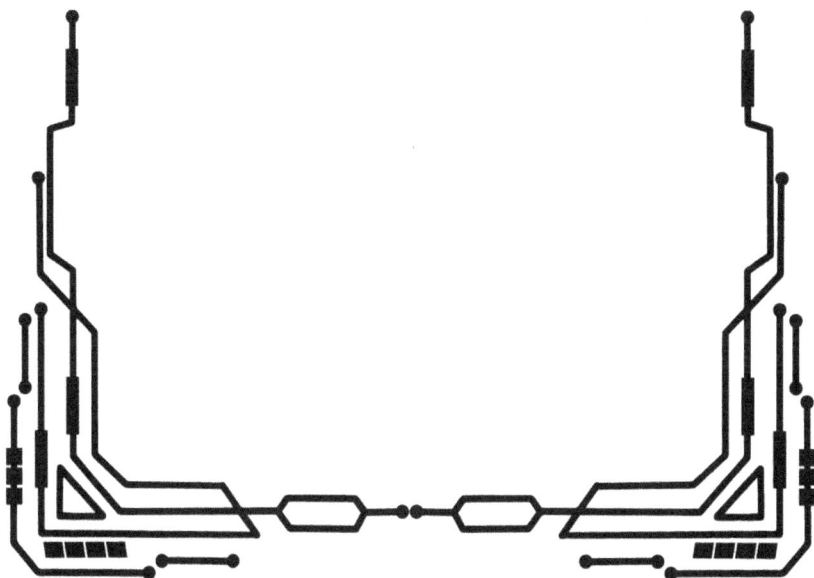

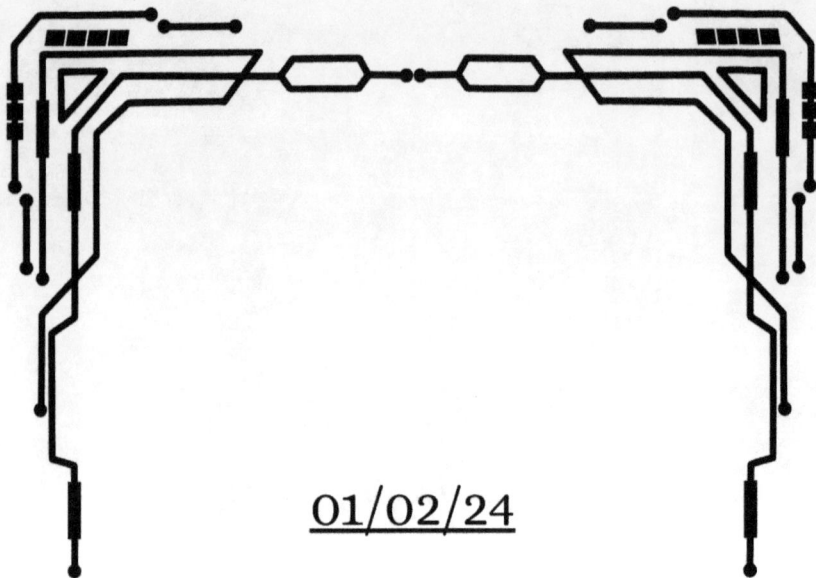

<u>01/02/24</u>

there was one woman
with type two diabetes
and twenty four cats

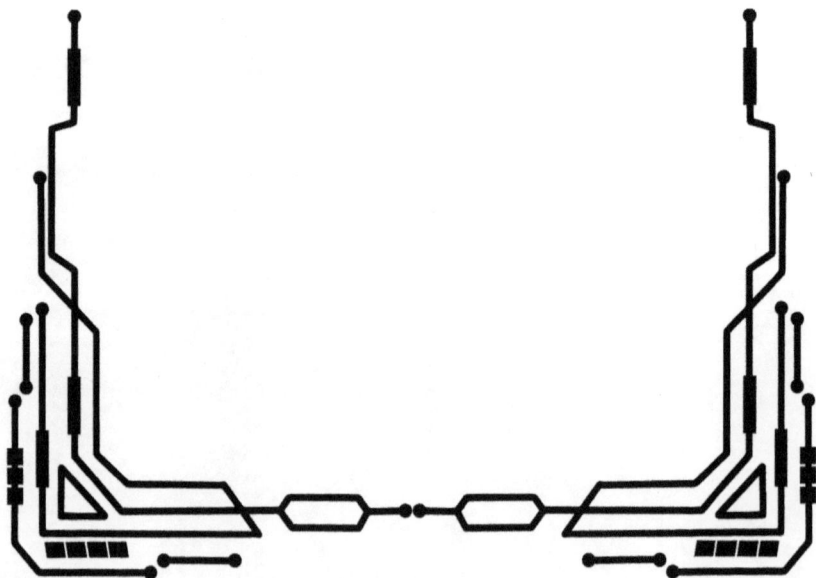

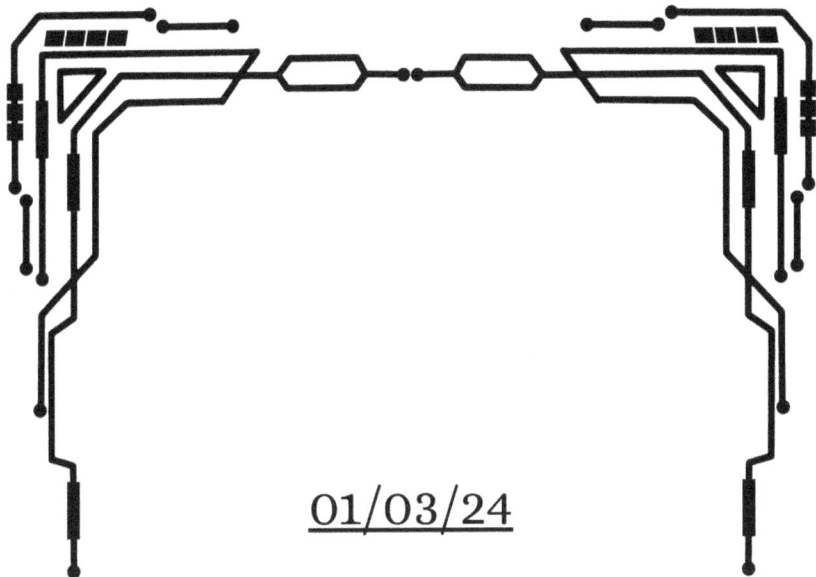

<u>01/03/24</u>

roll up a fat one
burritos won't get you high
but you will be full

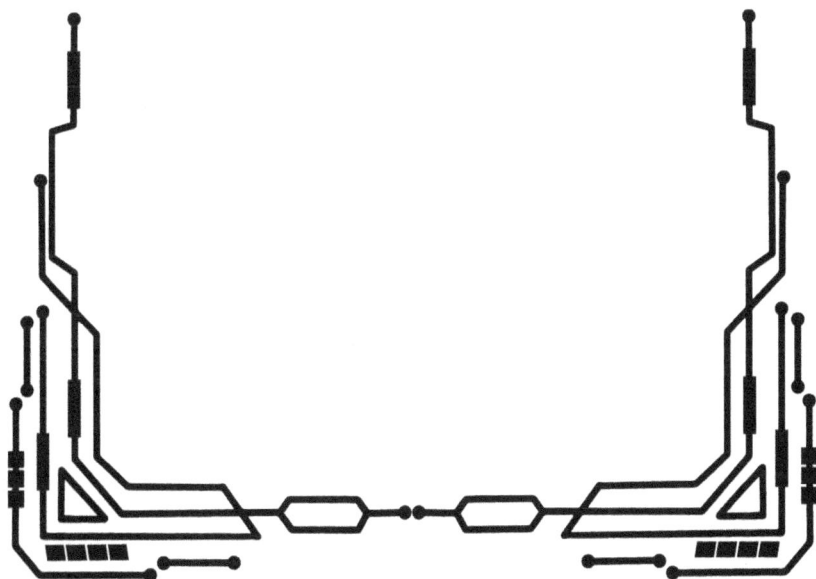

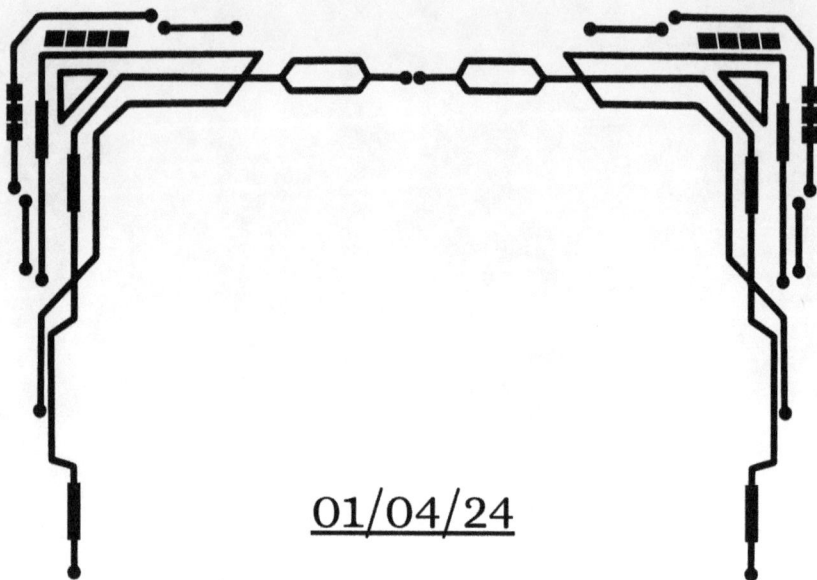

<u>01/04/24</u>

sometimes a tree falls
and it doesn't make a sound
dying in the wind

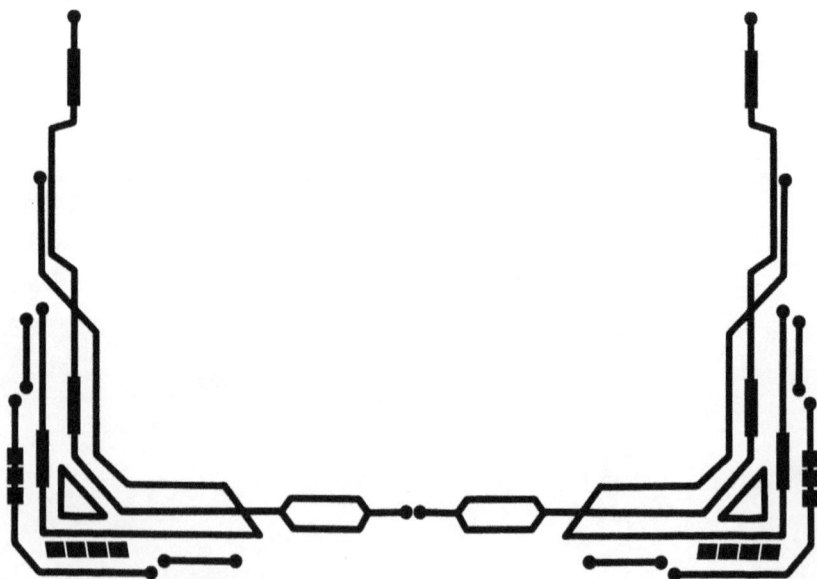

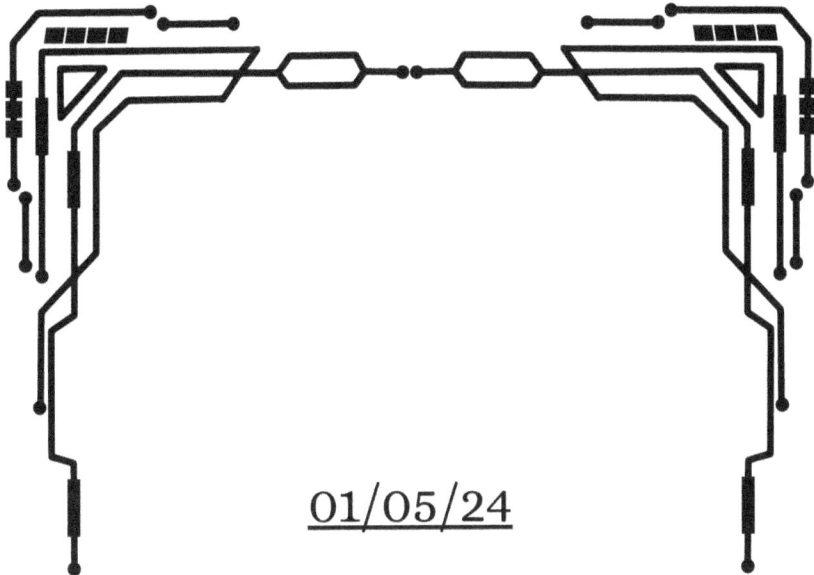

<u>01/05/24</u>

january sucks
the earth's angle is all wrong
god's protractor broke

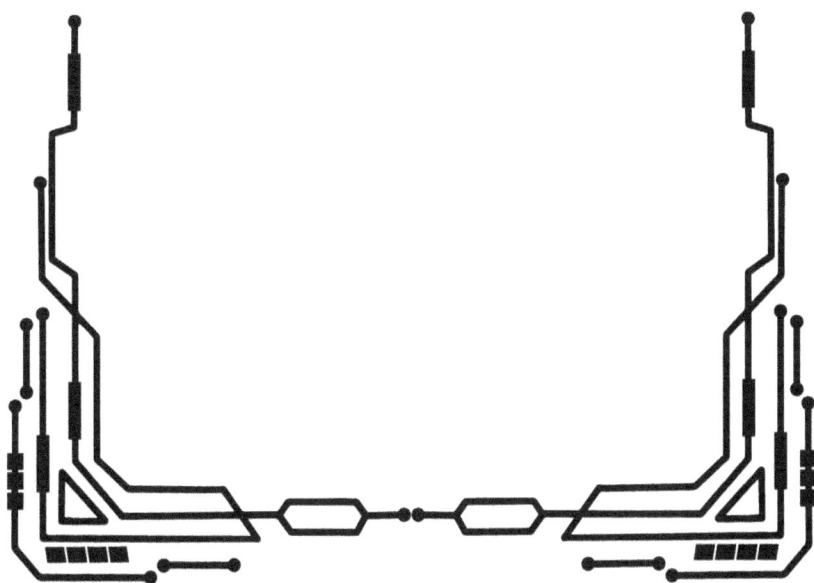

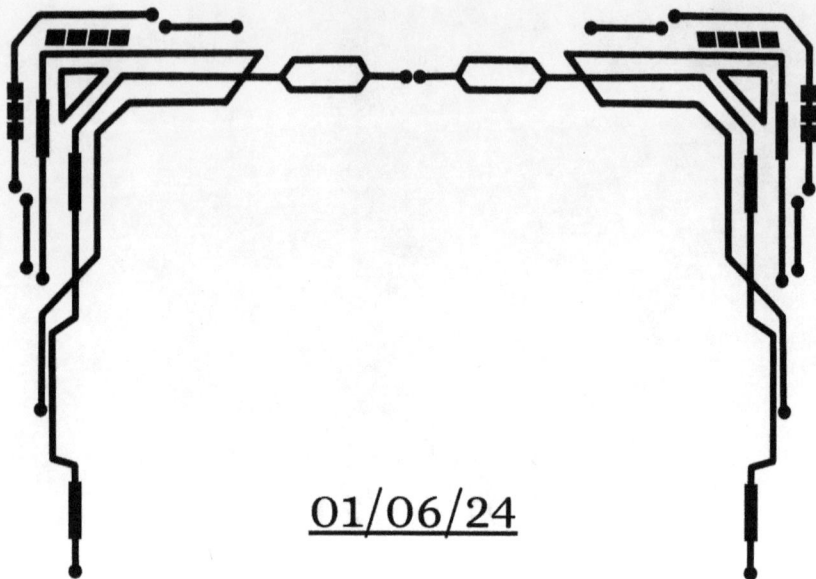

<u>01/06/24</u>

pretend there isn't
cold amidst the bitterness
something is awry

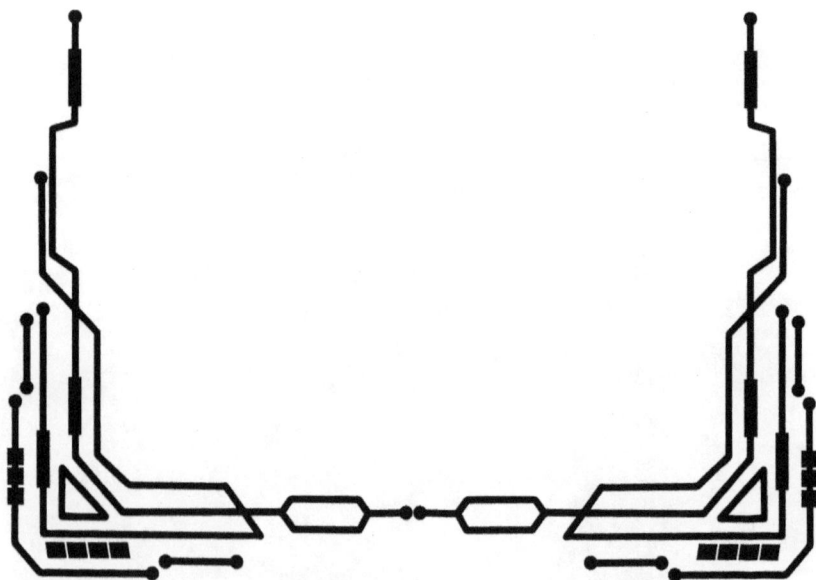

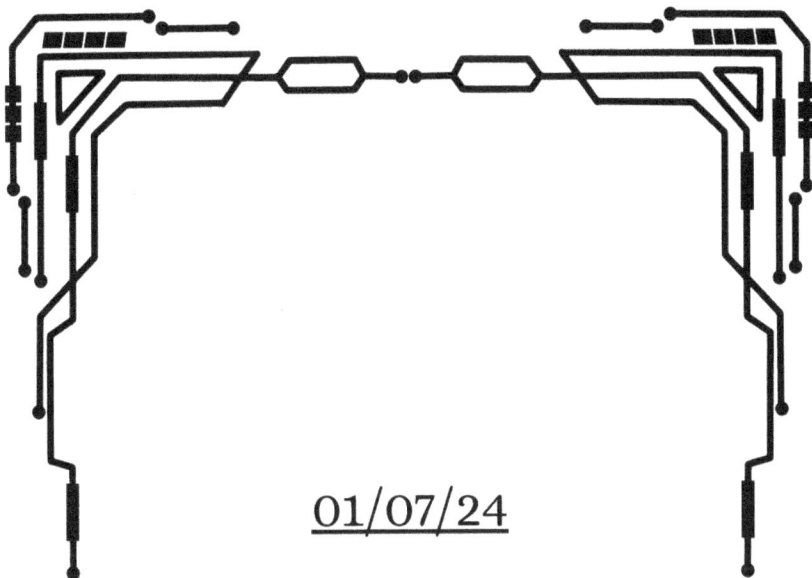

<u>01/07/24</u>

frosty tipped tree branch
hanging low for the big moose
tasty leaves for lunch

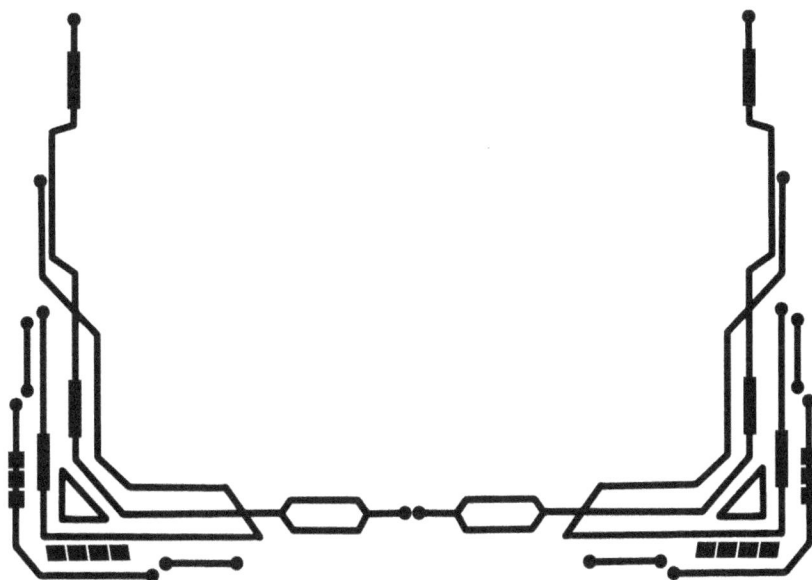

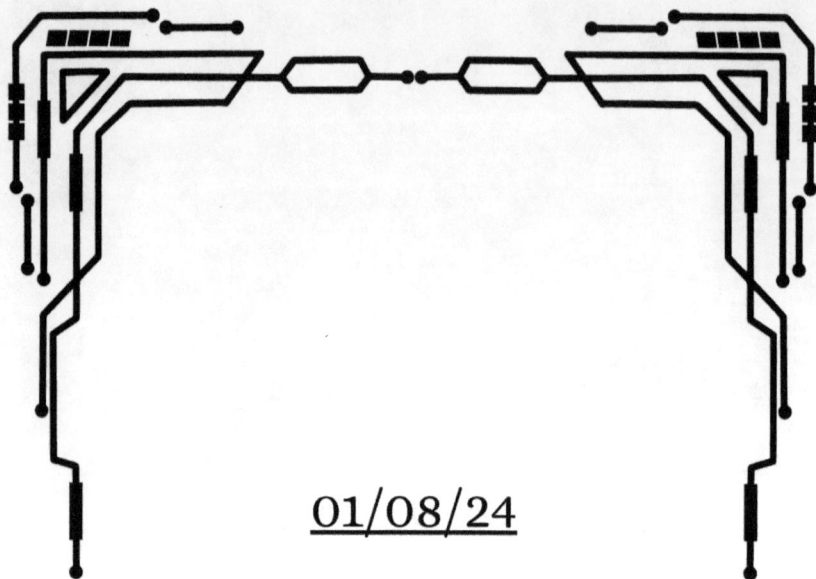

<u>01/08/24</u>

the sun was awake
for a little bit today
then it went to bed

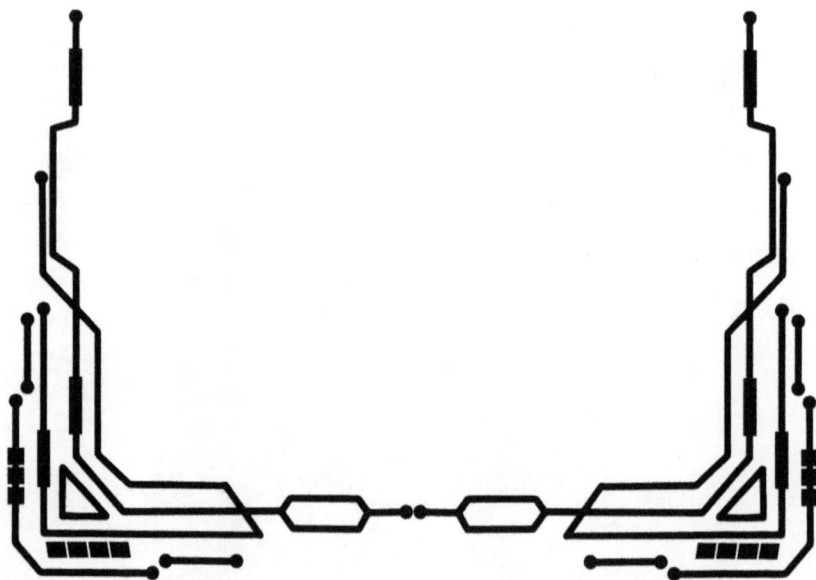

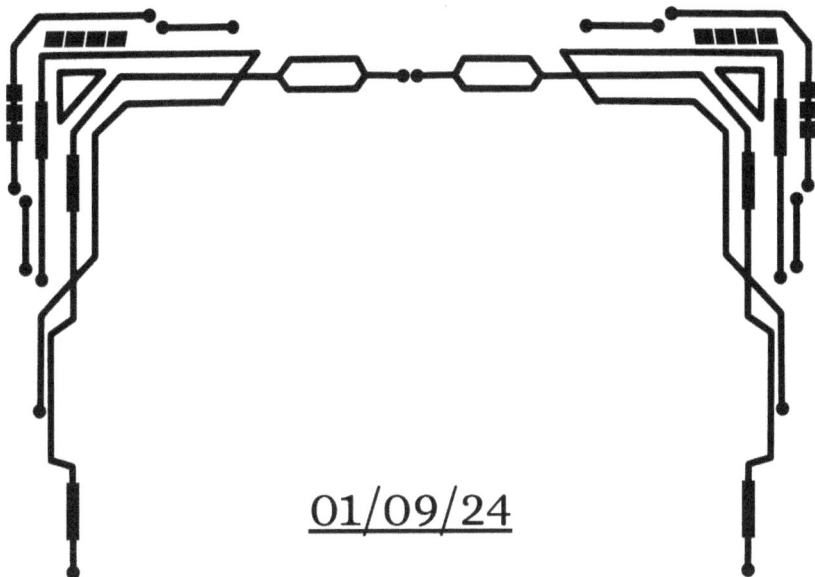

<u>01/09/24</u>

lebowski penguins
wobble like a bowling pin
delicious i bet

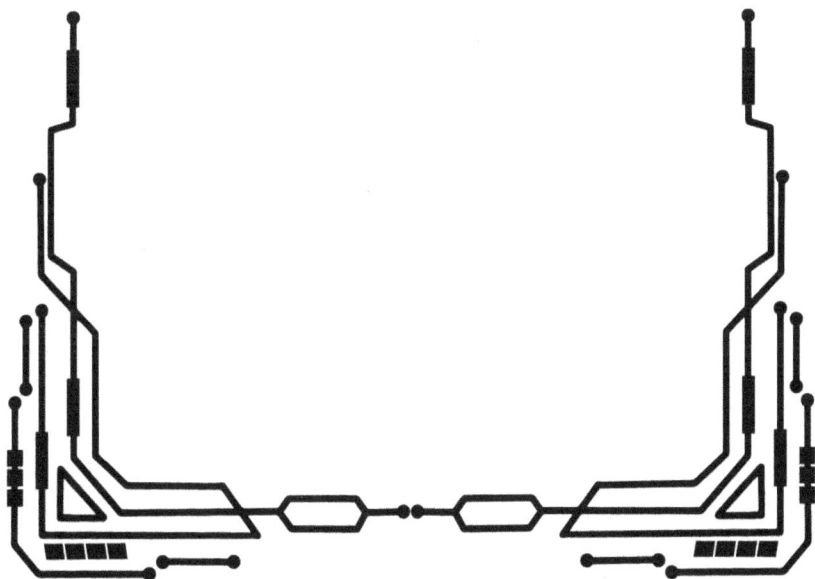

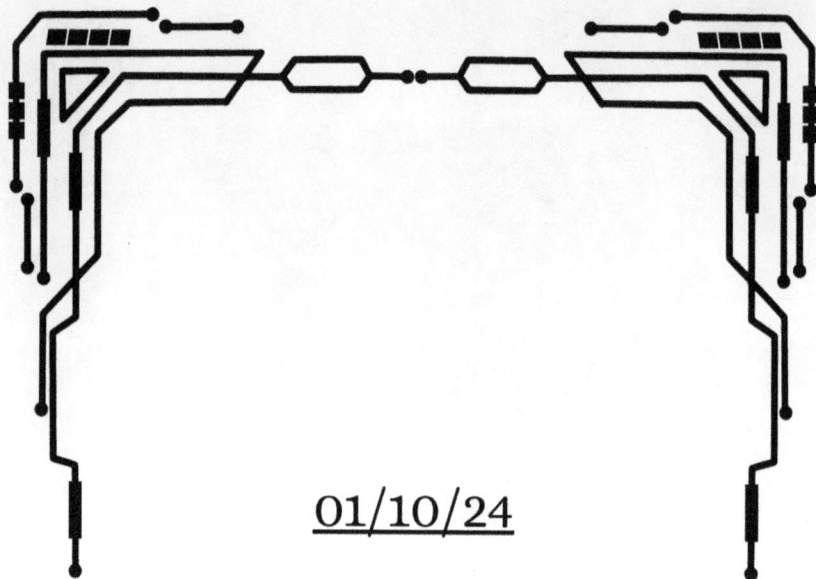

<u>01/10/24</u>

i see the icee
gas station beverage machine
is broken again

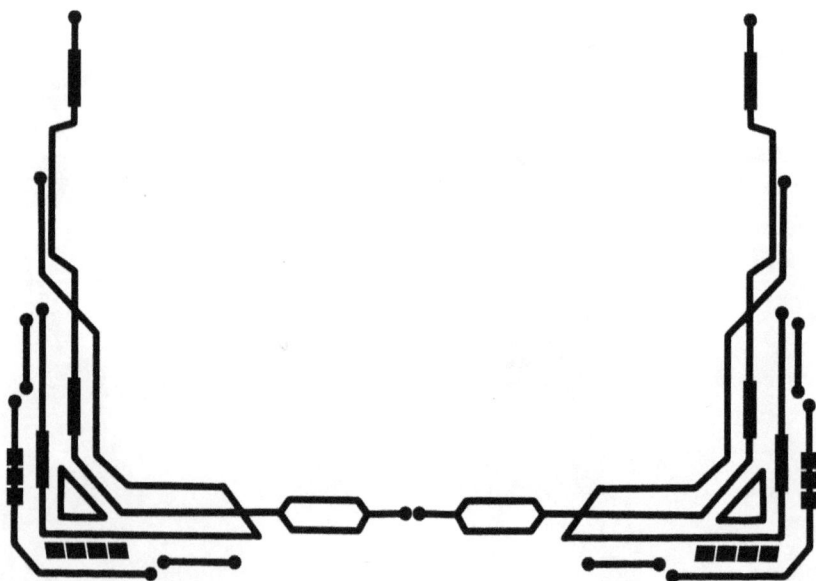

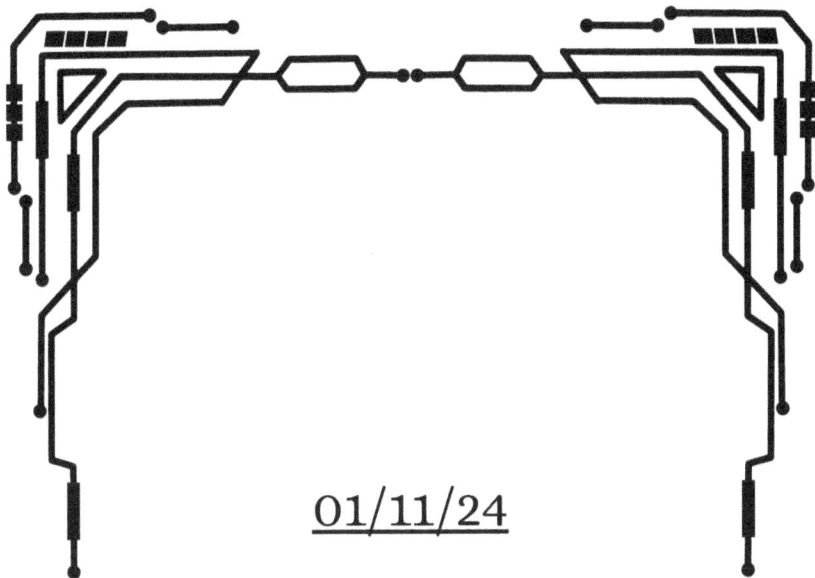

<u>01/11/24</u>

it's cold out today
gonna get colder i think
cold tomorrow too

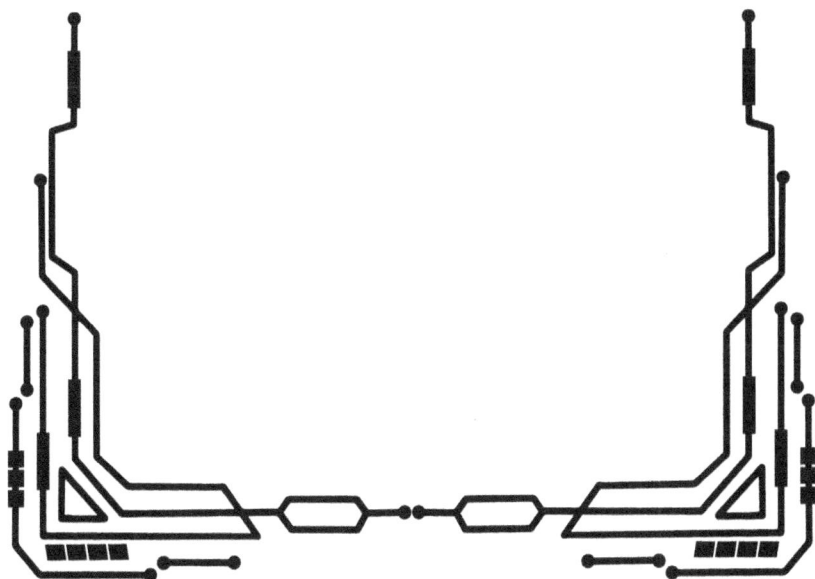

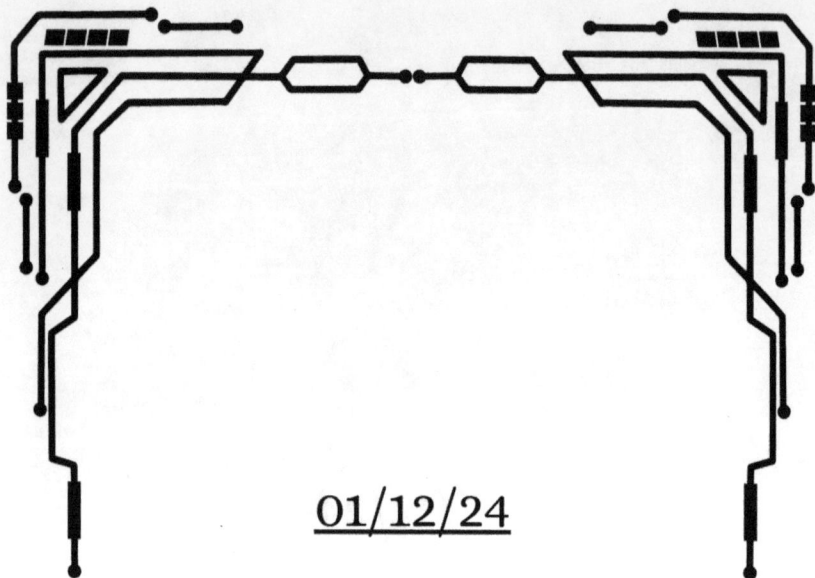

<u>01/12/24</u>

the day is short now
the spoon is long overdue
for chicken pot pie

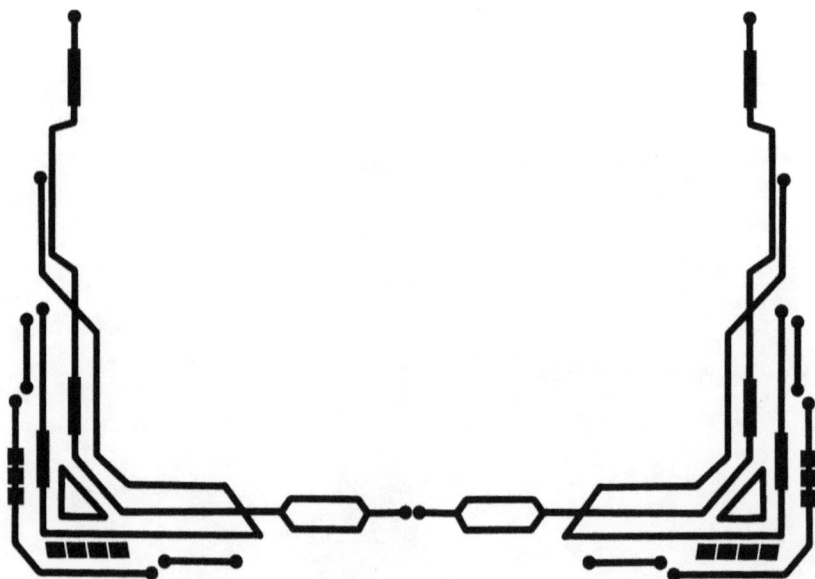

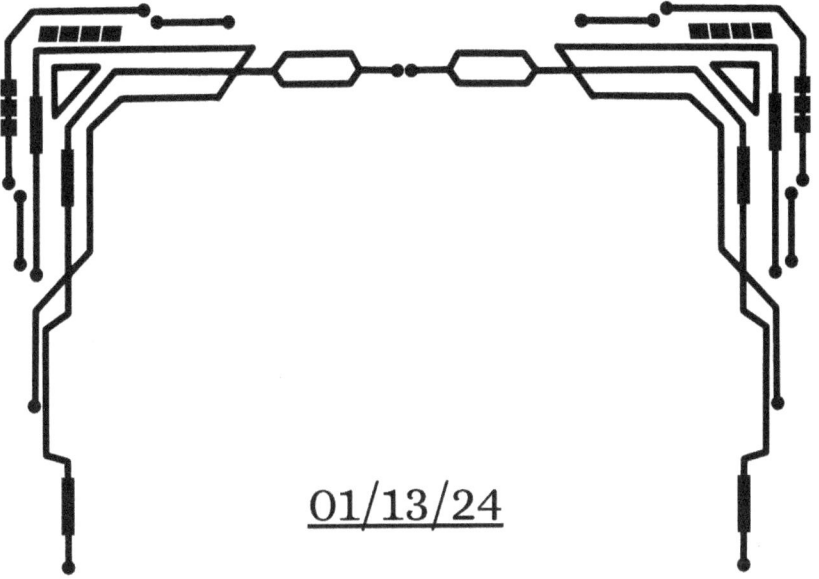

<u>01/13/24</u>

fire sprinkler alarm
waking up at six am
frozen pipes explode

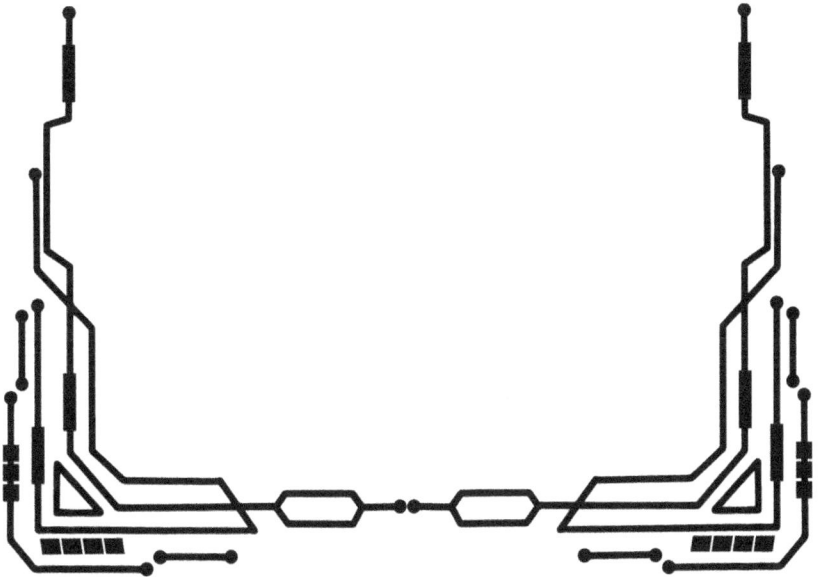

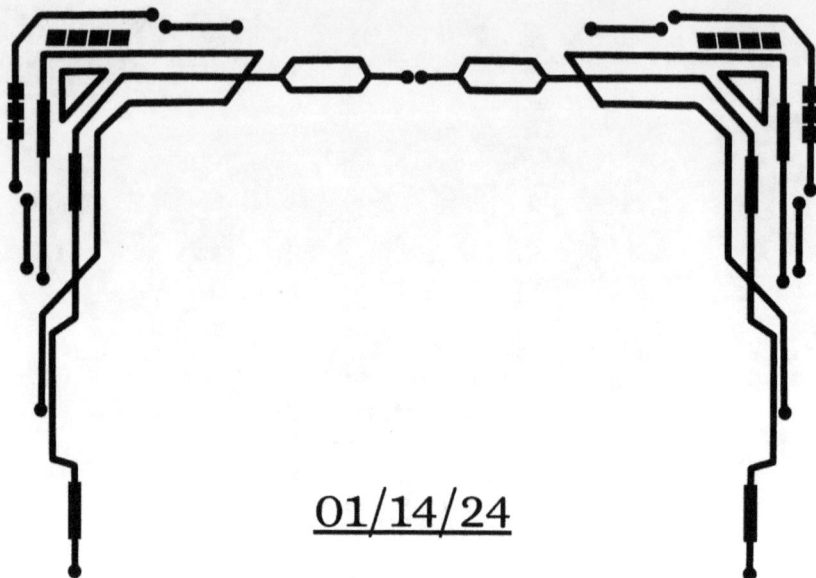

<u>01/14/24</u>

twenty below here
fifty below over there
the soup is frozen

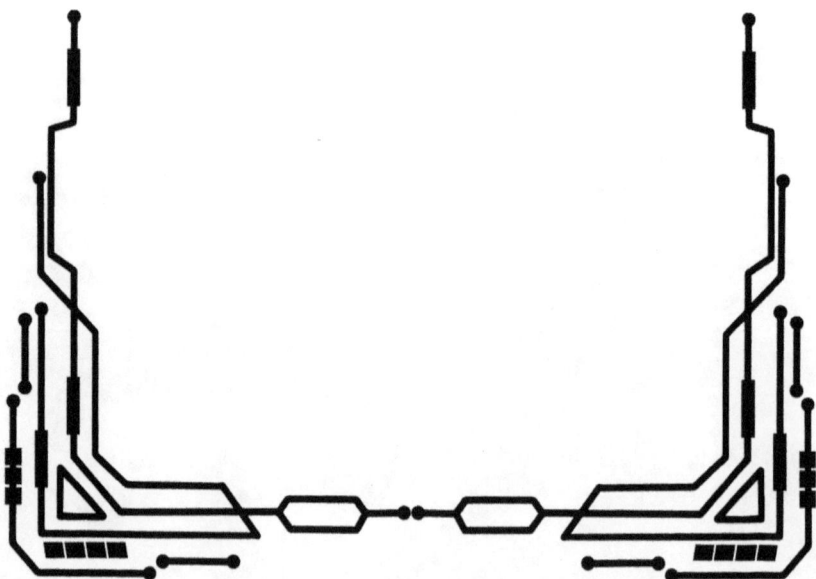

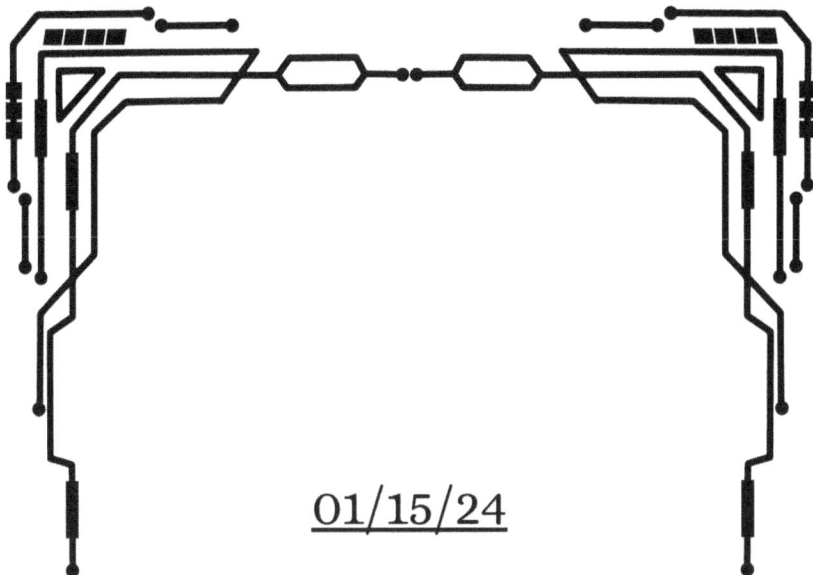

<u>01/15/24</u>

blanket in the wash
have to use the other one
it's a good blanket

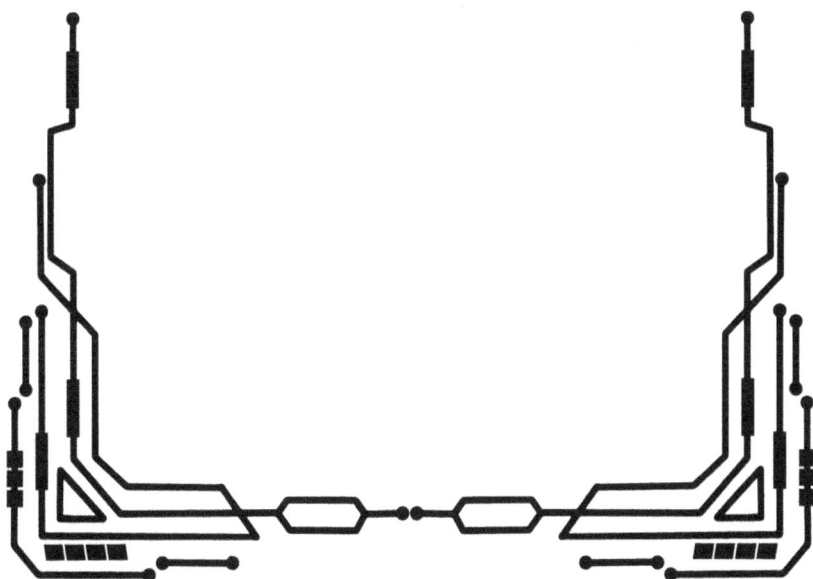

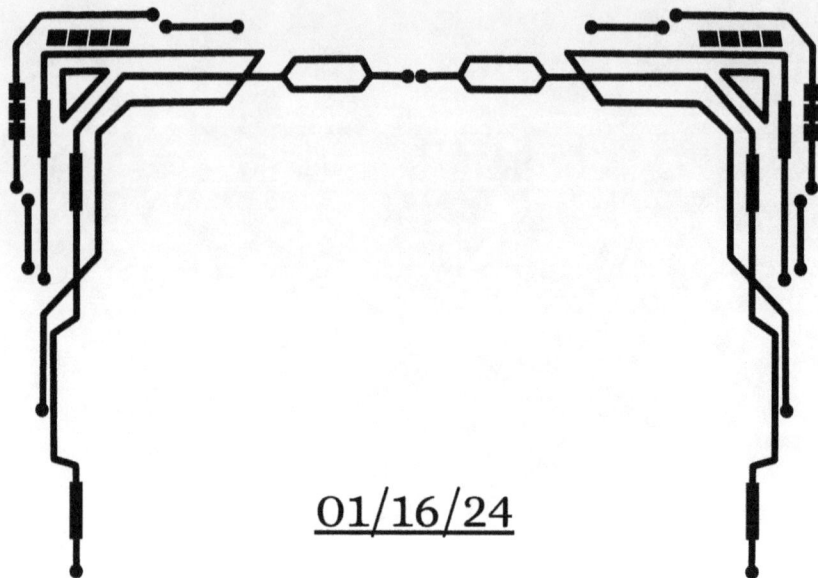

<u>01/16/24</u>

time to pay taxes
tally the granola beans
uncle sam gets his

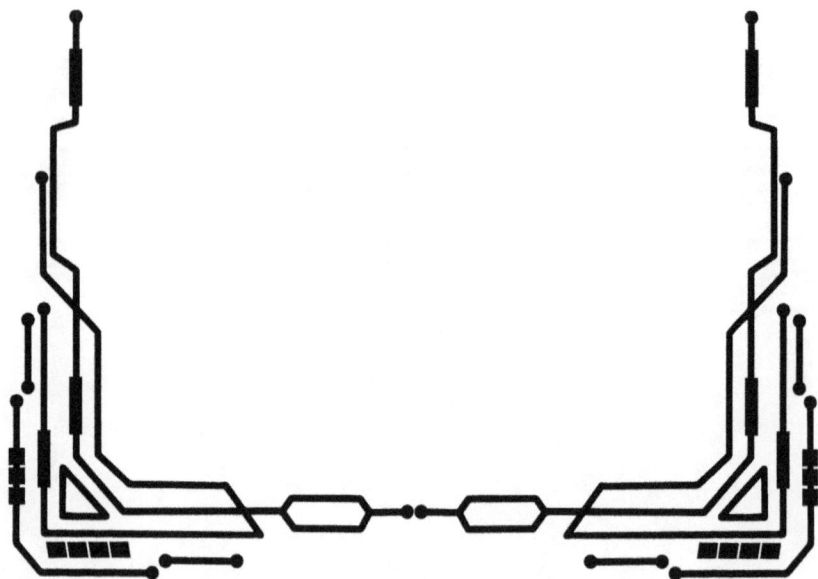

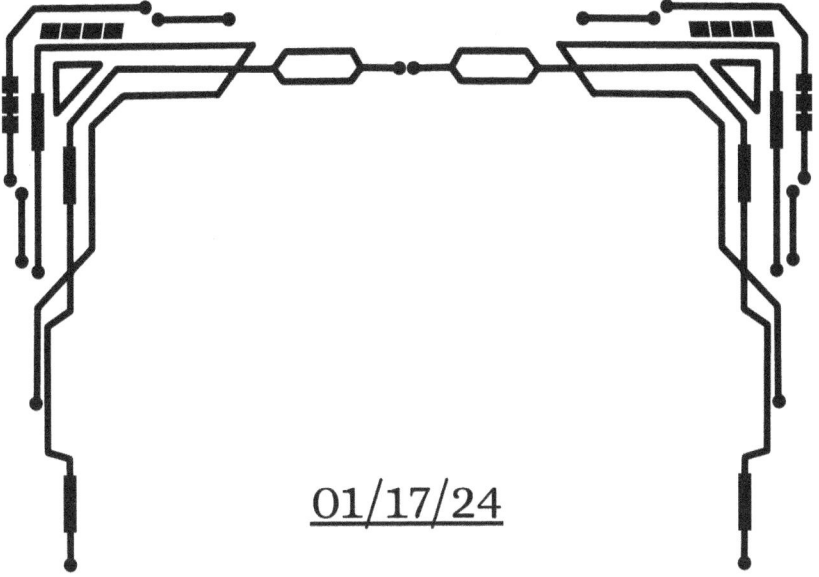

<u>01/17/24</u>

it's a casserole
except in minnesota
then it's a hotdish

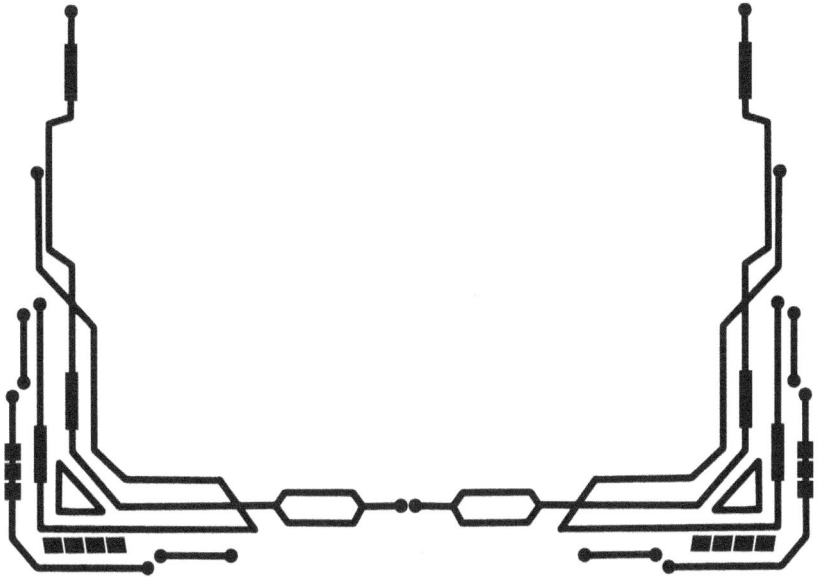

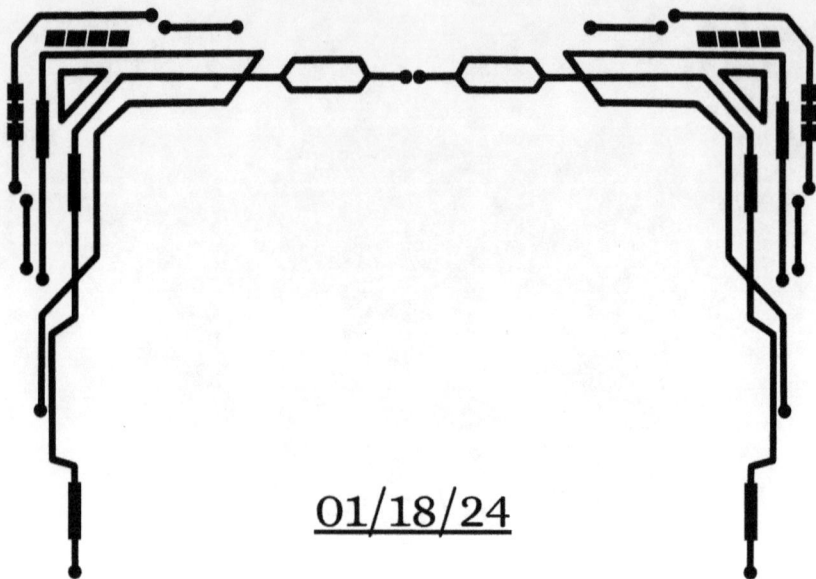

<u>01/18/24</u>

from a tiny sprout
there is a beautiful plant
where is my lighter

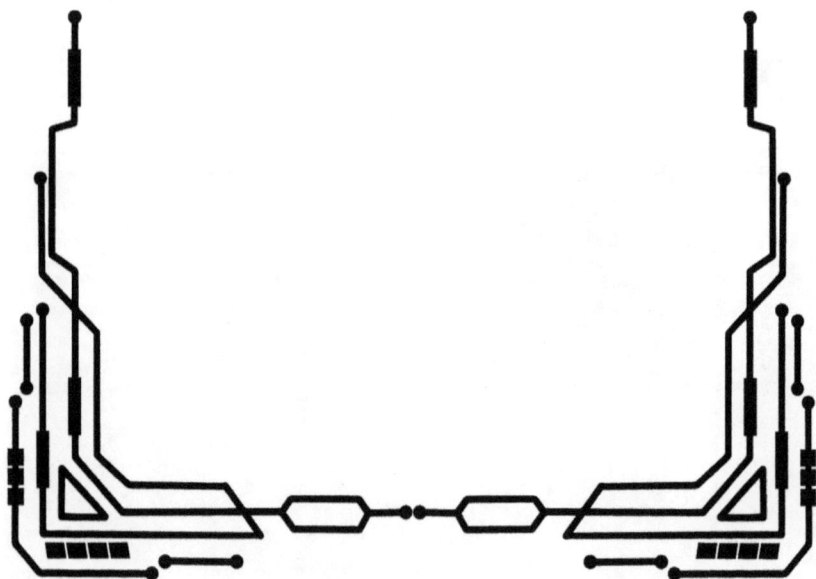

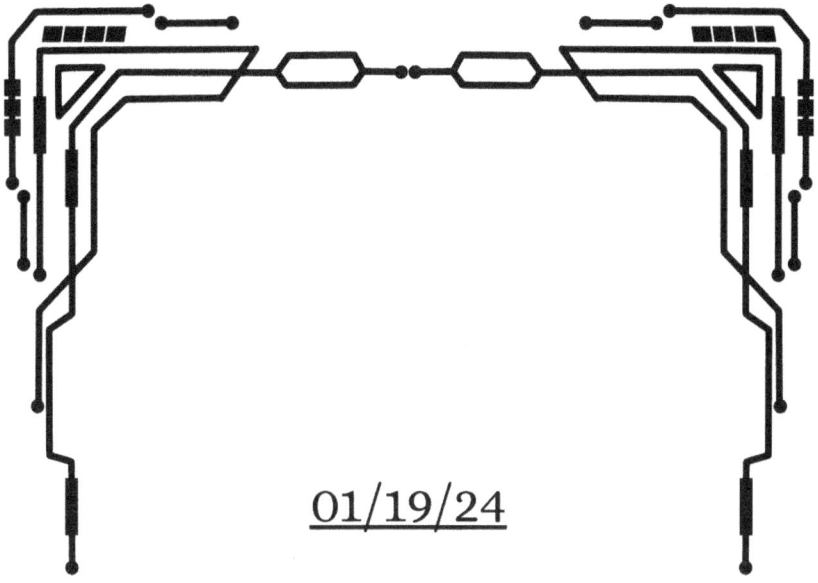

<u>01/19/24</u>

someday in this town
a baby mountain lion
will be the mayor

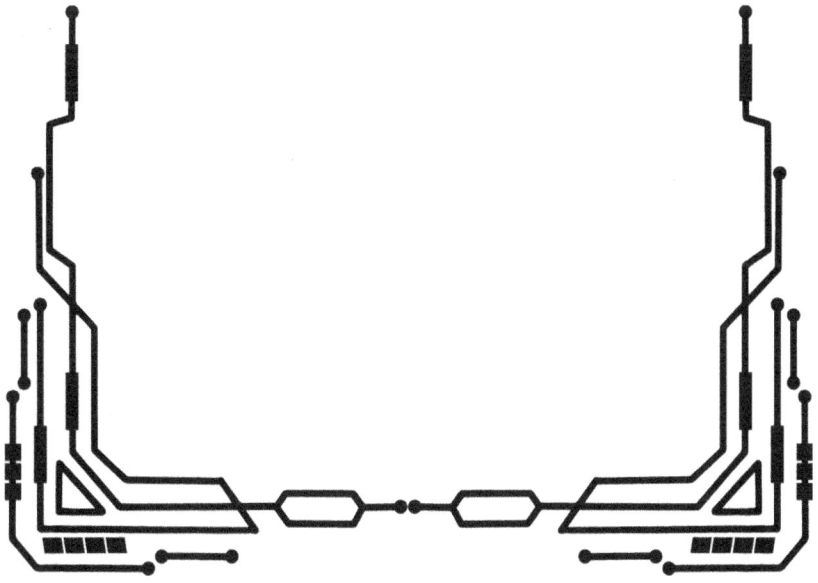

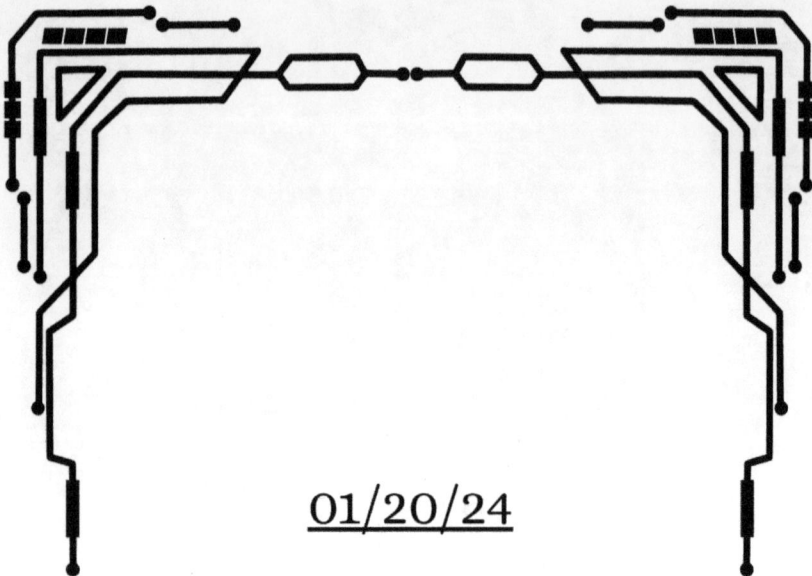

<u>01/20/24</u>

there's a secret club
where the frogs go in winter
a warm place indeed

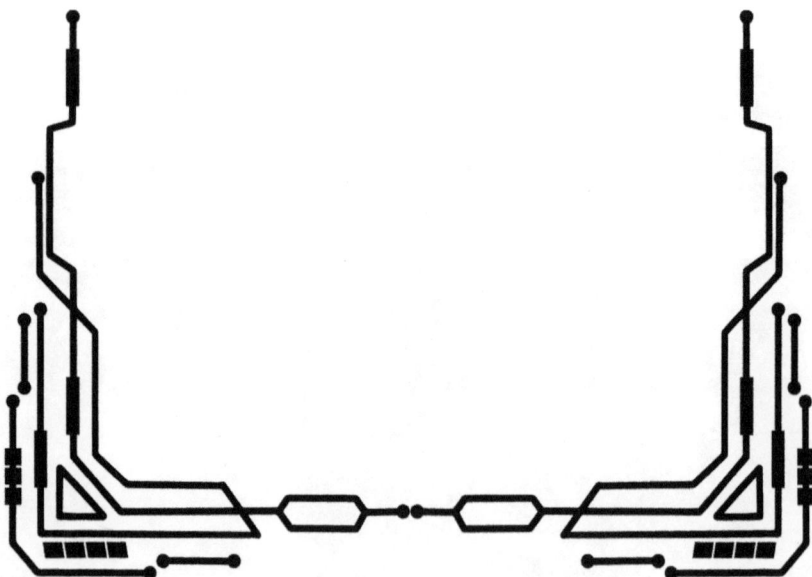

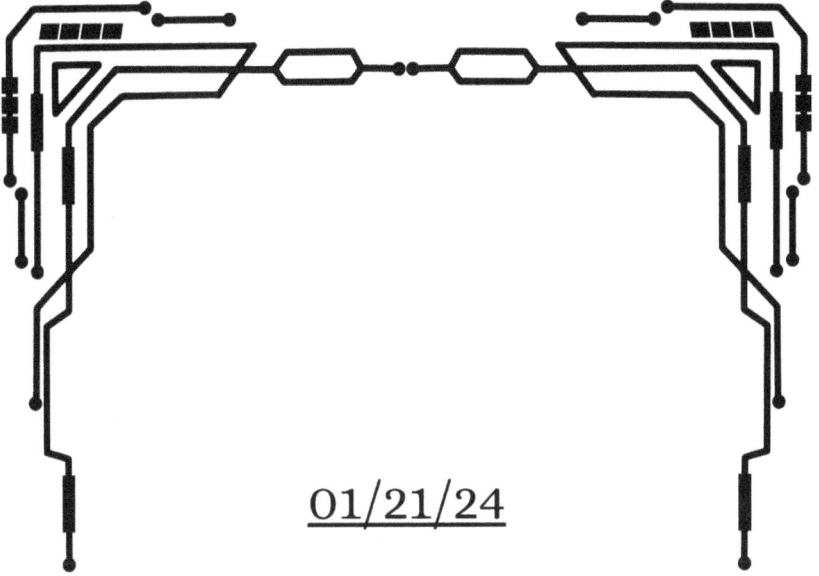

01/21/24

today feels a bit
like that lonely fallen branch
dead and brown and cold

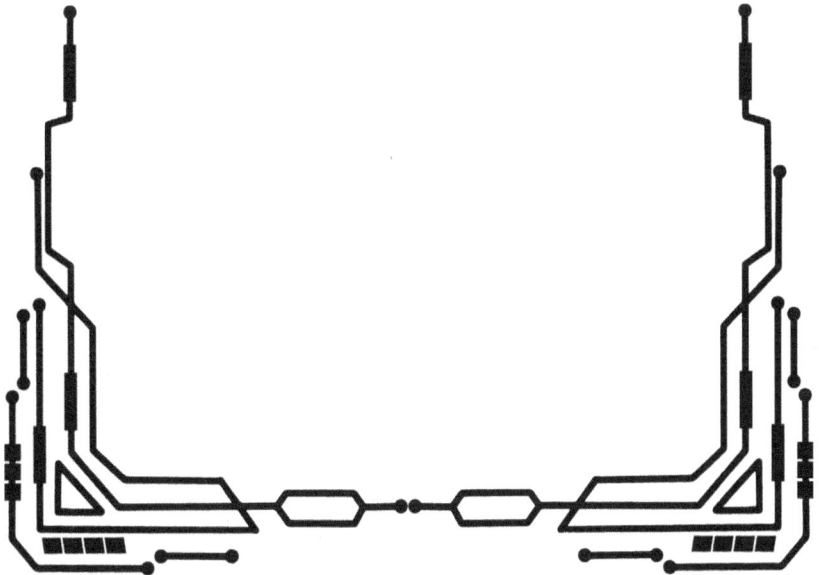

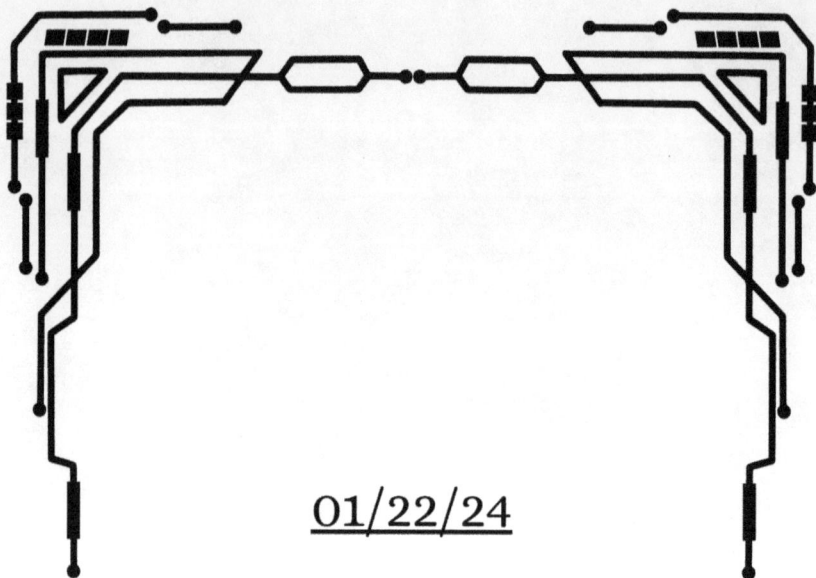

<u>01/22/24</u>

looking wet outside
let the nacho fountain rain
take the chip and dip

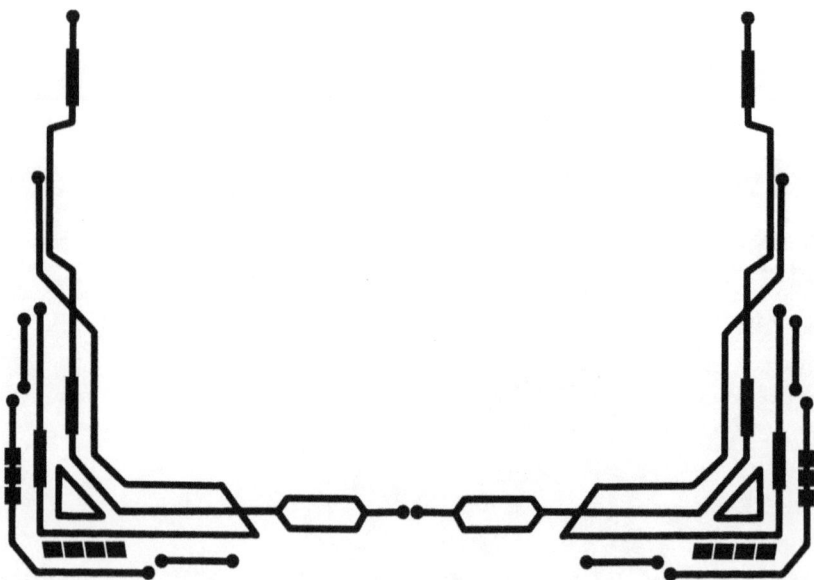

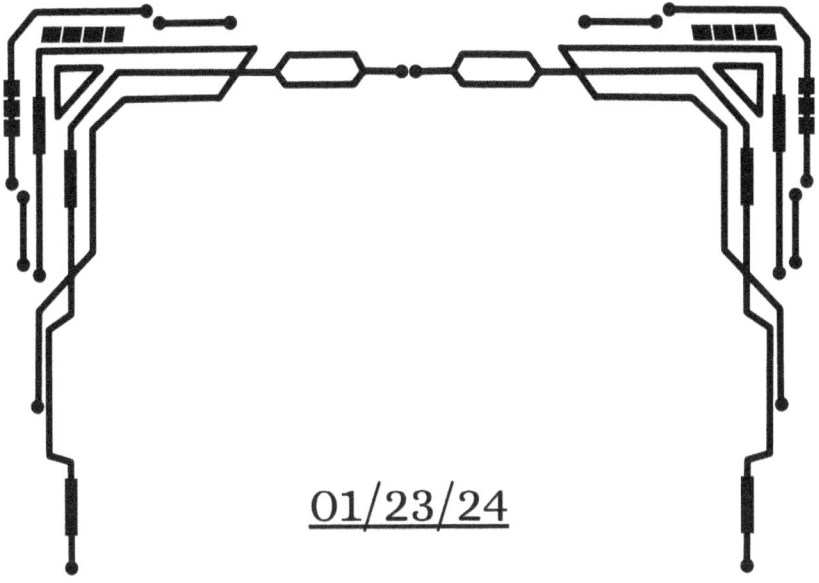

<u>01/23/24</u>

it looks delicious
cosmonaut candy bar sky
i want to go there

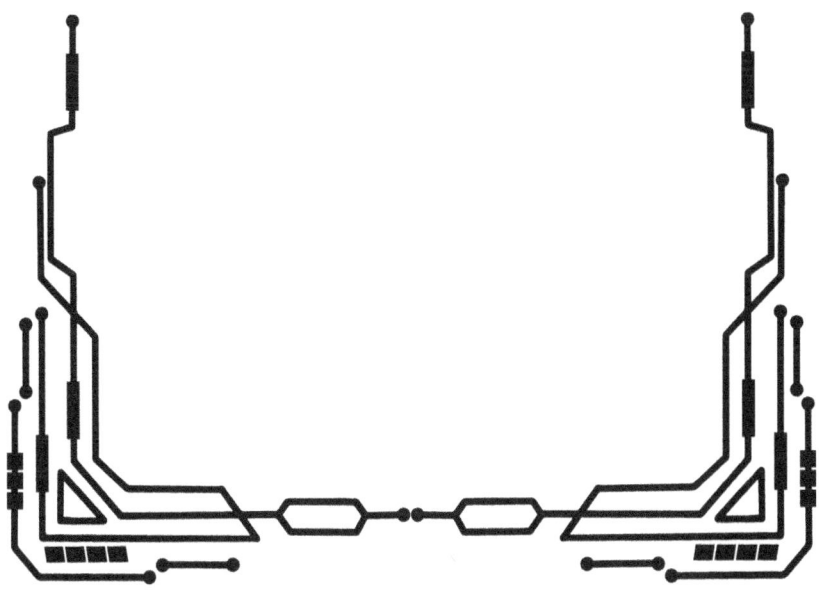

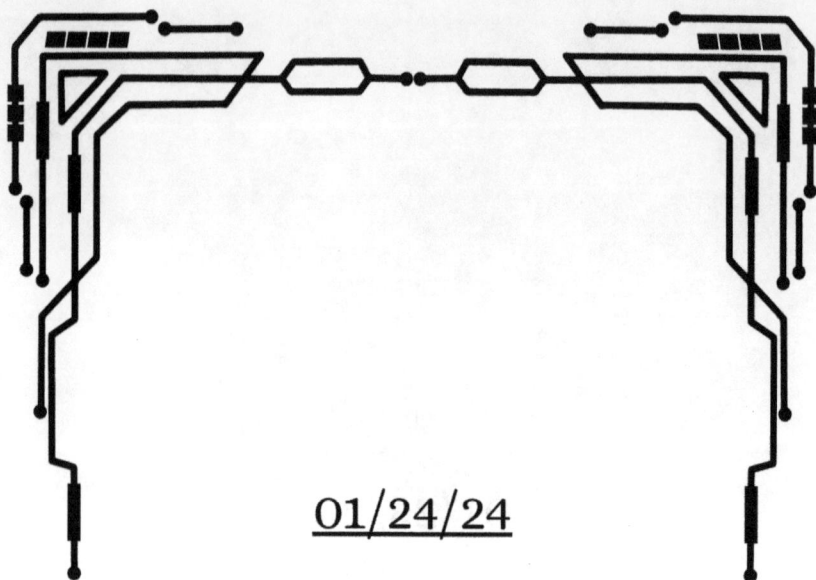

<u>01/24/24</u>

proper equipment
letter writing shower time
the paper towel

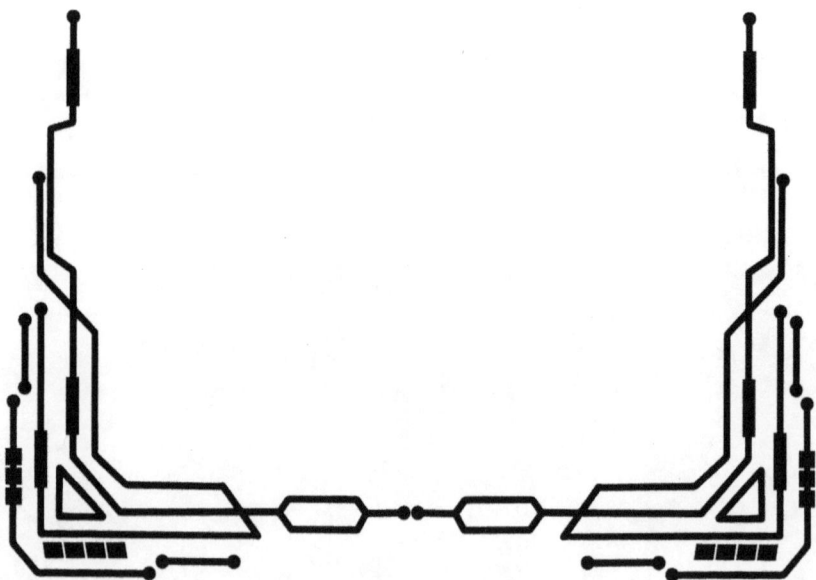

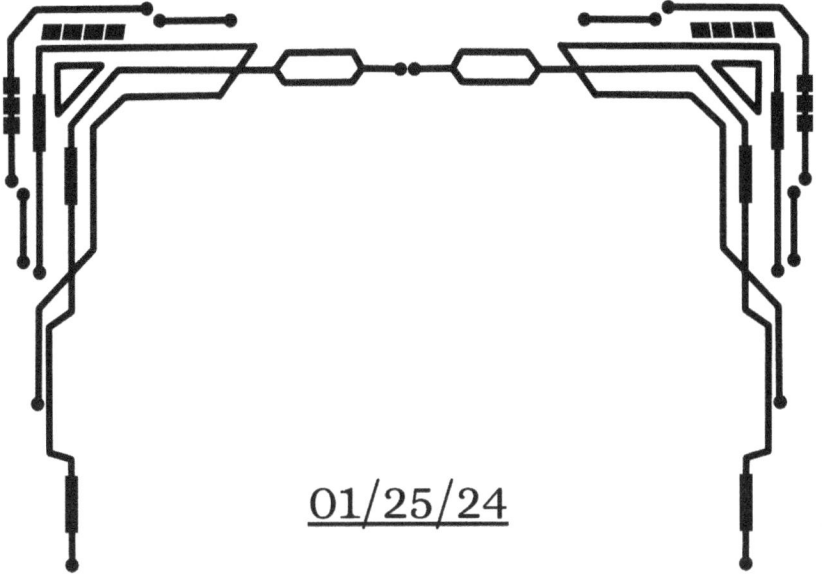

<u>01/25/24</u>

little italy
macaroni con queso
little mexico

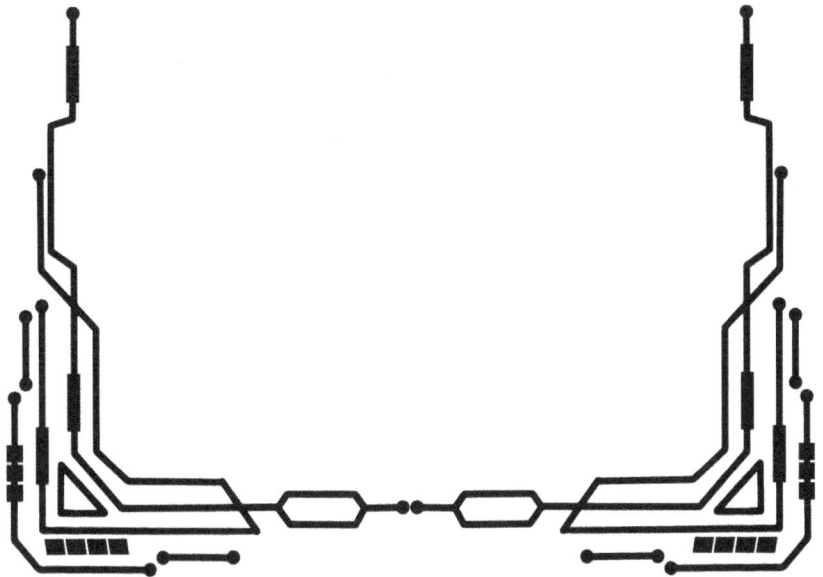

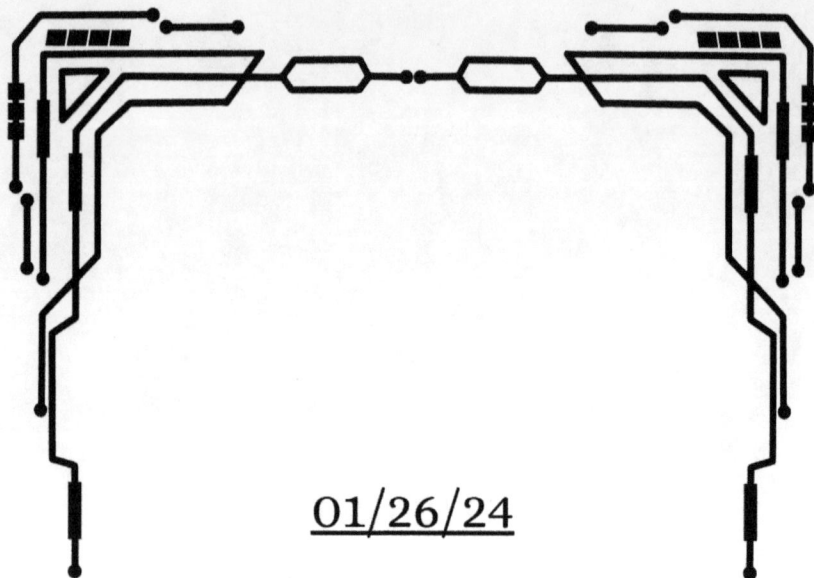

<u>01/26/24</u>

now it is over
at the end of everything
there is only dark

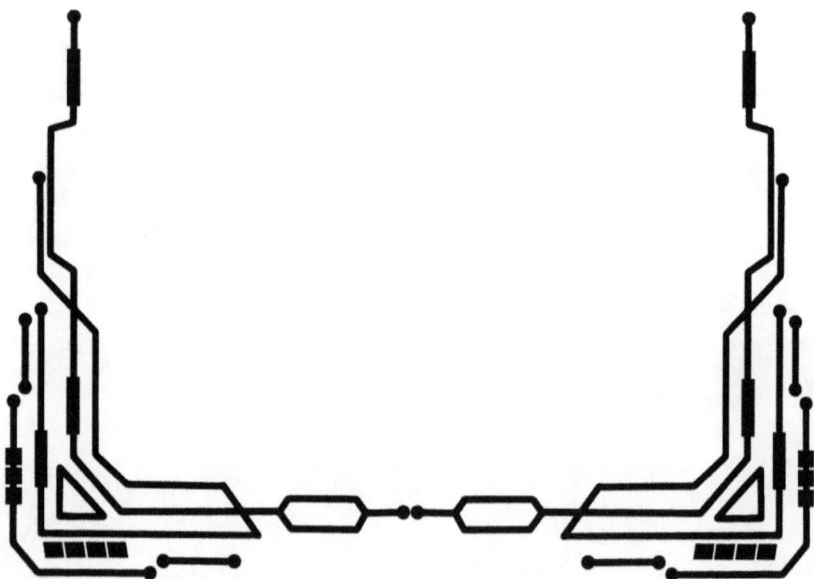

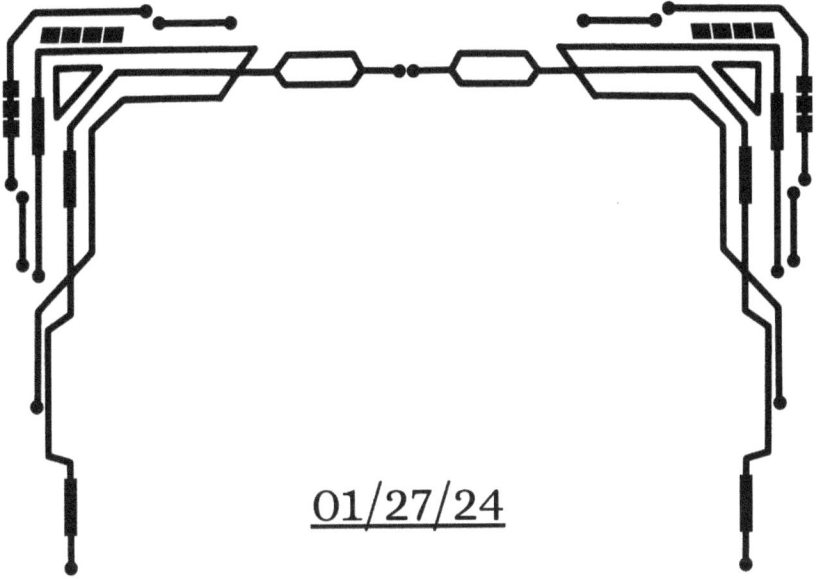

<u>01/27/24</u>

off to work again
i don't want to anymore
must win powerball

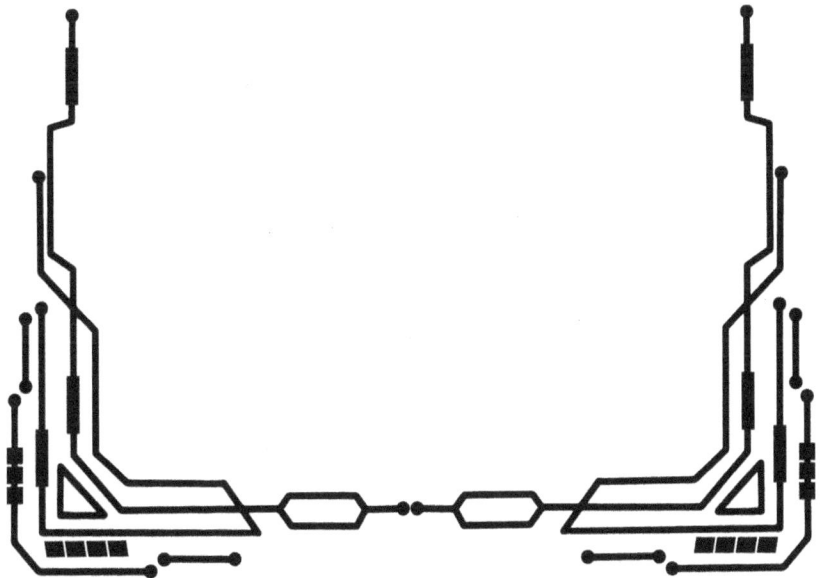

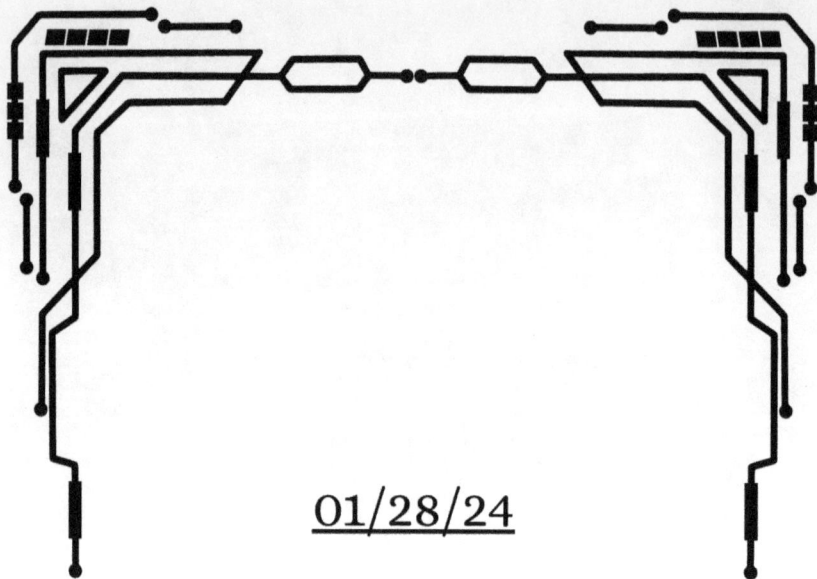

<u>01/28/24</u>

seems like there is some
suspicious activity
going on in here

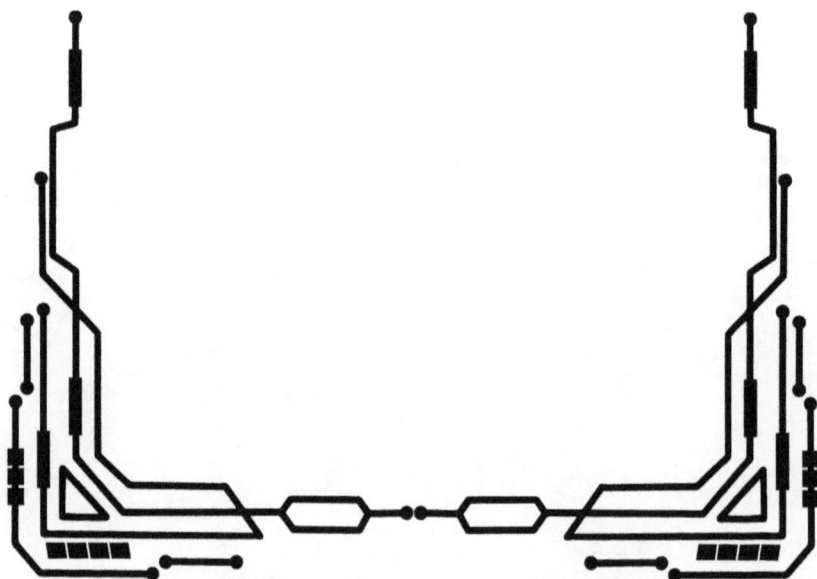

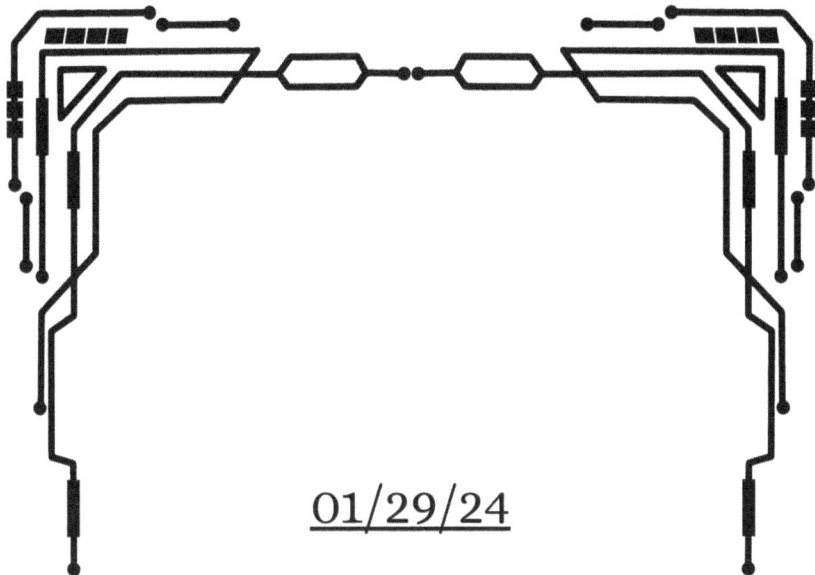

<u>01/29/24</u>

what to do today
sixty in january
sit on the front steps

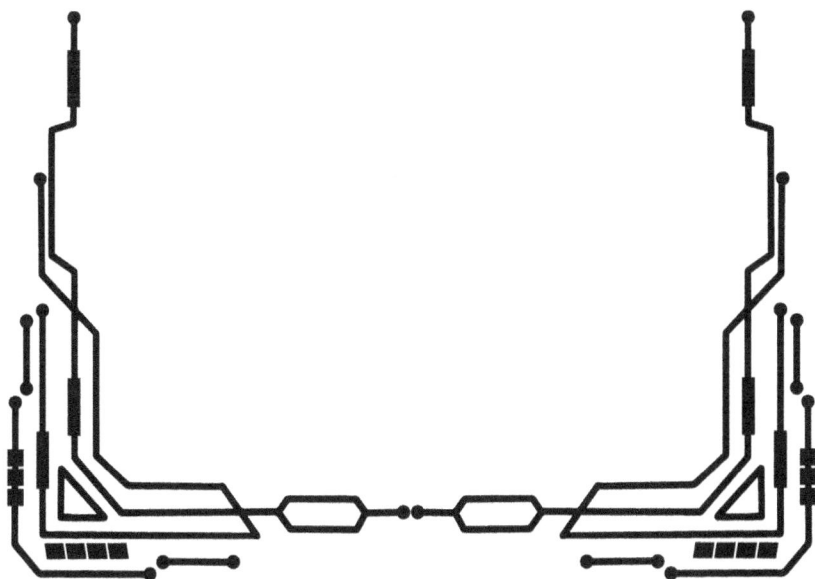

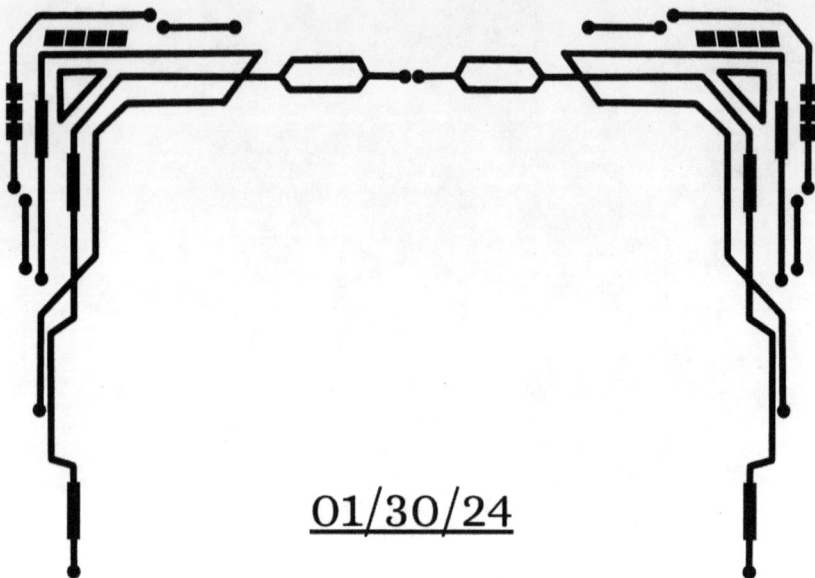

<u>01/30/24</u>

just got shot by cops
it's mayhem in the city
here in los santos

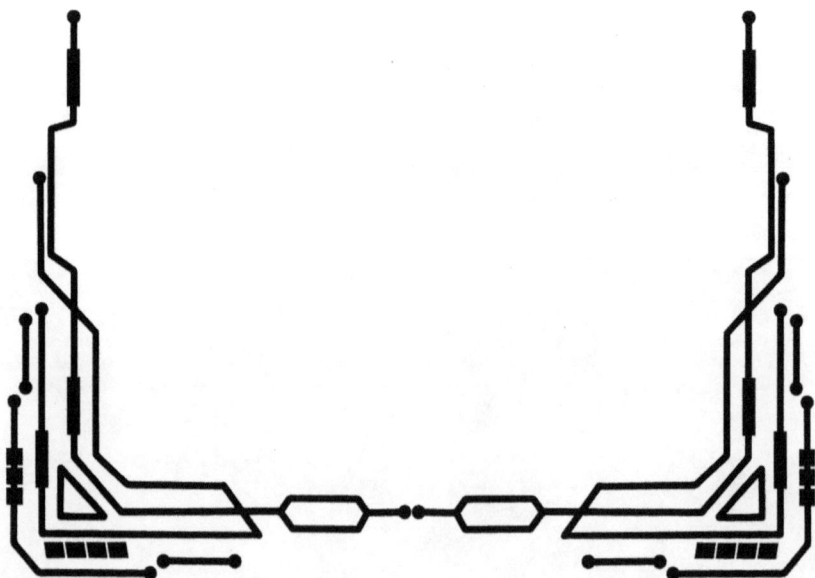

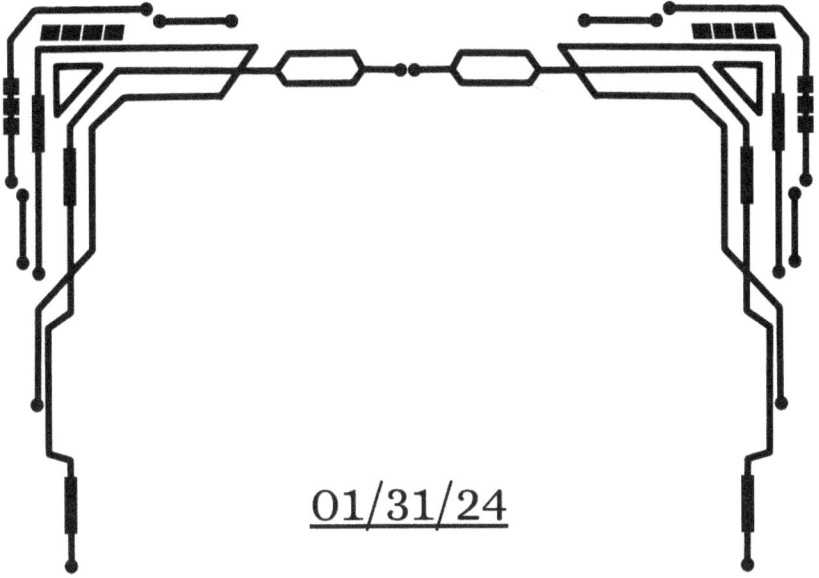

<u>01/31/24</u>

uncertainty now
predicted expectations
always a crossroads

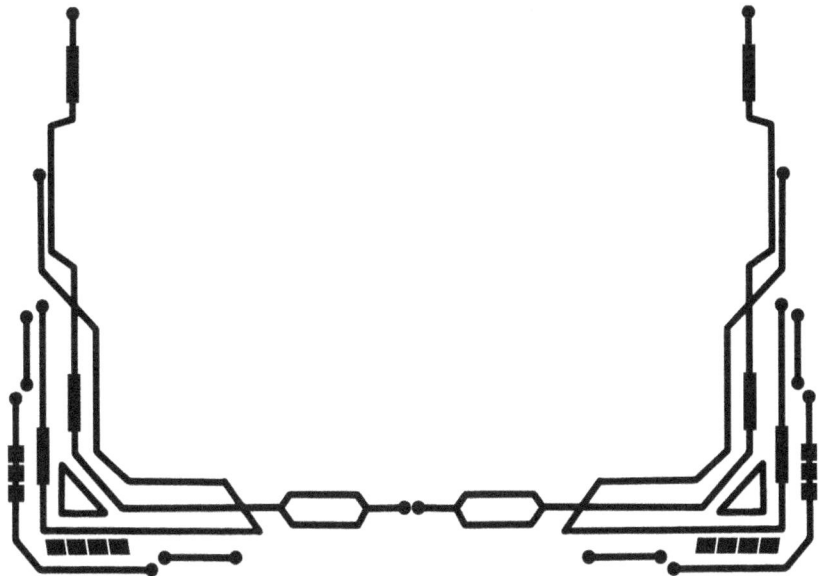

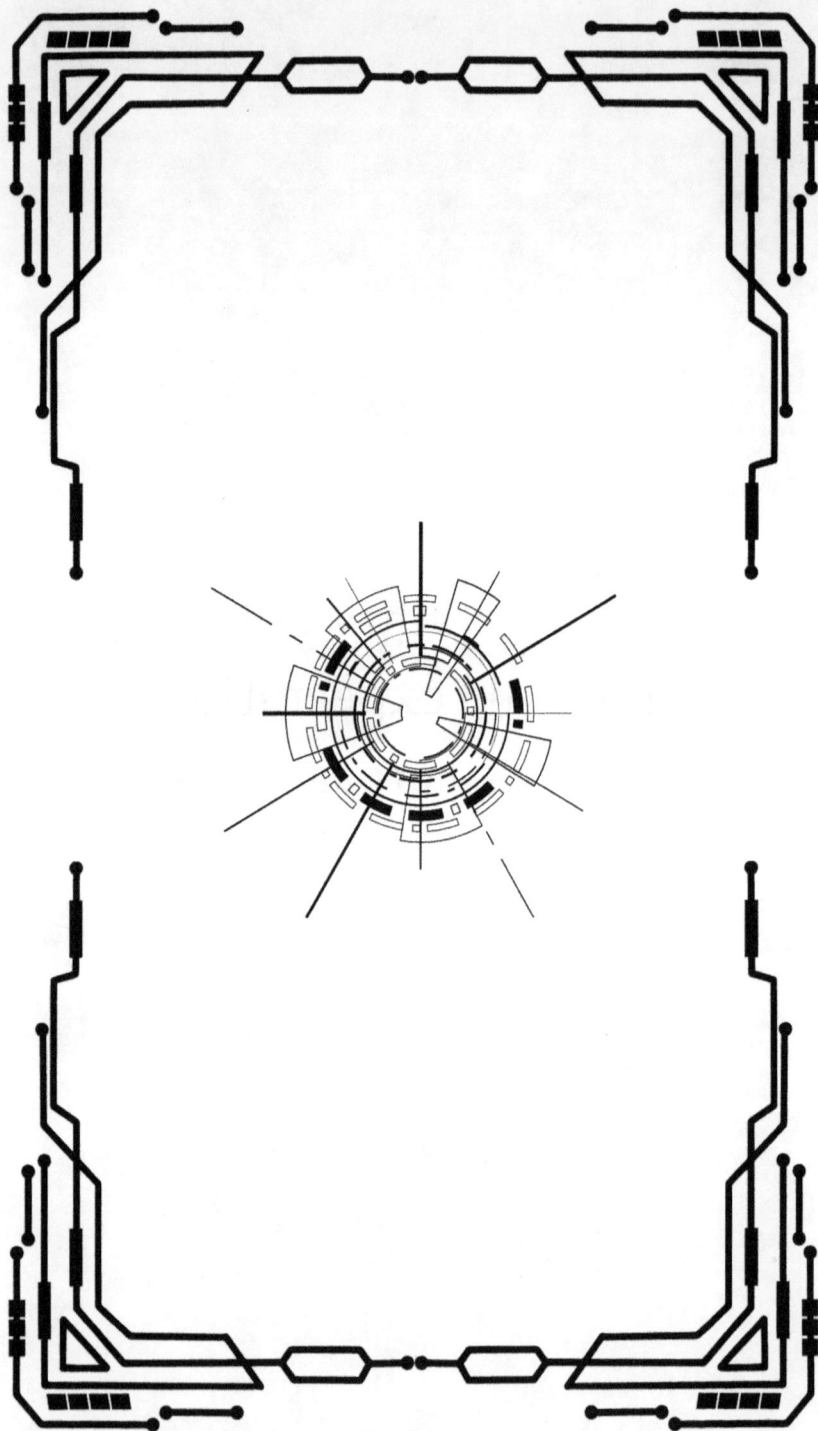

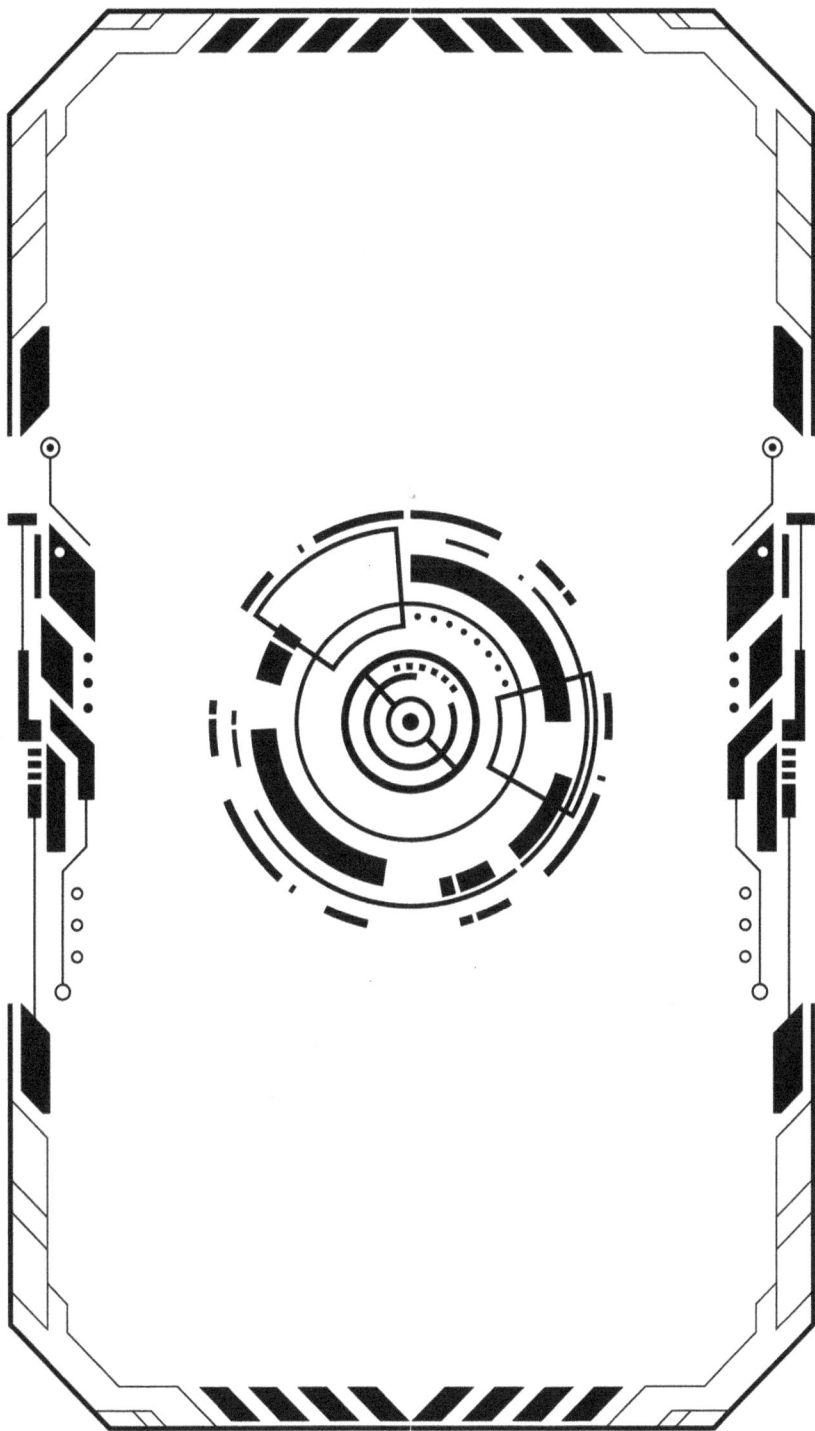

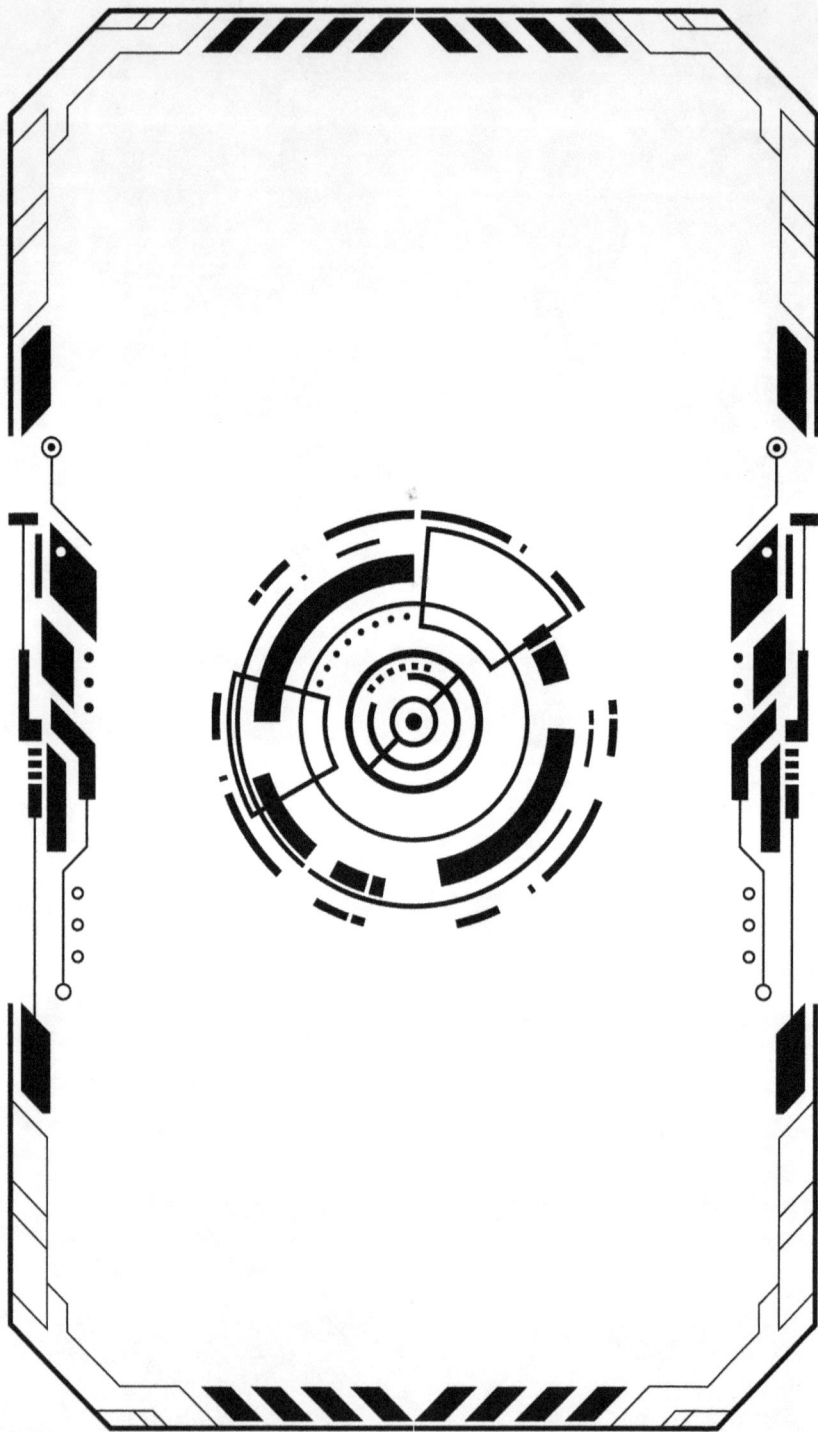

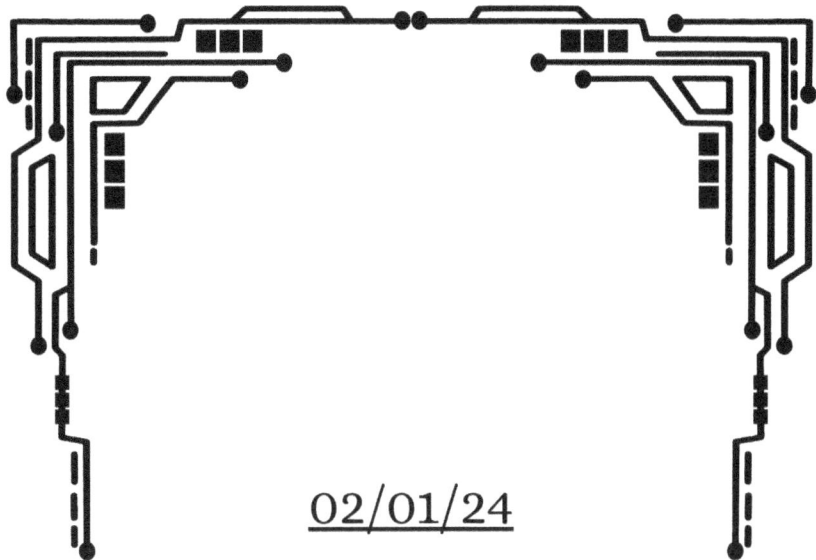

<u>02/01/24</u>

it's time for some toast
would you like jelly or jam
i'll give you a hint

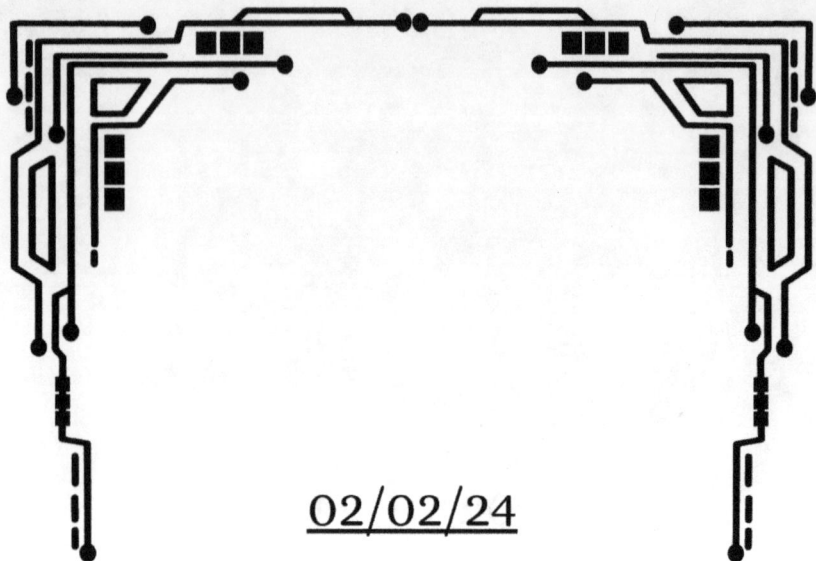

<u>02/02/24</u>

it's dark and cold now
this is my least favorite month
to do anything

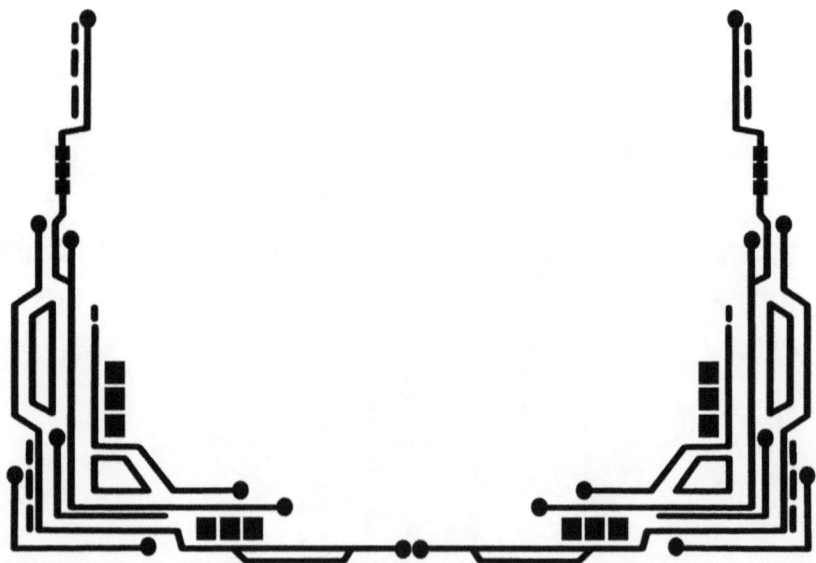

<u>02/03/24</u>

shimmering and white
crystals hanging on the tree
a living snow globe

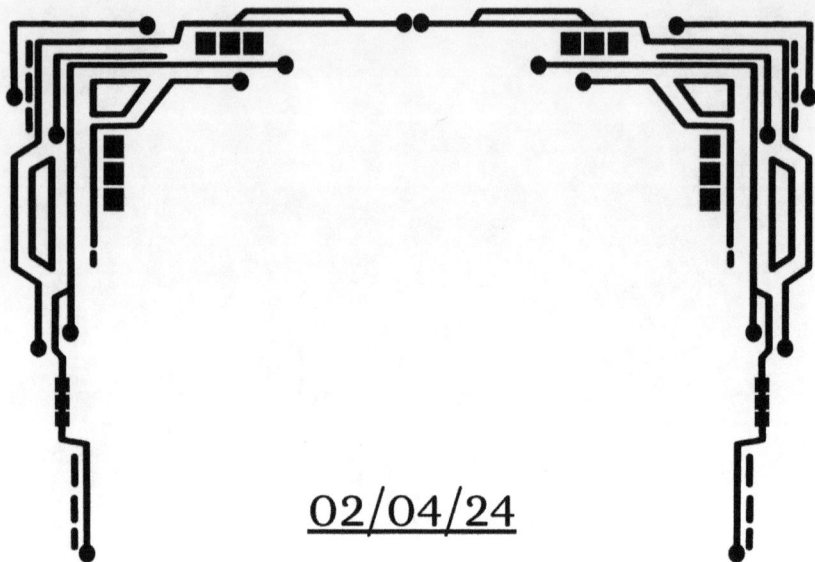

<u>02/04/24</u>

it gets dark early
i don't like it very much
in february

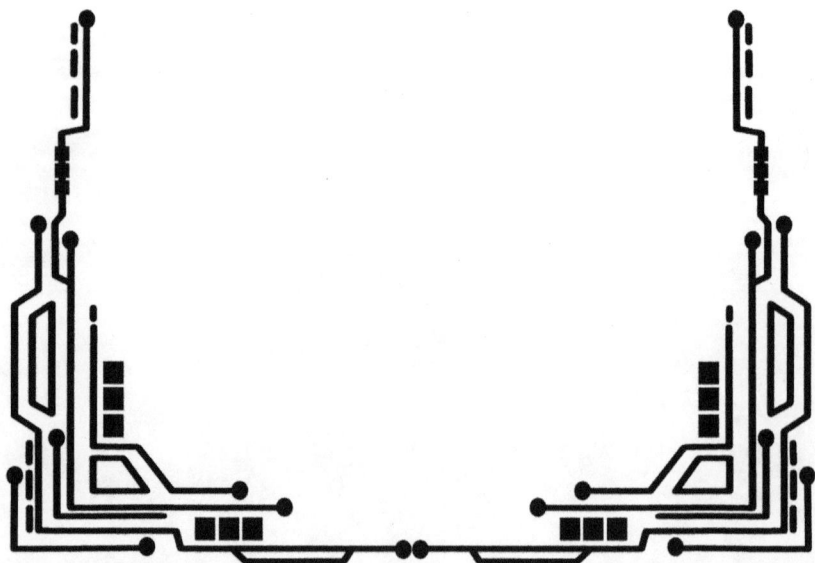

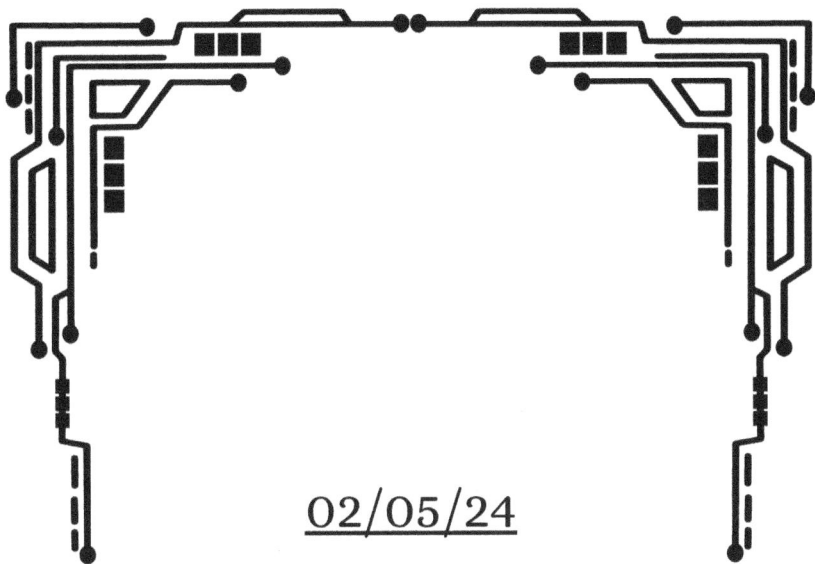

<u>02/05/24</u>

everything is dead
the brown compliments the gray
on the broken fence

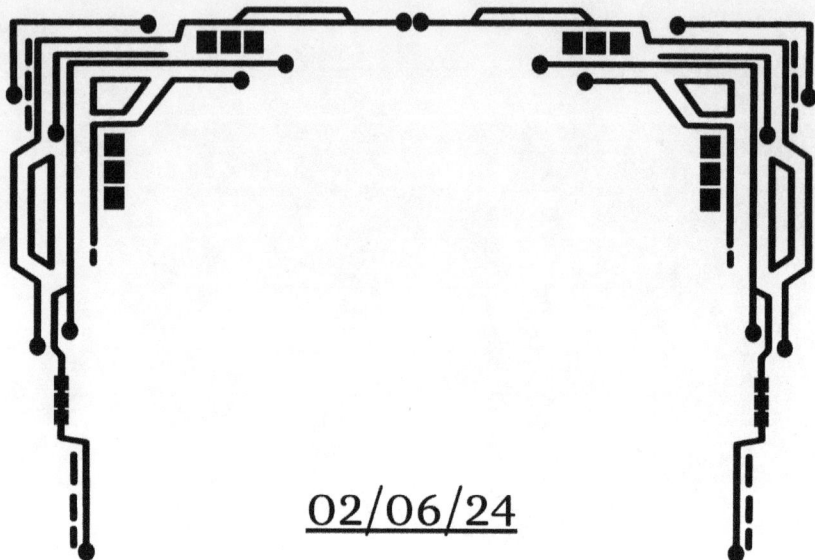

<u>02/06/24</u>

the wind only knows
where it's been as it flies by
momentarily

<u>02/07/24</u>

there used to be snow
and we used to dig tunnels
in the wintertime

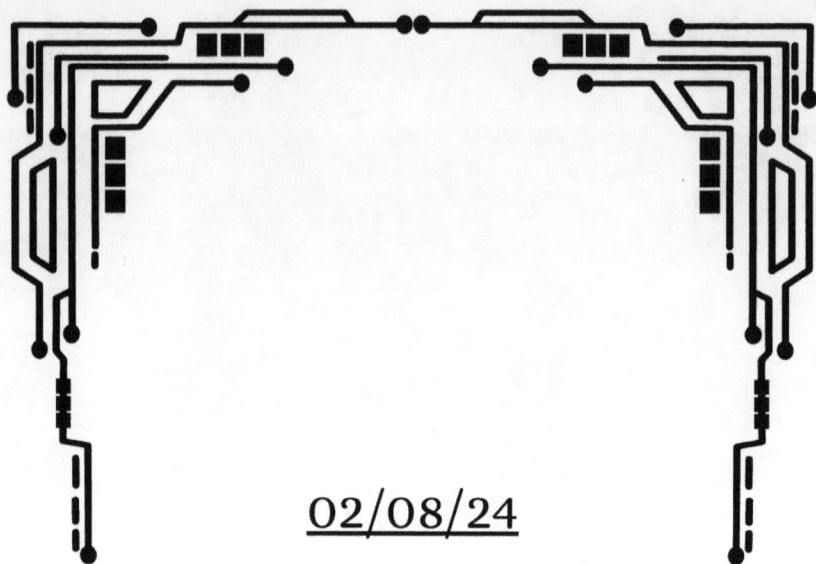

<u>02/08/24</u>

here we go again
the same dirty boulevard
someone should clean it

<u>02/09/24</u>

jacuzzi people
stir the human soup a bit
needs more paprika

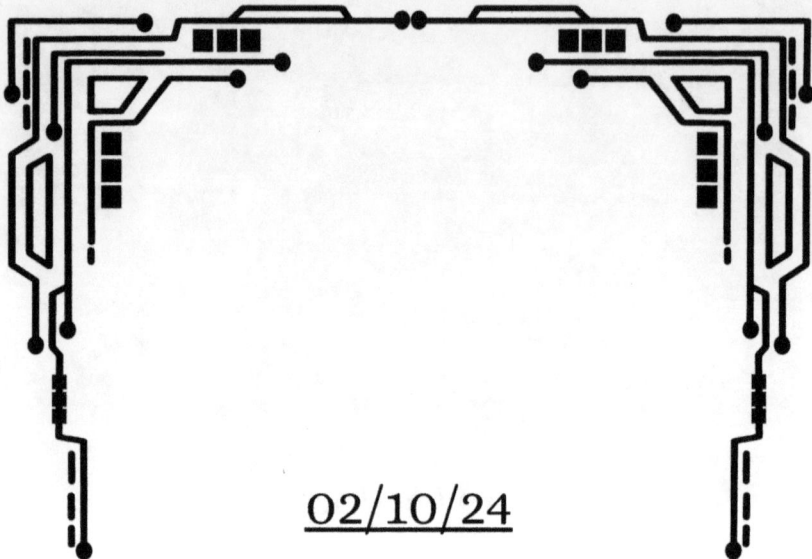

<u>02/10/24</u>

i don't like all these
decisions getting held up
in a committee

<u>02/11/24</u>

deep fried or pan fried
there is another option
within my skill set

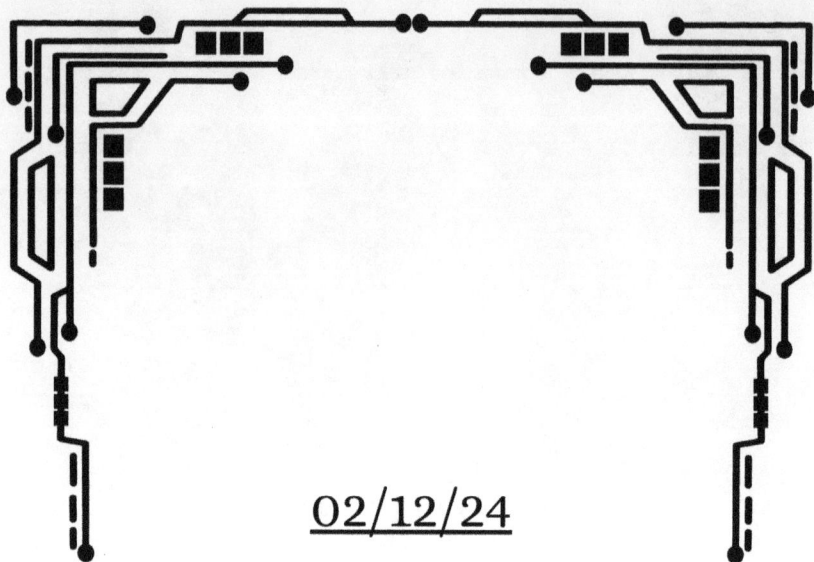

<u>02/12/24</u>

it just so happens
two times twelve is twenty four
and that is today

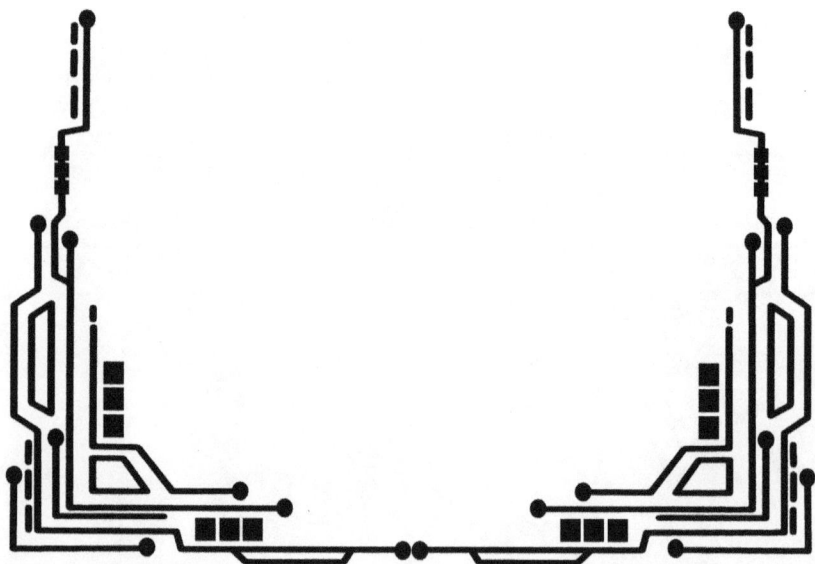

<u>02/13/24</u>

take a look at this
the curtains don't match in here
somebody fucked up

<u>02/14/24</u>

red roses are red
valentine's day is stupid
chocolate is ok

02/15/24

drink your water dude
push down into the dirt bed
grow little plant grow

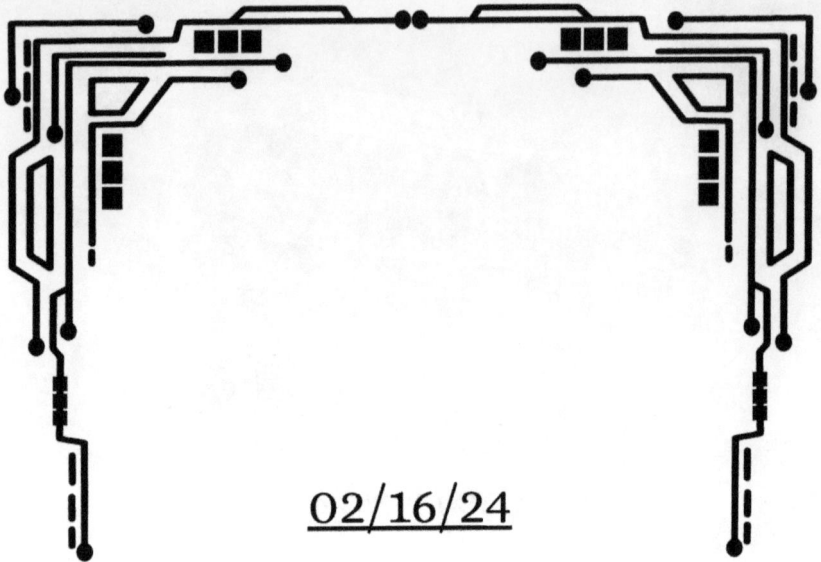

<u>02/16/24</u>

get the clam bucket
any day is a good day
for some fresh chowder

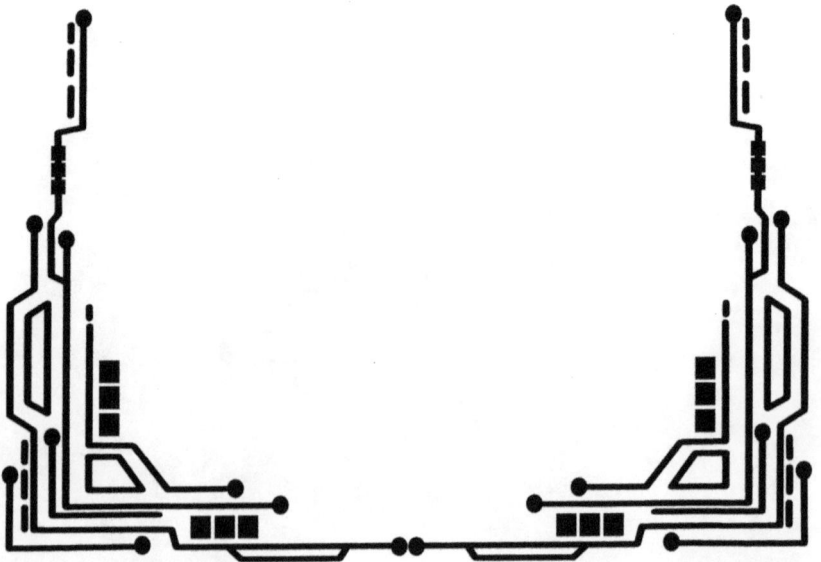

<u>02/17/24</u>

over the mountain
watercolors push the sun
into the morning

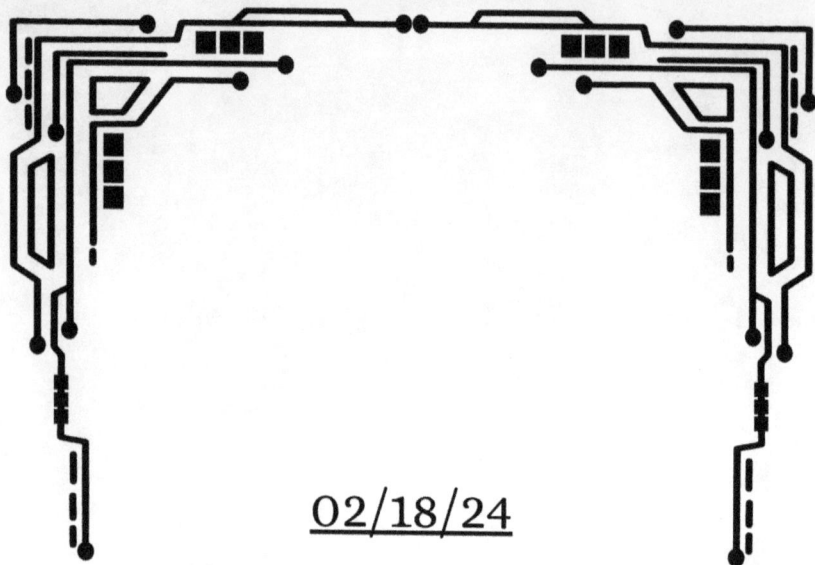

<u>02/18/24</u>

breath is cold and wet
disappearing icicle
dripping off tempo

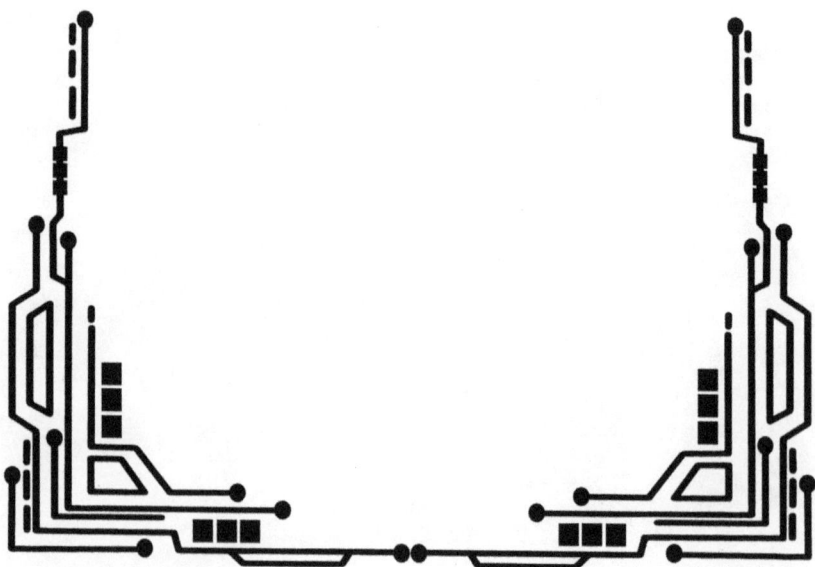

<u>02/19/24</u>

yes helen you can
have a dollop of cool whip
with your pecan pie

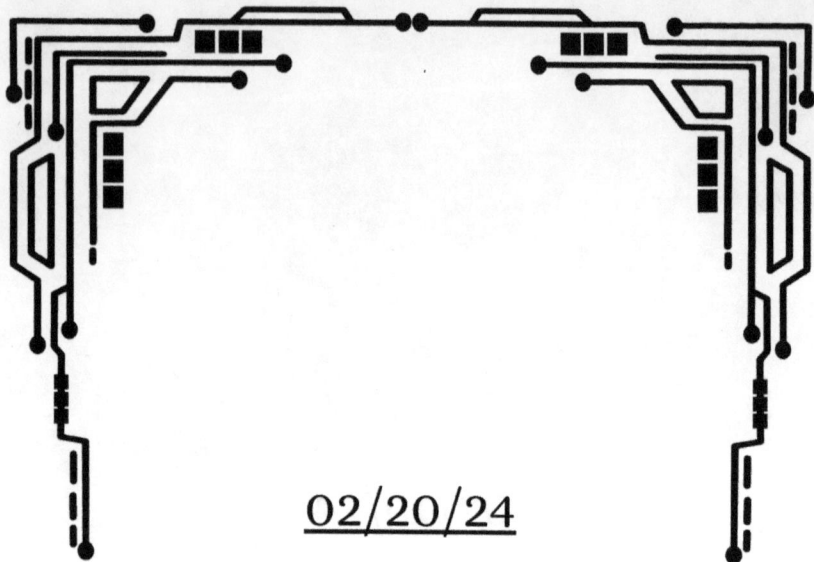

<u>02/20/24</u>

you are now aware
you only want it because
you can not have it

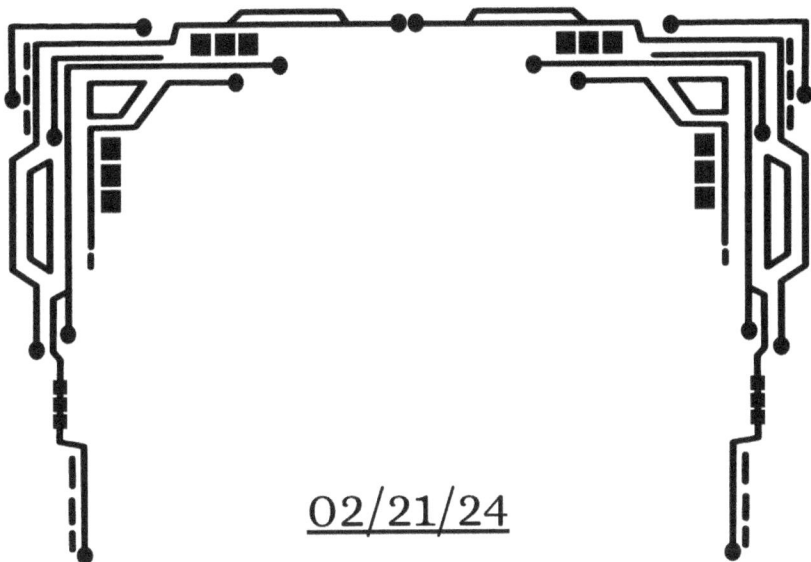

<u>02/21/24</u>

shadow people cry
listen close to hear the soft
whispers in the dark

<u>02/22/24</u>

is this over yet
almost time to wrap it up
haikus are stupid

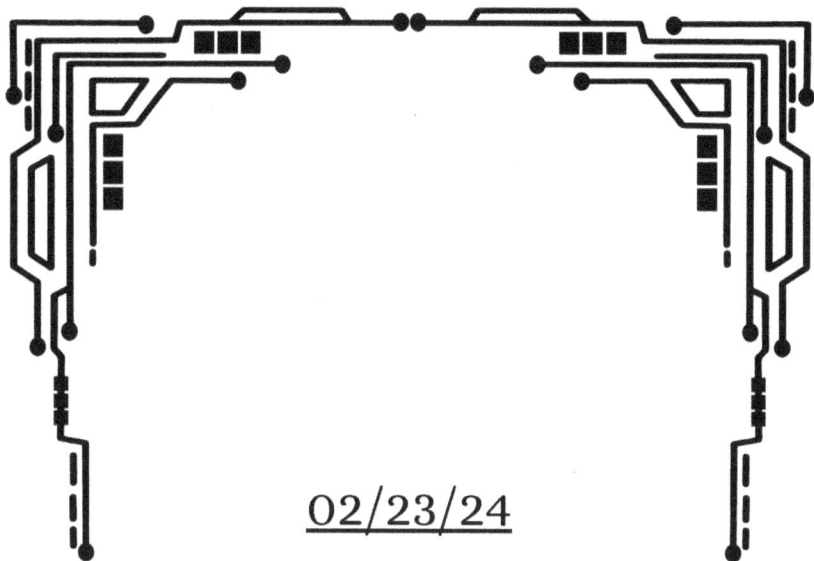

<u>02/23/24</u>

it's boring here now
things move slowly in the dark
in february

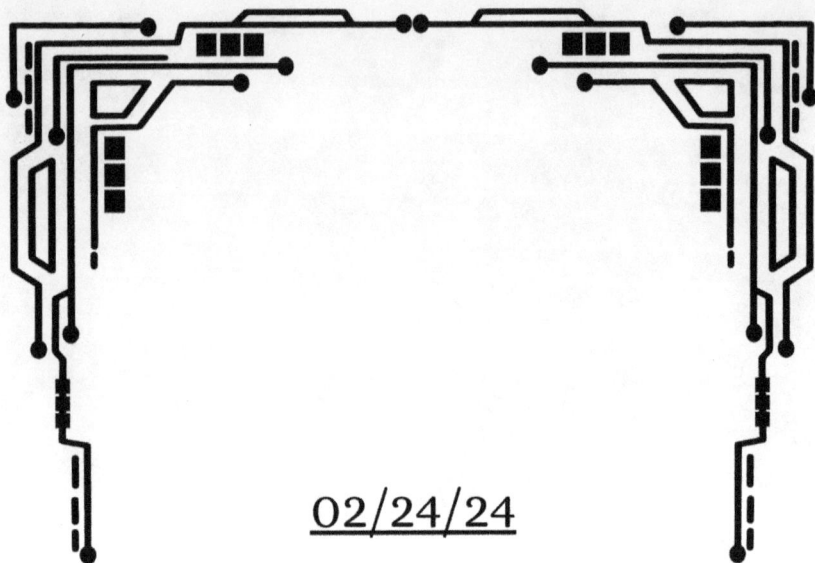

<u>02/24/24</u>

percussive weekend
with more emphasis indeed
on the twos and fours

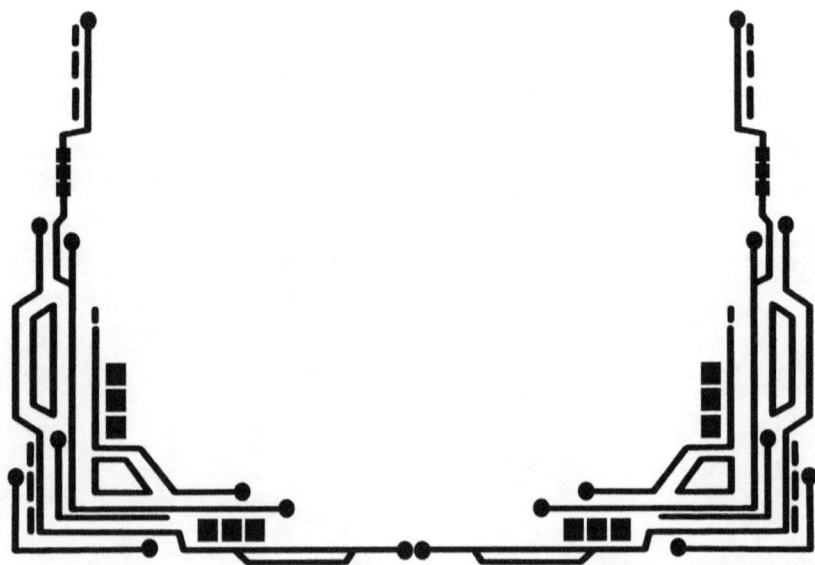

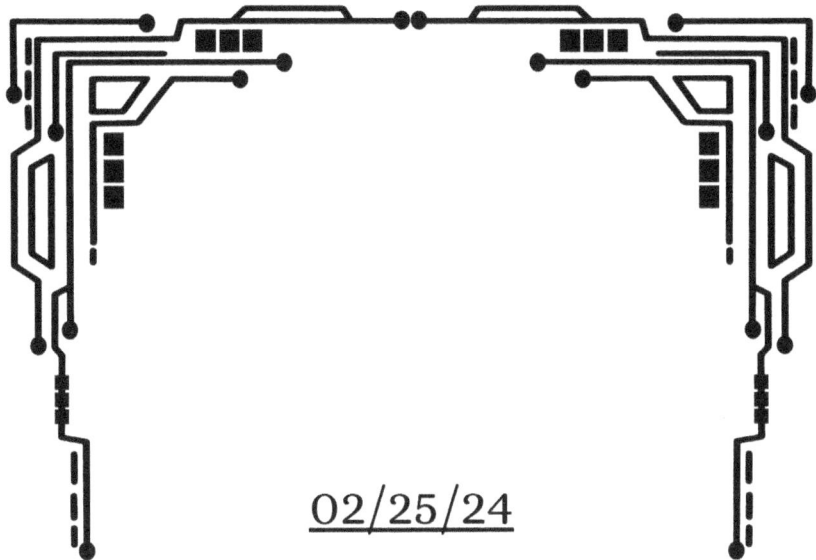

<u>02/25/24</u>

it's hard to daydream
when it's dark all of the time
so we have nightmares

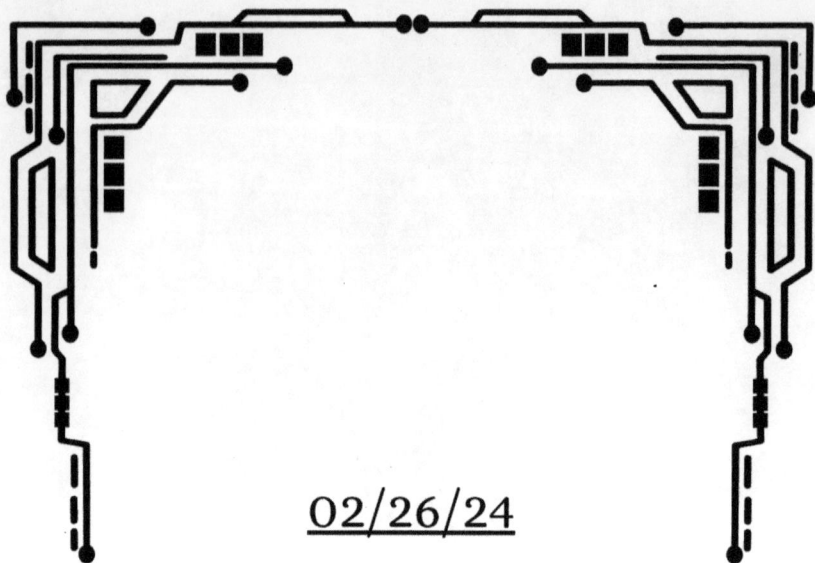

<u>02/26/24</u>

drifting from the north
where the cows eat their lunches
are the winds of shit

<u>02/27/24</u>

the end is in sight
i'm done with all these words now
one more month to go

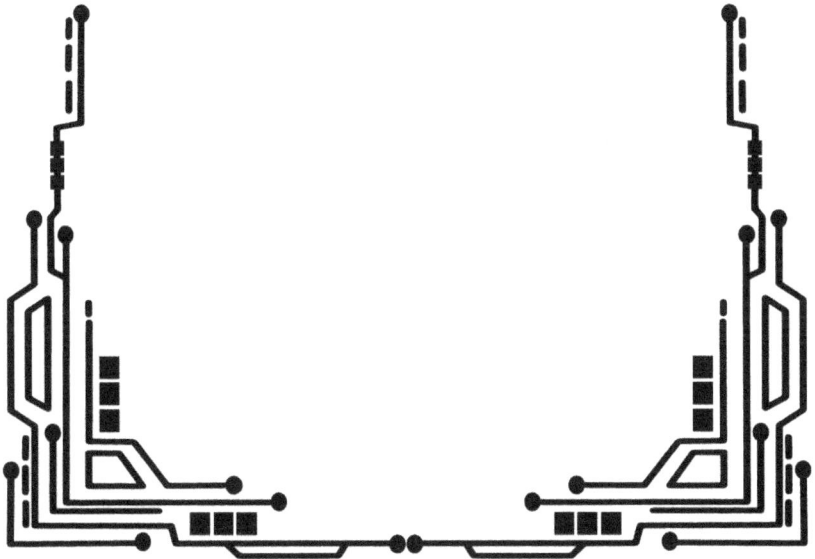

<u>02/28/24</u>

juicy flavor bombs
now i found them at safeway
golden berry snack

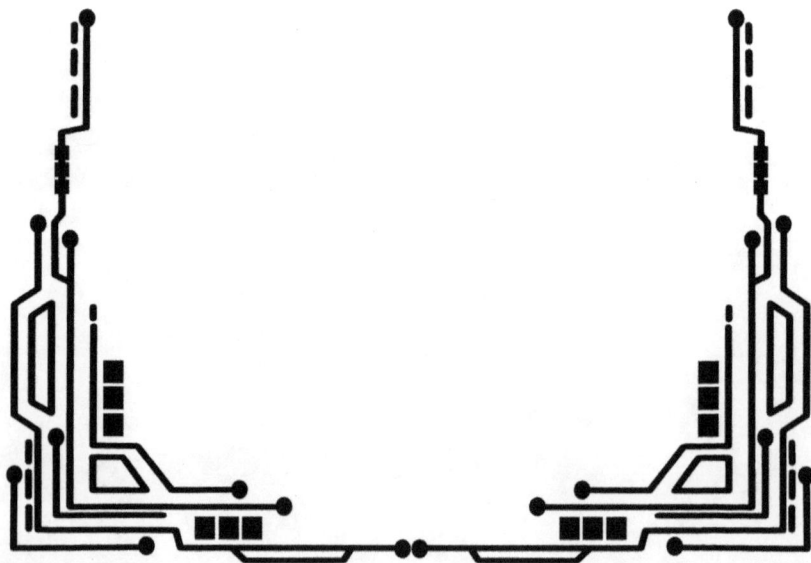

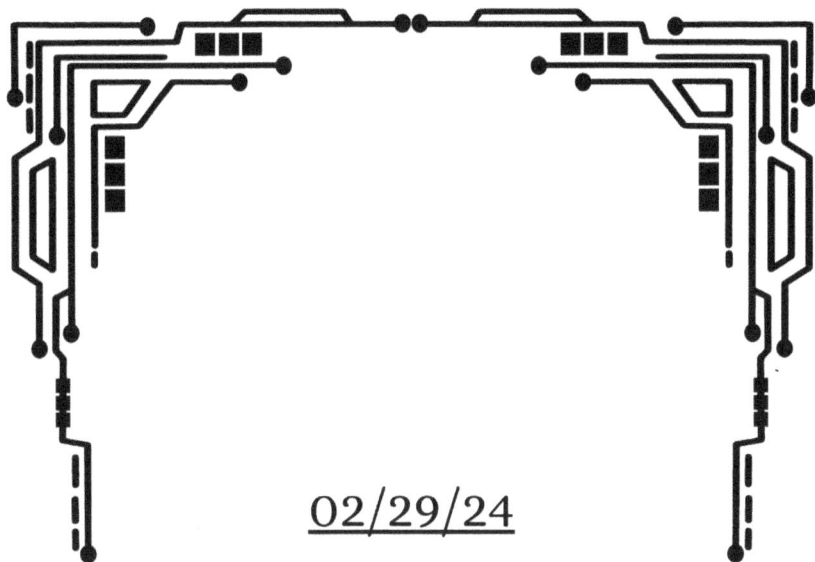

<u>02/29/24</u>

today is the day
final fantasy seven
on playstation five

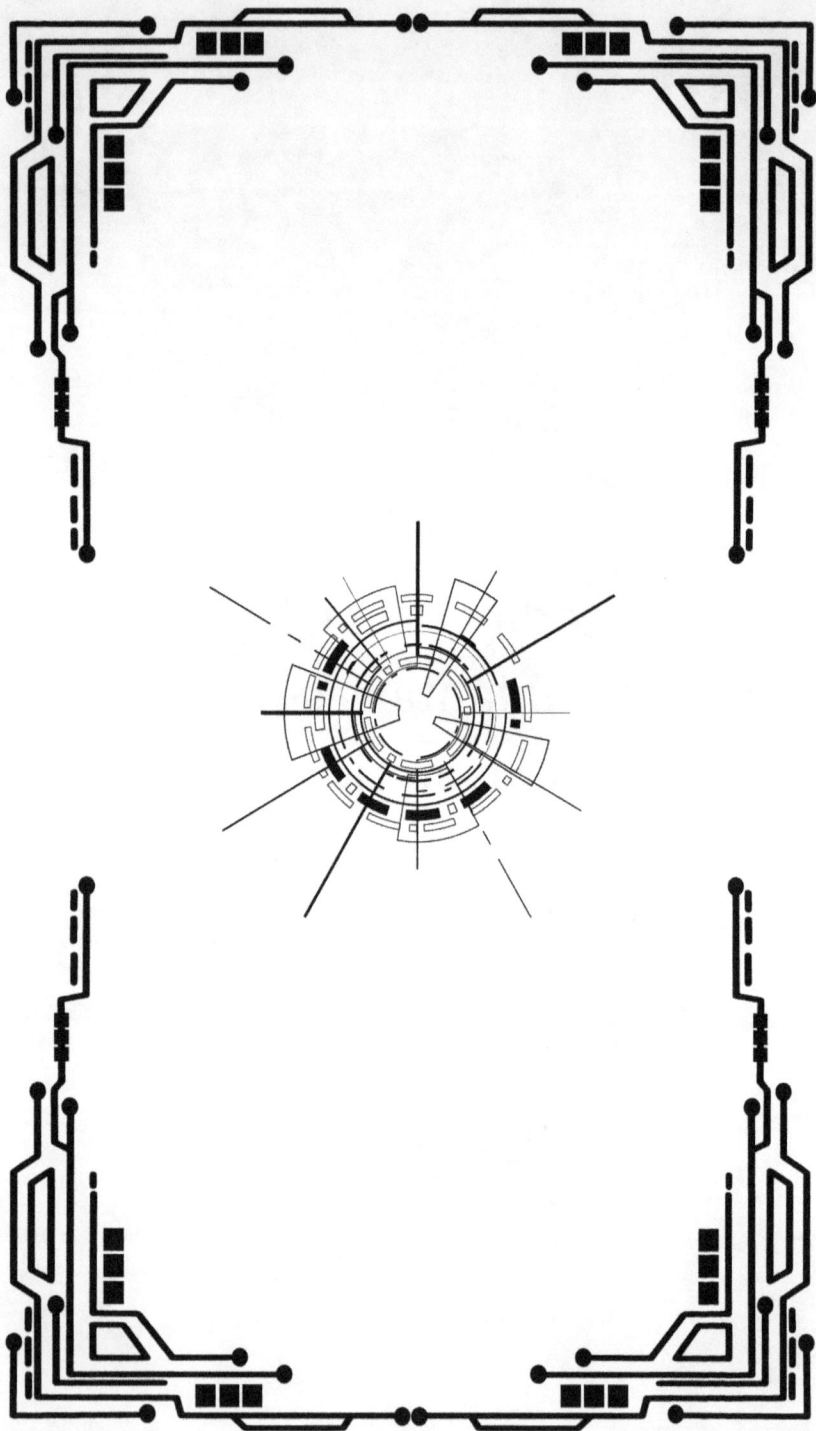

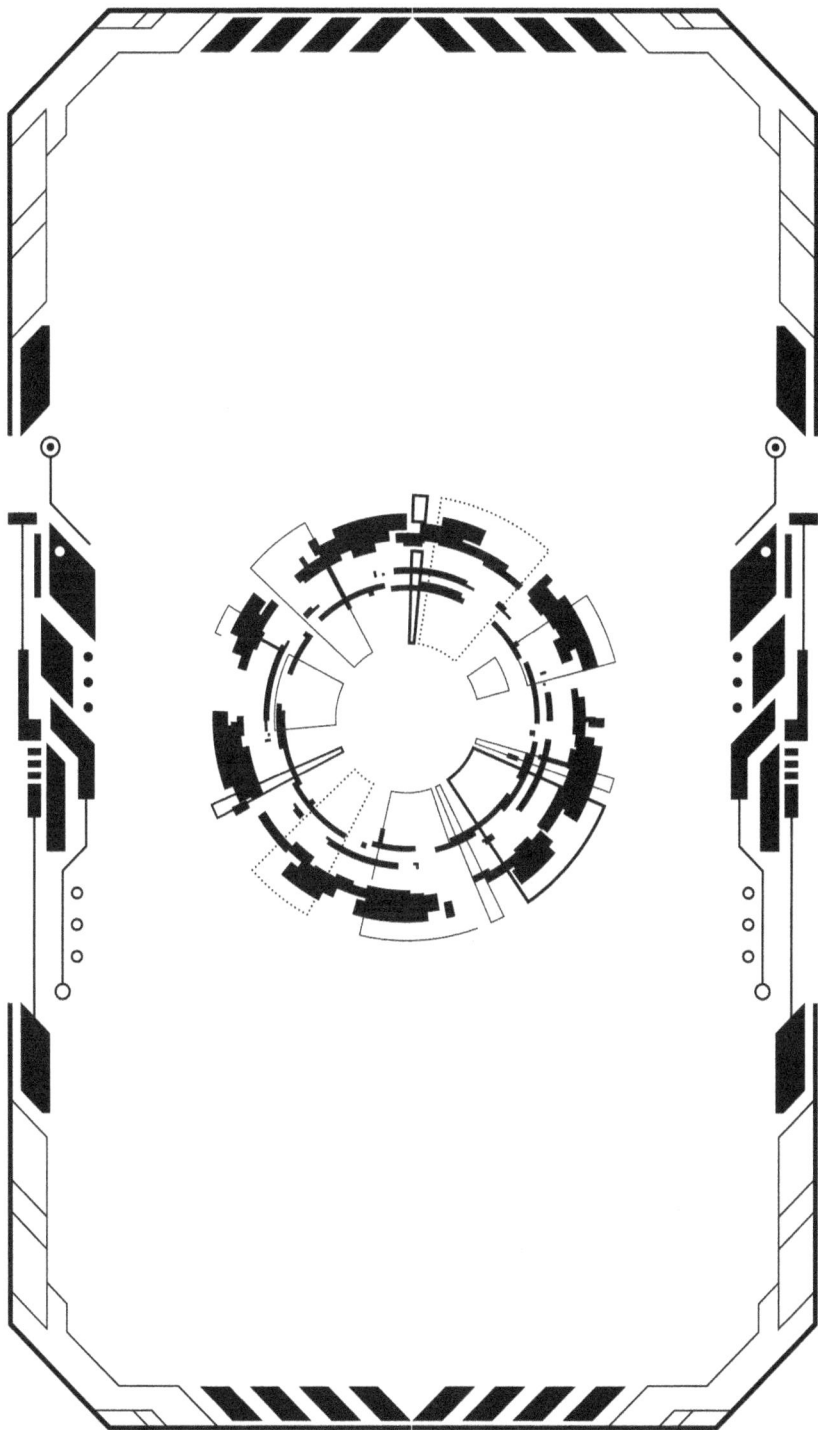

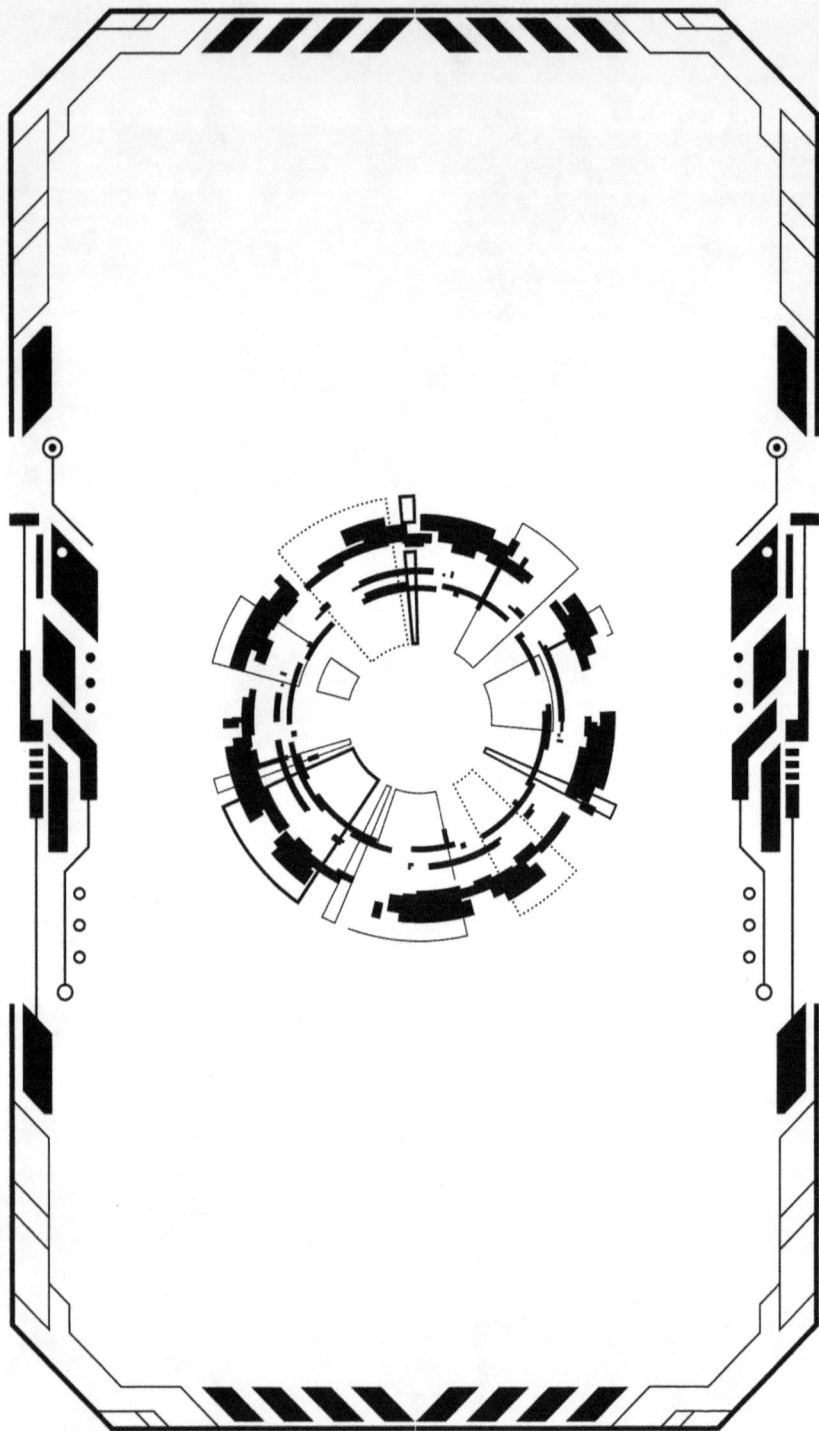

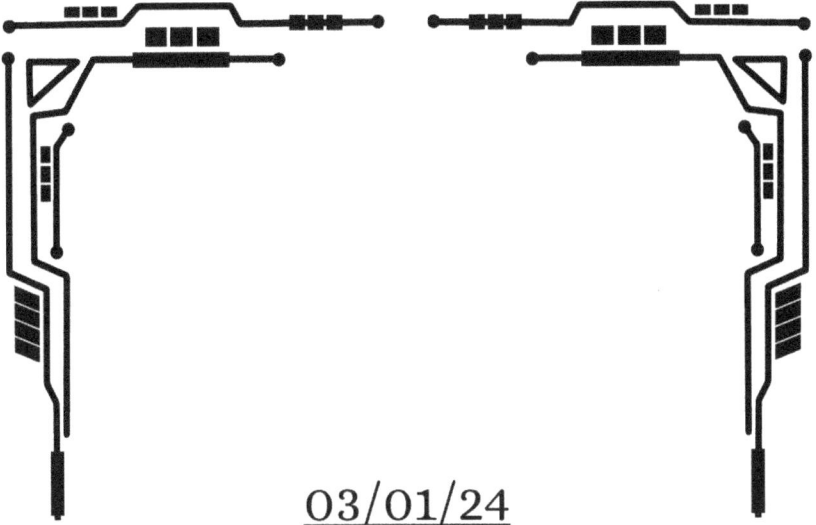

<u>03/01/24</u>

sunrise glowing fog
covering the mountain top
hiding in the clouds

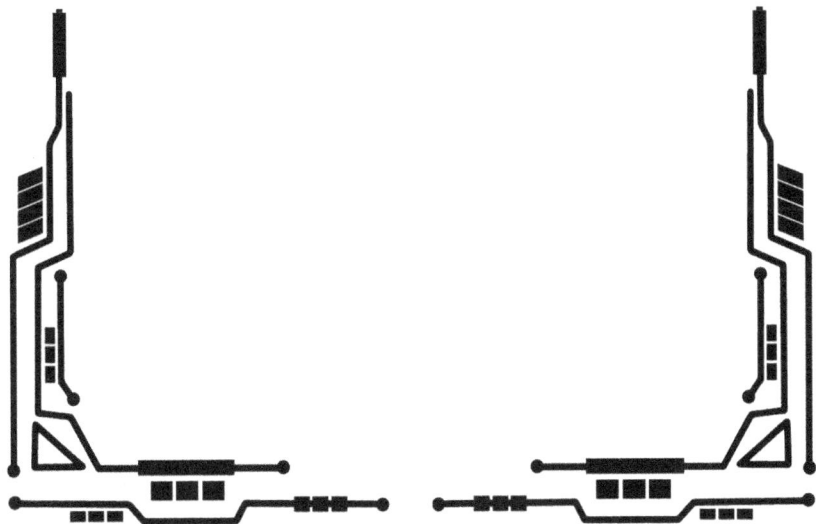

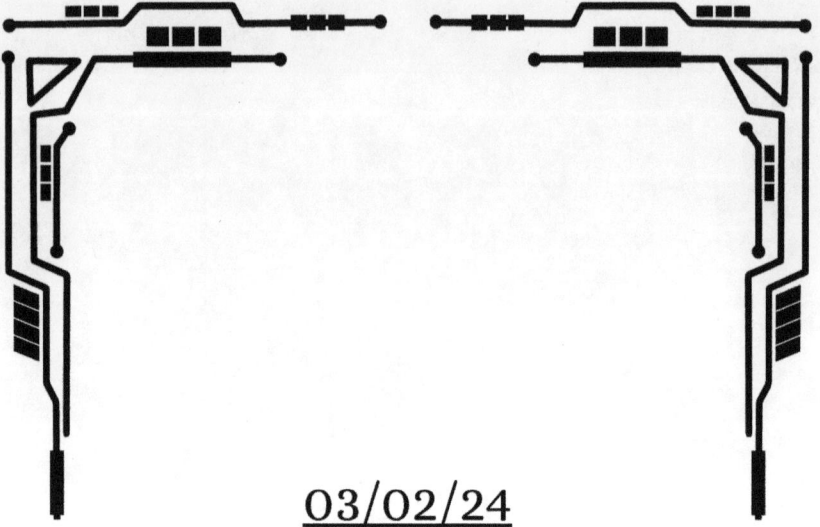

<u>03/02/24</u>

the last one was dumb
now this one will be better
than the other one

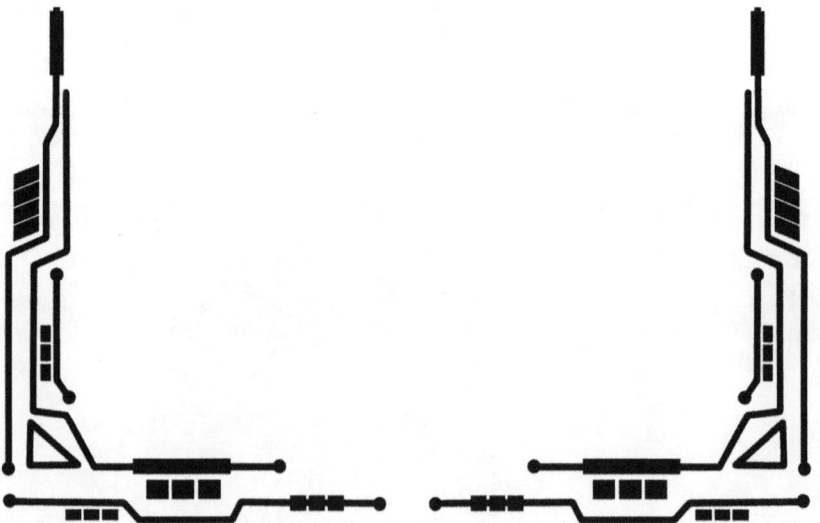

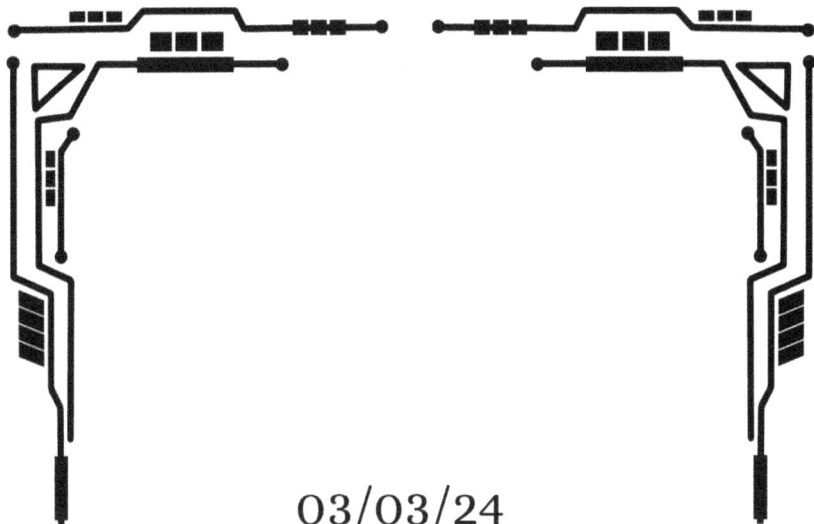

<u>03/03/24</u>

dog poop on the lawn
another day in the life
on the cul de sac

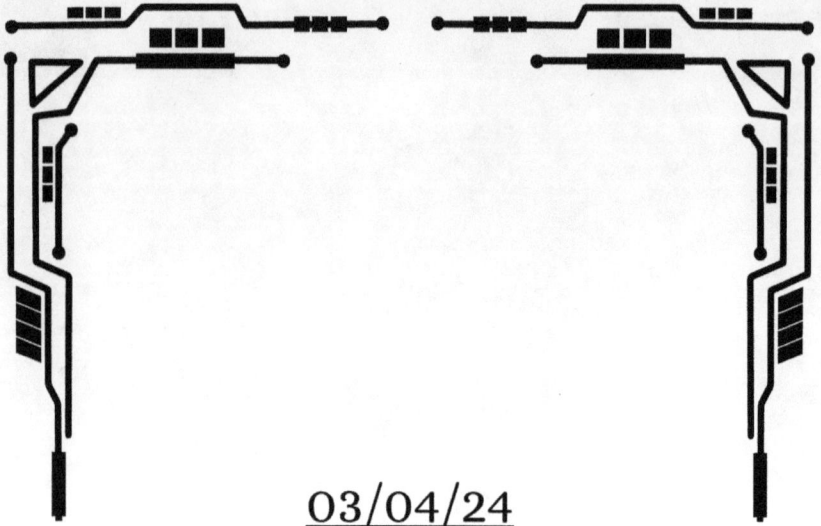

<u>03/04/24</u>

follow the leader
movements all in unison
let us now march fourth

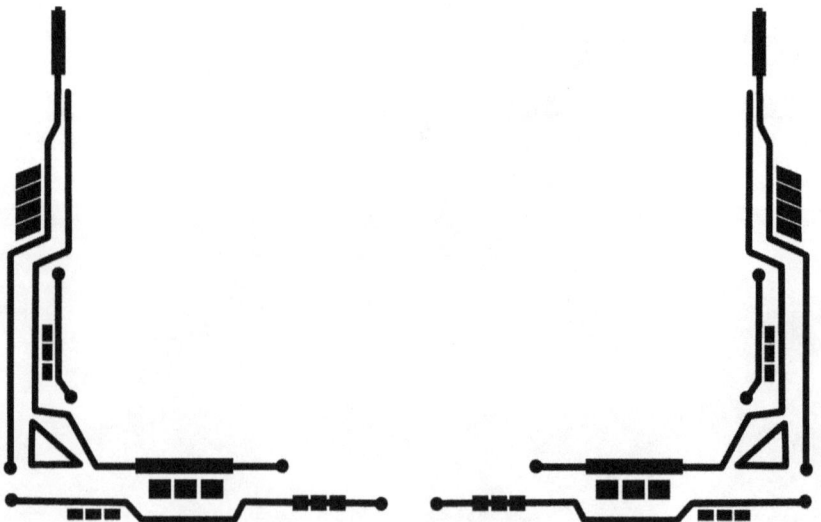

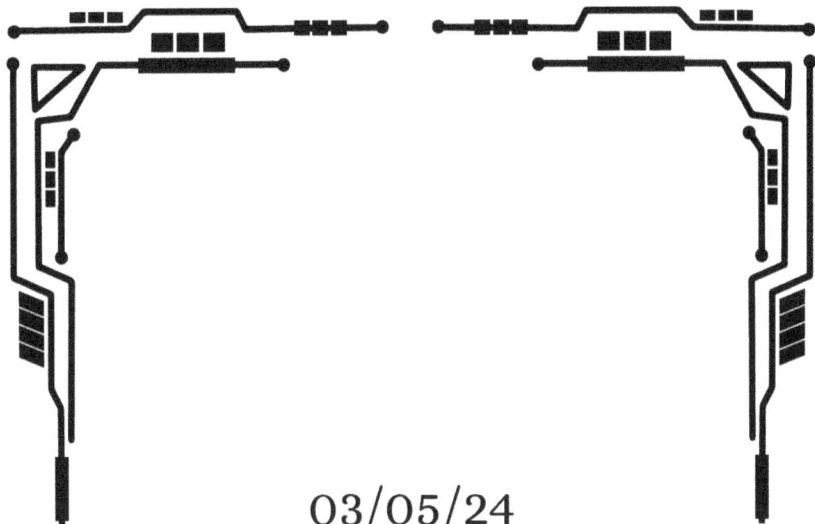

<u>03/05/24</u>

before it was not
right now it's temporary
later it will be

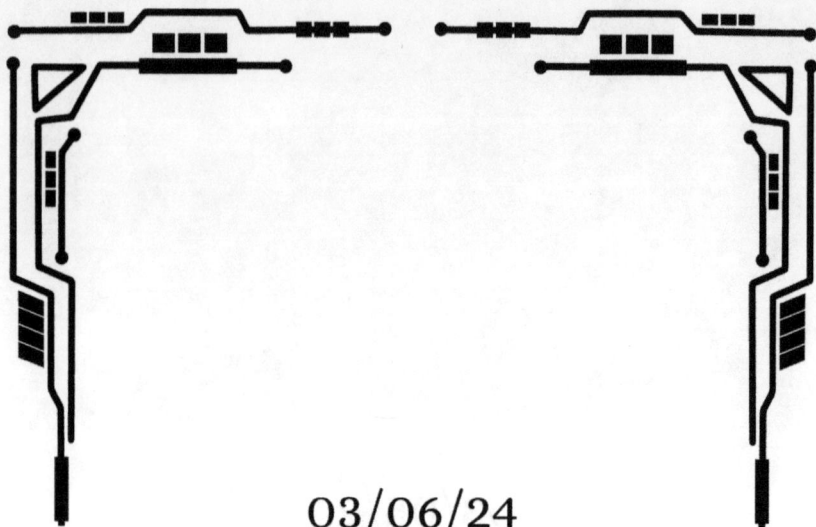

<u>03/06/24</u>

it is not nothing
the space between us is clear
my favorite color

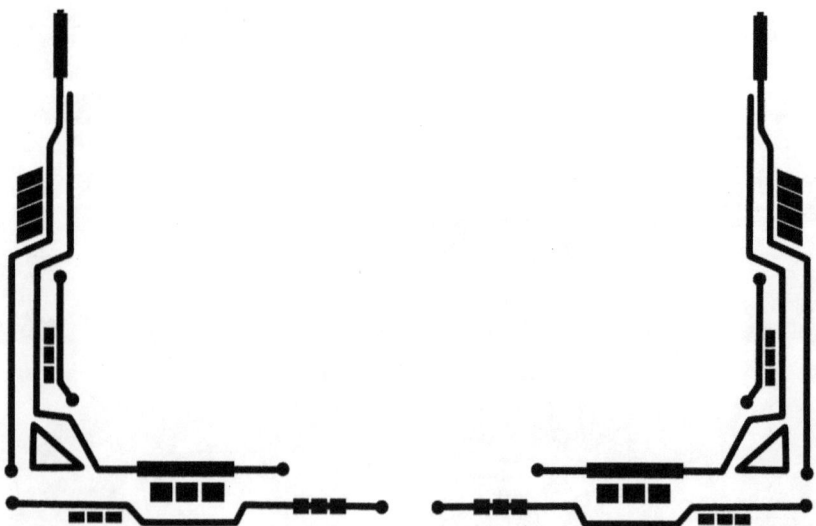

<u>03/07/24</u>

so many sunsets
a lot of things happen now
faster and faster

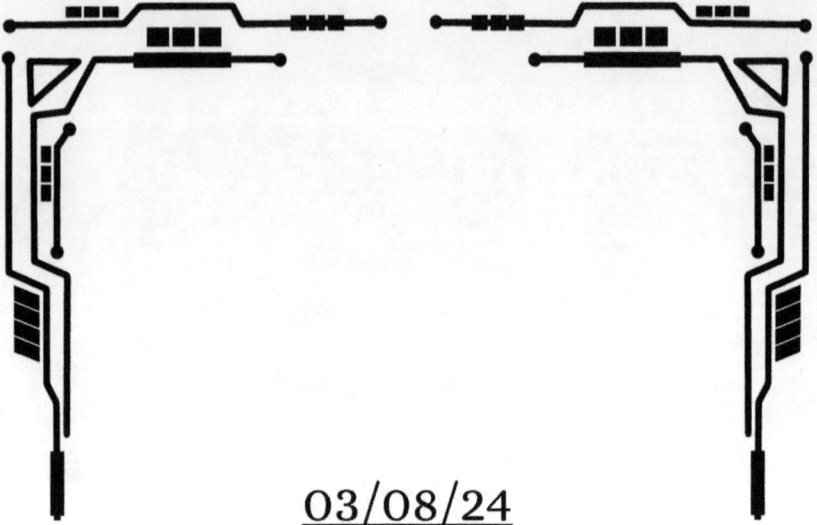

<u>03/08/24</u>

gigabyte gaia
a digital dilemma
downloading nature

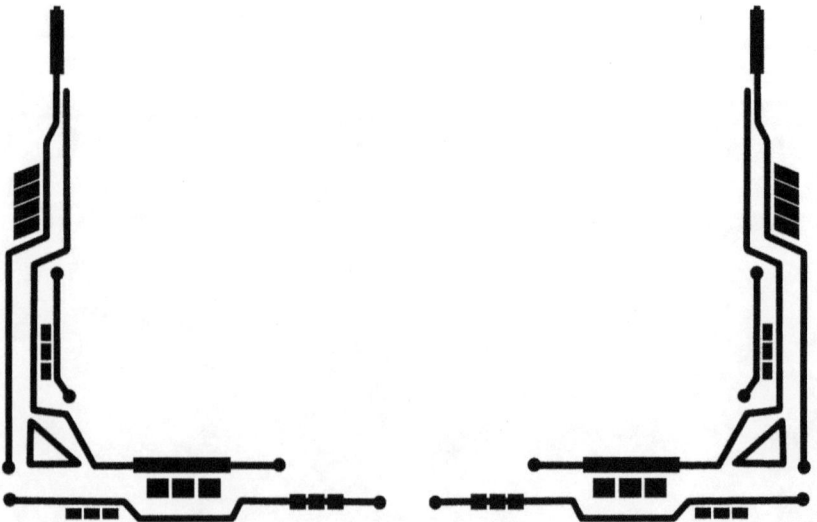

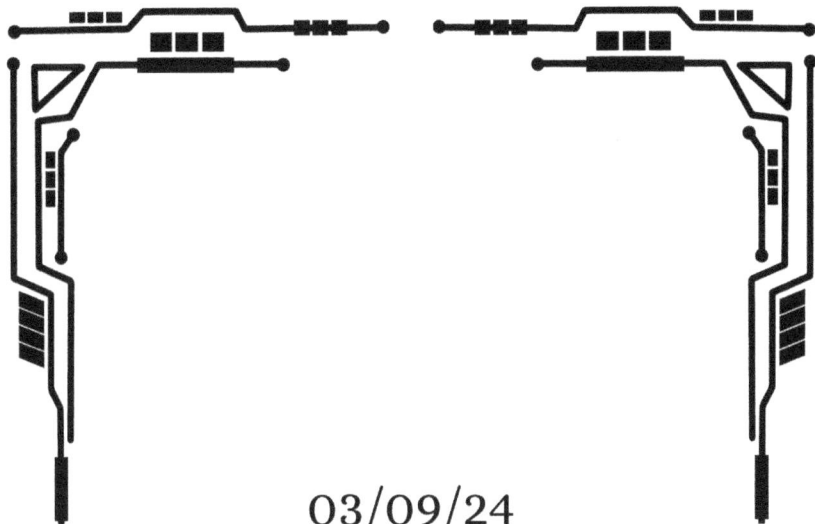

<u>03/09/24</u>

spots in the darkness
clouds of burning gasses or
the decepticons

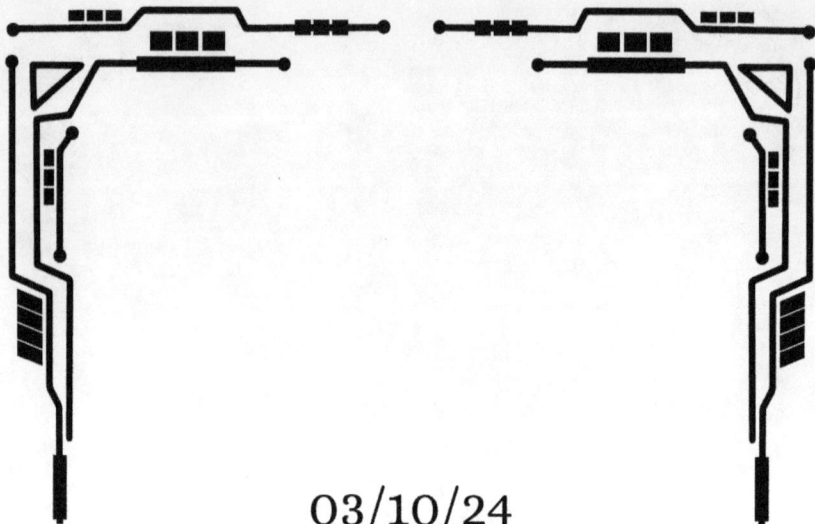

<u>03/10/24</u>

ascension declined
a pocket full of pockets
rest in misery

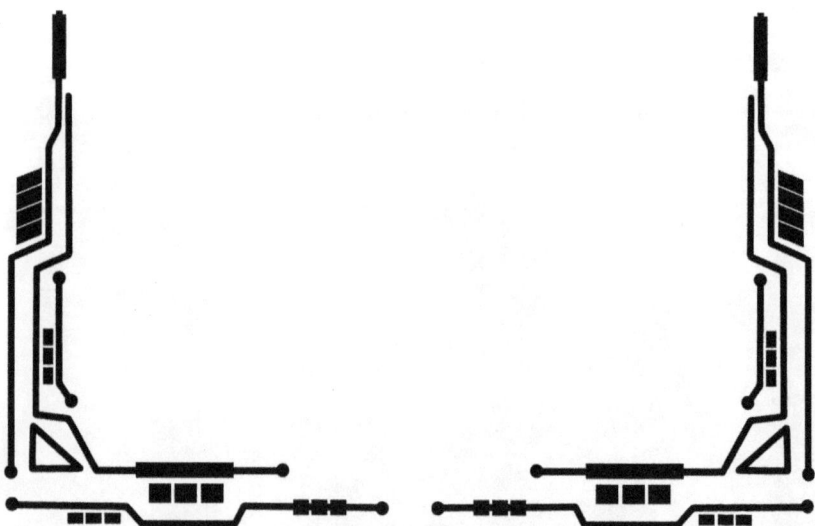

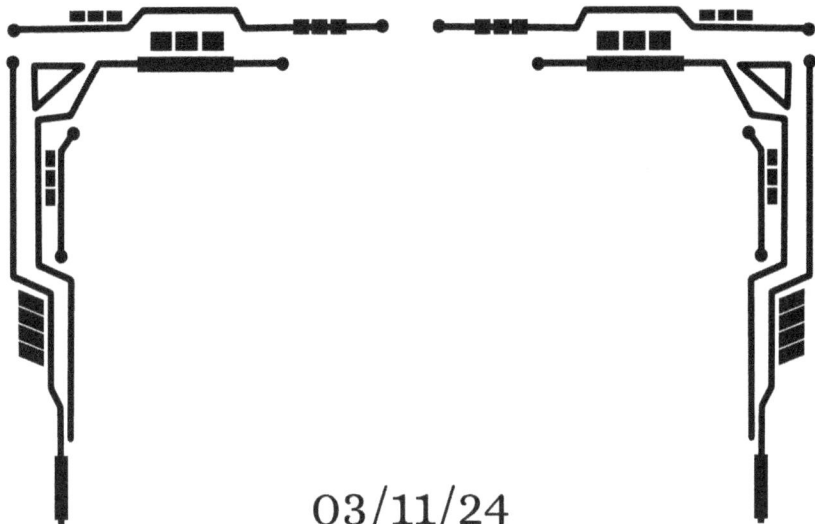

<u>03/11/24</u>

live stream the picket
fences being washed in black
we want more money

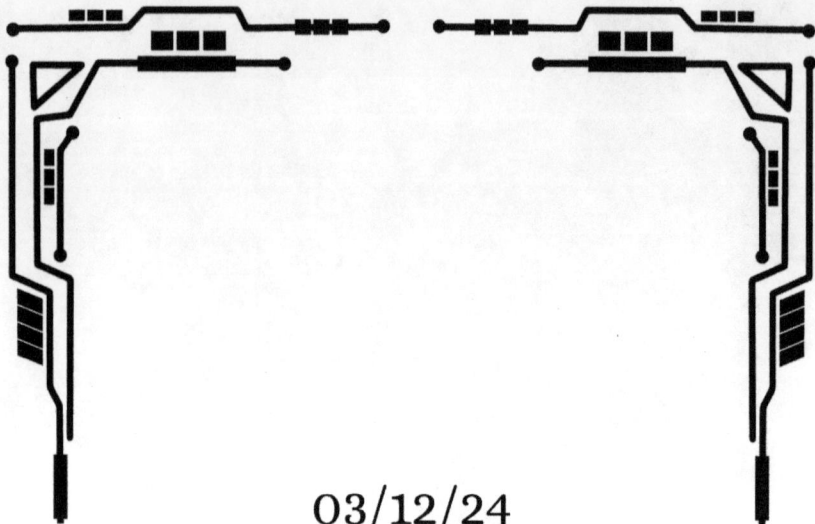

<u>03/12/24</u>

why does everyone
have an obsession with geese
it's fucking grey duck

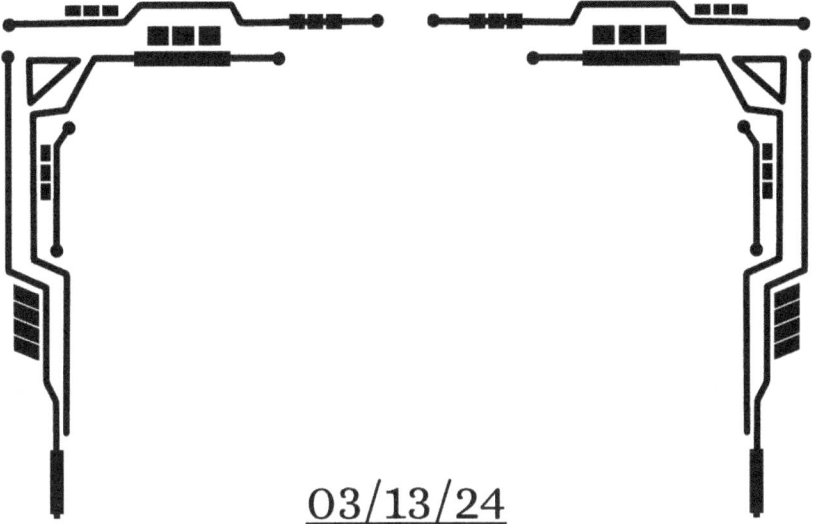

<u>03/13/24</u>

almost to the end
what will become of all these
words on the paper

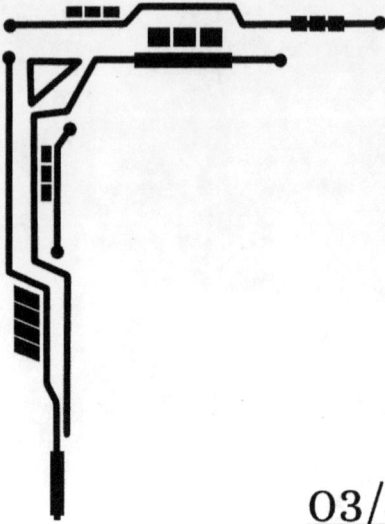

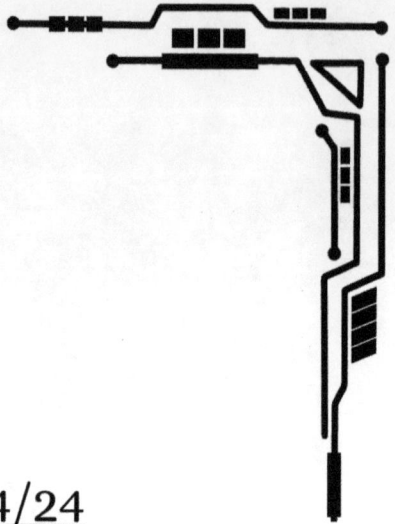

<u>03/14/24</u>

i don't want to sleep
maybe i'll just sit right here
and write a new poem

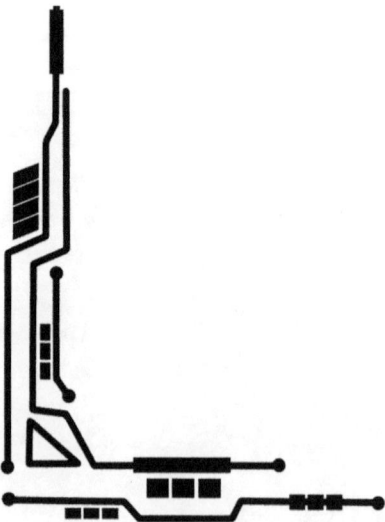

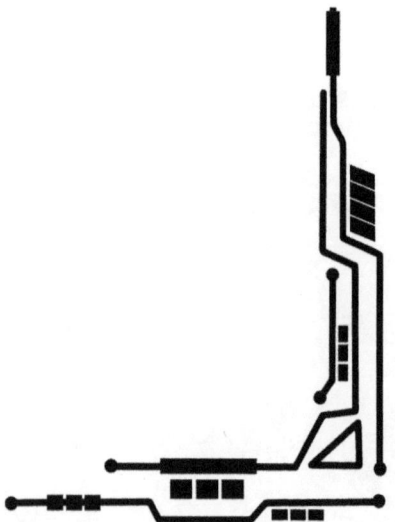

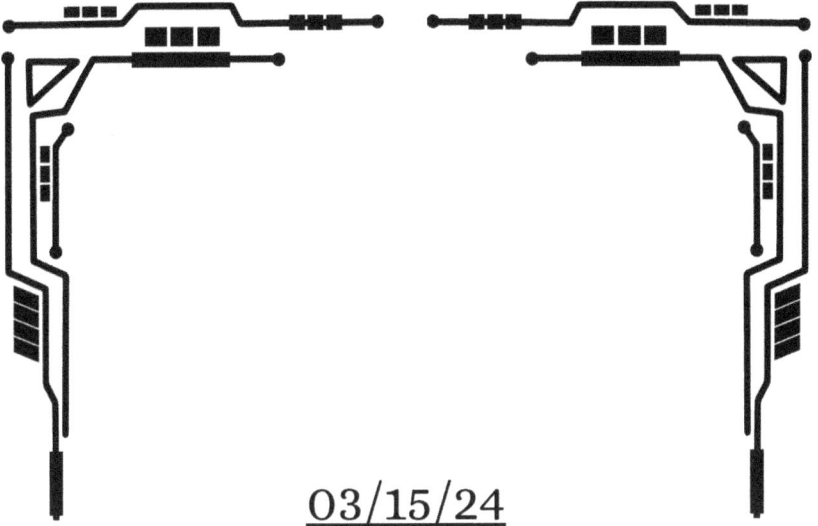

<u>03/15/24</u>

the old one is wise
the small one needs attention
the other one left

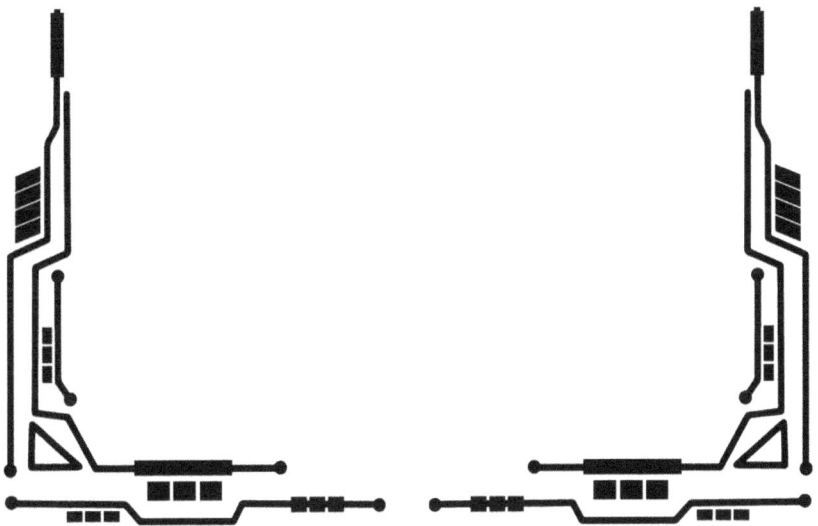

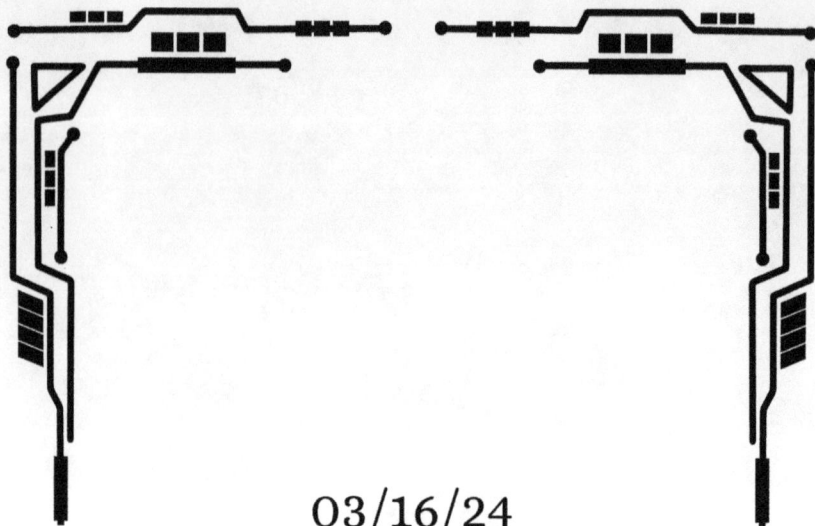

<u>03/16/24</u>

now what is that noise
i can't afford a new car
maybe i'll just walk

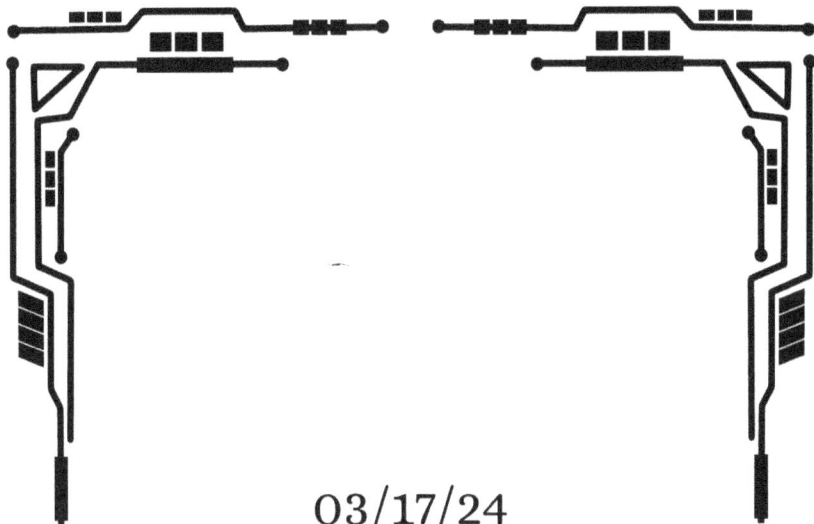

<u>03/17/24</u>

today is the day
we will make some reuben soup
and smoke a fat joint

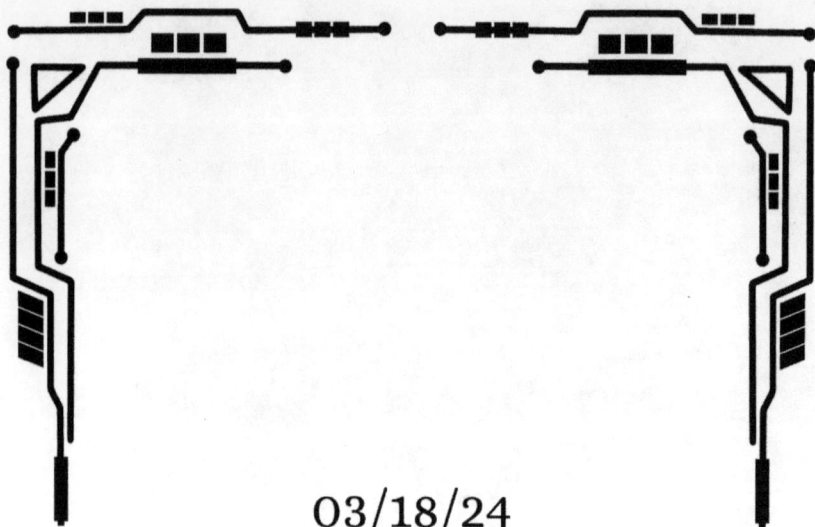

<u>03/18/24</u>

the traffic light broke
and there was a robbery
at the gas station

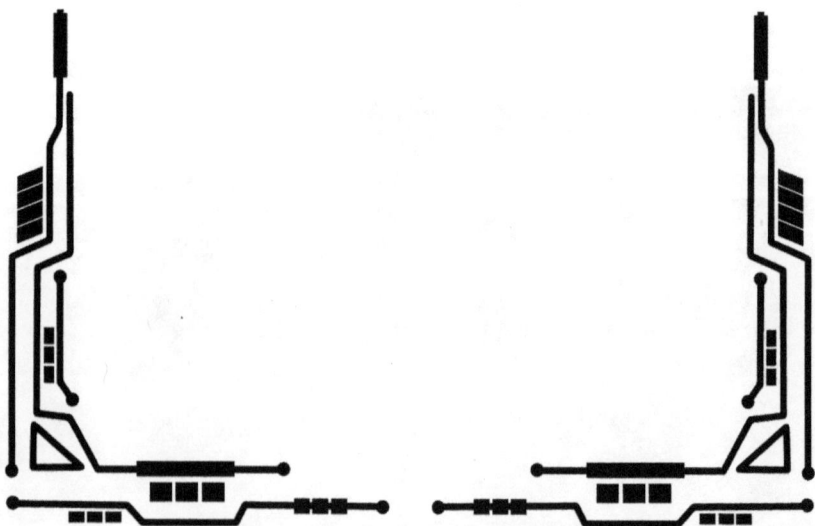

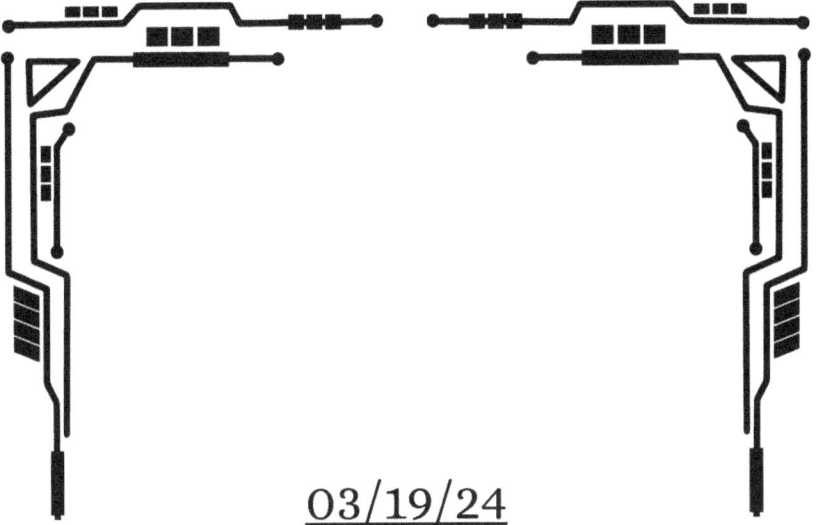

look it's empty now
where did all the money go
cars are expensive

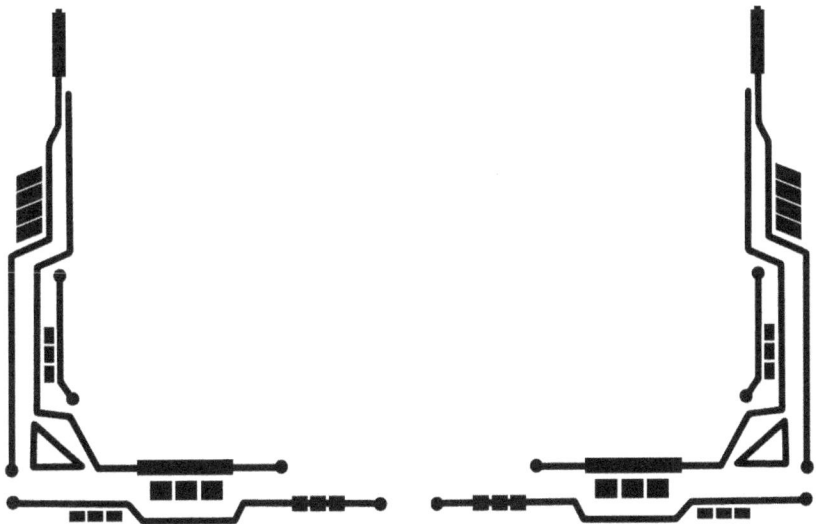

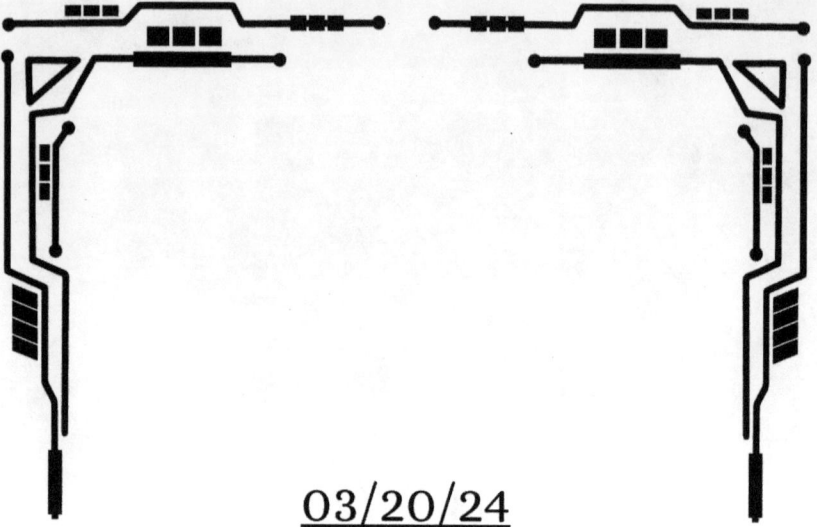

<u>03/20/24</u>

look at that coaster
protect the coffee table
nice work dude high five

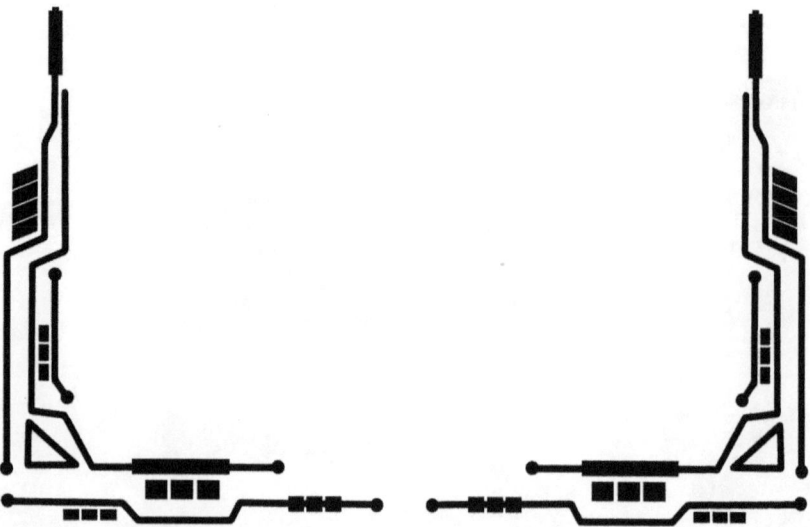

there was a fountain
it got everything all wet
twice a day sometimes

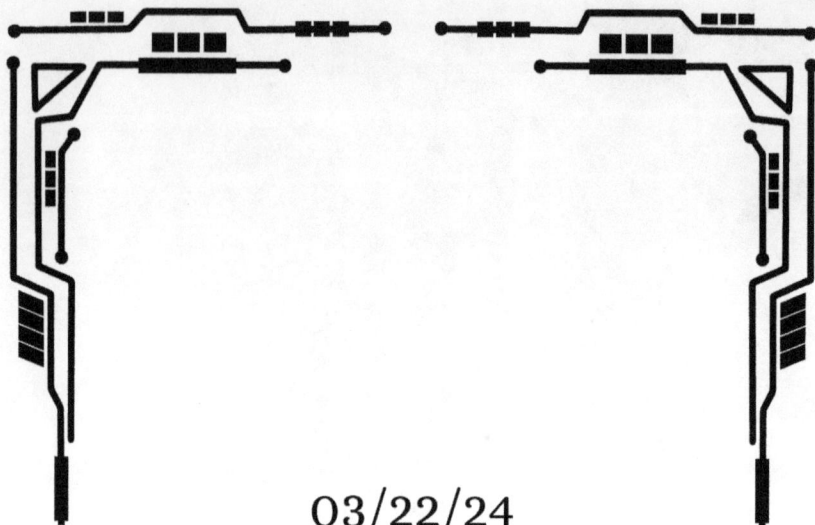

03/22/24

walking in the woods
a little bit in springtime
waiting for the rain

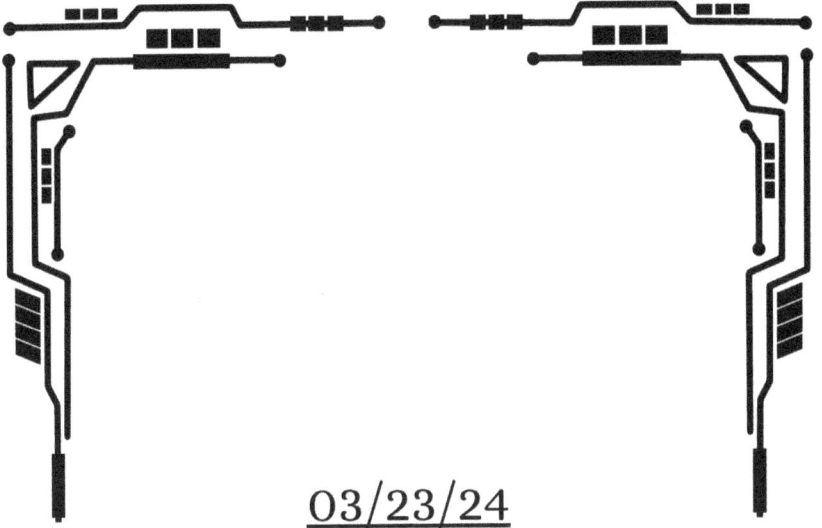

<u>03/23/24</u>

getting to the end
the days are almost over
it's time to end this

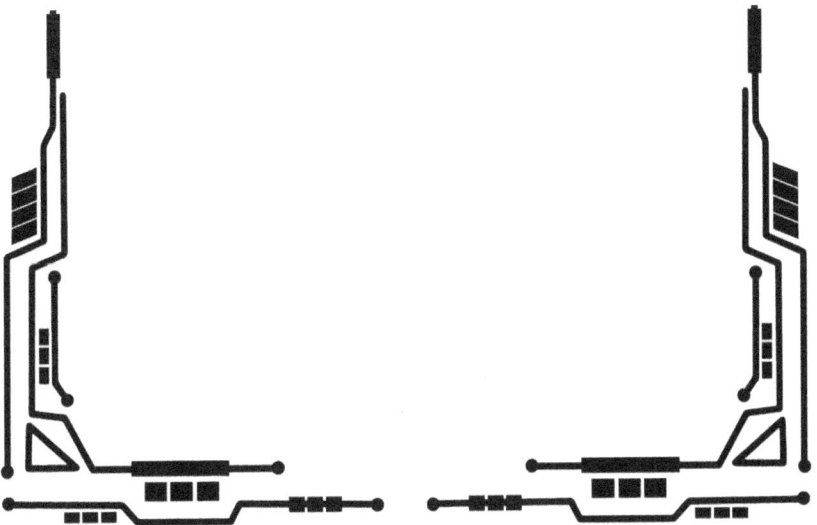

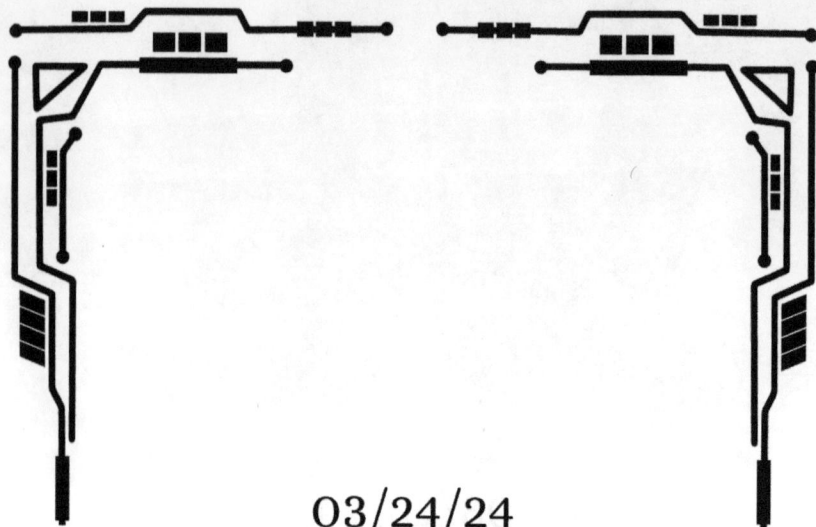

<u>03/24/24</u>

i see two of them
sometimes there are too many
but two is perfect

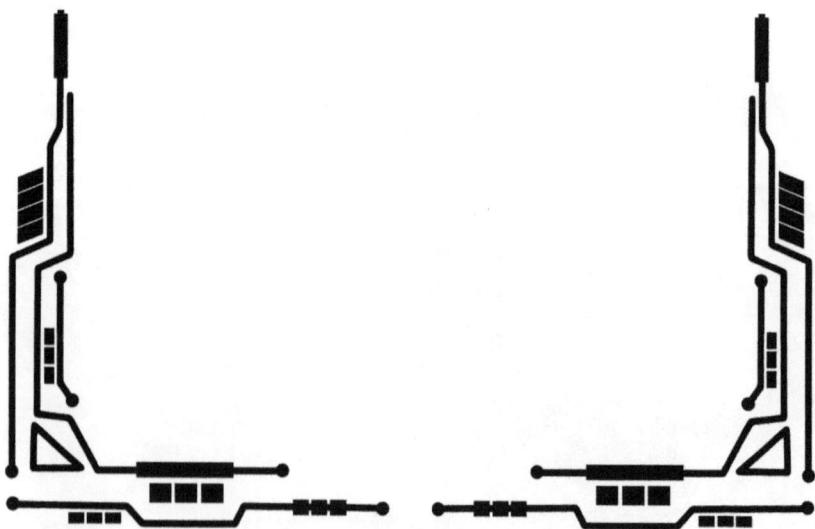

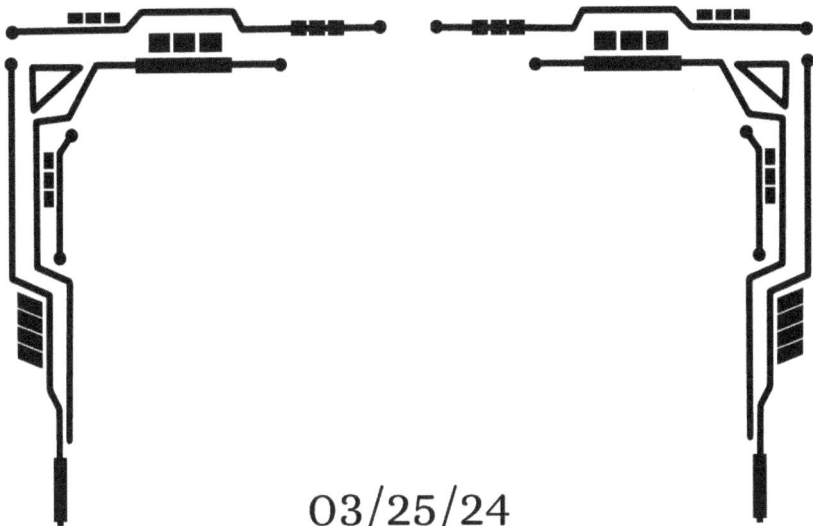

<u>03/25/24</u>

a lonely willow
dancing with the morning rain
beautiful and sad

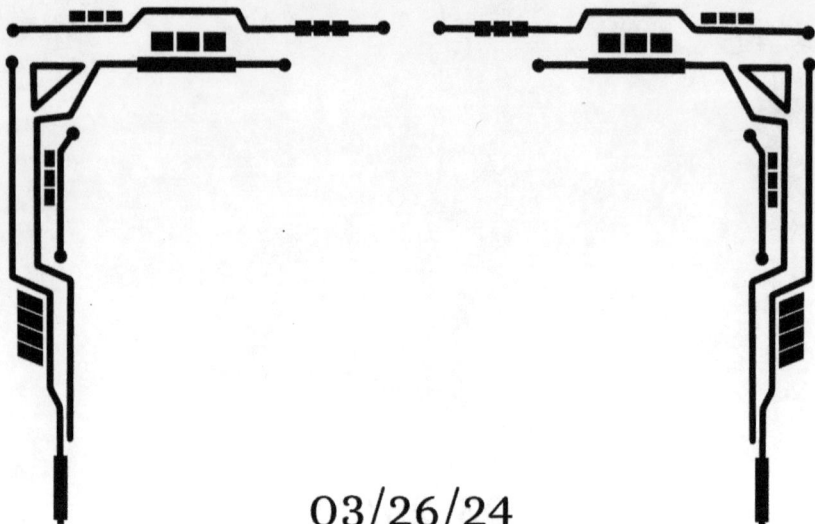

<u>03/26/24</u>

first there was the thought
then i wrote a haiku poem
now it ends like this

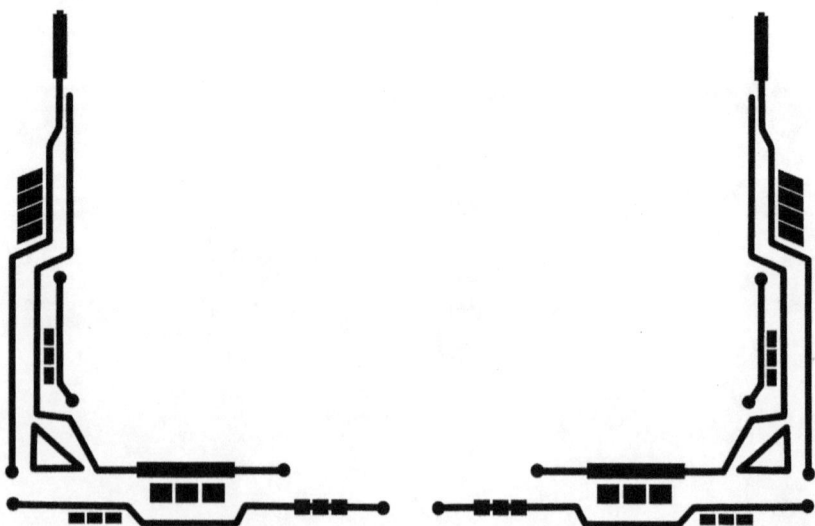

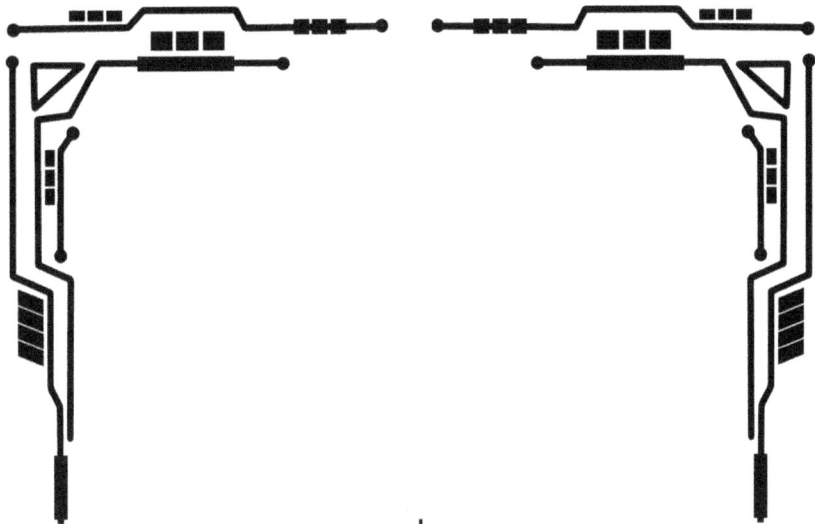

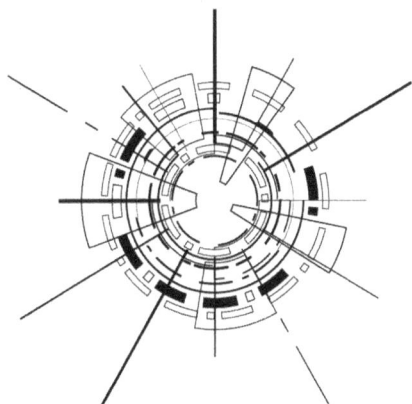

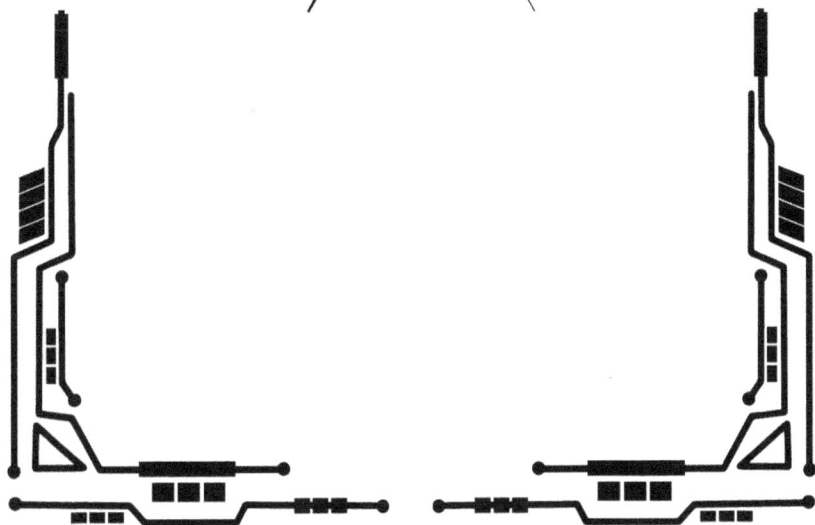

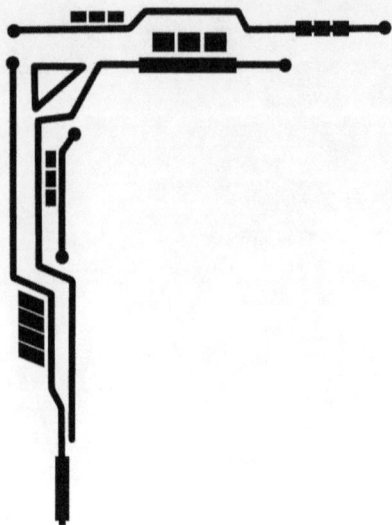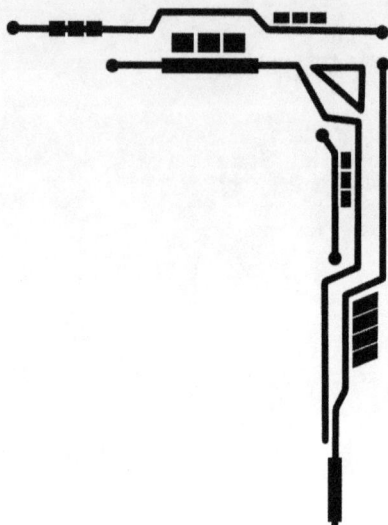

The End.

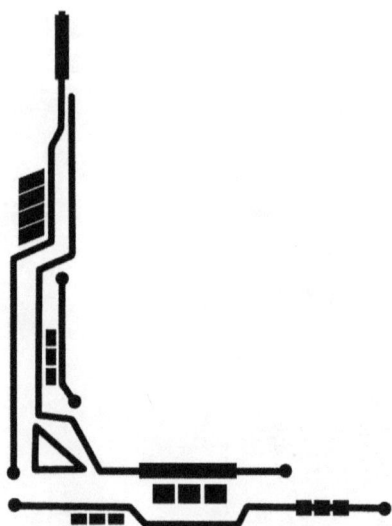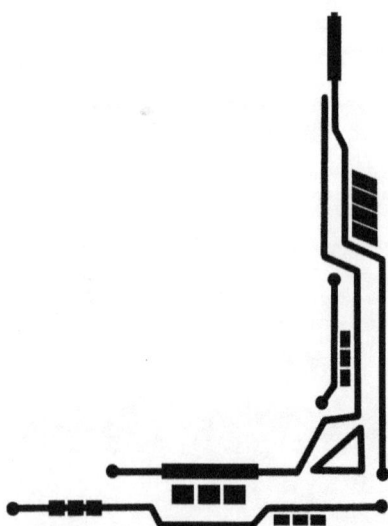

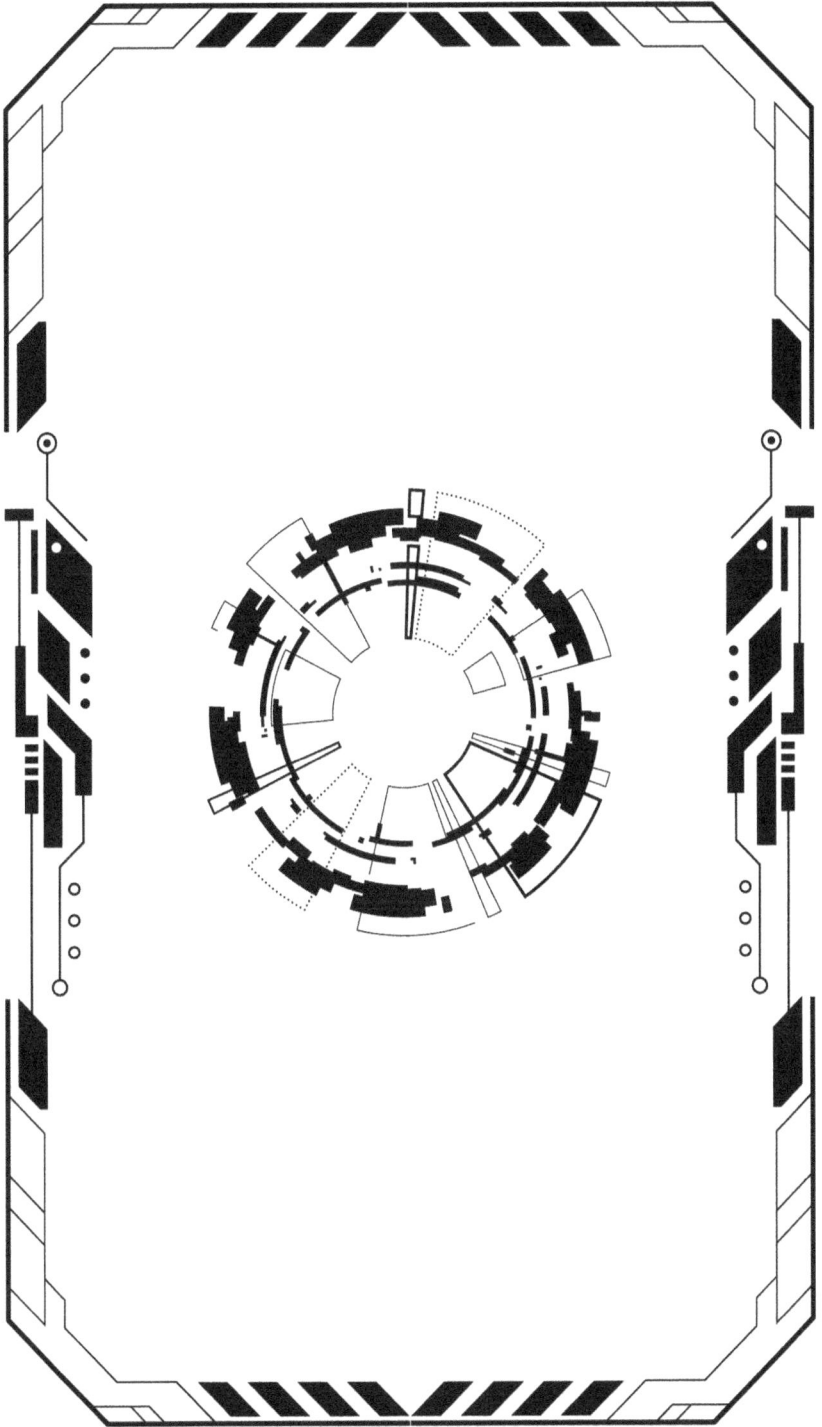

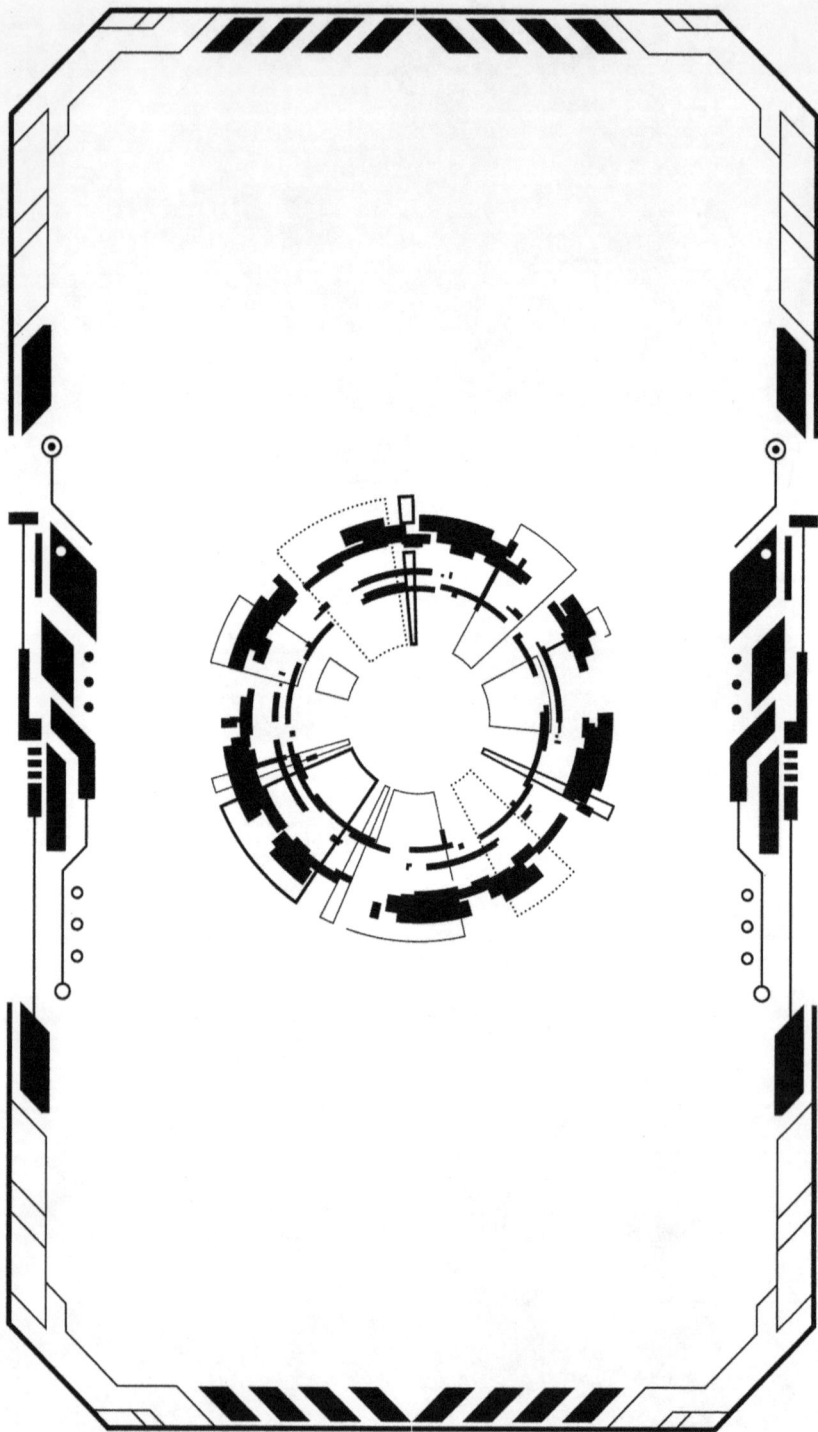

Travis Morgan Blunt was born in Medellín, Colombia on March 27th, 1983. He was raised in the rural farmlands of southern Minnesota, traveled the world on quests and adventures, and currently lives peacefully along Colorado's northern front range mountains.

He is an award winning chef, a former musician, an artist, a philosopher, a collector, an inventor, a small business owner, an outdoorsman, an indoorsman, and soon-to-be best-selling author.

Don't try to contact him. He has a people allergy.

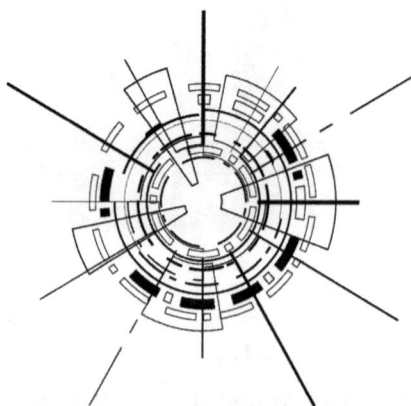

www.ingramcontent.com/pod-product-compliance
Lightning Source LLC
Chambersburg PA
CBHW022001090426
42741CB00007B/848